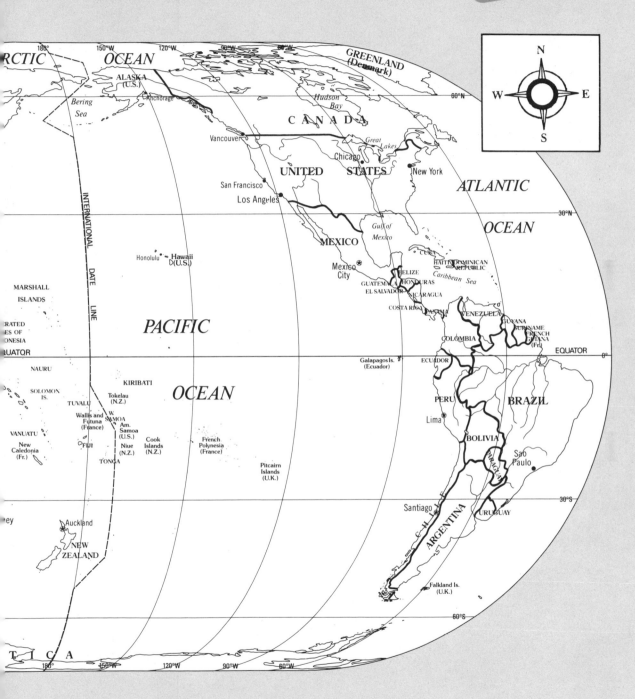

THE
PACIFIC
CENTURY

OTHER BOOKS BY FRANK GIBNEY

Five Gentlemen of Japan
The Operators
The Frozen Revolution
The Secret World (with Peter Deriabin)
The Khrushchev Pattern
The Reluctant Spacefarers
Japan: The Fragile Superpower
Miracle by Design
The Penkovskiy Papers (editor)

THE PACIFIC CENTURY

America and Asia in a Changing World

Frank Gibney

A Robert Stewart Book

Charles Scribner's Sons
New York

Maxwell Macmillan Canada
Toronto

Maxwell Macmillan International
New York   Oxford   Singapore   Sydney

Charles Scribner's Sons	Maxwell Macmillan Canada, Inc.
Macmillan Publishing Company	1200 Eglinton Avenue East,
866 Third Avenue	Suite 200
New York, NY 10022	Don Mills, Ontario M3C 3N1

Macmillan Publishing Company is part of the Maxwell Communication Group of Companies.

Library of Congress Cataloging-in-Publication Data
Gibney, Frank.
    The Pacific century: America and Asia in a changing world / Frank Gibney.
      p. cm.
    "A Robert Stewart book."
    Includes bibliographical references and index.
    ISBN 0-684-19349-3
    1. East Asia—History. 2. Pacific Area—Relations—United States.
    3. United States—Relations—Pacific Area. I. Title.
DS511.G54   1993
950—dc20   92-13862

Macmillan books are available at special discounts for bulk purchases for sales promotions, premiums, fund-raising, or educational use. For details, contact:

Special Sales Director
Macmillan Publishing Company
866 Third Avenue
New York, NY 10022

10 9 8 7 6 5 4 3 2 1

Printed in the United States of America

Dedication

This book is dedicated to the memory of Robert Doyle and Wilson Fielder—two friends and fellow correspondents in Asia who were killed in the line of duty. Bob Doyle was forced out of his jeep and shot by guerrilla fanatics on a lonely road in Indonesia on April 27, 1950. Wilson Fielder died on July 20, 1950, under a hail of bullets, as Kim Il Sung's brutal soldiery moved into Taejon, Korea. Doyle was thirty-one at the time of his death; Fielder was thirty-three. The two were both journalists and scholars, fluent in Mandarin and well acclimated to life in China and Southeast Asia. Bob had studied Asian languages and politics at Columbia and Yale. Wilson was raised in China. They made many friends among Chinese and other Asian peoples; and they were good analysts of the turbulent history in which they lived.

At the beginning of 1950 the three of us constituted *Time* magazine's reporting staff in East Asia. Bob and Wilson were based in Hong Kong and I in Tokyo. We kept in close touch and worked together on a variety of news assignments, from Korea to Indonesia. As the survivor of the three, I can only conjecture at the stories they would have covered, the books they would have written, and the projects they would have carried through. One legacy they left to me—and to many others—was a consuming journalistic curiosity combined with a deep sympathy and affection for East Asian peoples which transcended artificial boundaries of nationality and race. More than forty years afterward, I remain sad at the suddenness of their passing. We all face that final moment. Theirs came far too early.

> *Eheu fugaces, Postume, Postume,*
> *labuntur anni, nec pietas moram*
> *rugis et instanti senectae*
> *adferet indomitaeque morti . . .*
> (HORACE, *Odes* II, xiv)

Contents

Acknowledgments

The concept for this book came from a proposal which The Pacific Basin Institute advanced to The Annenberg/CPB Project for a television and text series entitled *The Pacific Century*. As I thought further about the various themes, this book quickly took on a life of its own. It neither grew out of the television series segments, nor did the series depend on the book. In fact, both were produced in very different sequences, although within the same general time frame.

The responsibility for what is in the book is mine alone. I was certainly influenced in its writing, however, by the impressions and insights gained from the producers of the series; and I believe they in turn found the various chapters of the book useful. In particular I owe a great debt to the executive producer of the series, Alex Gibney. Throughout production of both the book and the various segments of the series, he and I talked over the ideas and viewpoints ultimately expressed. Our discussions and comments on this work were extremely useful. Our viewpoints often differed, but I believe the end product of this book as well as the films was the better for this constant discussion and mutual examination.

I take this opportunity to thank the staff of Jigsaw Productions overseeing the entire series work—Kerry Neal, Alexandria Levitt, Andrea Malin, and David Mrazek—as well as the producers: Al Levin, Peter Bull, Steve Talley, Christopher Ralling, Alan Poul, Carl Byker, and Rachel Rosenthal. For access to their work and their comments I am most grateful.

I would also like to express my thanks to various members of the PBI scholarly advisory committee on *The Pacific Century* series. In the course of our meetings and individual talks, as we reviewed the basic themes of the television series, their comments, clarifications, and corrections were most useful. The book profited from this as well. In this connection I should like to thank in particular Chalmers Johnson, the chairman of our advisory committee, Don Emmerson, Michael Robinson, Leo Ou-fan Lee, Carol Gluck, David Halberstam, Haruhiro Fukui, Alan Liu, Lucie Cheng, Thomas Gold, and S. Gordon Redding, as well as my old friend Herbert Passin.

In Japan, during the course of this writing I profited greatly from the comments of Michio Nagai, Jiro Tokuyama, and in particular the late Takeo Kuwabara. Shigeki Hijino read much of the text and contributed valuable comments. In Korea I am grateful for the comments of Han Sun-joo and Han Changgi. Particular thanks is owed to Sarah Kim, senior editor of the Korean-language Britannica World Encyclopaedia, whose insights and comments on various chapters of the book were most valuable.

On matters dealing with China I would like to thank Frank Gibney, Jr., who was most helpful with his advice on people and events in the People's Republic of China as well as in Taiwan and Thailand. I also received valuable insights and support from Dale Hoiberg, my colleague at the Encyclopaedia Britannica and a Chinese scholar in his own right, as well as Suzhi Yan and Xu Weizeng in Beijing. Chia-Yun Yu also contributed useful research on China, Korea, Hong Kong, and Taiwan.

In the editing of the book I owe particular thanks to James S. Gibney, who reviewed all of the chapters, suggesting valuable editorial changes and pointing out many inconsistencies which otherwise might have seen the light of day. Readers may understandably wonder at the appearance of another Gibney name. As it happens, the three of my sons mentioned—documentary film producer, news magazine correspondent, and foreign service officer, respectively—have all lived and worked in Asia for some years. They are really knowledgeable about the area and its peoples. In an act of reverse nepotism— rare in these times—they have helped me greatly with this book.

Thanks are due to Maurice Mitchell, chairman of The Pacific Basin Institute for his support. Laura Omi and Melanie Zimmermann, project director and executive secretary, respectively, at The Pacific Basin Institute, were towers of strength in arranging and typing the editorial material and in helping with the procedure of picture selection. Here, Yukiko Honda in Tokyo and Louis Plummer in Washington were also most helpful.

Mark Borthwick, the director of research at The Pacific Basin Institute, was extremely helpful in many ways although understandably preoccupied with producing the textbook for this series at the same time. Gil Latz and Norton Ginsberg contributed interesting insights about the geographical aspects of this work.

Thanks is of course due to The Annenberg/CPB Project—represented by Dr. Mara Mayor and Dr. Hilda Moskowitz—for support of the television series, as well as NHK, the third major funder of the series. We are particularly grateful to the Ford Foundation for its generous and unstinting support of this project. Peter Stanley, then director of higher education at Ford (and now president of Pomona College), and Sheila Biddle and Andrea Taylor at Ford all provided us with invaluable help, guidance, and encouragement. They were also both extremely knowledgeable and understanding about the editorial content of the series. We can only hope that other American foundations will stir from their torpor on Asia-Pacific matters and join in the many excellent projects which follow this one.

Hiroko Gibney was a great help not only for translation assistance but also for the scholarly insights she offered me on Japan and China.

Finally I would like to express gratitude for the understanding and guidance of my editor at Scribners, Robert Stewart, and his assistant, Carol Cook, as well as the copy chief, Theresa Czajkowska. My agent, Leona Schecter, supported me not merely with her marketing skills but also with her editorial expertise.

Introduction

For many of us it began in war. Sailing through the mists of San Francisco's Golden Gate or the sunny waters off Coronado, heading out from the shipyards at Bremerton, or boarding the bucket-seat C-47s at Fairfield-Suisun air base for the flight westward, a generation of young Americans went off to battle, their anxious families knowing only that they would be somewhere in the "Pacific." There were soon names to fill out the map—Guadalcanal, Tarawa, Kwajalein, Ulithi, Port Moresby, and Brisbane; then, as the war years rushed by, Leyte, Lingayan Gulf, and Manila. Finally, Iwo Jima, Okinawa, and Tokyo came into view, with Shanghai and Seoul just over the horizon. By the mid-forties, victorious at last over the bombers and battleships of Japan's Greater East Asia Co-Prosperity Sphere, Americans began to think of the great ocean as an "American lake."

The flood of war reporting, set off by memorable TV and film panoramas like NBC's *Victory at Sea*, dramatized not merely the fact but the amazing scope of the Pacific war. Time and distances shrank; once trackless wastes of ocean became highways. No land on the ocean's littoral was beyond the reach of aircraft, cruisers, and troop transports. In the process our thinking about the great ocean and the Asian nations along its shores began to change. The same Pacific which had for so many years represented special, isolated aspects of exotica—Gauguin's Tahiti, Robert Louis Stevenson's Samoa, the ocean voyaging of Captain Cook, or the mutineers from the *Bounty*—gave way to an impression of one vast unity. American by right of conquest, the new Pacific world appeared to be a logical extension of our traditional westward progress. Hundreds of thousands of servicemen came back with real-life experiences to show how close to home it really was.

But the wars would not go away. Indeed the massive scale of World War II and the European Cold War confrontation that succeeded it served to mask only temporarily a wave of revolution, independence seeking, and anticolonialism that was spreading over East Asia. Just when the United States congratulated itself on General MacArthur's successful "democratization" of Japan—a seemingly satisfying vindication of the old missionary spirit—China turned resoundingly Communist. (How did we "lose" China? congressmen and commentators debated, as only Americans could.) Then came the Communist attack on Korea, the start of a series of very hot "postwar" wars in East Asia. Revolutionaries began to fight established regimes in the Philippines and Malaya, with Sukarno's newly belligerent Indonesia compounding the trouble.

By the mid-sixties U.S. Marines and Army troops were ashore in Vietnam in force. Once again the carriers, the transports, and the airlifts were on their way across the Pacific. If this was to be an American lake, our national responsibility, it was reasoned, was to defend and secure its hostile shores. If we saw the whole Asia-Pacific area as a unity, it remained the unity of a war theater, our most consistently explosive Cold War front. In this way a national tragedy began.

While the United States was thus meeting the military challenges of empire—real and fancied—something more fundamental and far-reaching was happening to the Pacific world. It would in the end prove more important than any of the postwar wars. A huge economic and social change was taking place in Asian countries along its western shores. The change was modern Asia's version of the West's Industrial Revolution and it would have an impact on the West comparable to the nineteenth-century assault of Western colonialism on China and Japan. Not only was the United States—economy, politics, and civilization—profoundly affected by this change; ironically, it was American aid and example that set the change in motion.

This central fact, although well known to Asians, would take an exasperatingly long time for Americans themselves to comprehend. As a nation, we remain singularly myopic. For all the superficial talk of internationalism, we still live largely within ourselves. If anywhere, we look most readily across the Atlantic to Europe or the Middle East as decisive to our foreign-policy making, or beyond that to the changing fortunes of the former Soviet Union, so long the object of our adversarial attention. However intrusive their penetration of our economy, the Asian countries on the far side of the western ocean remain culturally and traditionally remote to us. Yet we share a future with them. Their development and ours have a long history together.

Long before our contemporary concept of a Pacific world had dawned, Americans had forged strong links with the other Pacific peoples. The first clipper ships were designed for the lucrative trade routes to China (opium and coolie-labor traffic included). By the early nineteenth century Pacific whaling was a major American commercial endeavor; the modern Japanese whalers denounced by American ecologists were only following in our oceanic footsteps. Chinese labor helped build the first transcontinental American railroads, and the opium trade, truth to tell, was the foundation for some great New England fortunes.

Our mid-nineteenth-century ideas of Manifest Destiny took shape in the Pacific. Alaska, Hawaii, and the Philippines were the first U.S. colonies. It was Commodore Perry and his American squadron that "opened" Japan; and long before the World War II carrier task forces set sail, Teddy Roosevelt's Great White Fleet had carried our imperium into the Pacific.

Yet all these events seemed mere isolated happenings in the national consciousness—footnotes, as it were, to the mainstream of our history. It took a massive shift in the economic balance of power to make Americans take notice. Beyond trade and investment alternatives, we should realize that the postwar economic takeoff of the Pacific holds ever widening cultural and political significance for us as well.

The economic takeoff began with Japan in the early sixties. The combination of economic aid and political rehabilitation given earlier by the U.S. Occupation—and fueled by Korean War purchases—was a critical element in this first Pacific recovery.

Once independent again, however, the Japanese needed little further coaching. Starting with Prime Minister Ikeda Hayato's "double our income" policy, this remarkable nation turned itself away from ideological bickering and began a new era of economic expansion. Through the sixties Japan's GNP growth rates averaged over 10 percent annually. Thereafter, riding out the "oil shocks" of 1973 and 1979, export drives continued their headlong course. They escalated from electronics to automobiles to the present era of high tech. The seven million cars Japan turned out in 1983 exceeded U.S. output for the first time in history. By 1985 Japan's balance-of-payments surplus with the United States had swollen to over $50 billion, and capital-rich Japan was investing heavily in its American debtor.

The second phase of the Pacific takeoff began in the late sixties. The Republic of Korea—South Korea—switched from the standard developing country policy of import substitution to an intensive export drive, roughly following the Japanese example. Taiwan, Hong Kong, and Singapore took the same path. By the early seventies annual GNP growth figures of the four Little Tigers, as they were called, had exceeded Japan's performance in the decade preceding. Directed at first by authoritarian leaderships, Korea, Taiwan, and Singapore—Hong Kong remains a special case—exemplified even more than Japan a new factor in world economics: what the political economist Chalmers Johnson named "the capitalist developmental state."

Here too ideology was either downplayed or harnessed to economic objectives. Under the general direction of "technocrat" bureaucracies, business and finance worked hand in glove with government to expand existing export markets and research, create, and develop new ones. Although these were all market economies, featured by intense competition within themselves, their characteristically strong government "guidance" took them worlds away from the adversarial free enterprise of beloved American definition. American business competitors began to see "Japan, Inc." multiplied.

Other East Asian nations followed suit. After the formal union of ASEAN (Association of Southeast Asian Nations) in 1967, Thailand, Malaysia, and Indonesia began hitting increased growth figures in turn. Turning from political controversy toward economic concentration, they too entered the spiral of growing industrialization and rising consumer expectations.

This third stage of takeoff was climaxed by China's sudden turn toward economic modernization. Restored to power in 1978, Deng Xiaoping set the People's Republic of China on the same road toward an export-intensive market economy, which actively welcomed foreign investment. For ten years this "second revolution" of China—as Deng called it—was successful, in the case of agriculture dramatically so. Even in the nineties, despite the political freeze after the 1989 Tiananmen massacre, one doubts that it can ever be reversed. The force of economic incentive is too strong.

There are many reasons for the success and sweep of this Pacific takeoff. Export-directed economies, intensified agricultural production (fueled by land reform), and a high level of savings and capital investment are among them. Such economic factors have been grounded, interestingly enough, in traditional cultures. Asians, particularly those raised in the Confucian tradition, are strongly group-oriented. They have shown a willingness to respect authority, however oppressive, as long as family or other societal units are left alone. Traditionally unsteeped in Western concerns for individual human rights and win-or-lose legal justice, they have a relatively high political boiling point. They will work long and hard for the prospect of distant future gain. It is not for nothing that they have been called Confucian capitalists.

The Sinic peoples in particular—that is, Chinese, Japanese, Vietnamese, and Koreans—subscribe to an ethic which emphasizes mutual loyalties. They have an almost religious regard for scholarship and learning. The acquisition of knowledge is prized as an end in itself. In contrast to the universal and absolute values of ancient Western tradition, in the Confucian world wisdom, virtue, and authority were seen to intersect. Through the centuries its peoples have displayed an instinctive respect for the official, the person in authority, which makes the bureaucrat's role far more important than in most Western cultures.

This kind of "Confucian" culture has historically proved as much of a liability as an asset. The cultural smugness of the mandarins was largely responsible for their late start in modernization. Only Japan modernized itself. The other nations of East Asia slept through the West's Industrial Revolution, still dreaming of their own past glories. Finally awakened, by the mid-twentieth century their peoples had begun a massive "catch-up" effort. Suddenly plunged into a competitive but interlocking world economy, they found that their traditions of group loyalties and working patterns, their passion for education, their willingness to sacrifice individual preferences for common goals would become assets, not liabilities, in a world where the old economic verities of laissez-faire were fast changing.

The new world economy—and increasingly the new world politics—is the creation of modern discovery and adaptation. The individual Western capitalist of nineteenth-century folklore is as out of place in this new world as the eighteenth-century Manchu mandarin. Over the past thirty years we have experienced a technological revolution that humankind is still trying to sort out. Advances in telecommunications and transportation—from the jumbo jet to the fiber-optic cable—have transformed our traditional ideas of time and distance. Most notably, the huge increases in travel and communication throughout the Pacific region would have been impossible a half century ago.

The Pacific takeoff's spectacular gains in trade and investment, multiplied by communications efficiency, have resulted in an almost self-perpetuating expansion. One nation's economic growth helps others as well. By the mid-nineties, for example, American trade with the Pacific nations, now estimated at $250 billion annually, will probably be more than twice our commerce with trading partners across the Atlantic. As late as the 1960s such an economic projection would have seemed fantasy.

Trade and investment increases, however, are only part of an unexpected and quite irrepressible two-way transpacific traffic in ideas and ideals. The economic takeoff is only part of a cultural and political transformation. Along with the beginnings of affluence has come an increasingly strong desire for democracy and self-governance. We can hardly classify all the Pacific Basin nations as democracies. Some are still scarred by authoritarianism, in varying degrees. Yet economic success brings rising expectations with it. This in turn brings pressure for greater political and social freedom.

Not merely in Japan but throughout the Asia-Pacific countries a new middle class has developed, confident and self-assertive. In the late eighties popular protest toppled authoritarian regimes both in Korea and in the Philippines; increasing popular pressure is at last forcing the democratization of rich Taiwan. Nor are Asia's Communists impervious to change. In Vietnam and even Kim Il Sung's Stalinist satrapy in North Korea—as in China itself—the desperate police rule of old ideologues, the rear guard of twentieth-century despotism, cannot indefinitely dam up a rising tide of popular aspiration and discontent. As Japan's Socialist leader Eda Saburo said prophetically in the seventies: "The age of ideology is dead."

This era of Pacific growth could not have happened without the constant political participation and economic support of the United States. And for much of the Cold War era American military power has guaranteed the security of postwar East Asian polities. As Singapore's longtime leader, Lee Kuan Yew, attests, even the ultimately disastrous American intervention in Vietnam kept his and other Southeast Asian countries safe from threats of conquest or subversion during a critical period of economic growth.

More immediately, American aid and loans were a key factor in building up the economies of Korea, Taiwan, and the ASEAN countries, as well as Japan. The motive for aid was far from being purely altruistic. Throughout East Asia—from the sixties to the late eighties—Americans winked at these countries' economic protectionism and turned a blind eye to their political repression in return for loyalty to the anti-Communism of the Cold War.

The real hero of the Pacific economic takeoff was the American consumer. We bought and bought and bought. The huge trade imbalances that resulted surely gave the lie to the old dependency theory, so beloved by Marxist academics, whereby developed capitalist countries inexorably turn economically underdeveloped nations into helpless raw material suppliers and markets for their own manufactures.

Quite to the contrary, American consumers readily and greedily bought the manufactures of their Asian trading partners, with only minimal tariffs charged them. Similarly, American businesses, little concerned about their own work forces, were quick to build their plants offshore, wherever labor was cheap at the time. Any thought of reciprocity was long delayed. Thus the United States became the engine of growth for the whole Pacific area. From textiles to high tech the huge Asian GNP rises were generally based on expanding sales to North America.

Americans have been the leading instrument of the Asia-Pacific world's political and cultural modernization. Asian students have assiduously studied

English and gone for further training, wherever possible, to American universities. In their modernization efforts Asians have guided on American styles and art and rock music. More seriously, they have studied American—even more than British—ideas of law and democratic government.

Modernization, however, does not automatically mean Westernization. A knowledge of Copernicus, the *Divina Commedia,* and Kant is not necessary for learning the computer. Yet the Christian tradition, the optimism of the Enlightenment, and the empiricism of the scientific method are the legacy of all mankind; they cannot be ignored. The Japanese and Koreans, among others, have shown that they can be grafted onto older Asian thought and culture—or vice versa—without doing any damage to the local intellectual ecology.

It is a sign of our times that new Asian ideas and adaptations in business and the arts are being studied and followed by many Americans, as the Asian Industrial Revolution swings us back full circle. With this has come a healthy, if sudden appetite for traditional Asian culture, among at least some in this society.

Asian immigrants have been arriving in the United States in surging numbers. (More than 2.6 million came here in the eighties, comprising roughly one-third of U.S. immigration in that period.) By the 1990 census almost 10 percent of California's population was of Asian descent. A new element is being added to American culture—and not just in California. Cars, sushi bars, television sets, Buddhist philosophy, tai chi exercises, new Silicon Valley entrepreneurs, tennis rackets, video games, and financing for U.S. government bonds—all these come to us from across the Pacific, and become a part of the American lifestyle.

YET ON THE verge of the new Pacific century most Americans remain woefully ignorant of this strong and growing Pacific relationship, our own contribution to it, and the history behind it. Still prisoners of national self-sufficiency and Eurocentric education, we have barely begun to think of the Asian countries across the great ocean as neighbors, not curiosities. It is small wonder that the history of our Pacific interconnection has been characterized by appalling misconceptions, gross undervaluations, and needless wars. Our neighbors across the Pacific come from old cultures and confident traditions. We must begin to view them in context. Americans, for example, are generally all too aware of contemporary Japanese business successes. Yet few Americans even know the name of the Meiji Restoration, Japan's great self-modernization in the nineteenth century, which ranks as one of the modern world's five great revolutions; it remains indispensable background for understanding the dynamic of today's Japan.

This book has been written to examine and revalue the vital and increasingly close comity we share with the Asia-Pacific countries. It was first conceived as a companion piece to a ten-hour PBS television series. Although the book inevitably differs in scope and content from the films—if for no other reason than the nature of the media used—throughout its writing the producers and I shared our researches, impressions, and insights; the book is far richer for this collaboration. Both films and book bear the title *The Pacific Century*, because we believe that the next hundred years will demonstrate the truth of this statement. Judged from almost any angle, the American stake in this relationship can only increase. We are all actors on the same stage. We can no longer afford to be blinded by the shutters of race and cultural background, real or fancied, to the realities of our common destiny.

In his distinguished work on Mediterranean civilization, the French social historian Fernand Braudel wrote: "The Mediterranean has no unity but that created by the movements of men, the relationships they imply and the routes they follow."[1] Braudel's Mediterranean idea—with its sailing galleys, its Phoenician and Greek alphabets, and the religions of Christianity and Islam—took centuries to develop. In the world of the jet transport, the TV screen, and the semiconductor, the Pacific idea is by contrast coalescing suddenly, often explosively.

It has been my good fortune to have lived a good bit of the Pacific experience in my own lifetime. As a young Navy officer, I sailed west from San Francisco in early 1944, bound for first Pearl Harbor and thereafter duty as an intelligence officer in Peleliu, Okinawa, and the Occupation of Japan. I first visited Korea and the Southeast Asian countries in 1949 and 1950 as a news correspondent for *Time* magazine. (I flew to Seoul in June 1950 to cover my second Pacific war.) Since that day, as a journalist and part-time scholar, I have continued to study and visit the Asia-Pacific countries. For ten years during this time—from 1966 to 1976—I lived and worked in Japan as an editor and businessman for Encyclopaedia Britannica and its Asian affiliates. I continue to work and travel extensively in China, Korea, and Southeast Asia, as well as Japan and the United States.

In the chapters that follow, I have included some personal experiences and recollections. I have done so in the belief that the immediacy of personal experience may add something to the reader's understanding of people and events under discussion. They encompass a considerable time span, from talks

---

[1] A pioneering social historian, Braudel saw the Mediterranean civilization in terms of ecology, trade, and social mores as well as political events. His *The Mediterranean in the Age of Philip II* (New York: Collins, 1972), from which this passage is quoted, was followed by more ambitious writings on European and world civilization.

with Japan's Yoshida Shigeru and Vietnam's Ngo Dinh Diem in the fifties to interviews with Deng Xiaoping and Hu Yaobang in China in the eighties.

When we say "Pacific Basin" how much of the world are we talking about? A definable image would include, on the eastern shore of the ocean, the principal states of North America—Canada, the United States, and Mexico. On the western shore we have China, Japan, Russian Asia, Taiwan, Hong Kong and Macao, both South and North Korea, Indochina (Vietnam, Cambodia, and Laos included), and the ASEAN group—Indonesia, Malaysia, Singapore, Thailand, the Philippines, and Brunei. Australia, New Zealand, and the Pacific islands round out the list.

South American countries bordering the Pacific are not included, principally because their connection with the other Pacific nations has not been so close as the North Americans'. I am conscious of some injustice here, particularly in the case of Peru and Chile, as indeed I have worried over the relatively slight mention given to Australia, New Zealand, and the islands. This is, however, not an exercise in geography. Its treatment is thematic, as is the treatment of the television series that accompanies it. This is a book about relationships and interdependence in the Pacific region, most particularly about the relationships between my country, the United States, and the Asian countries on the other Pacific shore.

The book is also rooted in history, most particularly the history of the past 150 years. It was during this time that the interconnections between North America and East Asia developed. The history is one of conflict, challenge and response, featured by more than its share of misunderstanding and hostility. But this history we must learn. Without some knowledge of our immediate past, the present makes very little sense.

WE CAN GET a good feel for this recent history in the new international metropolises of the Pacific Basin, aggressive trading cities which, whatever their origins, increasingly belong to the region as a whole. There is something intrusive and raw about these great Pacific cities. They are a different sort from the grand metropolises of Europe. London, Paris, Rome, even faded Moscow are historic capitals that continue to do their venerable triple duty as traditional political centers, trading marts, and pieces of history. They have aged gracefully and on the whole gradually. They are old, but still serviceable and conscious of their traditional missions. They are above all European.

Not so Los Angeles, Seoul, Hong Kong, Sydney, Vancouver, and Singapore. They are new. Like the traders who built them up, they look outward—toward the ocean, the air lanes, the computer networks, and the fiber-optic cables. They are uncertain about tradition or culture. Even Tokyo, the archetypical Pacific metropolis, has managed to bury the past of old Edo under its canopy of cars and concrete. Even the new opera houses and cultural complexes seem a bit self-conscious in their surroundings, although their people can buy the best in pageants, paintings, or symphonies.

These are first and foremost business cities, dedicated to the pursuit of gain in its many forms and unashamedly pleased with the expanding lifestyles that come with heavy profits. The capitals of the Pacific takeoff, they serve as magnets to the people and goods of the hinterland, which is one reason for the almost universal spiraling of real estate prices to indecent levels.

The bulk of their trade and investments goes across the ocean that they face—east and west, north and south. And with the trade come the tides of people, hundreds of thousands of immigrants among them. The ubiquitous overseas Chinese—already dominant in the business communities of Southeast Asia—are now coming back to the hinterland that once exiled them. In Los Angeles's Koreatown or in Garden Grove, the suburban enclave of Vietnamese immigrants, you can walk for blocks without seeing anything but the street signs in English. Well-heeled Japanese businessmen buy condominiums to relax on Maui or in Newport Beach. Back home, despite long-standing restrictive fences against foreign immigration, a growing trickle of Asians comes in some-how to fill empty jobs in Japan's labor-short economy.

The transformation of these Pacific cities has taken place, explosively, over the past half century. When I first traveled to them, as a fledgling journalist in 1950, they had the look of asterisk items in a faded guidebook. Seoul was then, on the eve of the Korean War, a recently emancipated Japanese colonial city of 800,000, its most prominent landmarks the newly repossessed capitol build-ing and the bulb-towered headquarters of the old Bank of Chosun. Now, one war and twenty years of more than 6 percent annual GNP growth later, it is a forest of glass-and-steel high rises over an underbrush of gridlocked traffic. Its population of 10 million seems to increase hourly.

Singapore was a charming "picturesque" colonial city, with its tidy water-front buildings, the storied sprawl of the old Raffles Hotel, and cricket still played on the grassy *padang* near the Anglican cathedral. The *padang* is still there, but looking a bit like an environmental museum exhibit with the con-crete battlements of the huge new Raffles Center looming over it. Beyond it stretches an unending complex of gleaming office skyscrapers and lavish luxury hotels whose construction has almost obliterated the picturesque "world" amusement parks and colorful seamy streets that once constituted major tourist attractions.

Taipei, formerly Taihoku, was once another Japanese colonial town like Seoul. It is now metamorphosed in much the same way, its jumble of high-rise buildings, clogged highways, and air pollution a backhanded tribute to mod-ernization.

Only a few landmark office buildings and the moated Imperial Palace remain of the Tokyo where I lived then. They are now dwarfed by the revived glitter of Marunouchi's financial centers and the vast high-rise business palaces of Shinjuku and Ikebukuro on land once occupied by reservoirs and amusement centers.

Los Angeles has grown around and above its old precincts, in the process of turning itself from Hollywood Town into a world business center. With its swelling transoceanic air traffic and the largest harbor on the U.S. West Coast, Los Angeles has become America's major gateway to the Pacific. Heavy in the aerospace, refining, and electronics industries, the Los Angeles metropolitan area has become in recent years host to a complex of Japanese and other Asian banks and businesses. With its Asian population steadily on the increase, signs, advertisements, and TV programs in Chinese, Japanese, and Korean have become commonplace. All the Pacific peoples come here to trade and invest and drink in the heady drafts of the California culture. Seattle, smaller, has done the job more gracefully, but the city now shares the aspect of a Pacific metropolis.

Only San Francisco and Shanghai have kept their look of forty years ago relatively unchanged. But the Bay City too has its new monuments to modernity. In Shanghai it is a matter of time before the energy of the maritime Chinese breaks through the retaining wall of Confucian Communist restriction and makes the changes in mood, tempo, and appearance that have already happened to Canton (Guangzhou) in the south.

These bursting-at-the seams Pacific cities have a common denominator: in their present incarnation they have all come to prominence within the last 150 years. The cultures behind them may be properly ancient—Buddhism, Islam, and the Confucian ethic remain strong. So does the Christianity of the West. Seoul's and Manila's most abiding landmarks are the spires of Christian churches; Los Angeles itself, named after Our Lady Queen of Angels, is now the headquarters of the world's most flamboyant evangelists—Asian as well as American.

The Pacific civilization which these cities typify was hewed out over the past two centuries from the interaction—collision would be more apt—of East and West. Without the clash of ideas and armies, races and religions, traders, merchants, and mandarins in the past, there would be nothing even remotely resembling a community of economies and societies over the ocean that we might justly call a Pacific civilization today.

So it is with a look at this history that we begin our story.

1

The Seaborne Barbarians

It rolls the midmost waters of the world, the Indian Ocean and Atlantic being but its arms. The same waves wash the moles of the new-built California towns, but yesterday planted by the most recent race of men, and have the faded but still gorgeous skirts of Asiatic lands, older than Abraham; while all between float milky ways of coral isles and low-lying, endless, unknown Archipelagoes, and impenetrable Japans. Thus this mysterious divine Pacific zones the world's whole bulk about; makes all coasts bay to it; seems the tide-beating of the earth.

HERMAN MELVILLE

Let us examine the traditional geography of the Pacific Basin. A look at any map confirms the impression of a vast expanse of water, a trackless waste colored blue. There are scattered island dots in the middle and more west of the Hawaiian group. Turning farther westward, we see a chain of large islands bending south—Japan, Okinawa, Taiwan, the Philippines—masking the bays and capes of the Asian mainland. Farther south come the big and small patches of the Indonesian archipelago stretching east into the ocean.

Looking toward the distant eastern shore, past the midpoint of Hawaii, the North American coastline slopes off from the severed land bridge of Alaska and its mountainous island chains, backing away to the south along the receding coastline of California and Mexico, toward the twisted isthmus and the great canal. Still farther stretches the long coastline of South America, impossibly far away from New Zealand and the Australian continent that form the ocean's anchor on the far south and west.

The map does not exaggerate its distances. More than twice as large as the Atlantic, its huge undersea trenches almost seven miles deep, its currents, trade winds, and monsoons moving as relentlessly as the tides themselves, the Pacific—or Great Calm Sea, as the Chinese and Japanese call it—has historically mocked the image of serenity that Vasco Núñez de Balboa impulsively gave it when he "discovered" it in 1513. For centuries it has sustained its reputation as a daunting barrier, to be crossed only at one's peril, but at the same time an arena of challenge and adventure. For the sailor, perhaps, it epitomized what the naval historian Alfred Thayer Mahan called "a wide common, over which men may pass in all directions." But for the traveler embarking on the long months' voyage—the early Polynesian migrant, the Spanish missionary heading west from Acapulco on the Manila galleon, the Chinese laborer setting out from Xiamen east to find work in California goldfields or Hawaiian plantations, or for that matter the cruise-ship traveler of today—it has been a symbol of the Unknown or at best the exotic and remote. And the image of this traditional geography remains.

In contrast to the cultural successions of the Mediterranean—or even the impulsive journeyings of Vikings across the medieval Atlantic—the Pacific remained uncrossed by explorers or long-distance voyagers for long millennia. The cultures that grew up along its shores lived lives unto themselves. On the east there were only the Incas and the Mayas, farther inland, enjoying their brief periods of empire in isolation. Deep inland from the western shores the great seclusive civilizations of East Asia developed. But they fought their wars and built their cultures around the rivers or the islands offshore, notably incurious about taking to the open sea beyond.

Of these the greatest was, of course, China. Through more than four thousand years of recorded dynasties, built on the fortunes of warring kingdoms, the rulers of the Han peoples enjoyed the mandates of heaven, confident that their land was truly the world's center, where travelers and tributaries—"barbarians" all—would come to marvel. There was little incentive to go out and seek to pierce the Unknown. Even after the advent of Buddhism, which set out to be a universal faith, there was nothing in the leisurely travels of its scholarly emissaries to resemble the belligerent missionary zeal of the Christian or the Muslim. ,

South and west of China in the lush richness of the Mekong Basin, the Khmers built up their many-templed capital at Angkor, clusters of extraordinary monuments to ancestors and now forgotten gods, whose like will never be seen again. Here too was an inland stronghold—although Indic rather than Han in race—the center of warrior cults who battled for the land around them. Only the Srivijaya empire in the Indonesian archipelago looked seaward, from its port strongholds in Sumatra and Malaya, and dominated the trade with China that the contemporary Tang emperors disdained.

Even these seafarers stuck to their own islands or the north-south sea routes to China's and Vietnam's trading cities. About journeying into the great ocean on the east, they had little curiosity. Some Southeast Asians, driven by winds or circumstance, did sail eastward to people the islands of Polynesia and Melanesia. But where they landed, they stayed.

By the twelfth century Arab and Indian traders had long been sailing eastward with the favorable monsoons, to trade and pillage in the Southeast Asian archipelagoes they called "the lands below the winds." (A ninth-century Arab fleet had actually sailed north and sacked Canton.) They brought with them the teachings of Islam. When Marco Polo, in the course of his travels, stopped briefly at a town in northern Sumatra, he noted that the people there had been converted to the Muslim faith. It was then 1292. Within the centuries following more people on the coasts of Malaya and Indonesia accepted Islam, and traveling teachers took the word of Mohammed with them. But apparently there was no massive effort at conversion to Islam of the sort that took place in Africa, Europe, and the Middle East.

By the sixteenth century Muslim sultanates existed side by side with the older Hindu or Buddhist kingdoms. Elsewhere in what is now Malaysia and Indonesia some Chinese settlements had been established, dating from the Mongol dynasty's largely unsuccessful invasion attempts in the thirteenth century. But except for the short-lived Javanese empire of Madjapahit the sultanates and settlements were scattered, coexisting in relative peace. Japanese pirates fitfully harassed coastal shipping in the China Sea. But from China, the Middle Kingdom itself, the far-flung fleets and embassies so generally associated with empire were not forthcoming.

There was one remarkable exception. In seven great voyages, from 1405 to 1433, a Chinese admiral named Zheng He (Cheng Ho in the older Wade-Giles transliteration) led Chinese fleets south and west from the Celestial Kingdom. They voyaged systematically, stopping at Champa (what is now Vietnam) and Sumatra, then through the Strait of Malacca and into the Indian Ocean. They visited Bengal and Ceylon, going on as far west as Aden and the Strait of Hormuz before turning back to their home ports.

The scale of this undertaking was unprecedented in maritime history. Zheng's fleet numbered more than 300 vessels, with total crews of 28,000. The ships themselves were remarkable for that day, made the more seaworthy by watertight bulkheads and equipped with compasses and a variety of navigational aids long known to the Chinese. They even carried in their complement interpreters versed in local languages, for China had been trading with Indians and Arabs over past centuries.[1]

Zheng himself was a Muslim from the southern province of Yunnan and a

---

[1] For these insights on Zheng He's expedition I am indebted to Daniel Boorstin's *The Discoverers* (New York: Random House, 1983).

eunuch, a court favorite of the Ming Dynasty emperor Yong Le (Yung Lo). The object of his voyages was neither plunder nor military conquest. It was to impress people in far places with the power and glory of China's emperor, and to exact tribute from them. In a way they prefigured the "showing the flag" excursions of European and American navies centuries afterward. Thus they brought large quantities of presents with them, the better to persuade natives of the area to visit Beijing and acknowledge the world supremacy of the Middle Kingdom. They were peaceful, although one or two local potentates in Ceylon who objected to becoming Ming vassals were forcibly carted off to China. Zheng's only other concern, besides impressing the populations he met, was to gather interesting curios, local fauna, and other souvenirs for the emperor. (The giraffes he brought back to China proved to be particular imperial favorites.)

No people other than the Chinese would have sent such huge missions on this kind of errand. As the historian Daniel Boorstin writes: "The voyages became an institution in themselves, designed to display the splendor and power of the new Ming dynasty. And the voyages proved that ritualized and non-violent techniques of persuasion could extract tribute from remote states. The Chinese would not establish their own permanent bases within the tributary states, but instead hoped to make 'the whole world' into voluntary admirers of the one and only center of civilization."

Zheng's great voyages ended suddenly, shortly after the death of his emperor. With the maddening self-sufficiency that would remain their country's international trademark, the later Ming emperors totally reversed the policy of maritime expansion. On the advice of their Confucian mandarins, they decided that the country should henceforth live within itself. Zheng's fleets languished in their harbors, timbers rotting, as later emperors left seafaring to coastal traders and the inevitable pirates. (The admiral himself ended, as he began, as a court official.) "Fully equipped," Boorstin summarized, "with the technology, the intelligence and the national resources to become discoverers, the Chinese doomed themselves to be the discovered."

THE DISCOVERERS, as it turned out, were waiting in history's wings. In 1498, at the close of Zheng He's century, the Portuguese mariner Vasco da Gama made the first Western landing in India since Roman times, setting the seal on the Age of Exploration that would follow. By the first decade of the sixteenth century, European fleets were heading for East Asia in force, not only over the Indian Ocean but across the Pacific from the east.

These seaborne barbarians, as the Chinese would soon call them, operated from motives far different from Zheng's. They were bent on trade, exploration,

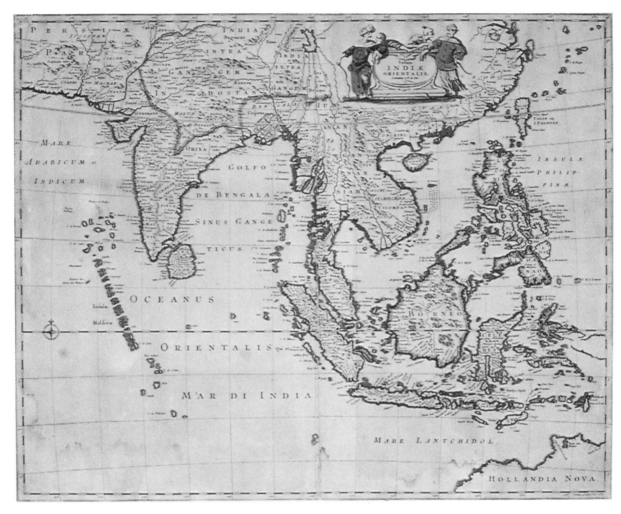

Sixteenth-century European map of the East Indies (Asia Orientalis). Gibney Collection

and conquest, in varying degrees. They wanted not tributaries, but money, goods, and power. Their own painfully acquired technology made them formidable. Besides compasses, charts, multiple masts and sails, they had developed the art of shipboard gunnery. The fruits of Renaissance discovery, their shipbuilding and navigation, if still primitive, had been aided by a century of exploration and warfare in the Atlantic and Mediterranean. With these militant explorers the man-made history of the Pacific began. For the next three hundred years the great ocean and most of its ports would belong to the Western seaman, the pirate or the trader who generally embodied a little bit of each.

Through most of the sixteenth century the Pacific itself was, as the eminent Australian geographer Oscar Spate has written, "a Spanish lake."[2] Having colonized Mexico, the Marianas, and the Philippines and built up their viceroyalties of silver, hemp, tobacco, and missionary cathedrals, the Castilian seafarers made the new Pacific sea lanes their own. In this they followed the example of their fellow Iberians, the Portuguese, who had come to Asia from the Indian Ocean on the west.

Well before the century ended they were joined by their more intrusive Northern European cousins, the Dutch and the British, with just a bit of French flavoring in the few fitful expeditions coming out from Brest. The Russians too, following the fur trade across Siberia, had begun to explore the waters off Kamchatka.

As we shall see, battles for trade supremacy and territory among the Europeans themselves became the order of the day. All of them were equally hostile to the Asian peoples in their path. The *mission civilisatrice* of that day—to use the well-worn French colonial phrase—was littered with chopped arms, severed noses, burned towns, and blown-up ships, as the European mariners extended their reach and temporary dominion over Asian and Pacific peoples. Among them were some truly great explorers, like Ferdinand Magellan, Abel Tasman, Vitus Bering, and the redoubtable Captain James Cook. But for most of them exploration was generally incidental to their main missions of trade and plunder.

Through those first three centuries of growing geographical knowledge—the Pacific coasts were not really adequately mapped until the late nineteenth century—the Asians on the western shores generally stayed at home. It is true that Malay seafarers and traders moved almost everywhere in Southeast Asian waters; Arab and Turkish fleets also occasionally journeyed eastward to support their Muslim co-religionists. From earliest times the north-south sea lanes

---

[2] *The Pacific Since Magellan* (Minneapolis: University of Minnesota Press, 1979, 1983, 1988), his monumental three-volume work, is an informative and most entertaining survey of Pacific geography and history through the age of exploration.

along Asia's coasts were well traveled. The first Europeans to attempt trading with China were harried by Japanese pirates, who were far-ranging and militarily quite effective. And even well-equipped Dutch warships on occasion found formidable maritime opponents in Asians like the Sino-Japanese pirate admiral Zheng Chenggong[3]—called Koxinga by the Europeans—who turned Taiwan into a private fief three hundred years before Chiang Kai-shek landed there.

There was, however, no national effort at exploration by the kingdoms of East Asia. China, the heart of Asia, remained self-centered and seclusive with a vengeance. Barely a century after Zheng He's voyages, the Ming emperors banned the construction of large ships and established the death penalty for would-be explorers to foreign parts.

This reluctance to venture eastward on the ocean cannot be attributed to scientific or technical backwardness. For all the development of European maritime technology, Asian mariners were by no means far behind them, either in long-distance seamanship or in maritime logistics. Zheng He's fleets were technologically ahead of the Europeans—who, of course, had never heard of him. In 1592, just four years after the repulse of the Spanish Armada in Europe, the heavily gunned and at least partly ironclad fleet of the Korean admiral Yi Sun-shin defeated the warships and transports of a Japanese invading army at Okpo, off Korea's southeastern coast, in a battle of far larger dimensions than the Armada's. (The 52,000 troops already landed in the first wave of the Japanese invasion were almost twice as many as the total of 31,000 Spanish soldiery who had been embarked in the Duke of Medina-Sidonia's troopships.)

The immediate reasons for Asia's self-imposed isolation were political. At different times during the seventeenth century both China and Japan had adopted seclusion as a national policy. Ming emperors and Japan's Tokugawa shoguns decided for a variety of reasons that they should shut off their people from further contact with a perceptively intrusive West. So had the monarchs of Korea's "Hermit Kingdom." Yet this tactical withdrawal was only part of a long-standing mind-set that had its origins in the dwarfing cultural and political superiority of China. That empire had dominated East Asia far longer than—to give an obvious example—Rome's preeminence over Europe and the Mediterranean. For Japan, Korea, and Vietnam, a well as other countries farther out on

---

[3] The son of a Chinese trader–pirate and a Japanese lady from the seaport island of Hirado, Zheng Chenggong was a skillful military leader who turned his father's possessions on Taiwan and the adjacent Fujian coast into a feudal satrapy. Loyal to the Ming Dynasty even after its overthrow by the Manchu Qing rulers in 1644, he several times invaded the mainland and fought off attempts by the Qing and their Dutch allies to dislodge him. Taiwan was finally overrun by the Manchu soldiery in 1683, after Koxinga's death.

the periphery, China embodied civilization and culture. Why look for any refinement or wisdom among the seaborne barbarians of the West?

There was another and more practical reason for China to look landward—one that a thirteenth-century caravan traveler like the Venetian Marco Polo could understand more readily than the sixteenth- and seventeenth-century European sailors who came after him. This was a matter of national or, more properly, civilizational security. From the earliest days of their empire, the Chinese fought a constant battle against nomadic invaders on their western and northern frontiers—much as imperial Rome had unceasingly fought the tribes pressing west and south on the far sides of the Rhine and Danube. These nomads, as they rode with their families and flocks in search of trade and pasturage, developed into the world's finest cavalry, as Europe discovered when Genghis Khan and the Mongols pushed their domains far to the west. For the Chinese, however, the tribes—Jurchen, Khitan, and above all the Mongols—presented an incessant problem.

Different dynasties had different solutions. The Tang emperors, who knew the nomads well, used a deft combination of military expeditions and tribute paying to keep the tribes at bay. Many, attracted by Chinese culture, accepted imperial rule. The Song rulers, more purely "Chinese," tended to retreat toward the security of the rich, agricultural south. But they fell to the Mongols, who under Genghis Khan's able grandson, Khublai, set up their capital at Beijing and became rather grandly Sinicized in the Yuan Dynasty.

Although the Mings later pushed the Mongols back into the steppes, their later emperors retreated under pressure of the northern and western tribes. The Great Wall of China, despite its earlier antecedents, was primarily a Ming artifact—a desperate attempt to hold back the continental barbarians by generals who no longer felt China's armies capable of defeating them in battle. When the Manchu armies rode down from the north in the seventeenth century, Beijing[4] was already a frontier city; the watchtowers of the Great Wall had long since been overrun.

Like the Mongols before them, the Manchus were conquered by the civilization whose armies they had destroyed. Their new Qing Dynasty, powerful

---

[4] For the purposes of consistency I have generally used the word Beijing when referring to China's ancient capital. Peking, while it occurs occasionally in quotations and comments, is merely an anglicized version of the original Chinese Beijing, which literally means "Northern Capital." It should be remembered, however, that at different periods in the city's history it was known by different names. During the Ming Dynasty, for example, the capital was shifted southward to Nanjing (Southern Capital) and Beijing was known as Beiping (meaning Northern Peace). Beiping remained the preferred term for the city under the rule of the Nationalists, whose capital was also situated at Nanjing. In 1949, however, after the Communists marched into the city, it was renamed Beijing and its status as the capital was confirmed.

Seventeenth-century Dutch fort. The Banda Islands in Indonesia became a stronghold of European explorers. Levie Isaacks

St. Paul's Church, Malacca
Noboru Komine/Pacific Press
Service

The Qianlong emperor. During his long reign (1736–99), the Ming ruler secured and expanded China's western frontiers but expressed little interest in British visitors to Beijing.
Encyclopedia of China

Old Peking. Gentlemen's grooming salon, as viewed by the Macartney Mission. Gibney Collection

Mongols on the march—film reenactment by Mongol Kino for the film Genghis Khan
Christopher Ralling

Chinese temple, Malacca
Ken Straiton/Pacific Press Service

and vigorous, secured the frontiers on the north and west and set out with the confidence of conquerors to enjoy their imperium. With the traditional invasion routes blocked, the Qing emperors and their Manchu bannermen settled down in the palaces of Beijing's Forbidden City and proceeded with considerable success to assimilate the Confucian culture and traditions of the Middle Kingdom.

To the Qing rulers, like the Chinese dynasts before them, the superiority and self-sufficiency of their realm seemed clear and beyond challenge. So the later Manchu emperor Qianlong explained in 1793 in his famous statement to the visiting British plenipotentiary Lord Macartney, who had come in search of trading concessions and normal European-style diplomatic relations. "Our celestial empire," he said, "possesses all things in abundance and wants for no product within its borders. There is, therefore, no need to import the manufactures of outside barbarians . . ."

In fact, the ancient capitals and temple cities of East Asia had never looked seaward. Changan, the present Xian, served as China's capital through various political incarnations for 2,000 years, reaching its great glory under the civilizing hand of the Tang emperors. It stands today where it always was, on the dusty Shaanxi flatland below the richly frescoed hill tombs of Tang princesses. Traditionally it looked westward, awaiting visitors from the caravan routes of the old Silk Road. It is 1,000 miles as the crow flies from the ocean. Old Beijing, which had succeeded Xian as the Ming and Manchu capital, lived within itself, now secure from traditional threats from the west and north. So did ancient Kyoto within its bowl of mountains and hills, its geometric network of broad boulevards modeled on those of Changan, secure and insular within monocultural Japan. Even the seafarers of the Indonesian islands found their spiritual focus in the lordly stone terraces of Borobudur, the Hindu-Buddhist monument of Java's ninth century, deep in the inland hills. There was no impulse to go out to meet the world in those traditions. The world was where they sat.

THIS TRADITIONAL smugness of the great Asian cultures only fed the desire of European explorers and traders to romanticize what they found on crossing the watery deserts of the Pacific or, as happened frequently, slipping from the Indian Ocean through the Strait of Malacca. It became embedded in the Western consciousness that the countries and people on the western shores of the Pacific were "exotic," remote, and, inevitably, "inscrutable." Strange races, incomprehensible languages, dark skins, slanted eyes, and infidel "pagans" to boot—these were people to be dealt with at arm's length, through compradors, interpreters, and, wherever necessary, the sword.

The Iberian explorers, firstcomers in the West's invasion, came to the East, as some of Vasco da Gama's companions tersely put it, "in search of spices and Christians." Throughout the sixteenth century they went after their dual objectives with tunnel-vision efficiency. The trade came rather easily. Eager to recover the storied Asian commerce in spices for Europe, they brushed aside the light craft of the Arab and Malay Muslim traders in a chain of sea fights dominated by their square-rigged and comparatively heavy-gunned vessels. In rapid succession they set up the fortified trading posts that would protect their buying and selling.

The Portuguese, led by their capable and farsighted admiral, Affonso d'Albuquerque, made their first land conquest when they occupied Goa on India's Malabar coast in 1510. They then moved on to capture the Malay and old Srivijayan port of Malacca the following year. In a speech to his men Albuquerque emphasized the crusading nature of their mission "in casting the Moors out of this country and quenching the fire of the sect of Mohammed so that it may never burst out again hereafter." He then added a thoughtful commercial consideration: ". . . if we take this trade of Malacca away from them Cairo and Mecca will be entirely ruined and Venice will receive no spiceries unless her merchants go and buy them in Portugal."[5]

IN THE DAYS of the seafaring explorers, Malacca, where the great monsoon winds meet, guarded the crossroads of Indian-Asian trade. It has long ceased to be a world trading port. Its once bustling river harbor is now a quiet stream. Land reclamation and accumulated silting have pushed some of the ancient waterfront streets back from the sea. Most of its maritime traffic is now coastal; the seaborne action has long been taken over by the huge tankers that pass through the strait almost hourly, on their way to and from Japan and its industrial motive power of Middle Eastern oil. But Malacca's old buildings and narrow, twisted streets remain as overlays of history—along with the descendants of the peoples who conquered and settled it in succession. It is one of those extraordinary living museums where the past is always available to revisit.

I first saw Malacca in 1950, before new roads and resort traffic made the car trip from Singapore something of a career. Some of the houses I visited then are now museums, but the aspect of the town has not changed much. The ruins of St. Paul's, the old Jesuit church, still stand on their hill near the last remaining gate of the old Portuguese fortress. The church was built in 1521, just a decade after Albuquerque's conquest. For a century and a half this was

[5] As quoted in K. M. Panikkar's *Asia and Western Dominance* (New York: John Day, 1958).

Portugal's stronghold, the midpoint for the fleets doing their work of trade and conquest between Goa across the Indian Ocean and Macao on the China coast. Albuquerque came to settle as well as destroy. After his troops defeated the local Malay sultan, he encouraged intermarriage with the local people; a Portuguese-speaking community remains to this day.

In 1641 the Dutch came to trade, shoot, and, as it turned out, to stay, at least for the next 150 years. Assisted by Atjehnese sailors from Sumatra—who had vainly attacked the Portuguese fort in the past—the Hollanders moved into the town, built their own town hall in 1650 and a new Reformed Christ Church with it, but with frugality overcoming dogmatic fastidiousness, buried their dead in the Portuguese churchyard. (I will never forget the clumsy weathered headstones with Dutch inscriptions carved on the opposite side from the original Portuguese.)

Early in the nineteenth century the British took over Malacca from the Dutch, making it one of the original Straits Settlements (with Penang and Singapore) that would later be folded into modern Singapore and Malaysia. But they were colonialists pure and simple and never put down roots. A classic comment from the old eleventh edition of the Encyclopaedia Britannica—"There is excellent snipe-shooting to be had in the vicinity of Malacca"—suggests the limitations of British interest.

It was the Chinese who came to stay for good. The interior decorations of the Cheng Hoon temple, built in 1645, were all painstakingly imported from the old country; to this day a wall plaque commemorates the visit of Admiral Zheng He to Malacca early in the fifteenth century. One of the admiral's duties, according to Chinese recollection, was to escort a Ming princess to Malacca for her marriage to the local Malay sultan. Since that time a sizable Chinese community has lived there, at the traditional heart of the so-called Straits Chinese population.

These "Baba Chinese" are the descendants of merchants who came originally from Fujian Province in the fourteenth and fifteenth centuries. The house of Tan Ching Lock, whom I visited in 1950, looked as if it had been transplanted from China. Yet his family and others like them had lived there, some of them for almost five hundred years, at peace with the Malay community but never a part of it. In the fifties Tan was the head of the Malayan Chinese Association, the social and political group representing the Chinese community in the new state of Malaysia. His son, Tan Siew Sin, later became head of the former British trading conglomerate Sime Darby and a powerful figure in Malaysian business and politics.

What still strikes the visitor to Malacca is the persistence with which the Chinese there have nurtured their distant heritage over the centuries, the while paying superficial respects to local religions and cultures. Much the same is true of overseas Chinese settlements throughout the Pacific area. Whether in Jakarta or Bangkok or Ho Chi Minh City (a.k.a. Saigon) their sense of cultural continuity has never dimmed. Nor has their business ability—as would-be Malay competitors can attest. Perhaps Zheng He's fleet, unlike the Portuguese and Dutch admirals, never needed to stay indefinitely in business. The Chinese traders and colonists did the job.

The Portuguese used their base at Malacca as a springboard for their trade and, on occasion, political aggrandizement in Pacific waters. By 1520 they had dispatched their first, albeit unsuccessful mission to the Ming court in Beijing. Finally, in 1557 the Chinese allowed them to establish a settlement at Macao (where they have remained to the present day). With logistical support from their older bases on the Indian coast, they ranged far and wide through what is now Indonesia, setting up strong outposts at Amboina and Macassar. As early as 1521 Malay sultans were complaining about Portuguese depredations to their nominal overlords in China. The *fidalgos* were rough traders, rarely averse to killing and looting when it served their purpose; but the profits of the Indies spice trade were good. In Lisbon the king and his courtiers were well pleased with the results. After all, they reasoned, the people they murdered were "heathen."

At making new Christians of these heathen they were, understandably, less successful. Although first Goa and then Macao were soon filled with ornate churches—funding a church in those days was a form of conscience money—sincere converts were few in number. Cannonading and pillaging were not very effective means of proselytizing. In India, it is true, Portuguese missionary efforts were favored by the presence of a large native Christian community, by tradition descended from the early preaching of St. Thomas the Apostle. But the work of effectively preaching the Christian gospel in China and Japan had to wait for the arrival of the Jesuits—Spanish, Italian, and Portuguese among them—later in the century.

The Jesuits, although of the same faith as Albuquerque and his bigoted chaplains, were a different breed. Determinedly intellectual, they were trained to be the polemicists and teachers of the Catholic Counter-Reformation in Europe. Their scholarship was formidable and rather broad-gauge. While rigid in doctrinal essentials, like everybody else in the sixteenth century, they tended to be flexible in their interpretation. In a sense mandarins themselves, they proved to be curiously well suited to the missionary work they now took up in Asia. The greatest of them was a priest named Matteo Ricci.

The offspring of an Italian noble family, Ricci joined the Society of Jesus in the late sixteenth century, just thirty years after Ignatius of Loyola had founded his order of learned (and militant) teachers. In 1582 he arrived at Macao, the Portuguese outpost on the fringe of China, to begin the study of Chinese. The following year he was allowed by the Chinese authorities to move to Guang-dong Province and afterward to Nanjing. In 1601, after years of patient travel and negotiation, he was permitted to reside in Beijing. He died there in 1610, at the age of fifty-eight.

Ricci was a man of prodigious energy, a rare combination of scholar, ac-tivist, and working saint. He gained a complete mastery of Chinese, wrote five books in that language, and earned the friendship of scholars and im-perial princes with a paradoxical blend of zeal and tolerance. In almost three decades of pastoral work in China, he built churches and gained hundreds of Christian converts, by example as much as doctrinal exposition. He attracted the Chinese intelligentsia by his wide knowledge of Renaissance science, mathematics, and geography. As he wrote in his *Journal:* "Whosoever may think that ethics, physics, and mathematics are not important in the work of the Church, is unacquainted with the taste of the Chinese, who are slow to take a salutary spiritual potion, unless it be seasoned with an intellectual flavoring."

Unlike the majority of his sanctimonious fellow Christians, Ricci perceived that the Chinese did a great many things better. "Though they have a well-equipped army and navy," he wrote, "that could easily conquer the neighboring nations, neither the King nor his people ever think of waging a war of con-quest. In this respect they are much different from the people of Europe, who are frequently discontented with their own governments and covetous of what others enjoy. While the nations of the West seem to be entirely consumed with the idea of supreme domination, they cannot even preserve what their ances-tors have bequeathed them, as the Chinese have done through a period of some thousands of years."

In years spent exchanging ideas with Confucian scholars—he dressed and talked like one—he developed a sneaking fondness for their ethic. "The ulti-mate purpose and the general intention of this sect, the Literati," he wrote, "is public peace and order in the kingdom. They likewise look toward the eco-nomic security of the family and the virtuous training of the individual. The precepts they formulate are quite in conformity with the light of conscience and with Christian truth."

The rationalist Chinese Literati,[6] in turn, liked and respected Father Ricci, even though his spiritual side made them a bit nervous. ("The superiority of the Western teaching," one scholar wrote, "lies in their calculations; their inferi-ority lies in their veneration of a Master of Heaven of a kind to upset men's

---

[6] Ricci used this Latinate term to indicate the Confucian scholars—the *jinshi (chin-shih),* literally "passed scholars"—who administered imperial China as an acknowledged mandarin class. Entry to the class could be gained only by passing severe examinations on the ancient classics.

Matteo Ricci with a Chinese associate, Li Paul. The Bettmann Archive

minds.")[7] He was, after all, a mandarin himself. After his death he was given a special burial place by the emperor, a rare privilege in the xenophobic Middle Kingdom. Far ahead of their own time, he and his fellow Jesuits had the wit to realize that preaching brotherhood in Asia had to rest on intellectual and social equality and interchange, not to mention mutual respect. The promise of a common future in heaven was not enough.

In 1549, St. Francis Xavier, Loyola's faithful lieutenant, had landed on the Japanese island of Kyushu to preach the gospel. He and the Jesuits who came after him were rather hospitably received, partly out of respect for their obvious sincerity and loyalty to their beliefs—two qualities more admired by the Japanese than most—but also because Oda Nobunaga, Japan's military dictator at that time, was engaged in what amounted to total warfare against the militant Buddhist clergy of that period, whose well-fortified monasteries were islands of secular as well as religious authority. To Oda and his courtiers these ascetic and determinedly otherworldly Christians looked like useful allies.

Often working hand in glove with Portuguese traders, the Jesuits attracted some highly placed converts because of the lucrative potential of a Portuguese connection. But their preaching also touched a vein of idealism and self-sacrifice in the Japanese spirit. Unlike the cross-and-sword missionaries who had accompanied the Spanish colonialists to the Philippines, the Jesuits in Japan, as in China, realized that they were dealing with highly sophisticated civilizations whose Buddhist and Confucian tradition could not be argued away by the Catholic equivalent of Bible thumping. So as prelude to their mission they studied a great deal. Their journals and reports on China and Japan remain valuable historical documents.

AT THE TIME another Italian of impressive intellect, Alessandro Valignano, was the superior of the Jesuits on the Japanese and the Chinese mission. Unlike the Spaniards in the Philippines—who scorned the idea of a native Malay clergy—Valignano insisted that the great hope of the Church in Asia was to ordain native priests and have them preach to their own people. It was in response to this that Ricci took up the study of Chinese. To appeal to the intellectual curiosity of the mandarinate, he and his fellow Jesuits taught them the latest learning of the Western Renaissance in mathematics, astronomy, and geography. With considerable subtlety, also, they endeavored to show that Confucian ethics and even ritual practices were by no means incompatible with a Christianity that, after all, was a universal, not merely a Western religion.

[7] As quoted in Jacques Gernet's *China and the Christian Impact* (New York: Cambridge University Press, 1985).

By the time he died, Ricci was a respected teacher among the Beijing mandarins. His Jesuit successors, Adam Schall von Bell and Ferdinand Verbiest, besides being allowed to preach their religion, were elevated to the highest orders of the mandarinate. By the beginning of the eighteenth century there were about 300,000 Christian converts in China, many of them members of the intelligentsia. In Japan, where the Jesuits had begun earlier, a similar number of Christians was estimated more than a half century before. As the great British historian of Asia, Sir George Sansom, wrote, speaking of China: "Had [Ricci's] successors been able to continue his policies, the Christian church in Japan might have been well established within another generation."

It was not to be. In Japan the obviously political activities of Spanish missionaries, newly arrived from Manila, cast a shadow over the work of the Jesuits before them, and fed the suspicions of Oda's successor, Hideyoshi, that Christian missions were merely a front for a possible Spanish invasion. A massive persecution of Christians began, on the eve of Japan's self-imposed isolation.

The work of Ricci and his Jesuit successors in accommodating Christianity to Chinese customs, already under attack by their critics, was ultimately condemned by the Vatican in 1742 after the celebrated "rites" controversy. The Chinese authorities, angered by this, needed little encouragement to proscribe Christian teaching in their turn. So ended the attempt of Matteo Ricci and his colleagues to reach the mind of Asia with the Christian message.[8] For all the impressive later missionary activity, Protestant and Catholic, of the nineteenth and twentieth centuries, the game had been lost 150 years before.

Ricci is buried in what is now Beijing. In 1986, in the course of a business trip there, I tried to find his grave. We located at last the graves of Ricci, Verbiest, and several other Jesuits—simple stone markers inside a fenced enclosure with a makeshift shed over it. The compound where we found the graves, ironically enough, was occupied by the Higher Party School for Communist cadres. The simple inscription on Ricci's grave read: "Li Ma Dou," in Chinese characters. Like other Westerners who had made their mark in China, he had been given the abiding honor of a Chinese name. No crosses, however, were visible, except those graven on the tombstones.

At the time none of the Party cadres who guided us knew who Li Ma Dou

---

[8] By contrast, the books written by Ricci and other Jesuits about their efforts in China were widely circulated in Europe. Voltaire, that professional freethinker, turned around the Jesuits' commentary to make the point that in China you had a highly cultured, rationalist civilization that did not need Christianity or any other organized religion. The German philosopher Gottfried von Leibnitz wrote his *Discourse on the Natural Theology of the Chinese* in support of Ricci's position and expended considerable effort to show that neo-Confucianism could be compatible with an ecumenical Christianity.

was. More recently, we were told that Beijing officials, noting the large numbers of Europeans to visit the graves, were contemplating construction of a small memorial park, with an eye on Christian elements in the hard-currency tourist trade. (In 1988 a friendly guide displayed an almost encyclopedic knowledge of Li Ma Dou and his fellow Jesuits as he showed us around the memorial.)

The Jesuits failed in their attempts to establish Christianity within the framework of the Confucian and feudalist-Confucian societies of China and Japan. They had realized, however, that if the Christian message was truly universal, it had to shed its carapace of conformity to Western European custom and institution and speak in the language of those spoken to. (Almost four centuries later most Westerners in Asia have yet to get this message.) At the same time, by preaching to China's mandarins and Japan's daimyo they tended to overlook the fact that Christianity's doctrine of universal brotherhood and individual free will was potentially subversive of Asian group-oriented societies.

Hideyoshi, the brilliant, if warped, despot of late-sixteenth-century Japan, summed up this problem very nicely in the letter he wrote to the Portuguese viceroy of the Indies in 1591. "Japan," he wrote, "is the realm of its native gods, the [Shinto] *kami* . . . the good order of the government which has been established here depends on the exact observance of the laws on which it is founded and whose authors are the *kami* themselves. They cannot be deviated from without involving the disappearance of the differences which ought to subsist between sovereign and subject, and of the subordination of wives to husbands, children to fathers, of vassals to lords and servants to their masters . . . The Fathers of the Society [Jesuits], as they are called, have come to these islands to teach another religion here . . . but this new law can only serve to introduce into Japan a diversity of cults prejudicial to the welfare of the state."

WHILE THE Jesuits conducted their dialogues in Kyoto and Beijing, their seafaring co-religionists from Portugal continued to build forts and factory complexes throughout the Indies. By the end of the century, however, armed trading fleets from the Netherlands were sailing into the Indies in force. The Dutch were better businessmen, on the whole, than the Portuguese, whose cumbersome state capitalism had a dampening effect on free enterprise. They also had more firepower, a puissant business consideration in that day. Under the banner of the highly profit-conscious United East India Company, the Dutch merchant-mariners concentrated their settlements in Southeast Asia. By the middle of the seventeenth century they had taken Malacca and other ports from the Portuguese and set up a chain of trading posts at key points in what is now Indonesia. The Dutch counterpart of Albuquerque was Jan Pieterszoon

Coen, a vigorous and appallingly aggressive governor-general. For all practical purposes he can be called the founder of Holland's East Indian empire, whose burgeoning trade in cloves, pepper, and nutmeg kept the shareholders in Amsterdam quite happy. In 1617, the same year he was confirmed as governor-general, Coen captured the old settlement of Jacatra from the local sultan and renamed it Batavia, after the old Latin name for the Netherlands. The following year he successively defeated first an English fleet, which had come to the city with the same idea as his, and then the Javanese troops of the sultan of Bantam. The name Batavia stuck; it would be almost three and a half centuries before a newly independent Indonesian government would change it back to Jakarta in 1950.

A rigidly pious Calvinist, Coen had the same contempt for Asians as the Catholic Portuguese, but unlike the Portuguese, Coen and his fellow Dutchmen had little patience for the work of Christianizing the local heathen. He had his own brand of certitude. (He once wrote: "There is nothing in the world that gives one a better right than power and force added to right.") He proved himself so brutal in his treatment of Javanese and Amboinans that even the hardheaded East India Company directors were moved to censure him. Before his death in 1627, however, he had sent one expedition to China and established a Dutch settlement on Taiwan, as a base for trade with China and Japan.

Both Coen and Albuquerque were colonizers and imperialists by nature. As Coen succinctly put it in one of his reports to the company directors in Amsterdam: "We cannot carry on trade without war nor war without trade." In their desire to establish settled (and militant) colonies of Europeans in Asia, they anticipated the nineteenth-century colonists. But neither man's country gave him much support. Albuquerque died in disgrace, unjustly accused of a palace intrigue. Coen was killed fighting the sultan of Mataram's army, after his directors had thrown cold water on his plans for granting special trading privileges to Dutch colonists.

Most of the Dutch and Portuguese, political leaders and merchants alike, were intent primarily on making money. Limited in manpower and resources, their directors in Amsterdam and Lisbon wanted to hold only enough settlements to safeguard the loading and processing of their cargoes. The Dutch in particular acted as single-minded predators. In Coen's tradition, succeeding proconsuls beggared whole populations in the interests of Amsterdam's profits. Throughout the once fertile Moluccas—the original Spice Islands—for example, Coen's successor as governor-general, Antonio Van Diemen, anxious to keep the company's monopoly, destroyed all clove trees outside the company's own plantations. He put down any resistance from the inhabitants with brutal force.

"The company made them change their clove gardens into rice fields and sago tree plantations," the Dutch historian Bernard Vlekke wrote. "The small mountainous islands could not produce food enough and the inhabitants were obliged to buy a supplement of rice from the company. It sold the commodity to them at too high a price, which made the situation still more desperate. Thus the economic system of the Moluccas was ruined and the population reduced to poverty."

THE SPANISH, for all their own greed for gold, were more territorialist than their Portuguese or Dutch contemporaries. With a colonizing zeal that, in sheer intensity, has never been equaled, they put down roots in the new worlds their explorers had discovered. By 1570, Spate tells us, there were an estimated 63,000 Europeans resident in New Spain, as the South American possessions were then called—including 18,000 in Mexico City, 25,000 in Lower Peru, and 7,000 in Upper Peru (now part of Bolivia).[9] By 1630 the total colonial population had more than doubled, and Mexico City's 48,000 equaled half the population of Madrid.

With increased populations came the churches and palaces that made Lima, Mexico City, Acapulco, and Panama mini-metropolises, while the British colonists in North America were still shivering within sight of Plymouth Rock. Craftsmen and manufacturers developed quickly in the service of the new urban centers, forced by the length and difficulties of the long voyages to Europe to become rapidly self-sufficient. And horses, sheep, and cattle imported from Europe, along with a wide variety of agricultural products, ultimately created a whole new world of ranch and farm wealth.

For the near term, however, the wealth came out of the ground, and in a profusion that even Cortes and Pizarro had not dreamed of. In 1545 the Spaniards discovered an extraordinary cone-shaped mountain in the Peruvian Andes rising more than 15,000 feet above sea level. Called Cerro Rico de Potosí, after an Indian word meaning "thunder," it was almost made of silver. Hundreds of mines were dug, to bring what at first seemed inexhaustible quantities of the precious ore out to the newly established processing centers.

Along with the already rich Mexican mines—and a fortuitously discovered source of mercury (for silver processing)—Potosí's silver dominated the world's monetary economy for the greater part of a century. It had a particularly wide influence in the Pacific. Since Roman times, China, which imported relatively little from the outside world, had been steadily siphoning off much of the West's bullion, in the form of gold and silver payments for its silks and porce-

[9] Spate, p. 179. I have relied on Spate's *The Spanish Lake* as the principal source for this portion.

lains, spices from the Indies, and other luxuries from Asia for which there was great European demand.

With Europe's Age of Exploration this demand only intensified. Both directly, on the transpacific galleons, and through the indirect offices of European bankers, roughly one-third of the silver mined in New Spain found its way to China, the "tomb of European moneys." Thus, centuries before the Age of Toyota and Sony, the first of many transpacific trade imbalances was born. So close was this economic connection that a mid-seventeenth-century recession in Europe had drastic inflationary effects on Ming China.[10] This did not, however, disturb the continuing trade imbalance in China's favor. It would only be rectified, rather unpleasantly, two centuries later when Chinese silver began to pay for the opium that European traders and gunboats brought to Canton.

With such wealth at their disposal Spain's rulers might have been able to establish a Pacific, if not a world monetary system four hundred years before anyone had ever heard of Bretton Woods. The Seville merchants who handled the bills and letters of credit at the nerve center of this Silver Standard were equal to the task, as were their backers in the financial centers of Italy and the Low Countries. Unfortunately, the dynasty was not. As Spate wrote: ". . . the returns, vast as they seemed for their day . . . were dissipated in the maelstrom of European politics." The silver coins themselves, however, had a long and rich life. Until well into the nineteenth century, the old Spanish "pieces of eight," later known as "dollars Mex," were the most common form of international currency used in China's port cities and other East Asian trading marts.

Apart from the follies of its rulers, Spain's colonial empire suffered from another mortal ill: the ruthless exploitation of the native populations. Labor for the mines, the fields, and the manufacturers was provided by Indians whom the Spaniards reduced to worse than serfdom. The spasmodic efforts of priests and religious in the colonies to better the natives' lot availed but little in that climate of political and economic greed. Worse yet, whole peoples were sickened and killed off by the spread of various communicable diseases that the Europeans had brought with them. It makes a cruel commentary on the Indians' treatment to note the efforts of the colonizers to import African slaves to supplement New Spain's dwindling labor supply.

Less obviously rich than the American colonies, but subject to the same intermittently profitable exploitation, was Spain's Asian outpost in the Philippines. Forty-one years after Spain's co-opted Portuguese explorer, Ferdinand

[10] This point is made not only in Braudel's great work, *The Mediterranean*, but also in Frederick Wakeman, Jr.'s *The Great Enterprise* (Berkeley: University of California Press, 1985).

The Levant *and the* Milo, *American ships anchored off the China coast. Smuggling boats may be seen in the foreground.* The Peabody Museum of Salem; photo by Mark Sexton

Magellan, landed on the island of Cebu in 1521,[11] a duly appointed Spanish viceroy from Mexico founded the city of Manila in 1565. Within the next decade Spanish troops had largely completed the conquest of the principal Philippine islands—they total 7,000—and begun a period of intensive colonization by soldiers, traders, and missionaries. The Dominican University of Santo Tomás, the first Western university in Asia, was founded in 1601 as an outpost of Hispanic learning. It was for Europeans only. Matteo Ricci's mandarin friends would not have been welcome.

Although the gold and spices which Magellan had promised the Habsburg emperor Charles V never materialized—as a royal consolation prize the islands were named after his son, Philip II—the Spanish colonists were able to work up a lucrative trade with the China mainland. At the juncture of the trade imbalance, they bought silks, damasks, porcelain, lacquerware, and pearls from visiting Chinese traders in return for silver shipped in from Mexico and Peru.

Manila grew into a sizable and rather impressive Spanish city on the proceeds of the round trips of the famed Manila galleon from Acapulco. Yet while most of the islanders were, broadly speaking, Christianized by the priests of Spanish religious orders, they continued to live on a bare subsistence economy of rice and fish until the late eighteenth century. By that time the development of cash crops like sugar, tobacco, and hemp finally brought a wider form of economic prosperity for the leisure-loving Spanish planters, if not for most of the native Filipinos who tilled their fields.

IN CURIOUSLY similar isolation from the rest of the world, the Dutch over the years developed their own colonial empire in Java, Sumatra, and other islands of *their* East Indies. Preferring to rule through local sultans, wherever possible, the Dutch fortuitously discovered the coffee trade, after some bold spirits had successfully transplanted coffee trees from southern India. Characteristically they made coffee a monopoly of the East India Company. Through most of the eighteenth century this new source of wealth more than made up for the falling revenues of the spice trade and inter-Asian commerce. Like the Spaniards in Manila and Potosí, they kept their tidily profitable empire to themselves.

---

[11] Fernão de Magalhães, to give his Portuguese name, had emigrated to Spain in 1517, at the age of thirty-seven, after an active career as a soldier and sometime explorer—he captained a ship in Albuquerque's invasion of Malacca. He sailed from Spain in 1518 and, after a heroic voyage around South America, first navigating the strait that now bears his name, entered the Pacific two years later. After a stopover on the island of Guam, he arrived in the Philippines and claimed them for the king of Spain. He was killed on Mactan Island in a fight with local Malay warriors and thus missed his surviving ship's triumphant return to Spain a year later, after making the first circumnavigation of the globe.

There was another East India Company at work in Asia during the seventeenth and eighteenth centuries, which we have yet to mention: the British. For most of this period the British concentrated on securing their commercial and, ultimately, political empire in India—the purpose for which the company had been founded. The efforts of Robert Clive, Warren Hastings, and others to frustrate the equally imperial designs of the French and the local Indian rulers, although a fascinating history, are not part of our Pacific story. But, like the Dutch and the Portuguese, the British early sought to expand their trading into the Pacific.

In 1580, Sir Francis Drake returned to his home port in Plymouth after almost three years at sea. Following roughly in Magellan's wake, he had sailed around the world on a voyage that combined exploration with what charitable historians called "freebooting"—in actual fact, a form of free-lance seaborne assault and battery. Before claiming a portion of the California coast (New Albion) for Queen Elizabeth—he apparently just missed San Francisco Bay—Drake had plundered some £600,000 worth of silver from a variety of Spanish ships. The amount he turned over to the queen equaled more than a year's tax revenue in those days. No less an authority than John Maynard Keynes was moved to comment: "The booty brought back by Drake may fairly be considered the fountain and origin of British foreign investment. Elizabeth paid out of the proceeds the whole of her foreign debt and invested a part of the balance in the Levant Company; largely out of the profits of the Levant Company was formed the East India Company, the profits of which during the seventeenth and eighteenth centuries were the main foundations of England's foreign connections . . ."[12]

The British East India Company was founded in 1600. By 1685, following earlier trading successes in India, the company's merchants had established a British "factory" at Canton and a second trading post down the coast at Ningbo. Before the eighteenth century was very old, British naval ships had effectively gained control of the China seas, displacing all their rivals. During the Napoleonic Wars, when the Netherlands itself was occupied by French troops, the British East India Company temporarily took control of the settlements established by its Dutch namesake in Sumatra and Java. It was at that point that a young Englishman emerged as the temporary civil governor of the occupation forces in Java. He went on to become, quite possibly, the most justly famous figure in the history of colonialism. He was certainly the best of the lot.

[12] From A Treatise on Money, as quoted by Spate and others.

2

The Merchant
Imperialists

*Great Britain owes it to herself and the civilized world to knock a little
reason into this besotted people and teach them to treat strangers with a
common decency.*

CAPTAIN WARREN DELANO, AMERICAN CHINA TRADER

Thomas Stamford Raffles first sailed into the Pacific two centuries after
Matteo Ricci's death in China. But he had the same determined, quest-
ing spirit; and he shared Ricci's respect for the cultures they found on the far
side of the Pacific. Both men differed sharply from others of their era in that
they tried to meet Asia and Asians at least somewhat on their own terms. Each
was the product of his time in a Europe obsessed with its own values and
verities. Yet each was gifted with the prescience to think of the world as one.

Ricci, a Renaissance man if there ever was one, looked toward a world of
multicultured Christianity, its peoples united by faith rather than nationality.
By contrast, Raffles came out of the European Enlightenment, with all the
Enlightenment faith in progress based on human reason. A self-taught scholar
of considerable ability, particularly in the natural sciences, he also spent much
time in studying both the Chinese and the Malay peoples. Like Ricci, he
regarded Asian civilization as equal to the European—a concept far more
shocking to nineteenth-century European nation-statists than it had been to
their forebears a century or two before. He saw the British colonies as latter-day
multicultural democracies. As such, he was a striking exception to colonial

37

European map of Japan, 1595. Gibney Collection

Jesuit memorial in Beijing. The tombstone monuments of Matteo Ricci and other Jesuit missionaries have become a tourist attraction in modern Beijing. Encyclopedia of China

Stamford Raffles, still a good name in Singapore
Singapore Promotion Board

Lin Zexu, China's antiopium czar
The Museum of the Revolution, Peking

Rev. Peter Parker, America's first medical missionary, who set up his practice in Hong Kong. The Peabody Museum of Salem

bigotry against Asians, which lay for centuries like a thick crust of sailor's dirt over the Pacific meetings of East and West.

Raffles, fittingly enough, was born at sea, his mother having accompanied his sea captain father on a homeward-bound trip from Jamaica. He went to work for the East India Company in London at the age of fourteen to help support his then widowed mother and his siblings at home. A hard worker and a prodigious reader, with a well-developed instinct for learning and power, he did well at his clerkship and was sent out to Penang, Britain's first outpost on the Malay Peninsula, in 1805 as secretary to the local colonial presidency. He was then twenty-three.

The Napoleonic Wars were at their height, and the French, having conquered the Netherlands, were attacking British commerce from their base in Java. Impressed by Raffles's useful research on the peoples of Malaya, Lord Minto, then governor-general of India, took him along on his staff for the British expedition against the French and their Dutch allies on Java in 1811. When Minto sailed away, he left Raffles behind in Batavia as the company's (and Britain's) lieutenant governor.

Raffles was a colonist and builder rather than a merchant predator. In this respect he belonged to the tradition of Albuquerque and Coen. He was free, however, from the blind intolerance and cruelty that had scarred their activities. On the contrary, he showed a great interest in the welfare of Britain's new Indonesian subjects as well as in their history and tradition. (His five-volume *History of Java* remains a classic.)

He attempted a sweeping reform of the existing Dutch colonial administration, going so far as attempting to establish trial by jury in the courts—a heroic gesture in view of past Dutch colonizing practices! But his advanced economic ideas failed to produce the quick profits demanded by the company's cost accountants in London. He was replaced after five years. Later, in the post-Napoleonic settlements, Java was returned to the Dutch.

Never one to accept defeat, Raffles sailed back to London, got himself a knighthood for his political and scholarly successes, and ultimately talked king and company into giving him another try, this time at setting up a permanent base for British trading and commerce in the neighborhood of the strategic Malacca Strait. Early in 1819 his six-ship squadron dropped anchor in the harbor of Singapore. It was then only a small Malay settlement named Temasek, living in the shadow of Malacca to the north. Raffles was fascinated, however, by ancient chronicles celebrating the fame of Singapura, the "lion city," as a center of Southeast Asian culture. It was in fact probably a small Malay tributary of the old Srivijaya empire, just as Malacca had once been.

Sir Stamford mapped out a new kind of Asian port city, in the best tradition of the European Enlightenment. A man of tremendous energies and wide tastes—he planned the design of Singapore's streets with the same detailed concern that he lavished on its administrative and legal systems—he saw the new island city as a beacon for free trade (England was then still stoutly protectionist). There, he reasoned, merchants of all nations would be safe to do business under the protection of sound laws and a benign government. He abolished slavery, then widespread throughout the area, restricted prostitution, gambling, and other vices, and set up a uniform code of justice, albeit informally administered. Almost unique among Westerners of his time in his appreciation of Asian cultures, he had a Confucian zeal for education. He hoped to make his island a center for "the moral and intellectual improvement of the Archipelago and the surrounding countries" and in particular a study center for Chinese and Malayan literature, which he felt were being debased by the Arabs, the Dutch, and the "robber religion" of Islam.

Raffles's last years were by no means happy ones. Three out of his four children died before him, and he expired of a brain tumor at the age of forty-five. Misunderstandings and various personal quarrels, some of his own making, caused him great pain. But as he wrote in 1823, the year he last left Singapore: "I have had everything to new-mould from first to last—to introduce a system of energy, purity and encouragement . . . to look for a century or two beforehand and provide for what Singapore may one day become."[1]

Raffles's settlement was an instant success—an idea, as a modern Singapore advertising man might say, whose time had come. Merchants of all nations— Chinese, Malays, Englishmen, other Europeans—flocked to the first protected trading mart and clearinghouse that the area had known. With trade and security came prosperity, a tribute not only to Raffles's vision but also to his early assistants, two sturdy British administrators named William Farquhar and John Crawfurd.

Over the years the noble and egalitarian part of Raffles's vision was lost sight of. Singapore's British colonial rulers gradually transformed themselves into a club lounge full of Colonel Blimps. Indeed, the colony's swift capture by General Yamashita in 1942, when fast-moving Japanese infantry columns overwhelmed the numerically superior but badly prepared British defenders, was an ironic monument to a century's lack of political and social foresight by Singapore's business-minded colonial managers. Yet the magic of Raffles's name lingers on. Whereas other imported colonial leaders of East Asia have long since been pulled from their pedestals, often quite literally, Stamford Raffles's bronze statue still dominates Empress Place in the waterfront heart of one of the modern world's great trading, manufacturing, and financial city-states. It is his town.

[1] As quoted in C. Mary Turnbull's *A History of Singapore* (New York: Oxford University Press, 1985).

* * *

RAFFLES'S VISION of an educated multiracial society in the colony, however, suffered much the same fate as Ricci's hopes for the conversion of Confucian China. For as the nineteenth century progressed, a new kind of Western colonialism lay siege to Asia, to replace the slapdash efforts of military explorers and their East India companies. The objectives of this European assault, its purposefulness and its intensity, reflected two great changes that Europe had undergone since the Age of Exploration.

The first was economic. The success of the Industrial Revolution, especially in Britain, had brought forth new factories with an increasing variety of manufactures to sell. Europe's new capitalists needed more markets. The countries of Asia, China in particular, seemed ideal for the purpose—if only they could be fully "opened" to European goods. Backed by the Pax Anglicana of Royal Navy supremacy on the seas, with the age of steam in the offing, British traders wanted to expand.

Cosmopolitan British consumers, meanwhile, had developed a huge appetite for tea and other Chinese goods. Yet only a trickle of their manufactures was allowed into China through the sole authorized trading port of Canton. Something had to be done to correct the growing imbalance.

The other big change was political. After Napoleon's defeat and their continent's remapping, Europe's nation-states were taking more or less permanent shape. Whether democracies or monarchies—in Britain's case, a good bit of both—the new polities were different in structure and aspirations from the old dynastic kingdoms that had preceded them. As part of the nationalist mystique, the nineteenth-century Europeans thirsted after empire. And expansion overseas at the expense of "lesser breeds outside the law" was far easier and less dangerous than attempts to change the military balance of power on the home continent. Intolerant and arrogant toward "Asiatics" the Europeans remained. But now they were organized nationalist predators, rather than the individual, company, or dynastic freebooters of past centuries.

With this new political imperialism came a movement, at once altruistic and patronizing, to bring the benefits of European civilization to the world. This conspicuously included the preaching of the Christian religion. A new generation of Christian missionaries—this time mostly Protestant—began planning how best to export their confident faith.

Along with these two changes came an important revision in the old Western cast of characters. The United States of America was becoming a new Pacific trading power—and very conscious of the fact. Yankee sailors had been active in the Pacific trade since 1784, when *The Empress of China* dropped anchor off Canton. A Pacific Squadron of the American Navy had existed since

1822. By the early 1800s American whalers were wintering at Lahaina Roads in the Hawaiian Islands.

A brisk and profitable commercial traffic quickly grew up between New England and the China coast. Elias "King" Derby, from Massachusetts's old seaport Salem, who died in 1799, was only the first American to make his million in the China trade. Soon Yankee firms like Perkins and Russell were crowding into what had once been a cozy British monopoly. In the trading season of 1833–34, for example, some 70 American ships put in at Canton, compared with 101 vessels of British or Indian registry, with considerably lesser numbers from other European countries.[2] These men were acquisitive and single-minded. As the Massachusetts merchant Robert Bennet Forbes once observed: "I had not come to China for health or pleasure, and I should remain at my post as long as I could sell a yard of goods or buy a pound of tea."

All three of these new factors came into play in 1840, when Britain fought the infamous Opium War with China. The British victory in that war began the semi-colonization of China. Although it brought a new colony (Hong Kong) under the Crown and provided a profitable future to numerous British (and American) traders, it cast a long and troubling shadow over the whole Pacific relationship. It is worth recalling in some detail. The memory is both pertinent and painful in an age when international drug trafficking has become a fact of our lives.

IN 1834 THE British government had abolished the East India Company's long-standing monopoly of the China trade. Coming soon after its Dutch counterpart was dissolved in 1798, the end of the British company makes a good milestone for the beginnings of European nationalist imperialism. For the successful eighteenth-century trading companies—what Braudel called "the multinationals of that age"—could no longer function as world commercial arbiters in the new era of international power politics.

The end of monopoly gave rise to a no-holds-barred competition among British and American merchants, almost all of them concentrating on the lucrative opium trade. The increased sale of this harmful narcotic to China resulted from an early East-West trade imbalance. European and American merchants, always eager to import from China, could get high prices at home for what were largely regarded as luxury products. But the textiles and other manufactures they had to sell were not much in demand among the Chinese, who had goods enough of their own. Thus the British and Americans had to

---

[2] As noted in Samuel Eliot Morison's *The Maritime History of Massachusetts* (Boston: Houghton Mifflin, 1961).

pay out good hard currency for the silks, tea, and chinaware they imported. This represented quite a cash drain. To solve the problem, British traders had to find some commodity which the Chinese wanted. Opium was the answer.

The supply was almost unlimited. Thanks to India's heavy manufacture of the drug, the old East India warehouses in Patna were bulging with freshly made cakes of opium. So British merchants cannily worked up a triangular traffic selling Indian opium to the Chinese. The Americans, not to be outdone, started up their own opium production in Turkey to supplement their dwindling supply of export furs from the Pacific Northwest, until then their principal export item to China.

By the 1830s, Jardine Mattheson Company of London, the creation of two shrewd Scots traders, was already doing a big business in importing Indian opium into China. It mattered not that the sale of opium was illegal in China, where the harmful effects of the drug were well known. "If the trade is ever legalized, it will cease to be profitable from that time," a company circular admonished. "The more difficulties that attend it, the better."

The opium was bought and distributed by Chinese merchant guilds in Canton. Although licensed by the imperial court in Beijing to deal with the foreigners in normal trading, these hong business houses were only too happy to join the opium traffic. Like the drug syndicates of our own century, they and their foreign partners had the money to pay for the illicit commerce. Everyone from venal government officials to semi-pirate boat crews shared in the almost inexhaustible take. Cargoes of the drug were unloaded at island way stations near Canton, then taken by fast boat into the city, to be sold all over China.

The benefits of this new trade were widely distributed in the young American cities, as well as in Manchester and London. While housewives in Boston and New York filled their mantelpieces and china closets with prized items of chinoiserie, New England sea captains rounded the Horn and sailed the Pacific with their lethal cargoes. The best families were involved. Peabodys, Russells, Forbeses, Lows, and Delanos all happily shared in the take. One of the leading opium profiteers, in fact, was Warren Delano—in other respects a God-fearing Christian. The grandfather of Franklin Delano Roosevelt, he was a leading figure in the American firm of Russell and Company. "I do not pretend to justify the prosecution of the opium trade from a moral and philanthropic point of view," he once said, "but as a merchant I insist that it has been a fair, honorable and legitimate trade . . . Besides, all the best people did it."

Only one of the Canton American traders refused to ship opium, the New York firm of Olyphant & Co. The Olyphant house was contemptuously called "Zion's Corner" by the others for its corporate fastidiousness. Few others in the foreign community shared Olyphant's scruples. One missionary, who earned extra money interpreting for the opium traders, was wont to throw out shipments of newly translated Chinese Bibles from one side of a ship while the drug was being unloaded on the other.

Although the opium vice was hardly unknown to the Chinese, the huge imports funneled through the foreign trading factories in Canton (and elsewhere through local smugglers) were causing profound dislocations in Chinese society. In addition the hard cash in silver paid for the opium created a serious economic problem. Faced with a drug abuse crisis on a national scale, the emperor Daoguang's councillors in Beijing argued whether to ban opium altogether or to regulate the sale of Chinese opium only, thereby freezing out the foreign traders—in a manner which strikingly foreshadowed the quandaries of the Reagan and Bush administrations in the United States 150 years later.

In the end the emperor appointed his own trade commissioner, a nineteenth-century version of a drug czar, in the person of a respected member of the mandarinate named Lin Zexu. A competent official in the Confucian tradition, Lin began with a campaign—just 150 years before Nancy Reagan's "Just say no" PR efforts—to educate people about the harmful effects of drug taking. Arrests were made, corrupt officials removed, and vast stores of opium confiscated.

Commissioner Lin then turned his attention to the traffickers—the Chinese trading companies that bought and distributed the "foreign mud," as the local circumlocution went, and their international suppliers. The Chinese distributors he shut down. He then went so far as to blockade the foreigners in their "factory" quarter in 1839. Faced finally with force majeure, the suppliers—mostly British—agreed to the confiscation of 20,000 chests of opium, almost a year's supply of their leading import. Lin ordered it dissolved in river trenches. "The foreigners," he summarized, "do not dare show any disrespect. Indeed, I should judge from their attitudes that they have the decency to feel ashamed."

He sadly overrated the consciences of the merchant imperialists. After angry protests by the affected merchants reached London, Lin's action was regarded as an affront to Empire. Captain Charles Eliot, the British official now in charge of the China trade, was empowered to move against the Chinese and avenge this presumed interference with the queen's authority. A fleet of sixteen warships was sent to assist him, with 4,000 troops abroad.

After capturing the island of Zhoushan and blockading the northern port of Tianjin, Eliot agreed to accept an indemnity from the Chinese and annex the almost deserted island of Hong Kong, whose port potential he appreciated.

But this was not enough for London. Britain's aggressive Foreign Secretary, Lord Palmerston, ordered further military action. The Chinese were helpless before the heavy firepower of the British. In 1841 a reinforced British squadron moved up the coast, its armed steamships sailing up the Yangtze to the junction of the Grand Canal, historically the key to China's inland trade. The Chinese were ultimately forced to sign the Treaty of Nanjing, by which the cession of

Opium factory, Patna, India, showing the stocking room where opium was packed and readied for shipment from the warehouses of the East India Company. The Illustrated London News Picture Library

Opium users, late nineteenth century. The Peabody Museum of Salem

*House of Augustine Heard &
Co., Macao.* The Peabody Museum
of Salem; photo by Mark Sexton

Canton Harbor
The Peabody Museum of Salem;
photo by Mark Sexton

*Napha (Naha) from the sea.
Perry stopped over at the capital
of Okinawa, then a tributary
kingdom, on his way to Japan.*
The Perry Expedition

Hong Kong was confirmed, among other things. (Palmerston, no one-worlder, dismissed this forthcoming jewel in London's colonial crown as nothing but a few "barren rocks.") Of equal significance, Shanghai (already captured by the British) and four other seaports (Canton, Fuzhou, Ningbo, and Xiamen) were opened to free residence and commercial use by British traders. Additional indemnities were stipulated.

Nothing was said in the treaty about opium; but the traders met with no further interference. Lin Zexu was sent to China's northwest provinces in exile, his antidrug campaign ended with the overwhelming triumph of the nineteenth century's "international drug cartel."

We can still hear Commissioner Lin's indignant voice echoing down the corridors of history. In his famous letter to Queen Victoria (which the British authorities did not deliver), Lin had denounced "a class of evil foreigner that makes opium and brings it to sale, tempting fools to destroy themselves merely to reap profit." He continued: "This poisonous article is manufactured in places subject to your rule . . . What is here forbidden to consume, your dependencies should be forbidden to manufacture."

Only a very few Englishmen agreed with him. One of them was a young Tory politician named William Ewart Gladstone. In a speech in Parliament the later Prime Minister denounced his merchants and his government for what they did. "[The Chinese] gave you notice," he said, "to abandon your contraband trade. When they found you would not do so, they had the right to drive you from their coasts . . . Justice, in my opinion, is with them. And whilst they, the Pagans, the semi-civilized barbarians have it on their side, we the enlightened and civilized Christians are pursuing objects at variance both with justice and with religion. A war more calculated in its progress to cover this country with permanent disgrace I do not know, and have not heard of."

In the vote that followed, Gladstone lost. Thereafter the spoliation of China by the Western powers began. France and the United States quickly signed similar treaties with the Qing court, to protect *their* rights, now that the British had opened the swinging door. Other European nations followed. In the face of growing antiforeign feeling among Chinese, their seizure of a British-registered ship, the *Arrow*, prompted an Anglo-French expedition to capture Canton in 1857. In 1860 a similar invasion force captured Beijing, forcing the emperor to flee.

At the time China was also in the throes of domestic turmoil. The wild Taiping Rebellion—an extraordinary movement of popular protest against the Qing Dynasty's rule—had begun its bloody course in 1851. Thus the Qing court had no choice but to grant the concessions that the Westerners demanded. The Western traders had themselves almost a captive market, while China was forbidden the right of protective tariffs. Fortified by the new principle of extraterritoriality, amounting to foreign-ruled enclaves in the Chinese port cities,

Western colonialism became a harsh fact of life in China, and in the life of those cities it enforced virtual caste distinctions between "Europeans" and Chinese.

The seaborne barbarians' attack from the coast had taken the Chinese court completely by surprise. Traditionally trouble on the frontier had meant land raids or invasions by hordes of nomad cavalry from the grasslands and steppes in the west and north. The Qings had themselves ridden southward from Manchuria to capture Beijing. Now, in the first half of the nineteenth century, China's policy on the western frontiers had proved a great success. The empire's armies had driven back the once feared Mongols, made tributaries out of the warlike Muslim emirates on the western marches, and served as protectors of a sort to Tibet against possible incursions by the British in India. They had checked even the southward movement of the Russians from Siberia, although a good trade was conducted over the borders—the Russians were as fond of tea as the British.

Helped by the Qing power, a continual stream of Han Chinese immigrants had poured into Mongolia and Xinjiang. More than at any time in the past, these vast lands to the west were being integrated in China. Thus, facing its traditional danger zones, the empire had never seemed more secure.

At first, therefore, the occasional trouble caused by Western traders and warships in coastal waters had seemed mere pinpricks to the mandarins in Beijing's Forbidden City. The Chinese had no comprehension whatsoever of seapower and the firepower that now went with it. The great maritime exploits of their own Admiral Zheng He were forgotten, buried in old chronicles. Even when the British Navy's guns leveled their forts and cities, the mandarins remained untroubled. Ships, they reasoned, would always sail away.

With only a few intellectuals' voices raised in favor of modernization, China's information about the West had been, to put it mildly, cloudy. As the Opium War began, as sophisticated a Confucianist as Lin Zexu could assure the emperor that the English, in the unlikely event they might land from their warships, were poor fighters on land. "Besides guns," he wrote, "the barbarian soldiers do not know how to use fists or swords. Also their legs are firmly bound with cloth and consequently it is extremely inconvenient for them to stretch . . . what is called their power can be controlled without difficulty."[3]

THE SUBJUGATION of China, Asia's ancient Rome, by Western military technology was repeated in areas around its periphery. Korea escaped a similar fate largely because of its remoteness. (Two small naval expeditions, one Amer-

[3] As quoted in *The Cambridge History of China*, Vol. 10.

ican and the other French, mounted punitive actions against Korea's west coast; their relative lack of success only served to harden the antiforeign isolationism of Korea's mandarinate.) Japan, as we shall see, took drastic action on its own. Thailand began a process of self-modernization in the 1860s—about the same time as Japan's—under the guidance of two shrewd Buddhist monarchs, Mongkut and his son Chulalongkorn. Not the least reason for Thailand's continued independence was its kings' success at playing off rival British and French colonialists against each other.

Vietnam, however, was ripe for the taking. French warships destroyed a Vietnamese squadron off Tourane, on the south coast, in 1857; they had sailed there to rescue an endangered missionary bishop. In the following year a landing party took possession of Saigon. Thereafter, in a series of slow bites, *la mission civilisatrice* was extended to the territories of Annam, Cochin, and Tonkin, all the peoples therein ultimately to be lumped under the convenient name of Indochina.

In Indonesia the Dutch had originally been content to rule indirectly, by controlling a hodgepodge of semi-independent sultanates. Gradually, however, as their plantation system spread, Batavia began to unify local administration, especially on the crowded island of Java. Quite the opposite of Raffles in their thinking, the Dutch authorities did almost nothing to educate the inhabitants of their island colonies. Islam began to fill the void. Just as the Japanese received most of their basic education in the Tokugawa era through local *terakoya*, "temple schools" as they were called, what primary education most Indonesians received came from Islamic teachers at the village mosques. In this way, as an ironic comment on Dutch colonialism, Islam spread far faster through Indonesia than it might have, gradually assimilating much of the local Hindu-Buddhist culture in the process.

In 1835, Prince Diponegoro, son of the sultan of Jogjakarta, declared a "holy war" against Holland in the best Muslim tradition, after the Dutch had ignored his claims to succeed his father. The Java War that resulted lasted five years and took more than 200,000 lives, most of them from starvation and disease. Diponegoro, a skillful guerrilla fighter, was finally overcome and sent into exile—to become a hero of the Indonesian resistance a century later.

Financially drained both by war in the colony and by the revolt of Belgium against Dutch rule, the Netherlanders adopted a new policy of Forced Cultivation, to squeeze the maximum return from their holdings. Villagers unable to pay the land rent would have to work part-time for the government, either in the fields or in the factories where cash crops were processed. Profits soared. Between 1831 and 1877 the Indies contributed an average of 18 million guilders a year—almost one-third of the Netherlands' budget.[4]

---

[4] As cited in Leslie Palmier's *Indonesia* (Walker, 1966).

On taking over direct administration of the East Indies from the now corrupt East India Company, the government had succinctly explained its policy: "The doctrines of liberty and equality cannot be transferred to or applied to the East Indian possessions of the State so long as the security of these possessions depends on the existing and necessary state of subordination" (that is, of the Indonesians).[5]

Jan Coen would surely have approved, although his language was less nicely phrased. "May not a man in Europe," he had written two centuries before, "do what he likes with his cattle? Even so does the master here to do with his men, for everywhere these and all that belong to them are as much the property of the master as are brute beasts in the Netherlands."

Understandably many Indonesians emigrated to Singapore, where conditions were immeasurably better. Raffles's city enjoyed a growing prosperity, and as colonies went, it offered good education opportunities to its multiracial population, at least at the primary school level. In 1867, after a half century under the Indian government, Singapore became a Crown Colony. Business grew better and better. The overseas Chinese businessmen in Malacca prospered, considerably safer than many of their relatives at home.

China itself remained the prey of the imperialist Europeans. When the combined Anglo-French expedition defeated the imperial army and occupied Beijing in 1860, the invaders committed a final act of arrogance. In what one might call Lord Macartney's revenge, they methodically burned the emperor's summer palace. Although the Taiping Rebellion was finally put down in 1864, the Manchu emperors were no longer able to resist foreign demands for unrestricted trade and, in the treaty ports, extraterritoriality.

Shanghai's famous International Settlement was only one of the foreign enclaves imposed on the Chinese. From the north the Russians now began moving into Manchuria. Later uprisings, notably the Boxer Rebellion (1898–1900) only provoked further Western reaction and the imposition of ever more indemnities and controls.

AMERICANS WOULD be the last of the Western colonialists to enter the Pacific. Reluctant imperialists, in a sense, they remained of two minds about the whole idea. On the one hand, several generations of American expansionists thoroughly believed in the idea of Manifest Destiny, first enunciated by a journalist named John O'Sullivan in 1845. This was, as he put it, a destiny "to overspread the continent allotted by Providence for the free development of our yearly multiplying millions." Yet throughout this expansive era many still felt that taking over someone else's rights or territory went against basic American principles.

[5] As quoted by K. M. Panikkar in *Asia and Western Dominance.*

Commodore Matthew C. Perry paying his farewell
visit to the Imperial Commissioners at Simoda
(Shimoda). *The Perry Expedition*

Warren Delano, Franklin D. Roosevelt's grandfather, was one of the early American China
traders. Here he appears in the center of a family picture at his eightieth birthday party, with
the young FDR (in sailor suit) on the right. The Estate of Frederic D. Grant, courtesy of Frederic D.
Grant, Jr., Executor

For most of the nineteenth century the expansionists had things their way. Even for good Christians the providential note in Manifest Destiny nicely fit into what was still a largely Calvinist religious tradition. This assumed that, irrespective of opium trafficking, high-pressure salesmanship, and the odd bit of gunboat diplomacy, the Deity remained firmly on the side of the United States.

At the same time the gospel had to be preached. Missionaries began their voyages across the Pacific in step with the merchants and the whalers. In 1820 a group of Congregational missionaries, fresh out of Boston, landed in Honolulu; only a few years afterward the Reverend Peter Parker, M.D., opened hospitals for the "natives" at Canton and Macao.

The victories of the Mexican War, an out-and-out adventure in imperialism, would have seemed to justify the faith of Manifest Destiny's true believers. In addition to Texas and the Southwest, the Treaty of Guadalupe Hidalgo in 1848 ceded all of California to the Americans. Just eight days before, in one of history's memorable coincidences, gold had been discovered at Sutter's Mill. The rush was on. The following year some 40,000 eager amateur miners arrived in San Francisco by sea, with 40,000 more traveling overland in wagon trains. Before the gold rush petered out in the mid-fifties, some $2 billion worth of the precious metal had been extracted from California's once virgin soil.

Apart from enriching many—most of them purveyors of various services to the miners—the gold rush and the maritime traffic around the Horn and into the Pacific made the entire country aware for the first time of its Pacific future. Americans in the mass were coming into contact with Chinese, Malays, Polynesians, and the other peoples of the Pacific Basin.

The New England and New York merchants of the early China trade and the sailors who served them were relatively few in number. The "devils of the flowery flag," as the Canton merchants familiarly called them, had not the slightest intention of putting down roots in China, where they lived a drab and sequestered, if comfortable existence confined to the foreign traders' quarter. Even the legendary John P. Cushing, Russell and Company's Canton agent, stayed in China only as long as it took to make his fortune. He finally retired to his Belmont estate outside of Boston in 1830, as the historian Samuel Morison tells us, "attended by a retinue of Chinese servants."

By midcentury, however, there was a substantial American colony in Honolulu, with a variety of shops, taverns, and inns catering to the considerable numbers of merchants, sailors, and whaling men visiting what many Americans still called the harbor of "Owhyhee." In 1844 some 400 whalers visited the islands. The missionaries built their churches there, brought more ministerial recruits from the mainland, converted many of the local Hawaiians, and did their best to counter the hedonistic impulses of whalers and traders.

More merchants came to use Hawaiian ports as bases for a trade that extended from China to Manila (for sugar and hemp) and Sumatra (for pepper and cloves), bringing manufactured goods from the American East Coast as well as hides from California, which had replaced furs from the Northwest as an export staple.

With business expanding and ever more competitive, a ship's speedy turn-around time meant money. To meet this pressure New England designers developed the clipper ship. With its sleek hull and expanded sail area, the clipper could beat normal sailing times by more than a third. Some could make from 17 to 20 knots with the right winds. The far-ranging clippers helped build a new mystique of the Pacific in the American mind. Its laureates were Herman Melville, who dramatized its ideals and conflicts in books like *Moby Dick* and *Typee,* and the more prosaic Richard Henry Dana (*Two Years Before the Mast*), who in the 1850s could salute San Francisco—two decades before only a village—"its wharves and harbor, with their thousand-ton clipper ships, more in number than London or Liverpool sheltered that day, itself one of the capitals of the American republic and the sole emporium of a new world, the awakened Pacific."

With trade thus expanded and colonies perhaps in the offing, the U.S. government decided to make its own overtures for a Pacific "opening." A treaty with China had already been signed, following Britain's lead. There remained the problem of Japan. The Shogun's government there had not been hospitable to American sailors shipwrecked on Japanese shores. Whaling ships were par-ticularly active in northeastern Pacific waters off Japan, and whaling had be-come an important American industry. In addition, the age of steam had begun. One of its by-products was a new demand for coaling stations for the Pacific trade.

By 1851 American plans for a Japan expedition had crystalized. No less a personage than the Massachusetts orator Daniel Webster, then serving as Sec-retary of State, drew up the basic instructions. Coaling facilities particularly interested him and he knew where coal was to be had. "A gift of Providence," as he phrased it, "[was] deposited by the Creator of all things in the depths of the Japanese islands for the benefit of the human family." All the government needed was someone to convey this sentiment to the coalfields' owners.

After considerable searching Washington found its man. It was a rare case of serendipity. When Matthew Calbraith Perry got his orders to command the East India Squadron in Asian waters, he was fifty-seven years old with a dis-tinguished naval career already behind him. He came from a Navy family. His father, Christopher, had been one of the first to command a ship in the new Continental Navy. His older brother, Oliver Hazard Perry, had won the de-cisive battle of Lake Erie over the British in the War of 1812; Matthew had served as a midshipman aboard his brother's ship. A rather large, bearlike man—he was known in the Navy with semi-affection as "Old Bruin"—Matthew Perry had served with distinction as commodore of the Gulf Squadron during the Mexican War. Later he became commodore (the American Navy had no admirals until Civil War times) of the Africa Squadron, watching for slave traders off the West African coast. Apart from the coveted leadership of the Mediterranean Squadron, which he never got, he had served ashore and afloat in almost all of the small Navy's commands.

He was far from being a conventional sailor, however. One of the first advocates of steam over sail, he had personally supervised the construction and commissioning of the USS *Fulton,* America's first steam warship, in 1837. He was called "the father of the steam navy." He instituted an engineering officers' corps for the new steam age. Dissatisfied with the slapdash system of midshipmen's on-the-job training, he spent years lobbying for a U.S. Naval Academy (finally established in 1845). Far ahead of his time in his concern over health and sanitation, he set new standards for nutrition and health care aboard ship (although he opposed the abolition of flogging as a shipboard punishment).[6]

Although highly conventional in his social views and behavior as a vested member of New York's Wasp ascendancy, he was a man of deep humanitarian instincts, with a talent for getting along with unfamiliar peoples, as had been borne out by his experience as an improvised diplomat in Europe, Mexico, and Africa. In his sailing directions for the Japan mission (which he may have had a hand in drafting) it was noted that the American commander "should be courteous and conciliatory, but at the same time firm and decided. He will therefore submit with patience and forbearance to acts of discourtesy to which he may be subjected by a people whose usages it will not do to test by our standard of propriety . . . [yet he will] do everything to impress them with a just sense of the power and greatness of this country."

The instructions went on prophetically: "Recent events—the navigation of the ocean by steam, the acquisition and settlement by this country of vast territory on the Pacific, the discovery of gold in that region, the rapid communication across the isthmus which separates the two oceans—have practically brought the countries of the East in closer proximity to our own; although the consequences of these events have scarcely begun to be felt, the intercourse between them has already greatly increased and no limits can be assigned to its future extension."

Old Bruin, whose nickname correctly conveyed a classic "bluff but kindly" image, was no Matteo Ricci with his soaring desire to convert the Asians on their own terms. Nor was he an Enlightenment colonial proconsul like Sir

[6] I am indebted to Morison's excellent biography of Perry, *Old Bruin* (Boston: Little, Brown, 1967), for much of this material.

Stamford Raffles. (Perry's foreign territorial ambitions were limited to naval bases.) He did represent, at its best, a purely American idea of international statesmanship. Perry's ideals may have been flawed by an entrenched Anglo-Saxon Protestant cosmology and an excess of frontier optimism, yet these were sources of strength as well. They surely represented an advance over the old European colonial order. There was in Perry the same instinct for teaching democracy, for sharing the benefits of the American experience—so manifest to him—that later generations of Japanese would encounter in the person of another old-fashioned American military man named Douglas MacArthur. There was also a good bit of imperiousness, a keen sense of theater, and the pomposity that some people acquire for the habit of command. In so many ways, the commodore and the general were the same man.

A Postscript on the Colonial Experience

From the vantage point of almost half a century later it is almost impossible to re-create the old European colonial mind-set in Asia, even for the purposes of explication. Modern humankind at the close of the twentieth century certainly has its quota of racial oppressions, religious intolerances, and social inequalities, but they are more or less on the run. And the rule of one political class or clique over another—whether apartheid racists, Khomeini theocrats, or New Class Communist apparatchiks—is fast fading. But in the world that ended somewhere between 1939 and 1945 this was not the case.

I had a glimpse of that old colonial world, at least as it was lived in the Asia-Pacific region, in the middle and late forties, shortly before it was forever closed down. It was a world of people called Europeans and people called Asiatics. If a self-proclaimed bastion of Western culture, dedicated to the preservation of classic "Western" standards, it was also at heart a crude and cruel world of color, with the whites on top and apparently running things. We were all some variety of imperialist then, Americans as well as Europeans—for those were the days when Hawaii was as much the white man's colony as Singapore or Batavia and the only job a black or a Filipino American could get in the U.S. Navy was that of a messboy.

Nor were the self-styled egalitarians of Communism much different. When they "went East," they were as much Russian as their tsarist forebears. (I remember walking onto the courts at the Tokyo Lawn Tennis Club in 1946 to play doubles with two Japanese members. "Ah," said Captain Smirnov, my Soviet partner, "now it's the whites against the others.")

Dinner given to the Japanese commissioners on board the USS Powhatan. *The Perry Expedition*

It was an accepted article of faith that "European" institutions were simply superior. Be it law, engineering, table manners, or—above all—religion, "we" had the Truth. The "lesser breeds outside the law," as Kipling not so ironically put it, might be acclaimed for special virtues or the beauties of moldering monuments. It was Frenchmen who rediscovered and preserved the temples of Angkor Wat, and the vocal admiration of British colonials for the sturdy Malays and other Muslims always made me suspect some secret fascination for Islam buried deep within the Church of Englander's mind-set. But to the simplistic "European" the other races were inferiors. And that was that. The tensions of E. M. Forster's *A Passage to India*, racial though they were, seem mild compared with the ironbound prejudices of the average colonial administrator. George Orwell's *Burmese Days* gives a good picture.

Colonial clubland epitomized the gulf between the automatically elite colonials and the various native or "subject" populations. The whited sepulchers of the old European watering places mostly remain, in various stages of preservation. The Palladian columns of Shanghai's French Club were first turned into a new International Club and then a high-rise hotel by enterprising tourist attractors in the People's Republic of China, while the storied long bar of the Shanghai Club on the Bund has long since been covered by various furnishings of the seamen's hostel into which the club was converted. The graceful façade of the old Harmonie Club in Batavia, where the Dutch administrators of the Indies used to play billiards and drink their *genever,* now fronts a half-used warehouse on a street in modern Jakarta. Others have survived under new auspices. The tennis and squash courts of the Tanglin Club in Singapore, once a rigidly segregated "whites only" enclave, are now the playground of Singapore's multiracial elite, who have cheerfully assimilated the old British club traditions, rather like the Egyptian clientele of the Gezirah Sporting Club in Cairo. Other establishments of the sort have similarly adapted to change. But the memory of that colonial era dies hard.

World War II, of course, shattered the myth of European superiority for good. The sight of British, French, Dutch, and American soldiers, sick and starving, being kicked and beaten by the temporarily victorious Japanese in the streets of Singapore, Hong Kong, and Jakarta was enough to end all that nineteenth-century thinking. As the British historian C. M. Turnbull wrote, commenting on the war's end in her *A History of Singapore:* "The only ultimate justification for a colonial power was its ability to protect and in this the British colonial regime had been tried and found wanting."

Of course, the Japanese wartime reputation was far worse. While proclaiming their idea of "Asia for the Asiatics" and soliciting cooperation in a new antiwhite brotherhood, the proconsuls of the Greater East Asia Co-Prosperity Sphere displayed an extraordinary combination of casual cruelty and administrative ineptness, not to mention a totally selfish attitude of Japan First. This has not been forgotten. If they were the last of the colonialists in Asia, the Japanese were far from the best.

Before dismissing the carriers of the "White Man's Burden" as unrelievedly bad, however, two points must be made in their favor. They left behind them a growing interest in democratic institutions—and the individual values on which they were based—however flawed they worked these out in colonial practice. At the same time all the colonialists—Japanese conspicuously included—made a beginning at economic and social modernization in their fiefs. They put in place at least some of the structures on which all the later modernizations of the Asia-Pacific nations developed. For sharing at least some of their homeland institutions and values, credit belongs to the missionaries, the teachers, and in some cases the colonial political administrators. For the second area of modernization we must give at least one cheer for the Western traders and merchants—and the foundations of free-enterprise business and modern technology that they created.

To begin with the merchants. They were certainly not altruists. In profiting so greedily from the opium trade that they initiated, the British and Americans, as we have seen, were little better than the Colombian cocaine cartels of our day. But they were also the inheritors of Europe's Industrial Revolution, which gained momentum as the nineteenth century deepened. Increasingly their interest turned to manufactures. In their characteristically self-centered Europeanism, they saw the East as a vast market for the textile factories and ultimately the steel mills that were going up in Europe and America.

Selling a mix of commodities, however, was a more complex business than trading opium for silks and silver with the old Canton hongs. For manufactured goods they needed modern ships and docking facilities and local transportation. The ships had to be bunkered and repaired. Money could no longer simply change hands. Banks were needed, and with them some form of insurance for protecting the merchandise they financed. As the British political economist G. C. Allen has noted,[7] "Western merchants were drawn also into [local] manufacturing industry . . . because supplies of merchandise of the right quality were not forthcoming unless the merchants made provision for the inspection of materials and the processing of the goods for export."

The next steps involved construction of large factories, railways, and a whole system of international concessions and settlements to channel and protect their investments. The need for local workers and functionaries led to a certain development of education, or at least worker training. All of which

[7] In his *Japan's Economic Policy* (London: Macmillan, 1980).

had to be done against the entrenched opposition of an ineffectual, but stub-born local bureaucracy.

Allen was writing specifically about China, but what he said would hold for most of the other coastal areas of the Asia-Pacific countries, including those like Indonesia and Vietnam where the European colonial administrators had the backing of political and military force. Unpalatable though their tactics were, the Western merchants and their political and military protectors were forcing on Asians the modernization that would otherwise have taken an extra century to effect. In Korea and Taiwan, Japanese colonialists did much the same thing. All of the colonialists ran a hard school and treated their pupils like backward second-class citizens. But the lessons they taught took.

The legacy of the missionaries and the teachers is more difficult to place, particularly when seen in a contemporary perspective. To the modern academic mind, generally areligious if not aggressively secular, the Bible-toting clergy-men who came "out East" in the nineteenth and early twentieth centuries represented a kind of spiritual bounty hunter, their progress measured by the numbers they converted, as they destroyed local cultures in the name of Christ. To many critics the "social gospel" trappings of modernization—medical care, the teaching of reading and mathematics, and instruction in simple technical skills—were simply efforts to build up ever bigger numbers of "rice Christians" to impress cost-conscious mission boards in the United States. Far from mixing with their local flocks, it is argued, the missionaries and their families lived apart, in the same comfortable world as the other "Europeans."

There was some truth to such charges, but a lot of mistaken oversimplifi-cation as well. While some of the missionaries did lead the soft colonial life in the port cities of Asia, the greater number of them lived with the people they had come to Christianize. Priest, nuns, and ministers shared the life of the farming villages and the poorer quarters of the increasingly industrialized cities. Despite their hard work and obvious sincerity, the number of actual converts they made were few. Except for the Philippines, Korea, and parts of Vietnam, where there was a comparatively wide popular acceptance of Christianity, the Victorian-era missionaries and their successors remained largely outsiders, un-able to penetrate the Confucian societies of East Asia the way the sixteenth- and seventeenth-century Jesuits had almost succeeded in China and Japan.

Their influence on people's ways of life, however, was appreciable. Whether through Catholicism—especially strong in Vietnam and the Philippines—or Protestantism as vigorously preached in Korea and parts of China, something of Western culture managed to make its mark. Among the intelligentsia of Asian-Pacific countries—many of whom attended college at "mission schools"—the idea of individual responsibility, the supremacy of the individual conscience, and the superiority of the rule of law to either government caprice or Confucian connections exercised a powerful appeal. Even the inherited Christian sense of time—as a measurable span between Christ's birth and the anticipated final judgment—represented something novel, part of the mind-set that had produced the new machines that were changing history. To learn even a crude form of Christianity is to learn a great deal about Western culture—and vice versa. So in a sense the preachers of the social gospel were right to link belief in the Resurrection to the understanding of Western technology. The machines by themselves made little sense without some feeling for the culture of which they were a by-product.

This cultural connection puzzled many in Asia, particularly during the nineteenth-century heyday of European colonialism. Indeed, the eighteenth-century Western philosophy of the Enlightenment was far more congenial to the practical mind of Asians seeking both truth and improvement. But that too depended much on the Greek, the Roman, and the Christian thinkers who had gone before it.

Which is where the teachers come in. From Stamford Raffles's first grand design of a teaching institution for his new city of Singapore, the transplanted schools of the West in Asia represented the good and the useful part of a Western imperialism and colonialism that in other ways showed itself to be so rapacious and exploitative.

The great majority of these schools and colleges were founded on Christian effort—although with some outstanding secular exceptions like the Rockefeller benefactions in China. Through the twentieth century, they educated generations of young Asians in the learning and ways of the West, pausing en route to learn a good bit about the East themselves. Yanjing in Beijing, St. John's in Shanghai, Doshisha in Kyoto, and Rikkyo (St. Paul's) in Tokyo were the Protestant teachers of Communists, freethinkers, Buddhists, and Christians alike—and most relied on America, not Europe, for both funding and intellectual inspiration. Sophia in Tokyo—by the late twentieth century one of Japan's premier universities—commemorates the enterprise of the Catholic Jesuits, as does Sogang in Seoul and the Ateneo de Manila in the Philippines. Also in Seoul is Yonsei, possibly the most impressive of all the "mission schools," its international faculty and 40,000 students a monument to Horace Underwood, the pioneer Presbyterian missionary who founded it as a small school for Christian converts in 1915.

The Christian teachings did not take deep root. But they were studied throughout the Asia-Pacific nations. They offered insight, as well, into the new technology of the West and Western ideas of law and government, which were studied most intensively.

*   *   *

IF THESE IDEAS were attractive, they were also complex. As the body of Western learning, as it was called, became more accessible to East Asians, it became clear that the artifacts and inventions of the West's Industrial Revolution could not be learned without some study of the culture that created them. This was not, as some of the enlightened Qing mandarins had thought, merely a case of combining Western mechanical skill with superior Eastern culture and civilization. Western culture itself had to be studied, dealt with, and—where need be—adapted, if Asia's own Industrial Revolution were to be realized.

Of all the Asia-Pacific nations, only one was able to accomplish this, and it did so swiftly, dramatically, and almost on its own terms. Which is the story of the next chapter.

3

The Meiji Revolution: Asia's Response to the West

Knowledge shall be sought throughout the world so as to strengthen the foundations of imperial rule.

EMPEROR MEIJI, FROM THE CHARTER OATH OF 1868

Like a bow tautly strung, the islands of Japan stretched athwart the northeast of Asia.[1] Steep with mountains, thick with forests, and thin of soil, they were watered by swift-running rivers and covered by a fretting of overworked fields. In terms of traditional geography—before its fundamental alterations by modern technology—they bore the same relation to their continent as the British Isles did to Europe. A bit out of the way, easy to reach but very difficult to invade, the Japanese islanders, like their British counterparts, liked to keep the kings and armies of the continent at a safe arm's length.

By the second century A.D. they had emerged as a recognizable society. They called themselves the people of Yamato. From the early mists of nationhood they developed a mythos of uniqueness, with the islander's sense of nervous exclusivity. Their first contacts with the Korean mainland nearest them were in the form of private raids. The already overcivilized Chinese (whom the Japa-

---

[1] These words and some of the thoughts in the following paragraphs are borrowed from my first book, *Five Gentlemen of Japan* (New York: Farrar, Straus and Young, 1953; Rutland, Vt.: Charles E. Tuttle, 1973).

nese also raided, on occasion) patronizingly called them the "dwarf people."

Where the Japanese came from remains a matter of conjecture. Many undoubtedly crossed over from Korea. (Structurally, the Japanese and Korean languages bear a striking resemblance.) Other progenitors, it is believed, had migrated from southern China and some, perhaps, from the Asia-Pacific islands. No one who has visited the Grand Shrine of Izumo, with its crossed roof beams and raised platforms, can lightly dismiss this presumed proto-Malay inheritance. In any case, they entered Japan from the south. Over the years, as they pushed back the indigenous Caucasoid aborigines—the noble white man of their folklore, one might say—they developed a tight island ethos, with its own gods, creation myths, and self-centeredness. They thought themselves to be a God-favored country.

Like the ancient Britons, however, they borrowed their civilization from the adjacent continent. From Korea they imported a written language, in Chinese characters, and the beginnings of a court culture. From China and Korea came the teachings of Confucius and the Buddha, which supplemented—although they did not replace—the native animism of Shinto. By the eighth century the Japanese emperors presided over a sophisticated society of poets, priests, and scholar-warriors, modeled on that of Tang China.

In the space of one hundred years, from 645 to 745, they had adopted for themselves a new religion, a new notion of ethics, new theories of government and administration, and a system of organized laws. They also imported refined arts of painting and sculpture and a fast-developing literature to go with their recently adopted written language. The success of this colossal mass borrowing has few parallels in world history.

The remarkable thing about the age of the "Great Change," the name the Japanese gave to the beginnings of their massive importation, was their rare facility for controlling their acquisitions. Having imported the civilization of Tang China, they slowly and smoothly rejected some of it, took some of it within their own culture, and changed other parts out of all recognition. A more speculative people might have failed to do so. But here, for the first time, the historian could watch the adaptive genius of the Japanese. Facing new ideas and institutions, they judged all things only by their two instinctive questions: "How well does it work?" and "How good is it for us?"

The idea of a Confucian bureaucracy, for one thing, had to compromise with the inherited feudalism of the Yamato clan society. Unlike the rest of Asia, they had no vast areas to be irrigated and controlled perforce by central authority. The narrow valleys and plains of this mountain country, although first ruled by hereditary court nobility, in the end became the holdings of local barons and their vassals, who quarreled continually.

Only the emperor in Kyoto was by definition above the battle. Unlike in

China, where dynasties could be removed when they had lost the mandate of heaven, the Japanese imperial line was thought to be a living link with heaven itself, too important to sever. The emperors emerged more pontiffs than kings, however. Most of their ruling was done for them by military surrogates, the shoguns, who in time created family dynasties of their own.

Until the early nineteenth century, the Japanese lived by themselves on their islands, relatively untroubled by the storms of invasion and conquest that broke over the Asian continent to the west and south. China remained their great cultural treasury, the same role Rome played to the blue-painted British of early times. But China for Japan was Rome, Greece, and Christianity together. Which is to say, it gave the Japanese religion, arts, language, and a sense of laws. Not particularly anxious to force their self-sufficient culture on others, the Chinese served as a nearby cultural emporium, condescending to loan or sell its goods to those who came for them. So to a great extent did their Korean neighbors.

Japan's arts and literature were largely adaptive, but they could not be dismissed as derivative. They developed their own highly distinctive styles of art and architecture, animated by an intense feeling for harmony with nature and what the cultural historian Sir George Sansom termed "a thirst for beauty of color and form." If the courtly arts of Japan's eighth-century Heian period borrowed from Tang China, they also rivaled it. Throughout the centuries, whether in the written words of a Genji,[2] the austere beauty of a Zen scroll, the splashy colors of a Momoyama screen or an Edo print, the quiet splendor of temples in Kyoto or Kamakura, Japanese culture developed its own arresting style—not to be confused with anyone else's.

There were only two periods when this tight island civilization was seriously threatened by outside intruders. The first threat took the form of outright military attack. Twice, in 1274 and 1281, the Mongol emperor Khublai Khan, his invading dynasty securely in control of China, sailed his armadas against Japan. Their ships were manned by Chinese, Mongol, and tributary Korean troops. Khublai's project ended in disaster. On both occasions his ships were scattered by typhoon storms which the Japanese piously called *kamikaze*, the "divine winds." The troops who had landed, cut off from seaborne reinforcement, were fought to a standstill by Japan's samurai soldiery on the beaches of Kyushu.

Three hundred years later there came a cultural and commercial invasion from the West, which Japan's rulers found more menacing: bands of dedicated Christian missionaries and European traders who brought galleons and gun-

---

[2] *The Tale of Genji*, written in the eleventh century by Lady Murasaki Shikibu, was perhaps the world's first real novel—and remains one of its greatest.

powder with them. Both the religion and the military science of the West found receptive students. By 1600, fifty years after the first missionary landed, there were about 300,000 practicing Catholics in Japan. Churches were built in Kyoto and other leading cities. Jesuits, some of them newly ordained Japanese, preached at the court of Japan's military rulers. That same year, at the battle of Sekigahara, which decided the control of the country, a significant portion of the samurai on both sides were equipped with European-style harquebuses, locally manufactured—and said to be improvements on the originals. In 1615 explosive mines were used in the siege of Osaka Castle.

If the new Western ideas had followed the pattern of earlier cultural imports from China, one might have expected that the Japanese, after first enthusiasms had passed, would have begun a leisurely process of digesting and adapting them. Instead, after less than a century's exposure to contemporary European culture, they threw it all out. Christians were in the end cruelly persecuted. Trade with foreign countries was banned. In 1636 the government decreed that no Japanese ship would be allowed to sail to a foreign port. A new dynasty of Japanese shoguns—ruling, as always, in the emperor's name—deeply feared the impact of Western culture on their people.

The success of this negative policy was almost unparalleled. For the next two centuries Japan lived the life of *sakoku,* "the closed country." Its people, its politics, its economy developed in almost total isolation. Because of past services to the shoguns, only the Dutch were allowed to send two trading ships a year to Japan. That was all. As late as 1811 Stamford Raffles, although eager for trading prospects, had to advise his superiors in India, regretfully, that "the Japanese have on every occasion . . . rejected in the most peremptory manner the various overtures of different nations of Europe, refusing equally to have any intercourse, negotiations or commerce with any of them."

In the middle of the nineteenth century this artificially made chrysalis was shattered by outside events: the spoliation of China, the old cultural motherland, by European colonists and the demands of a new Pacific power, the United States, that Japan unlock its gates. Far from collapsing under Western pressure, the Japanese—oddly energized by their long isolation—made drastic changes in their political and social structure and reached out to the West in a purposeful frenzy of self-modernization.

They called it the Meiji Restoration, in honor of the young emperor who presided over it. But in fact it was a cultural revolution, one of the great national transformations in history. In the space of a single generation the Japanese, by their own efforts, changed themselves from a backward-seeming feudal society, powerless to defend itself against the newly mechanized civilization of the West, into a modern world power, vital and vigorous, the arbiter of Asia's future.

Their example was electrifying. The tradition-bound island borrowers of other people's cultures turned into the pacesetters and dispensers of modernity. If the circumstances of their transformation were unique, no one could ignore the pervasiveness of its results. From Manchuria to the Moluccas, Asians watched and hoped to learn from the Meiji experience in order to build new eras of their own. Slowly at first, the nations of the West grasped the significance of Japan's emergence. They would come to realize that "modern civilization" need not be spelled in Roman letters.

Meiji was Asia's challenging response to the West. It is our purpose here to show how this great cultural revolution came about, who made it, what it entailed, and what effects it had—on Japan, Asia, and the West. Those effects are still with us. They are a part of everybody's world. Along with the American Revolution, the French Revolution, and the Russian Revolution, Meiji stands as a milestone in modern history. Without examining Meiji and its implications it is difficult to understand the civilization of the twentieth century—still less that of the twenty-first.

LET US BEGIN by taking a closer look at Tokugawa Ieyasu, the founder of the shogunate that Meiji displaced. It is only logical to start an account of any revolution with a description of the old regime and the institutions it destroyed. To most of the young reformers the name Tokugawa was as anathema as Bourbon was to the French revolutionaries. Yet the whole Meiji modernization would have been impossible without the Tokugawa achievement—goods and bads—that preceded it. "Our history begins today," the reformers of 1868 were fond of saying. Their statement was a piece of historical hyperbole. They were no more able to eradicate the Tokugawa heritage than the French revolutionaries could stamp out the various legacies of Louis XIV's state, or the Soviet revolutionaries cancel the tsarist heritage of secret police and authoritarian rule. Tokugawa's shogunate and its organization may have been superseded by the Meiji Restoration, but its roots were too deep to be cut. He continued to cast a long shadow across Japanese society, and his imprint is even more noticeable in late-twentieth-century Japan than it was in the hundred years before.

Tokugawa seized power in 1600, after more than a century and a half of feudal warring in Japan. The emperors continued their formal reigns from their Kyoto palaces, but real power had by the twelfth century passed to a series of military family dictators—the shoguns—who ruled in the imperial name. But these too had weakened, and the Ashikaga, the last of the early shoguns, were more famous for architecture than arms. Fifteenth-century Japan was effectively parceled out among local barons called daimyo who ran their domains with small armies of vassals and retainers. Almost alone in Asia, the Japanese had developed on their own a military feudal society like that of medieval Europe. And like the Europeans, their specialty was fighting each other. By the middle of the fifteenth century—fittingly called by the Japanese *Sengoku Jidai*, "the era of warring countries"—the country had become a battleground of constantly shifting feudal alliances.

Among them three potential dynasts emerged as leaders: Tokugawa, Oda Nobunaga, and the extraordinary commoner genius Toyotomi Hideyoshi. Contemporaries, they took power in rough—and I use the word advisedly—succession. Oda, a small landholding baron in central Japan, happened to be a born general. With a combination of shrewd tactics and firepower—he was one of the first Japanese leaders to exploit the muskets imported by Portuguese traders[3]—he captured the imperial capital of Kyoto (with the emperor in the bargain), ousted the last Ashikaga shogun, and seemed all-powerful until his untimely assassination by a disgruntled henchman in 1582.

Oda's successor, Hideyoshi, was neither daimyo nor samurai, but a farmer's son whose sheer ability had made him Oda's chief lieutenant. With Tokugawa's help he completed the subjugation of Oda's remaining rivals and installed himself as the country's regent (*kampaku*). Japan's first imperialist, he later dispatched a force of some 195,000 Japanese, the flower of the samurai armies, on a full-dress invasion of China. In 1592 they landed in Korea, the logical gateway to the mainland, and began their march northward. Although the brilliant Korean admiral Yi Sun-shin defeated the Japanese on the water several times, their troops ultimately swarmed over the peninsula, killing and burning wherever they marched. Ancient temples, public buildings, and monuments—a great portion of Korea's cultural heritage—were destroyed. Even today no sightseer in Korea can fail to notice the sad record of the invasion.

Since Korea was historically a tributary of the Chinese emperor, Chinese armies joined the battle. In 1597, after years of war, occupation, and parleying, Hideyoshi finally pulled his troops back to Japan. (They brought with them, as spoils of war, thousands of captive Korean artisans, who among other things were responsible for the revival of the potter's art in Japan.) They left behind them a shattered Korea, whose development as a nation had been cruelly set back by the experience. Hideyoshi himself died the following year, leaving his infant son in the hands of Tokugawa Ieyasu and four other vassal regents—a classic case of misplaced trust.

By 1615 Ieyasu had defeated Hideyoshi's last followers in the siege of Osaka

---

[3] About 1542 three Portuguese traders, traveling on a Chinese ship, were driven by storms to the island of Tanega, off the coast of Kyushu. Hospitably received, they demonstrated their firearms to their fascinated hosts. Other Portuguese merchants followed them. Very soon the Japanese were manufacturing their own harquebuses, called Tanega-island guns thereafter.

Castle, where Hideyoshi's wife and young son committed suicide. His hold on the country now secure, he set about the task of establishing his dynasty. There were to be no more risky foreign adventures like Korea; Ieyasu had strongly disapproved of Hideyoshi's empire building. Going to the opposite extreme, the Tokugawa house banned foreign trade altogether, except for one strictly watched Dutch trading post in Nagasaki harbor. The death penalty was decreed for any foreigner attempting to enter Japan.

The new shogunate also set in motion a rigorous persecution of Japan's surviving Christians. In this respect Ieyasu continued Hideyoshi's policy. Both men, after initially viewing the Catholic missionaries with favor, came to see a moral threat to Japan's particularist feudal loyalties in a religion with such uncompromising claims to universal truth.

With Japan now formally isolated, Tokugawa redistributed the country's feudal domains, some three hundred in all, among the daimyo, on a strict winner-loser basis. Those barons who had sided with Tokugawa at the crucial battle of Sekigahara (1600) were rewarded with rich fiefs. (The Tokugawa family holdings in themselves increased to 25 percent of Japan's revenue-producing land.) Those who had fought against him—the so-called *tozama*, "outsider" daimyo—were allowed to keep some land, mostly on the periphery. Distant clan chieftains like the Mori of Choshu, at the extreme southwestern tip of Honshu, or the Shimazu of Satsuma, in the remote south of Kyushu, were easier to negotiate with than to conquer.

While allowing the daimyo to reign as virtual rulers within their territories, Tokugawa kept them subservient to his court at Edo (the old name for Tokyo) through a rigidly enforced system of taxes, tributes, ceremonial, and hostage taking. Following Hideyoshi's example, he cut off the sword-bearing samurai from their original rural landholdings and forced them into the castle towns of the daimyo. There they lived as soldier-bureaucrats, dependent for their livelihood on portions of the fiefs' land revenues, allocated at the local daimyo's discretion. The peasantry who remained on the land were forbidden the use of weapons altogether.

The Tokugawa shoguns, following ancient Chinese models, compartmentalized Japan's feudal society into four distinct classes: the samurai (*shi*), who included bureaucrats and scholars; farmers (*no*); artisans (*ko*); and, at the base of the feudal totem pole, merchants (*sho*). Internal emigration was banned. Without special permission from the shogunate no one could leave the fief in which he dwelled. The daimyo themselves were kept in line by a network of shogunal officials and informers; at the slightest sign of disloyalty to the Edo regime, a clan baron risked losing his fief. In this way Ieyasu and his heirs froze the society beneath them, prefiguring the coercive devices of twentieth-century totalitarian states.

Like their later Communist or fascist look-alikes, the Tokugawa needed an ideology to justify their power. Ieyasu himself found this in the doctrines of the Zhu Xi school of neo-Confucianism. A Sung Dynasty Chinese scholar, Zhu Xi had taught that the same principle of order bound both the natural world and human political society; hence a strong and harmonious state, organized in a hierarchy of Confucian relationships, was in itself a reflection of heaven's law, something not to be transgressed. In a word, every man had his place.

For more than a century Tokugawa's system seemed to work. Above all, it had brought Japan peace, with the security of a strong central government. There were no abrasive outside influences to disturb a rural society recovering from the convulsions of civil war. Yet over the decades enforced conformity and isolation began to work against themselves, particularly with such a restless, dynamic people as the Japanese.

Writing many years later, in his *Outline of Civilization*, the great Meiji era reformer Fukuzawa Yukichi etched an unforgettable portrait of Tokugawa society:

"The millions of Japanese at that time were closed up inside millions of individual boxes. They were separated from one another by walls with little room to move around. The four-level class structure of warriors, farmers, artisans and tradesmen froze human relationships along prescribed lines. Even within the samurai class there were distinctions in terms of stipends and offices. At one extreme, the occupations of Confucian teachers and doctors became hereditary, too. Each of the other classes of society also had its own determining patterns of behavior. The walls separating them were as strong as iron and could not be broken by any amount of force. Having no motivation to employ their talents in order to progress forward, people simply retreated into the safety of their own shells. Over the course of several hundred years this routine became second nature to them. Their spirit of initiative, as it is called, was lost completely."

It took economic pressure to break Tokugawa's iron walls. By the middle of the eighteenth century the basic annual rice yield—the foundation of Ieyasu's feudal economy—had not increased, but the needs of people were expanding and changing. The shogunate's policy of concentrating the samurai class in the cities, with daimyo forced to spend half of their time as virtual hostages in the capital at Edo, had developed a new urban consumer society.[4] Prices fluctuated wildly. For one thing, there were no imports to take up the slack when crop harvests were bad. Even in good times, daimyo and their retainers, all of them

---

[4] During the period when a daimyo remained in his own fief, his wife and children were obligated to stay in Edo. With some members of each baronial family in residence throughout the year, complete with swarms of retainers, the daimyo residences grew into virtual palaces, whose inhabitants demanded the services of tradesmen, artisans, and merchants. Edo's growth as a metropolis was thus assured, with a court society rivaling any of Europe's.

on fixed incomes, were mortgaging their rice stipends for the new goods and services in the cities.

The tax burden on the farmers became crushing; and many fled the land to find work in the cities. The samurai were little better off. With no wars to fight, a warrior class two million strong—about 7 percent of Japan's total population—risked becoming parasites on their society. Most served as retainers or small bureaucrats for the local barons. Some were virtual menials. Others, in desperation, went back to the land or sought jobs—Confucian class distinctions be damned—as merchants or craftsmen.

The merchants meanwhile were doing very well. Starting as humble purveyors of goods and services to the shogun and the daimyo, the townspeople of Edo and Osaka had developed into successful commodity traders and business operators. While the daimyo mortgaged their rice income to build mansions and acquire luxurious creature comforts, the city businessmen inexorably turned Tokugawa's primitive rural rice economy into a hustling money economy. In Osaka and even more in Edo, the stronghold of Tokugawa power, they turned the money they acquired by trading into an instrument of power over their social betters. Inexorably, peddlers became dry-goods merchants and loan sharks became bankers (rarely a difficult transition in any society). The more money they loaned, the greater hold they had over their highborn borrowers.

Vainly the shogun's councillors enacted ordinances demanding a return to Confucian morality and the austerity of the uncorrupt old-fashioned *bushi* (warrior). It was like holding back the tides. Their command economy proved as sievelike as Marxist command economies two centuries later. The merchants in effect controlled the shogun's treasury. They borrowed and loaned among themselves through the great commodity houses formed to handle their trading, and stimulated the growth of commodity buying. A few of them, like the House of Mitsui, carried on into the modern business world.

The culture of the country showed the merchants' touch. Like the townsmen of Elizabethan England, albeit without the stimulus of overseas trade and exploration, they developed a vigorous consumer market in art, literature, and the theater. Japan was one of the first countries, Occidental or Oriental, to fashion a truly middle-class culture—lusty, affluent, and fickle—which prefigured that of later centuries. The theatrical caricatures of Sharaku or the flashy beauties of Kunisada and Kuniyoshi—sensual-mouthed women dressed in gaudy clothes—are monuments of their great patron: the prosperous town merchant, who was little interested in politics, higher art, or what went on outside the trading marts, the kabuki theaters, or the gorgeous brothels of the Japanese city. For Shakespeare and Marlowe these Edo Elizabethans had the broad-brush theatrics of Chikamatsu, the biting wit of Ihara Saikaku, or the irreverent buffoonery of Kita and Yaji, the roistering scoundrels of *Hizakurige* (literally,

Shank's Mare), a picaresque satire on life under the shogun. As the Tokugawa "box" society started to crumble, a lot of loose and critical talk was getting past the shogun's censors.

There had begun also an increasingly active trade in ideas. This was paradoxically intensified by Japan's isolation. For if Tokugawa had been able to impose conformity on the country's political and social systems, his attempt at totalitarianism could not stifle the ideas and discourse of a new class of Japanese intellectual, whose thoughts Ieyasu would have found appallingly subversive. The new thinkers were far different from the type of docile Confucian philosopher whom the Tokugawa favored. They were mostly practical people, untroubled by philosopher's logic, but animated by an intense idealism. In fact, the modern term "political activist" would best describe them.

Although some were merchants and commoners, by far the great majority of these activists came from the very class of people whom the shogunate relied on to keep the status quo: the low-ranking samurai. Now concentrated in the castle towns of the daimyo, they served both these barons and the shogunate as an increasingly indispensable bureaucracy. For during the long Tokugawa peace, actual military activity was largely restricted to training and swordsmanship classes. By the beginning of the nineteenth century most of the warrior class had become teachers, doctors, or official civil servants. It was unique to Japan—in contrast to its Confucian neighbors, China and Korea—that the warrior class began to double in the role of the Confucian scholar-bureaucrat, in the process merging both sets of ideals and traditions. As the high-ranking *bushi* and shogunal officials busied themselves with pleasures and ceremonies, almost all the actual work of political and economic administration was done by these people of low, often even marginal samurai rank.

Even more than the new generation of townsmen, these functionaries had received a considerable amount of education. There were some 17,000 schools of various sorts in Tokugawa Japan, ranging from academies of Confucian learning to the small *terakoya* (temple schools) where children of all classes were educated. More than 40 percent of the male population was literate (although only 15 percent of the female)—a far higher literacy rate, for example, than Russia could claim on the eve of the 1917 revolution.

A publishing industry grew up—large for its time—capable of disseminating literature on a nationwide scale. Thus Japan's incubation under the shogunate, far from producing a peaceful intellectual vacuum, had fostered controversy and dissent. Thanks to a certain uniformity of culture, something like a sense of nationhood developed during the Tokugawa isolation. New ideas and discontents were rapidly communicated across the country.

* * *

THE SEEDBED OF revolution proved to be the discontent of the low-ranking samurai, as they became increasingly impatient with the old order of the ritualized Tokugawa establishment. Comparatively well educated but frustrated by the frozen rituals of Tokugawa rule, they were the angry young men of that day.

Two schools of thought seized their imagination. They were, on their face, wildly contradictory. The first was Western learning. Starting with a trickle of books through the single Dutch trading post in Nagasaki harbor, the writings of the European Enlightenment slowly worked their chemistry on Japanese minds. In 1771 a samurai physician named Sugita Genpaku, at great personal risk, purchased and published a translation of a standard European anatomy textbook—translated from the German via Dutch! Reprinted and passed from hand to hand throughout the country, it revolutionized the study of medicine in Japan. Other useful handbooks followed—on geography, shipbuilding, and the making of armaments. These made young Japanese warrior-scholars painfully aware of how much the Tokugawa isolation had cost them. In the early 1800s a whole school of *Rangakusha*, "Dutch scholars," sprang up through all the feudal domains. These men disseminated the knowledge found in newly translated Western books, in Sugita's words, "as a drop of oil spreads across the surface of a lake."

The impact of the new Western science was intensified by the distant thunder of European guns to the south and west. Like flashes of lightning on the horizon, news of the incursions of British and French fleets into China's ports made its way into Japan. The few Japanese visitors to China were deeply disturbed by the new subservience of the Chinese to Western proconsuls and traders in Chinese treaty ports like Shanghai, which they found "an Anglo-French dependency." The shock waves of the Opium War and later European incursions into China made this new generation of Japanese scholars realize that they had some intensive catching up to do if they wished to avoid being similarly colonized by the West.

This sense of present danger combined with another line of thinking that had also incubated during the Tokugawa isolation. Led by the eighteenth-century scholar Motoori Norinaga, a new school of nativist philosophy, or theology, had developed. The Japanese began to reflect on their origins. As they delved into the old chronicles and reflected on them, the idea of a supreme emperor ruling a God-favored country came out of the shadows. It took only a slight leap of faith to deduce that the problems afflicting Japan's body politic could be attributed to the shogunate's usurpation of power. Could not these ills be cured—and the foreigners repulsed in the bargain—by a return to direct imperial rule? "The people of the divine land," the historian Ohashi Tatsuo expressed it, "are men among men, while the barbarians are like the bird and the beast."

* * *

UNTIL FIVE O'CLOCK in the afternoon of July 8, 1853, the tensions and discontents, incentives and aspirations of Western scholars, underemployed samurai, expanding merchants, desperate farmers, and a born-again generation of emperor worshipers had smoldered beneath the façade of Tokugawa's troubled shogunate. Now they exploded. For at that moment Commodore Matthew Calbraith Perry's East India Squadron—two steam frigates and their accompanying sloops—anchored off Uraga, just down the bay from the shogun's capital at Edo.

Sent by President Millard Fillmore—whose farsighted interest in transpacific expansion stood out in contrast to his cautious handling of domestic issues—Perry had been ordered to effect the "opening" of Japan to foreign trade. He was also to make provision for coaling and watering facilities for America's whalers. Ten years earlier, Commodore James Biddle had anchored off Japan to negotiate good treatment for shipwrecked American sailors. He had been dismissed with insults by the shogunate. This time the Americans were prepared to use force.

When the shogun's officers temporized, Perry returned the following year with eight ships (comprising at that time fully one-fourth of the U.S. Navy). The firepower from his *kurofune*—"black ships"—represented a threat that nothing in Japan could resist. This much the Edo officials knew, for they had received reports of the disastrous bombardments of Chinese cities some years before. To demonstrate further evidence of the West's technological superiority, Perry—a great showman in his way—had brought along a complete miniature railway, which his engineers set up and operated, along with a telegraph line, which they temporarily set up between Yokohama and Kanagawa. Both items the Japanese found fascinating. To supplement his educational efforts, the commodore and his officers gave them a complete tour of the "black ships," with interpreters providing detailed explanations of their engines and guns.

After a complex series of discussions, interspersed with ceremonial parades and considerable banqueting, the decision came down from Edo Castle to the Japanese negotiators on the beach. Abandoning its two-hundred-year-old policy of antiforeign seclusion, the once all-powerful shogunate now agreed to conclude a treaty with the "red-haired barbarians." The shogun, seeking to rally support for his action, now timidly asked the individual daimyo for their advice and consent.

This marked the effective end of Tokugawa power in Japan. Based on fear and force, it quickly lost its credibility. As Katsu Kaishu, a loyal follower of the shogun—although also one of Japan's early modernizers—wrote later: "From the day of Perry's arrival, for more than ten years, our country was in a state of indescribable confusion. The government was weak and irresolute, without fixed policy or power of decision."

For some years the country had been at once stimulated and terrorized by sword-wielding samurai scholars, hostile both to the shogunate and to foreigners, who mobilized under the slogan of *Sonno joi*—"Revere the emperor and destroy the barbarians." In China a similar breed of xenophobes would continue agitation and acts of violence against foreigners until the beginning of the twentieth century. The practical Japanese were different. It was these very activists who, paradoxically, turned their minds to study and adapt for Japan the "barbarian" civilization behind Perry's guns.

Within fifteen years of Perry's arrival a group of them had restored the emperor Meiji to power and taken over the governance and modernization of Japan. Their leaders came from the south and west, the very "outsider" clans of Choshu and Satsuma which Ieyasu had beaten centuries before. Their political capital was the walled castle town of Hagi, where so much of the Meiji revolution began.

THE CITY OF Hagi (population: 51,000) sits quietly alongside a small, storybook bay on the Japan Sea coast, close to the southwestern tip of the island of Honshu. It is some 450 miles as the crow flies from Tokyo, but it is divided from the capital by a lot more than distance. The ring of hill and mountain surrounding it have cut Hagi off from easy concourse with the populous metropolitan belt of Japan that extends from Tokyo southwestward through Osaka as far as Hiroshima. Few industries have sprouted in Hagi. It is rather a place for tourists to visit, although few non-Japanese tourists come. The local pottery is well known in Japan. And the unadorned cuisine of Hagi restaurants, serving fish taken out of the bay, is unrivaled.

Like similar towns in many countries, Hagi lives in and for its history. When the camera crews for *The Pacific Century* were doing the story of the Meiji revolution, they were stumped about what portion of contemporary Japan to photograph. Except for the remains of Tokyo's Central Station, parts of a few towns in the southwest, and the relocated buildings of Meiji-mura, a Japanese Colonial Williamsburg, there are few Meiji era survivals. Japan's modern beginnings, as our chief producer noted, had been "paved over in concrete." But in Hagi the spirit of the Meiji beginnings lingers on. Blocks of the austere-looking *buke yashiki*—the dwellings of the once sequestered samurai class—still cluster around the ruins of Hagi Castle. Walking through the narrow streets of the old town—taking care to ignore the odd motorbike, tradesman's cart, or Toyota station wagon parked alongside—it is easy for a visitor to imagine the last days of the old shogunate. It was in these houses, now slumbering behind

Tokugawa Ieyasu, founder of the Tokugawa shogunate, who began Japan's 250-year-long isolation

Yoshida Shoin. Shoin Jinja (shrine)

Hagi today. Houses in the old samurai quarter (buke yashiki) are virtually unchanged from Shoin's time. K. K. Fūkōsha

their façades of austere wooden fences, that the young samurai of Choshu plotted to destroy the shogun's government, playing local politics in an effort to gain their daimyo's support for the sequestered emperor's cause.

Hagi was the old capital of Choshu, the domain that included the busy port of Shimonoseki, commanding the straits between Honshu and Kyushu and the hills and farmland stretching south to the Inland Sea. The local daimyo, the Mori family, had once been the second-largest feudal landholders in Japan. But they had guessed wrong in 1600, lining up against Ieyasu at the battle of Sekigahara. Along with the rustic Shimazu daimyo from Satsuma, in the far south of Kyushu, the Mori lost part of their holdings. They were packed off to their shrunken domains and told to mind their conduct, their revenues diminished and their vassals watched carefully by the overseers and spies of the shogunate.

It was only natural, therefore, that the soldier-bureaucrats of Choshu, by clan tradition still thirsting for vengeance against the Tokugawa, would be among the first to act out their dreams of modernization, emperor revival, and revolt. In the event, many survived the post-Perry turmoil to become, first, leaders of the Meiji revolt, then the Prime Ministers and generals of the new Meiji state.

Their birthplaces and old homesteads are now scrupulously preserved, exactly as they were, for the schoolchildren who come from all over Japan to view them. Among them is a drab, unpretentious structure, with outbuildings around it and a small exhibit hall. This is the famous *Shoka Sonjuku*—"the Village Academy under the Pines"—where Yoshida Shoin, the great protestor of that time and still Choshu's favorite son, taught his eager pupils, and through them began Japan's new era.

Yoshida's life was stormy and short, and he lived it in a hurry. The heir of hereditary teachers of military tactics at the Mori clan court, he began lecturing there in his early teens. His studies made him acutely aware of the new Western sciences, but he remained nonetheless an ardent Confucian. His students learned from the Confucian classics, along with scraps of technology from painfully translated manuals on Western gunnery and fortification.

From the first he espoused the revived study of Japan as the God-favored country of the old Shinto chronicles. No one yielded to him in his denunciation of the foreign aggressors threatening Japan. He helped foster the xenophobic philosophy of *Sonno joi*. Yet he had rowed out to Perry's ships in 1854 and begged to be allowed passage to the United States, in order to study the foreigners, so to speak, in their native habitat.

"In studying the learning of Europe and America," he wrote, "to adore and idolize the barbarians . . . must be rejected absolutely. But the barbarians' artillery and ship-building, all can be of use to us—these should properly be adopted."[5]

Yoshida was a bitter foe of the shogunate. Throughout his short life, he did his best to inculcate a spirit of national unity, under a restored emperor, among the hitherto scattered and mutually suspicious feudal clans. He advocated a national university for Japan, to be administered by Japanese who had studied in the West. Most tellingly, he demanded that individual merit, not birth, be the qualification for official preferment. Not only the lower samurai but farmers and merchants, if they were able, should be allowed to advance. Here, Confucian though he was, he set out to undermine the rigid class distinctions of Tokugawa's "box" society. In his ideal army, notably, he made no restrictions of class or background.

A small, slightly built man with violent emotions—he referred to himself as the archetypal "fierce warrior" (*moshi*)—he was at the same time a kind, attentive, and charismatic teacher and a prolific writer. (His collected works encompass twelve volumes.) Yet he was always the activist, telling his charges that scholarship was only a steppingstone to their real work in the world. He lived out his own advice. Despite jailing and house arrest for unauthorized travel and political activity, he continued to plot against the shogunate. He was finally imprisoned in Edo and beheaded, after cheerfully admitting to an assassination plot against a leading shogunate official. At his death he was all of twenty-nine.

Hagi is still Yoshida's town, just as Williamsburg is Jefferson's and Inverness is Bonnie Prince Charlie's. When I last visited there, in the mid-eighties, the children in primary school were still reciting Shoin's memorable words in their classroom: "From now on I shall put away my childish thoughts and go the way of a *shishi*—a man of high purpose."

With the help of a cooperative teacher we asked one class about the significance of Yoshida's life. They were quick to reply. "Because of the efforts of Yoshida Shoin," one child began, "the country was opened up, and from that time on foreigners could come and go." Another pupil continued: "Before he died, Yoshida Shoin said, 'If I'm dying for the sake of Japan, then I'll gladly give up my own life—if it will help people.' He was that kind of a person." A third child added, more practically: "Shoin opened Japan to trade with the outside world and helped make Japan a big country. Without him, we'd all be eating nothing but rice."

Yoshida has gone into Japan's pantheon—as the equivalent, in American terms, of something between Tom Paine and an intellectual version of George

[5] As quoted in W. G. Beasley, *The Meiji Restoration* (Stanford, Calif.: Stanford University Press, 1972).

Armstrong Custer. But modern Japanese adults find some difficulty in placing him. "He was something," one of my friends, a senior Foreign Office official, once observed. "He was either a genius-hero or some kind of monumental nut. I've never really figured out which."

Whichever, Yoshida left an indelible mark on his pupils and through them on his time. A good portion of the men who made up the later Meiji government—including Prime Ministers Ito and Yamagata and the immensely talented Kido Koin—were products of his Village Academy. Like the other "men of high purpose," the Choshu militants were violent in denouncing both the foreign barbarians and the weak shogunate that had let them in. But thanks to Shoin they demonstrated a group solidarity and intellectual purposefulness which many others lacked. The *kiheitai,* a group of local shock troops that they organized, were unique in that—following Shoin's tradition—they enlisted both samurai and commoners and mixed them irrespective of social rank. This was a forerunner of the conscript army that proved to be the ultimate solvent of Tokugawa's old class society.

FOR ALMOST A DECADE after Shoin's death Japan remained in turmoil. The signing of a formal treaty in 1858, opening several Japanese ports to trade, provoked a wave of clashes and demonstrations throughout the country. The shogunate's chief official, Ii Naosuke, was assassinated by angry clan samurai in 1860. As the shogunate weakened, the militant "outsider" domains, with the help of the *shishi* activists, set about to make the antiforeign *Sonno joi* slogan a fact.

Mobilizing support for the emperor was not difficult. Choshu troops for a time occupied the imperial city of Kyoto. They were supported by the younger court nobility, now anxious to return the emperor to power. But driving out the "barbarians" posed a tougher problem. Throughout the early 1860s foreigners in the newly opened cities were repeatedly attacked by hot-blooded samurai swordsmen. Reacting to the murder of an Englishman by Satsuma retainers, a British naval squadron bombarded and demolished much of the city of Kagoshima in 1863. The following year, after repeated Choshu attacks on Western shipping, a combined fleet of American, British, Dutch, and French warships destroyed the Choshu forts at Shimonoseki.

Such object lessons in power politics were reinforced by the testimony of the first Japanese missions to visit Europe and the United States. The young clan bureaucrats were practical people. A consensus quickly developed among them that further antiforeign demonstrations against "barbarian" firepower would be at this time manifestly counterproductive. Instead they agreed to make common cause against the shogunate.

On January 3, 1868, troops from the five clans of Satsuma, Tosa, Echizen, Aki, and Owari took up guard positions around the Gosho, the imperial palace in Kyoto. A few hours later the young emperor Mutsuhito, then aged sixteen, read a proclamation dismissing the Tokugawa shoguns as imperial surrogates. Later that month, assisted by troops from Choshu, the combined forces defeated the shogun's army near Osaka and marched victoriously on Tokyo. *Kateba kangun,* the old Japanese proverb has it: "If you win, you are the emperor's army."

In November 1869, Mutsuhito, great-grandfather of the present emperor, Akihito, himself made the long trip from Kyoto to Edo over the Tokaido, Japan's historic Eastern Sea Road. His vehicle was a lacquered palanquin, hung with silk-gauze curtains to keep the roadside crowds from seeing his face. Four bearers of equal height and equal strength carried the palanquin on their shoulders, jogging along the coastal plain of Shizuoka and the bare hill barriers north of the Izu peninsula at a fairly uniform rate of twelve miles a day. About a thousand soldiers marched around the palanquin, in ragged groups of from forty to two hundred, some wearing snippets of Western uniforms, others dressed in the cloaks and flowing *hakama* trousers of the traditional samurai costume, the two swords of their rank fastened at their waists. Several groups of bandsmen played odd patches of music, which no one recognized. (The national anthem had yet to be composed—as it happened, by an imported German bandmaster.)

The emperor, accompanied by Prince Iwakura, his principal adviser, and the retinues of various court nobles and provincial daimyo, was on his way to take up permanent residence in Tokugawa Ieyasu's old capital of Edo, now to be renamed Tokyo—"Eastern Capital." Mutsuhito himself had assumed the reign name of Meiji, which means "Enlightened Rule."

The beginnings of Meiji, however, looked very dark and gloomy. Fighting against Tokugawa loyalists had continued, especially in the northwest. Government administration had crumbled. With the old Tokugawa tax system shattered, the treasury was empty. And foreign trade, newly permitted, had severely dislocated the economy. The shogunate's ratio of gold to silver, for example, fixed a century before, was still 1:5; the going rate in the outside world was about 1:15. When foreign businessmen found out about this, they began a gold rush of their own, converting at the Japanese price until the gold reserve in Tokyo was almost gone. Outside the capital, meanwhile, the rising discontent of farmers, merchants, and samurai alike threatened a state of anarchy.

The young Meiji government acted swiftly to face these emergencies. Installed in their new capital, the samurai bureaucrats who had impelled the Restoration from below now moved to enforce it from above. At their urging, the reform-minded daimyo of Satsuma, Choshu, Tosa, and Saga offered to give up their clan domains to the emperor. By 1871 an Imperial Guard, the nucleus of Japan's new standing army, had been formed from the troops of Choshu, Satsuma, and Tosa. The feudal domains were reorganized into prefectures, to be run directly from Tokyo. By 1872 a nationwide system of compulsory primary education was authorized, two years behind Britain's and fully forty-six years ahead of national (as opposed to state) compulsory education in the United States.

By 1873 a national land tax system was set up, based on monetary values and assessments. By 1874 the conscript army was a reality. In 1870 commoners were allowed to use surnames—for the first time in Japanese history. In 1875 they were ordered to do so. By the end of the decade the samurai class had been formally dissolved, and wearing swords became illegal. With this the samurai bureaucrats destroyed their own class, prefiguring a similar movement by the Russian intelligentsia in a twentieth-century revolution.

Keeping pace with his reformers, the Emperor Meiji discarded his old regalia for a Victorian frock coat, substituted a ceremonial coach-and-four for the old palanquin, and ordered the court ladies to start wearing skirts and bustles and stop blackening their teeth, thus eliminating an allegedly cosmetic practice in vogue since the eighth century.

Economic modernization kept pace with the political. The old "Drive out the barbarians" sloganeering was replaced by the newer goal of *Fukoku kyohei*— "Enrich the country and strengthen the military." In 1872, with the help of foreign engineers, Japan built its first railroad, from Tokyo to Yokohama; it was barely twenty years since the shogun's samurai had taken their rides on the miniature train that Commodore Perry had thoughtfully brought along with him for exhibition purposes.

By 1870 a Ministry of Industry had been established in Tokyo. The new bureaucrats began the task of building up a modern economy—steamships, textiles, steel mills, public utilities—from scratch. Inevitably the government and the newly founded banking system had to help. And when Japan's old-line merchants seemed too risk-conscious to take the plunge into modern manufacturing, the government built the plants, then turned them over to like-minded former samurai to manage. With this "privatization" policy, far ahead of its time, the Meiji reformers saved themselves from the temptation of forming huge, unwieldy state-run industries, which were to cause trouble for developing nations in the next century.

Thus it fell out, for instance, that a young Tosa samurai named Iwasaki Yataro, the founder of the Mitsubishi conglomerate, started his company with thirteen ships which the government let him have, on favorable terms, for ferrying troops to Taiwan, in one of the first overseas actions of the new army.

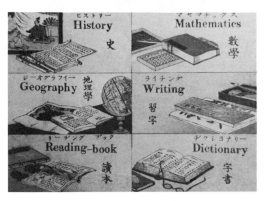

English reader of the Meiji era
Print Collection, Miriam and Ira D. Wallach Division
of Art, Prints and Photographs, The New York Public
Library, Astor, Lenox and Tilden Foundations

An American sailor partying with a geisha, 1861.
The Kanagawa Prefectural Museum

*Commodore Perry as a Japanese
artist saw him*
Yokohama Kaiko Shiryokan

Prints of an early Meiji train. Asai Collection

Perry's ships. Kurofune Kan

Another Meiji businessman, Shibusawa Eiichi, after a short turn in the new Meiji Finance Ministry, left to found the Dai-Ichi Bank—now the Dai-Ichi Kangyo. He went on to start the country's modern textile industry, in the process introducing the joint-stock company to Japan. He ultimately founded about five hundred of them, many still active today.

One of Shibusawa's early borrowers, a merchant named Furukawa Ichibei, bought the Ashio copper mines from the government, on highly favorable terms, in 1877. He parlayed his success there into a network of related companies—mining, cable manufacture, tractors, rubber—which ultimately became one of Japan's huge *zaibatsu* conglomerates and, among other things, the ancestor of the modern Fujitsu computer group.

Such success stories were by no means atypical. The Meiji government's privatization policy on the whole worked spectacularly well. This pattern of close collaboration among government, business, and finance continues to this day. It was the beginning of what Commodore Perry's fellow countrymen would later, in competitive exasperation, come to call "Japan, Inc."

4

Japan in the World

Japan today stands at the point of contact between the civilizations of the East and the West. Our great ideal lies in effecting the harmony of these civilizations.

OKUMA SHIGENOBU, 1913

The Emperor Meiji's reign lasted from 1868 to 1912. Within this span Japan transformed itself from a semi-feudal society into a modern nation-state. This work of nation building was accomplished by a remarkable group of men—for the most part the same kind of discontented samurai bureaucrats and rising young merchants who had brought down the shogunate in the first place. Although the three "outsider" clans of Satsuma, Choshu, and Tosa at first predominated, they were quick to invite talented people from other domains to join them, including many onetime Tokugawa supporters.

They were strikingly young. Almost all of them were in their thirties and twenties at the time of the Restoration. Saigo Takamori, the eldest, was forty-three. Born mostly in the Tenpo era (1830–43), they grew up to become activists in the turbulent last years of the shogunate. They were born fighters who prized their samurai tradition. Ito Hirobumi, who went on to become Japan's constitution maker, started his political career by burning down the new British embassy in Tokyo. Goto Shojiro, shortly after becoming the new government's Foreign Minister, remained enough of a swordsman to personally cut down a samurai troublemaker who had tried to carve up Sir Harry Parkes, the British envoy.

The Meiji leaders were crisis people. In more settled times many of them would have been shunted aside as noisy nuisances or fanatics. Certainly they do not fit the modern stereotype of the Japanese as talented groupies. Their modern descendants admire them all the more for that perhaps. The term "Meiji man"—which now covers people born in that era—still evokes in Japan the image of a pioneer: resourceful, confident, fearless, larger than life. Even in Japan's hyped-up Disneyland, young visitors flock to the Meiji exhibit, called, fittingly enough, "Meet the World," where they hear appropriate words of wisdom from the "audio animatronic figures" of Ito, the scholar Fukuzawa, and Sakamoto Ryoma, the samurai political activist who helped make the Restoration possible.

Meet the world they did. Just as Yoshida Shoin stifled his anti-"barbarian" feelings to beg passage to America with Perry, the Meiji reformers—many of them Yoshida's students—made the acquisition of foreign learning their first priority. In 1871, despite the crises facing the new government, most of the Meiji leaders, led by the court adviser Iwakura Tomomi—the same man who had escorted the emperor to Tokyo—went off for a year and a half to study the political and social institutions of Europe and the United States. Not so incidentally, they hoped also to persuade Western statesmen to ameliorate the low-tariff "unequal treaties" that Perry and the Europeans had forced on them.

They failed to annul the treaties, which remained in force almost until the end of the century. They did, however, gain invaluable insights into the workings of modern nation-states, in the process seeking advice from everyone from Otto von Bismarck to Ulysses S. Grant. Back in Japan, they imported hundreds of foreign experts in various fields, from Western philosophy to lighthouse construction, in an intensified effort to modernize and, if possible, transform the culture of the emperor's country.

While a recital of their accomplishments would seem to suggest a coordinated "master plan," there was none. The three leaders of the group were Okubo Toshimichi and Saigo Takamori from Satsuma and Kido Koin from Choshu. Of the three Kido was probably the most liberal in his views of popular government, while Saigo, who had led the imperial armies to victory, was, as we shall see, the most conservative. But it was Okubo, a master statesman, who called the shots. By welding together a coalition of the fractious "outsider" clans, Okubo staged the military coup in Kyoto that actually brought the shogunate down. It was he who later alternately cajoled and pressured the reluctant daimyo to hand their fiefs over to the emperor's government. It was he who decreed the national conscript army and pushed for rapid industrialization.

For all his audacity, Okubo rarely moved without first making sure of his power bases. He was an improviser with lightning-fast political reflexes. His display of political gymnastics evokes comparison with the contemporary tight-rope activity of Russia's Mikhail Gorbachev in the late eighties. Yet, as he directed his reforms, Okubo was careful to keep allies satisfied and opponents just a bit off balance. Also, he had several important factors in his favor: a clear goal, an emperor's authority to invoke (or hide behind), a homogeneous population, and the rising tide of a national cultural revolution.

"TAP A HALF-SHAVED head," ran the popular saying of Meiji days, "and you will hear the sound of temporizing conservatism. Tap a full head of hair and you will hear 'Restore imperial rule.' Tap a close-cropped head and you will hear 'Civilization and Enlightenment.' "

The popular aphorism referred to the speed with which modern-minded Japanese citizens were changing their hairstyles to fit new Western ideas of barbering—discarding in the process the old samurai-fashion hairstyle in which a portion of the hair was shaved off and the remainder was piled into a topknot. But it also symbolized the way people's daily life and culture were being meta-morphosed around them. It was not only the telegraph and the railroads. There was the new Gregorian calendar, adopted in 1873. Lamps and horse-drawn carriages became commonplace. Mustaches and beards sprouted along with the new Western-style uniforms. Eating beef had now become fashionable in this nation of determined fish fanciers. For gentlemen who had hitherto possessed only a vague notion of hourly time, large pocket watches were now de rigueur.

In the Meiji polity, "Civilization and Enlightenment"—the Japanese slogan *Bunmei Kaika* is handier-sounding—had become a national commitment. It was pursued with a vigor and consistency that later modernizers would forever envy. In 1871 the Meiji emperor actually issued an edict encouraging meat eating, Western clothing, and Western hairstyles. "It is our firm wish," he wrote, "that you, our subjects, change your way of dress and your manners and enhance the national polity."[1]

Behind such insistence on changing the national lifestyle—form has been traditionally almost as important as content in the Japanese cosmos—lay the conviction of the Meiji reformers that only by a massive cultural revolution could they catch up with the "advanced nations" of the West. The term "Meiji Restoration," still generally used in the history books, hardly describes what went on. In its connotation of imperial restoration and national "renewal" too, it refers only to political phenomena. The cultural transformation that took place had a seismic effect on Japanese society. In the end the modernization

---

[1] As quoted by the late Kuwabara Takeo in *Japan and Western Civilization* (Tokyo: University of Tokyo Press, 1983).

Fukuzawa in Western dress. Fukuzawa Memorial
Center for Modern Japanese Studies, Keio University

*Meiji cabinet ministers, 1887. (From top, clockwise:)
Tani Kanjo (agriculture and forestry), Saigo
Tsugumichi (navy); (center:) Enomoto Buyo (post
and communication); Matsukata Masayoshi
(finance), and Mori Arinori (education).*
Gibney Collection

Emperor Meiji. Mainichi Shimbun

Okubo Toshimichi. Mainichi Shimbun

became adaptive, as Western customs and practices were selectively used, altered, or rejected. This took time, however. The first Meiji decades saw a wholesale, pell-mell import of European and American culture, technology, and tastes by an emerging modernizing middle class.

The scope of the changeover was staggering. The reformers, for example, quickly set out to produce a whole system of Western-style laws and courts, at a time when crucifixion and impalement on spears were still on the books as standard punishments.[2] Torture during judicial interrogation was not abolished until 1876. An urban police force had to be started from scratch, since the very idea of public security had hitherto been enmeshed in a welter of feudal disciplinary ideas. The new officers of the law, in fact, were first called *purisu* (police), since at the time no words to express this concept existed in Japanese.

The same craving for Westernization that gave Japan *purisu*, beef eating, and Vandyke beards also for a time played havoc with artistic tastes. Classic Japanese paintings and sculpture went begging, as young artists tried to go Western. A visiting British watercolorist who had arrived in Yokohama as a staff artist for the *London Illustrated News* was soon busy teaching Western art, while the directorship of the Official Painting Office, traditionally held by a representative of the shogunate's favorite Kano school, was now assumed by a Meiji reformer named Kawakami Togai, who had taught himself Western oil painting after first learning Dutch.[3]

The great pioneer of Japan's modernization was Fukuzawa Yukichi, the same indignant samurai who had denounced the "box" society of Tokugawa days. Although known today to most non-Japanese by virtue of his picture on the face of the 10,000-yen bill, Fukuzawa was one of the movers and shakers of the modern era. Almost single-handedly he introduced and popularized the intellectual culture of the West—along with the whole body of ideas in the Western Enlightenment. Frequently called the Japanese da Vinci, he deserves the comparison.

Fukuzawa began his scholarly career, as many contemporaries did, by studying Dutch. In his memorable *Autobiography,* one of Japan's seminal books, he tells how he and his fellow students in Osaka would stay up all night copying briefly borrowed Dutch books on electricity, iron plating, and a variety of practical subjects. In Edo he switched his language studies to English, on finding that most foreigners he encountered could converse only in English or

---

[2] Not the least of their motives here was to convince the Western powers that they could now safely give up the principle of extraterritoriality, by which—as in China until well into the twentieth century—foreigners had to be tried by their own judges. Extraterritoriality was finally abolished by treaty in the 1890s.

[3] As described in Michael Sullivan's authoritative *The Meeting of Eastern and Western Art* (Berkeley: University of California Press, 1989).

French. In 1860 he accompanied the shogunate's first mission to the United States, sailing on the *Kanrin Maru*—the first Japanese ship, by the way, to cross the Pacific under its own steam. He visited Europe in 1862 and 1867, just before the Meiji revolution. On the basis of these trips and his further study, he produced a series of books on Western learning—*Conditions in the West* (*Seiyo Jijo*) and *The Advancement of Learning* (*Gakumon no Susume*) among them. They had a circulation in the hundreds of thousands, were used as school textbooks, and powerfully influenced two entire generations.

Part of his work was purely expository. It included instruction in geography and chemistry, public speaking and double-entry bookkeeping. But at its core was a shrewd analysis of Western philosophy and rational ways of thinking. This he contrasted favorably to Japan's established Confucian philosophy, based as it was on rote learning and the explication of ancient texts. He contemptuously dismissed the old Confucian scholars as "rice-eating dictionaries."

Fukuzawa did his best to lead Japan toward empirical learning and democracy. Students and young officials alike were fascinated by the Enlightenment ideas epitomized in the first sentence of *The Advancement of Learning*: "Heaven never created one man above another; when people are born, therefore, Heaven's idea is that all should be equal."

In the course of an intensely productive life Fukuzawa founded Keio University, one of Japan's great private educational institutions, and *Jiji Shimpo,* one of the country's first newspapers. Intensely nonpolitical, he consistently refused to join the government, but his teachings were responsible for a new and revolutionary emphasis on human rights and representative government in Japan.

He was ably seconded by others. By the late 1860s a whole generation of activist scholars was reading widely in Locke, Rousseau, and John Stuart Mill, as well as Herbert Spencer and other advocates of "scientific" progress. Most of these people shared Fukuzawa's view that Japanese must abandon Confucian studies to concentrate on "the laws of number and reason," as they were understood in the West.

For their first exemplars of "number and reason" it was only natural that Japan's cultural revolutionaries look to Commodore Perry's homeland, the United States. In 1871, when the government selected several hundred students to study in the West, more than half were sent to America. The Iwakura mission, begun in the same year, went first to the United States before going on to Europe. Mori Arinori, one of Fukuzawa's strongest supporters, was sent to Washington as ambassador by the new government at the age of twenty-five. Despite his youth—or perhaps because of it—he was quick to realize the sweeping cultural implications of the Meiji takeover. He advocated immediate, sweeping modernization. His older friend Ito called him, admiringly, a Westerner born in Japan ("*Nihon no unda seiyojin*").

Mori was in fact one of the first Japanese to use the term "revolution" in describing the Meiji experience. "Progress," he wrote in 1870, "can only be achieved through revolutions and trials." Obsessed by Japan's need to catch up with the industrialized West, Mori at first advocated that Japanese be abolished in favor of English as the national language. Going further, he proposed at one point that Japanese men should take foreign wives and breed a new race. (Mori's attempt to pioneer this movement by marrying an American woman ended in a rather swift divorce.) His book *Education in Japan,* based on letters of advice he received from prominent Americans, was an appeal for the rapid Westernization of Japan's school system.[4]

In this respect he was preaching to the converted. As a member of the Iwakura mission, Kido Koin paid particular attention to American schools. None of the reformers better typifies the Meiji emphasis on education as the life force behind modernization. When he saw the wide extent of American education—even if organized on the state and local levels—Kido was flabbergasted; but he resolved that Japan should have the same. "The civilization we have in our country now," he wrote, "is not true civilization . . . To prevent trouble ten years from now, [we must] establish schools worthy of the name . . . We have to develop universal adherence to the moral principles of loyalty, justice, humanity and decorum . . . The creation of such public morals depends entirely on people. And the supply of people in endless numbers over a long period of time clearly depends on education . . . Our people are no different from the Americans or Europeans of today; it is all a matter of education or lack of education."

For at least the first decade of the Meiji era, textbooks used in the new schools were translations of American models. The most influential of the foreign educators in those days were Americans. David Murray, a Rutgers University professor, was invited to Tokyo in 1872 to supervise the new national school system. The Declaration of Independence, the Constitution, and Washington's Farewell Address were among the first foreign documents to be translated.

The reformers were quick to make parallels with the American Revolution, which they understandably viewed in Japanese terms. As Nakaoka Shintaro's history of the American Revolution had it: "The oppression of the English king became more heavy each day and the American people suffered. At that point

---

[4] Mori's impatience with tradition and ceremony from Japan's past ultimately proved fatal. In 1889, after only four years in office, he was stabbed to death by a right-wing fanatic for having two years before walked up the steps of the imperial shrine at Ise with his shoes on.

a man named Washington complained of the people's hardships . . . He carried out an exclusion policy and expelled the barbarians."

There was some substance to the comparison. Both in their youth and in their broad intellectual interests, the Meiji reformers recalled the American Founding Fathers of almost a century before. No other revolutionary leaderships combined the same goals of building a nationalist ethos out of sectionalized populations under the banner of egalitarian reform. In Tokyo as in Philadelphia, the ideas of Rousseau, Locke, and the Enlightenment set the political tone.

Fukuzawa's *Conditions in the West* included copious explanations of American society and government. The *Federalist Papers* were well known among the reformers. In 1870 Kato Hiroyuki's widely read *Outline of Practical Politics* enthusiastically expounded the idea of the natural law as developed by the American Founding Fathers. Another scholar wrote a lengthy treatise on "the pursuit of happiness"—an idea with which even the most broad-minded of the reformers had difficulty. In 1876 the Meiji empress, joining the American fashion, scrolled out a series of poems in praise of Benjamin Franklin's famous maxims.

With new freedom-of-religion laws now in force—the Tokugawa anti-Christian proscriptions were revoked in 1873—American missionaries began arriving to join the teachers. Since most of the clergymen were educators as well as preachers, they gave their scholars a liberal dose of practical learning along with their Bible classes. A whole generation of Japanese students grew up admiring the famous admonition of the redoubtable William Clark, who had come from Massachusetts to teach agricultural know-how in Hokkaido: "Boys, be ambitious."

The new Imperial University in Tokyo, Japan's first, included practical subjects like agriculture, engineering, and medicine in its curriculum, in the American tradition. And the famous Protestant "mission schools" of this generation—such as Doshisha in Kyoto and Aoyama and Meiji Gakuin in Tokyo—had their beginnings in this period. Their founders, American-educated Japanese and American educators both, preached God and Progress with equal enthusiasm.

SUCH WHOLESALE and sudden modernizing was bound to provoke a conservative reaction. The first rumblings of protest came from the peasantry, who had already suffered heavily under the shogunate. The enforcement of the new conscription laws pulled able hands off the land, where they were badly needed. Farmers in the provinces denounced this "blood tax," which recalled for many the iniquities of the old Tokugawa corvée. The new Meiji land tax, designed as a systematic alternative to the Tokugawa regime's haphazard financing methods, weighed even more heavily on the poorer farmers, although the more prosperous profited considerably from the registration of land and ownership.

Protests and complaints led often to riots and open revolt. Whole prefectures—Fukuoka in particular—rose up against the new government. Although the uprisings were brought under control, it seemed only prudent to revise the land tax's harsher provisions in 1878.

The cultural backlash was as serious as the economic. The reformers' new separation of church and state, the new Western-style calendar, and the substitution of centralized government for the old feudal rules and observances evoked angry demonstrations. Compulsory schooling was at first particularly unpopular. Not only did the schools take badly needed hands from the family farms but the new primary school readers were often translations of foreign books and as such suspicious. Old prejudices die hard. While the enlightened townspeople were applauding the abolition of the old feudal classes and the legalized equality of all Japanese, angry mobs were torching settlements of the *burakumin*—the traditional outcast class—in protest against the rights of full citizenship now given them.[5] There was more to "Civilization and Enlightenment," the reformers were finding out, than simply proclaiming and legislating them.

A more obvious and concentrated threat came from another quarter. Not all the lower samurai were reformers like Okubo, Ito, and Kido, cheerfully ready to destroy their own class in the interests of modernization. On the contrary, the loss of both privilege and stipends at one fell swoop was for most of the old knightly order bitter medicine. Even during Tokugawa days many samurai had grown accustomed to fending for themselves and earning a living as farmers or small businessmen. That came from economic necessity. Now, however, they were not so ready to abandon cherished customs—the whole edifice of Tokugawa Confucianism among them—in favor of foreign practices. The old "destroy the barbarian" spirit of *Sonno joi* could not be abandoned merely by shaving off the traditional samurai topknot and substituting a Victorian coach for the imperial palanquin. Traditionalists were particularly chagrined, so soon after the Restoration began, to find their leaders fraternizing with foreigners and openly copying their institutions, instead of attempting to destroy them.

Ironically, it was Saigo Takamori, the victorious commander of the Meiji emperor's army against the shogunate, who finally led an open revolt against the emperor's new government. Satsuma, the same province that helped lead the Restoration, was its center. Although a Meiji loyalist, Saigo was no West-

---

[5] It says much for the strength of folk prejudice that, despite their new equal legal status, the *burakumin*, whose origins as an outcast group lie deep in Japan's history, continued to suffer the most vicious discrimination in practice. They do to this day.

ernizer. Basically, all he wished to import from Europe and America was military equipment. He dramatized the central problem of the Meiji revolution: how to reconcile the new dynamic of Westernization with the ancient and primitive cult of Japanese nationalism that the modernizers had invoked.

In 1875 Saigo had wanted to invade Korea. Okubo, Kido, and their modernist supporters stopped him, on the grounds that any such outward expansion was, for a newly modernizing Japan, at the least premature. The new national structure, they argued, was as yet too weak to support military adventuring overseas.

Leaving the government, Saigo returned to Satsuma, where he set up his own military academy. Saigo's academy became a focus for the growing reaction against all those foreign ideas emanating from Tokyo. The last straw for many old-fashioned samurai came in 1876, when the Meiji government outlawed the wearing of the traditional swords (along with the traditional stipends). By this time Saigo's restless students had begun to agitate openly against the Meiji government.

In 1877 some of his firebrand associates attacked and seized the government arsenal at Kagoshima. Forced by his own canons of feudal loyalty to support them, Saigo somewhat reluctantly took the field and led an army of some 40,000 Satsuma samurai soldiery against the emperor's troops. He lost. The winners were the infantry and artillery of Okubo's new conscript army—despised by Saigo as "dirt farmers," unworthy of fighting against real samurai. (The same conscripts had earlier put down a revolt by another antiforeign extremist among the reformers, Eto Shimpei.) After repulsing Saigo's forces from their siege of Kumamoto, the imperial troops, well armed and better trained than Saigo's men, drove them steadily back toward the Satsuma stronghold of Kagoshima.

In September 1877, his anachronistic swordsmen cut down in their last battle, Saigo committed suicide near Kagoshima. With him died the last real challenge to the new government's authority. Although he was a rebel and traitor by the standards of modern nation-states, Saigo's avowed aim had been to save the emperor from his advisers, in the old Japanese tradition. Even in defeat, he remained a heroic figure. Huge for a Japanese of that time—at 200 pounds and almost six feet tall, he had the look of a slimmed-down sumo wrestler—he was known for his generous and courtly character. His image lived on in the national mythos as a symbol of old samurai loyalty.[6]

---

[6] Japanese have a weakness for noble losers. Despite his apparent break with the government—but in the emperor's name—Meiji honored his family with a special patent of nobility only shortly afterward. He remains one of the country's national heroes—a Japanese edition, if you will, of Chevalier Bayard, the classic French knight "without fear or reproach."

Siege of Kumamoto. Meiji conscript troops defeat Saigo's samurai. Asai Collection

Saigo's two great colleagues did not significantly outlast him. Kido, wasted by his political exertions, died of tuberculosis in the same year, 1877. The following May, Okubo, the guiding genius of the Meiji revolution, was assaulted by some of Saigo's die-hard supporters at Shimizudani in Tokyo, a small district quite close to the present New Otani Hotel. He was mercilessly hacked to death before help could come.

OKUBO'S LOGICAL successor was already in place. With the Meiji era now into its second decade, Ito Hirobumi assumed increasing prominence as the leader in the small group of reformers who governed in the emperor's name. In some ways he was typical of this so-called Meiji oligarchy. He had come into the government with Kido and Yamagata Aritomo, all three of them products of Yoshida Shoin's Choshu school. Originally Ito lacked samurai rank. A poor farmer's boy, he was adopted by a low-ranking samurai family only a few years before the Restoration. He was an enthusiastic advocate of immediate Westernization and progress, sometimes to a fault. As Prime Minister in the 1880s, his fondness for the elaborate Western-style dances and parties at the new Rokumeikan ballroom led political opponents to denounce the "dancing cabinet."[7] Yet he had more than his share of political caution. While he advocated the principle of Japanese democracy, the idea of popular party rule, based on adversary debating, made his bureaucrat's mind rather nervous. Four times Prime Minister, he consistently and skillfully steered a tricky course between populism and the conservative reaction against it.

On the one hand the people's rights movement continued to gain momentum. Nor could it be dismissed as a foreign import or a "top-down" imposition. Over the centuries a certain tradition of rough "consensus" democracy had grown up in Japan's villages. Farmers and townspeople in the provinces were studying the new translations of Western books and passing them around. As the historian Irokawa Daikichi has written: "The movement toward a modern consciousness and thought took place through people's original and independent reinterpretations of ruling class thought, through a radical regeneration of tradition, based on the experiences of ordinary people . . . Japanese people were trying to modernize from the bottom up, trying to work toward greater democracy and freedom."

By way of proving his point, Irokawa in the 1970s searched out in old farmers' warehouses various copies of draft "constitutions" which had been written and debated by people in the provinces far from Tokyo. With them

_____

[7] Ito carried his socializing beyond the dance floor. At one point his strenuous pursuit of the empress's ladies-in-waiting brought on a gentle, but firm imperial rebuke.

were carefully preserved translations of the Declaration of Independence, Rousseau's *Social Contract,* and similar pieces of political literature, all dating from the late 1870s.

The country people who wrote these down were part of a growing agitation for representative government. Political parties began to emerge. The first of them, founded by the Tosa samurai Itagaki Taisuke in 1881, was appropriately named the Freedom Party (*Jiyuto*). "Freedom" advocates played an increasingly active role in the public political dialogue, organizing mass meetings and demonstrations throughout the country. They had their problems with the conservative opposition. Itagaki himself was the target of an assassin in 1890, but survived—having prematurely delivered himself of the classic last line after he was stabbed: "Itagaki dies, but freedom lives."

More important was the Meiji liberal Okuma Shigenobu, who first proposed a constitution to the emperor in 1881. For this he was frozen out of the governing establishment. But through his Progressive Party, he assumed a key role in Meiji parliamentary politics. An internationalist and a political gradualist, he tried his best to make Japan a European-style democracy. The founder of Waseda University, he finally became Prime Minister during World War I.

The movement for people's rights found an increasingly high-decibel voice in the newspapers, which by the mid-1870s were proliferating in the country. Although they were held down by government restrictions, the combination of strongly felt opinions and the use of Western-style presses produced something resembling a free press by the 1880s. *Yomiuri,* founded in 1874, was the first really popular newspaper, with features designed to sell papers as well as disseminate opinions. (In the 1990s *Yomiuri* remains Japan's largest national daily.) Japanese were getting the newspaper habit. Widely read by an expanding readership, the emerging national press was soon outrunning the government's efforts to control it.

More ominously, the new Meiji bureaucracy was harried by a series of populist revolts, as angry farmers, denied representation in Tokyo, took the law into their own hands and rioted in protest against the economic dislocations of the day. The Chichibu uprising of 1884 was only the most famous of a dozen armed disturbances, symptoms of political frustration as much as economic inequities.

Against the new populism were ranged conservatives like Yamagata Aritomo, a military man through and through, who wanted a continuation of tight bureaucratic rule from the capital. The emperor himself, whose liberalism did not go much beyond the enthusiastic wearing of Western uniforms, was part of this authoritarian backlash. Although a firm believer in education—he faithfully attended each annual graduation ceremony at Tokyo's new Imperial University—Meiji wanted teaching without questioning or dissent. One of the last

influential Confucian scholars in Japan, unfortunately, was the emperor's tutor, Motoda Eifu, who demanded heavy school indoctrination in "Japanese" morality and the family system, to offset the influence of the new Western learning. "Efforts are being made," he complained, "to convert Japanese into facsimiles of Europeans and Americans."

In the end, Ito, ever the cautious democrat, produced a constitution that treaded carefully between what he felt were two extremes. It was the product of long study. In the Meiji reformers' tradition Ito spent the year 1882 traveling in Europe to examine the governments of that day. Although one of his closest advisers, Kaneko Kentaro, had studied at Harvard under Oliver Wendell Holmes, Ito and those around him grew more and more worried about the American ideas of free popular democracy they had at first accepted.

The Germany of Bismarck seemed far more attractive, especially after the victory in the Franco-Prussian War of 1870. Like Okubo before him, Ito was impressed by the interesting combination of democracy, welfare, and authoritarianism present in Bismarckian Germany—a newly created modern empire whose recent unification of various states under the Hohenzollern Kaiser bore no small similarity to Meiji Japan. In Berlin, despite the presence of political parties, the real power seemed firmly in the hands of the Kaiser's loyal bureaucracy.

In many ways the Meiji constitution of 1889 was a great step forward. It guaranteed basic individual freedoms. It set up a bicameral legislature based on male suffrage—Japanese women had to wait until 1946 and the U.S. Occupation to get the vote. The legislature was given broad powers, including the right to approve and enact the national budget. Japan's general election of July 1890—the first in Asia's history—was justly hailed by advocates of human rights. "It is the year," Itagaki crowed, "in which we emerge from despotism and slavery and are born a people of constitutional liberty."

Yet the emperor was left as the centerpiece and final authority of the state, with a loyal bureaucracy responsible ultimately to the throne. This central role of the emperor was confirmed by the reactionary Imperial Rescript on Education, which also appeared in 1890. Ito did not oppose this. In his studies of European nation-states he had been troubled by Japan's lack of a universal religion like Christianity, which seemed to be the cornerstone of so many Western values.

"If there is no cornerstone," he had written, "politics will fall into the hands of the uncontrollable masses, the government will become powerless and the country ruined . . . in our country the one institution which can become the cornerstone of the Constitution is the Imperial House."[8]

[8] As cited in *Political Thought in Early Meiji Japan* by Joseph Pittau, S.J. (Cambridge: Harvard University Press, 1967).

Just a year later the Christian scholar Uchimura Kanzo was forced to resign his post as a teacher in Tokyo's elite First Higher School. He was accused of public disrespect—that is, he had refused to bow to a framed copy of the Imperial Rescript as it was being ceremonially carried into a school assembly!

AS MEIJI JAPAN moved into the 1890s, successive governments rarely lost sight of the reformers' early priority: "Enrich the country and strengthen the military." Since Ito's first turn as Minister of Industry, the civilian leadership kept a close watch on industrial development. A centralized banking system, with the government's Bank of Japan at its apex, turned to the task of capital formation. Consumption and excise taxes, along with various forms of indirect taxation, relieved the crushing pressure of the original land tax, which had penalized the countryside in the interests of hasty industrialization.

The Meiji government did not leave industrial growth to chance, however. Family silk farms led to heavy development of a silk export trade. Textile factories sprouted over the landscape. As with later developing countries, the local machine age began with cotton manufacturers. (Nonetheless, silk remained Japan's major export earner until the 1930s.) Thousands of young Japanese women were engaged to work in the new factories, many of them little more than sweatshops. Underrated and underpaid as they were, and often exploited by greedy overseers, the careful, painstaking labor of these *kojo*—"factory girls"—played a crucial, if unheralded role in developing Meiji Japan's industrial base.

Steel production and shipbuilding were to follow. To stimulate large-scale output and develop technology, the government established the Yawata Steel Works in 1901. Work was intensified on the national railroad network. By 1900—a bit more than twenty years after completion of the Tokyo–Yokohama railway—some 40,000 miles of track linked Japan's major cities. And Mitsui Bussan, the first of the great trading companies, was established as early as 1876, the better to compete with Western companies in acquiring commodities for manufacture.

The mining industry was heavily developed—especially in extracting coal, of which Japan had then a large supply (just as Daniel Webster had suspected). But the new mines and factories took a heavy toll in human lives and hardships. Girls as young as eleven or twelve worked long hours in stifling sweatshops for minuscule wages. The costs of rapid, forced industrialization were very high. Bad, unhealthy conditions in the new mines and factories recalled the worst of Europe's early Industrial Revolution.

Four miles outside of Nagasaki harbor sits the abandoned mine of Gunkanjima—"Battleship Island"—a ghastly relic of the costs of Japan's modernization. In the Meiji days the island was one huge Mitsubishi coal mine. Its scores of dormitories, now abandoned, once housed an overflow population of drafted workers—prisoners, outcasts, and impoverished farmers. Whole families were raised here, under virtual prison conditions. Few were allowed to escape their servitude. Places of this sort, in fact, were responsible for a whole school of "proletarian" protest literature.

As a natural protest against the sweatshops of Japan's new industry, labor unions began to emerge. They were led mostly by intellectuals and activists like Katayama Sen, who had learned about the union movement when he was an immigrant laborer in the United States.[9] But they were generally repressed by a nervous government. The persecution of socialists and other radicals—real or suspected—was tragically exemplified by the wrongful arrest and execution of the socialist Kotoku Shosui in 1911, charged with plotting the assassination of the emperor.

The pioneers of women's rights had equally rough sledding. Although reformers like Fukuzawa and Mori Arinori had spoken out loudly against the traditional Confucian disparagement of women, progress was very slow. Yet higher education for women was established by the early 1900s, which at least put Japan far ahead of other Asian countries in this respect. And the emergence of female publicists and political activists like Fukuda Hideko, Yamada Waka, and Hiratsuka Raiko suggested at least the beginnings of a new consciousness.

For all the human tragedies in its wake, Japan's industrialization went on. Toward the close of the 1890s, the economy was at the "takeoff" stage, as it now would be called. The foundations of a modern industrial society were in place, buttressed by the *zaibatsu* conglomerates that were to play such a large part in Japan's economic future. Foreign capital investment was severely restricted, however. The Meiji government had learned a great deal from the economic colonization of China. To compensate for the lack of foreign money, the bureaucrat and the businessman worked closely together, with new development organs like the Industrial Bank of Japan ready to provide financing. In building up the economy, the "coercive instrumentalities of government," as William Lockwood nicely put it,[10] were used to the full.

Increasingly, all roads led to Tokyo. With the ties between business and bureaucracy so strong, it was inevitable that the country's economic leadership would move closer to the political hub. Osaka and the Kansai area around it, under Tokugawa rule the trading center of Japan, had begun its long slide into

[9] Katayama later repudiated Christianity in favor of Marxism. He became a Communist organizer and by the 1930s a leading figure in the Comintern's Asia section. Highly regarded in Moscow, he was buried near Lenin in the Kremlin wall.

[10] In his *The Economic Development of Japan* (Princeton, N.J.: Princeton University Press, 1954), which remains a classic on this subject.

Saigo Takamori prepares for suicide. Asai Collection

Japan's steel industry—the Meiji beginnings. Mainichi Shimbun

Gunkanjima, site of the Mitsubishi coal mines. Mainichi Shimbun

Coal miners at Gunkanjima. *Mainichi Shimbun*

Ci Xi, *the dowager empress.* Pacific Asia Museum

Women at work in an early textile mill. *Mainichi Shimbun*

a less decisive, if still important economic role. Most ironically, Choshu and Satsuma, where the Meiji revolution began, were becoming quiet backwaters, to be visited only on ceremonial occasions. The men who led the Restoration had all gone on to Tokyo.

WHILE THE NEW factories hummed, Yamagata Aritomo, since 1878 Chief of the General Staff, worked to develop the armed services. Like Ito, he was a product of Yoshida Shoin's school, but his vision of Japan's future was far narrower. The second part of the Meiji watchword, "strengthen the military," was his purpose in life. He had introduced nationwide conscription as early as 1872. By the 1890s his army and navy were ready for action. The same troops who had overcome Saigo's last resistance were committed to the Sino-Japanese War in 1894, in a fight that began over which neighbor—Japan or China—would hegemonize the Hermit Kingdom of Korea. This war was in itself another piece of irony, since Saigo's plan to attack Korea twenty years earlier, opposed by Yamagata and Ito, had been among the causes of the early samurai uprising.

Yamagata's troops quickly overran Korea and went on to attack the ill-equipped Chinese armies in Manchuria. The decisive battle of the war, however, was fought at sea. Off the mouth of the Yalu River, on September 17, 1895, the new Japanese Navy smashed the vaunted Northern Fleet of China, which most foreign observers had expected would win. The implications of this victory would guide Japanese policy in Asia for almost the next half century.

Yamagata returned from the China front to become Prime Minister, but he later resigned to assume the Chief of Staff's position in 1904. Again he presided over a war, this time against the Russians, but, as before, it was fought for control of Korea and China's semi-captive province of Manchuria.

Ito and others in the Meiji government had tried to avoid hostilities, since they were by no means sure that Japan was ready for a full-scale war with a major European power. But Russia had already moved troops into Manchuria, as part of an increasingly belligerent Far Eastern policy. The Japanese popular press, equally jingoist in tone, denounced Prime Minister Katsura Taro as "a traitor and a coward" for seeking to avoid a conflict. War became inevitable.

In February 1904, Japan—prefiguring the Pearl Harbor sortie decades later—began the fighting with a surprise torpedo attack on the Russian fleet at Port Arthur. Two days afterward Tokyo declared war. With control of the sea, Yamagata landed army reinforcements above the Russian naval base at Port Arthur. At the same time Japanese troops already deployed in Korea moved against the Russians in Manchuria.

In January 1905, Port Arthur fell to General Nogi Maresuke's Third Army, after a protracted and bloody six-month siege, in which the victorious Japanese sustained some 90,000 casualties. In March the Japanese captured the Russian stronghold at Mukden in a large-scale battle, with more than 300,000 engaged on each side.

Despite Japan's victories, the final outcome of the war remained in doubt. As Ito had feared, the support of such huge naval and military forces had strained the Meiji economy to the breaking point. Japan had only been able to borrow money in the international market piecemeal, on the strength of successive victories, as they were won. Several hundred thousand fresh Russian troops were on their way to Manchuria from Europe, while Japan's reserves were seriously depleted. Now, as Admiral Zenovi Rozhdestvensky's Baltic Fleet steamed halfway around the world toward Vladivostok, many thought this final Russian reinforcement might change the odds.

It was not to be. On May 27, 1905, Admiral Togo Heihachiro's fleet won a brilliant engagement off Tsushima, the island lying between Korea and Japan. Togo's ships had trained well, both in gunnery and in navigation. They responded nobly to Togo's epic signal to the fleet, flown from the mast of his flagship, *Mikasa*: "The fate of the empire lies in this one action. All hands, do your utmost."

In the event, he brought off the classic naval maneuver of "crossing the T," in which a fleet masses all its firepower broadside against an enemy advancing in single columns. A hundred years after Trafalgar, Togo's victory had implications as profound as Nelson's. It was also something of a tribute to British naval tradition. Togo himself had trained as a naval cadet in Britain. His navy was modeled on the British Navy and lessons learned from it.

Just forty-two years before, aged fifteen and wearing a samurai's two swords, Togo had served the Satsuma guns during the punitive British bombardment of his hometown, Kagoshima. Ever loyal to his traditional roots, Togo led his officers after the battle of Tsushima to pay respects at the grave of Satsuma's noble loser, Saigo Takamori. His aide on that occasion was Lieutenant Yamamoto Isoroku, later to gain fame as commander of the attack on Pearl Harbor.

The Russo-Japanese War was sign and seal of the Meiji revolution's success. It was the dream of Yoshida Shoin come true. Japan had caught the fire of Western learning and used the new science to beat a major Western power at its own game. To millions of the colonially weak and oppressed throughout Asia, Togo's victorious guns came as a message of hope. Speaking more than a half century later, Mochtar Lubis, the distinguished Indonesian journalist, fairly summarized a reaction that transcended national boundaries. "One of the factors which pushed our nationalist movement," he told us, "was the defeat of Russia by the Japanese. An Asian country, an Asian power had been able to defeat a European power. That gave us more hope and courage in our own struggle."

Yet the victory and the example given belonged at least as much to the cultural modernizer Fukuzawa as to the militarist Yamagata or to the traditionalist spirit of Yoshida Shoin. The navigators and gunners who had beaten the Russians were products of a modernizing society, whose people—thanks to an unprecedented program of mass education—had quite convincingly mastered the disciplines of "reason and number" that Fukuzawa's Confucian colleagues found so difficult to understand.

It was a war, furthermore, that brought all the disparate and contradictory currents of the Meiji revolution together. Populists and bureaucrats, peasants and intelligentsia cheered and worried together. As Irokawa explained:[11] "The Japanese thought that if they lost the war, they would lose their independence as a nation, and all the successes of the Meiji Restoration would have come to naught. This fostered a tremendous nationalism. About a million Japanese soldiers went to war. When you look at the diaries they kept and the letters they sent home from Manchuria, you can see that they thought this was *their* war. They felt they were fighting it for themselves—all of them. I think this was the last war in Japanese history that was fought with this kind of 'spiritual' feeling. After that they were all wars of invasion, of conquest."

The peace treaty that ended the war was signed in Portsmouth, New Hampshire, in September, under the auspices of the President of the United States. Theodore Roosevelt liked the Japanese. He had read widely about Japan. Contrary to the popular image of the flag-waving Rough Rider, he was a scholar and historian of highly intellectual tastes. (An inveterate bodybuilder, he had also enthusiastically taken judo lessons from a Japanese embassy expert.) Early in the war, he announced his sympathies. "I have done all that I could," he said, "consistent with international law, to advance [Japan's] interests." Well aware of Japan's lack of economic and military reserves, he offered himself as a peacemaker, to help Japan preserve her gains.

Ito and the worried Meiji establishment were grateful for his intervention. But the Japanese public saw only the military victory, not the economic problems behind it. The newspapers demanded Russian-occupied territory and a heavy Russian indemnity to pay for the war. Forgetting what Japan gained by the treaty—control of Korea and virtual hegemony in Manchuria—mobs shouting "betrayal" rioted in Tokyo, threatened foreigners, and burned down fifteen Christian churches. Not for the first time, resentment swelled at the thought that the United States, the home of Perry's "black ships," seemed to have set itself up as the arbiter of the Pacific.

[11] In an interview in 1989 with the editors of the television series *The Pacific Century.*

The resentment did not last long. Only three years later the much celebrated visit of U.S. battleships to Japan in 1908—Teddy Roosevelt's famous Great White Fleet—officially marked a new high point in Japanese-American relations. The American sailors received a rousing welcome in Yokohama, with much favorable comment on the new Pacific *entente cordiale* in the press on both sides of the Pacific. Japanese observers did not fail to notice, however, that the professional objective of the American fleet was prolonged gunnery exercises off the Philippines. Shortly after the festive visit was over, Admiral Togo and his staff departed for Hiroshima, from where they would preside over Japanese fleet exercises aimed at countering the attack of a hypothetical enemy force heading toward Japan from the south.

JAPAN WAS HARDLY the only Asian nation to study and adopt the science of the West in the interest of modernization. In the mid-nineteenth century nationalist modernizers were at work in China, Korea, the Philippines, and Vietnam. In 1868, the same year the Meiji revolution began, King Chulalongkorn began in Thailand his own version of political reform based on Western models. No other country's modernization, however, even approached the sweeping nature of Japan's—or achieved anything like Japan's success.

In some cases the lag was due to colonialism. It is hardly possible to modernize a country already occupied by a foreign army and run by foreign colonizers. Where considerable modernization and Western education took place, notably in the Philippines, it was inevitably guided and hence limited by the American occupiers. But not all Asian nations were thus colonized. To understand why Japan succeeded at cultural revolution and why others did not, a comparison with China comes first to mind.

Europeans had come to China and Japan at about the same time. In China, as we have seen, their impact was at first greater and longer-lasting. Matteo Ricci's Jesuit successors were preaching and running the Manchu emperors' observatories in Beijing long after the Tokugawa shoguns had expelled the foreigners from Japan. The missionaries were proscribed early in the eighteenth century. During the reign of the Qianlong emperor (1736–99), when foreign traders were restricted to the port of Canton, all forms of Western learning had also come under official disapproval. This was, coincidentally, the very time when Sugita Genpaku and the other "Dutch scholars" in Japan were beginning to translate Western books into Japanese.

Much of the Japanese samurai scholars' early knowledge of the West was gained from books already published in China. Even their bold reformist slogans were borrowed. The slogan "Enrich the country and strengthen the military" was coined by the Chinese scholar Wang Anshi in the eleventh century;

the title "men of high purpose" (*shishi*), which Yoshida Shoin and his contemporaries proudly bore, was first used to describe the Ming Dynasty's last defenders against the Manchu invaders (*you zhi zhi shi*) in the late seventeenth century.

Nor were the nineteenth-century Chinese all that resistant to learning from the West. Those two farseeing mandarins, Zeng Guofan and Li Hongzhang, had built shipyards and arsenals in Shanghai and Fuzhou when the Meiji reformers were just starting their work. Their "self-strengthening" movement had the same basic objectives.

Yet the Chinese effort at modernization was spasmodic and far from intense. When Fukuzawa was studying in London in the early 1860s he met a Chinese scholar, there for the same purpose. They talked about their common concern for modernization. The Chinese asked Fukuzawa how many people in Japan were capable of reading and teaching from foreign books at that time. "About five hundred," Fukuzawa answered. "Now tell me how many scholars of this sort you have in China." The Chinese scholar, brow furrowed, gave the matter some thought. "About eleven," he finally replied.

There were several reasons why China lagged behind. In contrast to Japan's isolation and relative tranquillity under the Tokugawa, China was wracked by war and invasion—both connected with the impact of the West. In 1850 a failed candidate for a scholar's degree named Hong Xiuquan, imaginatively influenced by Christian missionary teaching, set out to build a new Heavenly Kingdom of Great Peace (*Taiping Tienquo*). Gathering about him a surprisingly large force of the poor and discontented, he attacked the Qing troops and captured city after city in southern China, setting up an avowedly (though hardly orthodox) Christian, anti-Confucian, and at first puritanical community. The Taiping rebels established a program of land reform and enforced a ban on opium sales (thus losing the support of the European traders in China and their governments). The hordes of people Hong and his lieutenants attracted to their banners evidenced the wide discontent with Qing Dynasty rule. They were finally subdued by regular Qing troops in 1864, but only after the slaughter of millions and the wasting of huge areas of the country.

Led by the British, the European powers, not content with their victories during the Opium War, attacked the beleaguered Qing government again during this period. British troops seized Canton and finally captured Beijing in 1860, burning the summer palace in the process. The news of their activity, quickly relayed to Japan, gave added impetus to the militant Meiji reformers.

Aside from civil war and Western attacks there was a deeper reason for China's resistance to Western learning. Confucian learning was deeply embedded in China. In China of the Qing era, there were no nationalist scholars like those in Japan whose researches made them impatient with Tokugawa Confucianism and eager for the alternative learning system that the West offered. To the mandarinate, Confucian learning and China were synonymous. It would require another half century of defeat before the supremacy of the ancient classics could be seriously questioned.

Thus the Chinese bureaucracy, thinking its culture totally self-sufficient, felt that merely the successful construction of Western ships and guns, based on imported technology, would be enough to counter the impact of the Industrial Revolution. They believed that their orthodox Confucian philosophy already made them intellectually and spiritually superior. The pragmatic Japanese, who had journeyed to the West and understood something of modern politics and economics, knew better.

Ci Xi (Tzu Hsi), the redoubtable empress dowager, took power in 1861 and remained the actual ruler of China until her death in 1908 at the age of seventy-three. Born Yehonala, the daughter of a disgraced Manchu captain in Beijing, she was selected because of her beauty as one of the twenty-eight concubines of the then reigning emperor. By her early twenties, having borne the emperor one son, she had become most influential at court. For nearly a half century, through the lives of three emperors—husband, son (who died young), and nephew—she, for all practical purposes, ruled China. Ill educated but extraordinarily shrewd, with a lethal grasp of dynastic power politics—her scorecard of depositions, imprisonments, executions, and suspected assassinations would rival the storied Renaissance prodigies of Lucrezia Borgia—the dowager empress Ci Xi proved a disaster for her country.

Where her Japanese opposite number, the Meiji emperor, became a living symbol of modernizing change, she resisted it. Although she allowed Li Hongzhang, a palace favorite, a certain amount of latitude in his "self-strengthening" programs, she intervened decisively against Liang Qichao, Kang Yuwei, and the other Chinese reformers in 1898, imprisoning her son, the progressive young emperor Guangxu, in the process. Like her Communist successors almost a century later, Ci Xi's primary object was to preserve her political dynasty. Modernization, not to mention democratization, would always take second place.

Despite China's obvious weakness after the Sino-Japanese War, Ci Xi secretly encouraged the movement known to Western historians as the Boxer Rebellion, which ran its course in 1898–1900. Starting with a group of secret societies in Shandong Province, known as the Righteous Boxers (*Yi He Duan*), armed bands of discontented peasants, believing themselves possessed of magical powers, began to sweep through the Chinese countryside, killing Christian missionaries and ripping up railroads—the other most obvious sign of foreign penetration—in a riot of xenophobia. The emotions driving them were similar to the mix of patriotism and anti-Western reaction that had preceded the Meiji

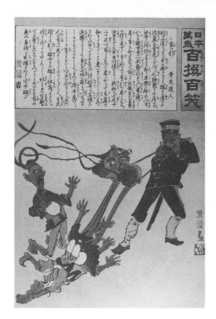

Anti-Chinese cartoons from the Sino-Japanese
War (1894–95). Leserman/Adler Collection

Chinese envoys seeking peace after their
defeat. Leserman/Adler Collection

A company of Boxer Irregulars
Library of Congress

revolution in Japan. Even the Boxers' slogan—"Support the Qing [Dynasty] and wipe out the foreigners"—echoed the *Sonno joi* slogan of pre-Meiji days. But there was no one in China to channel their indignation into a constructive political movement.

In June 1900, after slaughtering groups of missionaries in the provinces, thousands of Boxers massed in Beijing and besieged the foreign legation quarter, guarded by a small force of European, American, and Japanese troops. They were at first supported by violent antiforeign pronouncements from the dowager empress, who somewhat naively felt that by eliminating the foreigners in the capital ("They are like fish in a stewpot," she wrote one of her princes) she could end Western penetration into China. Although some units of China's regular armies were sent into action against the legations and a relief force coming to their aid, most of Ci Xi's provincial commanders held back from what was obviously a piece of monumental folly.

Inevitably, the Western powers and Japan retaliated. A 20,000-man expeditionary force captured Beijing, ordered the executions of Boxers and other Chinese leaders, and forced a huge indemnity on the hapless Chinese. Brazen, unpunished, and a trouper to the last, Ci Xi returned to the Forbidden City in 1902, where she smilingly hosted a tea party for the ladies of the foreign community. Poor Li Hongzhang, China's own battered modernizer, was left to negotiate what peace terms he could with China's latest set of foreign conquerors.

JAPAN'S NEARER neighbor, Korea, played out the same drama of tradition versus modernization as China, but in even more extreme and unsuccessful form. There, another imperial regent, the *taewongun*, emboldened by the repulse of two abortive Western punitive expeditions, insisted that primitive guns and Confucian thinking could turn back any invader. Here too the Japanese knew better. Having solved the problem of tradition versus modernization by harnessing them together, they gradually put pressure on the Koreans to accept, in 1876, a treaty with Japan opening two Korean ports to Japanese commerce.

This was another interesting sign of progress. Barely two decades after the 1858 treaty with the United States, the Japanese were themselves "opening" another Asian country, backed by their own modern military power. At first they hoped to install a Korean reform government headed by Kim Ok-kyun, who had studied under Fukuzawa in Tokyo. When the local Chinese garrison forestalled this maneuver, the Meiji government decided on strong-arm tactics. The Sino-Japanese War was the inevitable result.

The victories over China and Russia established Japan as the leading military power in Asia—and for the first time in Japan's history a force to be reckoned with in the Western world as well. For the Meiji people this sudden rise to prominence was exhilarating and rather unsettling—like the "bends" of deep-sea divers too quickly pulled to the surface. It produced a curious ambivalence of attitude, which remains to this day.

Something happened to the Japanese mind as people read the newspaper accounts of victories over the Chinese. For centuries Japan had looked up to China as the mother civilization. Yet here they fought the Chinese—and found them weak. They began to look on the Chinese with contempt. *Changoro* or *chang-chang* they would call them in the writings and popular caricatures of the day—the equivalent of the American deprecatory word "Chinks." Even so lofty a thinker as Fukuzawa could call the China war "a battle for world culture."

The Japanese attitude toward their Korean cousins was even worse, however. In 1905 Japan's elder statesman, Prince Ito—a suave diplomatist at home—marched into King Kojong's palace in Seoul at the head of armed Japanese troops. When the Korean Prime Minister refused to sign the treaty "asking" for a Japanese protectorate—the Japanese had thoughtfully drawn one up—he was muscled out of the audience room by their soldiers.

Yet at the same time many Japanese ideologues saw their country as the leader and champion of a new Asia, rising united against the Western colonial oppressors. This pan-Asianism remained as a major factor in Japanese attitudes. "Asia," as the cultural arbiter Okakura Tenshin had it, "is one."

Despite the wounds of the late war, Chinese nationalists and revolutionaries flocked to Japan. In 1898, the young emperor Guangxu inaugurated a bold series of reforms patterned on those of Meiji Japan. When the dowager empress moved troops in to suppress the reformers, their leaders, Liang Qichao and Kang Yuwei, were welcomed in Tokyo. So later was Sun Yat-sen, who planned for his more successful 1911 revolution with Japanese help. ("We are the *shishi* of the Meiji Restoration," Sun told his Japanese friends.) Yet life in Japan was never really comfortable for the Chinese leaders, who were alternately courted and snubbed by their Japanese hosts.

The same ambivalence governed Japan's relations with the West. After their two successful wars the Japanese became full members of the colonial predators' club. Happy to be invited, they proceeded to carve up pieces of China side by side with the Western powers. They continued their efforts to "catch up" with the West, conscious of a basic mechanical and "scientific" inferiority. They remained eager learners. At the same time, the legatees of the pre-Meiji "Destroy the barbarians" slogan harbored a basic suspicion of the West, fostered by a kind of inner cultural contempt.

These strong ambivalences made the Japanese bad teachers for the rest of Asia. Where they taught successfully, in matters of technology or assimilated scholarship, it was mostly by example, and all too often the example was the

Ito Hirobumi and young Korean Prince Ri (Yi).
As Japan's governor general in Korea, Ito first
advocated a conciliatory policy, assuming the role
of "protector" to the last princes of the Yi dynasty.
Library of Congress

Yamagata Aritomo. The archetypical
Japanese militarist, he was Ito's great
rival. Mainichi Shimbun

gunfire of a cruiser or an artillery battery. Goods and machines they could send overseas, but Japan's particular brand of cultural revolution was not a successful export item.

In 1909, just after resigning as Japan's first resident-general in Korea, Ito Hirobumi was assassinated by a Korean patriot, An Chung-gun, in the railroad station at Harbin. More than any of the other reformers, Ito typified the great strengths of the Meiji man, along with some stellar weaknesses. An overweening egotist, excessively fond of wine, women, expensive cigars, and his own oratory, he was also extraordinarily fair-minded, incorruptible, and dedicated to his nation. The Meiji emperor, a close friend of Ito but no fool, once commented: "Ito assumes that what Bismarck is to Germany or Li Hongzhang to China, he is to Japan. This makes things very difficult. I would like to find an able person who could act as a foil to Ito, but I cannot think of one."[12]

Ito himself, having brought Japan out of its past, worried about the future. Talking to his secretary late in his life, on a steamship sailing between the United States and Europe, Japan's great modernizer expressed his concerns: "Our nation has made great progress in barely forty years. Even more than we ourselves expected. But how will things go from now on? One cannot see two or three centuries ahead. We can only hope . . . that we will be succeeded by a new generation of able men. Even so, I am concerned about the attitudes of our people . . . If the Yamato race thinks of itself as unique and outside the laws of human rise and decline, if it ignores the proper interests of other nations and behaves outrageously, then national ruin is certain. They said in olden times that 'the proud man is short-lived.' This is true not only of individuals."

The emperor did not long outlive Ito. It is said that he aged perceptibly after his minister's death. Meiji died on July 30, 1912. The day was a page mark in history. As the author Natsume Soseki wrote (in his novel *Kokoro*): "I felt as though the spirit of the Meiji era had begun with the emperor and had ended with him. I was overcome with the feeling that I and the others who had been brought up in that era were now left behind to live as anachronisms."

In Retrospect

At the close of World War I, just fifty years after the Meiji revolution, Japan could look back with some pride on its achievement. If an era had ended, a new

---

[12] For this and the following quotation I am indebted to Oka Yoshitake's excellent *Five Political Leaders of Modern Japan* (Tokyo: University of Tokyo Press, 1979).

one seemed well on the way. Its promise far exceeded the reformers' most hopeful dreams. Japan was now universally accorded the status of a great power; and would be one of the five major decision makers at the Treaty of Versailles the following year.

The unequal treaties with the European powers and the United States were wiped off the books. Indeed, the colonial ruler of Korea, Taiwan, and a leading foreign concession in China had taken its place along with the Western predators. Japan's armed forces, having won an easy victory over Germany's few Pacific possessions, were holding them in fief.

Just under twenty years since Ito's constitution was promulgated, Japan was, by the standards of the day, a working democracy, with its national Diet, its prefectural assemblies, and its courts of law. Hara Kei, the country's ablest party politician, had just become Prime Minister. This was further evidence that a government of party politics, quite like those in the West, was in place. With a well-developed system of universal education and an increasingly independent press conscious of its rights, an informed public opinion had become a force to be reckoned with. The popular culture was developing, as people began to take the new communications media and creature comforts for granted.

Industry continued to grow. There were now some 1,800,000 factory workers in the spreading urban areas, producing the wide variety of goods, from bicycles and dresses to locomotives and cruisers, that befitted a modern economy. The close cooperation of government, business, and finance, begun by the Meiji reformers, continued to set the tone for Japan's business expansion. With wealth increased, the consumer economy became ever more of a factor. In 1918, thanks to rapid wartime expansion, Japan enjoyed a favorable balance of payments for the first time in its history.

The Japanese merchant marine, having profited greatly from wartime losses in European shipping, ranked fourth in the world. While raw silk remained a key Japanese export, textiles and light manufactures were beginning to pour out of Japan's factories. Worried European competitors were already hurling charges of "cheap goods" and "dumping" practices, as the "Made in Japan" label became popular in other Asian markets.

Despite the brutal aggressions against China and Korea, Asian revolutionaries continued to look toward Japan as the exemplar of modernization. Chinese students were not the only ones. Following in the footsteps of the Filipino hero José Rizal, who had spent a year in Tokyo studying, other young people from Southeast Asia came to learn there. Phan Boi Chau, an early leader of Vietnamese nationalism, had already helped to found an East Asia United League composed of like-minded spirits from China, Korea, and the Philippines. Anticolonialists from as far off as India joined them.

Caught up in their own ego trip of growth and aggrandizement, Americans across the Pacific already showed signs of their own ambivalence toward Japan. Increasing Japanese emigration to the West Coast had prompted a wave of anti-Japanese sentiment in California. Ugly riots took place. As early as 1906, with only a few thousand Japanese immigrants in the state, Japanese children were cruelly segregated in the San Francisco schools. More enlightened Americans, outside of California, continued to express admiration and respect for Japan's extraordinary self-modernization. Theodore Roosevelt, for one, saw "nothing ruinous to civilization in the advent of the Japanese to power among the great nations."

Yet within the legacy of Meiji success and power lurked some deep and unresolved contradictions. Both political transformation and cultural revolution had occurred with bewildering speed. In a sense Japan had combined Renaissance, Reformation, and Industrial Revolution—movements and trends played out in Europe over a period of centuries—and jammed them all into a crowded fifty years.

True, the timing had been critical to Japan's success. The Meiji era coincided with a great upsurge in modern technology in the West, a tremendous increase in economic achievement and consequent human expectations. As Eric Hobsbawn pointed out in his *The Age of Capital*:[13] "The most obvious drama of this period was economic and technological . . . it was the drama of progress, that key word of the age: massive and right and sure of itself." Yet in the various national drives for progress, many people's rights, concerns, and aspirations had been ignored or trampled on.

While the Meiji reformers had worked to equalize Japan's society, once so hopelessly stratified, they had also revived the primitive myth of a God-descended emperor who personified the national destiny. In the wrong hands, this body of national belief could be disastrously exploited. For it enabled politicians or militarists to bypass the whole democratic process in the monarch's name. If this emperor mystique was the unique factor in the Meiji success, it also carried within it the seeds of disaster.

OVER THE YEARS I have talked with a great many people about the Meiji revolution. Americans and Europeans still have difficulty placing it. In our Eurocentric historical cosmos, full of "significant" happenings like the Congress of Vienna and the Treaty of Westphalia, Meiji has yet to be programmed. Non-Westerners, however, know a lot about it. Most have studied it and envied it, as they attempt over the years similar transformations in their own countries. I have myself discussed the Meiji achievement with a variety of

[13] Published by Charles Scribner's Sons (1977) and New American Library (1989).

world statesmen and scholars. In China, Deng Xiaoping and Zhao Ziyang both recalled it with great interest. For them, as with all thinking Chinese, the comparison of Japan's success and China's failure at modernization still rankled. Korea's Park Chung Hee, as he planned his country's authoritarian "economic miracle," constantly cited the Meiji example. (The better to remind himself, he kept a Japanese-language encyclopedia in his private office.) In Egypt, talking in the roomy living room of his suburban house outside Cairo, Anwar el-Sadat told me how much he and other Arab nationalists, knowing almost nothing about Japan, had nonetheless gained inspiration from the Meiji experience. At a 1983 United Nations University conference in Tokyo, visiting Latin American scholars paid tribute to Japan's success. "Japan and Mexico both had revolutions in 1868," one Mexican scholar wryly observed. "Now look at them—and we are bankrupt."

Only the Japanese, an innately pessimistic people, seemed more at home talking about Meiji's flaws than its successes. In the early seventies I had begun my own researches on the Meiji period. Talking at that time over dinner in the garden of a famous Tokyo inn not far from the moated palace, I asked an old Japanese friend, himself a Meiji era product, where the reformers had gone wrong.

He answered without hesitation: "It was when they made the Army and the Navy directly responsible to the emperor. That gave a green light to a whole new generation of militarists. They were ignorant people, most of them. They were almost totally lacking in that sense of public responsibility which distinguished the old Meiji leaders. The colonels and the generals made their own interests identical with the emperor's and took us all into a disastrous war.

"The Imperial Rescript on Education, which Meiji himself sponsored, strengthened the myth of Japan as the emperor's country. He was above the law, accountable to no one—not the symbol of the country, like the European constitutional monarchs. He was the country itself. How could people argue against that?"

While the reformers installed all the externals of a working democracy, most of them never lost their basic Confucian feeling that they knew what was best for people. In an Asian context they had re-created Plato's old idea of the ruling Guardians of the State. Thus with the growth of free speech came a proclivity for state censorship of the press, the arts, and public morals. Similarly, trade unions were first permitted, then brutally repressed as a danger to public order. People, it was reasoned, could easily get out of control.

As in the old Tokugawa days—ironically enough—the expression of public concern or protest was gradually pushed underground, to surface only in sporadic riots or outbursts of discrimination against Koreans or the still outcast *burakumin* or other less favored elements of the population.

This dark side of Meiji grew worse as the pace of industry and technology quickened. Behind the façade of new industrial power clustered the factory sweatshops and the city tenements, where families newly uprooted from a poor, but culturally secure countryside tried to cope with urban civilization. Yet, as the tax burdens of modernization increased, the farmers at home also suffered, their grievances rarely heard.

If the revolution was a success, it was thus badly flawed. Throughout the twentieth century, in one form or another, the basic contradictions of patriotism and reform that the Meiji reformers had so brilliantly woven together began to unravel within the Japanese psyche. A tendency toward total uncritical modernization—Westernization at first—fought with an equally strong pull toward xenophobic, racist nationalism—what the modern social critic Yamamoto Shichihei labeled *Nihonshugi* ("Japanism") for want of a better word. It was the battle of *Bunmei Kaika* ("Civilization and Englightenment") versus *Sonno joi* ("Revere the emperor and destroy the barbarians") all over again, with no Okubo or Ito to call a truce that would bring the combatants together.

Nowhere was this battle fought more poignantly than in the writings of the Meiji intelligentsia. The flowering of Japanese literature and the other arts in the late nineteenth and early twentieth centuries was extraordinary. Few countries could boast of such a concentrated cultural renascence. But the mood of their writing was generally gloomy and introspective, marked by a gnawing intellectual discomfort. Suicides of talented writers were commonplace—people like Akutagawa Ryunosuke and Arishima Takeo come to mind—as the Meiji and post-Meiji intellectuals tried desperately, if often brilliantly, to reconcile the values of Japanese and Western culture.

Natsume Soseki saw this split personality all too clearly. "Western culture," he wrote in 1911, "has drawn its impulse from within, naturally. But at present Japan feeds itself from without and thus depends on the strength of others, not fulfilling itself . . . This leads me to feel great pessimism about Japan's future."

He added later, in another context: "Loneliness is the price we pay for living in the modern age."

5

Five Nationalists and How They Grew

There is a strong feeling that the end of the year marks the end of an age. The new year will be upon us soon. I have a sense that we will for the first time step into a world of our own.
EDITORIAL IN *NEW WORLD* (*SHIN SEKAI*), TOKYO, MAY 1, 1919

I n the middle of Seoul's Chongno district, just across from the pleasant antique shops and restaurants of Insadong, sits a small public park. Called Pagoda Park, it takes it name from an unusual thirteen-tiered pagoda that dates from the fourteenth century. Once an older temple stood there. What is left is not very prepossessing—only a few trees, shaded gravel walks, and some low gates. In the spring and summer old men gather there to play board games of *janggi* and talk about past days. Ladies from local charity organizations periodically bring around food and refreshments; groups of schoolchildren visit there on perfunctory guided tours. Only in March each year, on Korean Independence Day, does Pagoda Park come to life.

On March 1, 1919, two days before a planned nationwide funeral observance for their dethroned king, Kojong, several thousand Korean activists, mostly students, gathered in Pagoda Park for the public reading of a Declaration of Independence against Japanese rule. Crying out, *"Tongnip manse"*—"Long live independence"—and carrying the forbidden national flag, the demonstrators marched through the streets of Seoul. Tens of thousands joined them, setting the stage for similar mass meetings throughout Korea. Their scale was unprecedented. Over the next three months some two million Koreans turned out for meetings and protest marches.

The immediate inspiration for this national passive resistance movement came from America and Europe. Ground down after almost a decade of Japan's new colonialism, a whole generation of Koreans took heart from Woodrow Wilson's Fourteen Points and his brave talk at Versailles about the "self-determination of nations."

They were not alone. World War I, "the war to end all wars," and the Versailles Treaty that followed it, were European in origin; except for the Americans, the new reshaping of that continent—and its dependencies—had seemed to be an all-European matter. The idealism that Wilson brought to the peace deliberations may have been expressed in global, if not celestial terms ("The hand of God is laid upon the nations," he had said at the Armistice). But when he spoke of self-determination and people's rights, he was generally referring to the rights of Czechs, Serbs, and Poles—not Koreans, Chinese, and Southeast Asians in European colonies. Nonetheless, the principles he set forth at Versailles had in the end a massive effect on Asia. The currents of discontent they released gave way ultimately to a political and social flood that revolutionized the Pacific world.

In Asia as fully as in Europe—among Chinese and Japanese, Vietnamese and Indonesians as well as Koreans—the year 1919 was a watershed of history. For out of World War I and its aftermath flowed some thirty years of change—violent, confused, and often contradictory—which reached a culmination only after World War II. During these three decades a new generation of Asians—thinkers, traders, and bomb throwers among them—sought to alter old civilizations and build new nations out of their collision with the ideals, achievements, and prejudices of the West.

Through its Meiji self-regeneration, Japan had built itself, on the European model, into Asia's first modern nation-state. In spite of Japan's own rising colonialism, other Asians had begun making the pilgrimage to Tokyo. They were all trying to grapple with the problems that Japan's Meiji reformers claimed to have solved: how to use Western knowledge without becoming hopelessly dominated by its European and American proprietors.

For the immediate future, Versailles only strengthened the hold of the imperialist powers—Japan newly among them—on their dependencies in East Asia. But the creation of new European states in 1919 lent added urgency to the debates of Asian modernists and traditionalists over a better direction for their own ancient societies. While a majority of the new Asian intellectuals were antiforeign and anticolonialist, only a few obscurantists continued to believe that Western influences could be kept out.

This did not mean that the civilization of the modern West should be uncritically adopted. Even the most modern-minded of young Asians were shocked by the pointless mutual slaughter of "modern" European armies throughout World War I. And the almost complete disregard of the frock-coated Versailles peacemakers for people outside their continent was discouraging. Wilson's "self-determination," like the British clubs in Shanghai and Singapore, was for Europeans only. Even Japan's proposal for a mild racial equality clause, which Wilson at first supported, was quickly smothered by his European peers at Versailles. Japan, however—in the interests of "stability," as Wilson put it—was given a hunting license by the Western treaty makers for the spoliation of China.

Looming over the Versailles conferences was the shadow of the Russian Revolution. By 1919 the Red Guards of Lenin and Trotsky had made the Soviet Union a reality. Their success and their avowed internationalism dramatized the possibilities of armed popular struggle as nothing else could have. Yet Wilson's message of popular self-government, rooted in Western-style democracy, remained a powerful one. His vision of a just peace and his plan for a powerful League of Nations outlasted his repeated failures to realize them.[1] Over the next half century the nations on the western Pacific littoral, as they emerged from colonialism, would become a battleground between the ideals of a collectivist Communism, the individualist democracy of the Americans, and the intermittent Pan-Asianism of Japan. During this period the new world of the Pacific Basin came into being.

FOR THE TWENTIETH-CENTURY Asian nationalist revolutionaries, freedom came only after a succession of failures. None was more bitter than the suppression of the Korean patriots. The original group of thirty-three signers—sixteen of them Christians—had modeled their Declaration of Independence partly on the American. Its appeal for "the equality of nations" was full of lofty Wilsonian phrases; two copies were prepared, to be sent to the State Department in Washington and the treaty makers at Versailles. Seeking a public arrest, they reported their deed to the Japanese authorities, who promptly obliged by putting them all in jail. The polite Korean revolutionaries had not reckoned, however, with the brutality of the Japanese response.

---

[1] The League of Nations, which resulted from the initiative of Wilson and others at this time, was actually set up in 1919, with its international headquarters at Geneva. Despite the League's inability to take collective action against the aggressions of Nazi Germany and others during the thirties, it survived until 1946, when it was superseded by the newly founded United Nations. But the League was crippled from the beginning by the refusal of the United States Congress to ratify American participation—despite Wilson's strenuous effort, he had failed to "sell" the idea of the League to his isolationist countrymen.

Delegates to the Korean Congress meeting in Philadelphia, April 16, 1919. Syngman Rhee is third from the left.
Rhee Family

Syngman Rhee as provisional president of Korea, 1919. Dong-A Ilbo

Dutch colonial court in Indonesia about 1870. Dutch officials traditionally heard cases with local dignitaries, but the decision of the Dutch was final.
Royal Tropical Institute

The March First demonstrations were determinedly nonviolent. Fearing retaliation, the well-organized Korean underground had sent out circulars warning: "Whatever you do, do not insult the Japanese." But the Japanese administration, shocked at the extent of the demonstrations, reacted violently. Police and gendarmerie fired on the marchers, and then, in an orgy of vengeance, burned down churches, schools, and homes believed to serve as revolutionary headquarters. Demonstrators were arrested, cruelly tortured, and often executed. According to Japanese records of the time, some 46,000 demonstrators were arrested and 7,500 killed. (The actual death toll was presumed to be far greater.) Forty-seven churches were destroyed.[2]

Despite the bloody Japanese reaction to the demonstrations, plotting and secret meetings continued for a time. In April representatives from all the Korean provinces met secretly in Seoul to select a provisional government. An exiled political leader named Syngman Rhee—ironically a former doctoral student under Wilson at Princeton—was chosen President. Intensified Japanese police control made it impossible for Rhee or the other Koreans in exile to return. By the end of the year most nationalist leaders were either in jail or outside the country, plotting, propagandizing, or fund raising in Shanghai, Honolulu, or Vladivostok. A few guerrilla groups continued armed resistance in the northeastern border country. For the most part the Korean people sadly reconciled themselves to several generations of passive resistance to or acceptance, in various ways, of Japanese rule. But the year 1919 remained etched in the national memory.

As a background to the monument in Pagoda Park a series of bronze friezes depicts Japanese soldiers shooting and bayoneting Korean men, women, and children at that time. Major atrocities are painstakingly recorded. More than seventy years after those events, the severe design of the monument contrasts with the bloody scenes it portrays. At night it makes an ironic counterpoint to the garish advertising signs of various Japanese electronics makers glittering across the street.

IN CHINA, RAGE and resistance exploded two months later in 1919, but for similar reasons. On May 4 some 3,000 university students gathered before Tiananmen—the Gate of Heavenly Peace—at the entrance to the old imperial Forbidden City, to protest the sellout of Chinese territory to Japan by the Great Powers at Versailles. Just a few days before, the Versailles peacemakers, Woodrow Wilson included, had overruled the protests of the Chinese delegates and

[2] As noted in *A New History of Korea* by the distinguished historian Lee Ki-baik (published in English translation by Harvard University Press, 1989).

confirmed Japan's hegemony over China's important Shandong Province, the home of Confucius as well as the center of a rich industrial and trading complex. The concession to the Japanese confirmed the "settlement" they had forced on China during World War I, backed up both by military strength and by large-scale bribery of Chinese government officials. It was, as Wilson sanctimoniously observed, "the best that could be got out of a dirty past."

To the Chinese students it looked as if the dirty past was being imposed on their future. They had been watching the Versailles negotiations for some time; long before that they had shared the growing shame of the country's newly modernizing intelligentsia at Japan's increasing demands for a colonial role in China. Worst of all for the students was the disclosure that high Chinese officials, well paid off by Japan, were instrumental in the secret negotiations that preceded the treaty. The Chinese delegation to the peace treaty had sailed for France, in fact, without knowledge of the secret sellout. Thus the impetus for the Tiananmen mass meeting, the first of many demonstrations in that very spot, was intensified by the students' mounting indignation. Representatives of thirteen Chinese universities attended, led by Beijing (Peking) University, whose liberal faculty gave the students strong support.

In a statement handed out at the meeting, they cited telling international comparisons: "The French in their struggle for Alsace-Lorraine cried, 'Give us our wish or give us death.' The Italians in their struggle for the Adriatic straits cried, 'Give us our wish or give us death.' The Koreans in their struggle for independence also cried, 'Give us our wish or give us death.'. . .

"Our country is in imminent peril. Its fate hangs on a thread. We appeal to you to join our struggle."

A good part of the country did. During the first day the originally peaceful protest quickly escalated into violence. The students burned down the house of Zao Julin, Minister of Communications and a leading Japanese collaborator, and almost beat to death the Chinese minister to Japan. They were cheered by onlookers in their march on the foreign-policed legation quarter. And over the next few days the students won the support not only of university professors but of businessmen, urban workers, and a mixed bag of political leaders.

By contrast the relatively moderate reaction of the authorities reflected divisions inside the weak government. (In the end the Chinese delegation to Versailles refused to sign the treaty, their resolve decisively strengthened by Chinese students blockading their Paris hotel.) When more people heard the news and read the manifesto—written not in the old literary language of the mandarins but in relatively simple modern Chinese—more meetings and demonstrations followed. Shanghai workers went on protest strikes. Businessmen started to organize anti-Japanese boycotts. Despite spasmodic repressive actions by the government and local warlords, the agitation spread throughout the country. Nor did it abate, as other student demonstrations had done in the past.

The May Fourth movement, named for the day it began, ultimately built up a tidal wave of support for modernization and independence that transcended barriers of geography or class distinction. It grew into a revolution which spelled the end of old mandarin China, however difficult it proved to build a new nation on its ruins.

The revolution was as much cultural as political. In fact the cultural aspect of the May Fourth movement proved to have as strong and lasting an effect as the fragile political revolution of Sun Yat-sen in 1911. The demonstrating students were both the creators and the products of an angry new literature of protest. Their indignation at China's new republic, already crumbling around them, was fueled by the writings of a young bureaucrat in the Education Ministry named Zhou Shuren. Zhou took the pen name of Lu Xun, which he soon made famous. In the brilliant, bitter satire "The Diary of a Madman"—his first short story—Lu Xun denounced the old China as a culture of people eaters, constantly devouring its children with its cruel and archaic conventions. Both culture and politics, he argued, must be overturned. In the process writers must become political activists.

"The words of the writer," he wrote, "must be daggers and javelins that can hew out a blood-stained path to a new life."

Inspired by the iconoclastic thinking of Lu Xun and others like him, a whole generation set out to modernize. Their announced goal was to free their society from the ossified classical teaching and hierarchical posturings left over from the days of the dowager empress Ci Xi and her overthrown Qing Dynasty. In no other country did cultural rethinking become such a basic premise for political change.

FROM A DIPLOMAT'S point of view, Japan had done very well at Versailles. No one at the treaty conferences, preoccupied with the problems of European boundary making, seemed to have noticed the shootings in Seoul or the arrests in Beijing. Its colonization of Korea already tacitly confirmed by Europe and the United States, Japan had now received a green light to exact further concessions from a weak China. Then Japan annexed Germany's Pacific island possessions under the guise of a League of Nations mandate and gained a privileged position as one of the powers on the League's Council. The Meiji statesmen's plans for making Japan a world power seemed close to fruition.

For the Japanese people this seemed a hollow victory. Nothing rankled within them so much as the defeat of the racial equality amendment to the new League charter at Versailles, which was widely publicized in the sensitively nationalist press. Despite Wilson's early support, in the end it was the United States and the British Commonwealth, bowing to their various racist farm blocs, which voted racial equality down. Australia's Attorney General, in fact, with as much prescience as prejudice, had earlier explained: "As competitors they are the most dangerous of the Asians . . . we exclude the Japanese not because they are an inferior race, but because they are a superior one."

But it was Japan's internal problems that made 1919 a year of crisis in Tokyo. They were fully as intense as those of the Chinese and Koreans whom Japan was brutalizing. Just the year before, the country had been wracked by a series of rice riots. Starting with a women's protest in Toyama Prefecture, hundreds of thousands took to the streets throughout the country, denouncing the hoarding and profiteering of the wartime *narikin*—newly rich merchants. Worse yet for the economy was the collapse of the wartime export boom, as the European allies moved to get back the markets they had lost to Japan during the war. The depression that resulted brought to a head a festering discontent among Japanese workers and the newly urbanized city poor. The exploitation of women and children in the huge textile mills—with high death rates attributable to working conditions—was becoming a national scandal.

In 1919, despite laws and police regulations against union activity, there were 497 strikes in Japan (as against an average of 50 in 1914). The Yuaikai, a fraternal workers' organization, went militant at its 1919 convention and transformed itself into the All-Japan Federation of Labor. In September of that year 15,000 workers struck the Kawasaki shipyards in Kobe—to gain Japan's first guaranteed eight-hour day.

Walkouts in the factories, riots among consumers and tenant farmers in the countryside—these were symptomatic of a breakdown behind the façade of the great Meiji modernization. A rapidly industrializing and better-educated population was growing restive under the consensus of the Meiji reformers, who were now old and rather self-satisfied princes and viscounts. The *Far Eastern Economist* editorialized: "Unfortunately the political process in our country works only for the property-owning minority, while the classes without property are hardly given any security at all."

It was in 1919, incidentally, just a few months after this editorial appeared, that the first attempt to expand Japan's system of restricted male suffrage failed.

Japan's self-conscious intelligentsia had from the first been fascinated by the soggy profundities of early Marxist rhetoric. It took the successes of the Russian Revolution, however, to turn socialist researchers into Leninist activists. *Shin Sekai*'s editorial comment, quoted at the head of this chapter, was typical of the new intellectual journals "flying the flag of Marxism."

The social and economic tremors then shaking Japan seemed to fulfill the abundant Soviet prophecies about the end of capitalism. Although the Japanese Communist Party would not be founded until 1922, that archetypal Japanese socialist Katayama Sen arrived in Moscow in March 1919 at the head of a Japanese delegation specially invited to the first World Congress of the Comintern. Flattered by Soviet encouragement, Japan's bookish *interi* began a love affair with Marxism that lasted well into the seventies. Despite constant police harassment, they were able to build up a formidable network of publications, union groups, and university study centers.

There was also another kind of socialism in the air, which we might call authoritarian populism. Its exponents, also spin-offs from the broad intellectual crosscurrents of Meiji, were as indignant as the Marxists at the plight of tenant farmers and workers and the excesses of Japan's greedy establishment capitalists. They were traditionalists rather than Marxian materialists, however. For them the Japanese state should represent a compact between the emperor and the people, enforced by a loyal and responsive army. Most of them also saw Japan as the protector of Asia against the West, happily assuming the leadership of Asia for the good of all in a kind of commonwealth (whose virtues Chinese and Koreans had understandable difficulties in perceiving).

In 1919, just after his return from China, a brooding, seclusive Japanese Buddhist intellectual named Kita Ikki busied himself writing a variety of essays and letters on current problems. The Versailles settlement in particular disturbed him. "Self-determination" he denounced as Western trickery; for him Wilson was an archvillain. Finally putting many of his ideas together, that year he completed his magnum opus—a book called *An Outline for the Reconstruction of Japan* (*Nihon Kaizo Hoan Taiko*).

Kita's "reconstruction" managed to combine anticapitalism, bits and pieces of Marxist ideology, and devotion to Japan's army and emperor in an amazing way. Perhaps its appeal to many lay in its very illogic. It appealed to manifold discontents. Kita's writing became, in any case, a kind of handbook for young officers of the twenties and thirties, with fateful consequences for their country's—and Asia's—future. For the next quarter century Japan's genuinely democratic liberals (and there were quite a few of them) would be gradually ground down between homegrown populist-fascists like Kita Ikki, on the one hand, and would-be Marxist revolutionaries on the other.

IN FRANCE, at the peace conference, another Asian intellectual was politely but vainly knocking at the delegates' doors. Barely comfortable in a rented black suit, a young Vietnamese who had taken the ambitious name of Nguyen Ai Quoc (Nguyen the Patriot, literally translated) roamed the corridors of Versailles carrying an eight-point proposal for representative government in Vietnam. Its preamble—"All subject peoples are filled with hope by the prospect that an era of right and justice is opening to them"—recalled the brave words of the proclamations in Seoul and Beijing. Nguyen's was received in the West with the same massive indifference. Only a few French socialists listened to him. They were enough impressed to invite him to a conference at Tours the following year, where Nguyen—better known by his later pseudonym of Ho Chi Minh—became one of the founders of the French Communist Party.

Ho and his fellow radicals had a good bit to complain about. During the war the French had drafted 43,000 Vietnamese soldiers and almost 50,000 laborers for the war effort in Europe. Now that it was over, they intensified their efforts to squeeze as much profit as possible out of their colony. The work force more than doubled in the mines and on the rubber plantations, as well as in light industry, since the colony had had to make many of its own manufactured goods due to the falloff in wartime imports from France. Yet conditions grew worse rather than better; strikes and stoppages began to occur. And groups of French-educated intellectuals like Ho started to talk seriously about independence.

THE ISLANDS OF the Netherlands East Indies—which had yet to acquire the name Indonesia—were so tightly run by their Dutch administrators as to make the French in Indochina seem egalitarian by contrast. But here too the rumblings of European revolution were heard. The lessons of Japanese and Chinese modernizers were also influential, as was the drastic modernization of Mustafa Kemal, now taking place in another Muslim country, Turkey. As the historian Bernhard Dahm later wrote: "In 1919 a revolutionary situation prevailed throughout Java."[3]

The most important and numerous of the various Indonesian peoples, the Javanese chafed under the old forced-labor system of the Dutch, a carryover from the days of the East India Company. Labor riots and the burning of sugar plantations were commonplace. But this time there was a native organization to channel, if not to instigate them. Sarekat Islam—the Islamic Association—had grown from a Javanese membership of 4,500 in 1912 to almost 370,000 by 1914. By the time of its national congress in 1919 Sarekat Islam could count on more than a million members.

Thanks to the influence of Dutch as well as Indonesian Marxists, the Muslim religious tone of their resolutions was spiced with a strong dose of socialism, and resolutions denouncing both capitalism and colonialism were added to Islamic exhortation. In the end, however, Islam and the new Leninism proved incompatible; by 1921 the new Communist Party of Indonesia (PKI) was forced to go its own way.

[3] In his *History of Indonesia in the Twentieth Century* (New York: Praeger, 1971).

Even compared with the education offered in the other European colonies in Asia, that of the Indonesians had been cruelly restricted. According to a 1920 survey, for example, 1,344 Europeans attended secondary school there, out of a European population of 169,708. Out of 854,508 Chinese in the islands, 145 went to secondary schools. For the 48 million Indonesians of Malayan, Javanese, Sumatran, and other ancestries there was a grand total of 78 students. Although most people knew Javanese or Malay, many other languages and dialects were spoken. The national language of Bahasa Indonesia had yet to be invented. Which partly explains why Indonesians were so late in joining the outcry against colonialism.

One reason for the sudden growth of Sarekat Islam at this time was the dynamism of the magnetic Muslim leader Tjokroaminoto. Even after the original popularity of Sarekat Islam ebbed in the face of Dutch repression, a new generation of Indonesian students found a continuing inspiration in this religious statesman and his marvelous oratory. Among them was a precocious teenager who boarded at Tjokroaminoto's house in Surabaya and thought of the older man as a hoped-for "mirror" of behavior. His name was Sukarno.

ONE DATE OF importance remains in this watershed year of 1919. That is the March meeting of the Communist World International in Moscow. The International, thereafter familiarly known by its acronym of Comintern, had been planned by Lenin and his co-founders of the new Soviet state as the organ which would spread their revolution throughout the world. For Lenin, a pronounced Europeanist, this meant to carry the message of the Soviet "workers" to Germany and Poland and ultimately to France, Britain, and the United States, spreading the "world proletarian revolution" in the industrialized nation-states where Marx had predicted ultimate victory. As early as 1919, it was becoming clear that this strategy was in trouble. That year marked the total failure of the German Communist revolutionaries. In 1920, after Pilsudski's near-annihilation of the invading Soviet armies in Poland, Lenin commented, with rueful understatement: "The revolution which we had counted on in Poland did not take place." A similar fate had overtaken Béla Kun's attempted Communist takeover of Hungary in 1919, leaving little left of the original Leninist thesis.

Nothing abashed, the Communist hierarchy switched vestments to devise an intensified strategy for capturing Asia. As self-proclaimed "anticolonialists" and preachers of self-determination for all peoples, they were in a good position to exploit the expected surge of anti-Westernism in Asia. They hoped to construct, as Stalin put it, "a bridge between the socialist West and the enslaved East." Or as Lenin himself noted: "The infantry of the East will reinforce the cavalry of the West." (Typically, he had the Russians riding the horses.)

With this shift the Moscow International sent its best operatives to work in Asia. Hendrik Sneevliet, the Dutch socialist who had first organized Indonesia's Communists, went to China to do similar work. He was followed there by the famous Michael Borodin[4] and others. By the time the Comintern's second meeting convened, delegates from thirty-seven countries were present, including the peripatetic Ho Chi Minh and a recent Marxist convert from China, Li Dazhao. Li, Beijing University's activist head librarian, had already organized an influential Communist study group in Beijing. An assistant librarian, one Mao Zedong, was among its members.

Following their meetings the Comintern delegates moved quickly to start local branches. The Indonesian Party was organized in 1920, the Chinese Party in 1921, the Japanese Party in 1922. A clandestine Korean Party took shape in 1925, as did Ho Chi Minh's Association of Annamite Revolutionary Youth, for the moment based in Canton. In 1926 a regional South Seas Communist Group had its first meeting in Singapore.

The continuity in most of these organizations was impressive. Later support from the Comintern was spasmodic, reflecting the shifts and turnings of Joseph Stalin's domestic Russian policies, but local Communist parties soon began to serve as nuclei around which anticolonial and anti-Western sentiment could crystallize. Their resort to violence and extreme tactics over the ensuing decades exercised a strong appeal to two generations of young Asian intellectuals, repressed as they were by foreign colonial masters.

The Comintern's work could have been countered, if not offset by an active Asian policy from the United States, which was, after all, the home of anticolonialism and "self-determination." This was not to be. Instead, after Congress had rejected Wilson's brand of idealism along with the League of Nations, the Americans retreated into a policy of isolationism in foreign affairs and frantically reactive "anti-Communist" campaigns at home. About the only national interests the American public showed in the Pacific Basin were the strategic concerns of the naval limitations treaties, organized to counter Japan's expansion, and spasmodic, ineffectual pronouncements about an "Open Door" in China. By the early twenties racist bitterness in California had been literally codified by the Exclusion Acts directed against Japanese and Chinese. A new

---

[4] Mikhail Markovich Grusenberg, known best to history by the alias Borodin, learned his socialism in Poland as a member of the Jewish workers' bund there. He became an early follower of Lenin and the Bolsheviks, however, and after the Revolution was sent to direct the tactics of Communism in China. Although he was a commanding, fascinating figure—André Malraux immortalized him in his novel *Man's Fate* (*La Condition Humaine*)—his attempt to incite an urban workers' revolution in China failed disastrously. Originally befriended by Stalin, he worked faithfully in Moscow after his return from China, only to die in a labor camp in 1951, the victim of Stalin's later purges.

era of protectionism, typified by the renewed high tariffs of the Smoot-Hawley Act, showed the extremes of economic shortsightedness to which Americans could stoop.

It was only in the cultural sphere that the United States continued to exercise its influence. This, as we shall see, was considerable. Through the fog of local prejudices and meanspiritedness, American universities continued to open their doors to Asian students, while private American educators did much to assist the modernizing of schools and universities in East Asia. Despite the lack of official policies to project it, the glittering, selfish, altruistic, provocative civilization of modern America—literature, business, Hollywood, missionaries, Model T's, and general workaday know-how included—increasingly served as a magnet for Asian modernizers to whom the old Europe spelled only oppression, condescension, and deceit.

THE DECADES between the Versailles Treaty and World War II were a time of gestation. Governments superficially changed but little. One Japanese Prime Minister succeeded another, leading democratic parliamentary majorities responsible to the voters; but the emperor continued to review his troops. In China the Nanjing government declared its authority over the provincial warlords, while Nationalists and Communists began their fight over the heritage of the deceased Sun Yat-sen. The rest—except for the independent kingdom of Siam—was all colonies, variously colored on the map British, French, Dutch, or Japanese. Only the United States publicly promised its Philippine colony independence, partly out of altruism, largely out of impatience at long-distance colonial administration. Apart from periodic reaffirmations of the Open Door in China, Americans themselves remained practical isolationists.

Beneath the surface of established polities, however, a great many people were talking revolution, modernization, and change. While the majority in East Asia, mostly rural peasantry, concerned themselves with basic problems of subsistence, a new generation of intellectuals had begun to plot and plan for a variety of different futures. The discontent that had exploded before still smoldered; it was fed by increased economic development. First in Japan and later in China and Korea, a new urban society was slowly growing. New entrepreneurs were breaking surface, and workers were pressing for a fairer share of what they produced. Even in the European colonies communications and education were spreading; Asians came back from study or work in the West aggressively anticolonialist. They brooded over their people's backwardness in the new technology, the while wondering how to reactivate their old cultures.

The few people capable of bringing in a new era came from the relatively small mandarinate of the educated. Most had either direct or indirect experience of the West. Some demanded outright violent revolution; others preferred gradual reform. All wanted independence—either from foreign rule or from ruling oligarchies in their own countries. All were nationalists, with a deep sense of their own patriotic and cultural identity. They were revolutionaries as well. They sought to overturn what they saw as a bad existing system, whether it was foreign oppression, capitalist domination, or cultural stultification.

Five of such leaders we have already mentioned: Sukarno, Ho Chi Minh, Lu Xun, Kita Ikki, and Syngman Rhee. They are the subjects of this and subsequent chapters. Sukarno in Indonesia was a brilliant political opportunist who created a new nation. Ho Chi Minh was a dedicated Leninist, but withal a nationalist who put his restored country together through war and violence. Lu Xun was the ultimate artist engagé, an intensely activist writer whose moral indignation aroused his countrymen to work for a new, modern, independent China. Syngman Rhee fought through thirty years of exile for his own vision of an independent Korea, only to see it shattered by war and dissension; he would not live to see its later success. Kita Ikki's eccentric mix of social welfare and emperor worship failed to inspire a new populist Japan. In the end his work was used only as an incentive to aggression.

Each of these men typifies at least one aspect of the Asia-Pacific revolution. Each in his way provoked turmoil and radical change—for better or for worse. Their experiences sometimes intersected, sometimes contradicted one another. Through them, however, we may gain a better feel for the changes of that day.

LIKE MANY Chinese students of his day, the writer Lu Xun had journeyed to Japan, in 1905, to study at the medical college in Sendai. Despite China's defeat by Japan in the Sino-Japanese War in 1895, Chinese students, intellectuals, and would-be politicians continued to stay and work in Japan, as the Meiji exemplar of modernization. (It made, in fact, an ironic commentary on China's relative backwardness that new modern terms like "telegraph," "economics," and "philosophy" had to be recycled into Chinese from Japanese because China's still classical vocabulary contained no equivalents.) While their Japanese teachers watched with some condescension Chinese flocked to Tokyo and other Japanese cities for intensive study in modern Western learning, as apprehended and filtered by their aggressive Japanese neighbors.

One day in the classroom, after the teacher had exhausted his supply of lantern slides of microbiology specimens, he ran off a series of patriotic slides, scenes from the Russo-Japanese War then in progress. Perforce Lu Xun joined in the clapping and cheers of his Japanese fellow students. But he was brought up short by one film showing some Chinese captured in the war zone. One man was being accused of spying for the Russians. Hands bound, he was about to be beheaded; other Chinese in the picture stood by watching. They exhibited no anger, only curiosity. This was too much for Lu Xun.

He later wrote: ". . . after this film I felt that medical science was not so important after all. The people of a weak and backward country, however strong and healthy they may be, can only serve to be made examples of, or to witness such futile spectacles; and it doesn't really matter how many of them die of illness. The most important thing, therefore, was to change their spirit; and since at that time I felt that literature was the best means to this end, I determined to promote a literary movement."

After an unsuccessful effort to launch a new magazine in Tokyo, Lu Xun returned to China in 1907. He spent some humdrum years working as a high school principal and sometime translator of foreign literature (mainly German and Russian) into Chinese. Then he went to work for the Education Ministry in Beijing. In Beijing he began to write. "The Diary of a Madman" was published in 1918, on the eve of the May Fourth demonstrations. It was not only China's first short story, but also the first to be written in popular Chinese. Lu Xun, although well educated in the classical tradition, broke with it to write in colloquial, understandable Chinese, which could be read by almost anyone. For someone brought up in a family of literati in Zhejiang Province, this was a far more revolutionary act than merely joining a political movement. Writings of this sort signaled the real beginnings of China's modern era.

Lu Xun's stories bore a strong message. Most of them were allegories about the current state of China, whose people, without any sense of national unity, continued to feed on each other. Living for the moment, they ignored their real oppression by cruel, venal leaders and their hirelings. In Meiji Japan, novelists like Natsume Soseki and Shiga Naoya had enlarged the consciousness of people who were already in the midst of sweeping reform. By contrast Lu Xun and other young Chinese writers and scholars had a far more difficult task. They had to create an awareness of national identity that had hardly existed.

China's revolution in 1911, led by the American-educated doctor turned political philosopher Sun Yat-sen, was strong enough to topple the decadent Qing Dynasty. But Sun and his collaborators, who had spent most of their time plotting revolution overseas, lacked the military strength to retain power. They were quickly thrust into the background by the former imperial general Yuan Shikai, who had himself declared "president for life." After Yuan's death in 1916, real power in the republic was taken over by corrupt warlords, who ruled under the thinnest veneer of democratic forms. Sun bided his time from his own precarious power base in Canton, where he was assisted by an ambitious young general named Chiang Kai-shek.

Meanwhile the country drifted on political debris, its economy largely directed by foreign interests. "The revolution had changed nothing," Lu Xun

Ho Chi Minh's mausoleum in Hanoi Steve Talley

Sukarno as President. Royal Tropical Institute

Ho's picture is the centerpiece for worshippers at a local Vietnamese shrine. Steve Talley

Syngman Rhee before the League of Nations in Geneva, 1933 Rhee Family

Lu Xun and his wife, Xu Guangping
Encyclopedia of China

Shaoxing. This north China city, Lu Xun's native place, was the setting for his most famous short story, "Ah Q." Levie Isaacks

Lu Xun in Shanghai, 1935
Encyclopedia of China

wrote. "Beggars eat scraps by the roadside, half-starved children are sold for eight coppers a pound, and in the countryside men are starving to death. Our vaunted Chinese civilization is only a feast for the rich and the mighty."

In "The True Tale of Ah Q," Lu Xun etched the story of a petty crook masquerading as a revolutionary, but done in by more powerful "revolutionaries," equally fake and crooked. In this and other stories of biting realism, he stripped aside the pretense of ancient classics and Confucian custom to show the reality of a China ignorant, defenseless, and disunited, but a China that he loved.

"Imagine an iron house without windows, absolutely indestructible, with many people fast asleep inside who will soon die of suffocation. But you know since they will die in their sleep, they will not feel the pain of death. Now, if you cry aloud to wake a few of the lighter sleepers, making these unfortunate few suffer the agony of irrevocable death, do you think you are doing them a good turn?"

In this way Lu Xun mordantly posed the question: was it even possible to awaken China? Fukuzawa Yukichi had used somewhat similar language in describing Tokugawa Japan—"millions of Japanese closed up inside millions of boxes"—but that was Japan of seventy years before. What tortured Chinese intellectuals like Lu Xun was the thought that all their warnings about shaking the iron box of old China might be coming too late. Yet his very iconoclasm, his satiric wit, and above all the total lack of pretense in his writings agitated and moved a whole generation of Chinese. He became the lodestar and the conscience of the whole May Fourth movement, whose intellectual leaders, in their writings, lectures, and mass meetings, continued the students' 1919 goal of modernizing China.

Of course, there were others. Chen Duxiu was dean of Beijing University and editor of the magazine *New Youth*, which published many of Lu Xun's essays and stories. Beginning as an apostle of individualism—he gave his students lectures on adapting "Mr. Science" and "Mr. Democracy" instead of the outworn Confucian ethics—he later turned to Marxism and became one of the founders of the Chinese Communist Party. Hu Shi, professor of philosophy at Beijing University, had studied for seven years in the United States and had worked at Columbia under the progressive educator John Dewey. He resolutely remained a pragmatic liberal in the American tradition. (He was instrumental in organizing Dewey's Chinese lecture tour in 1919.) In a famous essay titled "More Talk of Problems, Less Talk of Isms," Hu brilliantly criticized the tendency of Chinese intellectuals to waste their time in abstract theorizing, generally on Western ideas swallowed whole. As a poet, philosopher, and teacher, Hu made as great a contribution as Lu Xun toward modernizing the Chinese language.

In this effort Hu, Chen, and Lu Xun were united. It was critical to China's progress as a modern society. For the classical written language of the Qing days, we must remember, was impenetrable to all but the tiny minority of Chinese with a classical education—as impenetrable as Latin would have been to a modern Frenchman or Italian.

There were other issues on which all of the May Fourth people could make common cause, liberals and reformist conservatives as well as leftists: the development of public education, the extension of democratic practice, and, in particular, the emancipation of women. For a time Lu Xun was particularly interested in the egalitarian "new village" movement. Russian writers also intrigued him, and he produced various translations from modern Russian; the Soviet Union seemed to point the way to the future. In the end, although hardly an ideologue, Lu Xun cast his lot with the more obvious revolutionaries on the left.

By then he had given up a good bit of his cynicism to join the struggle for China's modernization. Like others in the May Fourth group, he had been shocked by the increasing violence of police and soldiers against unarmed demonstrators. In 1925 Sikh troops from the International Settlement in Shanghai had fired on a procession of students and workers. Twelve were killed. On March 18, 1926, warlord troops in Beijing fired on a group of student demonstrators protesting new foreign demands on China. This time forty-seven died—all of them university students, both male and female.

"The students," Lu Xun wrote, "died for China. If China is not to perish, then the future holds a surprise for the murderers. . . . Blood debts must be repaid in kind. The longer the delay, the greater the interest."

Until 1927, Communists and other leftists had cooperated with the right-wing Nationalists under the umbrella of the Guomindang, the Nationalist Party, which Sun Yatsen had founded. But it grew increasingly difficult to paper over their differences. The last shreds of unity in the Guomindang were ripped apart that year after a bloodbath in Shanghai and other cities in which Chiang Kai-shek (Jiang Jesui) and his stronger military forces attempted to exterminate the Communists and their allies. This time the dead had to be reckoned in the thousands.

Faced with these outbreaks on the right, Lu Xun turned political. In 1930 he became president of the Communist-backed League of the Left-Wing Writers. "The brave man," he wrote, "draws his sword against the strong . . . I have always thought it important to train a younger generation of warriors . . ."

Yet in the midst of his militancy, he retained a basic pessimism about what activists could achieve. As he wrote: "Revolutionaries want to kindle a fire in men's hearts and create a blaze which may ignite the nation. But if men refuse to be kindled, sparks can only burn themselves out, just as paper images and carriages burn themselves out during funerals."

Lu Xun seemed a great catch for the Communists, for he immediately attracted many bright young writers to his group. But he proved hard to manage. His healthy distaste for all politicians included leftists as well as rightists. Surely the principal reason for his leftist alignment was the alternative. For by the early 1930s Chinese politics had polarized. There were many sincere and dedicated public servants working for the government, now dominated by the Nationalists. Yet, politically speaking, China's options seemed to narrow to a choice between the Communists and other left groups and Chiang Kai-shek's mixed bag of right-wing ideologues, big businessmen, and warlords, who now comprised the Nationalist leadership. Against this harsh rightist reality the expansive promises and apparent incorruptibility of the Communists had a powerful appeal.

Although his commitment to Communist causes helped gain them credibility, Lu Xun never joined the Party. Indeed, he became involved in some serious disputes with Party leaders largely because of his conviction that politics had no place in literature, including the literature of protest. In a speech entitled "The Divergent Roads of Literature and Politics"—prophetic, in view of the cruelties that Chinese Communism later inflicted on intellectuals—he had said: "After the success of revolution the revolutionary politician implements the same old methods which he opposed before. Such an act will arouse opposition again from the writer who would likewise be driven out and killed. . . . The fate of the writer, however, has not been changed by virtue of his participation in revolution. Everywhere he still knocks against nails. . . . Revolutionary writers and revolutionists can be said to be two entirely different kinds of beings."

Lu Xun died on October 19, 1936, wasted by tuberculosis. His funeral in Shanghai was a massive one. At least 10,000 people marched in a straggling procession. All of literary China seemed to be there, along with a large representation of students, schoolchildren, and simple citizens from the neighborhood where he then lived. Large floral wreaths bore the inscription: "Soul of the Nation."

There was not too much exaggeration in that. The effect on China's culture of the May Fourth movement, which Lu Xun so well epitomized, was more permanent than Chiang's calls to arms or Mao Zedong's Red Book of a later day. More than any politician could have, the realistic icon smashing of Lu Xun and others like him forced thinking Chinese to reappraise their basic ethic and moral values, as well as cultural ones. You could not build a modern nation, however old its civilization, in a society that makes serfs of its farmers and forces women to bind their feet.

The year after Lu Xun died, a precocious twelve-year-old named Liu Binyan began to read his books. Liu went on to join the Communist Party and became perhaps contemporary China's most distinguished journalist. But he never lost the spirit of honest criticism and hatred of injustice he learned from Lu Xun's writings. Despite long-standing Party loyalties, he became a severe critic of Chinese Communism's corruption and oppression. For this he was first silenced and persecuted by Mao Zedong and ultimately driven into exile by Deng Xiaoping. To Liu and to most Chinese intellectuals, Lu Xun remains an expression of "the national soul." "Lu Xun was profound," he wrote in 1990. "I was deeply affected by his concern with politics and his critical spirit. His merciless critique of Chinese culture deeply influenced me. It could be said that he determined the path for my life. Among Chinese writers he alone reached a unique depth in his understanding and analysis of our society."

Even such honest praise would have made Lu Xun a bit nervous as he sat in his small house in Shanghai,[5] a slightly built man in a tattered Chinese scholar's gown, cigarette smoke spilling over his mustache. He was not much of a talker. As his wife, Xu Guangpin, later recalled: "Mr. Lu Xun once said, 'In reality I have no need to say anything more, for everything I've ever wanted to say is all there, in tens of volumes of writings.' He didn't admit to having genius and said on another occasion, 'Where's the genius in it? I simply use the time for work that other people take drinking coffee.' "

EAST ASIANS—OR at least those of Han and related lineage—have always tended to apotheosize numbers. The five relationships of Confucius, the Seventeen-Article Constitution of Prince Shotoku, the Five-Article Charter Oath of Emperor Meiji, the Three Principles of Sun Yat-sen, the ghastly Four Olds of Mao Zedong's Cultural Revolution matched by Deng Xiaoping's Four Modernizations—the list is endless. Some ideas are so embedded in numbers that both seem of equal importance. It is the same with dates. Except for French city planners (Rue de 14 Juillet) or, possibly, American lawyers ("Where were you on the night of January 13?"), the fascination of Chinese and Japanese for remembering events by their exact times is unrivaled.

We have already noted the significance of March 1 and May 4, and the hopes they aroused. Now we turn to a more somber date: February 26, 1936. Called by the Japanese simply *Ni-ni-roku Jihen*—the February 26th Incident, its

[5] Although Lu Xun's Shanghai house still stands, most of the furnishings and memorabilia have been transferred to a museum, located near his tomb in Hong Kou Park. His former residence in Shaoxing has also been turned into a memorial hall. The inscription on the tomb, six gold characters, is written in the calligraphy of Mao Zedong, in ironic witness to the official Communist canonization of China's greatest modern freethinker.

mention even now evokes visions of cruelty, violence, and idealism tragically misplaced. Its consequences for Japan and the Pacific world were ominous, if almost totally unanticipated.

On the snowy early morning of February 26, 1936, some 1,400 soldiers of the Imperial Army's 1st Division, heavily armed with machine guns and light artillery, left their barracks and proceeded to occupy the key government buildings in the heart of Tokyo. Led by their company officers—the highest-ranking man was a captain—the mutineers dispatched detachments of picked men to systematically assassinate the Prime Minister and other government leaders in their homes. They managed to kill the Finance Minister, the Keeper of the Privy Seal, and the Army Inspector General; Prime Minister Okada Keisuke and others narrowly escaped. After dawn broke, detachments of the rebels handed out proclamations stating the purpose of their revolt. They were above all, they said, loyal to the emperor. They wished the country to expand its "national power and prestige." But to do this Japan must get rid of political and economic traitors.

"In recent years," the rebels continued, ". . . many persons have appeared whose chief aim in life has been to amass personal material wealth in disregard of the general welfare and prosperity of the Japanese people, with the result that the emperor's sovereignty has been violated. . . ."

"It is our duty to remove the evil retainers from around the throne and smash the group of senior statesmen. It is our duty as subjects of His Majesty the Emperor."

The script might almost have been written by Kita Ikki, who had, in fact, attended meetings with various of the plotters not so many weeks before. In his "Reconstruction" plan for Japan, which was first widely circulated in the twenties, Kita Ikki had argued that a swift military coup d'état was the best, if not the only way to restore direct imperial rule and get rid of the "evil" advisers. "The people are the main force," he wrote, "and the emperor their commander."[6] Barriers between them should be removed, he said. This is the way the young low-ranking samurai had seized power in the Meiji Restoration. It should do for the planned Showa Restoration as well.[7]

Kita's plan was an extraordinary mixture of socialism and a concern for human rights with a violent Japanese nationalism that was aggressive to the point of absurdity. Its economic section responded to the concerns of average people in the post–World War I era, bewildered by depression and apparently

[6] This translation is taken from *Kita Ikki: Radical Nationalist in Japan*, by George Wilson (Harvard, 1969). I am indebted to Wilson and the late Richard Storrey, author of *The Double Patriots*, for many insights into as well as information about Ikki's activities.

[7] Showa (literally "Shining Peace") was the era name chosen for Emperor Hirohito's reign (1925–89).

hopeless disparities between the kinds of life the "haves" and the "have-nots" were enjoying. He advocated sweeping land reform, in many ways anticipating the land reform of the U.S. Occupation more than two decades later. He called for breaking up the big-money *zaibatsu* conglomerates, with limits set on the size of companies. The rights of labor were to be protected, with profit sharing and worker participation in management.

Going further, he proposed to abolish the exploitation of women in industry—and he attacked the double standard that made it virtually impossible for a woman in Japan to obtain a divorce. He stopped short of advocating women's suffrage. He did, however, support general co-education. Private property was to be respected and the rights of criminal defendants protected—as part of a system providing broad guarantees of social welfare.

Along with these steps toward modernization, however, Kita advocated a general Japanese protectorate over most of East Asia. The Koreans ("incapable of self-determination") were to be assimilated; China was to be helped toward recovery by a protective Japan, which would "liberate" China and India, among others, from domination by the West. It was time for Japan to proclaim a "divine mission, an Asian Monroe Doctrine," backed by a successful war against the West. "England," he wrote, "is a multimillionaire standing over the whole world. Russia is the great landlord of the Northern Hemisphere. Japan is in the position of an international proletarian with a string of small islands for boundaries. Does Japan not have the right to go to war and seize their monopolies in the name of justice?"

Absurd though it may sound today, Kita Ikki's combination of Marx and *The Mikado* held a lot of appeal for the Japanese of that time. Although Japan had sat at the victors' table in Versailles, its world-power status finally guaranteed, the old Meiji Restoration goals of *Fukoku kyohei*—"Enrich the country and strengthen the military"—seemed far from realization. While the rural poor grew poorer, the tinsel of a new Hollywood civilization cast its glitter on the big cities. Jazz and flappers, chorus lines and splashy novels, touring cars and low-cut dresses, golf and stock-market plungers—all the superficialities of America's Roaring Twenties were imported into Japan. Or some of them at least. The new *mobo* and *moga* ("modern boy" and "modern girl") of the cities faced ubiquitous police "morals" surveillance, to the point where taxis in Tokyo had to keep their inside lights on to forestall any kissing by their passengers.

After the controlled democracy of the Meiji period, Japan now had "party government." It was the era of Taisho Democracy.[8] But considerable corruption came in along with the parliamentary system, despite the steadily widening

---

[8] So named after the emperor Taisho, son of Meiji and father of Hirohito, the Showa emperor, who reigned from 1912 to 1925.

franchise. With one of the major parties subsidized by the Mitsui interests and the other by Mitsubishi, collusion between party politicians and their big-business backers was all too obvious.

Kita Ikki began political life as a socialist. His first book, published when he was twenty-two, was an effort to show that the emperor's sovereignty really derived from the people. It got good notices from such socialist (and later Communist) stalwarts as Katayama Sen. After the Russo-Japanese War, how-ever, Kita fell in with several groups who were actively in support of Sun Yat-sen's revolutionary activities in China. He went to China himself, lived there for some time with his wife, and gradually became obsessed with the idea of helping the Chinese resist Western imperialism.

For years he participated in the various side dramas of plot and counterplot as Japanese China watchers tried to reconcile support for China's revolution and the "emancipation of Asia" from the Western powers with their growing conviction that any emancipation would have to be directed by Japan. Japanese have had a long-standing weakness for putting together study groups and fac-tions. Some of these were right-wing, some left-wing, although the distinctions were often not very clear. Most of the right-wingers had more than a streak of populism in them. Almost all of them were anti-Western. The failure of the racial equality clause at Versailles, the anti-Japanese Exclusion Acts in the United States, and, even in those days, protectionist measures against Japanese goods intensified their rancor.

The old Meiji establishment leaders, however, like Okuma Shigenobu, the former Prime Minister, and Prince Saionji Kinmoji, the last of the *Genro* (elder statesmen) continued to feel that Japan must keep up good relations with the West, if for no other reason than that it was "the new boy on the block" among the imperialist Great Powers. Accordingly, the conviction grew among the plot-happy zealots exchanging sake cups in the Tokyo teahouses that Japan needed a restorative housecleaning itself before going on to underwrite Asia's "protection." Which is where the Army enters the picture.

The Japanese officer corps in the twenties and thirties was no longer the stronghold of samurai family privilege it had been at the close of the Russo-Japanese War. Just as universal conscription had served as the instrument of literacy and basic education in Meiji times, the Taisho Army and Navy were offering an efficient, if limited, higher education to the sons of farmers and small tradesmen. More than 30 percent of the new officers came from relatively poor rural families. They were well indoctrinated with loyalty to the emperor and to Japan, the emperor's country—"Double Patriots" some of them called themselves. They also harbored two basic grievances: against the West outside and the rich moneyed aristocracy within the country.

It was these country boys who swallowed Kita's message whole. His idea of a military coup did not shock them. Had not Japan's early heroes of the pre-Meiji days resorted to assassination to make their protest? They were samurai too, even if they wore khaki uniforms.

They worked on two fronts. Disdaining the brother-Asian approach of old boys like Kita Ikki, the young officers were only too willing to carve out new conquests in China. On September 18, 1931, staff officers of the Kwantung Army arranged an "incident" at Mukden, giving them an excuse to fire on local Chinese units. The skirmishing thus begun quickly escalated into the military occupation of Manchuria. Later in 1932 aggressive Japanese officers provoked more fighting in China.

In 1931, angered by news of Japan's signing of the London Naval Limitations Treaty,[9] a right-wing zealot had mortally wounded Prime Minister Hamaguchi Osachi. The following year, in the infamous May 15th Incident, a small gang of Army and Navy cadets and junior officers murdered Prime Minister Inukai Tsuyoshi at his official residence. Two months before, some co-conspirators had shot down Dan Takuma, then head of the house of Mitsui.

Kita lived quietly through this period, spending a good bit of time in meditation and reading the Buddhist sutras. He was a philosopher, in his way, or at least a thinker. He was above all a loner. As he pored over old Buddhist tracts, he fancied himself a second Nichiren, with a mission to revive the consciousness of the twentieth century the way Nichiren, the militant founder of the sect that bears his name, strove to revitalize the Buddhist world of Japan's thirteenth century. Yet despite his personal seclusion his writings were still talked about. His disciples were busy plotting with the young military officers. If Kita Ikki took no part in the actual revolt of February 26, 1936, he had been told about it. He certainly knew that something was afoot.

In the event, the revolt was quickly suppressed. For a few days Tokyo—for which read Japan—lived in a state of suspended animation. Schoolchildren were told to be quiet and in some cases returned to their homes. Tens of thousands of Tokyo citizens walked through the snow to gaze at the rebel troops holding the government buildings, and later watched loyalist regiments brought up to surround and contain them. The rebels were disappointed; none of the senior military men they asked to lead them accepted the offer—however much they may have been in sympathy with their aims. The mutineering young officers, following Kita Ikki's scenario, had counted on gaining the sympathy of the generals by their forthright stand. With this, they hoped to gain imperial sanction. *Kateba kangun,* the familiar Japanese proverb ran: "If you win, you are the emperor's army."

This time the emperor conspicuously didn't want any reinforcements. In

---

[9] The London Treaty of 1930, a follow-up to the Washington Conference of 1921, had limited Japanese naval armament to slightly more than a 5-5-3 relationship with Great Britain and the United States. It was bitterly opposed by the Japanese military, who demanded total parity.

fact, he got quite cross. In a rare display of his authority, Hirohito, bolstered by Prince Saionji, ordered his generals to subdue the rebels. It was to be the last clear-cut decision he made until August 15, 1945.

Embarrassed by the emperor's hard line, the generals surrounded the rebels and demanded their surrender. After a simple appeal from headquarters ("Those who resist will be shot as rebels. Your parents and your brothers and sisters are weeping to think you are traitors") most of the rank and file laid down their arms. Some of the rebel officers committed suicide. Others were tried and executed.

So was Kita Ikki, one of two civilians to die. His book had been all too successful. Above all, his socialism—the very idea of an emperor system based on people's rights—made the more conventionally right-wing generals extremely uncomfortable.

Probably the most interesting modern evocation of those times—so hard for contemporary people, Japanese included, to visualize—is given in the novel *Runaway Horses* by Mishima Yukio. The novel's hero, one Iinuma Isao, a young Japanese martial arts champion, concocts a bizarre plot to assassinate leading Japanese capitalists and public officials, with the help of some like-minded amateur rightists. They are discovered and arrested. In his speech to the court young Iinuma denounces the big-money businessmen of that day. "The *zaibatsu*," he tells the judge, "have amassed vast sums through dollar buying and other policies ruinous to the nation. And no one pays any heed to the wretched misery of the masses."

The sympathetic judge lets Iinuma off. Whereupon he proceeds with at least part of his original plot. He stalks a prominent business leader at his villa, stabs him to death, then commits suicide himself, by slitting his stomach, in the best samurai tradition.[10]

WITH THE suppression of the young officers' revolt, the world's newspaper readers—or those few of them who cared—may have assumed that law, order, and peaceful civilian control had been restored to imperial Japan. Quite the opposite was true. The emotional rebels had lost their game, but in their place a tougher and far more professional gang of militarists now took over at Army headquarters. Called the Control Faction (*Tosei-ha*), they were led by a grimly

---

[10] Mishima fancied himself a modern revolutionary in the Kita Ikki tradition. In 1970 he attempted his own right-wing coup, with a small corps of like-minded zealots, by trying to provoke a rebellion at the headquarters of Japan's Self-Defense Forces in Tokyo. After failing abjectly in the effort—the soldiers of the new Japan laughed at his oratory—he committed suicide in the best samurai *seppuku* tradition, and one of his comrades-in-arms obligingly chopped off his head in the traditional samurai coup de grace. His book, therefore, bears more than a little verisimilitude.

Kita Ikki. Misuzu Shobo

On February 26, 1936, Japanese troops, led by
insurgent young officers in a military coup, took
up positions around government buildings in
Tokyo. NHK

*Rebel troops in front of their
Sanno Hotel headquarters,
February 26, 1936. During and
after the U.S. Occupation, the
Sanno Hotel was reserved for
American personnel.* NHK

efficient military bureaucrat named Tojo Hideki. The following year, after another contrived firefight with Chinese troops at the Marco Polo Bridge, the Japanese Army occupied Beijing and the China Incident began. The road to war lay clear ahead, and General Tojo, made Prime Minister in October 1941, was ready to lead the charge.

For many years it was fashionable to call Kita Ikki simply a "fascist," following the lead of Japan's eminent historian Maruyama Masao, and to regard the young officers' "rebellion from below" as a peculiarly Japanese phenomenon. Both are dangerous, if contrary generalizations. In the 1930s, Japan, for all its power, was socially and—if one can use the word lightly—emotionally speaking a still developing country, barely sixty years away from the days when its sword-wielding scholars cut off their topknots and set out to study the science and technology of the West. Fatally flawed by the lack of civilian control over the military, the young Japanese democracy ultimately became the Army's hostage. Spectacular Army and Navy successes made military rule easier. There was little popular opposition. In Japan, as in many other countries, people were proud of the parades.

Since the end of World War II we have seen the drama of the rebellious officers played over and over again in Korea, Thailand, Indonesia, and most recently the Philippines—not to mention the far cruder, in fact almost incessant examples of military takeovers in Africa and the Middle East. (Latin America seems largely to have outgrown it.)

The pattern is generally the same. The young officers have received something of an education. (In some countries the Army was for a time at least the only way poor boys could get higher schooling and make their mark in the world.) They are underdogs. Like their Japanese prototypes of the thirties, they resent excesses of wealth around them. They feel for the oppressed. They have grievances. They have guns.

As for Kita Ikki—part Marxist, part fascist, part populist—he was so muddled with injustices and concerns that he had a hard time focusing his literary rage. By contrast, Lu Xun knew exactly what he was mad about. So, as we shall see, did Sukarno, Ho Chi Minh, and Syngman Rhee.

6

Independence and the Postwar Wars

I have a government that is organized and ready to go. Your statesmen make eloquent speeches about helping those with self-determination. We are self-determined. Why not help us? Am I any different from Nehru, Quezon—even your George Washington? I, too, want to set my people free.

HO CHI MINH, TO AN AMERICAN OFFICER, 1945

We are happy to see so many Americans here. You have been with us in a most difficult time. You were perhaps misunderstood and unjustly criticized . . . but one great fact will remain and stand out prominently in history: you have come here to help us to restore our independence and you have accomplished it.

SYNGMAN RHEE, TO AMERICAN OFFICERS, 1948

On December 13, 1937, several divisions of the Japanese Army's Central China Command under General Matsui Iwane captured Nanjing, then the capital of Nationalist China. Over the next two weeks they perpetrated an orgy of killing, rape, and looting which has few parallels in modern history.[1] In Nanjing and its outskirts, by conservative estimate, Japanese troops murdered at least 150,000 Chinese civilians and war prisoners. More than 10,000 women were raped, most of them repeatedly; many were afterward killed. A third of the city was destroyed.

The rape and looting of the city went on for days; the systematic cruelties of

---

[1] The grim statistics of the Nanjing atrocities are taken from the postwar war crimes trials (International Ministry Tribunal for the Far East); they were amply confirmed from eyewitness accounts at that time. A summary is given in Robert Butow's *Tojo and the Coming of War* (Princeton, N.J.: Princeton University Press, 1961) and numerous other sources.

Interestingly enough, the affluent Japan of the early nineties is full of literary and scholarly apologists who contend that the Rape of Nanjing never happened, or that, if it did, it was a small incident that was greatly exaggerated by "anti-Japanese" propagandists. This appalling "incident" is barely mentioned in modern Japanese school textbooks.

Victory in Nanjing. Gen. Matsui Iwane leads Japanese parade through Nanjing, 1940. In this city, in December 1937, the armies under General Matsui's command perpetrated the Rape of Nanking. It was one of the worst atrocities in history. Mainichi Shimbun

some units, notably General Nakajima Kesago's 16th Division, rivaled the worst excesses of the Nazi SS. Nor was this a case of the troops "getting out of hand," as some apologists have said. Discipline in the Imperial Army was severe, administered by a chain of command that stretched tightly from division chiefs of staff to superior privates. (The only orders later unearthed about the incident were those forbidding any mention of what had happened.) Somewhere a decision had been taken to terrorize the Chinese by devastating their capital; the troops had, with appalling enthusiasm, obeyed.

Back in Tokyo, scholarly researchers like the members of Prime Minister Konoe Fumimaro's Showa Research Society continued to formulate plans for a peaceful pan-Asian union—under Japanese auspices. Ironically, General Matsui, the overall commander, was a pan-Asianist himself, but in fact he had little control over the field units from his Shanghai headquarters. (On the way to China, he had announced that he went "in the mood of a man trying to pacify his brother.") Peaceful union meant nothing, however, to the self-appointed praetorians of Japan's expeditionary forces in China and Manchuria, as they burned and killed their way through that vast country.

Chiang Kai-shek and his Nationalist government, all too conscious of their country's military weakness, somewhat reluctantly mobilized a national anti-Japanese resistance. The Communist forces of Mao Zedong and Zhu De mounted their own war in the countryside, against Japanese and Guomindang alike. Sadly for China, the Japanese invasion would become a three-cornered battle.

Intellectuals in both countries tended to polarize their thinking. Japanese internationalists like the later Prime Minister Yoshida Shigeru tried vainly for a peaceful settlement, but generally within the context of a Japanese protectorate. Socialist and Communist activists who might have worked against the China war to some effect were neutralized by police persecution. In fact, numbers of left-wing ideologues became turncoats (*tenkosha*) under police persuasion, handily rediscovering Japan's "divine mission" in Asia in time to stay out of jail. The peaceable emperor, presumably exhausted after quelling the 1936 rebels, had little trouble resigning himself to Army control. He spent a good bit of his time reviewing the troops on his attractive white horse, *Shira-yuki*.

Chinese intellectuals, equally angry at Japan and the domestic failings of the Guomindang Nationalists, found the idea of total revolution increasingly attractive. Communist Party cells began to multiply in publishing houses, newspapers, and universities—even the theatrical world. (One famous Shanghai actress could later boast that a good bit of the revolution was planned and plotted from her restaurant in the old French Concession.)

Most Americans regarded the struggle in Asia as a straight war of Japan against China, real but thankfully remote, something to cluck about sympathetically over breakfast. The struggles of the noble Chinese peasants in Pearl Buck's *The Good Earth* were touching enough to make the book (and the movie) immensely popular, but they were nothing so immediate as the spectacular aggressions of Nazis and fascists in Europe. Apart from the Sino-Japanese fighting, colonial Asia seemed peaceful. The Philippines had been promised independence by President Roosevelt, while in the British and Dutch colonies—virtually unknown to the American public—presumably contented natives continued to work in oil rigs, tin mines, and rubber plantations, faithfully offering their raw materials to the industrial West.

No one gave much thought at all to Korea and Vietnam (then known as French Indochina), those two ancient, troubled nations that were to play such a major role in American life after World War II. They had odd similarities to one another: Korea, the mountain-girt peninsula off northern China, and Vietnam, the singular complex of mountain, sea, and delta to China's south. Each was the home of a separate race, quite distinct from the loose homogeneity of Han China. Both had long histories of belligerent independence, with their own emperors and mandarinates, although both had continued to pay tribute to Beijing until almost the turn of the nineteenth century. Both shared China's Buddhist and Confucian heritage and entered the twentieth century encumbered by an incubus of ritualized thinking. What modernization they experienced was imposed. Vietnam, along with its neighbors Cambodia and Laos, had been a French colony since the 1880s. Korea had been turned into a Japanese government-general after the Russo-Japanese War in 1905.

Colonialism did not sit easily with these two peoples, who have over the centuries earned equally strong reputations as clannish, contentious, and competent societies. Each country had more than its share of strong nationalists, who continued to protest colonial oppression. But two men stand out as ultimately successful revolutionaries: Ho Chi Minh and Syngman Rhee. They were the same two who had unsuccessfully sought to gain a hearing for national self-determination with the Versailles peacemakers in 1919.

It would be hard to imagine more dissimilar idealists. Although both came from old mandarin families, they rejected that tradition. Each cast his lot with different Western ideologies. Ho became a convinced Communist in Europe, knew his way around Moscow, and served as a trusted official of the Comintern. Rhee became a Christian, got his education, and spent most of his life in the United States. Both lived most of their adult lives in exile, continually planning, plotting, and organizing. Both survived to lead their countries to independence, at the cost of violent, destructive warfare.

In contrast to the soul searchings of more introspective intellectuals like Lu Xun and Kita Ikki, Ho Chi Minh always seemed to know exactly what he wanted. After his father, an expert Chinese calligrapher, had been dismissed from his post at Vietnam's imperial court for his anti-French agitation, Ho found himself a job as a messboy on a French steamship bound for Marseilles. Earlier, family friends had offered him a chance to study in Japan, but Ho preferred to live in France. "I first heard the words *liberté, égalité, fraternité* as a boy of thirteen," he later told a Soviet interviewer. "I wanted to see French civilization and put my finger on whatever was behind those three words." He left Saigon in 1911.

Ho spent several years traveling in Europe and the United States. He did odd jobs; at one point he worked temporarily as an assistant chef to the great Escoffier at London's Carlton Hotel. Finally he settled in Paris, changed his name,[2] and sought out other expatriate anticolonials. By 1919, taking the lessons of the October Revolution to heart, he began to think of himself as a Communist. By 1920, as a founding member of the French Party, he was leading a Communist cell in Paris. In 1922 he made his first pilgrimage to Moscow, to attend the Fourth Comintern Congress. There he met Lenin.

Many American writers have given over a good deal of newsprint, particularly during the sixties, to speculation as to whether Ho was primarily a Communist or a "nationalist." For him there was never any conflict. He was, as Bernard Fall once wrote, "a dedicated Communist with Vietnamese reactions."[3]

Like the Dutchman Hendrik Sneevliet (alias Maring) and the almost legendary Michael Borodin in China and Nozaka Sanzo in Japan, Ho Chi Minh was a Party activist whose life was driven by an unshakable belief that the world's future lay with Communism. Whether or not Communism will be in the end accounted a Christian heresy, its early-twentieth-century apostles, in their combination of zeal and operational skill, certainly bore striking resemblance to Matteo Ricci and his fellow Jesuits of the seventeenth. Heedless of hardships, they ranged the world in pursuit of their unitary goal. Their dedication was supported by a ruthlessness that would have made the least scrupulous of Jesuits, however, seek the confessional. And the wide theater of their

[2] Born Nguyen Sinh Cung, he received the "scholarly" name of Nguyen Tat Thanh (literally, Nguyen the Triumphant) to celebrate his father's passing his official scholar's examination. In Paris he changed his name to Nguyen Ai Quoc (Nguyen the Patriot) to signify his revolutionary activity. He went to Moscow under the name of Tran Vang; while there he was generally known as Linov or Linh. He assumed the name of Ho Chi Minh (literally, He Who Brings Light) in 1941. Even after becoming president of Vietnam, he continued to use pseudonyms when writing articles. Questioned about these and other name changes in his life, Ho once commented: "You must allow an old man some mystery."

[3] As quoted in *The Two Vietnams* (New York: Praeger, 1963). For this section I have borrowed both information and insights from Fall and Jean Lacouture, whose biography of Ho remains the best obtainable.

activities, as they crossed from country to country to do the International's bidding, gave them an almost unequaled knowledge of international political dynamics. So a later generation of American political and military planners would discover.

Ho Chi Minh was almost a classic example of the breed, perhaps its greatest product. After a good basic education at Hue's Lycée Quoc Hoc, he picked up his political grounding in Marxism in Moscow during a year of intensive study in 1924. There he found time to turn out a few propaganda pieces, including a pamphlet titled *The Black Race,* dealing with racism among Americans and Europeans, not to mention the "barbarities and ugliness of American capitalism." The year before, at the French Communists' request, he had organized the Peasant International in Moscow.

At the end of 1924, Ho sailed for China, then the focus of the Comintern's efforts at provoking world revolution. For the next three years he had an organizer's paradise, thanks to the temporary alliance of the Nationalists and the Communists in the Guomindang. Operating out of Canton, he set up a League of Oppressed Peoples of Asia, the Comintern's front organization for the nascent Communist parties in Southeast Asia. But he did not fail to train and recruit for his abiding objective, the Communization of Vietnam. Promising fellow exiles were trained at special cadre schools in Canton, to be sent back to their homeland as leaders for an ultimate Communist takeover. (Anti-Communist exiles had a way of disappearing.) Some were given special courses at Chiang Kai-shek's Whampoa Military Academy under the direction of Soviet officers—a commentary on the strange political bedfellowship of that day.

All this collapsed when Chiang turned against the Communists in 1927. Ho had to cross the Gobi Desert in the course of a long, roundabout flight to safety in Moscow.

The rest of the years leading up to World War II he spent in a maze of underground activity and international intrigue—a living John le Carré plot with overtones of Eric Ambler and Maxim Gorki. As nearly as can be established,[4] he did political work in Berlin, attended an anti-imperialist conference in Brussels, and managed a brief visit to his beloved Paris—the cultural side at least of France's *mission civilisatrice* powerfully influenced this politically anti-French zealot—before returning to his "second home" in Moscow. Before 1930, give or take a year or two, Ho was back in Asia, hiding out in Thailand disguised as a Buddhist monk. Through it all he kept to his work of organizing, increasingly concentrating on building up Communist networks of Vietnamese.

In 1930 during a series of meetings in Hong Kong, Ho—this time posing as

[4] Here I have generally followed Bernard Fall as well as Stanley Karnow and Lacouture. Also useful in establishing Ho's devious chronology is *Ho Chi Minh* (Moscow: Progress Publishers, 1986) by Evgeny Kobalev, a former Tass correspondent in Vietnam.

a Chinese businessman—brought about the merger of different Marxist factions to form the Vietnamese Workers Party, the umbrella organization for the Communists. The following year he was arrested for his subversive activities by the British in Hong Kong, but he managed to escape prison, and extradition to French Indochina, after his British lawyer secured a writ of habeas corpus. Jailed a second time in Hong Kong, he made his escape from the prison infirmary and fled once more to Moscow, via Shanghai.

This time Ho—or Linov, to use his Moscow alias—spent four years studying and lecturing at the International Lenin School and working with old friends in the Comintern's Eastern secretariat. Dmitri Manuilsky, his Comintern mentor, Lenin's widow Krupskaya, France's Maurice Thorez, Czechoslovakia's Klement Gottwald, Germany's Wilhelm Pieck, and Japan's Nozaka Sanzo were friends and colleagues, part of the Red elite in which Ho held charter membership. His Moscow connections were probably unrivaled, good enough to let him escape the Stalinist purges then building up. By 1937 Ho had journeyed East again, this time to Yanan, where he did liaison work with Mao Zedong, Ho's junior in the international Communist hierarchy.

A deceptively frail-looking man whose wispy goatee became a trademark, Ho Chi Minh never altered his status or his objectives. A nationalist from the first, he combined his work as a very senior Communist international executive with his lifelong mission to revive a united Vietnam as a Communist state. Interestingly enough, he received far less support from Stalin's Russia and Mao's China than he might have expected, although in the end they provided the guns and munitions that sustained North Vietnam in its long war. The twists and turns of international Communist policies, as Moscow dictated them, were often more harmful than helpful to Asian Communists.

Yet life in the shadow world of the Comintern underground proved to be a great conditioner. For one thing, it taught Ho every variety of deception. At one point the Chinese Nationalists arrested him on grounds of being a Communist, and a French agent besides. Totally secure in his definition of what it meant to be Vietnamese and Communist, he dealt with opposition ruthlessly. ("All who do not follow the line which I have laid down will be broken," he once noted, commenting on the fate of a political opponent.) The friendly "Uncle Ho" figure so beloved by American antiwar protestors of the 1960s was a skillfully worn mask.

Ho could inspire and win people, the better to use them. In the course of his long struggle he managed to exploit Soviets and Chinese, Americans and French, with equal ease. Ho was fluent in Russian and Chinese. He wrote in French as well as his native tongue, and he handled English well. Well read and cosmopolitan, he could quote Stalin, Marx, Jefferson, and Molière when they served his purposes. Above all he had a longtime exile's patience.

Early in February 1941, Ho and a few aides hiked over the mountains of southern China into the northern Vietnamese province of Cao Bang. It was his first return to his homeland in thirty years. On May 10, sitting in a bamboo hut on piles deep in the jungle, he convened the Eighth Plenum of the Vietnam Party's Central Committee. For ten days they met, while torrents of rain poured down, making their hideaway almost uninhabitable. The decisions they made there shaped Vietnam's future.

Recent popular uprisings, Ho said, "show that our nation will take any opportunity to rise up in arms." With the example of the French Popular Front of the late thirties in mind, he urged a national movement, irrespective of class or politics, to drive out both the French and the Japanese, who had recently occupied part of the country. "The Party," he concluded, "should appeal to people's patriotic feelings, to win the support of all sections of society."

The Plenum decided on a broad, catchall name for their new movement: the League for the Independence of Vietnam (Vietnam Doc Lap Dong Minh). It would soon become known by its Vietnamese abbreviation Vietminh, however. Uncle Ho's political reflexes told him that Japan would ultimately be defeated in the Pacific war. His goal was to mobilize a Vietnamese "people's army" that could move in on both the Japanese and the French and fight for independence. Throughout World War II, Ho and his colleagues trained and organized, setting up bases of activists throughout Vietnam, preparing a coordinated plan of political and military action for the time *their* war began. In this work he was materially helped by a young history teacher, French-educated, with a fondness for military tactics, named Vo Nguyen Giap. Giap was as zealous an anticolonialist as Ho; his wife and sister-in-law had been executed by the French. He was also, as events were to prove, something of a homegrown military genius, with an unusual talent for both organization and attack.

The day after Japan's surrender in 1945, Ho and Giap assembled their cadres in the village of Tan Trao, in the backcountry outside Hanoi. As Giap recalls the day: "We met on the hill close to the banyan tree. Under the leadership of President Ho, the Central Committee decided that the time for the general uprising had come.

"On the evening of the sixteenth, I gathered the liberation forces under the trees in Tan Trao and I read out Military Order No. 1 . . . At that time the uprising began in many places in Vietnam."

On August 19, 1945, the Vietminh entered Hanoi and seized control of the city administration. As yet there was no effective French force to resist them. Japanese occupation troops stood apart, waiting to be disarmed by British troops, who were soon to arrive. On September 2, Ho read Vietnam's Declaration of Independence to a huge crowd in Hanoi. Its opening words—"All men are created equal . . . certain inviolable rights . . . Life, the right to be free and the right to happiness"—were taken from the American model.

Ho and Giap had indeed been assisted by American OSS agents who had parachuted into Vietnam before the war's end. It was well known, in Vietnam as in Washington, that President Roosevelt had opposed returning Indochina to French colonial status.

Forty-five years after, one of the surviving OSS officers, Allison Kent Thomas, recalled: "When I was with Ho and Giap in the field, I had the impression that they would fight no matter how long it would take to achieve their independence . . . There was a fierce rage against the French among the Vietnamese . . . In contrast, Ho was kindly disposed toward the Americans, because he felt we were against colonialism. He told me privately that he would welcome one million American soldiers, but not one Frenchman."[5]

Shortly thereafter Ho sent a letter to President Harry Truman asking American help in protecting Vietnamese independence from France. Truman does not seem to have sent a reply.

FITTINGLY ENOUGH for a Christian statesman, Syngman Rhee, first President of the Republic of Korea, began his political life as a near-martyr. A twenty-two-year-old protestor against the vacillating policies of the crumbling Korean imperial court, he was jailed in 1898, after reactionary courtiers smashed a demonstration of the Independence Club, a highly vocal group of young Koreans who demanded a speedy modernization of their ancient country.

Like Kang Yuwei and the young Chinese reformers, whose brief "Hundred Days" bid for power collapsed that same year, Rhee and his colleagues were essentially moderates. They hoped to achieve democracy within the framework of the Korean monarchy. There was nothing moderate about their punishment, however. From his cell window Rhee could hear the sounds of his closest friends' beheadings. He himself was brutally tortured and repeatedly caned and beaten in the course of six years' imprisonment.

While in prison Rhee wrote a series of essays called *The Spirit of Independence*. Essentially this was a plea for the Korean people to rise up and build themselves a working democracy based on principles then almost unknown in that archaic society of state Confucianism. "To live in this nation," he wrote, "is comparable to being a passenger on a ship in a cruel sea. How can you be so indifferent as not to be concerned with the affairs of your nation, but to insist that they are the business of high officials? The ship may be wrecked if you try to help yourself alone or are concerned only to save the captain of the ship. . . ."

By the time Rhee had these thoughts published, it was already too late. In

---

[5] From a filmed interview in 1990 with the producers of *The Pacific Century*.

1904, as the Russo-Japanese War drew to its close, Japan had already begun to make its de facto protectorate over Korea permanent. Freed from prison, Rhee sailed promptly for the United States. Powerfully influenced by his contacts with American missionaries in Korea—he would soon become a Christian himself—Rhee had learned English and spent some time reading up on American history and politics. The Americans, who had some years earlier signed a treaty with Korea, seemed the only source of deliverance from Japan.

In the summer of 1905, after intense discussions with fellow Koreans in Washington, Rhee hired a cutaway and took the train from New York out to Sagamore Hill, Theodore Roosevelt's Long Island estate. There he made a formal plea for Korean independence. Roosevelt was then occupied with preparations for the Treaty of Portsmouth, in which he negotiated the end of the Russo-Japanese War. Thus America's Rough Rider president was polite but evasive. He had already assured Japanese envoys that Japan should have a position with Korea "just like we have with Cuba." In the end the United States gave Japan a "free hand" in Korea in return for Japan's support of American annexation of the Philippines.

Nothing daunted, Rhee set out on what turned into a forty-year campaign to persuade Americans that Korea ought to be independent. His first goal was academic. With the help of missionary friends from Korea, he began his studies at George Washington University, later going on to Princeton. In 1910 he received his Ph.D. degree from Woodrow Wilson, who was then Princeton's president. Wilson knew Rhee and enjoyed introducing him around the college, half seriously, as "the future redeemer of Korean independence."

It was thus a double blow, after another nine years of Rhee's lecturing about Korea, writing newspaper articles, and seeking interviews with influential Washington politicians, when the same Woodrow Wilson, now in the White House, refused him even a visa to go to Versailles for the peace conference. He too seemed nervous about irritating the Japanese.

In the wake of the March First demonstrations a conference of Korean leaders was held later in 1919, and Syngman Rhee was elected president of a provisional government. Mass meetings to advocate Korean independence were held in Philadelphia and Hawaii, where by this time large numbers of Korean emigrants had settled. A Korean Commission was set up in Washington and various friendly congressmen inserted appeals for Korean independence in the *Congressional Record.*

In 1921, during negotiations for the Washington Disarmament Conference, Rhee managed to present his case to Charles Evans Hughes, then Secretary of State. (He would ultimately set an unofficial world's record for lecturing successive Secretaries of State, from John Hay in 1904 to John Foster Dulles in 1952.) Nothing happened. His visit to the League of Nations in Geneva in

1933 was equally fruitless, although a chance meeting in a Geneva hotel with a Miss Francesca Donner from Vienna resulted in a swift courtship and an abiding marriage.

Meanwhile, the thin strands that bound the government-in-exile together began to unravel. Koreans are not unjustly likened to bright, but internally contentious European peoples like the Irish and the Greeks. Radicals in the Shanghai organization denounced Rhee's gradualist, nonviolent approach, while Korean Communists from Ho Chi Minh's International, based in Manchuria and the Soviet Union's maritime provinces, began a series of guerrilla skirmishes against the Japanese occupiers. By the late 1930s the Korean independence movement was hopelessly fragmented into a mass of splinter organizations in Shanghai, Tokyo, and Hawaii, where Rhee made his headquarters.

When Japan's war on China intensified, Korean military units formed to fight, some with the Nationalists, some with the Communists. The only thing they all had in common was the enemy: Japan. In a book, *Japan Inside Out*, written in 1941, Rhee restated his faith in an American-style democracy, along with the conviction that war with Japan was inevitable. "Personal rights and personal freedom," he wrote, "are the fundamental basis on which the structure of the nation is built . . . A democracy insists that the people's rights should be protected against any possibility of the government's usurpation."

A scholar, a teacher, and in the best sense of the word a propagandist, Rhee had lived his life fighting for Korea's resurrection as an independent, democratic state. He was wholeheartedly, if a bit ostentatiously dedicated to Christian principles as well. (Every morning of their lives he and his wife began the day with a Bible reading. He did the reading, as one might suspect.) It is ironic that, when he finally came to power as President of the Republic of Korea, on the heels of the postwar occupation, he proved to be as grimly authoritarian a ruler as his Communist near-contemporary Ho Chi Minh.

It is true that by late 1945 the Soviet Union had helped set up a Communist dictatorship in the northern half of that sadly bisected country. But the need for being "anti-Communist" hardly excused the repressive apparatus of police and party controls that Rhee constructed from the very start of his presidency. He was, incidentally, seventy years old when he came back to Seoul after thirty-three years of exile. The iron in his soul had been hardening there for a long time.

I met Rhee myself for the first time in the spring of 1950, while visiting Korea as a *Time* correspondent. I saw a good deal of him over the next year, particularly in the hectic times after the North Korean invasion of June 1950. For a reporter looking for news Rhee proved a difficult customer. He was constantly surrounded by a tight group of retainers, one or two of them Amer-

Japanese paratroops attack
Palembang. The Japanese invasion of
the Netherlands East Indies took
place in 1942. *Mainichi Shimbun*

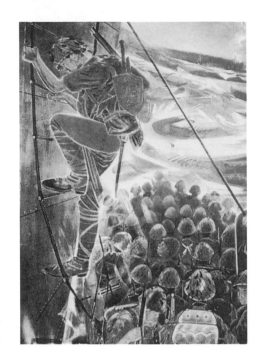

Japanese troops invading
Borneo, 1941. *Mainichi Shimbun*

Gen. Douglas MacArthur and Syngman
Rhee reviewing troops during the Korean
War. Dong-A Ilbo

Ulithi anchorage, 1945. The U.S. Fifth Fleet
assembled here, on the way to the invasion of
Okinawa. Library of Congress

ican. Getting through this palace guard was no easy matter. When one did, communication was not easy either.

If Rhee was a man who commanded respect, he was far from a likable person. Just when you began admiring his courage, he would repel you with his obstinacy and vindictiveness. Although a firm believer in democracy, in principle, he also believed that he was Korea's only real democrat—"the George Washington of Korea," he liked to style himself. Through long years of exile, pounding the corridors of Washington or Geneva in vain search for a hearing on Korea's problems, he came, understandably enough, to identify himself with the country. Once in power he saw an attack on himself as an attack on Korea. "Why should we create anything," he once told me, "between the President and the people?"

This attitude was at least consistent. On his return to Korea in 1946, as he took charge of the Society for Rapid Realization of Independence, Rhee had said: "I shall take over the society and run it on a purely democratic basis. I shall appoint all the other officials."

"POWER," AS Mao Zedong had it, "flows from the barrel of a gun." The guns and bombs of World War II shook the Asia-Pacific region like a series of volcanic eruptions. From Alaska and the Kuriles to the tropical north coast of Australia a man-made ring of fire engulfed the Pacific Basin, as fleets, armies, and air power fought for victory. Seen from America's ships and aircraft, it was Admiral Mahan's dream of sea power made real. I lived through part of the dream myself. Looking down from a Navy PBY patrol plane on the ringed waters of Ulithi Atoll in the western Pacific in March 1945, I could see the U.S. Navy's Fifth Fleet at anchor, on its way north toward Japan. From a Navy transport off Okinawa, just before the April 1 landing, I could watch the awesome spectacle of sea power in action, as heavy guns searched for the hidden Japanese defenses. At last in Japan, in September, I could see all around me the frightening lunar landscape of cities reduced by massed bombing. To those of us in the war the four years of Pacific fighting meant a final settlement. Japan had lost. The Allies, including China, had won. Through the gunfire of power, justice had been served.

But to Asians the war and its aftermath held different meanings. The settlement was yet to come. If Japan's Greater East Asia Co-Prosperity Sphere was smashed and discredited, the very fact of the Japanese conquests had changed East Asia's map forever. Already fading as powers in 1941, the European colonialists were doomed well before the war's end. General Abdul Haris Nasution, who led Indonesia's postwar liberating armies, eloquently summed up what had happened: "Before the Japanese came, Indonesians had literally to bow when any Dutch walked by. When the Japanese defeated the Dutch, they put them to work on road gangs, digging ditches. This was a powerful sight for me. Our colonial masters had been reduced to servants. And the new victors were Asians."

The same was of course true, if in varying degrees, in the British and French colonies. The British wisely relinquished most of their old possessions, just as they gave up India. The French and Dutch fought to keep theirs, and suffered for it.

With 1945 a new cast of characters was coming on stage. America would be more of a power than ever, its vast air and sea strength underlying the helter-skelter spread of its cultural and political ideas. So would the Soviet Union, a new factor in the equation—at least as long as Moscow could keep its unruly national Communist subsidiaries loyal to the head office. Japan, despite its defeat, would never quite go away. Within ten years the Japanese would be edging back on the stage, the Co-Prosperity Sphere turning economic. Ho Chi Minh, Syngman Rhee, and a host of local rivals and supporters were back in their countries, but moderates and democrats there and elsewhere were being swept along in an emerging war of extremes between left and right authoritarians. Hong Kong and Thailand were soon back doing business as usual, but in Malaya tension between Malays, Chinese, and British was building into a bloody military "emergency." The five "postwar" years were ironically named. There was no peace in them.

NOWHERE WAS THE political situation more confusing than in Indonesia. Here a battle had been building up for almost half a century, as yet another Asian people tried to carve out a new modern nation from a despised colonial past. But as compared with the struggles of Chinese and Korean or Vietnamese nationalists, the Indonesians were working in a brand-new historical time zone. The others could summon the weight of centuries-old traditions to help their cause. These traditions were unitary and they had continued. Vietnam and Korea, for all the divisions within them, contained the beginnings of modern nation-states. By contrast the Indonesian revolutionaries of the forties had to put together a collective of almost a dozen different races, with almost as many different cultures and traditions behind them.

Java was a civilization unto itself, with roots going back 1,500 years. The people in Sumatra were different, particularly the distinctively acculturated Menangkebau in the west. They could look back to the maritime Srivijaya empire of the eighth century, a worthy contemporary of Tang Dynasty China. The Hindu Balinese were equally distinctive. So were the people of the Celebes; by the twentieth century they had become heavily Christianized.

With such disparate components, the sense of unity was understandably late in developing. The very name "Indonesia" had been invented by European geographers in the nineteenth century. It was first used in a political context in the 1920s. A national language, Bahasa Indonesia, was barely coming into being. The Dutch colonial administrators, who ironically governed their Asian possessions even more harshly than Charles V's Spaniards had once governed the Dutch, were quick to point out, as Hendrik Colijn had said in the late twenties, that "the archipelago is a unity because it constitutes the Dutch East Indies and for no other reason."

Mochtar Lubis, Indonesia's premier journalist, once summed up this situation from another viewpoint: "We came to the realization that we really belonged to one nation only very late," he said. "I think it was in the twenties that the younger generation of Indonesians came to realize that we could never win back our independence without becoming united as one nation. That is why we proclaimed ourselves to be one nation, with one flag, with one language."[6]

Under the circumstances it fell to a small group of political intellectuals to breathe life into this new nation while they were fighting for it. Most of them were Sumatrans and Javanese. The most dynamic and politically charismatic among them was a Javanese engineering graduate named Sukarno. He was a man who lived by whims and contradictions. His brilliant political successes and his equally spectacular failures were almost a mirror reflection of his potential and the problems of the nation he helped create.

Although he graduated from the engineering college at Bandung, Sukarno spent almost all of his life in politics. As a student boarder in the household of Indonesia's leading Islamic nationalist, Tjokroaminoto—he married Tjokro's daughter—he gained a firsthand knowledge of the fledgling independence movement against the Dutch. He founded the Indonesian Nationalist Party (PNI) in 1926 when he was only twenty-five.

At the time, the gathering agitation against Dutch colonial rule was led mostly by intellectuals who had been allowed to study abroad—mostly in the Netherlands. Mohammed Hatta, an Islamic modernist, and Soetan Sjahrir, a secular-minded socialist, emerged as the leaders of this militant student generation. As with other Western-educated intellectuals—Syngman Rhee and Ho Chi Minh among them—their thinking reflected their European educations. Both Hatta and Sjahrir wanted Indonesia to become a parliamentary democracy, and at least for a time they were not opposed to some sort of dominion status within a Dutch commonwealth.

[6] Lubis's comments, as well as Nasution's before them, were made in interviews of editors of *The Pacific Century* television series.

Sukarno was different. Like Mao Zedong he was a homegrown product. Although his speeches quoted everyone from Friedrich Engels, Sun Yat-sen, and the French socialist Jean Jaurès to the Koran and the author of "Rule, Britannia," he was at heart a Javanese cultural nationalist who at the outbreak of World War II had yet to travel overseas. He never lost his fascination for the *wayang kulit*, the traditional puppet plays of Java, with their courtly all-mastering heroes based on the great Hindu epics of the *Mahayana* and the *Mahabharata*. For Sukarno, as for most of the *wayang* audiences, these Asian versions of Europe's medieval miracle plays came to symbolize Indonesia's struggle against European oppression. He often referred to himself as the *dalang*, the narrator and puppet-master of the plays.

"As the dalang manipulates the puppets," Lubis recalled, "so Sukarno manipulated his people. He could quote you Marx, he could quote you Jefferson and other Western philosophers very easily. He had them all in mind. But at the same time he used these old mythical symbols of Java and Bali. He used to tell the Balinese that he was a descendant of Vishnu, the Hindu god. So when he arrived in Bali and it was raining, he told his people, 'Look, I bring rain for your fields.' Just like that."

As an orator, he was a spellbinder. He could hold the attention of Indonesian audiences like a skilled *wayang* puppet-master. He had no problem reconciling Islam and Marxism as part of his eclectic nationalism.[7] The ancient Javanese maxim "All things are one" was the closest thing he had to a positive ideology. His enemies were imperialism and the domination of Europeans who had come to Asia as exploiters "only to fill their rumbling bellies." To support his crusade against them he was not above citing the ancient Javanese belief in the *ratu adil*—the righteous prince who would appear like a messiah to cast out Java's oppressors. No one could bring a crowd together in Java like Sukarno, and Java, by far the most populous and culturally the dominant island of the archipelago, was the arena where independence was fought and ultimately won.

Yet Sukarno spoke not only to Javanese but to all the diverse peoples of the archipelago. It was he, more than anyone, who created the hope of a united Indonesia. A skilled pamphleteer, he preached a racial war of the brown peoples against the whites. He was untroubled by any thoughts of compromise with European parliamentary institutions. The majority-rule principle behind them he thoroughly disliked. Real popular democracy for Indonesia, he argued, must

---

[7] When taxed with the contradictions between antireligious Communism and the all-embracing religious world of Islam, Sukarno would explain that Communism was hostile only to Christianity, which supported the upper classes in Europe, while Islam was "the religion of the oppressed in Indonesia."

be founded on a general consensus in which everyone's view would be respected, in the Javanese tradition. Time would prove the difficulties of melding the principle of "guided democracy" with his own dictatorial practice, but it sounded great in speeches.

THE DUTCH ARRESTED Sukarno twice, first in 1929 and then in 1933. On both occasions he was imprisoned and exiled for several years. The same rough treatment was handed out to Hatta, Sjahrir, and almost every other emerging political leader of that day. (Sjahrir's book *Out of Exile* contains a classic description of the hardships of those political prisoners.) What astonishes any observer in our time is the way the Dutch proconsuls in Indonesia, with rare exceptions, refused even the slightest compromise. Their suppression of any dissent, coming on top of Indonesia's economic spoliation, was what enabled a relatively small group of nationalist intellectuals to tap a huge reservoir of latent popular support for *merdeka*—"freedom"—among Indonesia's subject population.

There was one other powerful stimulus to independence: the Japanese. More than a century before the first Japanese troop landings in 1942, a famous folk prophecy, the *djoyoboyo*, had predicted that "yellow men will come out of the north to liberate the people."

Aware of the prophecy, if little else about Indonesia, Imperial Headquarters in Tokyo pounded home the message in radio broadcasts, leaflets, and official pronouncements before and during Japan's swift capture of the islands at the start of the Pacific war. Dutch resistance was overcome in less than three weeks. As Soedjatmoko, the distinguished Indonesian educator, later commented: "What really destroyed colonialism in Indonesia was the total failure of the Dutch to fight."

Very shortly, however, the Indonesians discovered that the "co-prosperity" in Japan's wartime Greater East Asia Co-Prosperity Sphere was strictly a one-way street. The oil and other raw materials of the Netherlands East Indies had been one of Japan's primary wartime objectives. To support their plundering the Japanese installed a military government which was just that. Behind the façade of pan-Asian propaganda ("Japan the light of Asia, the leader of Asia, the protector of Asia") the Japanese occupation proved to be more efficiently ruthless than the Dutch. The new flags and anthems of the Indonesian independence movement were banned. Instead Indonesians were ordered to bow ritually on all formal occasions in the direction of the Imperial Palace in Tokyo. Punishments for disobedience to occupation orders was brutal; it included flogging. Fully 250,000 Indonesians were drafted to serve Japan as laborers there and elsewhere in Southeast Asia. Only a small percentage of them returned home.

Sukarno, released by the Japanese after eight years of Dutch confinement, turned a blind eye toward Japanese atrocities. He still saw "Western imperialism" as the main enemy. Where leaders like Hatta and Sjahrir viewed the Japanese as yet another enemy, Sukarno enthusiastically joined the Japanese war effort, as if the *djoyoboyo* prophecy were real. "We'll flatten the Americans; we'll crush the English," he screamed in his speeches; and he organized "Heroes of Labor" send-offs for the hapless conscript workers. "Every drop of your sweat," he harangued them, "is poison in the veins of the enemy."

Many Indonesians, with the perspective of hindsight, insisted later that Sukarno was playing a double game. This is highly doubtful, for his support of the Japanese "partnership" was unstinting. The net effect of his collaboration, however, was to give him, uniquely, almost unlimited access to the people of Indonesia. He used the opportunity well. Along with Japan's Co-Prosperity Sphere, he preached Indonesian independence. In effect, the wartime occupation became the incubation period for the future Indonesian state.

Unquestionably, Sukarno and the other leaders were assisted by some Japanese officials, pan-Asianists in Kita Ikki's old tradition, who genuinely believed in Asian co-dependence. With their encouragement Sukarno worked out some of the basic plans for what ultimately became his "guided democracy." At a political rally in 1944, for example, he first set forth the Five Principles (*pantja sila*) that remain today the stated ideology of Indonesia: "nationalism, humanity, popular sovereignty, social justice, and faith in one God."[8]

The rising clamor of Indonesians for independence coincided with Japan's failing wartime fortunes. By 1945 Tokyo was ready to compromise with the independence movement it had previously rejected. Youth organizations and home guard military units put together by the Japanese now began to take matters into their own hands. On August 16, 1945, the day after Japan's formal surrender, Sukarno and Mohammed Hatta, under heavy pressure from the youth groups, issued a formal Declaration of Independence.

For all the cruelties of the Japanese occupation, Indonesia would not have gained its independence without it. As Bernhard Dahm later wrote: ". . . the years of occupation had done one thing: the Japanese, with their organization, their propaganda machine and their ever-increasing demands for increased production, labor and war volunteers, had mobilized the population and shaken it out of its previous indifference."

It took more than a month for the first Allied unit, a British brigade, to arrive and accept the Japanese surrender in Indonesia. In the intervening time, Sukarno, Hatta, and the other Indonesian leaders, although united by little more than the imperative for independence, managed to form a workable

---

[8] In my account of the Five Principles, as with other events of this period, I have followed Bernhard Dahm's *History of Indonesia in the Twentieth Century* (New York: Praeger, 1967).

government, with the active assistance of the Japanese. When the first Dutch troops arrived some weeks later, therefore, they found the situation drastically changed. They had left a restless colony. They returned to a hostile country.

The next four years turned into something of a nightmare for all concerned. By the end of 1945 the Indonesian National Army (TNI) was in action, at first hastily organized home guard forces armed with Japanese weapons. While the Dutch regular forces, some 140,000 strong, were far better trained and equipped, they were not strong enough to hold the countryside against the Indonesians. Foreshadowing the later success of the Viet Cong in Vietnam, Nasution and his guerrillas fought the Dutch to a standstill. "We were in our own country," he recalled. "The terrain is ours, the people are ours."

The two heavy Dutch "police actions," in 1946 and 1948, succeeded in occupying the major cities and, indeed, capturing key Indonesian leaders, but in the end they proved unsuccessful. Meanwhile a bewildering sequence of truces and negotiations continued. A Three Nations Commission—comprising representatives of Australia, Belgium, and the United States—was nominated by the newly formed United Nations to arrange a compromise between outright independence and some form of federation with the Netherlands. The Dutch rejected the commission's authority; nor were the Indonesians eager to continue in a Dutch federation.

In September 1948 the military situation was further complicated by the attempt of Indonesian Communists to seize power in a coup. When Indonesian troops, by themselves, put down the Communist revolt, American observers were most favorably impressed. The United States had always favored Indonesia's independence in principle. Independence plus anti-Communism looked ever more practical. Now, in contrast to their early indecision over whom to support in Vietnam, the Americans came down hard against colonialism here. The American UN delegation helped push through a Security Council censure of the second Dutch military action. Going further, Washington told the Dutch that their continued military aggression in Indonesia would force a stoppage of Marshall Plan aid to the Netherlands.

By the end of 1949 it was all over. Alerted by the eloquent pleadings of Sjahrir at the United Nations, world opinion had swung to the Indonesian side. In the end it was American support that turned the tide by pressuring the Dutch, who needed Washington's Marshall Plan aid, to give up their old colonial dream. Australia also helped. The same country that fought against the racial equality clause in the Versailles Treaty was now turning its attention, ever so slowly, to its Asian neighbors. The same Pacific war that cemented Australia's new feeling of comity with the United States had made the people of that insular white continent forcibly aware of the evolving brown and yellow nations north of them.

Sukarno went on to become President of Indonesia, with Hatta as the first Vice President. He was to lead his country for the next fifteen years, until an abortive Communist coup d'état and its suppression by the Army put an end to his skillful balancing act between right and left. His effort at "guided democracy" proved a costly failure, as did his attempted military "confrontation" with Malaysia and the Philippines. In the end he showed himself as incapable as Syngman Rhee of tolerating political opposition. He jailed Sjahrir in 1962. Even his old collaborator Hatta was put under house arrest.

Sukarno's own political posturings, his costly monuments, including a luxury palace at Bogor, and his satyrlike affections for women—he had eight wives, more or less in succession—had heavily eroded his popularity. The economy of Indonesia, despite its vast natural resources, became a disaster area. Whether Sukarno had instigated the attempted Communist coup was never quite proven. He died under house arrest in 1970.

Without this master of the political *wayang* shadow-play, however, Indonesian independence might have been a far longer time in coming. Hardly an original thinker, he was a brilliant packager of ideas. Be it Marxism, Javanese tradition, Islam, Western political thinking, or Japanese pan-Asian slogans like the wartime *hakko ichiyu* (literally, "the earth's four corners into one")— Sukarno could use them for his own purposes. Contradictions never disturbed him. A political synthesizer as well as an orator of studied brilliance (he used to practice before a mirror), he had the knack of making every member of his diverse audiences think that Sukarno was preaching his (or her) word and singing their song. He knew his people well. He believed in their myths as well as, unfortunately, his own.

ON DECEMBER 27, 1949, I found myself standing at the edge of the newly named Merdeka Square in the center of Jakarta (until a few days before, Batavia), next to the men of the Siliwangi Division, as the Dutch flag came down and the new red-and-white flag of the Indonesian Republic went up. A crack unit, originally Sumatran, of General Nasution's Indonesian National Army (TNI), they had fought their way to the square and clearly enjoyed the moment. They were disciplined, but relaxed. All over the city the shouts and signs and slogans of "*Merdeka*" could be heard and seen those last few days of the year.

Sukarno arrived in triumph the next day. It was his first visit to the Dutch-held capital in four years. The city rocked with cheers as the radio voice of the occupation years materialized in the flesh. "I raised both hands high," Sukarno later recalled. "A stillness swept over the millions. There wasn't a sound. Except for the silent tears nothing moved. Thank God, we are free."

Ho Chi Minh and the Americans, Hanoi, 1945. Maj. Allison Kent Thomas is the tall man in the center. Vo Nguyen Giap (wearing fedora) is on the left and Ho to the right of Thomas. Pictured from right to left, standing, are: Hong Viet, Rene Defourneaux, Ho, Thomas, Giap, Henry Prunier, Dam Quang Trung, Nguyen Quy, and Paul Hoagland. Kneeling: Lawrence Vogt, Aaron Squires, and Thai Bach. Allison Kent Thomas

Raising the Indonesian flag on Independence Day, January 1, 1950. Troops of the veteran Siliwangi Division stand at attention. Gibney Collection

Dutch officials were still very much in evidence, however. Although most of those I met were working quite sincerely for an orderly transfer of authority, other Netherlanders in town were bitter. They blamed the Americans for the loss of their colony, and having drinks at the bar of the colonial Hotel des Indes was generally a pretty argumentative affair. We few Americans were not at all remorseful for taking the Dutch colony away. We were young and those were still the Roosevelt years—before we had begun to worry about Communist revolutionaries and the domino theory.

Conversely, Indonesians were not much grateful to the Americans. To many of them we were colonial imperialists too. The moderate's lot is not a happy one, particularly for a fair-haired *Time* magazine correspondent who could easily be mistaken for a Dutchman.

I had come to Indonesia from Singapore, after a long, meandering trip from my base in Tokyo which took me through the Philippines, North Borneo, Sarawak, and Malaya. Shortly after my return I would make my first visit to Korea and Hong Kong. The trip was not an easy one. The days of jiffy (if uncomfortable) air transportation were still ahead of us. The last airfield in the Philippines was at Jolo. From there I went first by island steamer, finally in a smugglers' sailboat, to Sandakan in what was still British North Borneo.

It is not easy to recall that time, forty years ago, in the perspective of the 1990s. In the Philippines, democracy was already in action. Alone of the former colonies, this country had already received independence. Throughout the travail of World War II, Filipinos and Filipinas had fought heroically against the Japanese oppressor, and the Americans had belatedly returned for the rescue. But although education was widespread, democracy was more formal than real. The old Spanish-Malay barons still controlled their fiefs.

At election time in November 1949, after I had had enough guns stuck into my midriff, in the process of seeking out polling places in Negros Occidental and other provincial strongholds, I realized that there were some basic flaws in the Philippine democracy. "Whom are you voting for?" I asked a Filipino cabdriver on my way into Manila from the airport. "I think all three of them are crooks, sir," he replied, "but I am voting for Avelino to preserve my rights as a citizen."[9]

[9] For the record, José Avelino was the Speaker of the Philippine House of Representatives. A notably corrupt politician, he was one of the few prominent figures in Filipino political life ever to be indicted for graft. His opponents were little better. José Laurel had been puppet "president" during the Japanese occupation. The incumbent, Elpidio Quirino, finally won in a 1949 election characterized by wholesale bribery and ballot stuffing, where "even the birds and the bees voted," as the saying went. Quirino established a record as the most inefficient president in the nation's history and the most corrupt (before Marcos).

Such outspokenness was rarely vouchsafed in Malaya, where the population was already polarizing between Malays, favored by the British colonialists, and the overseas Chinese, who harbored many Communist sympathizers in the course of running the colony's business. But it was the Chinese, mostly led by Communist cadres, who had also fought the Japanese consistently in the World War II underground. Singapore, then as now largely Chinese in population, superficially looked like the outpost of empire that it once was. The tea dances were back at Raffles and the various clubs, as the British Navy tried to reassemble the vast base which the Japanese had so rudely treated. The old merchants and trading companies were back in business, although there was a new restlessness running through the labor force.

Hong Kong too looked to the casual visitor as if there had never been a war and a cruel Japanese occupation. With that era behind it, the colony was now facing the novelty of a China that was militarily strong but gone Communist, with Mao Zedong now ruling from Beijing. Still it seemed very tidy, very British in its aspect, and the Yacht Club races ran on weekends and on schedule. Hordes of refugees from the mainland were yet to come, but the leaders of the maritime Chinese, the same bankers and businessmen who had made Shanghai famous, were now beginning to build a new business city-state.

Most Chinese in both port cities were waiting to see how Mao and the Communists would behave when in power. Chiang and the Nationalists had been discredited by their own inefficiency and corruption. When I asked a Singapore Chinese editor why he was leaning toward the Communists instead of the Nationalists now on Taiwan, he replied only: "If you have a dish of stinking fish in front of you and someone takes it away, you are naturally well disposed to what comes next."

Behind the façade of returning normalcy in East Asia, however, a new kind of war was being fought. Its model was the long march of Mao Zedong and his Communist militiamen to power. With their strength in the countryside, their peasant troops would blend with the local population like "fish swimming in the sea." So Mao, the frustrated poet, enjoyed putting it. Those of us who had lived through the positional warfare against the Japanese, where even jungle battles were fought by regiments and batteries, found ourselves covering a new kind of guerrilla war, in which the enemy by night melted into the kampongs of the countryside during the day, indistinguishable from peaceful farmers in their fields.

In the course of four weeks I witnessed two kinds of guerrilla battle. The first, on the island of Jolo (Sulu) in the Philippines, was traditional—the barely Filipinized Mohammedan Moros against the revived Philippine constabulary.

Death by ambush could come swiftly in those jungles, but the enemy was an old one, a known quantity.

In the new war in Malaya the enemy was both unseen and unknown. I tramped for hours through the moldy, steaming jungle of central Malaya, where you could barely see five yards in front of you, with a detachment of the 7th Gurkha Rifles, setting ambushes and looking for them. Their enemy was the tightly disciplined fighting cells of the Malayan Communists, who levied food, tribute, and recruits from scared villagers and plantation workers, in a total war by ambush and intimidation that came within an inch of success. The same tactics were being used by Communist and fanatic Muslim *Darul Islam* bands in Indonesia. And the French, putative reconquerors of their Indochina colony, were already suffering from the same treatment at the hands of Ho's inspired military right-hand man, General Giap.

The thought of today's burgeoning Asia-Pacific community—with its newly industrialized nations, its tightly woven networks of electronic communications, and its increasingly intense struggles for workable democratic governments—any of us at that time would have dismissed as fantasy. Economics we then thought of only in its prewar Asian context of commodity producers dependent on Europe or America for their manufactured imports. Even once industrialized Japan, still prostrate after the war, seemed like something of an economic basket case. The principal interest of a reporter in 1949 and 1950 was military and political. Would the guerrillas in the jungle ultimately capture the cities, as Mao had in China? Would Asia go Communist, as China had done? Would France hang on to Indochina? Would the British put down the revolt in Malaya? Would the United States now move into Asia, fulfilling Teddy Roosevelt's prophecy? Where were our new allies? Was there any hope for democracy—"anti-Communist" democracy, to be sure—in the Republic of Korea or the Philippines?

Could any of these countries "modernize"—to the point where they would be something more than exotic cultural backwaters living on obsolete traditions? That is to say, would they join the West or lapse back into Eastern "obscurantism"?

Such questions had been posed from a Western vantage point. They were no more correct than the famous slogan that Liang Qichao had used in his ill-fated modernizing efforts in China at the turn of the century: *Zhongxue wei ti sixue wei yung*—"Take Chinese learning as your base and use Western learning to serve it." Or, going back to the Meiji Restoration, the battle cry of *Wakon yosai*—"Japanese spirit, Western knowledge"—used by the young Meiji innovators to reassure their more conservative supporters.

By way of rebuttal it is worth quoting the comments on this assumed East-West dichotomy made by Soetan Sjahrir: "We want to have both Western science and Eastern philosophy, the Eastern 'spirit' in the culture. But what is this Eastern 'spirit'? It is, as they say, the sense of the higher, of spirituality, of the eternal and religious, as opposed to the materialism of the West. I have heard this a thousand times, but it has never convinced me. Did not Hitler say that the Aryan *Geist* was the sense of the higher, the spiritual, the moral, the religious? And is this spirituality such a preeminently Eastern attribute and ideal?"

One could easily imagine Lu Xun nodding in approval.

IN THE YEARS since 1919, Asians had shown how quickly they could learn the science and technology of the West. They could and did put this learning to good use in many areas, from economics and banking to the making and repair of the internal-combustion engine. But adjustment to the Western ideas that lay behind the factories, the airplanes, and the guns was quite another matter. To what extent was it all a Euro-American package deal? Or to what extent could the new technology coexist with the old and valuable Asian cultures and religions in which individualism, pragmatic questioning, and legal argument were not necessarily seen as goods?

While new modern nations were emerging, the modernization of societies— and I do not equate this with "Westernization"—was only skin deep. A relatively small group of intellectuals—reformers, traditionalists, and iconoclasts among them—continued to probe the ideas of "reason" and "number" that Fukuzawa Yukichi had found so difficult to teach in Japan's pre-Meiji days. But people in the mass, given choices, tended to follow the slogan makers, who promised ultimately satisfying (and immediately obvious) goals. "China's walls," Mao Zedong had written, with unconscious irony, "are built of old and new bricks."

Rationalists like Sjahrir and Lu Xun did not swim well in the emotional currents of new nationalisms and new ideologies. After his death the writings of Lu Xun, who held passionately that "the role of the writer is to criticize," were neatly expropriated by Mao Zedong and his Party bosses when the Communists came to power—along with the Forbidden City and vast stores of Nationalist military arms and equipment. "The chief commander of China's cultural revolution," Mao said of him, ". . . a great thinker and revolutionary." Whereupon Mao's house ideologues, carefully selecting and annotating his works, attempted with some success to turn China's fiercely independent social critic into an officially mummified defender of the Party line.

Sukarno and Syngman Rhee shared Mao's flair for despotism without the camouflage of a "scientific" and professedly omniscient ideology. Sukarno recognized the need to create a new secular political ideology for his country, but he chose to reject the West totally in devising and assembling it. He ended up in a web of brilliant mismanagement. Like Mao, who also hated the West, he repeated the error of the nineteenth-century "self-strengtheners" in China, who could not harness new technology to the needs of a personal obscurantist ruler.

Syngman Rhee, already an old man when he came to power, showed himself to be a traditional Korean court autocrat underneath his Western and Christian outer image. During his twelve years of power, before his eventual overthrow in 1960, he based much of his authority on American support. This he received and sustained by constantly invoking the menace of the monolithic Communist state in the north of the peninsula. A similar tactic worked for Chiang Kai-shek, even after the exposure of his government's wartime inefficiency and corruption.

For the Americans, only a few years after overwhelming Japan in the Pacific war, were now worried about Communism stealing their victory. In the chill of the new Cold War, the Soviet Union, having annexed most of Eastern Europe, was casting its shadow over Western Europe. With China now militantly Maoist, it became all too easy to classify other Asian countries as either "Communist" or "anti-Communist." One was dangerous. The other was safe. On this basis Washington's choice of allies was greatly simplified—even before the Korean War gave the Communist menace an added force.

Yet even at the height of emotional anti-Communism in the forties and fifties, most Americans felt uncomfortable with "colonialism" and wanted countries to have "democratic" rule. Hence their significant support for the emerging state of Indonesia, despite Sukarno's demagoguery. The idealism of Wilson and his Fourteen Points kept recurring in American policy making, most recently in the "self-determination" of nations and the Four Freedoms which Franklin D. Roosevelt wrote into the Atlantic Charter.

Thus, along with the Christian missionary fervor, the spread of business and technical know-how, and the urge to imperium went America's desire to protect democracy where it existed and to export it where it didn't. It was hard enough to find and foster democracy on familiar ground in Europe. But how did you identify it in Asia? To support democracy, you must first identify it.

Was Ho Chi Minh, quoting Jefferson in Hanoi, a democrat underneath his Communist protective coloration? Could he have been supported—instead of attacked? If so, how different a history this would have made. The answer to such questions could be as complex as Ho himself.

He was easily the most brilliant, the most talented, and the most many-sided of the new Asian leaders on the western shores of the Pacific. He was a man of the world, more like Lenin than a homegrown ideologue like Mao. If he had any role model, Lenin was it.

"There is a legend in our country," Ho once told his friends in Moscow, "about the magic Brocade Bag. When facing difficulties, one opens it and finds a way out . . . Leninism is not only a miraculous Brocade Bag, a compass, but also a radiant sun illuminating our path to final victory, to socialism and Communism."

Not too much of Jefferson in that.

As befits a master political tactician, Ho kept his own counsel, while saying a great many things. The same man who reminded American OSS officers of his American-style Declaration of Independence could say at the same time to the perennial puppet emperor Bao Dai that the Americans were only interested in replacing the French. "They want to reorganize our country in order to control it," he warned. "They are capitalists to the core."

A man with a long view of history, Ho was quite confident he could cope with the French and, if necessary, the American colonizers. When Chinese Nationalist troops came to "occupy" northern Vietnam, in accordance with some foggy wartime "trusteeship" proposals, he was only too happy to make a temporary deal with the French in order to keep China out. As he reminded his restive Vietminh colleagues: "Do you remember your history? The last time the Chinese came, they stayed a thousand years. The French are foreigners. The white man is finished in Asia. But if the Chinese stay now, they will never go. As for me, I prefer to eat French shit for five years than eat Chinese shit for the rest of my life."

His overtures to the Americans in 1945 and 1946, however, cannot be dismissed. He was congenial to the idea of a Popular Front, from his experience with Léon Blum's French model. That is why he brought on the shrewd, if dissolute Bao Dai as his "senior adviser" in Hanoi and offered a similar post to the man who later became his political adversary, the tightly wound Catholic nationalist Ngo Dinh Diem. He welcomed the Americans, at first, as a means of support and a valuable counter against both the colonial French and the Chinese, whether Nationalist or Communist. (A traditionalist in this regard, he no more liked the Chinese than his junior Chinese Communist brother, Deng Xiaoping, liked Vietnam.) Ho was Moscow's man, not Mao's.

Through the years of negotiations that followed Ho's Declaration of Independence, he showed himself continually ready to compromise with the French, as long as independence could be preserved. It was the French who generally broke the agreements, as they tried to reconquer Vietnam by military force. Only a few French realized that Ho, through the years, had set the groundwork

Wayang puppet show in Indonesia. Sukarno, it was said, was the master puppeteer. Dannielle Hayes

General Giap in 1990 (during an interview for the series The Pacific Century*).* Jigsaw Productions

for a political as well as military mobilization of Vietnam that could not be reversed.

So Bao Dai, the erstwhile French puppet, had written to Charles de Gaulle: "Even if you should manage to reestablish French administration here, it would no longer be obeyed. Each village would become a nest of resistance, each former collaborator an enemy." He sent a similar message to Harry Truman.

Such warnings were not heeded. As early as October 1945, the United States—going back on Roosevelt's ideas of trusteeship—assured the French of support in their effort to restore the old order in Vietnam. Although many Asia experts in Washington were worried by this and similar decisions later, Europe was judged the major theater—just as in World War II. France's survival as a colonial power—unlike Holland's—was linked to the protection of Western Europe from Communism. The first appropriations for military aid to the French were decided in 1949. Four years later almost $3 billion had already been expended by the United States in this losing cause.

Whatever the future of an American-supported Vietnam under Ho Chi Minh might have been, the alternative taken was disastrous. The road to American intervention, self-defeat, and pullout in Vietnam began in 1945 and 1946, when the United States—in the face of strong evidence against this course—chose to support France in its effort to turn back the clock in Asia. As in Woodrow Wilson's day, the European alliance was given first priority.

IF THE MAP of East Asia seemed to have stabilized by 1949, this was an illusion. Life within the new countries continued to be in turmoil. Two major international wars were on the way, not to mention a rash of revolts, confrontations, and border skirmishes. Through it all, Asian culture and tradition did not die. Both Buddhism and Confucianism would revive over the years, albeit in different guises. Yet the old feudal beliefs and hierarchies that had so long ossified them were dying, along with European colonialism. Where tradition was alive, it would be either reprocessed, as in Sukarno's Indonesia, or forced into a mold of garrison-state totalitarianism, as in Vietnam. In Korea, it would revive only after the devastation of war.

Ironically, it was Japan, the country that had thrown the Asia-Pacific world into chaos, that now began to seem an island of stability. Here the Americans had moved decisively. The war had, temporarily at least, destroyed Japan's self-confidence, but with it the arrogance that had come with its abuse of power. Now, in the spirit of the Meiji past, the Japanese were ready to learn again. The military populism of Kita Ikki and his young officer protégés was hopelessly discredited, if not totally forgotten, in a nation with a new antiwar constitution and a disinclination to follow losers. In its stead American policy, so vacillating and uncertain in most Asian postwar situations, was attempting a bold and unique cultural, political, and economic transformation.

It is to the U.S. Occupation of Japan that we now turn.

7

Reinventing Japan

The myth of an unbridgeable gulf between the ways of the East and the ways of the West has been thoroughly exploded by the lesson of experience.

GENERAL DOUGLAS MACARTHUR, JANUARY 1, 1950

L
ate one darkening September afternoon the LSD (for Landing Ship Dock) on which I had sailed from Pearl Harbor edged its way through the choppy waters of Sasebo's fjordlike port to pull up alongside a drab Japanese Navy dock. We had finally reached enemy country. On the way in the harbor we had passed ample evidence of Japan's defeat—in the form of half-sunk gray hulls, crippled warships docked or at anchor, and low bomb-battered buildings. On hand to welcome us were several Japanese Navy liaison officers who had been apprised of our errand. The Naval Technical Mission to Japan had been organized to examine and evaluate Japan's seaborne technology, as part of the U.S. Occupation's mission to disarm and pacify a surrendered population—and the military which had led it into battle.

As an intelligence officer whose particular job had been prisoner-of-war interrogation, I was aware of the breakdown of Japan's morale in the face of total defeat. Accustomed to dealing only with random survivors of units that had battled to the death rather than surrender, we had been amazed when Army and Navy remnants on Okinawa began to surrender by platoons and companies. This occurred even before the A-bombs fell and the emperor finally came out of his gilt closet to make his memorable exhortation to his people to "bear the unbearable"—*shinobigataki wo shinobi*—in accepting the enemy's final victory. Long before that time we had begun to meet Japanese who were bitterly disillusioned by their country's wartime adventure. From captured Korean laborers we heard the stored-up rage of an enslaved country. (Hundreds of thousands had been conscripted by the Japanese military to serve on work details in Japan and the occupied territories, while thousands of young Korean women were forced into Imperial Army brothels in the infamous "Comfort Corps"—*ianbu.*) There were even some merchant seamen from Taiwan we had captured who told me with some enthusiasm how they hoped for an independent future, tied neither to China nor to Japan.

All such experiences we had already relegated to the category of wartime memories. Along with the other members of the Naval Technical Mission— engineers, ordnance specialists, economists, and some Japanese-speaking intelligence officers like myself—we thought of the Sasebo trip as a kind of last wartime junket. It would be something to talk about after we had flown home, taken off our uniforms, and taken up the threads of our old lives. For Japan, we assumed, there would be a brief military occupation, whereupon the U.S. troops would depart, leaving behind our erstwhile enemies to pick up the pieces.

And pieces they were. For all its damage, Sasebo—a small town built around Japan's huge naval base—had gotten off easy compared with the almost total devastation of Japan's major cities. Hiroshima and Nagasaki were still contaminated by nuclear fallout; Tokyo had been firebombed out of all recognition, except for the few ferroconcrete downtown buildings at its core, around the Imperial Palace; and Nagoya was 90 percent gutted, only some husks of buildings and steel warehouse safes standing among the flattened ruins.

Wherever one moved, there was misery. Thousands packed the floors of railroad stations—men wearing shreds of wartime uniforms, women still cloaked in the shapeless *mompei* trousers of wartime austerity, children sick and sniveling—waiting for windowless trains that might take them somewhere to borrow food or shelter. We members of the Occupation forces picked our way across the bodies, going to the heated cleanliness of the local U.S. Army Railway Transportation Office. Well, they started the war, we could reflect. It was not our concern.

But as it turned out, it was our concern. The technical missions, the combat troops on occupation duty, the Navy transports offshore were all destined to become part of an extraordinary military occupation whose goal, as it developed, was nothing short of totally transforming a hostile and aggressively unique country into an Asian version of the United States of America. Nothing of the sort had ever been attempted before, and it will probably never be attempted again. The American reinvention of Japan was far from a planned transformation. In fact, its scope only widened with the unfolding of events. It included more than its share of failures, mistakes, misunderstandings, and real disasters. Yet on balance it must be judged a success. It produced one of modern history's most interesting and durable, if unanticipated alliances. It changed the economic map of the Pacific Basin, if not the world. It catalyzed, if it did not indeed create the extraordinary social, economic, and cultural phenomenon that is modern Japan—the country that stamped its own chop on the words "economic miracle."

History is full of instances where one nation strove to make over the institutions and the polity, if not the entire society of another. In modern times this has generally taken the form of colonization. The colonizer has generally been content, after the original conquest, to superimpose its version of law and order on a subject population, controlling its politics and its economy without, however, bothering to disturb the basic lifestyle and beliefs and culture of the colonized. Neither the French in Indochina nor the Dutch in the Netherlands East Indies were particularly interested in turning the local inhabitants into Frenchmen or Dutchmen. The British, in particular, were always quite content to leave local ways as they found them, as long as British justice was observed and a sizable portion of the local economy's profits and dividends flowed back to London. The Chinese, of course, had pioneered the institution of vassal or tributary states, as the Romans had in their corner of the ancient world, but the mandarins were even less interested in intruding on the national lifestyle of their vassals, as long as the latter did the requisite amount of kowtowing toward the Dragon Throne in Beijing.

The Americans, however, perhaps because of their own colonial (and revolutionary) origins, seemed to harbor a national missionary urge to make everybody as much like them as possible. The U.S. annexation of the Philippines was hardly peaceful, involving more than ten years of determined and often ruthless military activity before the Filipinos' resistance finally ended in 1912. But unlike the British or the French, the Americans proceeded to install a large school system in which young Filipinos would be taught the same lessons that their contemporaries were learning in Springfield or Sioux City. The urge to make Americans out of them was almost irresistible. One can hardly imagine a British proconsul in Asia using William Howard Taft's avuncular term "little brown brothers" with such serious benevolence in describing his charges.

In 1917, true to our tradition of combining a *Machtpolitik* idea of Manifest Destiny with a moralistic urge to reform our neighbors, Woodrow Wilson led the country into World War I. The much anticipated final peace settlement at Versailles produced a train of disasters, not least of all the emergence of the Hitler dictatorship that culminated in World War II. Asia as well as Europe was

Pulguksa Temple in Korea. Erected in the eighth century, it was rebuilt after Hideyoshi's sixteenth-century Japanese invasion. Korean Overseas Information Service

Mongols on the march. On the set at Mongol Kino's filming of Genghis Khan
Christopher Ralling

St. John's Fort in Malacca, Malaysia
Ken Straiton/Pacific Press Service

Entrance to Fort Santiago in Manila's Old City
Steve Vidler/Pacific Press Service

The United States in Salem Harbor, forerunner of the China trade. Oil painting by Robert Salmon, 1817. The Peabody Museum of Salem; photo by Mark Sexton

Night attack on the foreigners' Canton factories by Chinese troops. Oil painting, ca. 1842. The Peabody Museum of Salem; photo by Mark Sexton

Sixteenth-century Jesuit church in Macao. From F. L. Hawks, *Narrative of the [Perry] Expedition . . .* (Washington, D.C., 1856) (hereafter cited as *The Perry Expedition*)

Official mandarin's boat off Canton. Watercolor by unidentified Chinese artist. The Peabody Museum of Salem; photo by Mark Sexton

Western ship off the Japanese coast. A print by Hiroshige. Gibney Collection

British destruction of Chinese war junks in Anson's Bay, January 7, 1841. Engraving by E. Duncan.
National Maritime Museum

Taiping Rebellion. Chinese government troops assault the rebel stronghold.
Picture reproduced courtesy of The Kelton Foundation

Kurofune, Perry's "black ship," as seen by a mid-nineteenth-century Japanese artist
Leserman/Adler Collection

Tokyo modernizers. Steamships, carriages, and steam engines at the start of the Meiji era.
Asai Collection

Hong Kong, as seen from East Point, mid-nineteenth century. The Perry Expedition

Commodore Matthew C. Perry meets the shogun's commissioners at Yokohama, 1854.
The Perry Expedition

Dance of the Stars and Stripes. *Geisha in traditional costume celebrate the Japanese-American relationship (early Meiji period).* The Mary and Jackson Burke Collection

The Horrible Pit. *A Chinese artist shows his countrymen the perils of backsliding from the new Christian teachings (late nineteenth century).*
The Peabody Museum of Salem; photo by Mark Sexton

Turn Ye, Turn Ye. *Another piece of Christian missionary art urging Chinese converts to reject worldly blandishments and gain salvation.*
The Peabody Museum of Salem; photo by Mark Sexton

The Satsuma Rebellion. *Saigo Takamori's rebel samurai are beaten by the Meiji government's uniformed conscript army, 1878.*   Print Collection, Miriam and Ira D. Wallach Division of Art, Prints and Photographs, The New York Public Library, Astor, Lenox and Tilden Foundations

Japan's cavalry and infantrymen press the charge against China's less-disciplined soldiery.
Leserman/Adler Collection

The Sino-Japanese War—a bugler dies in battle. Gibney Collection

The Battle of Manila Bay (1898). *A somewhat idealized popular presentation of Admiral Dewey's victory over the Spanish fleet.* Library of Congress

Tokyo's new trains (late nineteenth century)
Print Collection, Miriam and Ira D. Wallach Division of Art, Prints and Photographs, The New York
Public Library, Astor, Lenox and Tilden Foundations

Perry's first landing at Gorahama
The Perry Expedition

Uncle Sam and John Bull—"Two Great Missioners of Civilization"—as seen by a turn-of-the-century satirist
Library of Congress

Confucian temple ceremony in Taiwan
Coordination Council for North American Affairs

The Emperor Meiji on his way to celebrate the inauguration of Japan's new constitution
Gibney Collection

Modern Singapore skyline
Singapore Tourist Promotion Board

Tokyo's Ginza, looking down
Harumi Avenue
Ken Straiton/Pacific Press Service

Downtown Tokyo—the skyline is dominated by Shinjuku's new City Hall.
Ken Straiton/Pacific Press Service

Hong Kong at night
Peter Bull

Seoul's ancient South Gate—Namdaemun—seen against the background of the city skyline
Korean Overseas Information Service

Opening of the Olympic Games at Seoul, 1988
Korean Overseas Information Service

*Indonesian Wayang puppet. The
classic puppet show based on
Ramayana legends has retained its
popularity among the people.*
Dannielle B. Hayes

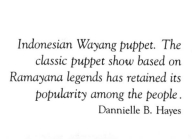

affected. For conspicuous among the Versailles Treaty failures, with its rejection of a racial equality clause and concern only for the colonial powers' hegemony over their subjects, was the approval the other Great Powers gave to Japan to continue its course of aggression and subjugation in China and Korea. This set in motion conflicts and confusions which led directly to the Pacific war.

WHETHER OR NOT prompted by a visceral memory of the Versailles failures, the leaders and planners of the United States military effort in World War II decided some two years before final victory that they should begin planning what to do with Germany and Japan after the war was won. It was with this in mind that General George Marshall, then U.S. Army Chief of Staff, called Major General John F. Hildring into his office in April 1943 and ordered him to take command of a new Civil Affairs Division on his staff. Hildring was distressed to lose the infantry division he had hoped to lead into battle. But he loyally obeyed and prepared to set up offices in Washington the following month. His recommendations about Germany and the European Theater do not concern us, except as they relate to Japan. His work in developing basic policy directives, however, was critical to everything that followed in Japan after August 15, 1945.

For more than two years Hildring and his staff beat the bureaucratic bushes in Washington, soliciting insights and opinions from every department and bureau that might be interested. Since this was to be a military occupation the War and Navy departments had a good bit to say, as did the relevant area experts at the State Department. The resultant State-War-Navy Coordinating Committee, known to archivists by the acronym SWNCC, cast a wide net to gather people's views. Some—old China hands in particular—advocated the draconian reduction of Japan to a bare subsistence level, along the lines of the Morgenthau Plan, which the Secretary of the Treasury had proposed for Germany. Against this were ranged the moderate ideas of the State Department's Japan experts; they wished to interfere as little as possible with Japanese institutions, as long as the pernicious military leadership was removed.

In the end the views of a representative "reform" faction predominated. Mostly New Dealers and generally untroubled by much detailed knowledge of Japan, they held that the militarists' influence on Japan ran deep and should be attacked at its roots. All agreed that the primary task of an occupation was to demilitarize Japan and destroy its military potential. But to do this well, it was argued, Japan's political structure and its economy needed a thorough overhaul. Forcible disarmament and policing were not enough. What was needed here, as in Germany, was a good dose of American democracy. All the trappings of

Japan's "feudal" society should be removed, the reformers argued, and Emperor Hirohito along with them. It was he who had inspired the military war criminals who served him.

Here the old Japan hands drew the line. Joseph C. Grew, who had spent the ten troubled years from 1931 to 1941 as ambassador to Japan, had returned to the State Department after repatriation and in 1944 became under secretary. A courtly conservative who had made many friends in Japan, he was convinced that retaining the emperor, at least as a symbolic figure, was essential to Japan's stability in the confusion that would follow national surrender. He was probably right. Grew put his personal prestige on the line in support of his views, including his acquaintance with his fellow Groton School alumnus Franklin D. Roosevelt. Backed by the other State Department people with experience in Japan, Grew held out for the emperor's retention.

For the rest, the reformers won the day. A memorable document known simply as JCS 1380/15—the policy directive of the Joint Chiefs of Staff to the Supreme Commander for the Allied Powers—set forth the outlines of a hoped-for Japanese democracy on the American model. If the emperor were retained, he was to play a purely symbolic role as a figurehead. Broad guarantees of civil rights and personal freedoms were to be enforced, if necessary by a new constitution that would do away with the restrictions on citizens' rights permitted under the old Meiji Constitution. Universal suffrage was to be guaranteed, including women's right to vote. Along with the abolition of the military and the old restrictive police laws, the huge *zaibatsu* business cartels were to be disestablished, in the best American trust-busting tradition. Labor unions were to be revived and the rights of unionists protected. Overall the Occupation was "to encourage the development within Japan of economic ways and institutions of a type that will contribute to the growth of peaceful and democratic forces in Japan."

In this connection business executives in charge of Japan's leading companies—along with military and political leaders, local government officials, many teachers and publishers, and all "active exponents of militant nationalism and aggression"—were to be removed from their offices.

The directive amounted to the total recasting of an ingrown and singularly stubborn nation-society, on the model of Franklin D. Roosevelt's open and optimistic America. Japan had managed such a massive change twice before in its history—first with the seventh- and eighth-century mass import of Chinese culture and institutions and more recently with the Meiji Restoration. But both of these transformations had been self-generated. Here the changes were to be effected by an alien occupying army.

*　　*　　*

SUCH A FORMIDABLE script of political theater called for a masterful director to present it and an actor of rare talent to read the lines. In the person of Douglas MacArthur the United States had both. Although the Commander in Chief of Allied Forces in the Southwest Pacific Theater was by no means the only architect of victory,[1] he was certainly the most visible. He was also the oldest. When war broke out in 1941 MacArthur was already sixty-one. Retired from the Army after a classic career—the youngest general officer in the Army in World War I, superintendent of West Point, and finally Chief of Staff—he had moved in 1935 to Manila, where his father, General Arthur MacArthur, had been military governor more than thirty years before him, to take command of President Manuel Quezon's new army there.

He was recalled to active U.S. Army duty in 1941 by President Roosevelt. Thereafter he presided over the unsuccessful defense of the Philippines against the attacking Japanese, escaping from Corregidor to Australia on Washington's orders. From there, after Bataan fell, he led U.S. and Australian forces on the long road back, capturing island after island until his troops successfully invaded and recaptured the Philippines in 1944. A master of overblown rhetoric, he had a gift for making his victories sound a lot better than they were. Yet no one denied his talents as a strong military leader, with a brilliant, if often erratic sense of strategy and timing.

His politics were hard to pin down. On the surface he was a conservative Republican. (From his vantage point in Japan, he later would continuously and unsuccessfully attempt to put himself in the running for the GOP presidential nomination.) He also had a broad streak of old-fashioned American populism in him. He was instinctively opposed to monopolies, restraint of trade, and restrictions on individual freedoms.

He could be arrogant, petty, and vindictive. Incapable of taking constructive criticism—his palace guard of military yes-men was notorious—he could also inspire great loyalty and reciprocate it. His roots and education were in a simple nineteenth-century America where words like "duty," "honor," and "country" were not said with a smile. This heritage gave him a swollen, almost oppressive sense of America's national mission in the tradition of past proconsuls. In fact, his showman's sense of pomp and glitter recalled no one so much as that temporary old Japan hand of a century before, Matthew Calbraith Perry.

---

[1] In fact, Fleet Admiral Chester Nimitz, as Commander in Chief Central Pacific, had a considerably more valid claim. Not only had Nimitz's forces defeated and virtually destroyed the Japanese fleet in several major actions; they had carried through their island-hopping strategy to the successful capture of Okinawa, one of Japan's home prefectures; in addition, submarines under Nimitz's command had imposed such an effective blockade of Japan's main islands that they were cut off from vitally needed imports of food, raw materials, and manufactured goods from other areas of what was then the Japanese Empire.

General MacArthur and Emperor Hirohito. National Archives

*General MacArthur and Maj. Gen.
Courtney Whitney leaving their Dai
Ichi Building headquarters, Tokyo.
Whitney was the head of the
Government Section and ordered the
new constitution to be drafted.*
National Archives

MacArthur's self-confidence was as lofty as his new title of Supreme Commander. Well grounded in the Western classics, he displayed a vision and a sense of history rare among his countrymen. And however patronizing his feelings for his Japanese subjects, he had none of the meanspirited racism that scarred so many of his Regular Army and Navy associates. On the contrary, he was capable of projecting the enthusiasm and missionary optimism which are America's best qualities and using them to inspire a nation of traditional pessimists.

AT THIS POINT in their history, the Japanese needed a man like him. For almost a full century, since the successful self-modernization of the Meiji Restoration, Japan's march to great-power status had been something of a triumphal progress. Reinforced by military victory, colonization, and industrial expansion, Japan's old myths of racial uniqueness and imperial mission had been increasingly accepted as facts. For more than a decade, since the rapacious Japanese military had advanced into Manchuria, national leadership had been taken over by a military-bureaucratic oligarchy which had stifled all public opposition and proclaimed itself unbeatable.

After four years of deepening privation during World War II the shock of total defeat had paralyzed the nation. Virtually the whole structure of authority had crumbled, except for the symbol of the emperor. And even he, responding to one of the earliest Occupation suggestions, had issued on January 1, 1946, a special proclamation renouncing his alleged divinity. ("The ties between us and our people have always stood upon mutual trust and affection . . . They are not predicated on the false assumption that the emperor is divine.")

Japan's military leaders had given their country a decade of purposeless hardships, escalating defeats, and deceitful communiqués. By 1945 they were thoroughly discredited. The disillusionment that I had noticed among prisoners of war, as they found out what was really happening, had spread to the entire nation. A whole people had been lied to. In a state of national depression after the surrender, most Japanese expected a brutal, vengeful military occupation. Thus they responded with hope and a few stirrings of reassurance when the U.S. occupiers announced that their goal was to democratize Japan, not destroy it.

In the towering figure of MacArthur, as he stood next to their own diminutive Showa emperor, they instinctively sensed a modern revival of the old shoguns, the all-powerful and masterful military leaders who had always taken care to send out their edicts under the emperor's name. For this people, at that time in their history, the eloquent bombast of the general's pronouncements sounded just about right. As a young Japanese of that day recalled: "MacArthur was like a force of nature. He was like the river that flows or the wind that blows. . . . Very few people thought of him as the enemy. It was as if a new emperor had arrived."

Add to this the spontaneously friendly attitude of the American troops—once they saw they were not to be attacked—and the rough-and-ready kindness they showed. Some bad actors there were. But in general the good behavior of the occupying army was a far cry from the ruthlessness with which most Japanese knew their own troops had behaved in *their* occupations.

"POLITICALLY," Douglas MacArthur once remarked, "the Japanese are young and plastic enough to copy anything." It was in this spirit, one assumes, that SCAP (for Supreme Commander for the Allied Powers) issued to the postwar Japanese government of Prime Minister Shidehara Kijuro a series of sweeping orders, designed to execute the basic political directive (JCS 1308/15) that he had brought to Japan. Over the last four months of 1945 the Japanese were ordered to establish general civil rights, including the vote for women, release political prisoners, abolish censorship and the system of police surveillance, break up the huge *zaibatsu* holding companies, promote unrestricted unionization of workers, enact a land reform program to eliminate the exploitation of tenant farmers, "democratize" the economy, and reform and "democratize" education. Besides arresting specifically named war criminals, the government was directed also to purge from office, in business as well as government, anyone who had played a substantial role in the war effort—a definition which might well include most of the national leadership.

The Japanese people who read these directives responded to them positively. But they were not actually so young and plastic as MacArthur suggested. Nor were they unused to the idea of democracy and citizens' responsibility in government. Despite the flaws of the Meiji Constitution, Japan had enjoyed parliamentary government and debated democratic freedoms for fifty-five years before MacArthur discovered it for them. The Emperor Meiji had convened the first Diet in 1890. By the 1920s, the period called Taisho Democracy, the country had been well on its way toward becoming a working democracy, complete with labor unions, strikes, socialists, a relatively free press, and a great deal of public debate about democratic reform.

The increasing power of the militarists and their allies may have smothered this growing democracy, but its memory was not erased. People hang on to values even under severe repression, as events in Eastern Europe in the late eighties have shown us. The Japanese were no exceptions to this rule. Without their own democratic tradition, however circumscribed, it is highly doubtful that the Japanese would have understood the reforms the Occupation was talking about. Still less would they have supported them.

Most of the young American occupiers, however, took the support of the local population for granted. (All that smiling and bowing, we thought, had to be sincere.) Following the general's lead, we regarded the 70 million survivors of this old and unique nation-society as "young" and "plastic" copiers. ("Wasn't Japanese business already known for the way they copied our machines?") For Occupation planners in Tokyo and grass-roots military governors in the prefectures, the relationship was to be that of eager teacher to attentive and presumably grateful student.

There was an infectious, if often exasperating enthusiasm about the way the young secular missionaries of SCAP preached their political doctrine. Recalling the breathless lectures of the YMCA missionaries in China in the twenties—and foreshadowing the up-and-at-'em zeal of the Kennedy Peace Corps in the sixties—MacArthur's scratch team of recently demobilized servicemen and hastily recruited Washington experts set out to make Japan over.

Few of them knew much about Japan—the Supreme Commander among the notably ignorant. ("There were only about sixty Japanese MacArthur ever met," one of his aides remarked, "and none lower in rank than a Supreme Court justice.") There was a good bit of truth in the tart comment later made by Prime Minister Yoshida in his memoirs: "The Occupation, with all the power and authority behind its operation, was hampered by its lack of knowledge of the people it had come to govern, and even more so, perhaps, by its generally happy ignorance of the amount of requisite knowledge it lacked."

This may have been all to the good. Many gross affronts to local history and custom were given. But if the occupiers had fully understood the tradition of the demons they set out to exorcise, the attempt might never have been made.

By April 1946, some 1,550 officers and government civilians were working for SCAP in Tokyo, along with a supporting staff of Army enlisted men and Japanese and "third country" nationals. By 1948, the high-water mark of the "reform" Occupation, the number had increased to about 3,200. Of these, some 900 could properly be called "decision makers"[2]

Recruitment at the Tokyo headquarters was often by happenstance. Time was of the essence. There was no room for leisurely evaluation. While hundreds of presumably qualified graduates of military government schools in the United States were kept cooling their heels—MacArthur characteristically liked to hire on his own—thousands more applied from among Army and Navy service personnel already in the Far East Theater. In general, military amenities were observed, but rank often took a back seat to qualification. Junior officers or enlisted men with the desired technical or professional training found them-

[2] This figure is taken from Theodore Cohen's *Remaking Japan*, as edited by Herbert Passin (New York: Free Press, 1986); it accords with my own recollections of that period.

selves hired and quickly sent back to the SCAP offices to command officers who may have been, just a few days before, one or two ranks senior.

Research facilities were scarce, and except for a few language officers and noncoms in intelligence and elsewhere, the occupiers' command of Japanese was minimal or nonexistent. Inescapably officers in the various Occupation departments formed symbiotic relationships with their opposite numbers in the Japanese government ministries or bureaus under their direction.

Less formal, although more intense boy-girl relationships also developed. In fact, once the original cultural shock was over, there was a great deal of social contact at almost all levels between occupiers and the occupied. One of the abiding blots on the Occupation's record was the effort of meanspirited and quite obviously racist Army officers at the Chief of Staff and G-1 level in MacArthur's headquarters later in the Occupation to prohibit "fraternization," to the extent that even Japanese and Americans eating together in restaurants was regarded as illegal. Although the nonfraternization directives ultimately collapsed of their own weight (they were canceled late in 1949), they sowed much misunderstanding and distrust, in sharp contrast to the unexpected harmony of the early Occupation days.

I PARTICIPATED in the Occupation during two periods. The first was spent largely in Tokyo, where I was assigned as Flag Lieutenant to Vice Admiral Robert M. Griffin after my duty with the Naval Technical Mission to Japan had ended. This lasted from September 1945 to July 1946. My second Occupation "tour" extended from March 1949, when I returned to Tokyo as a very young *Time* magazine bureau chief, to September 1950, when I left Tokyo for New York after having covered the first stages of the Korean War.

In each of these incarnations I served as a kind of well-placed fly on the wall. I knew most of the players in the Occupation, Americans and Japanese. Because of my language ability I saw a good bit of the latter, and was in the business of describing and evaluating their performance.[3] Considering the circumstances it was remarkably good. Although the Occupation had its share of fat cats and misfits, its keynote was a kind of contagious idealism. Most of us were spiritually New Dealers. Having grown up under Roosevelt, we were confident that the government that fixed the Great Depression could solve most problems. Just as the Pacific war—atolls, bugs, beaches, landing craft, and knee mortars—had become in a peculiar way our war, an exotic country that we had barely heard of before 1941 became ours by adoption.

Even in its devastation and defeat Japan worked its strong cultural gravita-

[3] Most of my observations of that time are contained in my first book, *Five Gentlemen of Japan*.

tional pull upon us. Those of us who spoke the language, in particular, found it the key to a culture. The mannered lifestyle we met, its grace, and indeed its humor were all the more fascinating in their contrast with the massed brutishness of the Japanese soldiery overseas. But for almost everyone the growing attractiveness of the country and its people made us all the more want to make them just like us. Democracy was our gift, we thought, and we were eager to share it.

Of the SCAP reformers three continue to stand out: Charles L. Kades, Theodore Cohen, and Wolf Ladejinsky. All three, interestingly enough, had worked in General Hildring's Civil Affairs Division in Washington and helped write some of the specific subject guides that gave rise to the basic Occupation directive. Each one exemplified one of the three major achievements of the U.S. Occupation: land reform, the revival of the labor movement, and the new postwar constitution.

Ladejinsky, a Russian-American from the Department of Agriculture, worked out the plan that ultimately, in December 1945, resulted in an eloquent memo from MacArthur ordering the Japanese government to "destroy the economic bondage which has enslaved the Japanese farmer for centuries of feudal oppression." Bills had already been presented in the Diet to correct the iniquitous absentee-landlord system and the preponderance of below-subsistence tenant farmers. Indeed, Ladejinsky's original proposal acknowledged its debt to the work of Japanese agricultural economists like Nasu Shiroshi. Agronomists, rural activists, and bureaucrats had worked for years to solve the tenant-farming problem. This was one Occupation reform which received strong support from the Japanese bureaucracy. But it took the power of a military occupation to overcome the political opposition of local landlords.

The combination of Ladejinsky's expertise and MacArthur's personal interest—here exceeding the scope of his Washington directive—resulted in a sweeping enforced sale and redistribution of farm property. More than one-third of Japan's agricultural land was affected. The Japanese countryside was transformed. By all accounts the most successful of the Occupation reforms, the peaceful legal transfer of farmland stood in contrast to the bloody Communist takeovers of land in China and Vietnam under Mao Zedong and Ho Chi Minh. Ladejinsky himself later went to Taiwan and helped direct a similar reform under an economically progressive Guomindang government. As in Japan, the Taiwan reform was accelerated by strong American pressure.[4]

*   *   *

[4] Ronald Dore's *Land Reform in Japan* (New York: Shocken, 1985 [new edition]) offers a comprehensive treatment of this subject.

THEODORE COHEN, WHO had written his graduate school thesis at Columbia on the subject of the Japanese labor movement, found himself, through bureaucratic serendipity, in charge of the Labor Division of the Economic and Scientific Section of SCAP headquarters. At the time he was only twenty-eight years old. The basic Trade Union Law, founded on the pro-labor American Wagner Act, was put together before his arrival in Tokyo. But it was Cohen who shepherded the Labor Relations Adjustment Law and the Labor Standards Law through Occupation directive and the legislative approval of a reluctant Japanese Diet.

"The pillars of the legal framework for labor relations in present-day Japan," as Tokyo University's law authority Ariizumi Toru noted, they amounted to a Magna Charta for Japan's emerging unions. Without this basic legal framework, supported by the watchdog regard of Cohen and his Occupation colleagues for labor rights, the Japanese labor movement could never have revived after its wartime suppression. This ranks with the land reform as a major Occupation achievement.

Cohen and his colleagues in the Labor Division were strong activists. Many had been American union members and organizers; some had worked with unions as bureaucrats in the U.S. Department of Labor. They toured the country tirelessly, visiting with Japanese workers and learning about their problems at first hand. Japanese unionists were pleasantly surprised by this official attention. MacArthur himself had pointedly told Prime Minister Shidehara that he regarded labor unions as essential "in safeguarding the workman from exploitation and abuse." Encouraged, a stream of new Japanese union leaders came to seek advice and encouragement at the Labor Division's offices. Almost every industry was represented, from miners and steelworkers to a delegation from the newly formed geisha union in Tokyo.

THE WRITING OF the New Japanese Constitution is of course the third major achievement. Worth a book in itself, the story of Colonel Charles E. Kades and his colleagues in SCAP's Government Section offers a fascinating case study of the Occupation reformers at work.

In line with his mission to democratize Japan, MacArthur had asked the Japanese government to prepare a significant revision of the Meiji Constitution of 1889. While thought of as liberal in its time, this charter for a constitutional monarchy had its built-in defects. Those clauses centering sovereignty in the emperor had the effect of putting the emperor's advisers beyond the law. The limits on voting rights and civil liberties now looked far from democratic, after years of use and abuse by autocratic Japanese cabinets. With revision in the air, various Japanese groups put together drafts, which they offered to the Occupation officers. Some of these were surprisingly liberal. One proposal provided for an elective President (to replace the emperor) an initiative and referendum system, and a mandatory eight-hour day.

Not so, however, the official draft offered by Baron Shidehara's cabinet. The fruit of four months' work, it was vintage Meiji, but rebottled. At this the SCAP command lost patience. On February 4, 1946, Major General Courtney Whitney, chief of the Government Section and MacArthur's only really close confidant, called a group of his officers and civilians into a large empty area, formerly a ballroom, on the sixth floor of the Dai-Ichi Insurance Building, MacArthur's Tokyo headquarters. He announced that they had just become a "constituent assembly," with every man and woman a Thomas Jefferson. He gave them six days to study, research, confer, and come up with a suitable draft. Strict secrecy was imposed, since their draft ultimately had to be presented to the Japanese Diet as the work of the Japanese government.

There were only twenty-four people involved. They were a mixed bag of eight civilians and sixteen military reservists—among them one congressman, five lawyers, a novelist, a newspaperman, a doctor, and two academics. None of them was a career officer. Their ages were generally twenties to early forties—which at least kept them in the tradition of Japanese constitution making. (Kaneko Kentaro and Ito Hirobumi's other key aides in writing the 1890 Constitution were in their early thirties.) It is a tribute to the intelligence and adaptability of these constitutional ghostwriters that the end product turned out so well.

For this, Kades, then Whitney's executive officer, deserves great credit. A lawyer in civilian life who had worked before the war in Washington's New Deal government agencies, Kades was assigned first to Hildring's Civil Affairs Division and finally to SCAP in Tokyo. He got along well with Whitney and the other "Bataan boys" on the general's staff, and soon became next to indispensable as the vital link between the original Washington planners of Japan's reform and the headquarters that was to carry it out. His role in the improvised constitutional committee was even more critical; he was the leader and the spark plug of the group as well as its conduit to higher authority.

After hastily borrowing what constitutional literature they could pick up in various Tokyo libraries (under a variety of pretexts), the constitution writers set to work. They were understandably awed by their task. "You couldn't help but ponder the role of a young ensign drafting provisions that would govern the functions of the emperor and the imperial throne," said one of them, Richard Poole, recalling the event. "It was a large order." They had no time for reflection, however. Working in nine committees—judiciary, emperor, civil rights, finance, etc.—they relied for guidance on basic SWNCC directives and examples of constitutions available to them. There was, in addition, a handwritten set of guidelines that came from MacArthur and Whitney.

Understandably, the MacArthur Constitution relied very little on its German-influenced Meiji forerunner. On the contrary, there was a prominent "Made in 1789" stamp on it. Sovereignty was shifted from the emperor to the people. The cabinet was made responsible to the legislative body. An independent Supreme Court was set up as the capstone of the judiciary. Local democratic government was guaranteed, as were basic personal freedoms. These included academic freedom and unprecedented guarantees of women's rights.

The women's rights clauses were the work of Beate Sirota, a twenty-two-year-old Austrian-American and a recent addition to the Government Section. A fluent Japanese linguist who had been brought up in Tokyo, she knew at first hand the discrimination against women in Japanese society. "A woman couldn't decide whom she wanted to marry," she explained. "She couldn't divorce a man. She really had no property rights. I wrote in many specific rights, such as even prenatal care, maternity leave, and things of that sort which appear in other constitutions—but not in the American. So our steering committee—all of them men—said these were too specific."[5]

In the end Kades and his fellows on the steering committee agreed to incorporate women's rights guarantees along with other basic freedoms. The draft that resulted was and remains a liberal, farsighted document with revolutionary implications. Not the least of these was Article 9, the famous antiwar clause—"War as a sovereign right of the nation is abolished"—which MacArthur had written out in his own hand. (Much support for this measure had come from Kades, a great admirer of the well-intentioned, if unsuccessful Kellogg-Briand peace pact in the 1920s.)

When Whitney and Kades unveiled their new constitution to Yoshida Shigeru, then the Foreign Minister, and his own constitution-drafting group, the Japanese statesmen reacted with predictable shock. Yoshida for one was strongly opposed. Whitney and Kades had walked out into the garden of the official Foreign Minister's residence, to give Yoshida and his aides time to read the document. When they returned, they made it clear that SCAP would go to the people in a national referendum if the government balked at acceptance.

At which point, by coincidence, a B-29 flew low over the residence. "I thought this had a certain persuasive element," Kades later recalled. Bowing to the inevitable, the Japanese accepted, but persisted along with SCAP in maintaining to all who would listen that the new constitution was a Japanese document.

[5] The comments from Beate Gordon (née Sirota), Richard Poole, and others on the committee were recorded for the film version of *The Pacific Century*.

The Constitution has remained controversial to this day. "We should have done it ourselves," former Prime Minister Nakasone Yasuhiro recently commented. "True freedom, true democracy must come from within. I agree with many of the ideas, but the process was wrong."[6]

For all the opposition to the new constitution, many Japanese supported it. As political scientist Milton Esman, one of the original twenty-four drafters, noted: "Democratic ideas were not something that we brought to Japan. These democratic ideas were there. Many people had already paid heavily for espousing them—the intelligentsia, writers, teachers, artists, women, the labor unions. Over the years there has been, I think, a tacit coalition among such groups to resist any basic change in that constitution which would have the effect of recentralizing the society—or limiting in any way the freedom of expression."

For despite the coolness of the Japanese establishment toward the "Made in the U.S.A." democracy of the Occupation, Japan's people responded to it. After the years of dictation and privation, most Japanese were ready for something new. Some 381,000 workers had joined the newly freed unions by December 1945. By June 1948, the number of union members had grown to 6.5 million. Once banned political groups like socialists and Communists were now being listened to. In fact, many Japanese assumed that the MacArthur democracy was some new kind of Communism or socialism. This was an impression that the small but capable core of Communist leaders—just recently freed by SCAP from their jail cells—did little to dispel.

A flood of new ideas, new songs, new writing, even new news—now that the Japanese police and military censorship had been lifted from the big metropolitan papers[7]—was proof positive that the "democracy" message was getting through. Jazz, swing, and baseball—deemphasized during the war as a foreign sport—were now played up by the Occupation's democratizers. On national radio, SCAP promoted an "Amateur Hour" on the American model to search out new talent. Hollywood movies were imported to promote free expression. Kissing, long banned by Japan's military censors, was now encouraged by film importers. People were urged to "speak their minds."

But it was just here, in the early days of the Occupation, that the American reformers came to grips with the first of three basic contradictions that were to underlie the U.S. Occupation of Japan.

The first was a matter of ideals versus subsistence. The Occupation was commanded to accomplish the demilitarization of Japan, keep order, destroy its

---

[6] From an interview for *The Pacific Century* in Tokyo, 1991.

[7] Of course, the Occupation brought with it a military censorship of its own, which could be onerous, although it relaxed with the passage of time.

Bombed-out aircraft factory, Yokohama. Horace Bristol

Transportation (pre-Toyota): Tokyo rickshaw stand. Horace Bristol

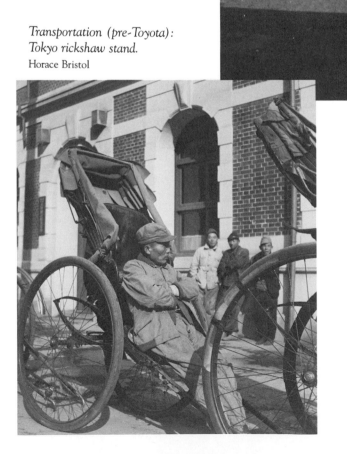

Shacks rising out of Tokyo rubble Horace Bristol

JAPAN UNDER U.S. OCCUPATION, 1946

Their cities ruined and their industry in pieces, the Japanese people picked themselves up and began to build for the future. These photographs were taken in 1946 by the distinguished photographer Horace Bristol, one of the first American photojournalists to spend some time in postwar Japan.

Posting the returns in the first postwar elections. Horace Bristol

Steelworker loading furnace, Kawasaki. Horace Bristol

Shipbuilding begins again.
Horace Bristol

war potential, and punish war criminals—the atrocities perpetrated by the Japanese armed forces throughout Asia were a matter of awful record. Punitive damages, in the form of economic reparations, were to be paid by transferring whole factories as well as products from Japan to various Asian and other countries which the Japanese had despoiled over almost a decade of aggression. SCAP was to do everything possible to democratize the enemy country. At the same time, the Basic Initial Post-Surrender Directive ordered General Mac-Arthur: "You will not assume any responsibility for the economic rehabilitation of Japan or the strengthening of the Japanese economy. You will make it clear to the Japanese people that you assume no obligation to maintain any particular standard of living in Japan."

Yet when MacArthur and his staff officers landed at Atsugi airfield at the end of August 1945, they found a country on the edge of mass starvation. Its industry was smashed, its cities leveled, and millions left homeless. In addition, fully 7 million Japanese, military and civilians alike, were stranded in China, Manchuria, Korea, and elsewhere in Asia, relicts of the vanished empire. Within a year most of these people had been repatriated, to return to bombed-out homes and factories. By the end of 1946 there were some 13 million unemployed.

Interpreting his various directives freely, as was his custom, the Supreme Commander first assured the Japanese that the peace would not be punitive. ("If the talents of the [Japanese] race are turned into constructive channels, the country can lift itself from its present deplorable state into a position of dignity.") Stocks of food and other U.S. military supplies that had been earmarked for the invasion of Japan were now released for Japanese civilian use. As the destitution of the country became apparent, the Occupation even imported raw materials to prime the pump of Japanese industry. In all, the United States spent fully $2 billion (in 1950 dollars) in direct aid between 1945 and 1952 to bring Japan back, most of it during the Occupation's first few years. In the Occupation's first year 800,000 tons of U.S. military food rations were given to Japan's civilians. For how can people appreciate democracy on empty stomachs?

A planned massive reparations program had looked neat and tidy in Washington's perspective. It was first stalled, then systematically sabotaged by SCAP as destructive and hopelessly impractical, in the face of Japanese economic realities. Nor could the countries destined to receive reparations agree on a program. The Soviet Union, for example, after its armies systematically looted plant and equipment in Japan's industrialized colony of Manchuria, insisted that these removals should be classed as "war trophies," hence outside the general reparations pot.

Although the Japanese later settled reparations directly with several countries—for example, Indonesia and the Philippines—the original program of huge material transfers was officially ended in May 1949. It was simply not in accord with the Occupation's plans for democracy and economic rehabilitation, as they evolved.

THE SECOND contradiction was rooted in the very structure of the Occupation. It required a large leap of faith, to begin with, to assume that an entire people could be "educated for democracy" within a few short years. But how could such an education be handled by occupiers working under military discipline and accustomed to issuing directives—and being promptly obeyed? It was one thing to congratulate the Japanese on their release from the military censorship of the Imperial Army and the much feared wartime *tokkotai*, or special police. Yet here was a new set of directives preventing anyone from criticizing the U.S. Occupation. This basic contradiction was never really solved. Postwar Japanese revisionist historians have used it in their athletic efforts to equate postwar American and their own wartime Japanese "militarism."

A classic example of the Occupation's dilemma was the general strike which Japanese unions threatened in early 1947. Charged with developing democratic trade unions, even at the cost of some unrest and disturbance, the Occupation consistently refused to intervene against planned strikes or slowdowns; a massive railroad workers' strike in September 1946 was averted only by the Japanese government's almost total capitulation to the strikers' wage demands.

The general strike called for February 1, 1947, however, was political in nature. Liberated from jail by Occupation order, Japan's Communist Party executive, led by a restless, dynamic, and brilliant Party activist, Tokuda Kyuichi, had concentrated its efforts on infiltrating and taking control of various nationwide union "struggle" committees. While the Occupation's labor experts were trying to encourage economic trade unionism on the American model, the Japanese labor movement had retained a strong Marxist flavor from the prewar days. Understandably reacting to brutal police suppression and business managements that were at best oppressively paternalistic but generally contemptuous of labor's rights, the leaders of Japan's prewar labor movement had advocated revolutionary class warfare as the only way to overthrow the militarists' rule. Taking advantage of this heritage—and in a sense riding on the Occupation's coattails—the Communists, their spokesmen argued, were merely the militant defenders of *demokurashi*.

Tokuda's intensively "political" union sympathizers, supported by a 10,000-man Youth Action Corps of strong-arm gangsters, gained control of the large

Sanbetsu union executive[8] and pressured other union leaders to join the massive general strike. Its purpose was frankly political—to bring down the Japanese government. So Tokuda and other spellbinders explained to a cheering crowd of some 400,000 gathered in the Imperial Plaza on a late January day.

As the planned strike's political direction grew obvious, MacArthur with great reluctance moved to order the strike canceled as too disruptive of public peace and order. The union leaders obeyed, after a last show of defiance. The strike was called off, with a consequent diminution of the Communists' prestige. But this action had also forced the U.S. Occupation into an official frontal collision with people and organizations whose rights to free activism and self-expression it was pledged to develop.

THE THIRD contradiction within the Occupation was the most serious. It involved changes in Japan and the United States. Changes in the world situation, in fact, between 1945 and 1948 were to force a serious rethinking of the entire reform mission. Called the "reverse course" by many Japanese and American historians, it was not, however, the simple clear change in direction and policy that the name implied. Nor did it roll back and nullify Japan's "democratization." The changes induced by the Occupation were too basic to be reversed with any ease, and most of the real reforming work had been done in the Occupation's first two and a half years. Yet the shift in emphasis was real and significant. No one can deny the far-reaching nature of the "reverse course" and its effects.

WHEN I RETURNED to Tokyo in March 1949, the Occupation democratizers were still at work. The SCAP sections remained; in fact, most were significantly larger than they had been in 1946. Sheltered by a barrage of grandiloquent Occupation directives, the economists in General William Marquat's Economic and Scientific Section were still trying to "democratize" Japan's

---

[8] At the beginning of the U.S. Occupation most of the new Japanese unions were divided into two rival groups, *Sodomei* (the Japanese Federation of Labor) and the leftist *Sanbetsu* (the Japanese Congress of Industrial Unions). Although initially fast-growing, *Sanbetsu* lost most of its membership because of its strong Communist Party affiliations. A new union, *Sohyo* (the General Council of Trade Unions) was organized by a merger of *Sodomei* and *Mindo* (the Alliance for Democratization), which had deserted *Sanbetsu* because of its Communist orientation. Later, after Sohyo itself turned to the left, anti-Communist unions broke off to form *Domei* (the Federation of Labor). Over the years Sohyo remained leftist, while Domei stayed right of center; but after the sixties Communist influence in the unions greatly decreased.

business structure. A new trust buster from Washington had arrived to complete the ruin, as it was thought, of the purged *zaibatsu*. A revitalized judiciary was being put in place, under the guidance of SCAP's Legal Division, and the Education Ministry's bureaucrats were being prodded to institute not only the 6-6-3 system of schools, modeled on America's, but the local management of education, fortified by an invigorated Parent-Teacher Association network. In addition, U.S. education experts had ordered the sweeping, if ill-advised transformation of virtually all Japan's technical and other postsecondary colleges into four-year universities.

Yet the context within which SCAP worked had changed. The Occupation's reformers had seen Japan as a kind of isolated political laboratory where a variety of "Made in America" ideas and institutions, if not a whole new democratic lifestyle, could be grafted onto an alien culture. They had been encouraged by the enthusiasm with which the Japanese were apparently willing to learn. But as the rather guileless optimism of the immediate postwar period gave way to the suspicions and aggressions of the Cold War, the laboratory technicians found themselves serving a lot closer to a new line of trenches.

My own perspective had certainly changed. Over the last year and a half, as a *Time* correspondent in Europe, I had been fortunate to cover the Berlin airlift, the beginnings of the Marshall Plan for Western Europe's recovery, and the escalating acrimony of the debates between the United States and its allies and the Soviet Union at the European meetings of the United Nations in Paris. From the vantage points of London and Paris, and the West's solitary outpost in Berlin, I had watched the Soviet Army tighten its grip on Eastern Europe. After Stalin's brutal Sovietization of Poland, Hungary, and East Germany, Czechoslovakia was swallowed up in turn.

The tragic suicide of Jan Masaryk in 1948, falling (or thrown) from the windows of Hradčany Castle in Prague, somehow dramatized Stalin's attempted takeover of Europe, just a decade after the Munich surrender had given Hitler the springboard for doing the same. Masaryk, the son of the first President of Czechoslovakia, was then his country's Foreign Minister. Almost until the end he had tried to persuade the Western powers that some sort of political compromise would be acceptable to the Russians.

RETURNING TO JAPAN, I brought with me unforgettable images of a new war building in Europe—the violent, if often entertaining histrionics of Andrei Vyshinsky, the vicious prosecutor of the Moscow purge trials of the 1930s, who brought the same uncompromising executioner's rhetoric into the UN debates inside the graceful Palais de Chaillot;[9] the suspense over the Italian elections of 1948, when the victory of Alcide De Gasperi's Christian Democrats, backed by every resource—visible and clandestine—that the United States could muster, stopped the tide of Communism in the West; the sight of ragged Berliners standing on their city's ruins and cheering as the huge (for that day) transports of the U.S. Air Force's Berlin airlift thundered over the city like trains on a timetable delivering the food and fuel that ultimately broke the Russians' blockade.

In Tokyo, by contrast, there were few outward changes. MacArthur still reigned from his sanctum in the Dai-Ichi Building. Occupation directives continued to be imposed on a subservient Japanese government the way the U.S. Army's convenient wooden signboards—Avenue A, 40th Street, etc.—had preempted the few visible Japanese identifiers to explain Tokyo's bewildering urban geography to its foreign occupiers. At key intersections MPs in khaki stood beside Japanese traffic policemen (by now equipped with U.S. infantrymen's combat boots). Apart from the few Soviet staff people serving General Kuzma Derevyanko, who sputtered periodic denunciations of SCAP policy at meetings of the figurehead Allied Control Council for Japan, there wasn't a Russian in town.

Yet around Japan's insulated islands the political map of Asia was changing. Mao Zedong and his Communist generals had virtually completed their conquest of China "out of the barrel of a gun," as Chiang Kai-shek prepared to remove his defeated and discredited remnants to the once Japanese colony of Taiwan offshore. North Korea's Soviet proconsul, Colonel General Terenti Shtikov, stonewalled any moves for meaningful democratic elections throughout the peninsula, while Kim Il Sung and his Soviet-trained army implanted a local Stalinist regime north of the 38th parallel demarcation line. Ho Chi Minh, having given up hope of any accommodation with the Americans, had begun the Communization of Vietnam.

The first major story I covered for *Time* in Japan, as it happened, was the return of the prisoners of war from the Soviet Union. Beginning in the summer of 1949, the Soviets shipped back some 95,000 surviving Japanese war prisoners interned in Siberian camps since 1945 (out of a total of 360,000 listed in Japanese demobilization records). The repatriates who were sent back had been thoroughly indoctrinated by their captors. Marching in lockstep, shouting So-

---

[9] Vyshinsky himself incorporated a bundle of ironies. Originally a Menshevik, with his roots in the Polish minor nobility, he made himself useful to Stalin because of his slavishness in supporting the Party line. Yet because of his background and education he had a thorough grounding in both the Russian and the Western classics. His speeches, for all the vitriol they contained, were models of Ciceronian rhetoric, replete with Latin and Greek tags as well as more homely references to Russian folk sayings and proverbs.

viet songs and slogans, and mocking the registration requests of repatriation officials, the returned men gave Japan its first exhibition of brainwashing, Soviet style. They were lionized by local Communists, who mobilized every available Party sympathizer to take over the welcoming celebrations in various Japanese cities. Understandably the repatriates readily signed up with local Party organizations, under the impression that Japan was already half Communized.

Ultimately all but a few repatriates lost their enthusiasm for militant Marxism and picked up the threads of their lives with their families. The demonstrations and disturbances backfired badly on the Communists—the Japan of 1949 was thoroughly sick of uniformed slogan shouting. But the whole episode was yet another sign that Japan was being drawn into the Cold War.

SMALL WONDER that policy makers in Washington had begun to have searching second thoughts about where Japan's reform democratization should stop and where security, economic stability, and indeed some form of military alliance should begin. In the July 1947 issue of *Foreign Affairs*, then almost the official journal of the Washington establishment, George Kennan, writing anonymously as "X," had set forth his now famous thesis on the need for the United States to contain Soviet expansion. Less than a year later, after an intensive fact-finding visit to Tokyo in March 1948, Kennan concluded that the Occupation reforms were "paving the way for a Communist takeover." He then made a seminal set of recommendations to the Secretary of State.

"The regime of control by SCAP over the Japanese government should, I recommended, be relaxed," he recalled later in his *Memoirs*. "The Japanese should be encouraged to develop independent responsibility. No further reform legislation should be pressed. The emphasis should be shifted from reform to economic recovery. The purges should be tempered, tapered off and terminated at an early date . . . The indiscriminate purging of whole categories of individuals, sickeningly similar to totalitarian practices, was in conflict with the civil rights provision of the new constitution we had ourselves imposed on the Japanese."[10]

The objective of Kennan and his State Department colleagues was world-political: to keep Japan and its great industrial potential out of the hands of the Soviets and the Chinese Communists and, going beyond this, to utilize Japan ultimately as the anchor of an island chain of U.S. allies off the Asian mainland.

The goals of William H. Draper, Jr., Under Secretary of the Army, were

[10] George F. Kennan, *Memoirs, 1925–1950* (Boston: Atlantic–Little, Brown, 1967).

similar, but a bit closer to the ground. Draper, like his superior, Defense Secretary James V. Forrestal, was an investment banker from New York's Dillon Read & Company. Along with Army Secretary Kenneth Royall, they wanted to start up the Japanese economy, with no further fuss about democratizing it, and make Japan economically self-sufficient and hence off the back of the American taxpayer. Japan's industry was to be revived and set to producing for trade with Southeast Asia, while some degree of rearmament, as Kennan had suggested, was to be considered.

Draper and the other banker-businessmen wanted no more trust busting. For them big Japanese companies, just like big American companies, made obvious business sense. They opposed the continuing purge of leading Japanese businessmen as well. (Some of them they knew.) With such thoughts in mind Draper sent several missions of U.S. businessmen to Tokyo to see how quickly the economy could be put back on a paying basis.

On December 12, 1948, therefore, a new directive from Washington arrived at SCAP headquarters in Tokyo, with specific orders to balance the budget and set up a single yen-dollar exchange rate, among other things. As Theodore Cohen wrote: "The target of this directive was not policy but performance . . . It was a massive vote of distrust in [MacArthur's] economic stewardship, confirmed by the President. From here on Washington intended to call the shots."

To supervise the shot-calling on the spot, Washington sent the president of the Detroit Bank, Joseph W. Dodge, to Tokyo as President Truman's personal representative. Dodge, who later became Director of the Budget in Eisenhower's administration, was part of the new environment in Washington. Most of the New Dealers had departed with the end of the wartime economy—except for the bridgehead left behind in Tokyo. The bankers and businessmen who now began to take over American economic policy were numbers men first and idealists second. And they were preoccupied by the staggering problems of world economic recovery. While the Marshall Plan was proving successful in Europe; it was also a drain on the U.S. economy, for all the American business it stimulated. So was the prospect of what seemed like unending outlays to put Japan on its feet.

Spurred on by an increasingly Republican Congress, whose ritual howls about "fiscal responsibility" would only increase, Washington's new objective was to reduce American aid as soon as possible and help local free enterprisers help themselves. This was completely in line with Dodge's own convictions as an old-fashioned budget balancer and investment-firster. He had already presided over the currency reform in occupied Germany. For Japan's economy he intended a similarly drastic solution.

"The economy," he told his new charges, "has traveled the early part of this road in a damaged and unrepaired vehicle, but the vehicle and the passengers

Charles Kades, now a Boston lawyer,
who led the task force that wrote
the new Japanese constitution
National Archives

Impounding stock certificates. As part of the
Occupation's "purge," the old zaibatsu conglomerates
were taken away from their family owners and the
stock put up for public sale. National Archives

George Kennan (left, shown with Ambassador William
Sebald, State Department representative at MacArthur's
headquarters.) Kennan, then head of policy planning at
State, was instrumental in launching the Occupation's
reverse course. National Archives

have been protected from road shocks by the cushion of U.S. aid. It is time the Japanese began to face up to the unalterable facts of their own life . . . Wealth must be created before it can be divided."

Dodge's immediate target was inflation. Despite the government's efforts to control prices, they had skyrocketed. If one took the prewar normalcy of 1936 as 100, the commodity price index in 1946 had passed the 1,800 figure. It reached 5,908 in 1947, 14,956 in 1948, and an astounding 24,336 in 1949!

There were many reasons for this, including huge Japanese government disbursements to pay off wartime commitments, procurement contracts, and production loans. Basically it was a matter of too much money in circulation and a pitiful lack of food and goods. With stockpiled military supplies simply stolen or diverted to illegal use, the black market thrived. By 1946 prices on the black market were fully seven times the official rate, which made it virtually impossible to live on legal rations.

In October 1947, Judge Yamaguchi Yoshitada of the Tokyo District Court was found dead of starvation because he had refused to eat black-market rice. In a note he left behind, he had written: "Even bad laws are the law and I am pledged to defend the law." The resultant outcry in the press underlined public outrage at the floundering efforts of the government to control the price of goods.[11]

Dodge moved quickly. A stalwart believer in free enterprise without government interference, he insisted that the Japanese government abandon subsidies to various key industries and cut back on a variety of pump-priming lending programs, which had up to that time at least raised production in coal and some manufacturing areas. He urged the government to turn its back on deficit financing and balance the budget—in fact, "overbalance" it to produce a surplus. He also put through a single exchange rate of 360 yen to $1.00 to replace the complex tangle of rates used by the Japanese government in its limited import and export trade.

Japanese business reacted to the purgations of the Dodge Plan, as it was called, in the manner of a patient who has received a dose of semi-lethal medicine. Thousands of firms went bankrupt in this first "rationalization" (*gori-ka*) of the postwar Japanese economy. Wholesale layoffs took place in both public and private sectors. The Japanese National Railways alone dismissed 100,000 employees. Thousands of laid-off workers streamed back to the countryside to become, for the time being, surplus workers on their family farms. Indeed, it is difficult to overestimate how much the strength of the Japanese family system at that time saved the country from serious social unrest.

[11] I am indebted for this anecdote to Chalmers Johnson's *MITI and the Japanese Miracle* (Stanford, Calif.: Stanford University Press, 1982), as well as for other insights into the economy of this period.

But the fifteen-year inflation was stopped. It was the first step toward Japan's postwar recovery. According to Joseph Dodge's brand of free-enterprise economics, it was just a matter of time before the good companies started prospering again, the country began to export, and consumers started to put their savings into capital investment. (One of Dodge's long-lasting legacies to Japan was his enthusiastic sponsorship of the law exempting from taxation the interest earned on individual Postal Savings Bank deposits up to 3 million yen.)

Strong though the medicine was, it took a long time to work. In fact, no one can be sure that Japan's economy would in fact have made the comeback that Dodge confidently predicted. In June 1950, the economy was still becalmed, with bankruptcies and government surpluses continuing to increase. Then, on June 25, the Soviet-backed armies of Kim Il Sung invaded South Korea—and gave Japan's sick economy a life-giving injection.

They called it the *Tokujo* (Special Procurements) Boom. As the U.S. and later the United Nations forces mobilized to fight on the Korean peninsula, special procurement orders from the U.S. military and expenditures of military personnel pumped almost $600 million into Japan in 1951. Some $800 million was spent in 1952 and about the same amount in 1953.

Becoming an impromptu "arsenal of democracy" in a hurry did wonders for Japan's balance of payments. As Japan's distinguished economist Nakamura Takafusa wrote: "To the Japanese economy, which had been doing its level best just to import something less than one billion dollars' worth of goods in 1949 and 1950, $2 billion in imports meant that the key industries which depended on imports of raw materials could virtually double their scale of production."[12]

As we shall see, the economic momentum gained was well used.

[12] In *The Postwar Japanese Economy* (Tokyo: University of Tokyo Press, 1981).

8

Income Doubling and the Economic Miracle

History offers examples of winning in diplomacy after losing in war.
PRIME MINISTER YOSHIDA SHIGERU, 1946

Isn't it all a matter of economic policy?
PRIME MINISTER IKEDA HAYATO, 1960

I n the preceding chapter we spoke of the U.S. Occupation of Japan largely in American terms, more or less in the way one describes a surgeon operating on an anesthetized patient. The analogy may have been apt for the first few months of MacArthur's reign, while democracy and SCAP directives were dropping on a population numbed by defeat and adversity. But it would not stick. Unlike the postwar occupation of Germany, where military government actually governed, the occupiers of Japan worked through an existing government. Weak as that government was, their directives inescapably went through a considerable filtration process.

After the caretaker cabinet of Baron Shidehara had resigned, the first postwar general election was held on April 10, 1946, and the conservative Liberal Party won a plurality. Its first nominee, Hatoyama Ichiro, was promptly purged by SCAP as a member of the wartime government. Whereupon a crusty prewar diplomat named Yoshida Shigeru became Prime Minister, as a thin second choice.

Yoshida stayed on the job for a year, sat out the next year in favor of two "opposition" leaders, one a Socialist and the other a Democrat, but returned to office on October 15, 1948. He led the combined Liberal-Democratic Party to a decisive victory in January 1949 and remained as Prime Minister until December 1954, two years after the U.S. Occupation ended.

If it took defeat and an occupation to bring Yoshida to power, he became almost indispensable in its exercise. A patriot and in his way an idealist, he was also a preeminent exemplar of the old truism that politics is "the art of the possible." Like MacArthur—and perhaps more so—he put his stamp on postwar Japan. Some would say he created it.

Yoshida was sixty-eight when he became Prime Minister. Until his retirement eight years before, he had been a professional diplomat. His last post—and surely the most congenial to him—had been as ambassador to London. He came into office out of relative obscurity, as a temporary caretaker, to do a job few people coveted. In this role he strikingly resembled those two old European Christian Democrats, Konrad Adenauer and Alcide De Gasperi, who assumed office in Germany and Italy at the ages of seventy and sixty-four, respectively. He played the same decisive role as they did in rehabilitating a defeated country.

A small, rather rotund man, seemingly locked into his pince-nez and old-fashioned wing collar, Yoshida had the look of a political trustee, a man chosen more for respectability than vigor to preside over a bankrupt national corporation during the tricky phases of receivership and reconstruction. Antimilitarist and from the first an opponent of the Pacific war, he had lobbied everyone in the Japanese establishment, from the emperor down, in an effort to move toward a negotiated peace. In April 1945, the Army's *Kempeitai* security police imprisoned him for ten weeks, after a long period of surveillance, for this very reason. Better equipped than most Japanese to deal with Westerners, he spoke English well and had a considerable acquaintanceship with foreigners. All in all, it would seem, the perfect man to take orders from an American Occupation.

He had, however, a mind of his own and very definite objectives. His admiration for long Havana cigars, British clubs, polite English conversation, and Churchillian phrases was superimposed upon rather than subtracted from his Japanese tastes and the old-fashioned code he lived by. He was a product of the Meiji Restoration. In fact, he was literally an extension of the old Meiji leadership. He was the son-in-law and protégé of Count Makino Nobuaki, who himself was the second son of Okubo Toshimichi, the leading architect of the Meiji changes. Like MacArthur, he held to a set of nineteenth-century political ideals. The phrase "Gladstonian liberal" comes to mind. He felt that Japan was best governed by an enlightened higher bureaucracy, in the Meiji tradition, and he did his best to make this goal a reality.

In one sense Yoshida's goals were the opposite of the young Occupation reformers'. They were intent on breaking up the old Japan, which they saw as feudal, militarist, dominated by authoritarian business cartels, and resolutely undemocratic. Yoshida wanted to put the old Japan back together. But his perspective was quite a different one. Yoshida's old Japan was a tightly knit country with a strong sense of imperial and national loyalties, its people working together in a web of interlocking commitments and responsibilities—a democratic society, yes, but ever to be guided by a benevolent, respected group of higher officials.

This harked back to the samurai ideal. Yoshida's political ethic was based on the same neo-Confucian principles that Tokugawa Ieyasu and his successors had adopted for Japan almost three centuries before. Both country and culture had been significantly altered by modernizing Meiji oligarchs like Okubo and enlightened businessmen like Shibusawa Eiichi. Yet the old leadership's yard-stick of conduct remained Confucianism, Japanese style, with its strong, almost familial sense of loyalty to the throne and the nation-society it symbolized.

As a political realist, Yoshida appreciated many of the Occupation reforms. At least he realized that they could never be totally rolled back. For one thing, he hated the militarists. It was their arrogance and cruelty which had destroyed much of Yoshida's old Japan by plunging it into a war that was bound to be lost. Thus he was dead set against rearmament that could lead back to the military authoritarianism of the 1930s. No one prized Article 9 of the MacArthur constitution more than Yoshida.

A conservative to the core, however, he was nervous about the sweeping democratizations of the Occupation. He was not above lobbying quietly against them with like-minded U.S. generals on MacArthur's staff. ("Mr. Yoshida understands what liberalism is," one of his younger supporters once told me. "I don't think he understands what democracy is.") Although shocked by bold initiatives like the new constitution and the wholesale purges of politicians and company presidents, he was enough of an internationalist and a free trader to support the drastic Dodge reforms. At least, he was willing to take the political heat for them. Without him and his handpicked Finance Minister, Ikeda Hayato, they would have been far more difficult to realize.

"We did not find much to propose to the Occupation authorities," he wrote wryly in his memoirs,[1] "for the zeal of the men and women of the Occupation took care of practically everything, so that it was sufficient (and rather more than sufficient) for us to take the directives as they were issued, one by one, and to strive to assert ourselves, as the government, whenever they seemed to err

---

[1] *The Yoshida Memoirs* (Boston: Houghton Mifflin, 1962) were translated into English and edited by his son, Yoshida Kenichi, an honor student in classics at Cambridge, who was in his own right a distinguished essayist in Japanese.

on the side of impracticability." As things turned out, his definition of impracticability was quite broad.

Yoshida's first order of business was to get a peace treaty. This would automatically end the Occupation and restore Japan to independence. Independence would mean the ability to modify, if not to repeal some of the more drastic Occupation reforms. He found a kindred spirit in a Wall Street lawyer named John Foster Dulles, who had been appointed by Washington to handle treaty negotiations.

Dulles, like Draper and the other Washington businessmen, was all for making Japan economically self-sufficient and strong. But in addition Dulles wished Japan to rearm, just as Germany would do, and enter a firm alliance with the United States. A devout Calvinist, he tended to identify God's interests with those of the United States of America and the sound establishment lawyers in charge of it. (He would go to heaven, one assumed, wearing his homburg.) Dulles was also an uncompromising and inflexible anti-Communist. He saw the world as a simple lineup of good guys versus bad guys, with middlemen automatically objects of suspicion.

Yoshida was with him in his antipathy to Communists, a category which for Yoshida included, possibly, some of the U.S. Occupation reformers. He also approved the idea of a firm alliance with the Americans. As he later wrote in his final work, *Japan's Decisive Century: 1867–1967*: "Ever since the opening of Japan's doors to the West more than a century ago, the basic principle of Japanese policy has been the maintenance of close and cordial political and economic ties with Great Britain and the United States. That Japan parted from this principle and became allied with Germany and Italy was the prime cause for my country being pushed headlong into a reckless war."[2]

But rearmament was another thing. Not only did Yoshida distrust anything that smacked of a new Japanese military establishment. He held, in addition, that "to equip the nation with an effective means of defense would have been tantamount to crippling Japan's convalescent economy."

After some horse trading, a compromise was reached. Japan's defense was to be guaranteed by a security treaty with the United States; in line with the treaty U.S. troops would continue to be stationed in Japan, on military bases, at Japan's request. The matter of Japanese defense forces in itself was a dicey problem; there was the antiwar Article 9 in the new constitution. In January 1950, Yoshida issued a classic compromise statement in the best Foreign Office

[2] This book (New York: Praeger, 1967) was a slight expansion of an article that Yoshida wrote at my request for Encyclopaedia Britannica's Book of the Year for 1967. In the writing he was materially assisted by Hessel Tiltman, a distinguished British journalist, who was a longtime friend of Yoshida's and prepared the first draft, in English, at Yoshida's request. A Japanese translation followed later.

tradition: "To abide fully by the renunciation of war does not mean the re-nunciation of the right of self-defense." Later that year, after the outbreak of war in Korea, his government authorized creation of a 75,000-man National Police Reserve, which ultimately grew into the Self-Defense Forces (*Jieitai*). Yoshida agreed to this inevitable evolution, but did not accelerate it. His ambivalence on this matter became the policy (or nonpolicy) of the Japanese government over the next quarter century.

There was another controversial matter to be handled. Japan agreed to sign a peace treaty with the Nationalist government of Chiang Kai-shek on Taiwan, ignoring the Communist mainland, thereby underlining the Japanese commit-ment to follow American foreign policy. Yoshida was reluctant to do this. Japanese businessmen still yearned for a resumption of their traditional China trade. He himself wanted to keep Japan's options open for future dealings with China. Beijing's entry into the Korean War impelled his acceptance, but Japan made it clear that this did not mean recognizing Taiwan's sovereignty over the Chinese mainland.

In return for these concessions Dulles assured Yoshida that the reforms initiated by the U.S. Occupation in Japan "need not be permanent." So much for the New Dealers.

ON A CRISP September morning in San Francisco during the 1951 treaty conference, I walked Prime Minister Yoshida down the back stairs of the Mark Hopkins Hotel, surrounded by a heavy complement of security people, Foreign Office attachés, and assorted PR supernumeraries, to an improvised TV studio, where I interviewed him for a CBS-TV special prepared by *Time* magazine. It was hot under the studio lights, and Yoshida, never one to suffer real or fancied fools gladly, complained about the inconvenience. In other respects he was extremely gracious. To dramatize the internationalism of its correspondents, I presume, my editors at *Time* asked me to interview Yoshida in Japanese. His English was far more sophisticated than my Japanese, but he went along with the game and let me interpret his answers to my not very tough questions. The televised exchange was important to him. He had two messages for the Amer-ican public, whom he here addressed for the first time. One was to pledge Japan's continuing friendship with the United States as the cornerstone of its foreign policy. The other was a statement of Yoshida's great remaining concern now that the peace treaty was a fact. "Japan has regained political indepen-dence," he said. "Now we must see to it that economic independence is achieved. Without this, political independence has little meaning."

Having secured Japan's political independence by means of the treaty, Yoshida had to set about the more complex task of bringing about economic recovery. To do so he needed a great deal of help—help in the form of talent, experience, dedication, and follow-through. He and his economics lieutenant, Ikeda Hayato, found all of this right at home, and in place, in the government bureaucracy to which they both belonged.[3] The story of Japan's growth into an economic superpower is a complex one with many factors responsible, Japan's recent wartime experiences and the reforms of the U.S. Occupation conspicuous among them. It was during the two decades between 1946 and 1965 that the designs and institutions of the superpower took shape—that is to say, beginning with the first Yoshida cabinet and ending shortly after the resignation of Ikeda, who himself became Prime Minister in 1960. Since Yoshida's bureaucrats were the agents and catalyzers of this growth, it is best to start with them.[4]

Prewar and wartime Japan was run by several entrenched groups. There were the *gunbatsu,* or militarists, the *zaibatsu,* or the big-business interests, and finally the *kanryo,* or bureaucracy. The U.S. Occupation effectively destroyed the militarists. The entrenched big-business groups of family corporations were shattered as well. (Although their components and many of their leading executives later regrouped to form so-called *keiretsu* combines later, those were quite different.) The absentee landlords were casualties of the land reform. But the bureaucrats remained. They had to.

Since the Occupation could work its will only through existing Japanese government channels, the keepers of the channels were essential cogs in the Occupation's own administrative machinery. Some civil officials were individually "purged" by Occupation directives forcing the retirement of those heavily involved in Japan's war effort. A good case could have been made for purging many others. At least the infamous Home Ministry, responsible for the police among its other activities, was abolished. But despite a variety of investigations and fact-finding missions SCAP headquarters did little to change the shape and consistency of Japan's civil service, other than to advocate increased "efficiency."

Unquestionably the bureaucracy embodied the sense of continuity in Japan's recent history. From the days of the Meiji Restoration, when the young samurai reformers took off their swords to settle down at the desks of the new modern ministries, the government official had stood at the respected top of Japan's very Confucian society. A consciously elite mandarinate, this bureaucracy continued to include, in the Meiji tradition, the best and the brightest in

[3] A career bureaucrat in the Finance Ministry, Ikeda served both as Finance Minister and as Minister of International Trade and Industry in the Yoshida cabinets and later during the premierships of Ishibashi Tanzan and Kishi Nobosuke, whom he succeeded as Prime Minister in 1960.

[4] In the following account I have leaned on the impressive scholarship of Chalmers Johnson, Nakamura Takafusa, and Leon Hollerman, who have charted the rise of Japan's economy most impressively, as well as my own experience and observations.

Yoshida Shigeru, the Grand Old Man of Japan's postwar politics, photographed at his villa in Oiso in the 1960s, after his retirement from office. Senzo Yoshioka

Yoshida in prewar days. As ambassador in Rome and later in London, during the thirties, Yoshida opposed Japan's Tripartite Pact with Germany and Italy. Here he is shown with Benito Mussolini and Japanese and Italian naval officers after a Rome meeting. At the close of World War II, Yoshida's antiwar record made him acceptable to the U.S. Occupation. Kazuko Aso

Anti-Yoshida union demonstrations demanded his resignation. Placard in left foreground of this December 1946 rally says, "Yoshida, quit!" Mainichi Shimbun

Prime Minister Yoshida Shigeru signing the peace treaty, San Francisco, September 8, 1951. Finance Minister Ikeda is second from the right. Dean Acheson is at the podium. Mainichi Shimbun

Police battle demonstrators at 1952 "Bloody May Day" mass meeting protesting the Anti-Subversive Activities Act. Mainichi Shimbun

Ikeda Hayato, first as Yoshida's Finance Minister and later as Japan's Prime Minister, helped engineer Japan's postwar economic "miracle" with his "income-doubling" policy. Here Ikeda is pictured at home shortly after his resignation. Mainichi Shimbun

Prime Minister Sato Eisaku (left), who held office between 1964 and 1972, was one of Yoshida's protégés. Yoshida's cigar, pince-nez, and old-fashioned collar became something of a trademark.

Japan. Somewhat comparable to their French and German counterparts, they constituted the peak intellectual product of the country's stiff, meritocratic university system. As such, they looked down on rich businessmen, crude soldiery, and grafting politicians alike.

For more than a decade, however, the bureaucrats had taken a long-sustained beating from the military and their political representatives. This was particularly true of the Foreign Ministry people like Yoshida, who as internationalists had vainly tried to curb the excesses of the military and some of their big-business accomplices. Finance Ministry officials, for their part, had looked disapprovingly at the economic dislocations caused by huge military expenditures.

The past two decades of economic turmoil had taught them all something. If wasteful competing free enterprisers might temporarily damage an economy, military ineptitude could destroy it. As the war continued, bureaucrats in the ministries became the arbiters, if not the controllers of the economic effort. The soldiers deferred to their expertise, as production and procurement problems multiplied. The businessmen became accustomed to their "guidance." In wartime Japan the old party politicians, bypassed and discredited, hardly counted at all.

When Yoshida became Prime Minister, he was determined to put the formal as well as the actual governance in the bureaucracy's hands. Almost fifty of the new Liberal Party representatives elected to the Diet in 1949 were former government officials. Although an even larger number were businessmen of various sorts—Yoshida had many friends in the business community—it was the bureaucrats who formed the party's cutting edge on policy. Their preponderance was and remains comparable to that of lawyers in the U.S. Congress.

The Prime Minister himself personally persuaded scores of younger officials to enter politics. The so-called Yoshida School became famous. It included among its more promising students four later Prime Ministers—his protégé Ikeda, Sato Eisaku, the ill-starred Tanaka Kakuei, and Miyazawa Kiichi—as well as scores of high-level economic movers and shakers.

In 1949 the Yoshida cabinet, with Diet approval, created a new government organ, the Ministry of International Trade and Industry, to be known familiarly henceforth as MITI. This was done by combining the existing Board of Trade with the Ministry of Commerce and Industry (itself the successor of the wartime Munitions Ministry). MITI and its bureaucrats soon transformed themselves into what Chalmers Johnson terms an "economic general staff."[5] Inevitably, as years of aggressive economic planning assumed an almost military

[5] Johnson's *MITI and the Japanese Miracle* (Stanford, Calif.: Stanford University Press, 1982) remains the classic exposition of this subject.

aspect, it came to be known among Japan's wounded trading partners as the Japanese Pentagon.

After the Occupation folded its tents in 1952, MITI and the other economic agencies took over the whole apparatus of controls which SCAP had used to run the economy. Instead of dismantling them, they kept almost all of them in place. And the economic bureaucrats, without either the Japanese or the American Army to bother them, set out to show the world how a growth economy could be jump-started and, wherever possible, steered.

A new set of circumstances at once restricted the bureaucrats' authority and increased their chances of success. Thanks to the Occupation's reforms, the farm economy was looking healthier than it had ever been before. Thanks to the labor "bill of rights" forced into law by the Occupation, the unions were a power to be reckoned with. Stimulated by the Occupation's imported business experts and a native urge to "catch up," a ripple of technology transfer was starting that would turn into a wave. Japanese business would pay out close to $3 billion in royalty and licensing fees between the end of the Occupation and 1970.

Most interestingly, the economic purge, despite its unfairnesses, had left unexpected room at the top in Japan's industry. With their chairmen and managing directors on the sidelines,[6] a whole new generation of managers was moved into jobs that they might normally have waited ten or fifteen years to reach—if indeed they would ever have been able to pierce the charmed circle of *zaibatsu* family and retainers. With this the stratified prewar world of Japanese business began to break up. In its place came a more practical new management elite who had a better understanding of the workers under them. Hanamura Nihachiro, vice chairman of the powerful Keidanren (Federation of Economic Organizations), the mouthpiece of Japan's big business, recalled this many years later: "As a result [of the Occupation's economic democratization] every Japanese stood at the same starting point and an environment was provided in which everyone was rewarded according to the effort he exerted. This generated in every Japanese a willingness to study and work hard, just as in the frontier days of the United States."

To buy the wares of the new managers' factories a broadly based consumer society was emerging that would supply both savings for capital investment and ready markets for consumer goods. In 1956, Ikeda, back in the Finance Min-

---

[6] The original Occupation directives ordered that all "standing directors" of major Japanese companies were to be purged. The Japanese bureaucracy took advantage of the ambiguity in this phrase to conclude that only actual managing directors and above had to go, mere directors being spared. "Which shows," Yoshida wrote puckishly in his memoirs, "that upon occasion mistranslations serve their turn."

istry after Yoshida's departure, primed the pump with a massive 100 billion yen tax cut. Domestic spending increased. Wages were still low, but the historically parsimonious Japanese consumer, confronted for the first time by an array of new and affordable goodies—transistor radios, washing machines, cameras, and now television sets—began to buy in quantity. Increased sales at home helped businesses to step up their export volume, with the economics of scale so beloved by Japanese executives. Exporters in turn were further aided by government tax breaks and other forms of subsidies—including the newly founded Japan External Trade Organization (JETRO), designed to provide a combined reconnaissance and intelligence-gathering service outside Japan for export-oriented businesses.

Yoshida's new economic general staff could not order an increasingly complex society by decree. Working alliances had to be made, at various levels, with the new generation of managers chosen for their skills rather than their position in the old company hierarchies, with the big "city" banks for their financing power, and with the new postwar politicians, many of them former bureaucrats, whose task it was to reign and keep the public happy while the bureaucrats planned and, they hoped, ruled.

As Chalmers Johnson explains it: "The new constitution and other reforms such as the fostering of the labor movement made state control politically impossible except as a short-term expedient. The economic bureaucrats might rule on the basis of their intrinsic talents, but they could never reign openly under Japan's new democratic system. Thus both government and industry recognized the need for a political division of labor."

Such cooperation had ample precedent. When Japan modernized itself in the Meiji Restoration, there was a scarcity of resources and no long-established business sector to work with. The young Meiji reformers, after setting up the government, had to find money for the banks and start up modern industries all at once. In the process they had created a tradition of close cooperation and interaction between government, industry, and the financial world. This very concept, while well known in Europe, was totally foreign to the ideas of Americans like the SCAP reformers, who thought of government and business as basically adversarial. It was against this background that Japan's capitalist development state was formed.

SUCH GATHERING harmony at the top did not, however, communicate itself readily to the nation as a whole. Through most of the fifties, despite its material gains, Japan was rocked by massive social discontent and political dissension. Riots and demonstrations were the order of the day. The acrimony between business and labor and right and left seemed capable of turning Japan into a class-warfare society. There were three major issues: (1) rearmament and the

U.S. security connection; (2) capitalism versus socialism; and finally (3) how to make the economy work. They were interrelated.

Among the forty-eight signers of the San Francisco Peace Treaty, the Soviet Union and the People's Republic of China were conspicuous by their absence. Their abstention from the treaty was understandable. The Russians had refused even to discuss giving up the northern islands they had held and garrisoned off the coast of Hokkaido. The Chinese were busy fighting UN forces in Korea. Many Japanese were left nonetheless with the uneaseful feeling that their country was being committed to a Cold War alliance with the Americans. Here Japan was the exposed party, facing its two large Red neighbors.

The Security Treaty of 1952 with the United States only deepened their concern, as the Police Reserve of 1950 began to assume the look of an army. On May Day, 1952, well organized gangs of Communist and leftist student rioters (many of the students in their thirties) turned a vocal but peaceful trade union demonstration against Japan's "rearmament" into a series of violent melees in which police and foreign passersby and newsmen were repeatedly attacked. This was only the first of similar outbursts which continued over the next eight years.

On the issue of rearmament, ironically, Yoshida stood right in the middle. He was attacked by the left for fostering a new "militarism"; he was under fire from his own right wing for deliberately going slow on their hoped-for military buildup. In the media Japan's *interi* (local shorthand for intelligentsia) began a twenty-year campaign of sniper attacks on the alleged American attempt to turn Japan into a client "puppet state."

Their charges were given some credibility by the high-handed tactics of the later Occupation people. Badly shaken by the Korean War, SCAP's ever vigilant security specialists had instigated a variety of punitive actions against Communists and other leftists. (Yoshida needed no encouragement to cooperate with the Occupation in this activity.) Freed at last in 1952 from the admonitory grease pencil of the SCAP censors, the *Asahi*, Japan's leading national newspaper, saw this "Red baiting" as a cover for the resurgence of Japanese and American militarism. With their memories of World War II all too poignant, many people were worried.

They were not reassured by the return to power of political leaders like Kishi Nobosuke, who ultimately became Prime Minister in 1957, some time after he had been "de-purged." During World War II, Kishi had served as Minister of Munitions. He was a leading figure in the wartime development of Manchuria, where he had worked hand in glove with General Tojo and the Japanese military. When he pressed for Japanese rearmament and a strengthened U.S. Security Treaty, his arbitrary behavior lent credence to leftist charges that the Americans were trying to revive Japanese militarism. With friends like Kishi, the Americans hardly needed enemies.

In the summer of 1948, following the counsel of a naive labor advisory mission from Washington, the Occupation had reneged on earlier guarantees and outlawed the right to strike for all government employees, including railway workers and employees at other government-run corporations. This crystallized labor's growing discontent both with SCAP and with the Yoshida government. Some 800,000 people were affected. ("Mad dog Yoshida," the Communist daily *Akahata* commented with its normal hyperbole, "has sunk his teeth into the National Railways, mastedon of the working class.") The massive layoffs that followed less than a year later gave rise to some ugly incidents of violence on the Japan National Railways. They were climaxed by the brutal murder of the JNR president, Shimoyama Sadanori, whose body was found run over by a train just outside of Tokyo in July 1949.[7]

Through the fifties, labor-management struggles grew more intense. Although fueled by political differences—in some cases, such as the strike against Toho films, Communist control of the unions involved led to destructive violence—the underlying problem was one of gathering mutual distrust. Many union leaders wished to expand their power even to the extent of crippling the companies involved. Many managements, for their part, encouraged by Yoshida's antilabor attitude, set out to break the power of the unions entirely. Some undoubtedly hoped to restore the pre-Occupation status quo.

Against this the unions, now led by Sohyo (the abbreviated Japanese title of the General Council of Trade Unions), began to link normal economic demands with an increasingly political stance. Along with wage increases Sohyo's representatives called for Japanese neutrality and an end to U.S. bases. The downfall of the conservative government was also a prime objective. The familiar chant *Yoshida naikaku butsubuse*—"Smash the Yoshida cabinet"—sung, incidentally, to the tune of a once popular Japanese war song, became No. 1 on the labor hit parade.

In 1953, Sohyo, working through the All-Japan Automobile Industry Union, went after all three large carmakers, Toyota, Isuzu, and Nissan, in a concerted labor offensive reminiscent of UAW contract negotiations in Detroit. While the two other companies settled in short order, Nissan chose to fight. In the course of a bitter five-month-long strike the company locked out the strikers and finally concluded an agreement with a second, company-approved union. The company was massively supported by its banks and, covertly, by the other car makers. Ultimately many workers left the autowork-

---

[7] The perpetrators of the crime were never really determined. Chalmers Johnson's *Conspiracy at Matsukawa* (Berkeley: University of California Press, 1972), which takes its name from this incident, is a fascinating study of the impact of the U.S. Occupation on Japanese laws and labor practices in this period.

ers' union for fear of losing their livelihood. Some were probably affected by the allegedly far-left political positions taken by the Nissan union's leaders. A second union, largely of white-collar employees, was formed in collusion with management. It eventually displaced the first one, and its leader, Shioji Ichiro, became for some years the de facto boss of Nissan.

The failure of the Nissan strike—coming after a similarly disastrous three-month walkout by the electric power workers' union (Densan Roso)—was a kind of high-water mark for industry-wide unions in Japan's private sector. Sohyo itself for a time turned toward the center politically in 1955, as private-sector unions went back to the single-company enterprise union with which history had made them familiar.[8] Many far-left union leaders were fired from their jobs, victims of the government's "Red purge."

"There is a Japanese bird called the *tanchozu*," labor economist Mikio Sumiya explained, "a sacred crane with a red head and a white body. The Japanese labor movement was like that in those days. The leadership was Red, but not the rank and file. They were moderate. So when the Red head was chopped off in anti-Communist 'purges,' the labor movement lost its radical direction."

There was one last surge of violence in 1960. It was fueled by growing concern over Cold War tensions and incidents like the death of crew members of a Japanese fishing boat, the *Lucky Dragon*, who suffered radiation burns on sailing into an American nuclear test area in the Central Pacific. In Tokyo a rising murmur of protest against Prime Minister Kishi's proposed extension of the Security Treaty with the United States escalated into violent demonstrations during May and June. The demonstrations were purportedly spearheaded by students, particularly the semi-professional "student" leftists of the Zengakuren and other extremist campus organizations, but there was heavy participation by the Socialist Party, the Communists, and the Socialist-affiliated labor unions. (Sohyo itself, increasingly based on public-sector workers, had swung back toward the left, away from economic union issues in favor of political agitation.)

The demonstrators were backed up by a crescendo of exhortation from newspaper editorialists and the ever present Greek chorus of *interi*, largely university professors, for whom anti-Americanism had become almost a ritual posture. In a series of barely controlled riots, they swarmed over the car of

---

[8] In the sixties the All-Japan Confederation of Labor (known familiarly by its Japanese acronym, Domei), further to the right than Sohyo, attracted a heavy membership among unions in private industry, Nissan's union included. Sohyo, again veering toward leftist political objectives, kept its principal strength in unions of civil servants and other government employees. As against the 7 million members of Sohyo and Domei, an additional 7 million-plus workers belonged to private enterprise unions. Increasingly, the enterprise union called the tune in labor; by the early eighties, Sohyo's power had waned.

James Haggerty, President Dwight Eisenhower's press secretary, in Japan to prepare for an Eisenhower visit, on the road from Haneda Airport to Tokyo. Mobs of demonstrators rampaged through downtown Tokyo. On June 15 they attacked and partially occupied the Diet building itself.

As a result, Eisenhower's planned July trip to Japan was canceled. Kishi himself resigned from office, but only after his Liberal Democrats had rammed the Security Treaty revision through the Diet.

The Tokyo riots of 1960 were not an isolated phenomenon. They reflected a general discontent with an apparent tendency by the majority party to rearm Japan as an American ally. Kishi himself, Tojo's old right-wing partner, was seen as an embarrassing anachronism. Many Japanese were worried about the future. To a public just about to turn the corner into prosperity, any foreign entanglement brought back bad wartime memories. And a backlash of latent anti-Americanism was inevitable after so much order taking during the Occupation years.

Since January of the same year trouble had been building up at the Miike coal mines in Kyushu. There a militant union had struck the Mitsui Mining Company after a wave of dismissals and a company lockout. For eleven months the strike continued. Its local issues were exacerbated by an apparent decision among government and business leaders to phase out the mines in favor of increased reliance on oil as the basic industrial fuel. The violence escalated. Rival groups of unionists and company guards fought pitched battles in which many were injured and some killed. In the end the union lost, although the whole incident revealed the total inadequacy of Mitsui's labor policies.

IN JULY 1960, Ikeda Hayato succeeded Kishi as Prime Minister. A blunt-spoken man whose bluff candor contrasted with Kishi's aloof authoritarian manner, Ikeda set out to keep a "low posture" administration politically. One of his first acts in office was to mediate and settle the disastrous Miike strike.

His platform was simple, if provocative, economics: double the national income (*Shotoku baizo*) over the next ten years. To this end he deliberately underplayed politics, ignoring ideological differences to concentrate on a steady growth rate of 7 percent a year. Capital investment was already booming, as companies plowed their profits back into plant improvement. Ikeda now offered lower taxes, more capital investment incentives, and foreign trade liberalization to push exports. His objectives were clearly stated: ". . . to move ahead toward a conspicuous increase in the national standard of living and the achievement of full employment. To that end the maximal stable growth of the economy must be contrived."

In this cause Ikeda asked Japan's business managers and workers alike to use all of their ingenuity, hard work, and competitive strength. The government, he promised, would help all it could.

Ikeda's simple slogans and objectives struck a responsive chord with most people. The mainstream of Japanese public opinion is something like a slow-flowing subterranean river, whose waters are notably hard to sample. Slow to speak out and naturally pessimistic, Japan's public takes a long time to lock on an idea. Once it does, try to dislodge it! In a changing time people had been waiting for a national goal, subliminally impatient meanwhile with the various ideological panaceas that had been spooned out to them.

As the economist Kosai Yutaka put it in his book *The Era of High Speed Growth*: "The Security Treaty and Miike were rites of passage into Japan's period of modernization in the 1960s; they were an exorcism for that purpose, a rite of purification. The society that emerged from the disturbances consisted of, on the one hand, a minority of fragmented radical factions that placed themselves outside society and, on the other, the new middle-class majority, who were both the promoters of rapid growth and its beneficiaries. Indifference to the decline of statism and class ideology was the social consequence of the Japanese economy's approach to full employment."

Speaking from another standpoint, Takaragi Fumihiko, a former chairman of the Postal Workers' Union, now sees the Miike strike as "a struggle against the energy revolution which was converting from the age of coal to the age of petroleum. The coal workers felt they should fight to the end or lose their jobs. And the unions of Japan, Sohyo especially, fought very hard on behalf of the workers. Yet the change was inevitable, given the limited supply of resources. And in our thinking about this a lot of wisdom was gained. And among the unions an impetus grew to stop simply making noise and opposing everything, but rather to work out a mutually constructive position. And through trial and error they came to see that it wasn't enough just to look inside Japan—but that whether it was ships or electronics or steel or cars they had to take a more international view. In this way the private-sector unions developed a larger frame of reference. That's how the stability among labor and management in Japanese industry was born."

IKEDA IS JUSTLY called the father of Japan's high-growth "miracle." As has been remarked elsewhere, it was a miracle by design.[9] Many practices regarded as postwar business innovation, like the seniority system (*nenko joretsu*) and guarantees of lifetime employment, were the result of government restrictions

[9] The rationale behind the "miracle" and the factors comprising it are more fully discussed in my book *Miracle by Design: The Real Reasons for Japan's Economic Success* (New York: Times Books, 1982).

during World War II, as was the reliance on enterprise rather than trade unions. Other reforms essential to Japan's postwar economic success had been enacted by the U.S. Occupation; Ikeda himself had pushed through the Dodge Plan. But it remained for Ikeda acting on his own, a political executive with a technician's stubbornness, to make the fast-growth program a reality.

As Finance Minister in previous cabinets, he had in 1951 created the Japan Development Bank, the Export-Import Bank, and other instruments of financial and industrial policy. His unprecedented tax cut in 1956 went a long way toward stimulating both investment and consumer spending. As Prime Minister he helped MITI set up the mechanisms for the protection of designated industries—e.g., electronics, steel, automobiles—that exemplified Japan's success at government "targeting" and "nurturing" particular industries. That is to say, government would provide help in the form of various tax breaks, research and development assistance, and export subsidies.

Other tools in the hands of Ikeda's bureaucrats, as Chalmers Johnson has enumerated, included "control over foreign exchange and imports of technology, which gave them the power to choose industries for development; the ability to dispense preferential financing, tax breaks and protection from foreign competition, which gave them the power to lower the costs of the chosen industries and the authority to order the creation of cartels and bank-based industrial conglomerates (a new and rationalized version of the *zaibatsu*, now made totally dependent on government largesse), which gave them the power to supervise competition."[10]

All this is not to suggest that MITI's decisions were made in the form of peremptory orders. On the contrary, Ikeda and his aides set up various committees and structural advisory boards of businessmen, which interrelated and communicated with MITI and the other economic ministries at various levels. Communication was furthered over the years by the practice of government officials moving, after their retirement, into working directorships in Japanese corporations. Other high-level bureaucrats passed over into politics, in the best Yoshida tradition.

Europeans were already familiar with strong bureaucracies. Toward the end of the sixties Eisenhower was to issue his famous warning to Americans about the strength of the "military-industrial complex." Here in Japan there already existed a far more powerful, because more flexible, bureaucrat-industrial-financial complex. In a sense it was a military command system that had everything but a war. Not that it was compulsory. The system worked because the whole nation-society of Japan was united behind Ikeda's policy. It was, in a sense, the Meiji compact of the past century of *Fukoku kyohei*—"Enrich the country and

[10] *MITI and the Japanese Miracle.*

strengthen the military"—writ large and new, but with the "strengthen the military" portion deleted. It took Japan's international business competitors the greater part of the next two decades to realize what Ikeda had wrought.

The growth program was, of course, based on heavy capital investment. By 1961, Japan was putting 23 percent of its gross national product (GNP) into building up a new industrial infrastructure. Personal savings rates moved to more than 20 percent of income. Fortified by a lump-sum bonus system, tax breaks on savings interest, and other factors—economists disagree on which— the Japanese public became the foot soldiery of this new national mobilization. In the heady air of the sixties, the national GNP figures were headlined in the newspapers and followed more religiously than the sports pages.

Electronics and steel—fueled by the new boom in shipbuilding—were the first industries to take off. At the cost of totally new plant and massive innovation, Japan's steel plants built themselves into the world's cheapest and most efficient producers. Instead of longing after colonies, as their unfortunate fathers had, the new generation of sixties managers built tight networks of communication and transportation, and thus turned the crowding of their narrow islands into a modern economic asset. By the midpoint of the sixties, Japan's GNP was No. 3 in the world (if the Soviet Union could be taken as No. 2). Japanese steel, ships, and electronics were world leaders.

Successive economic booms were led by the aggressive buying and selling of Japan's big international trading companies, acting as scouts and brokers for businesses back home. Helped also by the government's almost embarrassingly vigorous support of "targeted" export industries—"Who is that transistor salesman?" de Gaulle had asked after meeting Ikeda in Paris—Japanese companies moved into international marketing.

Sony, unconventional in other respects, was typical of this new breed of company in its emphasis on export markets. Its management combined aggressive technology research and development with an acute feel for what the world's consumer market wanted. Started by some engineers and former Navy reservists just after the war ended, the company began making small transistor radios in a little shed building outside of Tokyo, with an initial capitalization of 190,000 yen ($500 at the time). Its sales were pushing the $1 billion mark by the sixties. Its expansion, like that of so many Japanese companies, was based on a greed for market share, which, as its chairman, Morita Akio, enjoyed pointing out, "often takes precedence over profits."

PROBABLY THE GREATEST factor in the high-growth equation was a new working equilibrium between management and labor. As we have seen, this did not come easily. Not only were there the bitter strikes and lockouts of the fifties and early sixties. Behind that was a long tradition of worker repression and bad treatment. It was a far cry from the image in American business school folklore of Japanese workers trooping along like a platoon of Snow White's dwarfs, happily whistling the company song as they march out of the company dormitory on their way to another day of overtime quality control. It is correct to say, however, that Japan's labor-management harmony of the sixties emerged as a trade-off of job security, information sharing, and steady pay increases in return for working with management within the framework of the enterprise union. Both sides have seemed happy with the bargain.

Other "people" factors were at work. The rise in living standards of the new consumer society was swift and steep. The three sacred treasures, so called, of Japan's lifestyle in the fifties were radios, motorbikes, and sewing machines. In Ikeda's sixties they had escalated to refrigerators, washing machines, TV sets, and other refinements. (When I first met Ikeda, he was proudly wearing his new Parker pens in his top pocket.) By the seventies Japanese households resolutely took for granted the air conditioner, color TV, and the family car. Everyone had a stake in what the business society was doing.

Thanks to the postwar leveling, the new managers of the sixties lived not too differently from the workers. Gone were the huge discrepancies between management and employee compensation that used to prevail in Japan—and still do in the United States. (Even in the affluent eighties, the pay packets of CEOs in Japanese companies were about 15 times that of the average worker; as contrasted to something like an 80:1 ratio in American corporations.) The sense of company solidarity was furthered by having white- and blue-collar staff in the same unions. It became common in Japanese companies for management to promote good union leaders into executive jobs—partly to utilize their talents, partly to get them out of the union. (By the 1980s fully one-third of Japan's company directors had once been members of their local union's executive committee.)

There was also some social adhesive at work. As Japan became an urban society, the old mutually supportive (and confining) web of social obligation in the village often came to reside in the company. Like a kind of urban village, the company was thought of as a community in itself. In Japan's emerging "people-centered" capitalism, the company's self-perpetuation became as important as profits (although there is an obvious linkage). Shareholders—many of them banks and related corporations—consciously took a back seat, content to forgo high dividends in the interests of continuing capital investment.

More and more the company was seen as the creature of loyal management and its loyal, if at times restive workers. Even now it would be impossible for the shareholders to sell any Japanese company without a vote of the board of directors—and in Japan most boards are largely composed of management. So much for the possibility of takeovers and unfriendly mergers in Japan.

Through the high-growth period Japanese companies relied principally on bank financing. A company's main bank, which often held shares in the company, was interested in its progress over the long pull, rather than its current-quarter profitability and the current price of its stock. This kind of security was understandably envied by American company managers, whose financing was more often dependent on the whims of shareholders—and the stock-market analysts who guide them. Hence the average large Japanese company could afford to take the long view.

Most employees were in for the long term as well. As Sony's Morita once told me: "In Japan when we hire a research and development man, we hire him for the long pull. He is with us probably for the rest of his life. We have the benefit of his skill, knowledge, and experience, and it is stored up for us.

"This is in contrast to the short-term considerations you have for hiring and firing in America."

This sense of solidarity in Japanese business may be changing now, albeit slowly. But it was an essential element in the high-growth economy of the sixties.

AS A BUSINESSMAN in Japan in the latter half of the sixties and the early half of the seventies, I was struck by this sense of worker participation in the company. Admittedly, it gave rise to what we Americans thought of as time-wasting procedures. Interminable consultations and constant antennae rubbing seem to be essential to the process of group decision making. "We know you will make the decision in the end yourself," said one of our Japanese vice presidents, giving me a bit of advice. "But at least let everybody have his say, so you get their views first. Then they will know they are contributing."

The difference of philosophy was and remains immense. Although this view of the company as a living organism has been held by various organizations in the United States, it is generally denounced as paternalism. In Japan it has become part of the warp and woof of business. It was a key factor in the high-growth success of Japanese business.

With the same degree of awe I watched the way businesses would take their "window guidance" from the bureaucracy, without the benefit of laws, ordinances, or acts of Congress. This system has been in place now for many years. It too was a vital component in Japan's high-growth progress.

I would not personally like to work in most Japanese companies. The amount of hierarchical posturing and almost professional self-effacement is difficult for an American to take. So is the almost military veneration of the company leadership—even though there is enough workaday democracy for the union members to ritually jeer at the bosses during their annual "spring struggle" demonstrations (thereby proving that they could be really independent if they wanted to). Nonetheless, I came out of ten years in Japan with a lively appreciation of the difference between a company where people are hired and fired like chattels and a company where everyone thinks he is a partner—and where indeed firings or layoffs are thought of as only a bitter last resort.

It is not that the Japanese businessmen, whether managers or workers, are particularly bright. Brilliance is rarely encouraged in Japanese business. But they do have a strong cooperative spirit by which bright talents are content to work with those less bright and happy to share their knowledge. The great quality of the Japanese company is not brilliance, but perseverance. It is this constant sense of follow-through and a sense of building for the far future that have put them so far ahead in a technological world where constructive adaptation seems more important than either innovation or mass-production ability. The sense of quality tends to permeate the Japanese company. At least it did in the high-growth era.

It is said that the idea of seniority and job security works only for some 30 percent of Japanese business, the so-called top-tier companies. But the other 70 percent, which exist as part of this time-honored two-tier relationship—a mass of small businesses, suppliers, and hangers-on of the large *keiretsu* conglomerates—are resigned to this system, adapting to it as fully as they can.

An executive in Singapore once said to me, "We have the highest level of mediocrity in the world." He was too exclusive in his definition. He might equally have been referring to Japan, which for many years has been Singapore's exemplar and model. Japanese workers have a basic high common denominator of education, skill, and garden-variety intelligence. Even when not gifted with excessive imagination, Japanese company employees are able to follow well and participate in their daily round with a sense that the work they are doing is not only the company's but also their own. That makes for very successful business over the long pull.

THE LAST YEAR of Ikeda's time as Prime Minister encapsulated a kind of coming of age for the new Japan. On October 1, 1961, the *Shinkansen* ("New Trunk Line"), familiarly known as the Bullet Train, was ceremonially opened by its creator, Sogo Shinji, the president of Japan National Railways. Almost single-handedly, he had pushed through to triumphant execution the idea of a high-speed train linking the metropolitan cities of Tokyo, Nagoya, Kyoto, and Osaka. There was nothing like it in the world. This was no copy of a foreign model, and proud Japanese were quick to say so.

Barely ten days later the Tokyo Olympics opened. Here at last in the glare of worldwide attention was the great public purgation that would wipe out the shame of defeat after a brutal war. With its new stadiums and vast swimming pools and a whole network of thruways ready for the occasion, Tokyo almost exploded in an enthusiastic feast of hospitality for the world's athletes and their accompanying fans. Ichikawa Kon's spectacular movie about the 1964 Olympics, one of the great sports documentaries of all time, captured the spirit of the moment.

By this time Japan was also in the midst of a great postwar cultural and literary revival. Begun after the Occupation finally broke the long-lasting fetters of militarist censorship, a flood of impressive books began to distill the long-suppressed national experience of the thirties and forties. Mishima Yukio burst on a literary scene that was already crowded, with brilliant modern talents like Abe Kobo challenging the primacy of more conventional Japanese writers like Tanizaki and Kawabata. In the film world Kurosawa Akira had already made history in 1946 with his bitter indictment of wartime Japanese village life, *Waga Seishun ni Kui Nashi* (*No Regrets for Our Youth*), the powerful story of one woman fighting for individual freedom against conformist pressures. This was followed by the memorable *Rashomon*, which gained international success, and in turn was rivaled by younger directors like Oshima and Imamura. Bookstores and movie houses were equally crowded, although Japanese film audiences continued to favor Hollywood productions over their own masterpieces.

For Ikeda Hayato himself, probably the happiest moment of that year came in September, when he addressed the first Tokyo general meeting of the World Bank and the International Monetary Fund. There he could report to his peers on the sense of material prosperity and almost personal satisfaction that the income-doubling plan had given his countrymen.

"With the nineteen postwar years of rapid growth," he said, "Japan's national income is approaching the Western European level. We are attempting to do in twenty postwar years what we were unable to do in the eighty years before the war and what made this possible are the efforts of our people and international cooperation."

It was his last public speech. Terminally ill with cancer of the throat, he resigned his premiership in November 1964 in favor of his Tokyo University classmate Sato Eisaku, another diligent ex-bureaucrat scholar of the Yoshida School.

In July 1965, in the course of a brief reporting trip to Japan, I stopped in to see Ikeda at his house in the Yotsuya district of Tokyo. Ikeda's house was the sort of place old-fashioned Japanese like to come home to—a walled, rambling structure with a beautifully arranged garden behind it, complete with pools, miniature waterfalls, and Ikeda's special rock collection, a variety of interesting stones and rocks taken from almost every corner of Japan. It was a world away from the boomtown selling marts of Marunouchi and Ginza, although some-

The Miike strike. This bloody confrontation at the Kyushu coal mines in 1960 climaxed a decade of management-labor struggle in Japan. NHK

Prime Minister Tanaka Kakuei (shown here with the author) was another member of the "Yoshida school" who learned his politics in Yoshida's Liberal Democratic Party. An aggressive politician, with a vast program to "rebuild the Japanese archipelago," he was involved in the Lockheed bribery scandal and forced to resign. Gibney Collection

The Shinkansen (New Trunk Line) Bullet Train entering Tokyo station. Opened for service on October 1, 1961, the last year of Ikeda's prime ministership, the new high-speed train symbolized Japan's high-growth era, which Ikeda began.
Ken Straiton/Pacific Press Service

what less removed from the government offices in Kasumigaseki where Ikeda had spent most of his working life.

I had known Ikeda for almost the greater part of two decades. I met him first in 1949 when he was Yoshida's Finance Minister. A friend brought me to visit with him in the cabinet room of the Diet building, where I found him eating a rather spartan *obento* lunch with some of his peers. We had become friends. Over the years, as an inveterate Japan watcher, I had come to appreciate Ikeda's gruff honesty, which made him stand out from the crowd of rising postwar politicians. He could on occasion be abrasive. In fact, he had once had to resign his post as MITI minister in 1952 after a casual remark. Commenting on the Dodge-induced depression, which was causing thousands of business bankruptcies, Ikeda opined that if "five or ten small businessmen" went bankrupt and committed suicide, their loss was not much to weigh against the country's economic salvation.

For Ikeda, an old Finance Ministry economist, was little influenced by public opinion or editorial denunciation. He held throughout to his and Yoshida's belief that, as he put it, "real political freedom and independence cannot be hoped for where there is no economic independence."

By the time of my visit, Ikeda was in the last stages of his final sickness. He was to die only a month later, on August 13, 1965. He brought me into his study, where he was lounging in a plain, rather rough *yukata* kimono, and took me on a short tour of the garden before we sat down. It was hard for him to talk and I tried to press him as little as possible. What he said, however, he was anxious to say.

Japan, at that time, was enduring something of a recession, an inevitable by-product of the Ikeda booms. Bankruptcies had again multiplied. One of Japan's big-four security companies—Yamaichi—had almost gone under. Ikeda told me he was confident that joint action by government and business could cool off the overheated economy: "It is simply the problem of adjustment in the midst of a rapid economic growth period. I do not think that most people are seriously worried about it. Inevitably, we developed an overcapacity for production in many basic industries—steel, textiles, and cement among them—and this we must correct." (Indeed, in the months after we met, the economy righted itself and prepared to go into yet another of the postwar "booms.")

We talked a bit about Japan's growth. By this time, industrial production was more than three times what it had been ten years before. By way of underlining the success of the "double your income" plan, the annual growth rates now exceeded 12 percent. (With the final goal set for 1971, the actual doubling was attained in 1968.)

Ikeda agreed that it was time for Japan to think of a better aid program for the underdeveloped nations, particularly those in Asia. "This is something we are well suited to do," he said. "But we need assistance, especially in the foreign currency area, to accomplish any real meaningful plan. It is a sobering thought to contemplate how much of Japan's raw materials have to be imported."

I reminded Ikeda that Japan was already approaching the catch-up stage, and had some major international economic responsibilities to discharge. It was no longer a question of depending on the United States to handle the major share of aid to underdeveloped countries, since U.S. resources, as the Vietnam War proceeded, looked increasingly limited. At this, Ikeda shook his head and chuckled a bit. "You Americans are all talking the same," he said. "It's just the rich man crying poor."

It was ironic that twenty years later Japan would seem to fit the role of the poor-mouthing rich man far more than the Americans. Ikeda probably would have enjoyed savoring that moment.

But for his time, Japan's premier economic bureaucrat had achieved extraordinary success. The signs of a new affluent society were all around us—barely twenty years since I had landed at the old Imperial Navy docks in Sasebo, to see a country almost unique in its devastation.

Over the years to come, one success would follow another. With the successes would come an increasing clamor against Japan, as the country continued to play the high-growth game, consistently reluctant to soften an industrial policy that verged perilously on the edge of beggar-your-neighbor autarchy. But these problems would wait for others to decide. For his moment in history, Ikeda had done the job.

9

The Confucian Capitalists

The key factor of the military revolution was to effect an industrial revolution in Korea . . . My chief concern was economic revolution. One must eat and breathe before concerning himself with politics, social affairs, and culture.

PARK CHUNG HEE, 1970

I n the mid-1960s, shortly after the makers of Japan's "economic miracle" had set their course for the future, a similar set of transformations was taking place in four other East Asian economies: the Republic of Korea, Taiwan, and the two city-states of Singapore and Hong Kong. Hardly noticed by Americans or Europeans at the beginning of the sixties—and generally regarded, when thought of at all, more as political problem children than as economic *Wunderkinder*—these countries began to attract attention to themselves by a growing volume of exports to the United States and Europe. Travelers observed some bustle and the gradual appearance of new buildings in their cities. New factories and a few export parks appeared; American corporations began to give some thought to their use as promising sites for offshore production, rather like Mexico. International bankers pondered their creditworthiness.

By international consensus, however, they were judged to be, if anything, pale lunar reflections of Japan. Their businessmen and bureaucrats were presumably content to follow along by imitating Japan's successful example. The cute journalistic names given them—the Four Little Tigers or the Four Little

Dragons—added to the impression of quaint "Asiatic" imitators, interesting if a bit second-rate.

By the eighties, however, after two decades of double-digit rises in GNP, the four had become major players in the Pacific economy, and the world's. Korea's big steel complex at Pohang was turning out the world's cheapest steel at arguably the world's most technologically advanced plants; Korean construction engineers were putting up buildings on four continents, while Korean ships and low-cost cars were actively competing with Japan's. Taiwan's burgeoning export trade had piled up the world's largest hard-currency reserve after Japan's. Singapore had become a world-class center for banking services and high-tech components manufacture. Hong Kong's traders, manufacturers, and investors were doing their best to bring a politically obscurantist China into the present economic century.

The statistics for all four were almost unbelievably good. Since 1963 the annual GNP growth rate of South Korea had averaged close to 10 percent, holding just under that figure into the nineties. By the eighties a Korean economy that had started with cheap textiles counted 60 percent of its exports in heavy industry and chemicals. Among the Fortune 500 largest international corporations reported in 1986, ten were from the Republic of Korea, as against seven from all the other developing countries.[1] Taiwan's growth rates were similarly spectacular, with corresponding structural changes in industry and exports. The national GNP in 1982 was twelve times that of 1952; by 1990, Taiwan's hard-currency reserves approached $70 billion.

The rise of the Hong Kong and Singapore city-states was, if anything, more dramatic. By 1990, Hong Kong was exporting fully $82 billion in goods and services. Its GNP had risen from less than $3 billion in 1958 to $55 billion in 1988. By 1992, Singapore's per capita GNP had passed the $15,000 mark, with Hong Kong's only slightly less. For their part, Korea, with just under $7,000 per capita, and Taiwan, with almost $10,000, had long since outstripped such nations as Argentina, Mexico, and Brazil.

Theirs was by no means a simple four-lane road to success. They had bumps, breakdowns, and detours on the way. The very speed with which these several economic miracles were achieved involved, as we shall note, some highly unpleasant social and political trade-offs, with long-term consequences. Nonetheless, the achievements were solid. By the time the nineties began, these Asian NICs—for Newly Industrializing Countries (or, out of deference to China's pending relationship to Hong Kong, Economies)—had placed

[1] This statistic, along with several others, I have taken from Alice Amsden's impressive book *Asia's Next Giant: South Korea and Late Industrialization* (New York: Oxford University Press, 1991). I have referred to many of her comments and assessments elsewhere.

The Pohang Iron and Steel Company's plant at Pohang, one of the world's most modern and efficient steel mills. Korean Overseas Information Service

Pohang in the 1960s. Thirty years ago the site of the steel mill was a tract of peaceful farmland, close to a small fishing port. The contrast dramatizes the swiftness of the industrial surge in Korea and the other three Asian "dragons." Korean Overseas Information Service

themselves far ahead of other Third World nations as models of economic progress.

In so doing they had stood on its head almost every rule of neoclassical economics and shattered the conventional wisdom of Western economists and sociologists about how underdeveloped, once colonial societies should logically evolve. If in many ways they followed in Japan's path, they had transformed themselves into significant economic powers in less than half the time that Meiji Japan took to do so. If their prosperity owed a huge debt to American aid and purchasing power, they had won it with an original mix of free enterprise, government direction, and cultural singularity which confounded a variety of American premises and preconceptions on these matters.

Other Third World nations, with similar objectives and often greater resources, had spectacularly failed to equal their achievement, although Asian developers like Indonesia, Malaysia, and Thailand would in time come close. African economic progress looked hopeless by comparison. (Julius Nyerere's Tanzania, once touted as a showcase for enlightened socialism, had a per capita GNP of $120 in 1992; its economy had shrunk steadily for more than two decades, despite some $10 billion in Western aid.) Latin American countries, although some made good growth progress in the seventies, bogged down in the eighties—their economies slowed by excessive borrowing, impulsive spending, and notably bumpy relationships between the public and private sectors. Yet only recently have Latin American specialists taken note of the contrasting Asian achievement.

It is our purpose here to discuss and, if possible, explain how the Asian NICs did it, what qualities and systems they shared, and the problems that economic success has brought them. They have dramatized, as no other modern exemplars have, what the great Austrian-American economist Joseph Schumpeter termed "the obsolescence of the entrepreneurial function" as the West has known it. But they have done so in ways that Schumpeter could hardly have anticipated. In the process they have displayed courage, imagination, marvelous cohesion, and a new, but striking kind of entrepreneurial skill themselves. Despite their considerable peculiarities and individual differences, they have, along with Japan and the United States, advanced in concert, in something of a pattern.

Japan's sturdy economist Okita Saburo was himself one of the authors of the Ikeda economic growth blueprints for his country in the sixties. He has spent a great deal of time since then analyzing the trends in Asia-Pacific economic development. Okita called this the "flying geese" pattern of shared growth. Taking his term from the theory of division of labor offered in the thirties by another Japanese economist, Akamatsu Kaname, Okita uses the image of V-formation flight to demonstrate how a latecomer country adapts the techniques of more industrially advanced economies to catch up, in the process using its own distinctiveness to support itself. As he points out, this is neither the horizontal type of integration of the European Economic Community nor the classic vertical relationship between industrialized countries and their colonies or other underdeveloped commodity suppliers so beloved by academic "dependency" theorists. It is, in fact, typical of the economic relationships at work in the Pacific Basin over the past three decades. Such is the "climate of international cooperation," as Okita put it, in which the region as a whole can develop by following the lead countries.

THE CURRENT history of these four countries began in the confused aftermath of war. All four were former colonies. Hong Kong and Singapore belonged to Britain. Korea and Taiwan had belonged to Japan. The word "belong" is used in its old colonial era meaning, in the same sense once used to describe those vast areas of Africa and Asia labeled on the map as "belonging" to Britain or France, with little or no reference to their peoples, cultures, or origins.

Hong Kong and Singapore in this context possessed very simple histories. Since its settlement by Sir Stamford Raffles in 1819, Singapore had evolved as the key portion of the Straits Settlements, a bustling entrepôt city ruled by the British Raj (until late in the nineteenth century, its colonial governors took directions from India) and run by the Straits Chinese. These originally impoverished emigrants from southern China had over the years established volatile, but lucrative networks of traders, moneymen, and small manufacturers. Hong Kong was a Crown Colony from the time Britain wrested it from China at the close of the Opium War in 1842. Despite sizable importations of Indians, Singhalese, and, in the case of Singapore, Malays, plus an overlay of non-British foreign traders, the economies of both colonies, while supervised by the British, were increasingly dependent on the maritime Chinese. These hardy émigrés had continued over the years to flee the oppressions of warlords and rich merchant employers in search of the opportunities that the Chinese hinterland denied them.

The former Japanese colonies of Korea and Taiwan, however, possessed pedigrees of a far different order. Taiwan was Japan's first overseas colony. Annexed in 1895 at the close of the Sino-Japanese War, this rich island of sugar, rice, and tea production was run by its Japanese masters with a comparatively loose hand. An enlightened Japanese administrator named Goto Shimpei, one of the later Meiji reformers, planned to re-create the Meiji modernization there, albeit on a basis of second-class citizenship.

He was fortunate in the citizenry he had to work with. The Chinese on Taiwan were largely descendants of relatively recent immigrants from the mainland, who had arrived there over the past three hundred years. (Before the seventeenth century the island had been generally left to its aboriginal tribal inhabitants.) The ties of the Taiwan Chinese to the Qing Dynasty rulers in Beijing were never very strong. Many families were descendants of the pirate-seafarers of Koxinga's time, who had fought the last battles of the fading Ming Dynasty against the Manchu invaders from the north. Traditionally independent and progressive in their thinking, the Taiwanese, before their annexation by Japan, had led China's mainland provinces in the development of railroads, steamship lines, communications, and public health facilities. Several governors of Taiwan were pioneers in China's efforts at modernization in the nineteenth century. So the population was by no means unreceptive to the heavy dose of modernization imposed by Japan.

Unquestionably Taiwan's economy improved under Japanese occupation. Order was established, private property was respected, and a network of elementary schools set up. Productivity—both in agriculture and in light industry—greatly increased. Yet the Chinese Taiwanese were consistently regarded as a subject people. Not only did all significant jobs and positions of authority go to Japanese—even assimilated Japanese-speaking natives could only rise to a certain subordinate level—but the island's basic crops of rice and sugar were incorporated into the Japanese economic pattern, in the worst European colonial tradition. As Thomas Gold writes:[2] "The Taiwanese in general were restricted to the periphery of the capitalist mode in their own society."

If the Taiwan Chinese were dominated by the Japanese colonialists, the Koreans were cruelly and brutally oppressed. Few peoples so close in language, culture, and societal patterns have maintained such a persistent adversary relationship as the Koreans and the Japanese. Since their late-sixteenth-century invasions the Japanese have been persistently cast as the aggressor. Japan's successful war with China in 1895 was fought over the issue of who would dominate Korea, and control of Korea was a focus of the rivalry that led to the Russo-Japanese War ten years later. After Japan's formal annexation of Korea in 1910, every effort was made to assimilate the Koreans as a useful, but subservient subject class within Japan's empire.

First regarded as a kind of granary to provide cheap rice for imperial Japan, Korea ultimately became the linchpin of Japanese colonialism in Manchuria and northern China. As in Taiwan, the lessons of Meiji modernization were transplanted to Korea. By the end of World War II the Japanese had built up a considerable industrial base in Korea's north. Some small Korean capitalists were allowed to participate in economic development, albeit as very junior partners. But modernization in Korea was inextricably tied to enforced Jap-

---

[2] In his excellent *State and Society in the Taiwan Miracle* (New York: M. E. Sharpe, 1986).

anization, to the point where Koreans were forced to take Japanese names. During World War II more than two million Koreans—women as well as men—were drafted to work in Japanese factories and as laborers (military civilians, or *gunzoku*) in occupied China or Japan's island possessions. The accumulated cruelties of a half century will not easily be forgotten or forgiven. Nonetheless, the fact remains that Japan's enforced modernization, although hardly done in Koreans' interest, did help lay the foundations of a modern economy, which an independent Korea had failed to develop on its own.

When I first visited these countries in 1950, the mark of colonialism was heavy upon them. Seoul looked and felt like a Japanese provincial town. The brown brick mass of the Chosen Hotel—known familiarly among visitors as the Frozen Chosen because of its idiosyncratic heating facilities—dominated the center, along with the Meiji-type cupolas of the old Bank of Chosen and the similarly Japanese construct of what had once been the governor-general's residence. An early generation of American economic advisers was pondering how the agrarian Korea south of the 38th parallel could possibly support itself after being sundered from the coal, minerals, and manufacturing plants of the Soviet-occupied north. Japanese was widely spoken. Many Koreans recently repatriated from Japan were hastily trying to relearn their own language. A flotsam of foreign businessmen, recent refugees from Shanghai, tried to put together deals with the few export products the new Korea had to offer. Outside their offices countrymen carried a few primitive manufactures in carts and on A-frames through dusty streets.

While Syngman Rhee and other long-exiled Korean politicians tried to settle scores with a hodgepodge of leftists, Communists, and sincere agrarian reformers, the newly created officers of the Republic of Korea's Army taught different varieties of discipline to their recruits. Some I visited, only a few years away from Japanese Army service, still hung their Japanese swords nostalgically behind their desks. The thought that Seoul could become a world-class business metropolis was at that time inconceivable.

Taiwan was even quieter. Although little touched by World War II, its people had had to endure, through the late forties, an equally traumatic experience: the arrival of some two million Nationalist Chinese soldiers and bureaucrats from the mainland to build a last redoubt for Chiang Kai-shek against the victorious Communists. In February 1947, rising tensions between new arrivals from the mainland and the native Taiwanese erupted in heavy rioting against mainland rule. What is still known as the February 28 Incident was actually a series of spontaneous protest demonstrations against the oppressive tactics of Chiang Kai-shek's carpetbaggers. Heavy and brutal retaliation followed, after more troops had been brought over from China. In May, Nationalist troops began a bloodbath that resulted in more than 10,000 deaths.

Singapore skyline. A rising center of the new knowledge industries, Singapore has virtually obliterated its old colonial past with a new image. Singapore Tourist Promotion Board

Downtown Taipei. Heavy traffic has become a tradition in the crowded metropolis, headquarters of Taiwan's spectacular economic growth.
Coordination Council for North American Affairs

The killing, carried out under the orders of Taiwan's Nationalist governor, was purposeful and selective. Most of Taiwan's intelligentsia and native leadership were slaughtered in their own streets.

After this Taiwan was, on the surface, quiet. With hundreds of thousands of Nationalist troops now garrisoned on the island after their defeat by the Communists, local dissidents had scant hope of success. Few people, however, believed the boasts of the defeated generalissimo that his army would soon go back to reconquer the mainland. Even many American supporters of Chiang, finally stung by well-confirmed accounts of Nationalist ineptitude and corruption, questioned the wisdom of pouring any more aid money into what seemed like a backwater of history.

In Hong Kong, still rebuilding after the atrocity-ridden Japanese occupation, tens of thousands of refugees from Mao Zedong's Communist "liberation" were flooding in, from penniless farmers to the survivors of Shanghai's businessmen and bankers, prepared to start up again in a different city. The center of the island was the scene of colonialist restoration, as the old British taipans and their associates came back from the Japanese prison camps. The Hong Kong Club was back in business. Once more only Europeans could buy apartments on the storied Peak. But just blocks away from the tidy business center packed tenements swarmed with new residents, as family after family made it over the border from a revolutionizing China. With Kowloon overflowing with people, there was an ample supply of labor for the textile factories now going up in the adjacent New Territories. By 1951, Hong Kong's postwar population of some 600,000 had swollen to 2,500,000. Visitors could justly wonder how this small island and the adjoining land could possibly absorb a new and largely destitute refugee population. One never thought of them as the tireless workers and entrepreneurs of a new international future.

Still less could a future be seen for Singapore. When I came there first, in the winter of 1949–50, the island seemed to have almost returned to its semi-sleep of the prewar colonial days. The British base was back in operation and the old trading companies were hiring again. But new political currents were swirling below the surface. Across the causeway in Malaya, the Communist insurgency had begun its attempt to wrest control of the peninsula through armed violence and terror tactics. Mostly Chinese, and including a large slice of the Straits Chinese intelligentsia, the Communists maintained an active underground in Singapore. For the next few years the fate of the city and Malaya would depend partly on the success of the military tactics the British used against them, but even more heavily on the efforts of Malay and Straits Chinese anti-Communist movements for independence.

*   *   *

ON JUNE 25, 1950, the Korean War began. Six months before, at a meeting in Moscow, Stalin had given his grudging consent to the plans of North Korea's Communist leader, Kim Il Sung, to invade the south with heavy Soviet support. Politically divided and thinly defended, the new Republic of Korea was almost overrun. Seoul fell after four days. Although American and other UN troops ultimately pushed the North Koreans back, MacArthur's subsequent invasion of the north and the massive Chinese reaction led to three years of fighting, which in turn both spread and intensified the Cold War in Asia.

The outbreak and progress of this grim conflict are treated in a later chapter. Here we are concerned only with its effect on the Asia-Pacific economy. South Korea was literally devastated. After the truce in 1953, wartime U.S. economic aid was greatly expanded. Over the first three postwar decades, the United States spent almost $13 billion on the Republic of Korea.

In the decade ending in 1962, American aid paid for 70 percent of South Korea's imports and accounted for fully 80 percent of fixed capital formation. Among other things, this helped put the fledgling Korean textile industry, the first big postwar dollar earner, on its feet.[3]

American aid goals were relatively modest, concentrated on commodity shipments, rebuilding the country's shattered infrastructure, and setting up some light industry. (No one in the late fifties was thinking in terms of Hyundai cars or supertankers.) Yet Washington's aid funds offered an indispensable base for Korea's later "economic miracle," as surely as the rush of Korean War procurement orders energized Japan's.

Taiwan also benefited from the Korean War, thanks largely to the prevalent American Cold War view that all anti-Communists were of a piece. Fearing a general Communist attack in Asia in 1950, President Harry Truman ordered the U.S. military to protect Taiwan from the Communists. A corollary of this move was a revived aid program for the Nationalist government on Taiwan. Although no Korean-type reconstruction effort was needed, the $1.5 billion in aid given Taiwan proved a powerful factor in righting its economy and preparing it for later expansion.

The war in Korea had another and rather odd by-product. A hugely successful Hong Kong smuggling operation brought badly needed goods into the People's Republic of China. After Chinese People's Liberation Army troops—the so-called volunteers—were ordered into the war on the North Korean side, the United States and other UN allies placed an embargo on exports to the PRC. Shrewd Chinese traders in the Crown Colony, however, were able to get

---

[3] The statistics are taken from *Korea Old and New: A History* (Cambridge: Harvard University Press, 1990), by Carter J. Eckert, Ki-baik Lee, Young Ick Lew, Michael Robinson, and Edward W. Wagner, an authoritative short history of Korea adapted from Lee Ki-baik's original.

around the embargo by transshipping to China, in the best entrepôt tradition. Not a few capitalist businesses in Hong Kong got their start in this manner.

On the subject of American aid programs in East Asia, one significant factor needs to be mentioned: their consistent emphasis on land reform. In part this was a direct result of the successful land reform undertaken by Wolf Ladejinsky and other idealistic agriculturalists in MacArthur's Occupation of Japan. Both in Taiwan and in Korea—in the midst of the otherwise spectacularly unsuccessful U.S. military occupation there—the Americans pushed land reform as a matter of commonsense policy. Neither Korean nor Taiwan officials needed much convincing on this score. During the Korean War, the Communists' drastic, if bloody land redistribution policies made some further postwar action by the South Korean government necessary. For their part, Chiang Kai-shek's surviving bureaucrats in Taipei had rueful memories of the successful colonization of China's peasantry by the Communists under the banner of *their* land reform. In addition, there were large tracts of formerly Japanese-owned land to be distributed in both countries. Nor did a large landlord class remain, comparable to that in Latin America. (Since landlords in Taiwan were all local people, Chiang Kai-shek's officials from the mainland felt little sense of obligation to them.)

The resultant rises in agricultural productivity paved the way for the intensive industrialization to come. This contrasts with the case of other Third World countries, where increases in manufacturing were bought at the price of losses in the farming sector.

Land reform and raised agricultural productivity are two of the reasons Okita Saburo gives for the success of the "flying geese" development economies in the Pacific Basin. The others include: (1) an aggressive private business sector operating within what is basically a free market system; (2) export-oriented policies, whereby a developing country abandons the path of import substitution—that is, attempted economic self-sufficiency—to rely instead on its own exports to other nations; (3) a high rate of investment, backed by ever higher domestic savings; (4) successful economic adjustment policies—that is, the capacity to make adjustments in a developing economy to deal with sudden change or other emergencies (a classic example being the way Japan handled the "oil shocks" of 1973 and 1978–79).[4]

These are analyses after the fact—academic postmortems, as it were. They do not fully explain why and how Korea, Taiwan, and Singapore—and, in its

[4] These enumerations of policies and principles appeared originally in Okita's essay, *Pacific Development and Its Implications for the World Economy*, published in New York in 1986 (American Academy of Political Science). They reflect longer treatments by Okita in *The Developing Economies and Japan* (Tokyo: University of Tokyo Press, 1980) and other works.

peculiar way, Hong Kong—evolved the way they did, so that in the end, following on Japan's example, they came to epitomize that late-twentieth-century phenomenon, the capitalist development state. Yet we cannot regard them as mere carbon-copy followers of Japan's modernization. They were in too much of a hurry to avail themselves of the longer incubation period which the Meiji experience had allowed Japan. In their urge for economic efficiency as much as in their funding, they borrowed directly from the United States. But in their manner of governance they relied, as we shall see, on far older traditions than those of capitalist America or imperial Meiji Japan.

THREE REMARKABLE men helped create the several economic miracles involved. In many ways they symbolize them, in their defects as well as their virtues. Park Chung Hee, President of the Republic of Korea, ruled his country from 1961, when he seized power in a military coup, until his death by shooting in 1979. Chiang Ching-kuo, President of the Republic of China on Taiwan, took over actual power from his aging father, Chiang Kai-shek, in the sixties, although he did not assume the presidency until 1978, ten years before his death. Lee Kuan Yew, Prime Minister of Singapore, led and dominated his island country from 1959 to his announced retirement in 1990.

Their history and backgrounds could not be more disparate. Park, a graduate of the Manchurian military academy, began life as a regular officer in the Imperial Japanese Army, joining the newly formed Republic of Korea Army at its inception after World War II. Chiang, the eldest son of the Nationalist Chinese leader, studied for ten years in the Soviet Union, thanks to the temporary rapprochement between the Nationalists and the Communists in the 1920s. After his return to China he became something of a specialist in secret police and security matters. Lee studied law at Cambridge and first practiced as a barrister when he returned to Singapore in 1950. Working with trade unions, intellectual leftists, and Communists, he maneuvered his way to the forefront of the anti-British independence movement. He became Prime Minister after the 1959 elections and continued to lead the city-state since independence was won in 1965.

In manner and accomplishment, however, Lee, Chiang, and Park showed themselves strikingly similar. All three were authoritarians, albeit in their way nationalist patriots. As military men, educated under the Japanese and the Soviets, respectively, Park and Chiang ruled in the manner of autocrats, with only minimal attention paid to maintaining legal and democratic forms. While far more subtle in his parliamentary tactics, Lee showed himself as ruthless as his onetime Communist colleagues when it came to suppressing opposition to his policies.

Yet these were no ordinary political despots. Along with Suharto in Indonesia and, indeed, Ikeda in Japan, Park, Lee, and Chiang represented a second generation of postwar Asian leaders. Their predecessors like Syngman Rhee and Sukarno were political jugglers. In their single-minded crusades for independence there was little room for economic planning and administrative structure building. By contrast Park, Lee, and Chiang were blueprint people. They were builders who wanted to leave stable and workable societies behind them.

To this end all three surrounded themselves with staffs of bright economists, political planners, and other "technocrats." Driven by the need to make a living for countries badly disadvantaged by circumstance, with foreign aid bound to diminish, all three put economics first. Unlike other Third World leaders, they recognized that the only salvation for their countries lay in a policy of dynamic economic growth, based on heavy exports and an abiding commitment to the international marketplace.

As long as they found their technocrats politically reliable, these leaders gave them a relatively free hand. In Taiwan, a keen-minded electrical engineer named Yin Chung-yung (most usually anglicized as K. Y. Yin), who had spent some years working and studying in the United States, played a major role in putting technically trained people in positions of authority in the new development efforts. Once he gained the Nationalist regime's confidence, he did much to keep the government from interfering with private businesses. Influenced by his American experience, Yin, along with his technocrat colleagues, realized that economic growth could best be attained through productive free enterprise companies competing in the international marketplace. Not for them the command economies of the Communists, which Mao Zedong was now putting into practice on the mainland.

Yet at the same time they insisted that free enterprise growth be guided by enlightened government policy. For both Yin and his successor, Li Kuo-ting (K. T. Li), a brilliant physicist turned bureaucrat, had also spent some time in Japan. They were much impressed by the "plan-rational" economic policy making of Japan's bureaucrats. Working in Taiwan at a far less sophisticated stage of economic development, they needed to spend more time on basic productivity problems. If Yin's technocrats, like Ikeda's bureaucrats in Japan, comprised a kind of mandarinate, they were a mandarinate of engineers. Economic modernization, as Li put it, is a "huge engineering system that requires extremely careful and elaborate planning."[5]

Such a close interconnection between business and bureaucracy flew in the face of American conventional wisdom. To the Asian governors of the NIC

[5] As quoted in Alan Liu's interesting study of Taiwan's modernization, *Phoenix and the Lame Lion* (Stanford, Calif.: The Hoover Institution/Stanford University Press, 1987).

economies, however, it seemed quite logical—given their countries' circumstances. So Park Chung Hee explained Korea's first Five-Year Plan in the sixties: "The basic economic system during the period of *enforcement* [my italics] of this plan respects as much as possible the freedom and creativity of private individuals. However, with regard to key industries, the government must take a direct or indirect part in the public sector. This is to stimulate voluntary activities and initiative on the part of private individuals. In other words, an enterprise leadership system has been adopted."

Although economic conditions in all three countries—not to mention Hong Kong—were quite different, the principles of this government engineering were basically the same. The goals far exceeded the modest aims of light industry self-sufficiency that the Washington planners at the Agency for International Development (AID) recommended. On the basis of their own studies of world markets the NIC planners charted their progress from elementary exports like cheap textiles and electronics through heavy industry to (perhaps) competitive high tech. With state planning, financing, and, on occasion, subsidy, their export industries would sell to the world as cheaply as possible, while keeping foreign products out of their home markets as long as possible.

By making their economies export-led, however, they broke with the tempting, but ultimately destructive Third World practice of simple import substitution. Protected industries have a tendency to grow flabby, uncompetitive, and, ultimately, prohibitively expensive for both producers and consumers. By contrast, export industries, exposed to the cut and thrust of international competition, are perforce competitive. Their greater efficiencies and economies in turn benefit the domestic market as well.

In their drive for economic success the technocrats in Seoul, Singapore, and Taipei were unimpressed by such time-honored economic laws as Ricardo's principle of comparative advantage. According to this neoclassical doctrine, nations should specialize in selling products which they can make with the greatest relative efficiency, while importing products in which others demonstrate greater relative productivity.[6] The planners in Seoul and Taipei, however, were in too much of a hurry to wait for such economic leveling laws to take effect. Taking a leaf from Japan's book, they practiced political warfare through economics wherever they could get away with it, restricting imports while they "targeted" exports.

"Whenever we wanted to do anything," a Korea Central Bank governor

---

[6] Even when one country can produce almost all commodities more efficiently than others, Ricardo held, international trade remains the best way to go, for every country will have a comparative advantage in making some products. He laid down this law in 1817, working on the assumption that governments would not interfere in the trading or pricing of goods.

once commented, "the advocates of comparative advantage told us we don't have comparative advantage. In the event we did everything we wanted, but whatever we did, we did well."[7]

Like the Japanese a decade before them, they borrowed widely and shamelessly. As Alice Amsden has noted, the young planners in Korea—a good portion of them products of graduate schools in the United States—practiced a "learning" type of industrialization. That is to say, where older capitalist countries like Britain, Germany, or the United States industrialized through invention and innovation, the Koreans caught up by borrowing and adapting from well-defined models. Where American universities turned out theoretical physicists, theirs, like Japan's, turned out engineers—and as quickly as possible. In the Republic of Korea alone, the number of engineering graduates shot up from some 4,500 in 1960 to almost 45,000 in 1980. Through government-sponsored think tanks like the Korean Institute of Science and Technology and its successor, the Advanced Institute (KAIST), they worked to build up their capacity both for professional training and for research.

THE GREAT EXTERNAL reason for the success of these "flying geese" economies was the American market. As Okita noted in his essay: ". . . the American market is the largest, most diverse and most accessible overseas market anywhere in the world—companies and traders everywhere have their sights set on it. At the same time American capital, technology and managerial know-how have made important contributions to Pacific development—all this in addition to the United States' key role in peacekeeping."

For many years Marxist economists and their followers contended that developed capitalist "core" countries kept underdeveloped Third World nations hopelessly dependent by buying up their commodities, turning them into manufactures, and selling them back to the underdeveloped, at great profit. In this way, the so-called dependency theory ran, the underdeveloped nations remained on the "periphery" of industrialization, their poverty deepening as the degree of dependence on the developed countries increased.

From the sixties on, the American consumer market offered a spectacular refutation of this theory. Operating on the principle of the free market, American consumers eagerly bought the new manufactures of Japan, Korea, Taiwan, and other NICs. Tariffs and other trade barriers remained low, in contrast to the protectionist walls that the East Asian governments threw around their

[7] As quoted by Robert Wade in *World Politics* (January 1992). Wade's book *Governing the Market: Economic Theory and the Role of Government in East Asian Industrialization* (Princeton, N.J.: Princeton University Press, 1990) is a standard work on this subject.

own fledgling industries. While American wholesalers found new sources of supply in Asian manufactures, American corporations, in their single-minded search for increased profits, took advantage of cheap labor (and strong central governments) in the Asian NICs to set up their own "offshore" plants. These then proceeded to ship goods back to the United States, for sale under familiar American brand names.

The rapid growth of industry in Taiwan, for example, owed much to this practice. Singer Sewing Machine opened its Taiwan plant in 1963. In the next two years, encouraged by cheap labor, tax breaks, and plans for a new export-processing zone, some twenty-five American firms set up shop in Taiwan. Others followed. So did a host of Japanese companies, attracted by much the same incentives. But in offshore manufacturing the Americans led the way.

Successive administrations in Washington supported this two-way Open Door policy for political reasons. Their desire to make anti-Communist Asian countries healthy and prosperous outweighed any economic concerns about cut-rate Asian competition. Nor did the neoclassical economic advisers in Washington adequately appreciate the intensity of government-backed export policies in these countries. The net result was to supply the Asian "flying geese" economies with a jet-assisted takeoff. From the sixties on, the "dependency" shoe was on the other foot.

There were, of course, important internal reasons for the Asian NICs' success. All of them have established rigorous and widespread educational systems; Taiwan, Korea, and Singapore have been spending fully 20 percent of their annual budgets on education, as against 5 percent or less in Western Europe and the United States. All have high personal savings rates. Taiwan's savings rate of 30 percent remains the highest in the world. And these savings are, of course, put at the disposal of government and private financial institutions for capital investment. In Singapore some 20 percent of a worker's salary is arbitrarily deposited into savings accounts by the government, not to be tapped except for the purchase of a house or some such worthy project.

To the Western mind, citizens' cooperation with this high-handed paternalism would seem either docile or obsessively patriotic. Yet people like Park or Chiang or Lee would not find such behavior strange. Lee, explaining Singapore's political rationale to some predictably puzzled Australian reporters, put it simply. Singapore's two core values, he said, are, first, "the basic attitude that the individual is lesser than the society . . . the notion of society as number one and the individual, as part of that society, as number two." The second, he added, was recognition that the family is the basic unit of society. (He has, not inconsistently, ticketed his son Brigadier General Lee Hsien Loong, to be his ultimate successor.)

There is no doubt but that all of these countries learned a great deal from Japan's example. The success of an export-oriented policy was there for all to see. As Japan raised the level of its exports in value and complexity—from textiles to electronics to automotive—Korea, Taiwan, Hong Kong, and Singapore stood ready to climb the next rungs of the industrial ladder after Japan. By the sixties, their textiles—and by the early seventies, Korean-built ships—were pushing more expensive Japanese products out of the market, as Japan's had once pushed those of the United States. In addition, increased Japanese investment in all four countries made them more familiar with Japanese business methods and provided them with a certain amount of technology transfer. (By the late seventies, however, Japanese steelmakers became increasingly reluctant to share technology with their new Korean competitors, so that most of Korea's steelmaking know-how was imported from Europe.)

A look at Japan's history also proved instructive. Both Korea and Taiwan, faced with organizing brand-new industrial economies, found useful examples in the Meiji modernization, when Japanese governments had to create industries and build financial structures for the first catch-up effort. Even in 1945, although devastated by an unsuccessful war, the Japanese had several generations of modern manufacturing experience behind them. The NICs of Asia, like Meiji Japan, were starting from scratch.

It was here that they had to draw on much the same cultural resources available to the Meiji reformers: a work ethic, a sense of family solidarity, a strong sense of group responsibility, and above all a disposition to accept the authority of the state, even where citizens were not represented in its governance. This ethic can justly be called Confucian.

It may seem ironic that a set of values widely regarded in the West as archaic and reactionary would play such a prominent part in the success of these new capitalist development states. But old values can be put to new uses. A word of explanation may be necessary to describe how a rethinking of Asia's ancient Confucian ethic could serve as the cement holding together dynamic new economies as they emerged.

THE MOST STRIKING thing about the traditional shrine of Confucianism is its utter formlessness. A sprawling complex of house, courtyard, audience chamber, and temple enfolds the original home of China's great teacher in Qufu. It seems endless to the visitor, who is all too easily lost. The temple of Confucius itself contains more than four hundred rooms, its chambers ranked so that in olden times officials and servants authorized to enter one hall might not be permitted to go on to the next. But there is no equivalent to the high altars and heaven-searching art that one associates with Buddhism or Christianity. There are inscriptions and scrolls and exhortations. Noble styles written in classic Chinese characters preach the virtues of learning, self-restraint, and above all filial piety. There are the rites—now faithfully observed by China's Communist hierarchy—with words, chants and ancient music, sacrifices, and involuted forms of respect; but they are more like a royal family's memorial service than a liturgy. For there is no God, no Savior, no Lord Buddha in this system of prescribed codes that is far more an ethic than a religion. But it is one of the most powerful and tenacious ethics in the world.

The way of Master Kong—the Chinese Kong Fuzi became the Westernized Confucius—is a cult of relationships and quietly enforced duties. The ideal of the Confucian sage is harmony, not justice. There is no supernatural power above, only people here below, but these must govern themselves and obey authority, in all its forms, if they wish to conform to the order of an unknowable heaven. Community is everything. The human condition can be improved, as the modern American Confucian scholar Tu Wei Ming tells us, "through personal cultivation as a communal act."

Confucius lived in the sixth and fifth centuries before the Christian era. While popular tradition sets his birth and death dates as 551 and 479, they are in fact unknown. His life was spent in the political and military turmoil of the Warring States period, before the unification of China under the emperor Qin Xi Huang-ti in 221 B.C. His wanderings and teachings were in fact a search for stability in the midst of war and confusion. His ideal of political and moral harmony he traced back to the past dynasty of Zhou. The ancient school of Chinese thought called the Legalists sought to restore peace through the enactment and firm enforcement of laws. By contrast, Confucius preached the need for social virtue, whereby people could regulate their behavior by practicing enlightened humaneness—called *jen* in Chinese—in their relationships with others.

In a sense Confucianism turned the human conscience outward. In contrast to the individualism of the single conscience in Christianity, he made virtue dependent on the fulfillment of a person's part in well-defined societal relationships. In the five basic relationships of Confucianism, little room was left for the single soul. Whether between ruler and subject, father and son, husband and wife, brother and brother, or friend and friend, the faith in Confucius was inseparable from belief in a particular community. Not man but his relationships became the measure of all things.

Even more than the ancient Greeks, the Confucians made the very act of learning into a moral virtue. If self-sacrifice, following Christ's example, is the key to the Christian message, then learning, after the fashion of the Master, is the vital ingredient of the Confucian message. As Xun Zi (Hsun Tzu) put it: "Learning continues until death and only then does it cease."[8]

---

[8] I have taken this comment from Raymond Dawson's excellent short study, *Confucius* (New York: Oxford University Press, 1989).

Continual study and the imitation of worthy models were the real path toward goodness, as displayed in the ever perfectible conduct of one's various relations. In the Confucian scheme of things you never learned by yourself; you learned from somebody or some model.

Another strong mark of the Confucian ethic is devotion to the family. It is around families that life is formed. It is within the context of families—and only in this context—that the lives of individuals have true meaning. As the Book of Filial Piety enjoins: "One should serve one's parents as one should serve heaven." The idea of the house, the family, the clan is dramatized by a web of ceremonies and prescribed rituals.

All of these stemmed from the belief of Confucius and his disciples that it is through the observance of rites (li), as well as the practice of humaneness toward others, that people can realize their true human potential. Patient and faithful observance of these rites helps even the most ordinary people follow the dictates of virtuous kings, who communicate their wishes through the agency of loyal scholar-ministers, all in minutely prescribed ways. "Instead of a code of morals," the historian Sir George Sansom commented, "the good citizen has a code of manners."

No visitor to the house of Confucius at Qufu can fail to be struck by the overpowering sense of family. Some thirty generations of Kongs have lived in the mansion complex. More, including the sage himself, are buried in the tombs at the nearby Forest of Confucius. Every level of the family relationship is painstakingly recorded. The Kongs naturally represent the pinnacle of the family cult; for wherever there are Han peoples, almost every family has its own annals and obeisances.

Confucius and his disciples saw the harmony of the family to be both a reflection of the harmony of the state and a contribution to it. But it was the state that made harmony possible. As the Japanese Confucian scholar Shimada Kenji had it: "The great distinguishing factor in Confucianist thinking is: *In the beginning there was government.*"

Over the centuries the teachings of Confucius spread throughout East Asia. In China they took deep root and grew into the fabric of society. Korean scholars were poring over the *Analects* and the other Confucian classics by the third century A.D. and Japanese students were learning them by the seventh. In Vietnam, Confucianism became as strong as in China. A nobility of thought and expression shone through many of the Confucian teachings, especially as great Confucianists like Mencius and Zhu Xi preached a doctrine of brotherhood and virtuous striving.

All Confucian thinking was by no means as authoritarian as a first impression suggests. Confucianists had their share of liberals, pure scholars, and defenders of people's rights. The Master himself was a great believer in gov-

Hong Kong. The old porticos of the Hong Kong Club are dwarfed by the new skyscraper Bank of China building, a portent of 1997. Peter Bull

Shanghai. The fabled Bund, once the business capital of Asia, is now quiet, its old buildings suggesting the contrast between the PRC's stagnating heavy industry and the new models of Koreans and maritime Chinese. Levie Isaacks

Presidential harvest. After land reforms, increased agricultural production greatly helped the progress of the NIC's economies. Here Korea's President Park Chung Hee harvests the new "miracle rice" strain. Dong-A Ilbo

Farm and factory are juxtaposed in Korea. A small cultivated tract contrasts with the Lucky-GoldStar computer plant in the background. Peter Bull

In Qufu, Confucius's ancestral home, China's Communist leadership staged an International Confucian Culture Festival in 1990. Celebrants are pictured going through some of the ritual dances in the ceremony. Levie Isaacks

Korean Confucians. Ryu Chan Yu (right), chairman of Pongsan Metals, continues to emphasize Confucian values among his employees. Here he is pictured after holding a Confucian ceremony. Peter Bull

ernment by meritocracy. Yet it was inevitable that a system which placed such reliance on the disinterested rational thinking of a "literati" elite could be manipulated. Emperors and mandarins over the centuries turned the sage's original inspirations into frozen codes of rituals and hierarchical deference to authority, whose principal role often seemed to be keeping the lower orders down and the upper orders up. Altruistic "Superior Men" turned into corrupt officeholders, taking advantage of the passivity of their subjects, who were taught to regard all authority as virtuous unless proved otherwise.

Korean and Chinese revolutionaries decried Confucian feudalism in their 1919 rebellions, just as Japanese pre-Meiji scholars had thrown away their Confucian texts in favor of Western learning. In his famous essay "Confucius in Modern China," Lu Xun wrote in disgust: "It was those in authority who boosted Confucius in modern China, making him the sage of the powerful . . .

"Admittedly Confucius devised outstanding methods of governing the state, but these were thought up to rule the people for the sake of those in authority; there was nothing of any value to the people . . .

"Try any time you like going in rags and barefoot to the sacrificial hall in the Confucian temple in Qufu to look around and you will probably be thrown out as fast as when you blunder into a high-class cinema or a first-class tram carriage in Shanghai. For these places, as everyone knows, are for bigwigs and gentlemen."

In academic circles the sociologist Max Weber, in his writings on the religion of China and elsewhere, was said to have the last word on Confucius. The author of *The Protestant Ethic and the Spirit of Capitalism* found very little support for capitalist entrepreneurship among the Chinese literati who formed a bureaucratic upper class in the traditional Confucian scheme of things. He contrasted their Confucian morality directly with the "Puritan morality" that he found to play such a leading role in Western capitalism's development.

I have no wish to take up the cudgels with either Weber or Lu Xun. I merely point out that each saw the Confucian ethic from a special point of view. Weber was judging both Confucianism and capitalism from a Western European perspective. Lu Xun was understandably outraged by the rigid formalism of state Confucianism as it had been ossified by the decadent Qing Dynasty. Qing mandarins had converted a noble rational ethic into a cloak for tyranny, much as some of the luxury-loving prince-bishops of pre-Reformation Europe had exploited the Christian message.

Certainly Weber, if not Lu Xun, could hardly have foreseen the appearance of the capitalist development state in East Asia. Yet it is in the context of this capitalist development state—through a combination of insight and serendipity—that traditional Confucian values have been revived, in fact almost reinvented, to serve as an adhesive for a modern economic phenomenon. By this

I do not mean to play down the tremendous effect of factors like U.S. aid and the American market, technological borrowing, the Japanese example, and changes in the international market. Such obvious economic and political factors, however, are not enough to explain these countries' successes. With all due respect to economists, political scientists, and other dedicated searchers for mechanical causation, we must not underrate the strong and pervasive influence of Confucian culture.

For these developing "flying geese" economies are not the mere products of Western societies, despite their apparent internationalization. Their peoples are distinguished by an obsessive, almost religious regard for education and learning. And in the Confucian tradition they see merit rather than disgrace in learning through the disciplined study of models. This is an ideal cast of mind for Amsden's "learning" economy, in which catching up is all-important.

The American idea of the school as equalizer and incentive to democratic thinking is not for them. While we may decry their concentration on "rote learning," a look at the superior comparative scores of Korean, Chinese, and Japanese students in mathematics and other basic disciplines is instructive. Their American counterparts, however advanced socially, have by far the poorest set of aptitudes.

The intense family consciousness of Asian peoples has been fostered—indeed, codified—by centuries of the Confucian tradition. Whether it is the direct blood-relation family solidarity of a Chinese business or the extended-house solidarity of the Japanese or Korean corporation, the propensity for group standards and group effort has proved a powerful asset to corporate productivity. In the modern factory and laboratory, group effort is critical to success. There are not many Edisons discovering new electric lights by themselves in modern inventors' workshops.

These old Confucian virtues lie behind the spectacular growth of current economic phenomena like the Korean *chaebol* conglomerates that have mushroomed since the sixties. (Literally meaning "money clique," *chaebol* is written with the same Chinese characters as the Japanese *zaibatsu*.) *Chaebol* groups like Hyundai and Samsung are complexes of different companies in different fields united under a strong leadership core. They are capable of heavy investment outlays and profitable economies of scale because of their very size and solidarity. Like the family business groups of Taiwan and Hong Kong—and the original prewar *zaibatsu* in Japan—they are run by fathers and sons and brothers in an old Confucian tradition. Excepting perhaps Indian family conglomerates, there is nothing quite like them in the West or other Third World nations. One can argue that in a non-Confucian society they would not be widely tolerated.

Other Third World countries, despite old cultures, cannot boast the heavy deployment of educated talent furnishing Asian NIC companies with managers and engineers. In no other region, also, do we find such strong tendencies to save and invest among private citizens, largely content to forgo individual returns and profits until the group has prospered. While notable in Taiwan and Korea, this is equally characteristic of the maritime Chinese, who dominate business not merely in Hong Kong and Singapore but also in other Southeast Asian countries.

This "capacity to cooperate," as the University of Hong Kong sociologist S. Gordon Redding writes, can justly be called Confucian. "Directly Confucian ideals," he continues, "and especially familism as a central tenet are still well enough embedded in the minds of most overseas Chinese to make Confucianism the most apposite single-word label for the values which govern most of their social behavior. This does not imply that they are unusually devout, consistent or narrow. It is simply a convenient label for a complex and changing set of values."[9]

Of all the attributes of family Confucianism, however, the most noteworthy has been the interesting relationship between these peoples and their governments. In each of these countries, as in Japan, governments have guided the development process. Asian bureaucrats have never been content to wait for Adam Smith's famous "invisible hand" to set their economies in the right direction. In describing the capitalist development state the word "state" is writ large. Government direction can be subtle, if pervasive, as in Japan. Or it can be spasmodic, arbitrary, and brutal in its authoritarianism, as in Korea a decade ago. Yet even the most authoritarian of the East Asian governments has respected the integrity of the private sector and the need for a competitive market economy. Even the most assertive of their businessmen have accepted the guiding hand of the bureaucracy—despite obvious tensions between public and private—with the obedience (or resignation) of a Confucian merchant heeding the words of the local mandarin. Cooperation is the watchword, even if it be the sort of cooperation that few American or European businessmen would accept.

PARK CHUNG HEE in Korea, Chiang Ching-kuo in Taiwan, and Lee Kuan Yew in Singapore very consciously fostered the Confucian aspects of their societies. Lee once told his Singapore university students: "The day Chinese lose their Confucianness . . . that day we become just another Third World society." Both Taiwan and Singapore have long taught Confucian ethics in their school systems, despite the growing disinclination of the new TV gener-

---

[9] In *The Spirit of Chinese Capitalism* (Berlin and New York: De Gruyter, 1990).

ation to cherish the Book of Filial Piety the way their grandfathers did. In Korea, traditionally the most hidebound of Confucian societies, these values are ingrained, even if ritual Confucian observances are now minimal. The second-class status of women in Korean society is a reminder of Confucianism's dark side.

We have noted that all three of these leaders acknowledged the primacy of free enterprise in building up their economies. Yet in stimulating what Park referred to as a new "industrial revolution," the visible hand of government was always at work—often about as unobtrusively as a mailed fist.

Describing Korea's situation, Park wrote in extenuation of his tough policies: "One of our big problems concerned the shaky foundations of private industry, which was unable to carry its share of the development burden. Furthermore, the market structure was not modernized. Consequently the government had to play the leading role in the development plan, though we knew well that, in the long run, such a plan must rely on the creativity and initiative of private industry. We hoped to encourage businessmen who could play leading roles in planning. On the other hand, rigid restrictions were put on business activities that ran against these efforts."

In the context of any developed industrial society such a statement would seem mere window dressing for the worst sort of government interference. Yet given the situation of Korea or the other NICs, it made sense. Although his and other governments made some bad mistakes in their policies, the end result was to build up new modern businesses that now stand on their own—despite some more than vestigial remains of government financial tinkering.

Perhaps we can better understand the problems of building a free economy by fiat—to any Western businessman a wildly contradictory concept—if we recall Japan's forced-draft construction of its catch-up economy in Meiji days. For the Meiji experience remains the model for all these capitalist development states.

Japan's self-imposed modernization was fortunate in its timing. Visiting Europe at the high tide of its second Industrial Revolution, the young Meiji reformers could witness the emergence of the modern industrialized nation-state. They were able to learn from ideas and technologies recently developed. They were indeed the prototype of the modern "learning" economy. Yet their reforms depended on two essential homegrown components. The more obvious was the existence of a dedicated group of managerial bureaucrats, the low-ranking samurai who had grown up managing the clans of Tokugawa Japan. The less obvious, but equally vital factor was a population comparatively well educated, with a growing class of merchants and businessmen who were accustomed to working together within the framework of a Confucian tradition.

In ordering up their cultural revolution, the Meiji reformers introduced a wave of new ideas and concepts to their people. Democracy, conscription, the franchise, and the notion of individual human rights were harder for late-nineteenth-century Japanese to get used to than railroads, newspapers, and Western-style haircuts. But with the imperative of economic modernization on their backs, the Meiji leaders tried to tamper as little as possible with the old Confucian work ethic they had inherited from Tokugawa days. To set up the railroads, steel mills, and banks of the world's first capitalist development state, they needed an industrious and fairly docile work force, people who would believe in the Meiji magnate Shibusawa's slogan that "productivity is a way of practicing virtue." With factories and ships to build, too much democracy might prove a distraction. In this dilemma, which Japan never quite solved, they prefigured the problems that Asia's NIC leaders were to face almost a century later.

The Japanese, however, enjoyed one short-term advantage that the late-twentieth-century Asian modernizers lacked. Their revival of the ancient imperial institution, with all its nationalist overtones, gave them a powerful, immanent legitimacy symbol, useful in justifying the popular mobilizations and sacrifices that the Meiji statesmen demanded.

The authoritarian leaders of Korea, Taiwan, and Singapore did not have this useful bit of political insulation. Instead they had to rely on personal or party authority, with often abrasive results. For if their cultures were old, the nations they led were new and unsure of themselves. It is small wonder that they evoked the ghost of Confucius, wherever possible, to encourage national and corporate effort.

In the following chapter we shall look more closely at the development economies of these countries, to see what different shapes they took.

10

The Business Society, Asian Style

We started with agricultural development, then light industry, then some import substitution industries, then export-oriented industry and then gradually heavy industry and high tech. We have a very cautious, step-by-step developmental program.

FREDERICK CHIEN, FOREIGN MINISTER, REPUBLIC OF CHINA

A Confucianist view of order between subject and ruler—this helps in the rapid transformation of a society . . . in other words, you fit yourself into society—the exact opposite of the American rights of the individual.

LEE KUAN YEW

Park Chung Hee, Chiang Ching-kuo, and Lee Kuan Yew faced a worse set of problems than the Meiji reformers of Japan almost a century before them. They assumed the leadership of countries devastated, weakened, or spoliated to some degree by war, bad or at best unenlightened management, and the effects of colonialism. (Some of these excesses, ironically, had been visited upon them by the Japanese imperialism of the Meiji reformers and their descendants.) Their greatest assets, like the Meiji leaders', lay in the sturdy work ethic of their people, their zeal for education, and their family solidarity. Add to this a traditional tendency to see government at best as a kind of father figure in the Confucian tradition, at worst as an impersonal power, to be placated or, preferably, avoided.

In this tradition government was regarded as the apex of a harmonious social order and its arbiter. Morally as much as politically, government was expected to guide as well as lead, playing the role of a stern, if ultimately benevolent parent-teacher. ("To rule," Confucius tells us, "is to rectify.")[1] People were

[1] *Analects*, XII:17.

expected to obey its guidance, preferably as personified by a father figure at the top. In East Asia, Lucian Pye and others have noted, paternalism is not a dirty word.[2] Except among the intelligentsia, the modern Western concept of government as a creature of its citizens does not fit comfortably with traditional Asian values.

In my own experience I have become accustomed to this difference of attitude, which explains much of the acquiescence to authoritarian rule. A Korean professor, incidentally an authority on Lincoln, once pointed out to me: "You talk of government of, by, and for the people. Here people have been used to government for the people, but definitely not *by* or *of* the people." In Jakarta a shrewd Chinese banker attempted to explain his attitude toward government. "In America," he said, "you can't be sure that Reagan will get another term. [Our conversation took place in the early eighties.] My English friends can't be sure that Mrs. Thatcher will be around next year—or Mitterrand in France. But here we know that Suharto will be around for a long time. In Singapore they know that Lee Kuan Yew will be around for a long time. You may not like them, but they impart a kind of stability to our countries. It's easier to plan that way."

All three leaders consciously exploited the latent Confucianism in their societies. In Taiwan and Singapore, various forms of Confucianism were taught formally in the schools. Koreans made similar efforts to develop group consciousness through "moral education" in the schools and company training courses stressing a Confucian work ethic. In Hong Kong and other cities where business was largely run by the overseas Chinese, the sheer strength of family Confucianism—without government sponsorship—played a major role in the rise of cohesive business organizations. Yet for all their cultural similarities and common influences from the United States and Japan, each of these rising economies marched to its own drum.

THE KOREANS were closest to the Japanese model. Coming to Seoul from Tokyo, a visitor would be struck immediately by obvious parallels. Companies would be organized on the same rigid hierarchical patterns. Korean company presidents would be called *sajang* instead of *shacho* and department heads *bujang* instead of *bucho*—both languages deploy their borrowed Chinese characters in much the same way—but the seniority systems, the complex of salary, bonus, and allowances, the heavy company indoctrinations of new people, and the

---

[2] In his stimulating book *Power and Politics in East Asia*, Pye wrote: "[In Asia] the relationship of power to the responsibilities of office accountability rests upon quite different concepts of power and authority."

inevitable university peeking order (for the top-dog Tokyo University or Keio graduates read Seoul National University or Korea University) were strikingly similar. This was partly from old tradition, partly from current observation and adaptation. If you have a business success story in the country next door, why bother to invent your own norms? In a catch-up "learning" economy there was little time for that. If the Japanese sold good electronic gear, cars, and ships, the Koreans could make them cheaper. Ultimately, if they worked hard enough, better.

In the mid-sixties, when I returned to Asia as a businessman, I had the peculiar fortune to serve at the same time as president of a Japanese company and as president of a Korean company, both of them subsidiaries of an American publisher, Encyclopaedia Britannica, Inc. At the time many Koreans still spoke Japanese. This was an inescapable heritage of their unpleasant colonial experience. (The use of *hangul*, the marvelously logical, if complex, Korean alphabet, was not yet compulsory.) So I could make myself reasonably well understood in Japanese. At least I could read the signs and a good bit of the newspapers. Our Korean employees were more obviously outgoing than the Japanese and more rough-hewn, somewhat lacking in the dogged administrative finesse I had come to count on in Tokyo. But they did work. If the crew in Tokyo would customarily stay at their posts an hour after closing time, the Koreans would stay two. I was not surprised when the Korean company, just a few years after it was founded, began to get awards for the best performance in the international Britannica network.

More than a decade later, on reporting trips to Korea, I was impressed by the same apparent dedication of company employees. At one construction company I visited, managers proudly pointed to their slogan—"Run, don't walk"—liberally placarded on the walls. And there remained the kind of determined hustle that was no longer so evident in Japan. After formal closing time, groups of engineers and technicians, wearing the same uniform jackets over their street clothes, were gathering for various on-the-job study sessions.

By the late eighties such wholesale dedication to work was wearing off. As government oppression relaxed and unions began to gain power, workers understandably began to campaign for their own betterment, as well as the company's. But for the sixties and seventies, the catch-up goals had been sufficient, even without official pressures, to produce a highly motivated work force whose members performed without complaint the tasks that management and a controlling government bureaucracy had set for the country.

Shortly after his military coup in 1961, Park Chung Hee gathered his group of technocrats about him and charted the first in a series of Five-Year Plans to put Korea's shaky, corruption-ridden economy on its feet. An appallingly dour man—one could not imagine telling him a joke—he was consumed by a sense

Lee Kuan Yew. Cambridge-educated barrister turned Confucian despot, Lee single-handedly directed Singapore's consistent prosperity. Jigsaw Productions

Park Chung Hee. A military autocrat, Park was the architect of Korea's high-growth economy. Here he is shown firing the first furnace at Korea's Pohang Steel Mill. Dong-A Ilbo

Seoul in 1950. When the UN forces first recaptured Korea's capital, it had been reduced to rubble—reflecting the entire country's devastation. The capitol building (left, center) was still standing. Korean Overseas Information Service

of mission, which grew with the years. When he wrote an article for the 1971 Britannica yearbook, which I helped edit, he modestly described his country as the soil and he, Park, as the "fertilizer." (It took a while to persuade him, for decency's sake, to change the term to "catalyst.")

In 1970 I had the opportunity to visit with Park in his office at the presidential Blue House in Seoul, in company with former U.S. Vice President Hubert Humphrey. Park was as friendly with Humphrey as he could be with any foreign visitor. (He remained grateful, interestingly enough, for Humphrey's personal intervention in speeding up shipments of kimchee, the spicy staple of Korean diets, to Korean troops fighting in Vietnam.) His talk centered on the American alliance with Korea, the ever present danger from the Communist north, and, above all, the economy. He spoke like a man with a mission, confident of his abilities after almost nine years in his job. He talked of mobilizing all Koreans in his "industrial revolution" and he meant it. Impressed by my Korean colleague, who had succeeded me in managing the local Britannica company, he asked him bluntly what *he* was doing for his country, and suggested that he might well consider government service. As the President looked sharply after us, going down the corridor, I could almost hear him snapping at a subordinate, "Lieutenant, get that man's name."

Over the years the general-President's attitude grew ever more dictatorial. Yet he was able to refrain from attempting the direct economic crisis management that was to lead so many other Third World authoritarians to disaster. Not only did he rely on his bureaucrats and newly founded think tanks for economic guidance. But, building on the foundations of existing Korean companies and some wealthy and well-connected businessmen, he fostered the development of that unique and uniquely dynamic Korean economic organism, the *chaebol* conglomerate.

More diversified than the American conglomerate, far more centrally directed than its Japanese counterpart, the modern *keiretsu* network of affiliated companies, or even its not so remote ancestor, the old prewar *zaibatsu*, the Korean *chaebol* are in a class by themselves. To begin with, they are huge. Between them, the four leading *chaebol*—Hyundai, Daewoo, Samsung, and Lucky-Goldstar—and their suppliers produce more than 30 percent of Korea's total gross national product.

Cars, ships, cosmetics, finance, electronics, construction, hotels, oil refineries—they make, refine, and sell a huge array of products and services. They are export-oriented. Until recently some 60 percent of the *chaebol* output was sold overseas, although Korea's own domestic market has lately got more of their attention. They are mostly family firms, in the Confucian tradition. The typical pattern has the chairman-patriarch sitting on top of the heap, with sons, brothers, nephews, and in-laws holding down as many important posts as possible. As of 1990, Chung Ju Yung, Hyundai's "honorary" chairman, had two brothers and seven sons working for him. Five of the sons were presidents of Hyundai companies.

In December 1990, I had a chance to visit with Chung at the Hyundai Group headquarters in Seoul. He arrived at the top-floor reception room—audience chamber might be a better term—accompanied by the usual screening force of international department heads and public relations people. The setting could have been duplicated at General Motors, Royal Dutch Shell, or Matsushita Electric Industries. But it was old Matsushita Konosuke, recently expired in his nineties, whom Chung reminded me of. Like Matsushita, he had received only a primary school education (although his profusion of honorary Ph.D.s and such could supply several academic wardrobes). He had the same natural ease of manner, reinforced by long-held authority. At seventy-five, Chung was already an industrial patriarch.

He had just come from Moscow, where he was in the middle of negotiations for a variety of joint business activities with the Russians. Earlier in that year he had been to North Korea, the first capitalist allowed (by both sides) to visit Kim Il Sung's tottering Workers' Paradise, for discussions about a possible infusion of capital and skills there.

Hyundai is a big company. In 1990 annual sales exceeded $30 billion. Its twenty-seven affiliates deal in everything from shipbuilding and petrochemicals to robotics. In 1973, barely a decade after starting its first manufacturing plant, a cement company, Hyundai built its first ship. A decade later it had become the world's largest shipbuilder. By 1986, Hyundai's new Excel sedans were pouring off the docks in North America.

Chairman Chung began this empire with a small trucking and auto repair business in the early forties. In 1947 he founded his first corporation, a construction company. "When I started," he reminisced, "I never imagined this growth. I was too busy taking care of immediate subsistence problems. We were all very poor."

The chaebol are new, as big companies go. A few trace their antecedents back to textile manufacture and other light industry during the Japanese occupation. Most, however, are postwar constructs. Hyundai's first job was repairing trucks for the U.S. Army. Lucky-GoldStar started off in the forties as a small cosmetics manufacturer, and went into plastics because it could not find adequate bottle caps for its products. Samsung's founder, P. C. Lee (Yi Pyong Chol), began with sugar, woolens, insurance, and, not so incidentally, heavy contributions to Syngman Rhee's government.

It was under Park Chung Hee's governance, however, after both Rhee and his successor, Chang Myon, had been overthrown, that the chaebol really began to take shape. From the first their relationship with his government was sym-

McDonald's in Taiwan—the ubiquitous sign of cultural "Californiazation" in Asia.
Peter Bull

Automobiles awaiting shipment. The Hyundai plant at Ulsan sends new cars overseas on its own shipping fleet. Hyundai Motor Company, Ltd.

Chung Ju Yung, Hyundai's long-time chairman, exemplified the power of chaebol industry.
Jigsaw Productions

biotic. Their peculiar shape—their sudden growth and their proliferation into so many different industries—was the product of necessity. Devastated by more than a decade of war and misgovernment, Korea in 1961 was a virtual bankrupt, kept going principally by American aid. The only choice was to export or go under. "We had no options," one *chaebol* executive told me. "We had to compete as a matter of survival."

In a jungle of rough new international players, with the Japanese economic miracle erupting on their doorstep, Koreans reasoned that only big companies, with concentrated resources and practicing economies of scale, could withstand international competition. One success, they predicted, would lead to another. And in many ways this proved correct.

Hyundai's Chung looks back on Park Chung Hee's rule with considerable respect. "He did many things that contradicted or deterred democracy—that's true," he said. "But he had strong and unique economic policies. Without them today's economy would not be possible. He motivated entrepreneurs to borrow money from the government to make profits. The government guaranteed the loans. Of course, if a businessman failed, he might even be imprisoned; so everyone worked hard. Most did well.

"Park did everything he could to bring people in Korea out of poverty. He came from a poor family himself. He entered the Japanese military school because he couldn't afford to go to teachers college. He hated corruption—so much so that people once thought him a Communist. But it was his concern for the poorness of this country that made him obsessed with economic growth."

There were failures as well as successes. In those cases the government would either bail out or close down, just as it would provide the financial muscle for the successes. For at least through the high-growth booms of the sixties and seventies, it was the government that called the turn. It was Park's boom. One of his first acts after taking power in 1961 was to nationalize Korea's banks. With this the government became the one source of corporate financing. That was just the way he wanted it. Park and his young bureaucrats used their funding power to force mergers, shut down losers, and urge winners to enter new lines of activity. The *chaebol* marched in line, for the orders and the pace were military. If Japan's was the bureaucrat's economic miracle, Korea's was that of the military man. There was no room here for dissidents. If a company wanted government help, its owners and managers had to be politically reliable. For Korean merchants it was a familiar bargain.

But Park had a lot of helpers. The national war effort in Korea had not only mobilized but educated. As in other Third World countries, the young bureaucrats as well as the company managers were fresh from the armed forces. Many owed their education to military academy, staff school, or specialized military training. After the military revolution the best talent in the Army turned themselves into bureaucrats, like the Meiji samurai in Japan before them. In Park's day some 70 percent of the government officials had military backgrounds. Plant managers and engineers in the companies—most of them war veterans—were used to obeying orders. None questioned the urgency of the economic effort.

This was equally true of the Korean labor force, the corporals and privates whose educated sweat made the Korean economic miracle a reality. They too remembered the horrors of the North Korean invasion and the privations of postwar political chaos. On the low rungs of the ladder of rising expectations, they could nonetheless glimpse a future far better than what they had. In an old tradition, they worked and waited, while productivity soared.

The meteoric rise of the Korean construction industry offers a classic case of this development strategy. It began with wartime and postwar reconstruction. A variety of Korean contractors, Hyundai included, set out to repair the shattered roads, reservoirs, and buildings of the peninsula; much of their know-how derived from contract work with U.S. Army Engineers and other aid projects.[3] From these sprang the Hyundai Cement Company, an obvious enough connection. Ssangyong Cement, now the country's largest, was founded in 1962, with government blessing—thanks to its chairman's strong political connections. Shortly afterward Ssangyong and other conglomerates began developing construction capabilities.

Desperate for hard-currency earnings, Korean construction firms began to export managers and crews to work on various projects elsewhere in Asia and, increasingly, in the Middle East. (After the 1973 "oil shock," the government pressed for Middle East business to earn money for soaring fuel costs.) As more trained engineers came out of Korean universities, the construction people built up their capabilities.

In 1976 the big break came for Korea's master builders: a billion-dollar contract from Saudi Arabia to build a huge harbor complex, starting from scratch, at the port of Jubail. Whereupon the Korean industry went determinedly international. Companies that had started out furnishing little more than mobile manpower to American and European contractors now aimed at turnkey contracts on their own for urban complexes, petrochemical installations, and solar-energy facilities throughout the world. It was high-risk business, financed ultimately by a staggering amount of government loans to overseas lenders. But it brought in handsome returns. By 1982 Korean construction companies were doing more than $13 billion annually, with projects

---

[3] For much of the Hyundai story I am indebted to Alice Amsden's *Asia's Next Giant* (New York: Oxford University Press, 1991), as well as my own reporting.

scattered over twenty countries, from the huge Congress Hall in Libya to the 71-story Raffles City Complex in Singapore.

In construction, as in electronics and shipbuilding, the Koreans' most obvious rivals were their old colonial masters, the Japanese. They relished the competition. "The Japanese can't begin to compete with us," a construction executive told me in 1983. "You can't get Japanese workers to endure the privations and long hours that Koreans take for granted. That is one big competitive edge."

Ultimately the overseas construction boom faded, but by the mid-eighties Korean engineers were busy with new projects for the Olympics and other work in an expanding domestic market. By the eighties also banks were largely returned to private hands. With this, corporations were doing more of their own financing. As in Japan a decade earlier, the hold of the bureaucrats on business had loosened. Korea was looking more like a real free enterprise society, with all the attendant problems of a strengthening labor movement, consumer complaints, and international pressure to cut down protectionist walls. The *chaebol* remained strong, even as they moved to meet new challenges and problems, both at home and in their markets overseas, which were beyond the power of government guidance to solve. Nonetheless, in outline at least, Korea's capitalist development economy was still the house that Park built.

Probably his greatest monument is the Pohang Iron and Steel Company, familiarly known as POSCO. With some $8.5 billion in annual sales this ultramodern plant complex in what was once a quiet east coast port city is now the world's third-biggest steelmaker and probably the most cost-effective producer. When POSCO was founded in 1968, international experts at the World Bank and elsewhere had advised against it. But Park needed a heavy steel producer to set the base for the country's heavy-industry expansion. The original funding came from Japanese war reparations, and the Japan Steel Company (Shin Nittetsu) for a time gave generous technical assistance. Its founding chairman, Park Tae Joon, was himself a former general. Park Chung Hee put him in his job and decided to make POSCO a government corporation—one of the few in Korean industry—because the heavy capital and technological investment required seemed beyond the capacity of any *chaebol* at that time. Nothing better exemplified the high-risk character of Korean investment.

Under Park Tae Joon, who has stayed on as chairman for more than two decades, POSCO installed modern equipment and antipollution devices far ahead of its time. Its labor policies were generous. In striking contrast to most large Korean companies, POSCO offered its workers company-supported housing and free college educations for their children. Its R&D work is facilitated by the Pohang Institute of Technology, a graduate-level research university founded for that purpose. Not only are POSCO's products competitive with the

best Japanese products but profits are high and consistent. In 1986, as an index
of its own development, POSCO began a joint-venture undertaking to modernize one of the plants of U.S. Steel (now known as USX) in California.

IN CONTRAST TO Korea's sprawling diversity, Lee Kuan Yew's Singapore is
almost incredibly tidy. Its 2.6 million people, hardworking, affluent, and at
least superficially self-satisfied, can boast the second-highest per capita income
in Asia (after Japan). The city is the world's second-largest port (after Rotter-
dam) and the world's third-largest oil-refining center. Local electronics production is formidable, and high-tech work is increasing. Fifty percent of the
disk drives used by the world's computer industry comes from Singapore. Some
3,000 multinational companies have offices or factories there, almost one-third
of them American.

Many multinationals have made the city-state their Asia-Pacific headquarters. (One Japanese company sends its outward-bound executives to Singapore
for training because of its "international" atmosphere.) Heavy business from
the world's bankers has made Singapore something of a "financial supermar-
ket," the way the establishment bureaucrats tell it. There is a contagious hustle
about the businesses, the banks, and the multinationals' assembly plants, not to
mention the ever present construction activity. But it is all very, very orderly.

Both the hustle and the order are the products of a unique modern one-man
show, albeit based on some ancient models. The city and its accomplishments
demonstrate what a hardworking British-educated barrister, Chinese by inheritance and inclination (who twenty years ago could not make a speech in
Mandarin), can do to re-create Confucius's version of an earthly paradise. For
his world of perfect harmony, governed by a wise but firm ruler, the Sage might
not have looked backward toward the Duke of Zhou if he could only have
known that Harry Lee's Singapore was just around history's bend, some 2,500
years in the future.

When Malaya, Singapore included, was about to gain independence from
the British, Lee and his young Straits Chinese colleagues first thought of their
city as the hub of a new multiracial Malayan nation. The Malays, worried
about possible Chinese domination of the whole peninsula, didn't see things
that way. They elected for the new state of Malaysia and Singapore to go
separate ways. So it fell out that, in 1965, Lee, who had earlier said that
"island nations are political jokes," found himself presiding over one.

He began with a strong political base. He and his People's Action Party had
destroyed the rival Communists, principally through clever use of Bolshevik
tactics. (Lee first made common cause with the Communists, to gain their
support, then elbowed them out of political control.) But the economic future

Seoul today, its city hall in the foreground. The modern metropolis contains only a few monuments to the past. Alan Barker

for an isolated Singapore seemed dim. The huge British military base, hitherto the island's principal employer, was being totally phased out. There was no local industry and few local entrepreneurs. No Matsushitas or Chungs were building embryo electronics or automobile companies behind their corner storefronts. Singapore's population was largely Chinese—although there were sizable Malay and Indian communities. The island's educational levels were modest. Most of its people were good at doing what overseas Chinese had always done, selling and trading on a small scale, in mostly family businesses.

With a few close associates—Goh Keng Swee and Sinnathamby Rajaratnam among them—Lee set out to transform the economy through a massive undertaking of social engineering. Their goal was first to confirm Singapore's status as port and entrepôt trader, emphasizing the security and order inherited from Stamford Raffles's colony. Building on this, they planned to turn their city-state into a financial and services center for all of Southeast Asia, as well as a manufacturer and supplier of goods—and workers to make them—for international companies. (Singapore was one Third World principality where "foreign multinational" was never a dirty word.) To achieve this, they had not only to educate and train their entire population in the ways of modern technology but also to keep them law-abiding, docile, and happy with the changes thrust upon them. Jobs, decent housing, and steadily rising living standards were stressed. A full-employment society was the government's first goal. To reach it, they needed the full cooperation of Singapore's unruly trade unions. They got it, thanks to the People's Action Party's long record of union support. As in Ikeda's "double your income" Japan of the same vintage, the unions exchanged independence for job security.

Although avowedly socialists, Lee and his lieutenants were firm believers in private enterprise, as long as the government could direct its energies. "More important than owning economic power," he had said, "is the direction, planning, and control of this power in the people's interests." Ridiculing the Communist "dogma" of egalitarianism, Lee opted instead for equal opportunity "so that those whose ability and application are better than the average can become more equal than the others."

Helped by the seventies boom in developed countries, Lee's full-employment goals were realized when Singaporeans showed their ability to do labor-intensive manufacturing far better than anyone else in Southeast Asia. But Singapore's work force was too limited, Lee and his colleagues reckoned, to squander on low-productivity work. Competition from the cheaper labor forces of neighboring countries threatened. By the end of the seventies, therefore, Singapore's bureaucrats drafted the blueprints for what they called "the second industrial revolution." This amounted to a national effort to move up to higher levels of industry. Lee's first step in this direction was to have his National Wage

Council arbitrarily raise wages in basic industries by 20 percent annually. As one of his officials told me, with some understatement: "This put tremendous pressure on employers to have high productivity and develop new plants."

Such a program called for an all-out effort at intensive education at home and constructive salesmanship overseas. Describing what happened, Chan Ching Bok, the alternate chairman of Singapore's Economic Development Board, told me later: "People outside thought of [Singapore] as a little low-cost place where you would go to save 50 percent on your labor costs making a simple product.

"On the contrary, as our people grew more proficient, Singapore's labor developed greatly in its technical skills. We had to teach our school leavers the discipline of sitting down at an assembly line, then expand their skills so that they can perform ever more complex tasks. Thus they graduated from the level of making electric irons to tool-and-die manufacture and lately to the higher forms of high-tech manufacture. Take the computer disk drive . . .

"At the beginning of the eighties we began to emphasize special services. In a sense the service sector of the economy was succeeding manufacturing. We have had great increases in our banking facilities, designer engineering studios, data processing, as well as more modest services."

WHEN I VISITED Singapore in 1984, it was the twenty-fifth anniversary of the city-state's independence—and, by an interesting coincidence, the title year of George Orwell's book about Big Brother. In the course of a long reporting trip, I had set myself the mission of finding out how many little brothers were helping the Prime Minister run this intensely paternalistic state. There were surprisingly few. Short of land and population, the island state has been understandably short of administrative talent. Again and again, in my interviews, I discovered that many of Singapore's leading civil servants held two or more jobs. An officer of Singapore Airlines would concurrently hold a job on the Development Board. A banker would also hold a post in the Monetary Authority. The director of the government shipyards might also play a leading role in public works projects. I estimated that about fifty senior bureaucrats ran the whole island country, presiding over an interlocking network of party, government, and semi-public activities. (The nominally independent labor unions, for example, were actually dominated by government or party administrators—with roughly the same amount of freedom as their counterparts in Beijing.)

Most of the senior people I met were bureaucrats of some years' standing; others had academic backgrounds. Some had come from business; nor was it unusual for a government official to be spun off into business when, as often happened, a government enterprise was privatized. All were predictably solid supporters of Lee Kuan Yew. They had few visible social graces. With rare exceptions they exhibited the smugness of modern-day mandarins who had passed their examinations and knew what was good for the people as thoroughly as their ancient Chinese predecessors. They had an embarrassing habit, in fact, of referring to Singapore's working population as "digits." ("Better not print that," one of them warned me. "It might be misinterpreted.")

Yet they were quite proud of their well-educated work force. More than one-third of all Singaporeans go on to the university or a technical college after they graduate from secondary school. Illiteracy, a formidable problem in 1950, is down to 4 percent today. (English is generally used, although the study of Mandarin Chinese is pushed by the government.) The education Singapore most prizes is not, however, the cultural sort that Raffles had in mind a century before; it is determinedly functional, addressed to developing good performance in special and professional skills. "We have here," a veteran economic planner confided with some pride, "the world's highest level of mediocrity."

At lunch one day with a group of young Singaporeans—bank employees, advertising men, junior officials, and other useful "digits"—I taxed them with what seemed to me to be a suffocating atmosphere of almost constant government regulation. In a city where chewing gum and long hair on males have been officially banned and people who forget to flush toilets are given summonses by the sanitary authorities, books and magazines are censored and the use of cars in the city is strictly regulated. Heavy fines ($300 to $500) are imposed for eating on the new subway system or littering the streets. The government's ever watchful Internal Security Department polices morals, subversion, and sanitary violations with equal zeal.

My informants agreed that such regulations were irritating and sometimes obnoxious. But they seemed notably untroubled by their well-regulated living arrangements. (Some 85 percent of the people, for example, live in public or semi-public housing, where apartments are allotted according to the wage earner's official rank—department heads in one block, assistant department heads in another, etc.) Their answer, and that of most Singaporeans I met, was to compare their own high level of creature comforts and consumer goods with the far lower levels in other Asian countries—or, for that matter, with life in Singapore a generation before them. It seemed to them a good trade-off.

I asked the women present whether they resented the Prime Minister's recent directive, supported by copious TV advertising, that college-educated females must have more children than women of lower intellectual levels, whom statistics have shown to be twice as fecund. ("If we continue to reproduce ourselves in this lopsided way," Lee said in a 1983 pronouncement, "we will be unable to maintain present standards.") None of the women liked Lee's idea much, with its overtones of state eugenics.[4] But to my surprise there were few serious complaints. "We have these little irritations," a consensus agreed, "but look at how well we are doing. And we can do better."

Thirty years before, I had been depressed by the colonial stuffiness and self-confidence of British Singapore. The pervasive Chinese self-confidence of the new Singapore was equally oppressive. Lee Kuan Yew knew his people well. Working with the advantage of a confined space, he had installed this new mandarinate of technocrats on top of a society of overseas Chinese, traditionally hardworking and eager to acquire more skills for economic advantage, but politically passive and quite happy to be ruled and directed, as long as its family structures and work potential were not interfered with.

An eloquent spokesman and a shrewd international statesman, quick to defend Western values and the rule of law (as long as neither interfered overmuch with his government's authority), Lee attracted investment and support—as well as worshipful editorials in the American and European press—because of his calculated openness and the obvious competence of his technocrats. In a sense Lee Kuan Yew had reinvented Confucianism, put it in modern dress, and turned its ancient stress on harmony and unity of the realm into a code of patriotism for his new nation. He will go down in history as one of the few brilliant politico-economic minds of his day. I would not like to live in his town, however.

Over the years Big Brother Lee's velvet-gloved rule has grown more capricious. People have been arrested and jailed without trial under the state's Internal Security Act, or tried and sentenced on trumped-up charges. (Trial by jury was abolished in Singapore in the late sixties.) The most vicious sort of vendettas have been waged against a few courageous souls who dared to oppose various acts of government oppression, from former Solicitor General Francis Seow and Joshua Jeyaretnam, for some years the single opposition member in Singapore's legislature, to a group of young Catholic social workers.[5]

[4] Whereas women college graduates who worked were allowed tax deductions for each child, women with little education were at one point offered financial incentives for submitting to sterilization. (This policy was later abandoned.)

[5] Both Seow and Jeyaretnam were victims of a systematic persecution that included everything from rigged legal "judgments" for tax evasion and libel to disbarment—also on dubious legal pretexts. Seow was hounded out of the country simply for having expressed opposition to various government policies. Jeyaretnam's "conviction" for alleged misappropriation of his party's funds was overturned by the Privy Council, to whom he had made a Commonwealth appeal, with the comment that he and a colleague had been "fined, imprisoned and publicly disgraced for offenses of which they were not guilty." (Subsequently, Lee's government denied the right of Singaporeans to appeal to the Privy Council in the future.) The Catholic social workers, who had tried to correct some abuses of human rights, were prosecuted in 1987 for being part of a "Marxist conspiracy."

Lee's control has extended to restricting the sales of Western newspapers and magazines—such as *The Wall Street Journal* and the *Far East Economic Review*—whose criticisms of Singapore government policy his bureaucrats found disturbing. Again there has been little complaint from Singapore's citizenry. There are signs, however, that foreign banks and businesses have begun to resent some of the mandarins' economic control activities.

Starting in the early eighties, Lee and his all-seeing bureaucracy have tried ever more energetically to formalize the cult of the Confucian society, by way of explaining why freedom must be limited in the interests of pursuing the good life for all. Lee's motives are the same, essentially, as those that inspired Tokugawa Ieyasu three centuries ago to set up his stabilizing four-class society of warrior, farmer, artisan, and merchant on the ruins of old feudal Japan. Lee's task has been more complex. (Tokugawa was untroubled by worldwide TV news and irritating foreigners talking about civil rights.) Yet Lee has done a fairly good job, according to his lights, with his three-tier cosmos—mandarin bureaucrats on top, hardworking "digits" on the bottom, leading merchants and businessmen and a closely watched professional class in between.

It cannot last forever. Nor could it have worked in a larger polity. But for the overseas Chinese who live in the ever more freshly poured concrete of the anachronistically named "Garden City," Singapore living is not bad. Their families prosper in a way they have not for long generations past. And if the ruler is wise, one puts up with his eccentricities. (How happy are the subjects of the Duke of Zhou!) It takes a docile electorate indeed to applaud pronouncements like the statement of Prime Minister Goh Chok Tong, Lee's anointed successor, who told his subjects before taking office in 1990: "If people behave in a way that threatens the wider interests of Singapore, they will feel the firm smack of the government. That must be so, because if you loosen the reins so much that people run all over Singapore, it can't be good for Singapore. Every jockey in a race carries a whip to goad his horse to perform better."

THE OTHER CHINESE city-state, Hong Kong, is everything that Singapore is not—and vice versa. Where Singapore makes a fetish of planning, Hong Kong relies more on enterpreneurship. Where Singapore's mandarins, like Japan's, constantly look over the businessman's shoulder, Hong Kong's colonial British bureaucrats and their Chinese understudies have preserved a cult of noninterference; theirs to maintain and protect the level playing field, not run on it. Where Singapore dotes on long-range plans, Hong Kong likes quick profits. As the late Richard Hughes, the expansive Australian journalist and Hong Kong chronicler, epitomized the Hong Kong formula for success: "low taxes, no controls, quick profits, hard work, laissez-faire."

Even more than Singapore, Hong Kong is a Chinese city. Its six million people, their numbers swollen in the sixties and seventies by a huge emigration from the Chinese mainland, turn out a bewildering variety of products from their small family-run companies—only a few of which have grown into large international corporations. The world's largest exporter of textiles and clothing, Hong Kong also makes significant amounts of electronics gear, plastics, toys, and ships. Its gross national product has soared from $1 billion in 1960 to some $63 billion in 1989—most of it exported.

Hong Kong is the largest container port in the world. Its network of financial services, from huge banks to street-corner moneylenders, has made it the world's fourth-ranking financial center, just below New York, London, and Tokyo. Its wealth is quickly gained and often just as quickly squandered. Joseph Schumpeter's principle of capitalism's "creative destruction" has no better exemplar. While its business and financial center, with its Babel of soaring high-rise office buildings and glitzy shopping palaces, makes even New York seem shopworn by comparison, most of its products are pounded out in squalid back-street workshops. At least half of its people are packed into rabbit-warren tenements, crowded and dirty.

Hong Kong got its start through cheap labor and hard, painstaking work. Its largely refugee population toiled long hours at just above subsistence wages in order to survive. Just as tourists first knew it as a place where a good suit could be made cheap and delivered within twenty-four hours of the fitting, American, European, and Japanese manufacturers came to know it as a place where goods could be manufactured at incredibly low cost but still meet quality standards.

This was only the beginning. As Hong Kong's little family companies prospered, they were quick to turn to more complex products. These they could export on their own, although their small size restricted them to products that could readily be mass-produced on assembly lines. The 100,000 workers in Hong Kong's rather rudimentary electronics industry were divided, as of 1990, among 1,500 companies!

Underlying the cheap labor and the good prices were two obvious "givens." They were the basic factors that transformed the placid Crown Colony of the fifties into the export prodigy of the eighties. One was the presence of British law and order. For all its old colonial stuffiness, this set a stable political flooring under the wild competitiveness of Hong Kong business. Their support did not approach the Big Brother government guidance to business found in Singapore, Korea, and Japan; yet British colonial governors nevertheless did their best to provide a favorable business climate. This included offering a far greater range of educational and other public services than China or, for that matter, any Southeast Asian country could have given them. Merchants, manufacturers, and international entrepreneurs alike were free to concentrate on their trades—

thanks to low taxes, no exchange controls, and a marvelously broad-minded attitude toward incorporation and overseas profit and capital remittances.

Not that the remnants of the British Raj inspired some kind of patriotic loyalty. That has always been a rare commodity in Hong Kong. And the original "Europeans first" racial discrimination of the British was hardly appealing to those supreme racists, the Chinese. But the stability of British rule and the predictability of British procedure were precious assets in themselves. They represented a vast improvement over the capricious rule of a distant Manchu or Maoist emperor. With the British you knew where you stood.

A second and unexpected gift to the island state was Mao Zedong's "liberation" of the Chinese mainland in 1949. Among other things, this represented the victory of an aroused xenophobic Chinese hinterland over the Westernized maritime Chinese businessmen and bankers of the coastal cities. No one knew this better than the Shanghai merchants and moneymen who fled to Hong Kong by the thousands. With them they brought a certain amount of capital, but far more importantly the stored knowledge and instincts of a people with business in their bones.

Over the ensuing decades, while their old offices and godowns stood stark and empty at home, the Shanghai bankers and traders built up an extraordinary economic transplant outside China's body politic. Virtually the whole textile industry, the foundation of Hong Kong's prosperity, was the work of Shanghai people. Other entrepreneurs and businesses followed. Many of Hong Kong's postwar tycoons—the fabled shipping magnate Sir Yue Kung Pao among them—were Shanghaiese who reconstructed their old companies or started new ones on what seemed to be safe ground. Others, like Pao's fellow billionaire, Li Ka-shing, who arrived in Hong Kong in 1941 as a penniless refugee from Guangdong Province, parlayed shrewd real estate acquisitions into a huge business conglomerate.

By the late eighties Pao and Li were international business players, with significant acquisitions in Europe, Canada, and the United States. Other Hong Kong businessmen, closer to home, were reacting to rising labor costs there by setting up acres of "sweatshop" factories across the border in the free-trade zones of Shenzhen and other Guangdong cities. They enjoyed the active help and patronage of Deng Xiaoping's Communist modernizers. Even before Deng's era, through the darkest hours of Mao's Cultural Revolution, Hong Kong had remained the one window on the world for a politically landlocked China.

DURING THE PAST forty years I have visited Hong Kong innumerable times, enjoyed its creature comforts, marveled at the glories of its harbor, shopped in its glittering malls and bargained with street-corner merchants, savored its many-splendored cooking. I have never felt comfortable there. Perhaps its growth has been too obviously explosive and expensive. (Good central office space in 1990, incidentally, sold for more than $1,000 per square meter, right behind Tokyo and London and twice as dear as New York.) Its business rhythm, with time counting as money, resembles a continuous reel of speeded-up film. Crowds are everywhere, but they are purposeful. Everyone is busy doing business, and nervous about it. The extremes of wealth and poverty rival New York's. And the high-risk content of most business arrangements would repel anyone but a Hong Kong banker.

Borrowed Place, Borrowed Time, the title of Dick Hughes's book about Hong Kong,[6] seemed to me to tell the story. How long could it last? How long could the house of cards hold up, its stability depending on so many factors out of Hong Kong's control? Not the least of these uncontrollables was the prospect of the colony's return in 1997 to a still grimly Communist China.

In the eighties the house of cards came close to collapsing of its own weight. A few years after widespread scandals in the police and bureaucracy had damaged its old image of official integrity, the colony was rocked by a series of major scandals involving real estate scams on a multimillion-dollar scale and the grossest sort of insider trading. With the spectacular stock-market collapse of 1987, following New York's, came revelations of what seemed to be endemic corruption in banking and company acquisitions.

Belatedly British authorities started to impose a system of government control and surveillance. They finally faced the fact that Hong Kong's growth as a world financial center had put too much stress on an easygoing financial control system originally designed for a small trading colony.[7] Hong Kong, for example, had never possessed anything like a central bank. It made one look wistfully at the close, but clean air of Singapore.

For all the financial explosions over their heads, Hong Kong's workers and traders kept doing their jobs and building for the future of their family firms; their children worked hard at school, so they could be better managers when their turn came. Theirs is as close as the modern world comes to a consistent religion of work—a vital cultural underpinning to their extraordinary business success. It is a success that has not been approached, in recent years, in better-favored work centers in Latin America, Europe, Africa, or, for that matter, North America. Yet it has its equals in Japan, Korea, and all those countries where overseas Chinese have come to work and live. For in their

---

[6] Published by André Deutsch, 1968. Hughes himself, as he notes in his book, borrowed the title from the imaginative Chinese political apologist Han Suyin.

[7] Kevin Rafferty's *City on the Rocks* (New York: Viking, 1990) provides an excellent account of Hong Kong's recent problems, along with a historical view of the city-state's modern evolution.

Confucian world, obedience and harmony count for more than individualism and legal rights. Paternalism and filial piety go hand in hand. Family ties and connection building are permanent realities, far more than citizenship or personal development.

In his book *The Spirit of Chinese Capitalism*, S. Gordon Redding, who knows Hong Kong well, has made an interesting analysis of how Chinese family Confucianism has proved so successful in building competitive modern economies. Historically wary of government authority, Chinese managers have built their self-contained worlds on the basis of family or corporate family solidarity and self-perpetuation. On the basis of intensive interviews with Chinese businesspeople in Hong Kong, Taiwan, and Singapore, he regards this as their primary value.

Following Max Weber, Redding contends that there can be no capitalist development without an entrepreneurial class, no entrepreneur group without a moral charter, no moral charter without religious premises. He summarizes: "Confucianism is a religion working to stabilize and provide meaning for much of Oriental life and society. Filial piety, human-heartedness, paternalism, reasonableness, compromise, propriety are in the Chinese context religious principles. They are essential to an understanding of the moral charter and that in turn is essential to an understanding of the emergence of this particular class of capitalists.

"The economic culture of the Chinese is the aggregate of the shared beliefs of the actors in the economic system . . . It is the spirit of their form of capitalism, and the latter cannot be understood in isolation from it."

THE TAIWAN growth story represents a kind of halfway house between the seclusive family capitalists of Hong Kong and the mandarinate of Singapore. Its impact on the economic world is more comparable to Korea's. Yet its structure and its pretensions are quite different. There are no Korean-type *chaebol* here, and only few really big combines like Formosa Plastics and Tainan Textile. Rather there is a forest of little or medium-sized companies, almost 90 percent of them family-run and many closely connected. Jostling for business, they expand or contract, appear or disappear as the market dictates. Over them presides a determinedly Confucian bureaucracy, still pushing the levers of financial and administrative control against the growing pressures of an internationalist market.

The whole story is visible in the crowded, hustling, and gaseous capital of Taipei. Here is surely the classic environmentalist's nightmare of growth running wild. The glass-and-concrete castling of new luxury hotels rises out of a complex of seedy office buildings, ramshackle tenements, and garish advertising billboards. Thousands of little stores, manned by hustling proprietors, do their best to pull in passersby. Everything is available, from genuine expensive to counterfeit cheap. Street peddlers and hucksters are part of the landscape. Restaurants, bars, and honky-tonks offer inexhaustible variety in cuisine and entertainment to the crowds of Chinese "salarymen" and well-dressed "office ladies," in the Japanese parlance, coming out of shiny new corporate head-quarters and fortresslike government bureaus. The packed streets come as close to total operational gridlock as I have experienced anywhere (Tokyo and Manila included). Double-parking makes a shambles of curbs and sidewalks, as Jaguars, Mercedeses, and top-of-the-line Toyotas bring the big traders and shoppers downtown from their hilltop residences on the city periphery.

There are other crowded Asian metropolises, but they hang together some-how. They are of a piece. Taipei suggests a curious split personality, a city that has yet to find an identity. Its hodgepodge of Japanese provincial architecture, sprawling South China construction, and stark public buildings in Chiang Kai-shek modern reflects a confusion of mind that has intensified rather than diminished with time. Is this the capital of a new independent island country? The headquarters of a world economic giant? The business metropolis of a reuniting China? Or is it the secluded fortress redoubt of an outlaw trader, scorned by outsiders but at the same time contemptuous of them, particularly when its bureaucrat guardians look at the $70 billion in hard-currency reserves safely tucked away in their vaults?

The basic problem of identity has yet to be solved. It is compounded by the gulf that still exists, forty-five years after Chiang Kai-shek's occupying troops moved in, between the native Taiwanese and the mainlanders. The gulf is being bridged. Lee Teng-hui, the astute Japanese-educated agronomist who is now Taiwan's President, is the first Taiwan-born person to hold that office. The old Kuomintang men in the Legislative Yuan who still stubbornly represent their old provinces on the Chinese mainland are dying off, inevitably if grad-ually—as reluctant to leave the planet as their spiritual counterparts, the an-cient Communists in Beijing.

The current generation of Taiwan people tends to be impatient with the old island versus mainland distinctions. Yet to many Taiwanese the Guomindang government had long represented an alien, repressive force. (Until 1945 Tai-wan people had lived apart from their mainland cousins longer than Americans have lived apart from England.)

I met my first Taiwanese during World War II. Seaman Ng had been picked up by a U.S. Navy submarine after his ship, a Japanese freighter, had been tor-pedoed. When I asked him his nationality at the Pearl Harbor interrogation cen-ter, he said he was Taiwanese; he was dedicated, he explained, to gaining Taiwan's independence from both Japan and China. This was news to me, as it

Daewoo Shipyard is a flourishing example of the drive that made Korea the world's largest shipbuilder. Korean Overseas Information Service

Chiang Ching-kuo, son of Chiang Kai-shek, realistically supported economic expansion for Taiwan, tacitly abandoning his father's goal to recapture the Chinese mainland militarily. Coordination Council for North American Affairs

Computer testing in Taipei. Small labor-intensive factories like this one were the key to Taiwan's postwar growth. Coordination Council for North American Affairs

would be to most Americans. It took some years of exposure to Asian realities before we began to realize that most Taiwanese shared Seaman Ng's sentiments.

For the first ten years or so of the Kuomintang[8] occupation the Taiwan people kept their heads down. In the manner of most maritime Chinese, they concentrated on starting up businesses and making some money. Their young people went into the newly established Chinese schools and colleges, along with the children of the emigrant Kuomintang officers and bureaucrats. Most of the males did conscript service in the large, well-equipped, American-trained Nationalist Army, formally dedicated to recapturing all of China from the Communist "bandits." Only one political party was allowed. Dissent from orders was suppressed by Chiang's secret police with the same efficiency displayed by their Maoist counterparts across the water. Taiwan, the official fiction held, was the temporary capital of the Republic of China, of which the island was merely one province.

About the middle of the 1960s, however, just when Ikeda's new economic drive was taking hold in Japan and Park Chung Hee's bureaucrats in Korea were developing their first Five-Year Plan, things began to change in Taiwan as well. Chiang Ching-kuo moved to the forefront, acting as support and then proxy for his ailing father. Already Vice Premier and boss of the security and defense forces, Chiang now took over as chairman of the Council for International Economic Cooperation and Development. This operational think tank, loaded to the gunwales with economists and other technocrats, was designed to move the economy into high gear. Now firmly in control, Chiang, an astute realist, edged his colleagues—or at least a significant portion of them—toward the decision that Taiwan had better start living on its own, shelving the dream of mainland invasion in favor of building a strong economy where they lived. Much underrated by his international contemporaries at the time, he is now justly respected as the Republic of China's "great reformer."

K. Y. Yin had already set the course for Taiwan's industrial growth, as noted above, by privatizing government-run corporations and encouraging the development of a new entrepreneurial class; by 1960, more than 7,000 new factories were in business. Following the same path, K. T. Li, as Minister for Economic Affairs, established the first Export Processing Zone at Kaohsiung in 1965, just as U.S. aid programs were being phased out. He and his economist colleagues were able to count on Chiang's active support in their economic restructuring.

Attracted by cheap land, duty-free imports, and cheap, but efficient labor—docile under Taipei's strong anti-union government—more American and Japanese transnationals began to set up plants on the island. There they could

---

[8] Although the pinyin orthography spells this Guomindang, I have used Kuomintang out of deference to the prevailing official Wade-Giles transliteration used in Taiwan.

assemble, process, or make products for export to the United States or other advanced countries, to be sold under a wide variety of local brand names. This marriage of convenience worked out well for all concerned. The foreign multinationals realized impressive profits. (Between 1965 and 1974 the Kaohsiung foreign investors earned some $930 million on their investment of $64 million.) In turn Taiwan's managers, workers, and bureaucrats gained a valuable exposure to modern industrial practice.

Offshore manufacturing has remained a useful prop for Taiwan's economy. Even today most Americans who complain about Taiwan's $18 billion annual trade imbalance with the United States fail to realize that a good bit of this comes from the cut-rate offshore manufacturing of American firms.

Local businesses began to piggyback on the foreigners, importing ever more techniques and ideas for Taiwan's version of the "learning" economy. U.S. government offshore purchasing for the Vietnam war effort also helped hugely. Now overseas Chinese businessmen in turn began to invest in Taiwan. Its banks growing on the gratifying savings rate of its people, the government began to assist new Taiwan companies more actively.

Before the sixties, capitalism had been something of a dirty foreign word in a Taiwan still committed to reconstructing the economy on the basis of Sun Yat-sen's original socialist principles. As the American-educated technocrats gained more influence, this attitude changed. Through the opening acts of Taiwan's peculiar economic "miracle play," however, the bureaucracy dictated both monetary and fiscal policy without any restraints.

Chiang's Nationalist government, it must be said, had learned a great deal from the economic disasters over which his father presided in his last years of power on the mainland. Inflation was a special bugaboo. Not for Taiwan, therefore, was the high-risk policy pursued by Park's technocrats in Seoul. Growth was carefully controlled and government reserves carefully husbanded. (Much investment had originally come from landlord compensation during land reform.) Nor was there anything like the wholesale borrowing from foreign banks which took place in Korea. Heavy borrowing from abroad had not helped the Nationalists hold the mainland. Financial self-support was a new imperative on Taiwan.

After the first flurry of import substitution subsided, exports became the name of the game—direct exports as well as the processed exports of the multinationals in the free-trade zones. For the next two decades Taiwan's trade figures, like Singapore's, would rival the sum of its gross domestic product. As their reputation grew internationally, the Taiwan manufacturers and assemblers were pressed into service to make brand-name products for American as well as Japanese companies. It is only in recent years that Taiwan products began selling under their own brand names.

The Walsin companies in Taipei are typical of the tightly run family businesses that have powered Taiwan's economy. Chiao Ting Biao, the chairman,
founded the Walsin wire and cable company in the mid-sixties, when the
business boom had barely started. "I was a worker's worker," he recalls. "I did
everything. I was the factory director, the chief engineer, the president . . . In
those days the country's economy was our top priority. Everything was done for
the sake of development, for economic advancement."

The company began manufacturing cables. The government offered them
tax breaks to get started—and waived duties on machinery they imported.
Today one-third of Taiwan's telephone calls are channeled through wires made
by Walsin. It is a family company. A few years ago, after twenty years in
charge, the chairman turned over management to his two sons. Although stock
is sold to the public, the family owns the controlling shares.

"We may have started as a cable company," said Chiao's son, Yu Lon, "but
we have diversified into many new areas, semiconductors and specialized steel
among them.

"We started out as a company for the domestic market. Now every time we
pick up the phone, it is some government official telling us to export more. There
seems to be an enormous amount of pressure to earn that foreign exchange."

THE EVER RISING trade figures—exports were pushing the $70 billion market
annually by 1991 (GNP for that year being $178 billion)—had for some years
posed serious imbalance problems with Taiwan's trading partners, notably the
United States. Despite the continuing purchases of Taiwan's goods by Americans and the massive jump start given the isolated republic's economy by U.S.
aid through the fifties, Taiwan's bureaucrats had been slow to drop their high
tariff walls against imports. Like their wing mates in East Asia's "flying geese"
school of economic catch-up, Taiwan's businessmen and bureaucrats had stood
neoclassical economic laws on their collective head in patterning their own
version of the capitalist development state.

As at first in Korea, they chose the option of fast, export-oriented growth for
Taiwan, but at the cost of neglecting to build up a stable economic (and social)
infrastructure. Less risk-taking than the Koreans, Taiwan planners relied on
often draconian financial controls to keep the economy from slipping its moor-
ings. Despite the government's support of medium-sized businesses, heavy industry and the beginnings of high tech were set up under official auspices. The
new China Steel Corporation, like POSCO in Korea, took shape as a government business, after private investors showed little enthusiasm for putting their
money in.

Until 1985 all of Taiwan remained under martial law, with political dissidence ruthlessly suppressed. As in Singapore, however, popular acquiescence—or resignation—to autocratic rule was a by-product of the country's growing affluence. For a society traditionally disposed to obey its mandarinate, this was not a hard bargain to strike. To shore up its claim to legitimacy, the government did its best to keep up the forms as well as the traditions of Confucius, down to employing Kong Decheng (Kung Teh-chen), the seventy-seventh direct descendant of Kong Fuzi (Kung Fu-tzu), as president of the Examination Yuan, in charge of all civil service appointments.

Still the identity crisis continued. Native Taiwanese had only grudgingly been let in the old Kuomintang establishment. And a younger generation, for whom "mainland" ties had progressively less meaning, was vocally impatient with the official fiction that the island state of Taiwan was still the Republic of China, a sovereign state with authority over all of China's billion people, waiting only for the moment when its 20 million people could liberate their mainland brothers. For four decades, this country—or, as its governors maintained, this one province—had been living a lie.

Only at the beginning of the nineties, under Lee Teng-hui's patient leadership, did the government move toward recognizing the status quo of two Chinas, without admitting it. With trade and investment across the Taiwan Strait swiftly increasing, time seemed to be working on Taiwan's side. In the 1991 elections, significantly, the sponsors of total Taiwan independence—without even the pretension of ultimate unification—lost heavily.

The low point in Taiwan's fortunes had been reached in 1979, after the United States, historically the Kuomintang's patron, withdrew formal recognition, in favor of rapprochement with Deng Xiaoping's modernizing People's Republic of China. For a time thereafter, consistent emigration, mainly to the United States, constituted a formidable brain drain. Some 230,000, including many of the island's "best and brightest," left the country between 1984 and 1989. The outflow of hard currency was equally significant. The Central Bank, for example, reported a $15 billion leakage in the two years 1988 and 1989, as people took their money out of the country.

The brain drain has now lessened. So has another by-product of Taiwan's isolation, the propensity of local merchants to counterfeit or pirate other people's products with a sense of impunity. The flouting of intellectual property rights was another symptom of a kind of outlaw mentality that developed among businesspeople living in Taiwan's political limbo. Nor was a government whose legitimacy was officially rejected by the major powers particularly anxious to protect foreigners' copyrights.

Over the past few years the climate has changed in Taiwan. Internally, since the abolition of martial law, the trend toward democracy has intensified. Given a per capita GNP of almost $9,000 annually, people have begun to worry about the quality of their life. Internationally, the sheer dynamics of its successful economy have brought Taiwan the respectability of wealth. It is a country to be courted.

In an ironic way the triumphs of the maritime Chinese on Taiwan may have begun a new chapter in economic history on the Chinese mainland. Since the Tiananmen massacre and the subsequent hard-line political policy of the People's Republic of China, Western business and investment, if not Japanese, has grown cautious about increasing its commitments in China. But Taiwan businesses, on the lookout for both cheap labor and investment growth possibilities, have moved in. It takes little imagination to project the economic colonization of nearby Fujian and Guangdong provinces by the Confucian capitalists from Taipei. In the end, economic power may succeed in at least a partial reconquest of the homeland that so decisively rejected Chiang Kaishek's generals.

ON SEPTEMBER 28, 1990, the same day that Mr. Kong Decheng, Taiwan's only hereditary official, was presiding over the official celebration of Confucius's Birthday, a similar observance was being held in Qufu. Past the bulky old stone statues along the Divine Road in the Forest of Confucius, into the Hall of Great Achievements, with its portraits of the Sage and his disciples, a Vice Premier of the People's Republic of China led a procession of officials and house intellectuals, in the best Chinese tradition, to view the rites within the shrine. The recitals and obeisances were made according to ancient prescription, with the oldest surviving Kong, Ms. Kong Demao, also of the 77th generation (she is Decheng's sister), in attendance. Outside, People's Liberation Army guards saluted. It had the pomp of official ceremony.

More than two decades ago, gangs of Mao Zedong's young Red Guards had surged through Qufu, smashing hallowed Confucian monuments, in obedience to Mao's denunciation of Confucius as the apotheosis of all the bad "olds" in China. During my visit to Qufu in 1984, my Chinese companions, all veteran Party loyalists, had mentioned with some caution the possibility that the Master's reputation just might be rehabilitated. In the end, they conceded, Confucius had "taught many good things as well as bad." With some embarrassment they had shown me traces of the Red Guards' vandalism. That six years later Confucius is now given official respect—for the government-sponsored conference at Qufu is to be an annual occurrence—underlined the erosion of Party authority in Deng Xiaoping's China. The soul of Mao, the "Great Helmsman," wherever it rests, must be spinning.

"When in trouble, call on Confucius." Faced with almost total popular disbelief in their Maoist-Leninist orthodoxy, Beijing's aged Communist autocrats, like other fading dynasts before them, hoped to bolster their legitimacy with ancient tradition. "Modern Confucian thinking works wonders in Taiwan, Korea, and Japan," one can almost hear them saying. "Why not here?"

Any businessman or bureaucrat in Seoul, Taipei, Hong Kong, or Singapore could have told them—or, for that matter, the nonideological business moneymakers in their own southern province of Guangdong. For the new Confucian capitalists had not venerated the Master so much as they used his teaching and tradition. "Confucianism," a Korean woman scholar had once said to me, disapprovingly, "is a way of controlling people."

In all of these countries, postwar government mandarinates had indeed exploited a tradition of family loyalty, education worship, and an ingrained subservience to political power to forge a compact between authority and enterprise. In return for accepting bureaucracy's guidance and control, workers and managers could make and build their companies on their own, work hard, learn more, and, with a bit of luck, grow rich. But they would not have ideology shoved down their throats. There would be no political tests by a professedly omniscient Party. And if they wished to join the ruling class, they need only keep dissident thoughts to themselves and pass the examinations. Justice may be ideal, but harmony and prosperity are better. So the rationalization ran.

This successful trade-off would not endure indefinitely. All of these countries are now moving through a political and social as well as economic spiral of rising expectations. But over the last half of the twentieth century it has produced a remarkable economic achievement. They had reinvented Confucian ideas to help craft the new phenomenon of the capitalist development state, in a manner almost beyond the ability of neoclassical economists or Third World governments in Africa or Latin America to understand.

Their compromises between enterprise and authority have been up to now successful. They would remain incomprehensible, however, to their remaining Marxist compatriots in Qufu, as they vainly postured before Confucius's empty shrine.

11

China's Continuing Revolution

Father is close, mother is close, but neither is as close as Chairman Mao.
CHINESE POPULAR SONG, CIRCA 1960

Bombard the headquarters . . . To rebel is justified.
MAO ZEDONG, 1966

"To rebel is justified," they said, means that you can beat people up, smash their houses, and loot their possessions.
DENG XIAOPING, 1979

O f all the empires of antiquity only two made a permanent mark on history: China and Rome. They were comparable in size. If we superimpose the Roman Empire at the time of Trajan in the early second century A.D. on a map of China and its possessions—whether in the Qin Dynasty (third century B.C.) or the Tang almost a thousand years later—we find that they encompass roughly comparable areas, with similarly wide variations of climate, topography, and humanity within them.

Both were world empires. Their boundaries set by a combination of geography and military conquest, Rome and China both produced enduring civilizations that outlasted emperors and generals. Their languages and their arts, their religions and philosophies, their ways of life and their systems of governance dominated two worlds. Conquered and conquerors alike sought out their cultures and submitted to them.

Yet the two civilizations persisted and perpetuated themselves in strikingly different ways. Rome fragmented itself politically. The nations of Europe, east and west, grew out of Rome's decline. Yet it was the urbanizing culture of Rome—its laws, its arts, its literature—that supplied the brick and mortar of their development. In the end it was practical Rome's espousal of universalist, otherwordly Christianity that made possible Roman culture's essential survival, albeit clothed in diverse political and social garments. From Madrid to Moscow, the West, as we have come to know it, built itself on Roman models—however much they differed in practice.

Rome itself is long gone. Although both Italians and Greeks can claim direct inheritance from Rome's citizens and the Greek-speaking Romaioi of Constantinople, they have evolved into separate modern nation-states. Italian is no more Latinate than Spanish. And modern Frenchmen, Germans, and Americans can all assert reasonable claims to Rome's culture and tradition. The monuments remain—the Colosseum, Hagia Sophia, the roads, the grammars, and the laws—but the singular people who made them have vanished into history.

China has remained China. For more than 5,000 years—however much its parts separated, however deep the cultural divides between the peoples of its north and south, east and west—the sense of an abiding Chinese identity has been preserved. The same people who walk past the Ming tombs outside of Beijing water their fields from Li Ping's 2,000-year-old irrigation system at Chengdu. The People's Liberation Army troops leaving Kunming to patrol the Vietnamese border are direct and conscious descendants of the mustached terra-cotta warriors standing at attention in the excavations of the old capital at Xian. They are all Han people. They are Chinese. For all the variations of dialect, they speak a common language, the same language that is written on the styles and tombs of Han emperors and the oracle bones of Shang priests before them, going back long millennia.

The genius of the Chinese was in cultural assertion and assimilation. As they spread out from their original home on the North China plain, they brought their crafts and culture to others and in turn made the faiths and ideas of others their own, Buddhism being a crowning example. Where Rome mostly left local creeds and cultures alone—covering all with the legal blanket of citizenship, the Chinese absorbed others into their civilization. All became part of a mantling Chinese whole.

As dynasties succeeded one another—whether native rulers like Han or Song or outsiders like the Mongol Yuan or the Manchu Qing—they maintained this sense of civilizational unity, too big for mere nationhood, that nonetheless insisted on a kind of political identity. More than citizens of a nation-state, the Chinese thought of themselves as dwellers in a world empire. Their very word for their country—*Zhongguo*, the "Middle Kingdom"—proclaimed a civilization that was at the center of things, giving of its riches, when necessary, to tributaries or, on occasion, to invaders.

The very bigness of the area and the obvious diversities of its people made it difficult for this unitary civilization to keep a comparably united political identity. It took the ruthless energy of the monstrous Qin ruler, Qin Xi Huang-ti, to force all of China into one administrative mold by 221 B.C. At that time Rome was still a rather small republic. Yet disastrous civil wars followed the Qin despot's reign, and later lines of emperors, for all their cultural achievements, had to devote most of their energies to keeping the vast country somehow together.

Some succeeded brilliantly. The Han emperors reigned for four centuries, sending their armies and their proconsuls south to conquer Vietnam and as far west as the Caspian Sea. The Tang Dynasty was even more glorious. The graceful pagodas and the still colorful tomb paintings in their old capital of Changan (the modern Xian) recall three centuries—from the seventh to the tenth—when Tang China might be called the center of world civilization. Civilized neighbors like Japan and Korea reflected the Tang culture in their own, and the always restless tribes to the west kept their distance, awed by Tang power.

Nonetheless, maintaining the unity of China was an ever present problem, unendingly magnified by the distances involved. As each dynasty weakened, local rulers sought autonomy. If successful, they aspired to empire themselves, but always within a Chinese context. From the northern and western frontiers, warlike peoples threatened. Farmers rebelled, squeezed beyond endurance, to make common cause with dissidents or usurpers. Over the centuries it was the Confucian bureaucracy, heavy with the legitimacy of rank and intellectual pretension, that kept succeeding dynasties in place, once strong hands had taken the power for themselves. By and large the people acquiesced, in their tradition. If an emperor had lost the mandate of heaven, there was always another one to come along. China remained.

IN MODERN TIMES the problem of keeping unity and order was tremendously complicated by the intrusion of the West, with its Industrial Revolution and its proselytizing modernism, on a China that centuries of cultural superiority had made complacent, self-centered, and resistant to change. The last imperial dynasty, the Qing, tried and failed. Successful at fending off the traditional attacks of "barbarians" from the lands to the west, the mandarins of Peking were confused by the new assaults from the Pacific. The guns of the Europeans and Americans had new factories to back them up. Li Hongzhang and the other perceptive mandarins who advocated "self-strengthening" by copying Western arms were unable to manage the popular awakening that China needed if it was to compete with the aggressive economies and polities of Rome's nation-state successors.

Throughout the nineteenth century, China suffered from internal turmoil as well. The Taiping Rebellion, in itself a backlash from the intrusion of Western ideas, animated the pent-up frustrations of China's peasantry against their rulers. Millions died in the ruins of sacked cities and burnt fields. And it took the firepower of the Westerners in Shanghai to put the Taipings down.

By the time the twentieth century began, an oddly mixed band of reformers, technocrats, revolutionaries, and warlords was trying to move China toward modernity. Chinese thinkers strove, often brilliantly, to devise ways for bringing both the technology of the West and its analytical thinking within the framework of their ancient culture. More pragmatically, generals and new politicians tried to duplicate modern nation building on their own by selling railroad concessions and buying guns.

Both the thinkers and the activists fell far short of their goals. The Qing government fell, but the revolution that toppled it collapsed in turn. Confronted by continuing Western economic imperialism as well as Japanese military attack, the Western-educated bureaucrats of Sun Yat-sen's new Guomindang republic failed as abjectly as the Qing dynasts before them to mobilize and educate the Chinese people to a workable politics and economics. Whatever successes Chiang Kai-shek's modernizers may have had were swamped in the tide of Japan's military invasion.

After 5,000 years of agglutinative civilization, China seemed to be choking on its own history. Was there no dynamism left in it either to resist or to assimilate the aggressive ideas of the West? Put another way, had the sense of national unity been worn too thin from the recurrent efforts to preserve it?

At this point—just before the midcentury mark—a new dynasty arose and wrested control of China from its custodians. The dynasty did not call itself that. Indeed, its original appeal was to overthrow all past dynasties and allegiances, to liberate the people of China now and forever from subservience to owners, landlords, "oppressive" philosophies, and old ways of governance. For the first time a Chinese government promised to institutionalize for public benefit all the angry revolutionary ideals that had periodically shaken China in the past—from the thirteenth-century Outlaws of the Marsh to the nineteenth-century Taiping rebels. Far from seeking the mandate of heaven, the new government relied for its legitimacy on its own interpretation of one type of Western thought—the dialectic of Marxism-Leninism.

Yet this same revolutionary government, after a brief few years of progress, ended by producing its own dynast. He was just as powerful and merciless in his way as Qin Xi Huang-ti. This new emperor was named Mao Zedong. He proclaimed a modern, socialist, enlightened rule of the people. But in the end he slaughtered opponents and burned their books as ruthlessly as the Qin emperor twenty-three centuries before him. In the name of the "people," determined to forge a unity for China on the basis of a new class ideology, he left China exhausted, impoverished, and embittered, with uncounted millions dead from famine, execution, and the warfare of his reign.

Mao Zedong died in 1976. After a brief interregnum a successor named Deng Xiaoping came forward and took control of the country. Aware of the disasters around him, Deng set about trying to heal divisions and to "modernize" his vast country effectively, in the tradition of other modernizers in the century past. He pledged himself to do so, however, without sacrificing the goals or the structure of the Communist dynasty he had inherited. A variety of emperors had tried the same thing before him.

In this and the following chapter I have attempted to tell the story of this last Chinese dynasty and the men who preside over it. Although the narrative covers the whole of China's explosive Communist half century, I have concentrated on the dozen years from 1979 to 1990 and my own experience of China in that period.

"WE ARE STANDING at another turning point in Chinese history. Starting last year we have launched a vast program of modernization, which in fact we call the Four Modernizations: the modernization of China's industry, agriculture, science and technology, and national defense . . .

"For us in China this is in a real sense a new revolution, and it is a socialist revolution. The purpose of revolution after all is to liberate the productive forces in a country and develop them. If a revolution is divorced from the development and modernization of production—on which the prosperity of any people depends—then the aims of this revolution are mere empty words.

"We were opposed to the old society in China because it oppressed people and held them back from developing the forces of production . . . The people of China chose socialism because they felt that socialism would bring China out of weakness and poverty . . .

"Now we are very clear in this view. But it was not always shared by everybody. For fully ten years the Gang of Four tried to edge China off its true course. They even had a slogan: "We would prefer a poor society under socialism to a rich society under capitalism.' That is absurd . . ."

The words are Deng Xiaoping's. Newly made Senior Vice Premier of the People's Republic of China, vice chairman of the ruling Communist Party, and Chief of Staff of the People's Liberation Army, he was describing to me the goal and scope of the reforms he promised to enact for China in the name of modernization. The date was November 26, 1979. Barely a year before, Deng had been summoned back from disgrace to lead his country. We sat in one of the audience chambers of the Great Hall of the People in Beijing, a spacious, but arid room ornamented by classic Chinese paintings of sea-and-mountain style with hydroelectric projects, in the best Maoist tradition. For an hour and a half, speaking with a poise and self-confidence that ignored his past years of arrest and harassment, China's new leader gave me a talking blueprint of his plans for the future.

My presence was almost accidental. After some months of long-distance negotiations, I had flown into Beijing to begin talks concerning a Chinese-language edition of the Encyclopaedia Britannica. This was just the kind of educational project that Deng wanted, for his policy, as he told me, of "opening our doors to the world." He had recently started the Encyclopedia of China, the organization that was to be Britannica's partner, as part of his program for reeducating his countrymen, and he was doubly pleased to give me an interview for the Britannica's yearbook. In the manner of an emperor granting an audience, he wished to go on record explaining his program to foreigners, and I happened to be there.

The very idea of a classic Western reference work appearing, free and uncensored, in the Chinese language in the stronghold of "Mao Zedong thought" seemed fantastic. And there were many people to tell me so. But the new socialist China of Deng Xiaoping was to be quite a different world from Mao's. Pragmatism would replace ideology. Economic modernization would replace Mao's "class struggle" as Chinese Communism's primary goal. Visiting newsmen and academics nodded approvingly as their Chinese hosts quoted Deng's famous aphorism: "Black cat, white cat, who cares as long as it catches rats."

Foreign businessmen saw a long-awaited green light for buying, selling, investment, and manufacture in Deng's assurances that China "must avail ourselves of foreign funding." Pentagon strategists began plans for military cooperation, hoping to play a new "China card" in their Manichaean Cold War struggles with the Soviet Union. In Deng's stated objectives to "make the mass of people better off and have them lead a happy life," Western and Chinese economists alike—many of the latter just released from Maoist jails—saw China moving toward a real market economy. There would be an end to the disastrous Communist planning of past years. Or so it seemed at the time.

There were good signs aplenty. Visiting China for the first time in 1979, after years of reading and hearing about its closed, unicellular Communist society, I caught a sense that the walls—or at least some of them—were now tumbling down. Beijing in late fall leaves much to be desired. Its heavy, coal-laden air is yet another environmentalist's nightmare. Its monolithic, neo-Stalinist public buildings surround and effectively stifle the still graceful survivals of faded imperium in the Winter Palace and the Forbidden City. Its traffic in 1979 was a confused mass of purposefully pedaling cyclists, looking cold, with only a few trucks and official cars pushing their way among them.

Sun Yat-sen brought off China's successful 1911 revolution, but his Kuomintang Party was unable in the end to control the country. Encyclopedia of China

Deng Xiaoping pictured during an interview (with the author) in Beijing, November 1979. Gibney Collection

Red Guards, 1966. Mao's Cultural Revolution was carried on by hundreds of thousands of fanatic young people; here some brandish Mao's Little Red Book at a rally. AP/Wide World Photos

(The imported cars and trucks of later years had yet to make their appearance.) Yet there was vitality in the air. The denunciatory Red Guard graffiti slogans of the sixties and the early seventies were being scrubbed off, to be replaced by Deng's new slogans for "the Four Modernizations."

Only Chairman Mao still glowered down from his huge picture facing the square at Tiananmen. His old companions, Messrs. Marx, Engel, and Stalin, had been removed, along with a good bit of the chairman's own pictures and statuary elsewhere. Down the street advertising billboards were going up in praise of Sony, Hitachi, and other foreign products now available. Women were wearing bright scarves and sweaters to vary the dull unisex Mao suits that until a few years ago had been compulsory dress. Now they could get permanents, use cosmetics, and even wear skirts without running the risk of censure for "bourgeois" habits. (Over the next ten years I was to find that changes in women's apparel offered the surest yardstick of "modernization's" progress.)

TV stations were featuring comedians (where they could find them), classic plays, and BBC English lessons instead of their old hortatory diet. After a long drought consumer goods were beginning to appear in the department stores. Food was more plentiful at street stands and in the markets. The countryside reported better harvests now that the Maoist agricultural commune system was being dismantled. The *People's Daily* and other official newspapers were saying good things about foreigners and international cooperation.

Above all, people were talking. Books and articles were appearing that would have brought condemnation or imprisonment just a few years before. Despite government disapproval, posters and manifestos were still being pasted up on the so-called Democracy Wall. Musicians were playing Beethoven again and artists were gingerly bringing some of their proscribed work to view.

There was an almost tangible sense of relief at the end of the Cultural Revolution, the ten years of destructive anarchy that Mao Zedong himself had instigated in 1966. Under Deng's new regime, China's intelligentsia—writers, scholars, artists, and bureaucrats—were coming back from exile or imprisonment. Tired but angry, they looked toward a new future, only too happy to blame all the sins of the past on Mao's widow, Jiang Qing, and her three colleagues, who had temporarily ruled China as the Gang of Four.[1]

The people I had to deal with at the Encyclopedia of China were a mixed bag. Some were veteran Communist Party officials. Others had come from teaching at Beida—the familiar term for Beijing University—or other institu-

---

[1] Jiang Qing's three partners were Yao Wenyuan, Zhang Chunqiao, and Wang Hongwen. All three came suddenly to power in the mid-sixties, riding on Mao's coattails, and were arrested in 1976. They received long prison sentences after a televised show trial in 1980. Zhang and Wang were Party politicians in Shanghai, while Yao, something of a cultural-political propagandist, worked closely with the widow Mao in Beijing.

tions. There were writers and translators among them, and some bright young people without much education. Casualties of China's educational shutdown in the Cultural Revolution sixties, they had been recommended for their jobs by Party insiders. The top editors and Party leaders had been carefully chosen by the Academy of Social Sciences, itself newly reorganized, for this was one of Deng's pet projects.

On returning to power, I was told, Deng one day received a presentation copy of a small encyclopedia from the Republic of San Marino, the small city-state in Italy nominally run by its local Communist leadership. "Isn't it a disgrace," the restored leader commented, "that San Marino has an encyclopedia, but we have nothing like this in China?"

Anxious to please, Academy scholars set out to plan a huge seventy-volume encyclopedia, to be completed in the nineties. While this huge work would serve ultimately as the country's standard scholarly reference work, the editors eagerly agreed to my suggestion that a ready reference section of the Britannica, the so-called Micropaedia, could be edited and translated in five years' time and made available to the public. After China's long isolation from the outside, a reliable information source with an international point of view seemed like a priority item.

And while I was in Beijing, the Encyclopedia of China management asked, would I give a lecture to their newly assembled staff on current politics and economic conditions in the United States, as well as my thoughts on the international situation? "Do you have any reservations on my topics?" I asked, quite mindful of the People's Republic's long record of propaganda politics and brainwashing. "No," was their answer, "say what you want to say."

So it was that, wrapped in my overcoat and muffler, I sat at the small speaker's table in the Encyclopedia of China's icebox of an auditorium, about to give a requested lecture on, essentially, what was going on in the world outside. There was one interpreter, a former political science professor at Beida, and he did his job well. As I spoke, looking at the intent faces before me, I could think of nothing so much as the days of Japan's Meiji Restoration, something over a century before, when foreign teachers were invited to "explain" the world of "Europe and America" to the eager young modernizers in newly named Tokyo. Like the Meiji Japanese—and in contrast to the rather homogenized groupies of modern Japan—these Chinese were not afraid to ask questions. They were good ones. And as we talked together over the next week, the editors conveyed a strong sense of urgency, like people trying to make up lost time.

This was understandable. For almost without exception the editors and administrators of the Chinese encyclopedia, like most of their intellectual peers, had only recently been released from jail. Most had been arrested and imprisoned during the late sixties, as the Cultural Revolution swept over China. Some had been accused even earlier and sent to work on state farms that were little more than prison camps, totally isolated from their families. Others spent from seven to eleven years in political prisons. Two of the editors had been held in solitary confinement for more than six years. Some still had no idea of why they were accused or who accused them. One or two of the leaders, released on Deng's orders, had the satisfaction of seeing their jailers thrown into their old cells. But for others rehabilitation came slowly, as Party committees searched through old records to reverse past Party judgments. One skilled editor, I was told, would be with us shortly, as soon as his civil rights had been restored. Others were being sent for, as their names were remembered.

Taking a brief excursion to visit the Great Wall one afternoon, Paul Armstrong, my colleague from Chicago, and I sat mesmerized as our new Chinese colleagues told us, quite calmly, their stories of prisons, exiles, beatings, and humiliations. And they were, by Communist standards, far from ordinary people. Some had headed important Party publications. One man, Yan Minfu, had been Mao's Russian interpreter and would later become a minister in the government. The editor in chief, Jiang Chunfang, was China's greatest authority on the works of Marx, Lenin, and the other Communist teachers. His deputy, Liu Zunqi, had been in charge of the Foreign Languages Press, a key Party propaganda organ. These were no "reactionary" enemies of Communism. For the Great Proletarian Cultural Revolution, as it unfolded in China, had the same effect, ultimately, as Stalin's purges in the Soviet Union. Here was dramatized the classic story of the revolution devouring its children—and itself.

THE GREAT PROLETARIAN Cultural Revolution was formally proclaimed on August 18, 1966, at a huge rally in Tiananmen Square, in the heart of Beijing. Before a cheering crowd of one million Red Guards—most of them in their teens and early twenties—Mao Zedong put on his own Red Guard armband as their Supreme Commander. Lin Biao, the Army leader recently anointed as Mao's successor, urged his volunteers to begin "a new era in Marxism-Leninism" by rooting out reactionary and bourgeois elements who had come to control the Communist Party leadership. "Bombard the headquarters," Mao had written days before in a "big character" poster. "How vicious they are," he anathematized, after a Party plenum in which he had begun to demote his supposed antagonists, Deng Xiaoping among them.

Screaming, cheering, crying hysterically as they waved their Little Red Books of Mao's quotations, the young Red Guards, who had come from all over China, shouted their loyalty to the Chairman. They were the first of some 12 million such who would be brought to Beijing in the next months by Lin Biao's Army transport units, to start on their return home a campaign of wholesale destruction of people and possessions, monuments and institutions almost without precedent in its random frenzy.

The Beijing mass meetings had been preceded for some months by a systematic campaign against intellectuals, university officials, and local Party bureaucrats in the press and at various meetings and rallies. Although the instigators varied, they all claimed to be acting on behalf of Chairman Mao, and they invoked his name with religious zeal. Many close to Mao, including his wife, Jiang Qing, had helped organize groups of the young and disconcerted all over China—students especially, in the best May Fourth tradition—to attack those in authority. This meant officials of the very Party that Mao led. His intuitive poet's leadership confined by the technocrats and planners of his own bureaucracy, Mao urged on the young his idea of a "continuing revolution" to uproot organizations, postpone technology, smash foreign influences or, as it turned out, anything "old." He was and remains the great reverse Luddite of the twentieth century.

Response came from a mass of discontented people for whom the promised revolutionary gains had been a disappointment. Misspent sacrifice had led to frustration. Now frustration was channeled into hatred, then violence—all apparently sanctioned by the highest authority. The worst in the Confucian tradition of obedience to the ruler, with all its historic confusion of morality and politics, was at once mobilized and perverted by the Communist emperor, who, in effect, authorized everyone to strike at his immediate superior.

Within two years China was on the verge of anarchy, as bands of Red Guards, shouting Mao's name, disrupted almost every type of organization— economic as well as political. By 1969, Lin Biao had brought in the People's Liberation Army to restore order, and to take over organizations with its own brand of violence. In 1971, Lin Biao, after apparently challenging the Great Helmsman himself, was done away with. He was succeeded by Jiang Qing and her propagandists, who continued to cause chaos for the next five years, settling thousands of private scores in Mao's name; they maintained a climate of national terrorism. It was mob rule. The crowds of people cheering at the humiliations and beatings of their fellows, as distinguished scholars, educators, and veteran officials were dragged out, dunce caps on their heads, to be abused, beaten, and often killed by kangaroo courts, ironically recalled the somber words that Lu Xun had written in "The Diary of a Madman" fifty years before: "I have only just realized that I have been living all these years in a place where for four thousand years they have been eating human flesh."

In the ten years that the Cultural Revolution raged over China, at least 20 million people were arrested, sent away to labor schools (for which read penal farms), arbitrarily relocated, dismissed from their jobs, or worse. (Deng Xiaoping's own estimate, which he gave me in 1979, was 19 million, but the actual toll may have been much greater.) At least 500,000 people were killed, generally after severe harassment or torture. Among them was Liu Shaoqi, Chairman of the People's Republic of China and (before Lin Biao) Mao's acknowledged successor, who died horribly in a solitary cell. Countless thousands of China's intellectuals committed suicide in despair. Like the massive earthquakes or famines that have visited China, this man-made catastrophe was on a scale too big for outsiders to imagine.

A whole generation—people now in their thirties or forties—was robbed of any chance for proper education or training. Millions of students and young wage earners in the cities were moved to the countryside, to gain "wisdom" from Mao's beloved peasants. Universities were either shut down or opened to people only on the basis of "political" qualifications. The mindlessness of the "anti-elitist" young Red Guards, encouraged by Mao's exhortations, had no bounds. Factories were smashed in fighting among rival Maoist groups. Taking as their text a Maoist denunciation of the Four Olds ("old ideas, customs, culture, and habits of the exploiting classes"), Red Guards ranged over the country in mobs, singling out not only monuments, temples, and libraries for vandalism but anything that seemed to them "bourgeois." Any grievance, it seemed, could be acted upon, once it caught the mob's attention. I once asked a Chinese educator about the widely circulated story that groups of Red Guards had smashed traffic lights because "red" should be a sign of progress—not a stop sign—in a Communist country. Surely that was a made-up story. "It was not," he answered. "It happened—and worse."

In a sense the pell-mell violence of the Cultural Revolution days resembled the bloodiest kind of religious war—but with the difference that orthodoxy was never defined for the combatants. Hence the warring sectarians continued to fractionalize themselves as they fought in smaller and smaller denominations, until the whole country was reduced to gang warfare. Mao's only command had been to "bombard" and "destroy." And as the gang warfare intensified, now with People's Liberation Army gangs and factory worker gangs participating, control was impossible.

Inevitably one compares the bloodletting of the Cultural Revolution with Stalin's massive purges, similarly destructive of Soviet life in the late thirties. But Stalin worked, as Hitler did, through organized terror, institutionalized, as it were, by the Chekists of the State Security. In China the terror was random. Its victims might be denounced by neighbors, by co-workers, or, worse yet, by people whom they never knew. Like Stalin's purges, however, the terror came from above. In her arresting book *Wild Swans*,[2] Jung Chang, herself a survivor of the Cultural Revolution, put responsibility where it belonged. Mao, she

[2] New York: Simon and Schuster, 1992.

wrote, "ruled by getting people to hate each other. In doing so, he got ordinary Chinese to carry out many of the tasks undertaken in other dictatorships by professional elites. Mao had managed to turn the people into the ultimate weapon of dictatorship. That was why under him there was no real equivalent of the KGB in China. There was no need."

AT OUR FIRST interview in Beijing, Deng ruefully summed up the damage done by the Cultural Revolution, as he saw it: "Their supporters often cited [Mao's] slogan 'To rebel is justified.' This was used as an excuse for mass violence. 'To rebel is justified,' they said, means that you can beat people up, smash their houses, and loot their possessions. Thus what the Gang of Four preached was literally anarchy. Before they finished they did incalculable harm to the social fabric and the economic system of China."

On October 6, 1976, just three weeks after Mao Zedong died, his widow, Jiang Qing, and her cohorts in the Gang of Four were arrested by security forces. In the orgy of relieved celebration that followed, all Beijing's liquor stocks were exhausted in two days. October, as it happened, was the Month of the Crab, a creature known in Chinese folklore for its selfish grabbiness. Crabs disappeared from Beijing as well, as households able to afford them prepared festive dinners of four crabs, preferably three male and one female, to celebrate Jiang Qing's downfall. Chinese like symbolism in their food.

One magnificent dinner, however, remained unserved. The day she was arrested, the widow Mao had ordered up an evening feast in the compact pavilion restaurant at the Winter Palace, her favorite and, coincidentally, the preferred dining place of the Winter Palace's most famous previous tenant, the archreactionary dowager empress of the Manchus, Ci Xi.

On a December evening three years later I sat down with some Chinese friends to a modest banquet on the same premises. (The chef had thoughtfully prepared for us some of Jiang Qing's favorite cakes.) The talk, as inevitably it did in China those days, turned to the misdeeds of the Gang of Four. Jiang Qing, a former Grade B actress in Shanghai's movie studios, had acted increasingly like a despot, while using Mao's name. ("I was Chairman Mao's dog," she later said at her trial. "When he told me to bite someone, I bit.") She settled old personal scores. One of our editors recalled that she insisted on signing his arrest order herself.

Thanks to her influence, the Cultural Revolution had begun as literally that, with carefully placed press criticisms of "bourgeois" cultural works. Through most of that period she personally censored China's art and drama. She banned Western music—for the Cultural Revolution's young enforcers, Bach was as much a dirty "old" as Confucius. She permitted only eight plays of her own choosing to be produced anywhere in China, where theatergoing, under whatever political auspices, is an engrained habit. "Eight plays in eight years for 800 million people," ran the post-Revolution comment. The Winter Palace itself was closed to the public for five years, because Jiang liked to enjoy her daily horseback ride in privacy on its grounds.

The Cultural Revolution, of course, signified far more than the realization of one woman's power trip. The Gang of Four and Mao's onetime designated successor, the doctrinaire soldier Lin Biao—Deng Xiaoping often bracketed them together in his conversation—were no more than its instruments, along with the Red Guards and their kangaroo courts. It was from the beginning Mao's idea. It was the last act of the Great Helmsman's efforts to keep his "continuous revolution" in ferment.[3] Mao's talk about harnessing "the boundless creative power of the masses" concealed his concern that *his* revolution might turn into an orderly authoritarian government by a Party bureaucracy, as had happened in the Soviet Union. His announced goal was to keep up a constant "class struggle" by workers and peasants, even if it meant disorganizing the very Communist Party that was partly his own construct.

There was no visible logic to Mao's power play. It sprang from the mind of an aging poet-dictator, in power for thirty years, who seemed to think of himself not merely as a revolutionary but more and more as a dynast, in the ancient Chinese tradition. To understand even partially this extraordinary psychodrama, played out on a vast scale, we must go back to the origins of Chinese Communism and Mao's rise to power at its head.

CHINESE COMMUNISM did not begin with Mao. The Party was founded in 1921 by two professors at Beijing University, Chen Duxiu and Li Dazhao, in a secret meeting at a girls' boarding school in Shanghai. It was a gathering of urban intellectuals, quite like its Russian prototype (which, incidentally, had itself set up shop at the Smolny Institute, a girls' boarding school in what was then Petrograd, only a few years before). Caught up in the frustrated idealism of the May Fourth movement, young Chinese were in angry revolt against the arid Confucianism of their traditionalist teachers and the rapacity of the warlord generals, who had made a mockery of Sun Yat-sen's 1911 revolution.

Attracted by Western science and "rational" thinking, they were nonetheless indignant at the continued spoliation of their country by Europeans and Americans. The revolutionary ideas of Lenin and the Bolsheviks seemed to

---

[3] The phrase recalled Leon Trotsky's much-discussed idea of "permanent revolution," which Stalin later denounced as dangerous. Mao, too, had distanced himself from the archheretic Trotsky in this regard.

offer a perfect answer. Here was Soviet Marxism, an avowedly scientific Western philosophy in action, which promised to destroy bourgeois Western governments as well as outmoded traditional thinking in a grand world socialist revolution.

Young intellectuals in Shanghai and Beijing as well as visiting Chinese students in Europe—Zhou Enlai and the teenage Deng Xiaoping among them—eagerly made contact with the new leaders in Moscow, ready to begin a revolution of their own in China. Mao was an early recruit. Then a fiercely independent-minded young scholar at Changsha in Hunan Province, he had made his way to Beijing, where he first got himself a job as a librarian assistant to Li Dazhao at Beida. He later returned to Changsha to help organize local Party committees. Already a budding poet, he had little formal schooling but had read widely both in Western revolutionary literature and in the Chinese classics—the Confucian books, the old historians, the strategist Sun Tzu, and *The Romance of the Three Kingdoms* among them. These mixed influences were to remain heavy on him throughout his life.

The Soviet leadership was eager to indoctrinate their new Chinese friends. If Lenin never actually said, "The road to Paris lies through Peking," he and his colleagues in the Comintern were thinking in that direction. For the next decade the Soviets were to exercise a strong, if in the end disastrous influence on their protégés, through a program of arms, money, and various expert revolutionary cadres dispatched from Comintern headquarters.

After Lenin's death in 1923, Stalin pushed the young Chinese Communist Party into an alliance with the Guomindang Nationalists. His primary concern being Soviet (for which read Russian) national interests, Stalin and his advisers felt that they could better control the *combined* Chinese revolutionary forces. Indeed, Sun Yat-sen, the Guomindang leader, was strongly influenced by Soviet thinking, especially in his later years. After Chiang Kai-shek succeeded to the Guomindang leadership—Sun Yat-sen died in 1925—the alliance wore thin on both sides. Alarmed by Communist successes in the Chinese countryside and, to a lesser extent, the cities, Chiang surprised both Stalin and the Chinese Communist leadership with bloody purges in 1927. In Shanghai and later in Canton, Guomindang troops and their street-gang allies almost destroyed the urban Communist Party.

It was here that Mao Zedong came to the fore. Unlike the intellectuals from the coastal cities, Mao had never accepted the conventional Marxist view that revolution must come through the urban proletariat. While China's Communist leadership, still obediently following the Soviet model, urged their scattered following into ever more fruitless uprisings in the cities, Mao and his military lieutenant, Zhu De, set up a Red republic at Jinggangshan (Chingkanshan), deep inland, an isolated mountain area on the Hunan border with

Guangxi. For three years they held out there, before being overwhelmed by Chiang Kai-shek's Nationalist forces.

Everywhere else in China the depleted Communist forces were in retreat before the Nationalist Guomindang. Backed by rural landowners and the businessmen of the prospering coastal cities, Chiang Kai-shek was fastening his hold on the country. In the autumn of 1934, Mao and Zhu De decided on a major retreat. Gathering up the surviving remnants of the Party and its armed forces—some 100,000 in all—they set out from Guangxi on the famous Long March farther west and north to the interior. A year later, some 8,000 survivors reached Yanan, in Shaanxi Province. There, finally safe from Chiang's pursuit, they set out to build a new revolutionary China, based on the peasant "masses" of the countryside.

Despite some verbal skirmishes with the Moscow-trained ideologues, it was now Mao who called the turn. In the years that followed, Mao developed further his idea that the "socialist activism" of the masses in the countryside was the great hope of the revolution. In the process he overturned all the accepted Marxist ideas of a socialism gained through the urban proletariat. He now set himself up, brilliant and overbearing as he was, as the leader of a new agrarian Communism. By the end of the thirties, after the privations of the Long March, there was no one to challenge him, and gradually Mao and Chinese Communism became almost synonymous.

It was in Yanan, an old, but poor city set among the barren hills of Shaanxi, that Mao developed his ideas of a new democratic revolution based on "proletarian consciousness."[4] Throwing away the classic stages of Marxist thinking, in which bourgeois capitalism inevitably preceded socialism—hardly an intent reader of the Marxist-Leninist scriptures, Mao was nonetheless always quick to throw the mantle of Marxist socialism over his own ideas—Mao outlined a new state and society based on the "dictatorship of a united front of all the revolutionary classes under the leadership of the proletariat." Who was to be a member of the revolutionary class and who should lead the proletariat? These Mao chose to define himself.

In 1937, Mao Zedong, now the Communist Party chairman, got his united front. In that year Japan's creeping aggression against China escalated into a full-dress war. Pressed by a wave of anti-Japanese feeling in China, Chiang finally agreed to cooperate with the Communists in the fight against a common enemy.

The war worked against the Nationalists, however, as the Japanese pushed back their armies and occupied Chiang's power base in the coastal cities. The

---

[4] Maurice Meisner's *Mao's China and After* (New York: Free Press, 1986) offers an excellent analysis of Mao's thinking in such matters.

Attacking "revisionists," Red Guards, here holding Marx's portrait, victimized older
Communist leaders in Mao's (and Marx's) name. AP/Wide World Photos

Mao Zedong at twenty-seven. In
1920 Mao was still working and
reading at Beijing University.
Encyclopedia of China

Chen Duxiu. A brilliant
academic at Beijing University,
he founded China's Communist
Party in 1921.
Encyclopedia of China

The Chinese civil war. PLA troops attacking the Nationalist-held city of Jinzlian, Liaoning Province. Encyclopedia of China

Victorious PLA troops march into Jinan, Shandung Province, in 1949. Encyclopedia of China

Communists, unhampered by the burdens of government, spread out over China's countryside with their guerrilla armies. Under cover of the united front, they preached the doctrine of peasant revolution, offering land, opportunity, and a bright future to China's poor and exploited rural underclass. Communist troops and Party cadres—under strict orders—proved to be models of rectitutde in their dealings with the people in their territory, in contrast to the often rapacious behavior of Chiang's soldiery.

At this stage reformist rather than revolutionary, the Communists worked to develop local youth leagues, farmers' groups, and neighborhood improvement associations. In the process they gained considerable popular support, particularly among rural people whom the Guomindang Nationalists had long neglected.

Even before the Japanese surrender in 1945, both sides in China were preparing for civil war. Despite a flawed effort at mediation by the United States,[5] heavy fighting was in progress by mid-1946, with the Communists strong in the north and northwest, while the Nationalists held the southern provinces. At first the Nationalists seemed the likely winner, with an obviously great superiority in trained soldiery and equipment. But their leadership was poor. And their morale weakened as the government in Nanjing proved unable to cope with rising problems of inflation, corruption, and failed efforts at economic reconstruction.

Meanwhile, Mao was mobilizing the countryside. Even inside the cities the Communists were helped by a spreading underground among China's intellectuals. By 1949, the issue was decided. Chiang Kai-shek fled to Taiwan with the remnant of his armies. On October 1, 1949, Mao stood for the first time in triumph at Tiananmen Square in Beijing. Surrounded by his old colleagues from the Long March—the diplomat Zhou Enlai, the Party organizer Liu Shao-qi, Zhu Deh, Peng Dehuai, and the other victorious generals, he proclaimed the founding of the People's Republic of China.

THE TASK AWAITING Mao and some four and a half million zealous Party members was a staggering one. They had to institutionalize their revolution and build China into a modern great power, where all previous efforts—from Li Hongzhang's self-strengthening to Chiang's Shanghai bankers—had failed. There was much in their favor. For the first time since the Taiping Rebellion

---

[5] The Communists were rightly incensed that heavy amounts of U.S. military aid were still being given to the Nationalists in 1946, at the same time that General George C. Marshall's mission to China was engaged in an avowedly neutral mediation effort. Aid ceased after the mission's final withdrawal in January 1947.

Mao in Beijing. On October 1, 1949, Mao Zedong announces the Communist liberation of China in Tiananmen Square. Zhou Enlai is standing at the far right. Encyclopedia of China

a regime had mobilized the latent populism of China's countryside. Rural China had won. The Western-oriented compradors of maritime China were for the moment disgraced—many already on their way to start over again in Taiwan or Hong Kong. The Communists' first sweeping land reform decrees were often brutally executed. Tens of thousands were killed as Communist cadres in the villages, their popular front tactics discarded, now declared open season on "rich peasants" and the landlord class. Yet in the light of China's history of rural oppression the reforms were undeniably popular. They were far less dislocating than Stalin's enforced collectivization a quarter century before.

The urban intelligentsia were singing Mao's praises. Even capitalists who remained in the cities were at first allowed to ply their old trades, although they were soon coaxed into "joint ventures" with the new government. For the common people of China—the workers and peasants in whose name the revolution was fought—life was better and the promise of an even brighter future beckoned. Resources may have been scarce, but for the first time in China's history a government was attempting to share them equally. With food evenly distributed, the incidence of famine decreased. New schools and medical care were promised, to improve the lot of China's people.

Mao and his generals even weathered a punishing war with the United States over Korea—albeit at the cost of almost one million casualties among their "people's volunteers." Thereafter they put their energies into building up a new heavy-industry economy on the Soviet model. Their Soviet allies offered considerable help. Led by the veteran Party bureaucrat Liu Shaoqi, Communist technocrats pushed to develop a modern industrial society, run by an orderly bureaucracy. Production figures burgeoned. Technical and professional people who had fled Communism in 1949 began to come back.

But this temporarily efficient central planning was only one part of Chinese Communism. For Mao had brought back with him from Yanan not merely trained Party workers but a myth. It was a myth that Mao had created, a myth of unending "class struggle" that would ultimately result in a perfect proletarian dictatorship. Although papered over with Marxist-Leninist terminology, the heart of the myth was the dream of an autocratic poet-philosopher from China's heartland, in his own right something of a political genius, to command a new people's empire, where ideological dedication, mass mobilization, and a united will would do the work of Western machines.

As a person alternately vengeful and compassionate, Mao had the charisma to attract and inspire millions, but he was never known to forgive a single enemy. He was a great hater. And for all his skill at strategy and planning, Mao remained at heart a romantic. The almost miraculous survivals of the early hardships, the Long March, and the Yanan encirclement had left him with a sense that people with the right "consciousness" could do just about anything—given, of course, the proper leader.

AT FIRST everything seemed to be going Mao's way. Thousands of Party-mobilized farmers worked on irrigation and land reclamation projects in the countryside, while crowds in the cities were mobilized against bird and insect pests, capitalists, foreigners, and other undesirables. The central government could pride itself on its tight control of the country. Thanks to a meshing network of local Party, government, and People's Liberation Army authorities, China's traditionally fractious provinces were for a time neatly under Beijing's thumb. But by the late fifties Mao had begun to worry that his Party was growing too complacent and bureaucratic, with a tendency to backslide away from true proletarian consciousness.

Some new spark was needed. Although never a friend of the intelligentsia—his Yanan speech on literature and art, punctuated by several writers' purges, remained an abiding statement that culture was suspect unless it served obvious "proletarian" objectives—he initiated in 1956 the so-called Hundred Flowers movement. "Let a hundred flowers bloom," ran the slogan, "let differing schools of thought contend." If he hoped to gain new revolutionary literary insights thereby, he was disappointed. Given apparent freedom to criticize, the writers did so, loudly complaining of oppressive Communist Party dictation. Mao and the Party's security forces reacted swiftly. In what became known as the antirightist campaign, hundreds of thousands of intellectuals were arrested and jailed, mainly on suspicion of having some ties with the West.

Nothing daunted, the Chairman announced in 1958 two other drastic steps on his continuing revolutionary road to Communism. The first was to march China's peasantry into communes, one lockstep beyond collectives. With this the entire countryside was turned into agricultural work brigades, with family entities sacrificed to mass living. Even tiny family plots were banned; child care became a commune responsibility. Farm workers were mobilized and directed like troops on the march.

The second, evolving from the communes, was the Great Leap Forward. Through careful ideological training—no "experts" allowed unless they were "Red" as well—Mao hoped to have China's peasantry produce industrial goods literally in their backyards, meanwhile vastly increasingly agricultural yields. This added farm production would support industrial expansion—and not so incidentally pay the Soviet Union in kind for its technical and industrial aid programs.

"Revolutionary enthusiasm," Mao said, would triumph over all obstacles, just as it had, presumably, during the Long March. And so began the period of mass meetings, slogan making, and exhortations to make tired people produce more. Overeager political agronomists set wildly unrealistic goals for the communes, while basics like fertilizer, irrigation, and adequate crop rotation were ignored. Almost half a billion people were mobilized on huge, but impractical rural construction projects, while the planting of basic crops was neglected. All the while, worried Party bosses sent in faked reports of huge productivity increases to keep Beijing happy and their jobs and privileges intact. Where disasters could not be hidden, they were blamed on "counterrevolutionary" sabotage, for which scapegoats could always be found.

The end result was a countryside scarred by tens of thousands of small backyard iron smelters that didn't work, fields that lay fallow, and dwindling productivity that resulted in famine. Precious reserves of coal and iron as well as food were squandered. In the three years following the Great Leap some 20 million Chinese died of hunger in their villages. Inland China was no closer to self-sufficiency than it had been before.

A huge people's militia had been created, however, as part of the Great Leap program. Those farmers who were not starving were urged by officials to try their hand at poetry, in another Maoist attempt to develop mass "revolutionary enthusiasm"! As Jonathan Spence writes: "Perhaps this aspect of the Great Leap came closest, briefly, to realizing a fragment of Mao's dream about developing fully rounded human beings with access to all their latent talents."[6]

While Mao burbled about the glories of people power ("Our nation is like an atom, capable of releasing tremendous force"), his loyal Party bureaucrats increasingly worried about what the Great Helmsman's efforts at reviving "proletarian consciousness" were doing to the country. Liu Shaoqi, whom Mao had named Chairman of the People's Republic, and Deng Xiaoping, since 1956 the Party's general secretary, now tried to repair the damage and put the economy together again. For a year or two they seemed to succeed. Mao kept temporarily in the background. But he found a new ally in Marshal Lin Biao, whom he soon installed as Chief of Staff of the People's Liberation Army. In the early sixties Lin set in motion an intensive campaign of indoctrination in "Mao Zedong thought" throughout the Army, first publishing the Little Red Book of Mao's quotations, a sort of poor man's Confucian *Analects*, that was to become the trademark of the Cultural Revolution.

For all his idealism a consummate bureaucratic infighter, Mao was by now convinced that Liu and Deng were taking his Communists down the bureaucratic road of "revisionism," following Nikita Khrushchev's Soviet model. He decided on a preemptive strike. He and his ambitious activist wife, Jiang Qing,

[6] Spence's *The Search for Modern China* (New York: Norton, 1990), from which this comment is taken, contains the most incisive and best-rounded account of this period.

used their influence in the media to instigate a series of attacks on "capitalist roaders" in the Party who were still fostering "bourgeois" tendencies.[7] Soon Liu Shaoqi and Deng were personally singled out as targets.

As Mao moved to dislodge his real (or fancied) opponents from the Central Committee, the first bands of young Red Guard enthusiasts were urged to purge the Party of "bourgeois elements" within it. Within months the Mao cult had intensified. Standing in Tiananmen Square, "the great teacher" acknowledged the cheers of the teenagers brandishing their Little Red Books and sent them out to attack Party leaders and virtually all official authority, intellectual "capitalist roaders" in particular. "Let loose the masses," the People's Daily editorialized. Mao's own handwritten poster—"Bomb the headquarters"—warned the young against a "white terror" of Party officials. The hate and resentment thus mobilized set the tone of the Cultural Revolution that followed. It strangely combined the active pent-up frustrations of a repressed youth with the passive inability of many old Communists to resist destruction at the hands of their own "great leader."

The term "cultural revolution" was not a new one. It had been used—by Mao, among others—to describe the intellectual stirrings of Lu Xun and his fellows in the May Fourth movement a half century before. They in turn had invoked the example of the European Enlightenment and, indeed, Japan's Meiji Restoration, a cultural revolution that was broadly successful. But May Fourth, like Meiji, was a movement of intellectuals, scholar-activists who tried to pull a nation along with them. Mao's revolution was totally anti-intellectual. Behind all his talk of the "masses" was a determined effort to destroy the intelligentsia, the same intelligentsia who had built up the Communist Party, and all the rational thinking and Western influence which, to Mao's shrewd peasant mind, they symbolized. His anti-intellectual witch hunts in Yanan, the "antirightist" purges of the late fifties, and the Great Proletarian Cultural Revolution were all of a piece. They would prefigure the anti-intellectual purge by his successors after the Tiananmen massacre in 1989.

Many things changed during the Cultural Revolution's stormy decade. The break with the onetime Soviet ally that happened in Khrushchev's time was

[7] A well-known historian, Wu Han, had written a play, called Hai Rui Is Dismissed from Office, about a Ming Dynasty official who had the courage to criticize an emperor for his tyrannical policies. Most Chinese readers readily assumed this was an attack on Mao, who had removed Lin Biao's predecessor, Marshal Peng Dehuai, for criticizing the disastrous policies of the Great Leap Forward. In November 1965, Yao Wenyuan, at Jiang Qing's urging, wrote a searing public criticism of Wu for attacking, by implication, the Maoist idea that the "masses" (for which read Mao) rather than single individuals controlled the course of history. The intra-Party arguments over Yao's critique set the stage for the Cultural Revolution. Wu Han was one of the Cultural Revolution's casualties. He died in prison in 1969.

intensified; in 1969, a small war broke out along the Soviet-Manchurian border. In 1971, Lin Biao, fleeing China after an as yet unexplained plot and counterplot sequence against his mentor, Mao, died in a mysterious plane crash in Mongolia. The following year, President Richard Nixon visited Mao in Beijing to start a new era in international politics.

In 1973, despite the international thaw, the Cultural Revolutionaries continued their confusing "class struggle." This time they turned their fury against Confucius, China's great intellectual exemplar. The sudden anti-Confucius drive was actually the beginning of an attack by Jiang Qing and her curious culturalists on Zhou Enlai, in Party circles the symbol of conservative "old" values, who as Premier had tried to modulate the excesses of the Red Guards and other "rebel" groups. As usual in such cases, the attack was made obliquely and its real target for the moment not mentioned. After mobs of Red Guards smashed priceless ornaments at the Kong mansion in Qufu, Party theoreticians obligingly resurrected the late Lin Biao to vilify as a prototype of feudal Confucianism. By contrast they lauded the ruthless emperor Qin Xi Huang-ti, who burned books and buried Confucian scholars alive, as the first unifier of China and the precursor of—as it happened—Chairman Mao. Mao, who was getting old and never liked scholars overmuch, was reportedly quite pleased, but he was not prepared to abandon the ever faithful Zhou Enlai.

Mao finally expired in September 1976. Apparently disillusioned by the Cultural Revolution he had provoked, he brooded over his unfulfilled efforts to make China great, powerful, and proletarian. The words he wrote in a poem for his old friend and perennial henchman Zhou Enlai, who had died almost a year before him, could almost serve as his own epitaph:[8]

> Loyal parents who sacrificed so much for the nation
> never feared the ultimate fate.
> Now that the country has become Red,
> Who will be its guardians?
> Our mission unfinished, may take a thousand years.
>
> The struggle tires us and our hair is gray.
> You and I, old friend, can we just watch our efforts being washed away?

A less poetic but quite realistic evaluation was left us by Nikita Khrushchev, who wrote before his death in 1971:

Today Mao is doing the same things in China that Stalin did in the Soviet Union. He gained strength in his victory over Chiang Kai-shek and the

---

[8] As quoted in Meisner's *Mao's China and After.*

counterrevolution. Once he was established, he started getting rid of those who had helped him achieve this goal. Mao couldn't brand his opponents "enemies of the people" the way Stalin did, because that had already been exposed at the 20th and 22nd [Soviet] Party Congresses. So he had to invent a new version—the Cultural Revolution.

The Great Leap Forward and the creation of communes caused a great decline in China's industry and agriculture, leading to famine. It was necessary for Mao to recognize his mistakes. But that was no more possible for him than for Stalin.[9]

---

[9] As quoted in *Khrushchev Remembers*, translated by Jerrold Schecter (Boston: Little, Brown, 1970).

12

Deng's Halfway House

We are standing at another turning point in Chinese history . . . we have launched a vast program of modernization

DENG XIAOPING, 1979

Everybody here is scared—the young, even more the old. That is why our technology is so far behind.

DENG XIAOPING, 1975

See that little man over there?" said Mao Zedong to Nikita Khrushchev in 1957 (when they were still speaking). "He's highly intelligent and has a great future ahead of him." The occasion, Mao's visit to Moscow in 1957, was an unusual one and Mao's observation was unusually prophetic. Mao regarded Deng as a trusted, faithful lieutenant, practical and good at problem solving, but whose place was always one or two steps back. When Deng began to grow prominent in the early sixties, Mao occasionally moved to put him down. ("Who is this emperor?" the aging dynast had remarked on hearing that Deng had initiated a policy without informing him.) But he prized Deng's abilities both as administrator and as adviser. On both of his Moscow visits Mao had Deng lecture the Russians on Communist orthodoxy.

Throughout the history of Chinese Communism, Deng was indeed the highly intelligent little man who was *always* there. Walking through the War Museum in Beijing, past the large colored maps of guerrilla campaigns and pictures of half-smiling men in rumpled uniforms standing by their weapons, a visitor can get a good idea of Deng's role. While the foreground of the pictures is dominated by the highly visible leaders—Mao, Zhu De, Zhou Enlai—in almost every scene, somewhere in a rear row or off to the side, Deng's short, stocky figure can be identified. He was one of the last survivors of the Long March generation. As a young radical student from Sichuan Province, son of a prosperous family of mandarins and local gentry, he went to France with Zhou Enlai and others in 1920 to do educational work among the 200,000 laborers sent by China as its contribution to the Allied war effort in World War I. The educational work-study programs they joined quickly developed into Communist propaganda and indoctrination projects. It was in France that Deng became a Party member, while working at the Creusot steel works. He visited Moscow for the first time in 1926.

Back in China by the late twenties, he spent five years as a guerrilla fighter, trying to organize the peasants to fight the Nationalists in Guangxi Province. They had few successes, and he was generally lucky to avoid capture. After barely fighting off encirclement by Nationalist forces in the south, he finally led the remnants of his troops to join Mao Zedong in the hard-pressed Jiangsu Soviet.

In the bitter intra-Party feuding of that day Deng allied himself with Mao against the original Moscow-trained Communist leadership. He was almost expelled for backing Mao's ideas on peasant revolution. Reinstated, Deng accompanied Mao, Zhou Enlai, and the other core leaders of Chinese Communism on the Long March to Yanan in 1934. Once Mao's leadership was reestablished, Deng as a loyal supporter was entrusted with the editorship of the Army newspaper, *Red Star*. Thereafter he continued his work as a political commissar with Army units.

During the civil war against the Nationalists he served variously with all of the regional Army districts. He was the only man in the leadership to have done so. But he did most of his military work in the south, as the political commissar for the Second Army, commanded by the redoubtable "one-eyed general," Marshal Liu Bocheng. After the Communist victory in 1949, Deng returned to his native province of Sichuan. For three years he bossed Sichuan and the other southwestern provinces and established Party control there.

In 1956, Mao had Deng appointed general secretary of the Party. Second only to Liu Shaoqi, he had emerged as one of Chinese Communism's leading Party bosses. For both of them building up a strong, disciplined Party machine took first priority. Known primarily as a competent administrator and efficiency expert, Deng was by no means regarded as a liberal. He was in fact one of the prime movers in the vicious "antirightist" purge of China's intellectuals after Mao's Hundred Flowers campaign was reversed—"rectified" was the approved Party word—at the end of 1957. China's great woman poet Ding Ling, the world-famous sociologist Fei Xiaotong, and an outspoken young physicist named Fang Lizhi were among the 300,000-odd teachers, editors, artists, and other professional people to be arrested, jailed, or exiled in this period. Many were driven to suicide. The survivors became Deng's fellow prisoners in the later Cultural Revolution.

Both Deng's and Liu Shaoqi's pragmatic souls were shocked, however, by the disasters of Chairman Mao's Great Leap Forward. Without openly attacking Mao they joined forces with Peng Zhen, Zhou Enlai, and other Party leaders in a general retreat and retrenchment, for editorial reports of "revolutionary" zeal and faked production figures could no longer disguise the economic disasters brought on by the combination of backyard industry and forced communization of the countryside. The withdrawal of Soviet technicians and scientific advisers, part of the growing rift with their ally, had further darkened the economic picture. The Chairman now moved to the background, in the process relinquishing his post as head of state to Liu, and China seemed on the way to becoming another Communist country run by "technocrats" and the entrenched Party bureaucracy. The Central Committee, it was said, had just authorized a new post of "honorary chairman."

Mao would not be bypassed for long, however. Using Lin Biao, the newly appointed Army Chief of Staff as his ally and agent, the Party's veteran alley fighter began to build up mass enthusiasm once more. It was Lin Biao, anxious to prove his loyalty, who had the Little Red Book of Mao's sayings distributed to all People's Liberation Army (PLA) troops. ("A spiritual atom bomb of infinite power," Lin called the book in his enthusiastic introduction.) By 1966, after Lin moved picked detachments to Beijing, Mao presided over a rigged Politburo meeting that promised to push a "cultural revolution" with new vigor. With this mandate behind him, the old dynast began to move against his own Party leaders.

Government ministers and local Party secretaries alike were subjected to mass kangaroo courts. Their names were given to the Red Guards by the Chairman's trusted agents. They were cruelly beaten before jeering crowds, then paraded through the streets. Many were killed. Few had the courage to resist the Chairman's anointed emissaries. Zhou Enlai himself barely escaped.

Deng Xiaoping and his family were roughly handled. His children were reviled and beaten up by Red Guards. His eldest son, Deng Pufang, was thrown from a window after a daylong beating by Red Guards, then denied medical aid for several years! (He remains partially paralyzed.) Ejected from their handsome quarters at Zhongnanhai, the elite government residential compound, and cut off from all communication, the family was sent under guard in 1969 to Jiangxi Province in the south. There Deng and his wife were given jobs in a tractor repair workshop.

For all the indignities his family suffered, Deng was spared the brutal beatings and humiliations which Mao visited on Liu Shaoqi and his family.[1] Some tie evidently remained with Mao, who allowed Deng at least to keep his Party membership.

By the end of 1973, Deng was released from his confinement and moved back to Beijing. Shortly afterward he was restored to power, through Zhou Enlai's intervention, as Vice Premier and Chief of Staff of the armed forces. Once more he took up the cudgels with Jiang Qing and her clique, trying to implement Zhou's modernization plans, but Mao, now weak and senile, remained in their hands. In the Chairman's name Deng was once more denounced and dismissed. In 1976 he fled south to Guangdong Province, where his Army friends protected him.

That same year both Zhou and Mao died. Zhou went first, wasted after a five-year battle with cancer. He remains an enigmatic figure. He alone of Mao's henchmen had stuck with the aged dynast to the end; he alone had worked to mitigate some of the gross excesses of the Cultural Revolution. If he typified the classic kind and honest official of Chinese tradition, he was nonetheless incapable of changing a bad system; publicly he supported the terror. Yet the people of China felt real affection for him. On April 5, 1976, at the annual mourning day of Qing Ming, tens of thousands of people carrying wreaths and flowers for Zhou crowded into Tiananmen Square in a massive and this time spontaneous demonstration. Hundreds of demonstrators were beaten by gangs of security police, in the last violent act of the Cultural Revolution—but they had signalized, at last, the country's protest.

In the confusion of Mao's last year the Chairman had named Hua Guofeng, a colorless Security Ministry official, as his successor. It was Hua who had the Gang of Four arrested in October, barely a month after Mao's death. Lacking any significant Party constituency of his own, however, Hua was forced by pressure from the Army, where Deng's allies were now in control, to rehabilitate Deng once more, this time as vice chairman of the Party.

By 1978, after skillfully isolating Hua in a series of back-room political moves, Deng found himself in effective control of China. During his successive reverses he had enjoyed ample time for reflection, so he moved cautiously. There was to be no Mao-like "cult of personality," no huge photographs or marble sculptures of Deng to be put on view. (Under Deng's direction, however, local officials saw to it that the late Chairman's memorials began to disappear.) Not until well into the eighties were the collected works of Deng Xiaoping served up to the public as inspirational reading.

Deng's first task, as Chinese Communism's classic organization man, was to

---

[1] After three years of brutal confinement, Liu died in Kaifeng, sick, naked, and alone in his cold cell, after medical aid had been withdrawn. Two of his sons died of their tortures. His wife, Wang Guangming, survived only after years of imprisonment.

reorder his confused and demoralized Party and give everyone a new set of goals for the new era. The goals were not hard to find. As appalled as anyone at the economic and social chaos left by Mao's Cultural Revolution, he revived the Four Modernizations program that his old mentor, Zhou, had begun some years back. Reversing Mao's past isolationism—and again taking his cue from the internationalist Zhou—Deng unhesitatingly proclaimed that China was now "open" to the world.

THAT WAS THE easy part. The deeper underlying problem was how to keep the Communist Party in charge. The virtual civil war between 1966 and 1976 had shattered the interlocking power structure of Party, Army, and government by which the Communists had ruled China. The People's Liberation Army was hopelessly politicized; the government bureaucracy was demoralized; and the Party cadres were worst hit of all. Of some 40 million Party members in 1978, roughly 17 million had become members during the Cultural Revolution. These were, to put it mildly, a mixed bag: anti-intellectuals, people of "pure" class peasant or worker background but with little education or intelligence, sincere Red Guards or other varieties of Maoist zealots, city boys who hated the country, country boys who hated the city, turncoats or informers who got their positions by vilifying neighbors or fellow workers, and varieties of hoodlums who in the unenlightened capitalist world would have been classified as gangsters.

China's best and brightest—the educated urban students who would normally have gone into Party work—had been scattered by the forced migrations of the Cultural Revolution. Some 15 million young people had been shipped off to the countryside to learn hard work and "antibourgeois" thinking from the peasantry, who hadn't much liked them. (The antipathy, one gathered from returned city kids, was generally mutual.)

All too many of the old-line Party people who remained had kept their jobs by denouncing their associates. Despite the immediate vengeance that Deng and his followers were to take on the most obvious of their persecutors, as one "rectification" purge followed the other, it would prove impossible to separate the good guys from the bad guys. There were too many exasperating shades of gray, too many layers of denunciation, too many kinds of compromise. Children had denounced parents, wives had divorced husbands—all for the glory of that marvelously indefinable body of Holy Writ called Mao Zedong thought. From that day until this, people would find themselves sitting in offices or living quarters next to the same "cadres" who had persecuted them. In the end, as with so many things in China's Confucian network, promotion on the job, if not survival itself, depended on whom you knew.

Throughout more than ten years of visiting Deng's China, I heard an unending series of horror stories with no discernible endings. "And what about the man you mentioned," I would ask, "who worked for your father at the ministry, then denounced him and turned your family out of its house? The man whose children beat you up at school as 'capitalist roaders'?"

Back came the answer: "He is now the ambassador to London. They never even bothered to apologize." This kind of exchange was repeated almost innumerable times, with many different people.

After two decades of systematic internal shock, from the Great Leap Forward through the Gang of Four, the credibility of the Party was shattered. It could never be put back together again. A bright young bureaucrat in Chengdu, herself a reformed Red Guard, recalled for me the Cultural Revolution's last, shattering days:

"In 1975, before Zhou Enlai died, Deng Xiaoping had begun to lead the Party again. He is from Sichuan. We were all full of hope. I was anxious to begin school again. The *People's Daily* articles no longer attacked Deng, but praised him. Then a few months later he was dismissed. The *People's Daily* denounced him as an 'unrepentant capitalist roader.' When I read that I wondered to myself: How can we ever believe the *People's Daily* again?"

The credibility problem remained to haunt Deng and the old Party stalwarts who had come back to rule with him. It ran like a fissure beneath all the pronouncements about building—yet again—the new socialist China. It was Mao's legacy. For Mao's own Cultural Revolution had destroyed the myth of Party infallibility which they had so carefully built up since the Long March and the now legendary days in Yanan. Throughout the next ten years Deng and his peers would try continually to rebuild the myth. They had already lost the young generations they were counting on.

IN DECEMBER 1987, a young Chinese worker named Wei Jingsheng, a former PLA soldier and Red Guard who now worked as an electrician, wrote himself a thoughtful, provocative essay. He pasted it up among the various manifestos, poems, and posters on the so-called Democracy Wall in Beijing's Xidan district. It became part of China's history. Under the title "The Fifth Modernization: Democracy," Wei's essay argued eloquently that no amount of modernization could ever work unless China freed itself from the reactionary Communist Party dictatorship. He made the same points for real representative government that other young Chinese had been writing about in wall posters, magazines, and crudely printed discussion papers since the fall of the Gang of Four. Angry, disillusioned, deprived of education and decent livelihoods, ordered from city to country in forced mass migrations, the young people in the cities now wanted a voice in their future, and the Communist Party was not what they had in mind.

Deng's rule, Wei said, was simply the substitution of "the Wise Leader" for "the Great Helmsman." He continued:

"The people need no longer suffer the wearisome drivel of 'class struggle.' Now it is the Four Modernizations that have become the new panacea. Nevertheless, we still must obey the orders of the central authorities. Follow the guide dutifully and all your beautiful dreams will materialize . . .

"I beg you all—do not let these political swindlers cheat you once again . . . The cruel experiences of the Cultural Revolution have opened our eyes . . . The people need democracy . . . Who can really believe that this socialist way contains any recipe for the happiness of the people . . ."

Wei was arrested, on faked charges of espionage. He received a fifteen-year sentence and has not been heard from since 1979. The Democracy Wall was closed down. Deng was furious at such challenges to Party authority. If reform came, it had to be at the Party's pace.

When I had my first long interview with Deng, he went to some pains to tell me about Wei's challenge to established authority. "You have doubtless heard of the so-called Democracy Wall in Beijing," he began, without any prompting from me. "I may have made a mistake in agreeing to let it last for so long. For despite the good intentions of some who put up posters on the wall, it has been used to manipulate public opinion with distorted rumors and outright false-hoods . . . The wall came to be controlled by people who preferred trouble-making to working at their jobs. Foreigners who regarded the activities at the Democracy Wall as a barometer of the political climate in China were quite deceived . . .

"There people did not represent the aspirations of the overwhelming majority of the Chinese people . . .

"What we call the April Fifth movement [April 5, 1976, as we noted, marked the Qing Ming demonstrations honoring Zhou Enlai and attacking the Gang of Four] was a movement launched by our young people. But a few troublemakers engage in ultra-individualism and anarchy. Toward this small number we must take a very stern attitude, for the purpose of educating the majority. That is why we passed such a heavy sentence on Wei Jingsheng.

"It is imperative that while emphasizing socialist democracy we must strengthen the application of socialist law . . . For the Four Modernizations to succeed we must maintain an attitude of unity and tranquillity . . . China has finally reached this stage of tranquillity and now a few people are making trouble!"

I have quoted Deng's comment on Wei Jingsheng's harsh treatment to illustrate the consistency of his views. The same man who had Wei sentenced in 1979 gave the final order to shoot down the student demonstrators in and around Tiananmen Square ten years later. No one can doubt either the initial success of Deng's reforms or their sweeping nature. No Communist leader of his era, Mikhail Gorbachev included, had shown himself so flexible in modifying the socialist system to meet practical needs and cope with long-suppressed human wants. But Deng was a reformer only within the framework of his own background and political premises. Some freedom of speech he could tolerate, and intellectual dissent within limits. None of China's Communist leaders had tried so hard to win back the country's intellectuals. But when the dynasty's grip on power was at stake, he would not compromise. He was as quick as his mentor (and persecutor) Mao Zedong in interpreting exactly what constituted "the aspirations of the overwhelming majority of the Chinese people."

If Deng had learned much compassion from the horrors of the Cultural Revolution, he had equally developed a horror of losing political control. Yet the very increase of economic and social freedom and aspiration in Deng's China made people all the more aware of how much real freedom they still lacked. As I visited China over the decade of Deng's rule, I could to some extent watch the pendulum's erratic swings between liberalization and reaction. Each step the liberals took forward brought the country nearer an ultimate confrontation with Deng's governance and Mao's ghost.

CHINESE SCHOLARS brought out the first approximation of an encyclopedia more than 2,000 years ago. For some time it was customary for a dynasty, as it began, to produce its own compendium of knowledge, to convey to posterity its particular view of history. Deng's sponsorship of the Encyclopedia of China— and our own shorter Chinese-language Concise Encyclopaedia Britannica—was in this tradition. China had been cut off from the world for too long, he had told me, and needed to get its people back in touch with contemporary knowledge. This we tried to do. In the process we gained some insight into the tensions between China's intelligentsia and its Party rulers.

"This Chinese Britannica," said the Encyclopedia of China's deputy editor in chief, Liu Zunqi, "is a kind of barometer of the changes China is going through as we move toward real modernization. As long as we are in business, modernization is safe."

The man who said this was in himself a living history of Chinese Communism. Born into a poor family in 1911, he worked his way through the American-sponsored Yanjing University in prewar Beijing, where he learned to speak fluent English and developed a strong sense of social consciousness. Indignant at the poverty and corruption he saw around him in China's cities, he joined the Communist Party at the age of twenty. He was arrested for Party activity the same year, 1931. Released from a Guomindang prison two years later, through the good offices of Madame Sun Yat-sen, he was back in jail by 1935. Released a second time, after a feigned recantation to the police, he worked thereafter as a journalist in China and Japan. But he kept up his underground Party activity.

During the latter part of World War II, after escaping Japanese capture in Singapore, Liu worked for the Americans, heading the Chinese staff at the Office of War Information's bureau in Chongqing. He got along well with the American diplomats and correspondents, although his Communist sympathies were hardly a secret. (Given a choice between Chiang Kai-shek's Guomindang and the Communists at that point in history, most Americans who knew anything about Asia would have preferred the latter.) He remained a firm admirer of the American idea, as he put it. He was particularly impressed by Leighton Stuart, later the U.S. ambassador to Nanjing, who had been president of Yanjing when Liu was a student there.

After the Communists took power in 1949, Liu's future seemed to have been assured. He became director of the Foreign Languages Press, in charge of most of the PRC's English-language publications, and founded the foreign-language division of the new Xinhua News Agency. When Chairman Mao needed an English-language interpreter, to talk to overseas visitors, it was Liu who did the honors. He and his first wife, also a veteran Party activist (she bore their first child while in prison), settled down after the "liberation" to raise their three children. Energetic, idealistic, and happy in a Party-planned future, Liu set out to live Mao's myth.

It quickly shattered on the realities of Mao's adventuring, compounded by Party infighting. In 1957, when the frantic "antirightist" campaign began, Liu was arrested for having been an "American spy" in Chongqing. (Interestingly, most victims of Mao's various "rectification" campaigns were jailed for past history, rather than present offenses.) He was sent to a labor camp in the north. The charge was baseless, but there was no trial. In 1960, Liu, now labeled a "rightist,"[2] and almost starving, was sent into internal exile in Hunan, where he worked as a translator and "librarian" on a state farm.

In 1968, as the Cultural Revolution spread over China, Liu was arrested again. For two weeks he was brutally interrogated, day and night, by a five-man team, who kept dredging up faked "charges" from his old Party record. As an old Communist, he was as obvious a target for Mao's self-appointed policemen

---

[2] Once a person was accused, jailed, or otherwise punished as a "rightist," this designation was put on his or her official record. People with obviously "bourgeois" backgrounds were similarly labeled, with similarly predictable effect on their chances for promotion or even employment.

Deng Xiaoping and Zhao Ziyang. When Deng moved back to power in Beijing in 1978, Zhao, then governor of Sichuan Province, was one of his closest aides. Zhao later became Prime Minister and, until the Tiananmen Square massacre, Party Chairman.
Encyclopedia of China

"Man of the Year." In 1980 Deng was chosen for Time magazine's preferred cover position. © 1978 Time Warner Inc. Reprinted by permission.

Chinese Britannica on sale. When the Concise Encyclopaedia Britannica, an abridged Chinese-language edition of the Encyclopaedia Britannica, was put on sale in 1984, eager buyers crowded the Xinhua bookstore in Beijing. It was a sign of Deng's modernization policies that this uncensored reference work could appear.
Encyclopedia of China

as Russia's "old Bolsheviks" who had suffered under Stalin two decades before.

"I was in prison again," he told friends later, "in Beijing in 1968 as I had been in 1931, in solitary confinement.

"When I was in the Guomindang prison that first time, I felt proud and confident. But now I was in the people's prison—in the *people's* prison. When they came for me, they handcuffed me. I was depressed, so depressed, I nearly cried. But I couldn't cry, I didn't want them to see me cry . . .

"From the middle of May 1968 to December 10, 1969, I was allowed no visitors, no letters . . . Food was brought to me in my cell. I could speak to no one. Even the jailer who brought the food made me lower my voice to a whisper when I asked for anything . . . I could hear nothing, nothing. There was a hole in the ceiling and a window high above my reach. But no sound, not even of birds, outside . . ."[3]

Over the next six years Liu was sent to several other maximum-security jails. His wife denounced him, to keep up her own Party status, as many did in those days. Liu never heard what the charges against him were. Suddenly released in 1975—after Deng Xiaoping had returned, briefly, to power—he remained in internal exile until 1977, when he was reassigned to the Academy of Social Sciences in Beijing. Another year was spent clearing his name and restoring his full civil rights and past salary. (Calculations for this were based only on his labor camp pay: 76 yuan per month, less 11 yuan deduction for prison food!) Finally he moved over to edit the Chinese encyclopedia, after twenty-one years of his life spent in his Party's prisons.

There were two extraordinary things we noticed about Lao Liu, or Uncle (literally "old") Liu, as elders in China are called. The first was the amazing enthusiasm and conviction he brought to his job. In this he was typical of so many old people, many of them with foreign educations and highly specialized training, who had been rehabilitated to make Deng's Modernizations program real. I have never known a more dedicated group. Liu's second quality was a sense of fairness and intellectual integrity, undimmed by the years of persecution. He was a Communist through and through. Even when he talked of dying, he spoke with a grin of "going to see Marx." Yet he was a Communist of an old, spartan, internationalist tradition—what the Germans used to call *ein alter Kämpfer*—an old battler. He was also dedicated to modernizing China; here the Western education Leighton Stuart imparted at Yanjing had stuck. No one better understood the need for a real "opening" of his country.

Encyclopedia making has traditionally been regarded as a dull, if honorable

[3] The quotation is excerpted from Harold Isaacs's moving book *Re-Encounters in China* (Armonk, N.Y.: M. E. Sharpe, 1985), which tells the stories of Liu and other victims of the Cultural Revolution.

craft, tedious work best performed in some secluded editorial attic. Making the Chinese Britannica was far from that. It involved intellectual and political risk taking of a high order. Editors, many of whom had themselves been censured or imprisoned for expressing their opinions, were charged with publishing, under Britannica's supervision, a basic reference work with *no* political additions or overtones.

At the editors' request, China's Concise Encyclopaedia Britannica was to be strictly a translation of the Britannica's Ready Reference (Micropaedia) section. Contrary to the practice followed in the Japanese and other translations, few local additions and no explanations or other concessions to Chinese readers would be made. (This was the safest way to avoid political tinkering with the text by the Party hierarchy.)

The sheer work of translation, however, was often overpoweringly difficult. How do you translate articles dealing with investment, stock exchanges, psychoanalysis, heaven, purgatory, cross-examination, and appeal—not to mention democracy, free enterprise, and private ownership—when the very words involved have been declared taboo in a society for more than a generation? How do you restore meanings that have been arbitrarily distorted and redefined in the name of Mao Zedong thought? How do you find translators in a society where even the study of Russian was only recently found dangerously "revisionist," if not actually rightist?

While the twenty- and thirty-year-olds laboriously began the study of English, the old men, survivors, came back to give on-the-job training in disciplines that they had been coerced into forgetting. Religion was particularly difficult. The editors finally found a small theological seminary, recently reestablished, whose professors, after some hesitation, consented to take on the task.

We had agreed to allow some 5,000 entries on Chinese subjects, provided Britannica had the right to an editorial veto. And here the worst problems predictably occurred. Through the shifts of Party policy, Chinese had been inured to stacking forcibly applied value-judgment adjectives on any political explanation. Thus the first articles had an always *vicious* Gang of Four or perennially *reactionary* Guomindang elements working against the *correct* Mao Zedong line. After some discussion we all agreed that adjectives must go. Surprising what a difference that made.

Some articles posed particular problems. It had long been an article of faith in the People's Republic that South Korea had started the Korean War. While privately recognizing the absurdity of this policy, the Chinese editors were not about to denounce it for the sake of encyclopedic accuracy. At the end of a hot summer's day of argument at the Guesthouse in Harbin (formerly the old warlord Wu Peifu's villa), all accepted a statement that, "after skirmishing and clashes on both sides of the 38th parallel, the North Korean forces pushed forward."

Nationalist statesmen and generals were at first roughly handled. Finally, using the distinguished scholar Hu Shi as a test case, we agreed that having been Nationalist ambassador to the United States did not invalidate his contribution to modernizing the Chinese language. Dethroned Communist leaders were in for even worse treatment. At first our Party advisers refused to include a biography of the former chairman Hua Guofeng, whom Deng had unceremoniously elbowed aside. We convinced them that even villains had to be given their place on history's stage. In the end we encountered total disagreement with the Chinese only over the Britannica article on Stalinism, which said embarrassing things about Stalin's (and Mao's) cult of personality. It was the only article to be omitted.

Through the first critical years of our work, the encyclopedia was kept on an even keel by the stubborn sense of fairness that Lao Liu transmitted to the younger editors. He was backed by the Academy of Social Sciences and, ultimately, by the authority of Deng Xiaoping. We were allowed, literally, "to seek truth from facts" in China, as the Britannica had done elsewhere. What the Academy's scholars had first seen, probably, as an effort to translate modern scientific and economic concepts into Chinese emerged as an invaluable popular educator, the first modern unbiased—and uncensored—reference work to be published in China since 1949.

THE WORK OF our Beijing encyclopedists was helped by the changes going on around them. For the first few years of Deng's rule produced a kaleidoscope of political and cultural as well as economic transformations. The new "opening" to the West not only brought in continuous planeloads of American and European tourists, with high-priced foreigners' hotels sprouting up to support them. It also attracted traders, entrepreneurs, representatives of American and Japanese transnational corporations—along with lawyers, investment bankers, accountants, consultants, and other varieties of commercial spear bearers. Academics from American universities arrived by platoons with new or revived China study programs, and they were more than balanced by the thousands of Chinese students now allowed, in fact encouraged to continue their studies in the United States. By the early eighties more than 12,000 university students annually were on their way to American campuses. They included the children of almost the entire Party hierarchy, Deng's son and daughter among them.

Only a few years after the shutdown of the Democracy Wall, newspapers and magazines were printing all manner of critical articles. Scholars and professional people advocated new political and economic directions. China's newly unregimented publishers were quick to translate foreign books of every variety, generally without the formality of royalty payments. (At one point five different publishers were in the stores with translations of Lee Iacocca's autobiography.) All of this increased the national appetite for just the sort of international learning that we were compiling. Politically speaking, the new official policy to court, rather than threaten, the separated brethren in Taiwan and Hong Kong made it increasingly easier for our China articles to rescue Nationalist officials and even generals from the demonology to which they had been consigned.

Social change was increasingly visible. Women in Beijing and Shanghai were now going to the hairdresser, buying newly available cosmetics by the bushel, and coming out in skirts and high heels. Boys and girls were walking together hand in hand. Party officials were appearing publicly in suits and ties, looking not very different from the foreigners on the numerous imported TV programs. English-language courses proliferated. Each time I came back to China I found more goods in the department stores, more outdoor markets, more small creature comforts, more food.

Such phenomena reflected Deng's policy to increase production of consumer goods, to develop joint ventures with foreign companies, to make factories more efficient by giving control to local managers rather than to government ministries and Party central committees. But at the base of it all was his successful reform of China's agriculture. From the moment he returned to power, Deng had moved to dismantle the dehumanized and massively ineffi-cient communization of the countryside that Mao had left behind him. Grad-ually but steadily he had restored rural enterprise, created new private marketplaces, and given greater control of the land back to the traditional bulwark of China's still rural economy, the family farmer.

The contented farmer, quick to climb the ladder of rising expectations, became the foundation of Deng's rule. Relatively undisturbed by intellectual oppression or students' calls for more democracy, the men and women of China's good earth worked and prospered, pushing up agricultural growth to an unprecedented 7 percent annually for the next decade. Many supplemented their income by starting businesses. That wise veteran bureaucrat Huan Xiang said to me early in the game, in his office at the Academy of Social Sciences: "The farmers are happy. And they are eighty-five percent of the people."

ONE OF THE happier by-products of my work with the Chinese encyclopedists was the chance it afforded me to visit different parts of China and see the farms and small towns that I was then reading about. Our hosts kindly arranged to have the periodic editorial board meetings held in different parts of the country. From Heilongjiang Province in the Manchurian north, rich in wheatlands and rebuilding industry, past the parched dusty plains of Shaanxi to the teeming business clutter of Guangzhou (Canton), whose increasingly free and easy trading practices made me think of it as "Hong Kong West," to the semitropical city of Kunming, not far from the terminus of the old World War II Burma Road supply line, we traveled, meeting a mixed bag of editors, publishers, scholars, and the inevitable Big Brotherly local Party greeters. While admiring the local scenery—it takes a visit to the extraordinary domed mountains of Guilin or the spectacular banks of the upper Yangtze to realize that so much of Chinese landscape painting is not imaginative but representational—I was struck by the two central facts of China's paradox. On the one hand there is a fierce devotion to the sweep of China's history (all too often manifested in an insistence that the visiting foreigner see as much of it each day as possible). The foibles and virtues of centuries-dead emperors are recalled constantly, used with some degree of safety to underline comments on current happenings. Poets and artists are revered, and the sages religiously quoted. Nowhere else in the world is there a thinner dividing line between past and present, a greater feeling of belonging to a unitary civilization.

Yet at the same time there is an equally strong sense of local identity. A person is described immediately as Shanghaiese or a Shandong man or a Hunanese woman. These are in a way countries rather than provinces, although all are within the same empire. The distinctions are fortified by dialects, still in some cases mutually unintelligible, temperament (real or fancied), and, inevitably, food.

To be a landsman in China is all-important to a relationship. In our encyclopedia work, we finally decided to publish a slightly expanded version of the Concise E.B. in Taiwan. One of the conditions of so doing, which both sides accepted, was to set up a joint editorial committee, which would have to settle any differences about sensitive political articles. The very existence of this committee was unprecedented. It remains the only such group to have met regularly, with both Beijing and Taipei participating. Although by the time the committee first met, a policy of conciliation on both sides had already eliminated many potential points of disagreement, I was worried about frictions developing. The worry was needless. It so happened that representatives from both sundered parts of China were from Shanghai and had many acquaintances in common. Once they lapsed into Shanghai dialect, no insuperable problems remained.

Of all the places we visited, Sichuan was for me the most fascinating. The Chang Jiang (Yangtze) and four other rivers flow through this great landlocked province; its name means "four rivers." Protected on all sides by mountains, its Red Basin contains some of the country's richest farmland, enough to feed its population of some 100 million and, in decent times, to export a surplus.

Separated from most of the country by its mountains and difficult river gorges, Sichuan constitutes a kingdom all its own—which indeed it was, starting deep in China's history. It is also, significantly, the place where Deng Xiaoping's economic reforms began.

Very consciously Deng's home province, Sichuan's independent-minded people put up more resistance than most to the Cultural Revolution. Self-contained and remote from Beijing, it seemed to Deng and his advisers a natural testing ground. In 1975, after Deng's first return to power, he had engineered the appointment of a veteran Party apparatchik named Zhao Ziyang as Sichuan's First Secretary.

A relatively young man among the aging Party leaders—he had become a Party member in 1938, at the age of nineteen—Zhao had spent most of his career as an agricultural specialist. By 1978, when Deng confirmed his Modernizations policy, Zhao set out to implement it with all possible speed. When I first visited Sichuan in 1980, the changes in farm policy were everywhere visible. Household farming had been restored, under a "responsibility" system that allowed farmers to sell a certain portion of their yield on the open market. They were encouraged in addition to set up the kind of sideline businesses—silk farms, small machine shops, restaurants, and retail stores—that had been previously suppressed. Mao's beloved communes themselves were soon to be disestablished, with work brigades once more becoming groups of households and villages returned to their old geographical identities.

Layer upon layer of overgrown Party and government bureaucracy had already been stripped away, with spectacular results. Between 1976 and 1979, Sichuan changed from an importer to an exporter of agricultural products. Similarly good results had been achieved with some one hundred "self-determination" enterprises, factories returned to the control of their managers and allowed to set their own work goals and retain a considerable portion of their profits. In September 1980, his Sichuan experiment a success, Zhao was called up to Beijing to become Premier of China.

When I interviewed Zhao Ziyang, almost four years later, his Sichuan example had spread across the country. "By now," he said, "ninety percent of the Chinese countryside has been drawn into this kind of a contract system, by which households undertake to produce a certain commodity in areas where they have particular competence. They are permitted to keep what they earn after the amount for which they contracted to the state has been achieved . . .

"We didn't really think that these reforms would work so fast. To start with, we were trying to solve the problems of some hundred million people throughout China who were living below the subsistence level in agricultural areas. Our experience with this exceeded our first perceptions. Poor areas quickly caught up with rich areas and the success really snowballed . . .

"It was inevitable, with people specializing in different things, that some households would do better than others . . . The contract system also led to changes in the labor force and in our social structure. Some peasants stayed on the land. Others left for towns and cities to do work in transportation, distribution, and other service occupations . . . As a result, we have a new trend: small cities and towns are becoming more prosperous, as against a steady decline in the past . . . Some families, moreover, are beginning to employ a few people to help them in their work activities."

Confident, assured, and almost exasperatingly fluent, Zhao gave me what amounted to a two-hour progress report on China's modernization economy. In the process he casually overturned two of modern Marxism's most sacred tenets, the ban on people hiring others to work in private enterprise (what the Party manuals used to call "the exploitation of man by man") and the prohibition of anything like private landownership. For here he explained that farmers could now sign work contracts for fifteen-year periods. ("Formerly peasants were nervous that they might lose the land because of policy changes.")

This was all done in the name of efficiency. Now, he predicted, even the traditional "iron rice bowl" was to go; instead, people would be paid for the amount and quality of their work. ("People who are good at management," he added, "would receive a larger share of the income.")

Reforming the old statist economies of the cities, he conceded, would pose more difficult problems. "We have to learn how to combine regulation by state planning with market regulation," he said. "That is a new experience for us. We must combine the experience of the United States and other Western countries in this, but without copying them. We must find an economic system suitable to the character of this country."

The difficulties he hinted at would of course come back to haunt him, as the realities of an approaching market economy began to pose a mortal threat to the Communist Party's political control. But what fascinated me then, and in a later meeting, was Zhao's obvious willingness to experiment, until he found the right formula, however much this conflicted with hitherto accepted Communist truths. This man had never been to a university, still less studied formal economics. His whole school had been work with the Party organization. Yet he seemed untroubled by worries over Party orthodoxy. He looked and talked like a politician trying to find new answers to new challenges. Unlike Deng, he did not emphasize Party ideology, apart from the normal ritual statements that China would remain socialist. This was in March 1984.

OTHERS IN THE Zhongnanhai compound in Beijing felt more strongly than Zhao about preserving the "Chinese road to socialism." Deng Xiaoping, we should remember, had not returned to power unaided. The same old Party comrades who had helped him to defeat the Gang of Four—Marshal Ye Jianying and Yang Shankun from the Army, the Party leader Peng Zhen, the economist Chen Yun—were far from reformists. They had all been growing nervous about the widening influence of Western customs and ideas on China's younger generation. They were nervous about the fashion shows, the new hairstyles, imported rock music, "decadent" art shows, uncensored books, and a new wave of entrepreneurial thinking. Go-getters who started new small businesses were praised as successful modernizers, whereas less than ten years ago they would have been jailed. This seemed to the Communist old guard an attack on the Party itself.

From their point of view they were more than a little right. New ideas from outside were sweeping through China, most particularly the universities and the study institutes where the intelligentsia gathered. Students at Beijing University now laughed at the once obligatory lectures on Marxism and "Mao Zedong thought." The children of high officials were asking "Why?" when their elders urged them to join the Party. Inevitably, criticism of the Gang of Four had extended to the Party that had nurtured their excesses. Sober Party veterans like the poet Ding Ling, still loyal after all her persecution, could write sorrowfully in the *People's Daily*: "We have reached the point where people laugh scornfully when someone sings, 'Without the Communist Party there would be no new China.' "

Throughout 1983 a variety of Party spokesmen waged a bitter campaign against what they called "spiritual pollution." Deng Xiaoping himself, recalling his harsh treatment of Wei Jingsheng and the Democracy Wall writers, denounced "all varieties of corrupt and decadent ideologies of the bourgeoisie and other exploiting classes" in an official statement in October 1983. Local Party officials, many of them Cultural Revolution products, hastened to chime in. For a while it was open season on long-haired young males, rock music festivals, and most particularly articles and films, like the now banned *Bitter Love* (*Kulian*),[4] that threatened the established order of things.

Such calls back to orthodoxy were not, however, supposed to hinder economic modernization and the new "opening" policies of the regime. Zhao tried to explain this in our conversation. By the end of 1983, in fact, the *People's Daily* was warning that "people should not confuse spiritual pollution with [laudable] changes in material and cultural life." Thus Deng, like the Qing

---

[4] Written by Bai Hua and produced in 1980, *Bitter Love* tells the story of an idealistic activist who returns to China after the Communist "liberation" and gives his life to the Party, only to face continual suspicion and persecution. In a touching ending, his sorrowing daughter asks, "What has the Party done for you?"

Zhao Ziyang, now Premier, greeting the author at Zhongnanhai in 1984. Liu Zunqi, deputy editor in chief of the Encyclopedia of China is standing in the center. Encyclopedia of China

Chinese delegation at Disneyland. Breaking with Mao's isolationism, Chinese scholars, officials, and tourists traveled widely in the eighties.

Minimills in Xiaoshing. Small enterprises did well in Deng's China, while the bloated state-run factories continued to lose money.
Photo by Levie Isaacks.

Hu Yaobang. Dismissed as Party Chairman in 1988, this feisty liberal leader died in 1989. His death set off national demonstrations that culminated at Tiananmen.
Encyclopedia of China

The Forbidden City, 1980s. Foreign tourists in turn poured into China, here visiting Beijing's great landmark. Photo by Levie Isaacks

mandarin Li Hongzhang a century before him, continued his pursuit of economic modernization with foreign help, hoping the while to keep up his dynasty's system of domestic thought control.

BEFORE AND AFTER my meeting with Zhao, I had a chance to observe quite closely the growing strains between modernization and Party orthodoxy, in a bit of micropolitics that made the macropolitical picture all the sharper. Early in 1983 the Party bosses from the Encyclopedia of China's Shanghai offices had journeyed to Beijing with a serious complaint. The Chinese-language Britannica, essentially a foreign product, was not only too difficult; it was becoming dangerous. It was "like a chicken bone stuck in the throat," one editor commented. "A cancer that should be cut out of the Encyclopedia of China's body," the Shanghai Party boss added. The people involved in the project, he warned, might end up regarded as "traitors." In Shanghai, it would seem, they took the spiritual pollution problem seriously. Why not change the agreement with Britannica, they argued, and keep the completed Chinese version under lock and key—for "internal use only."

Liu Zunqi reacted swiftly. With the Chinese Britannica's managing editor, Xu Weizeng, a skilled and fearless translator (who had also served almost twenty-one years in detention), Liu challenged his detractors to point out any specific faults with the project. He also reminded all concerned that the Chinese Britannica was being published on the explicit instructions of Deng Xiaoping, with obvious Party approval.

After some discussion Jiang Chunfang, the editor in chief, sided with Liu. He ruled that they would abide by the Britannica agreement. Editorial work moved forward, facilitated by the subsequent forced retirement of the "antipollution" editors from Shanghai. Some months later, at a banquet that we hosted for the Shanghai editors, Lao Liu laid down the law for all to hear. "Some of the comrades," he remarked, "have been complaining about this project. They have even used the phrase 'like a chicken bone stuck in the throat' to describe it. If anyone here has any objections to what Deng Xiaoping has supported, let him make them known now."

Dead silence followed. Casual conversation was at an end. There is a formidable quality to the use of the word "comrade" in such a context. Grateful for the support, although feeling a bit sorry for the timorous bad guys, I proposed several hasty rounds of *mao-tai* toasts.

On September 10, 1985, we all attended a banquet at the Great Hall of the People in Beijing to celebrate the publication of the Concise Encyclopaedia Britannica's first three volumes. The remaining seven were well on the way to completion. The finished product was something in which all took pride. Many problems had been ironed out. Staples of the Marxist-Maoist vocabulary like "right opportunist," "capitulationist," and "left adventurist" were rigorously pruned, and Chinese reviewers later applauded the encyclopedia's "factual" content. Articles on Harry S. Truman and Douglas MacArthur—neither a great popular favorite in the People's Republic—were in the end given adequate treatment. There was full coverage of Taiwan, listed as "under separate administration." As a final gesture of impartiality, a picture of a smiling Chiang Kai-shek appeared with a factual article on him. From our long conferences the Britannica editors had learned as much as our Chinese counterparts—we had our corrections to make as well.

At a morning meeting in the Great Hall of the People, Deng Xiaoping gave us his official blessing. "Your publication is extremely useful," he said. "This kind of information is needed in China and we are very pleased to have it."

Over the next few days we all watched with some satisfaction as queues of prospective buyers lined up in front of bookstores in Beijing and Shanghai to subscribe to the first of the 100,000 first-edition sets the Encyclopedia of China published.

During most of our interview, Deng had proudly pointed to China's impressive growth figures. Reiterating his conviction that China must remain socialist, he cited two principles of official economic guidance. The first was to have "public ownership of production. That is to say, the public section must predominate." The second was, as before, "to achieve common prosperity for all." He added one caveat. While he was happy that some people and regions were achieving prosperity ahead of others, "we do not want a polarization of incomes in this society."

Nothing was said about spiritual pollution. But there was one slightly jarring note. At our first meeting in 1979, Deng had made a point of his wish to retire within five years. This was part of his general plan for setting up rules and guidelines for orderly retirement procedures—as badly needed as incentive plans in his society. "People in my age bracket," he had said in 1979, "should be busy arranging for what comes after them. We must find good and reliable successors, so that once a succession takes place, new turmoil does not break out again. Our leadership is of one mind . . .

"As for myself, I have publicly declared that by 1985 I shall become only an adviser or consultant. At the moment what I have here upstairs"—he tapped his head—"is still functioning in good order. But by that time who knows what changes may come . . ."

I reminded him of this earlier statement. Almost everything he had prophesied in 1979 had come to pass, except for retirement. Had he misled us?

Deng answered with a wry smile, "Come back in five years." There was general laughter in the hall.

* * *

DENG'S APPARENT determination to retain power indefinitely was hardly a laughing matter. Had the old man, following in Mao's footsteps, decided that the dynasty was his, not in his time to be relinquished? Or was this masterful political manipulator still nervous about the house of cards he had put together over the ruins of Mao's mistakes? Over the next five years, as my visits to our successful encyclopedists continued, I had ample time to ponder these alternatives, and there was no dearth of bright, interesting people to discuss them with.

On the surface things went well. Deng's two carefully selected successors were in place: Zhao, the bureaucrat turned economic innovator, to push forward the modernization reforms, and Hu Yaobang, a small, scrappy veteran of Communist youth organizations, to reform and energize the Party as its general secretary. (An associate of Deng's since the post-liberation days in Sichuan, Hu was fond of saying that he owed his job to the fact that he was the only official in China who was shorter in stature than the five-foot-tall Deng.)

The GNP growth rate kept soaring, led by thousands of small private enterprises. The right to hire workers without restriction had been finally written into law. Tens of thousands of superannuated officials had been retired (although allowed to keep their cars and privileged apartments). Foreign investment was encouraged, with new Special Economic Zones set up in coastal areas to attract more.

A new legal system was being created, impelled by the need to regulate and safeguard foreign investments and joint ventures. (The same motive had impelled Japan's legal codification after the Meiji revolution.) Farmers and small rural enterprisers were doing better and better. Party newspapers now argued that getting rich was perfectly all right, as long as people worked hard and paid their taxes. The antispiritual pollution campaign seemed only a memory, as intellectual and cultural discussion and criticism blossomed. Visitors from Taiwan (especially business investors) were now welcome. And émigré publications like the *China Intellectual* were setting up offices in Beijing.

Yet some major problems remained, swelling like tumors beneath the skin of Deng's prosperity. There were four major causes of concern, all closely related: prices, public enterprises, pervasive corruption, and political freedom. Linking them all was the underlying source of rot: a Communist Party of some 42 million, faction-ridden, shorn of its credibility, united only in the desire of its members to hang on to power and perquisites.

With all the talk of a market economy, Zhao's economists were unable to effect anything like a real price reform. While a few commodities were allowed to find their own price level, the Party's well-entrenched central planners dug in their heels at the very thought of freeing prices. The existing system of fixed prices and subsidies remained imposed on a partly freed economy like a huge scaffolding, growing ever more creaky and inefficient. Stimulated by new investment, demand exceeded available goods; by 1988 the annual rate of inflation exceeded 20 percent.

The large public enterprises, swollen by subsidies and still dominated by Party politicians, perpetuated the myth of the iron rice bowl. All too frequently they turned out their products independent of markets or consumer demand—with little or no consideration of profit or service to the consumer.

Corruption riddled the society. Without a workable set of commercial laws and regulations—and with what were at best rudimentary fiscal and monetary policies—new growth and investment were funneled into under-the-counter gain. "We are now considering ways to overcome a variety of unhealthy tendencies in our economic affairs," Zhao told me at our second meeting in 1988. "We must make our Party and government workers clean and honest."

With the air of men expecting no tomorrow, Party bosses and officials grabbed whatever they could for themselves, in a sense transferring to a new money economy the networking of back-door favors they already lived by. Their ingenuity was impressive, if ill spent. In one of the world's more impressive modern scams, for example, a group of bureaucrats on Hainan Island, using borrowed bank credit, imported in one year (1984–85) some 90,000 automobiles, most of them Japanese—for a brief moment in history, the island was the world's largest Toyota importer. They added 3 million TV sets and 250,000 videotape recorders. Almost all of these imports were to be sold at huge profits to their comrades throughout China. When the scam was uncovered, the island's leading official, one Lei Yu, got off with a reprimand, and shortly afterward became vice mayor of Guangzhou.

This was only one case of the Communist "New Class" leadership protecting its own. Repeating the sins of the Cultural Revolution in another context, the children of the top leaders had grown notorious for their own back-door economic activity, using their families' political influence. Deng's and Zhao's sons were among those privately criticized. The fourteen Big Families of the Party leadership, as they have become known, have given a homey Mafia slant to Chinese Communism.[5]

Which brings us back to the Communist Party. For all Deng's "rectification" purges of overenthusiastic Maoists and other unrepentant leftists, the Party remained divided, but jealous of its authority. It was also hopelessly corrupt. (In

---

[5] Among them were the families of Deng, Zhao, the current Premier, Li Peng, and President Yang Shankun, as well as the heirs and descendants of Chen Yun, Li Xiannian, Peng Zhen, Hu Yaobang, Ye Jianying, Lo Ruixing, and the posthumously rehabilitated Liu Shaoqi.

1987 and 1988, fully 70 percent of the country's economic crimes were by official admission perpetrated by government, Party, and Army officials—Mao's old power trinity ironically at work under the counter.) As the reformers tried to decentralize old controls and put economic managers, not Party politicals, in charge of enterprises, the politicals at all levels fought for their jobs and perquisites. From Party bosses at a dissolving commune to the aging veterans in the leadership compound at Zhongnanhai, they clung to power with a death grip.

Many Party members counted themselves reformers. Disillusioned by the Maoist disasters, they were yet unable to repudiate them. That the Great Helmsman was 70 percent right and a mere 30 percent wrong had been Deng's public verdict. They went along with economic reform, but they grew increasingly worried as factory autonomy and the imminence of a market economy threatened Party control. If the people complained about market pricing, ran the leadership's conventional wisdom, hold off price reform and appease them. Twice in the past decade unruly crowds had gathered at Tiananmen Square. The next time, the veterans of the Long March warned each other, might bring not Deng's controlled "second revolution" but real revolution, possibly with an end to Party rule and privilege. As the conflict between economic modernization and the dynasty's power became more apparent, even progressive Party mandarins grew nervous.

An even greater number of the Party cadres—half, perhaps—had been opposed to reform in any case. They found it wise to pay lip service, at least, to Deng's programs. But the legacy of Mao's Cultural Revolution still lay hard upon them.

HU YAOBANG, a blunt and honest man, made this point when I talked with him in 1986. "Superficially speaking," he said, "we have put an end to the Cultural Revolution. That is, there is no more beating people. But psychologically, the wounds are far from healed. They go very, very deep in our society. Many people did very bad things in this Cultural Revolution. When I say 'many,' I am speaking of tens of millions. Yet we punished only a small minority according to legal procedures—only in the tens of thousands. The majority of wrongdoers have gone free.

"Do you think there will be no repetition of such evildoing? We are not sure. It will take twenty or thirty years before we completely remove the stigma of the wrongdoing in that time."

Neither official corruption nor the more obvious misdeeds escaped notice. From the students in particular, there came a rising chorus of demands for political as well as economic reform. Wei Jingsheng's cry for the Fifth Modernization was by no means forgotten.

Chinese are great communicators. The students who returned from overseas brought with them more information about the open societies outside. Widening dialogues with foreign scholars, principally American, were bringing the average Chinese university student into the world community. Gorbachev's era of *glasnost*, if not *perestroika*, in the Soviet Union was having a heavy impact, as was the breakdown of Communism in Eastern Europe.

But within the fastness at Zhongnanhai—Communism's version of the Qing Dynasty's Forbidden City—nothing moved. Although procedures had been set up for free voting in Party and local elections, they were generally canceled out by "administrative" measures. Hu Yaobang alone had given some support to the move for widening political as well as economic reform, but when I interviewed him about this at our September 1986 meeting, he pointedly ignored only that question. I was told later that this reflected a "leadership conflict."

The students were more expressive. Later that year, inspired by calls for academic freedom, freedom of expression, and popular democracy from Fang Lizhi, the courageous astrophysicist at Hefei's University of Science and Technology,[6] they began to hold demonstrations. "Chinese intellectual life, material civilization, moral fiber, and government are in dire straits," Fang had told them. "The truth is, every aspect of the Chinese world needs to be modernized."

In December 1986, a wave of protest meetings and demonstrations rolled over Chinese universities. Starting in Shanghai and Hefei, the protests spread to some one hundred institutions. It was the heaviest demonstration since the spontaneous public mourning rites for Zhou Enlai at Tiananmen Square just ten years before.

In January 1987, Deng Xiaoping and his gerontocracy reacted. In a kind of classic Communist coup d'état, recalling Leonid Brezhnev's overthrow of Nikita Khrushchev, Deng and his old Long March comrades—Chen Yun, Peng Zhen, Bo Yibo, Hu Xiaomu (Mao's former secretary), Army boss Yang Shankun, and others—convened an impromptu (and, even by Party standards, illegal) meeting to force Hu Yaobang's resignation.

The charges? Hu had "released a bourgeois liberal flood," "forced many old comrades to retire"—so much for Party housecleaning—and, amazingly, "used the law to punish the children of old comrades who had violated the law"! That is to say, he had dared to prosecute the Party bosses' children for their crooked business and financial dealings.

Fang Lizhi was expelled from the Communist Party, along with the writer Wang Ruowang and Liu Binyan, the fearless *People's Daily* reporter whose

---

[6] Later to be driven into exile for his uncompromising stand, Fang deserves the title of China's Andrei Sakharov.

exposé articles had revealed so much official corruption, both before and after the Cultural Revolution. A new umbrella organization was set up, ominously, to control all the country's publications, among other things allocating the already limited paper supply.

The 13th Party Congress seemed, briefly, to set the country back on the path toward greater economic freedom. Farmers were virtually given the right to buy and sell land and pass their holdings on to their children. More cuts in the bureaucracy were announced. And Zhao Ziyang, who had succeeded Hu Yaobang as Party general secretary, was encouraged in his drive to free market prices. But this was only a mirage.

Inflation began to skyrocket, exacerbated by subsidies for unproductive state industries and Party officials' crooked manipulation of fixed and market prices. In reaction, the cautious old men around Deng began plotting a return to the same centralized command economy that was the historic root of China's economic failings. (Their guiding spirit, Chen Yun, once Mao's favorite economist, had continually urged a brake on economic reform.) Deng temporized. Party insiders later noted that in the same week that the aging dynast gave Zhao the go-ahead on new plans for a market economy, his cronies, gathered at the Beidaihe resort, had complained about the market economy's dangers. Deng told them that they were at liberty to stop the whole thing. So much for decision making at the age of eighty-five.

Liberals were worried. The students grew angrier. But the old men in Zhongnanhai began to close ranks behind their new spokesman, the recently named Premier, Li Peng, a "technocrat," as the cadres contemptuously called him. Alarmed by an impending purge of the intelligentsia in the Maoist tradition, Fang Lizhi and other intellectuals issued manifestos and open letters calling on China's new "middle class" to demand political freedoms. There was no response from the leadership.

Hu Yaobang died suddenly, of a heart attack, on April 15, 1989. A few days later angry posters began to appear at Beijing University. ("Those who should die," one big-character inscription ran, "have not. Those who should not die, have.") That week some 20,000 students from Beida and Beijing Teachers University marched on Tiananmen Square to urge Hu's posthumous rehabilitation and an increase in political freedoms.

The authorities denounced the disturbance. Thereafter more came to demonstrate—some 150,000 strong. By May 18, one million had gathered in the vast square. More assembled in other cities, to produce what was clearly China's greatest surge of spontaneous protest since the memorable May 4 demonstrations in 1919.

For a time there was an uneasy stalemate. Zhao Ziyang and other Party liberals tried to persuade the students to disperse. They failed. Partly because of their very spontaneity of assembly, the crowds were almost impossible to control. The students had been joined by workers, bureaucrats, and groups from Party organizations. The whole city seemed to demonstrate, an act of popular protest amply recorded by TV cameramen from all over the world. The first soldiers sent to break up the crowds seemed to make common cause with the demonstrators. Other units were turned back by massed civilians and their barricades. Earlier, Mikhail Gorbachev's visiting delegation from the Soviet Union had to be rerouted for their official meetings. The crowds of demonstrators seemed to proliferate. In meetings and on the ubiquitous posters, Deng Xiaoping himself was singled out for attack.

After two weeks of stalemate, however, the crowds began to dissipate. Student leaders urged their followers to leave, as the informal dialogue with liberal government leaders continued. They had promised more democratization. "We are for you," one government minister had said.

It was too late for Deng and the other old men at Zhongnanhai. On June 4 the tanks and soldiers of the PLA's 27th Army were sent into the streets of Beijing to clear the square. Some demonstrators resisted. But most, their numbers dwindled, either fled or fell victim to the indiscriminate gunfire of the troops. In the end the Chinese people's protest was met by military massacre. Students, workers, and bystanders alike were shot down in the street; estimates of those killed ran as high as 2,000. Government officials, led by the obedient, conscienceless Li Peng, came out of their hiding places to denounce the peaceful demonstration, which Deng, with wild irony, called "a horrifying counter-revolutionary rebellion" perpetrated by "the dregs of society." A glossy brochure, called "The Beijing Riot," was quickly prepared to commemorate the Army's "victory."

On June 9, Deng Xiaoping, who gave the order to kill, smilingly congratulated his troops. After all, hadn't Chairman Mao said that "power flows out of the barrel of a gun"?

IN THE SUMMER of 1990, a year after the Tiananmen massacre, I returned to China. On my own business front all was well. Our editors at the Chinese-language Britannica were doing nicely, working with us on new plans for a revision. As always, I found them bright and stimulating colleagues. No one said much about the previous year's events, nor did I ask. Some 120 of the staff had marched in the Tiananmen demonstrations, under the enterprise flag, along with almost every other state enterprise in Beijing. But the new editor in chief had made a self-criticism on behalf of the group; there were no punishments. If the old men in Zhongnanhai had taken reprisals against all of the students' sympathizers, they would have no intellectual sector left.

In other respects it was not a happy time. Deng's two current vice regents—Li Peng as Premier and Jiang Zemin, a fast-talking apparatchik whom I

Crowds at Tiananmen. Peaceful students and worker demonstrators parade through Tiananmen Square on May 17, some half-million strong—days before the army massacre.
The Bettmann Archive

had met when he was mayor of Shanghai, as Party general secretary—bustled about making statements about normalcy and the Party's leading role, while telling the foreigners that good international business went on as usual. I recalled Fang Lizhi's comments, made the year before, about the Chinese Communist policy of "forgetting history." He had written: "In an effort to coerce all of society into a continuing forgetfulness, the policy requires that any detail of history that is not in the interests of the Chinese Communists cannot be expressed in any speech, book, document, or other medium."

The economy stagnated. Caught between the fading promise of a market economy and the present realities of revived central planning, industry marked time where it could. Foreign investment was quietly returning, but with little confidence. There had been too much bureaucracy, too much gouging of foreigners on the Chinese side. The large state enterprises, now heading back to the "iron rice bowl" era of full employment and dwindling productivity, were swallowing up their restored subsidies. The promising private sector was being officially harassed.

Only the coastal provinces in the south were doing well—very well, fueled by business ventures from Taiwan and Hong Kong. The maritime Chinese were carving out new production bases (and markets) for their economic empire by exploiting the mainland's reservoir of cheap and willing labor. Local Party bosses in Fujian and Guangdong provinces were happy to cooperate and profit thereby; Taiwan businessmen could play their game. Beijing was having an increasingly hard time reining them in. Economically speaking, Chiang Ching-kuo's free enterprise ghost was reconquering the China coast.[7]

The people were quiet, albeit for different reasons. The farmers continued to improve their lot. Compulsory grain quotas remained, however, and there was now some worry about whether the government would make its contract payments on time. The politicized communes were gone. Now, as long as the money came in, farm families showed a notable disinterest in politics. City workers, as opposed to intellectuals, were nervous about denouncing the established order. They had had enough of scarcities and interrogations. For a time they would settle for known, if limited job and price security, as against the uncertain promise of a burgeoning market economy. That was beyond their experience. For its part, the regime made available ample supplies of food and other basics, at least for the potentially rebellious urban centers of Beijing and Shanghai.

A year before the Tiananmen massacre, a poll conducted by the Citizens Political Psychology Organization and Research Group—in China you some-

[7] Ezra Vogel's *One Step Ahead in China: Guangdong under Reform* (Cambridge, Mass.: Harvard University Press, 1989) offers a fascinating study of this economic resurgence.

times have to spell things out—indicated that fully 74 percent of PRC citizens believed that it was best to have "little involvement in political affairs." Thirty years of denunciations had had their effect. Thus the 1989 killings left those who knew of them shocked, angry, but silent. All the combustibles for popular revolution were in place, but they would take some time to ignite.

In 1990, the security forces had tightened their hold on Beijing. Foreigners were closely watched, especially those in the press; the clicks of the ubiquitous listeners punctuated many telephone conversations. Even the one bar in the foreigners' high-rise ghetto was operated by the Public Security. Meeting old Chinese friends was difficult. One longtime Chinese personal friend canceled his dinner date with my wife and me after officials from his old ministry had begged him—for his own sake—not to show up.

Conversations tended to be rather formal, with the official propaganda prominently featured. One female publicist at the Xinhua News Agency, with a very straight face, gave me a stern lecture about Lei Feng, China's humorless version of the Good Soldier Schweik, whose alleged example of Party loyalty had been quoted for decades by Communist apologists. (After the Tiananmen massacre the "Learn from Lei Feng" posters had been dusted off once more by the Party bosses.) Lei's story was an "integral part" of Chinese culture, she assured me, which "foreigners couldn't possibly understand."

Presiding over this society in stasis were Deng Xiaoping and his fellow gerontocrats in Zhongnanhai. If their myths were shattered among their countrymen, their power seemed intact. Men in their high eighties don't abandon myths easily. It would be inaccurate to say that the "hard-liners," as American newsmen liked to call them, had won. There remained much reform sentiment among the government and the Party. (Not for nothing had Hu Yaobang seeded his people throughout the Communist hierarchy.) Zhao Ziyang, replaced as general secretary, was still in the Party and notably unpunished, as were other reformists.

Deng still kept up vocal commitments to modernization. In the Chinese fashion the new power alliance was a complex of individual personal connections as much as ideological bedfellows, a crazy-quilt version of a put-together Rubik's cube, cohesive for the moment but impossible to assemble again. Some time afterward, early in 1992, Deng apparently gave the signal for economic reform to move ahead once more. While Japanese investments in China now increased, latter-day American China lobbyists—President George Bush, notably—continued to argue for a friendly attitude toward Deng's regime.

AND SO THE LAST Chinese dynasty prepares for its end. Mao molders a bit in his mausoleum (apparently the 1976 morticians had done a poor job of preserving him), but the old men—his disciples and their followers—continue to mouth the old rituals, like tired shamans hoping to avert the chill of the night with their incantations. The sacred books remain in place—Marx, Lenin, and something called Mao Zedong thought—but no one in China believes in them. Hardly anyone reads them, outside of compulsory Party meetings. There is Deng and his writings on the Chinese road to socialism, but only the professional Party careerists have much concern over that. Among the intelligentsia they are a joke.

There remain the rites, hallowed by almost a half century of Chinese Communism: the Young Pioneers mobilized at mass meetings, the old comrades on the podium reviewing troops, workers, or any other specimens of mass humanity willing to stand at attention in a confined space, and of course the slogans: not only "Learn from Lei Feng" but also "Learn from Dazhai" or "Learn from Daqing," more cases of paragons of socialist workers whose alleged efficiency had long since been overtaken by contrary pessimistic statistics. But they are still repeated like talismans, for nothing new has come to replace them in the ritual.

Remaining official priests of the cult warned against the familiar demons, like devil statues in Taoist temples—"bourgeois liberalism," "capitalist exploitation," "Soviet revisionism," or "Japanese revanchism." But they are worn out and found out. Enough has appeared on television, enough has been read, enough has been seen—from visits to foreign countries or the example of foreign visitors—to make the fruits of capitalism and the open society all too attractive to the average Chinese.

Guangdong and Fujian provinces, physically and politically a part of China, are already regarded by some as the fifth Newly Industrializing Economy (NIE) with per capita GNP running at well over ten times that of the rest of the country.[8] Hong Kong, while its people nervously await their reversion to China in 1997, continues to serve as the financial brain of China, available in transplant form. It is more than that. For the wealth of Hong Kong and the other maritime Chinese strongholds exert a visible and powerful attraction for Li Peng's fellow citizens on the nearby mainland.

To quote some lyrics of a popular rock song current in China in 1992:

> *Hong Kong Hong Kong Hong Kong*
> *Why is the lure of this name so strong?*
> *Hong Kong Hong Kong Hong Kong*

---

[8] A good summary of economic progress in the south is given in several long articles by *Newsweek*'s Beijing bureau chief, Frank B. Gibney, Jr., which appeared in *Newsweek* and *Newsweek International Edition* in February 1992.

I have heard of the freedom and the markets
Let me go to see that glamorous world
Let me wear my fanciest clothes
Come soon, 1997, let me see the real Hong Kong
I can go to midnight films—and buy the fanciest clothes
Come soon, 1997 . . .

As Fang Lizhi and others have pointed out, the efforts of the old men in Beijing to shore up the crumbling edifice of their dynasty is like nothing so much as the posturing of the Confucian mandarins at the court of Ci Xi, the dowager empress, in the last years of the Manchu empire. It is no accident that the Communist leadership has revived the official celebration of the Confucian rites at Qufu. It is the last tree they have to lean against in a barren landscape. Indeed, with its sacred books, its rituals, and its band of dedicated (and corrupt) mandarins, Chinese Communism has revealed itself as a parody of Confucianism, just as European and in particular Soviet Communism showed up as a monstrous parody of Christianity—both of them pietistic political faiths that have long since lost any trace of the "scientific" rational dialectic that once made them so attractive to the world's intelligentsia.

Mao, the barefoot emperor, is of course long gone and discredited. But to whom shall we compare Deng, Mao's ultimate successor? Going back to the analogy with the Qing Dynasty's end at the beginning of this century, how do we place him? Is he another Kang Yuwei, who tried so hard to modernize China but within the framework of the dynasty? Or has he become another Ci Xi—smiling in frustration at the foreigners but sworn to keep them out? Is it best, perhaps, to think of Deng as another Li Hongzhang, eager for "self-strengthening" modernization but unwilling to pay the political and social price? Or does Deng really know the size of the stakes and the extent of his apparent failure?

However the change works itself, the genie in China is forever out of the bottle. Can this brilliant, contrary people who kept their brittle empire together while Rome fragmented, draw upon the strengths of their heritage—its love of learning, its understanding, its cohesive Confucian tradition, which the Chinese outside of China have so marvelously exploited—and take their rightful place as a leader among the world's peoples? To do this, can they borrow and adapt and compromise with the world outside, as China has never done before?

The question was best posed by the authors of *He Shang* (*River Elegy*), a brilliantly written six-part television series that was aired in China—to the accompaniment of controversy and strong official censure—in June 1988. Taking their theme from the Yellow River (Huang He), they described how its vastness, its pervasive riverine culture, and its long history of catastrophes tell the story of the Chinese nation. Chinese history throughout the centuries demonstrated the growth of an inland, continental culture, brilliant but hopelessly self-contained and self-satisfied. Protected by stone walls and a kind of societal arrogance, the Chinese lived the life of landbound river people.

Only in recent centuries did the challenge of the seaborne West make China look at last outward, to modernization across the blue water. While old river cities die—Mao's capital of Yanan among them—a new spirit in China, transcending ideologies, stands finally ready to accept the "opening" ideas of a Pacific civilization. How can the Chinese, the authors ask, rise above the aged culture, "decayed and impoverished," that has made them unique, but held them in its thrall?

"Today," they wrote in their script, "many Chinese can clearly see that reform does not mean 'changing from sweet potatoes to steamed bread' or a matter of 'bachelors taking a wife.' It does not simply mean color television, refrigerators, and higher wages. Nor does it mean leading a comparatively well-off life, with earnings of more than $1,000 a year [China's current per capita GNP hovers at something over $300].

"Under most circumstances reform entails deep, tremendous birth pains that signal the transmutation of society. This is an undertaking fraught with risks. The arduous course requires sacrifices from our own and several future generations. We are standing at a crossroads. Either we can allow our ancient civilization to continue to deteriorate forever—or we can endow it with new vitality. In no case can we decline this historic responsibility."

13

The Fight for Democracy

That this shall be, or we shall fall for it . . .

JULIUS CAESAR

*It is evident to all alike that a great democratic revolution is going on
among us, but all do not look at it in the same light. To some it appears
to be novel but accidental and, as such, they hope it may still be checked;
to others it seems irresistible, because it is the most uniform, the most
ancient and the most permanent tendency that is to be found in history.*

ALEXIS DE TOCQUEVILLE

At the center of Tiananmen Square, in the last days of May 1989,
the embattled Chinese students and workers of Beijing erected a
white plaster-and-cardboard statue called "The Goddess of Democracy." Modeled on New York's Statue of Liberty, her torch carried in high hope, the
Goddess reigned only briefly. She was demolished days later when the troops of
the ironically named People's Liberation Army shot and bayoneted their way
over the bodies of China's young. Imitations were quickly constructed in Hong
Kong, Taipei, Paris, New York, and wherever people gathered to commemorate the June 4 massacre—now known to all Chinese by the simple numerals
"6-4." Almost everywhere people of good will were at one with the bravery and
spirit of the Tiananmen demonstrators.

When the Goddess's far-flung worshipers began to discuss democracy's character, however, differences of definition were quite apparent. Egalitarianism,
pluralism, liberalization, free enterprise, freedom of expression—all had their
special pleaders. Some even held democracy to be a purer form of Communism.
Yet from Seoul to Singapore everyone could unite on certain basic prodemocracy demands: greater personal freedoms, the right to elect their leaders freely,

the end to the corrupting police control of governments. In authoritarian states, with the processes of law twisted against them, the only way people could hope to achieve democracy was by active public protest, as, ultimately, at Tiananmen.

The protests came. Throughout the latter half of the eighties, people all over East Asia—in Manila, Seoul, and Taipei as well as in Shanghai and Beijing—were taking to the streets in anger. Strikingly, the angry crowds recalled another wave of protesters almost seventy years before: the demonstrations of 1919, denouncing the colonialism and imperialist put-downs of Asian countries by the treaty makers at Versailles.

There was an important difference between them, however. In 1919, the May 4 marchers in Beijing, calling out for "Mr. Science" and "Mr. Democracy," followed in the footsteps of Korea's nationwide rallies of students and intellectuals on March 1. Along with kindred spirits in Indonesia and Vietnam they were protesting against foreign oppression of their countries—whether it was the active cruelty of Japanese occupying troops or the cynical neglect of the Western peacemakers as they reordered the world from the European palace at Versailles. By contrast, the demonstrators of the 1980s were citizens of countries independent for the past four decades. They were now denouncing, not foreigners, but the rule of their own dictatorial governments.

In Shanghai and Beijing the students and workers failed. They failed because a few years of economic democracy and openness to foreign influence were not enough to break the forty-year hold of Mao Zedong's imperial police state. But in Seoul, Taipei, and Manila, from 1986 to 1988, the people had won. They won unexpectedly—and by their own efforts. But they were powerfully helped by their exposure, over the past decades, to the tradition and example of democracy and popular freedom, however much they had been abused in practice.

Both the tradition and the example came principally from the United States. Just as Woodrow Wilson's Fourteen Points had excited the Chinese and Korean students of 1919 and the Occupation preachments of demokurashi kindled new hope in Japan's hungry repatriates of the late 1940s, the rallying cries of Asian demonstrators in the 1980s drew on the familiar language of the American rule of law and the Bill of Rights. Their countries had been helped by American economic aid and military assistance. But citizens' hopes for democracy had been let down over the years, as we have seen, by an American diplomacy that all too readily compromised with dictators as long as they were strong anti-Communists. Foreign policy and American remoteness from the scene were not the only problems. A matter of perception was involved.

The American idea of political democracy is rooted in the individualism of a pluralist society, growing out of the Christian faith and the later philosophy

The Goddess of Democracy. Chinese students cluster around their Statue of Liberty–like depiction of "Democracy" in the last days of the Tiananmen demonstrations in 1989. The Bettmann Archive

President Richard Nixon and Chairman Mao, 1972. Nixon's rapprochement with Mao, by ending Chiang Kai-shek's old dream of reconquering China with U.S. help, paved the way for more realistic and, ultimately, democratic policies in Taiwan. AP/Wide World Photos

Temple festival in Taipei, 1991. Although respectful of old traditions. Taiwan's rising middle class continues to press for greater democratization. Levie Isaacks

of the European Enlightenment. It has depended on respect for human rights and liberal values. This manifests itself through freedom of the press, freedom of speech, and above all the rule of law.

American economics, in its turn, was derived from a free enterprise capitalism developed in the West over several centuries by bourgeois entrepreneurs and the independent businesses they founded. When Americans in Asia said things like "democracy," "free elections," and "human rights," as well as "free enterprise," they were thinking in terms of their own history and traditions, despite the universal-sounding terms.

The East Asians had a strikingly different set of experiences behind them. In building their capitalist development states, as we have seen, they demonstrated a Confucian respect for administrative authority and a traditional inclination to think in terms of harmony and group accommodation rather than individual justice. Thanks to their history of political subservience and bare subsistence economies, they presented a rather high threshold of political indignation. People anywhere find it hard to worry about a free judiciary and an unpolluted environment when they have barely enough to eat. At that point any work is welcome, as is the guiding authority, however severe, that can point to a better and more secure future.

Growing affluence, however, gave people in these countries a greater sense of political independence. At least the feeling grew that choices were now available. A middle class was emerging, better educated and less inclined to condone the caprices of authority. These people began to complain that economic security was not enough. They began to grope for political alternatives to what they had, based on what they thought was attainable.

Americans who felt "free elections" were the panacea for any "undemocratic" situation often had trouble understanding that the very idea of a parliamentary process founded on debate and election was a new and imported concept in Asia. As one crossed the Pacific, historical time zones changed rapidly. Even the thoroughly "modernized" Japanese found it hard to keep their cultural equilibrium while condensing, for example, 150 years of Europe's Industrial Revolution into the forty-four years of the Meiji era. Imagine how much harder it was for Koreans to cope with the rubrics and responsibilities of democratic government in one short decade, after forty years of Japanese colonialism and centuries of obscurantist kingly rule before that.

For their part, Koreans, Filipinos, and Chinese (in Taiwan at least) tended to hold Americans responsible for backing up the postwar democracies which Americans had after all introduced. To the best and brightest in these countries, American "noninterference" in political affairs—as long as their governments remained publicly anti-Communist—seemed more like abdication and desertion. American-educated technocrats in these countries marveled in turn at the naiveté of Americans in assuming that the give-and-take of the democratic process which had taken two centuries of American living to develop—through slavery, restricted suffrage, sweatshop working conditions, and police firing on workers' protests—could be readily transplanted across the Pacific in the course of a few decades.

The effort was made, however. In many ways it proved surprisingly successful. In evaluating its success, we might do well to set aside the yardsticks of pluralism, liberalization, and the rule of law—in all these respects "democracy" in different countries has very different political spellings—and concentrate on the matter of democratic succession. Chalmers Johnson, with a bow to the political philosopher Karl Popper, has phrased the problem well. "What democracy requires," he writes, "is the institutionalization of a competitive process by which people choose their leaders. Competition involves a rule-bound contest in which both sides recognize the legitimacy of the other side's interests and strategies so long as both sides obey the rules . . . Democracy is the set of institutions that allows the citizens to hold their governments accountable for what they have done and what they propose to do. In a democracy, election day is judgment day."[1]

In all the countries under discussion, the problem of political succession proved to be the crisis point of the fight for democracy. This was as true for Korea, Taiwan, and the Philippines, where at least the structure of democratic institutions was in place, as it was for the People's Republic of China, groping its way out of totalitarianism.

BY THE BEGINNING of the eighties the high-rise economic success stories of the new Confucian capitalists and their governments could no longer hide from view the clouds of political and social discontent that now threatened their very base. This unrest was by no means general throughout the western Pacific nations. Japan in the north and Australia and New Zealand in the far south remained stable democracies—despite their sharply variant definitions of the word. All but one of the ASEAN powers looked stable, although local definitions of democracy were singular. Singapore was locked in the euphoria of ascending GNP, as was its city-state counterpart in Hong Kong, but in both places political discontent was gathering. Indonesia's petroleum-rich prosperity continued to grow under the guidance of the Pacific Basin's longest-reigning ruler, the low-key authoritarian President Suharto (a smoother, oil-rich version of Park Chung Hee). The other well-off commodity producers, Thailand and Malaysia, had relatively few problems with social unrest at that time, although

[1] From "South Korean Democratization: The Role of Economic Development," *The Pacific Review*, Vol. 2, No. 1, 1989.

problems were developing. The trouble in Korea and Taiwan, however, was growing serious; and in the Philippines it was approaching the boiling point. The magnitude of their discontent was directly affected by the increasingly high education level of their populations.

At the core of the crisis in all three countries was doubt over political succession. All three could boast well-educated and politically conscious populations with a growing urban middle class. All three, however, presented a similarly ugly picture of repression generating powerful political discontent.

In both Korea and Taiwan political unrest was ironically the by-product of spectacular economic growth. For prosperity was becoming highly selective. Increasingly, Korean workers were demonstrating against a government that not only repressed their rights to organize, but also kept wages at a low subsistence level while increasing capital investment and company profits. Park Chung Hee's authoritarian government was turning into a ruthless one-man dictatorship. A new 1975 edict ordered jail for anyone even criticizing the president. The parliamentary process was moribund and no succession to Park was provided for.

Taiwan chafed under the rule of Chiang Kai-shek's nationalist Kuomintang Party, whose one-party dictatorship, complete with propaganda organs and secret police, was in its way as total as its Communist enemy (and opposite number) on the mainland. Chiang's son, Chiang Ching-kuo, continued to rule Party and country under a martial law that dated from 1949.

Life in the Philippines was worst of all. Ferdinand Marcos, the self-styled "guerrilla hero" of World War II, having been elected president in 1965, proceeded to turn himself into a plausible imitation of a banana republic dictator. After proclaiming martial law in 1972, he and a group of rich cronies set out to loot the country, in the process driving thousands of Filipinos into a Communist-led insurgency. In addition, thanks to an ill-advised "import substitution" policy and primitive nationalist protectionism, the Philippine economy languished in a welter of corrupt and uncompetitive industries. So the Filipino people endured the pains of dictatorship without even the compensations of ascendant GNP.

The first succession crisis came in Korea. On October 26, 1979, after a year of increasingly violent strikes and student demonstrations, Park was shot and killed by a close associate, the director of the Korean CIA, Kim Chae-gyu, in a KCIA compound not far from the Blue House, Korea's presidential palace.[2]

---

[2] The Korean Central Intelligence Agency, founded in 1961 after Park's military coup d'état, was an "intelligence" organization with sweeping powers of investigation and surveillance over the country that approximated those of a secret police. Its resemblance to the American CIA was in name only. It was formally abolished in 1988, although some of its functions were transferred to other agencies.

The shooting came during a private dinner, after a bitter personal argument over whether the demonstrations should be suppressed by armed force. (The KCIA man had argued against this.)

Park's killing sent shock waves through the country. Despite his repression and power mania, he had been respected as the author of the Republic of Korea's postwar prosperity. Like Lee Kuan Yew in Singapore and Suharto in Indonesia, he had become a kind of political "given." Ruthless but personally incorrupt and in his way farseeing, he had led the country for eighteen years.

Park was succeeded as president by his Prime Minister, Choe Kyu-ha, thanks to a rubber-stamp vote of the National Council for Unification, Park's personally selected legislative substitute. Choe moved toward liberalization; one of his first acts was to release some 700 of Park's political prisoners, including the opposition leader, Kim Dae Jung. But he was not quick or decisive enough. In December, Major General Chun Doo Hwan, then in charge of Army Security forces, took over the government at the head of a military junta.

Chun's coup was totally illegal; he deposed the Army command only after seven hours of fighting. Chun next put himself in charge of the KCIA, using the same strong-arm tactics. In May 1980, after a wave of protesting student demonstrations, Chun had the hapless Choe government issue a decree of martial law. Strikes and demonstrations were banned. The universities were shut down, along with the National Assembly. Kim Dae Jung and other opposition leaders, after only a few months of freedom, were put back in jail.

On the morning of May 18, the day after martial law was declared, Chun's Special Forces troops brutally broke up a student demonstration in the city of Kwangju. Kwangju, the capital of Cholla Namdo Province, was Kim Dae Jung's stronghold. Since the early days of Park's regime, its people had opposed the central government and they had been victimized for it. For years Park's regime had starved the Cholla provinces of economic development, even as the rest of the nation prospered. No one knew better than the people of Kwangju what another round of military government would mean.

So they fought. They were probably provoked. As Kim Dae Jung asserted later: "Chun Doo Hwan intentionally provoked Kwangju people to fight against him, as an excuse for cracking down on them." But they seized weapons and in an extraordinary display of "people power" drove out the troops and took over the city. The students and workers armed themselves. Local police contributed their weapons. They held the city for three days, waiting for help from the outside. Some thought that the Americans would send troops in to aid them—or at least order Chun's troops back. (At the time a good portion of the Korean Army was under the unified U.S.-ROK Command.)

No help came. Instead Chun ordered more Army troops in to restore order.

Kim Dae Jung, Korea's most prominent opposition political leader, speaking at an antigovernment rally, Seoul, 1991. Peter Bull

Mourning at Kwangju. In May 1980, Maj. Gen. Chun Doo Hwan sent troops to suppress popular protest demonstrations in Kwangju, in southwestern Korea. In a brutal police action, hundreds of civilians were killed. Families and other mourners here honor their anniversaries.
Alan Barker

Seoul Rally. Students and middle-class professionals joined the protest. Peter Bull

Ignoring the efforts of Kwangju citizens to negotiate a truce, the 20th ROK Division (which had been detached from the American command structure) smashed its way into the city, killing and beating until all opposition was over. At least 300 civilians were massacred at Kwangju. Although the government's official death toll was 150, Asia Watch and other human rights groups estimate the number as closer to 2,000. Hundreds more were imprisoned; thousands managed to flee the country, many to the United States.

Kwangju was a grisly forerunner of the 1989 Tiananmen massacre in China, but here the deed was perpetrated by an American ally. To justify his action, Chun apparently told the Americans he had foiled a "Communist" plot. The United States continued to support his government. On February 2, 1981, President Chun, who had resigned from the Army to become the Republic of Korea's chief executive, was received at the White House by President Ronald Reagan. He was Reagan's first official foreign guest. "Our special bond of freedom and friendship," Reagan told him, "is as strong today as it was twenty years ago."

As the country's elected President, his victory facilitated by some handy revisions of the election laws, Chun presided over a military dictatorship more dangerous than Park's because it was more capricious and less intelligent. It was also corrupt. Although he shut down newspapers and TV stations, effectively muzzling what was left of Korea's free press, Chun was unable to hide the scandals of what quickly became a rule by venal cronyism. The economy continued to expand, thanks to the cooperation of government technocrats and the big *chaebol* conglomerates. The Korean people were cowed for the time being by Chun's police rule, but confidence in their government steadily eroded. Demonstrations continued and the students leading them grew increasingly radical. No apologies or reparations were ever made for the Kwangju massacre. But no one in Korea forgot it.

UNTIL THE LATE 1970s the people of Taiwan had been patient and docile under the rule of the monolithic Guomindang government. Few could forget the wholesale slaughter of the native Taiwan Chinese leadership by Chiang Kai-shek's troops in 1947. Thanks to the makeup of Taiwan's industry—a patchwork of thousands of small family-owned firms—the growth of a labor movement lagged far behind South Korea's. Strikes were almost unknown. Press and publications were under the tight censorship of the Government Information Office, an organization that traditionally suppressed more than it revealed.

Political activity was still almost totally regulated by the Guomindang, which continued its fiction that the government of Taiwan was the government of all China, including that 98 percent of the population "temporarily" under the rule of the "bandit" Communists in Beijing. Regularly deputies to the Legislative Yuan in Taipei took their seats representing Chinese provinces like Sichuan or Shandong which they had not seen since the Nationalist defeat in 1949. Yet the ultimate reconquest of the mainland was proclaimed as a matter of faith. No political parties other than the Guomindang were allowed. Native Taiwan Chinese were regarded as little better than second-class citizens. For more than three decades the mainlanders had remained in charge.

During the seventies, however, while business continued to grow, seismic political changes were taking place. President Richard Nixon's visit to Beijing in 1972 shattered the Guomindang illusion, based as it was on the continued anti-Communist militancy of the United States. Shortly thereafter, following the visit of Prime Minister Tanaka Kakuei, Beijing and Tokyo resumed relations. In 1979, after the United States reestablished formal diplomatic ties with the People's Republic of China, the American embassy in Taipei was closed.[3] Deng Xiaoping's return to power in Beijing began a far more conciliatory approach toward Taipei by the Communist regime. The Taiwan Chinese, understandably shaken by these events, began to look more critically at their Guomindang government.

In November 1977, some 10,000 angry demonstrators attacked a police station at Chung-Li, a town just five miles away from Taipei's Chiang Kai-shek airport; they burned vehicles and rioted through the streets. They did so in protest against Guomindang attempts to rig a local election—hardly an unusual occurrence in Taiwan politics. But their protest was unusual; it was the first case of public revolt against the government in thirty years!

The following year there was a mass demonstration in Kaohsiung for Taiwan independence. It was suppressed with violence and mass arrests. Over the next few years a rising number of articles and meetings began to publicly criticize the government. (The overworked censors could hardly keep up with them.) University campus demonstrations proliferated, after years of student quiescence. Cases of violence against antigovernment activists, one of them the 1984 murder of journalist Henry Liu in California by Guomindang agents, led to investigations of Taipei's formidable secret police network. Ten years after the death of Chiang Kai-shek, the lid he had fastened over the Nationalists' island was being pushed off.

COMPARED TO the Philippines, however, Guomindang oppression in Taiwan was light. After eighteen years of rule, not only had Ferdinand Marcos and his free-spending wife, Imelda, plundered the economy—they were venal on a

---

[3] It was succeeded by the American Institute in Taipei, a "shadow embassy" staffed by temporarily "retired" U.S. State Department officials. This arrangement, with a corresponding Taiwan presence in Washington, has remained and works effectively.

scale that Chun Doo Hwan would have envied—but goon squads from the police and the Marcos-dominated Army had instituted a continuing reign of terror, in which "salvaging," the kidnapping, torture, and murder of political opponents, had become commonplace.

On August 21, 1983, the regime resorted to public assassination. Benigno Aquino, a bright, well-read, extrovert politician known as Ninoy, was Marcos's one great political rival. After illegal imprisonment by Marcos, he had been released for medical treatment in the United States. But he kept up his highly vocal opposition to the dictatorship. Returning to the Philippines, he was hustled off his plane on arrival by military guards and shot in the head. The assassination plot's organizer, who has yet to be brought to trial, was most probably the then Army Chief of Staff (and Marcos's former bodyguard), General Fabian Ver.

Ninoy Aquino was an immensely popular man. Although a rich landowner in his own right—he belonged to one of the old *illustrado* families who had long made up the islands' power elite—he was widely traveled, had a strong intellectual bent, and presented believable plans for rehabilitating his country. On the few occasions I met him I was impressed, as were others who knew him better, by his wit, intelligence, and courage. To many Filipinos he represented their country's greatest hope for leadership since the untimely death of President Ramón Magsaysay twenty-five years before. Two million people joined the funeral procession for Aquino through Manila's streets.

Aquino's death set in motion a formidable chain of events. Led by the archbishop of Manila, Jaime Cardinal Sin, Catholic prelates now joined the chorus of priests and nuns who had long been attacking Marcos's brutal regime. Pressured by the embassy in Manila, U.S. government policy makers and politicians began to question American support of Marcos. The impoverished Filipino farmers were already against him, as their support for the Maoist New People's Army in the countryside indicated. Now well-dressed businessmen in the middle-class suburb of Makati began to demonstrate against him. When Marcos, trusting in his well-tested capacity for ballot-box stuffing, called for an immediate presidential election on February 7, 1986, he made a critical error.

Reluctantly responding to a million-signature write-in campaign, Aquino's widow, Cory, an American-educated housewife, agreed to run for President. After a dramatic "people power" campaign she and her running mate, Salvador Laurel, won almost 60 percent of the vote. Nonetheless, Marcos stole the election. His election commissioners sequestered the ballot boxes, then tampered with the totals; once the fix was in, the Marcos-controlled National Assembly declared his reelection.

With this the Philippines exploded. Protest marchers came out all over the country, two million of them in Manila alone. Aided by thousands of volunteer workers, Aquino toured the southern islands, making speeches and holding prayer rallies. (The nation's Catholic episcopate had denounced Marcos's vote fraud; bypassing the Marcos-controlled radio and TV channels, the news of the Aquino election majorities in the provinces had been carried over the radios of the Catholic Broadcasters Association.) Two days after the voting, a crowd of 500,000 gathered in Manila's Luneta Park to support Aquino's call for civil disobedience.

Although the armed forces at first held firm for Marcos, doubts began to develop in the face of what Lieutenant General Fidel Ramos, then Deputy Chief of Staff, would soon call "a revolution of the people." Ramos, a dour, honest, and incorruptible West Point graduate, had hoped to take over from Ver as Chief of Staff. He represented the new Army reform movement, mostly younger officers tired of rule by cronyism. Given the gathering popular support for Aquino and Marcos's evident reneging on Army reforms, Ramos and the Defense Minister, Juan Enrile, decided on open revolt. On February 22, they brought some 300 troops and reform Army leaders into the Defense Ministry and Camp Crame, in the heart of Manila, called a press conference, and publicly demanded Marcos's resignation in favor of Cory Aquino.

The next day Marcos and Ver sent a tank column of still loyal Marines to attack the insurgents. They were stopped effectively by tens of thousands of people who had massed in the streets around Camp Crame. Urged on by Cardinal Sin and Ramos's broadcasts over the Church's Radio Veritas, the people of Manila—shouting, cheering, praying—placed their bodies in front of the tanks. Civilian trucks and buses were piled up at improvised barricades. The tanks retreated. Shaken, Marcos went on TV to denounce the "rebels" and assure the country that he was still in charge. At 9:50 A.M. he suddenly went off the air. A column of Ramos's troops, after a brief firefight, had captured the Maharlika Broadcasting System complex, giving Ramos and Enrile access to the airwaves.

Broadcasts now urged the citizens of Manila to keep coming out in support of the new "people power." From around the country military commanders began calling in their support to Ramos. (It was later said that some Army waverers had been pressured by their wives to join the "New Armed Forces of the People.") Several jets buzzed the city to assure the insurgents of air support in the event of a military showdown. They included U.S. aircraft from the American base at Clark Field.

On February 25, Ramos's troops captured the TV stations still controlled by Marcos supporters. Crowds poured into the streets to force more of Marcos's tanks out of the area. At 10:45 A.M. on that day, Cory Aquino's informal inauguration as President was broadcast to the country. Marcos's own swearing-in ceremony was witnessed by only a small group of supporters at Malacañang Palace.

Shortly after 9 P.M., Ferdinand and Imelda Marcos and their immediate family left Malacañang by helicopter for Clark Field. From there they were flown to Hawaii, with very few options in the matter. Although the United States—making amends for its longtime support of Marcos's "anti-Communist" government—quickly recognized the Aquino government, the Americans had agreed to allow the Marcoses asylum in the United States.

The spectacular success of Filipino "people power" was a milestone for the spread of democracy. It marked a new dimension in politics. In this age of information, communications were all-important; the most valuable counters in a revolt were now not the arsenals but the television transmitters. There were, of course, other elements to consider. Ramos's military resistance, Marcos's own failing nerve, and the surprising political charisma of Corazon Aquino all counted heavily. (As the Tiananmen massacre later demonstrated, the lack of these elements could still give temporary victory to hard-line despots.) But it was the people who won.

The lessons of that Manila February were not lost on the rest of the world. They were both forerunner and model for what later happened in Eastern Europe and in Moscow itself. They were most quickly taken to heart in the Asia-Pacific countries. As a Thai Foreign Ministry statement put it: "Politics in the ASEAN countries is not as it was fifteen or twenty years ago, when one man could dictate."[4]

CITIZENS OF the Republic of China on Taiwan had been among the most interested watchers of Marcos's deposition and "people power's" victory in the Philippines. Their interest was shared by Taiwan's aging President, Chiang Ching-kuo. Now determined to go down in history as a political liberalizer, Chiang allowed an opposition party to enter candidates in the 1986 local elections, for the first time in Taiwan's history—or, for that matter, in all of China's. (The newly organized Democratic Progressive Party promptly won 30 percent of the vote.) In October of that year, the ruling Guomindang Party announced that marital law would be lifted in 1987. Chiang personally declared that no one in his family would hold high political office after his death.

He made good on both these commitments. In July 1987, martial law was repealed. When Chiang died in January 1988, he left behind him a country in transition toward democracy, with an increasing number of native Taiwan

[4] This statement was ironic in view of the trouble which later broke out in Bangkok. Authoritarian rule in Thailand was traditionally loose—an odd combination of monarchy, democracy, and militarism. But in May 1992 demonstrators were shot down on orders of Suchinda Kraprayoon, who was later forced to resign as Prime Minister.

Chinese now prominent in political positions. His successor as President was to be a native Taiwanese, Lee Teng-hui. Chiang had himself groomed Lee, an able agricultural expert, for the job.

ALMOST TWO years to the day after Marcos received his walking papers, Korea's President Chun Doo Hwan stepped down from office in disgrace. Although the political mechanics involved were very different, the atmospheres of their passing were strikingly similar. Understandably, reports of the popular uprising in the Philippines had the effect of a shock wave in Korea. To many Koreans it seemed as if Marcos and Chun Doo Hwan were the same man. Throughout 1986, with the effect of a chain reaction, violent demonstrations escalated. Pitched battles with police were fought in the streets of Seoul and other cities. At the end of the day, in Seoul as in Manila, it was not student demonstrators but the middle class, finally outraged and indignant, whose action proved decisive.

With his eye on the forthcoming 1988 Olympics, to be held for the first time in Seoul, Chun Doo Hwan had set out to keep the country quiet. Unlike Chiang Ching-kuo, however, he decided on tighter repression rather than conciliation. Here his own rough tactics worked against him. In January 1987, a student activist from Seoul National University, Park Chong Chol, died under police torture. This was not an isolated incident. Accustomed to arresting and interrogating "suspects" without warrant, the security police—elements of the former KCIA had been euphemistically renamed the National Security Planning Agency—had a long record of using torture during interrogations. This time Park's death was enough to force the resignation of the Home Affairs Minister and the national police chief. The Korean Federal Bar Association, not normally regarded as a civil rights activist, demanded publicly that "all practices of torture which have been either covered up or ignored by authorities should be thoroughly reviewed and brought to light."

Despite such criticism Chun decided to act tough. In the face of general opposition demands for a direct presidential election in 1988 (instead of selection by the Assembly), Chun suspended all debate on this matter; the status quo would not be changed. He announced that the ruling Democratic Justice Party's candidate—under the current electoral system, sure to win—would be Roh Tae Woo, a fellow general and Military Academy classmate of Chun's, whose troops had participated in the 1980 Kwangju suppression.

Street violence broke out on an unprecedented scale; private citizens—businesspeople and housewives as well as factory workers—were loud in their criticism. Fighting between police and student demonstrators spread from Seoul to all the country's major cities. This time middle-class white-collar workers supported the demonstrators. As in Manila the previous year, many turned out on the streets themselves. Church groups, both Catholic and Protestant, were prominent among the new activists—evidence of the strong influence of Korea's Christians, now almost 30 percent of the population, on the nation's moral issues. Rumors of a military crackdown filled the air. Chun's past behavior under pressure strongly suggested this.

On June 29, just three days after Seoul's midtown district had been torn up in a pitched battle between riot police and hard-line radical students, Chun's handpicked candidate, Roh Tae Woo, now chairman of the majority Democratic Justice Party, dramatically defused the impending explosion. In a statement that evidently had Chun's approval, he promised revision of the Constitution and the election laws to allow direct presidential elections in December. He promised amnesty for Kim Dae Jung (then under house arrest) and other political prisoners, freedom of the press, new guarantees for civil rights, local autonomy based on local elections, guarantees to allow "the free and democratic growth of political parties," and, finally, reforms to cope with "deep-seated" corruption. "The people," Roh summarized, "are the masters of the country and the people's will must come before everything else."

Popular reaction was instant and enthusiastic. Epitomizing the national mood, a midtown literary coffeehouse posted a sign outside its doors. "Free coffee to all. Today is a good day!"

Roh's statement signalized, to put it mildly, a new approach in Korean political leadership. When it was confirmed two days later by a tight-lipped Chun, the nation breathed a collective sigh of relief. What made the government give in? Part of the answer lay in the character of Roh himself. A shrewd political pragmatist, untainted by personal corruption, he saw the situation far more clearly than Chun and was prepared to act on what he saw.

There were other factors at work also. The entire governing establishment of the Republic of Korea had put its faith in making a great show of the 1988 Olympics. They were to mark Korea's coming of age as a postwar modern nation, just as the 1964 Olympics had marked Japan's. Continuing violence or its converse, a sullen peace enforced by the military, could bring on a cancellation of the Games. The Manila demonstrations against Marcos remained a disturbing example. With the Olympics barely a year away, even Chun grew nervous about a crackdown. "In a sense," as a Seoul journalist put it, "Chun was held hostage to the Olympic Games."

The attitude of the United States was an added imponderable. The Americans had not intervened against the violence at Kwangju in 1980. But they had intervened against Marcos in the Philippines, despite his well-publicized friendship with Ronald Reagan. In the midst of the 1987 crisis, just days before Roh's statement, Gaston Sigur, then Assistant Secretary of State for Asia/

Violence in Seoul. Student demonstrators throwing gasoline bombs fought continuing battles with police. Jigsaw Productions

Roh Tae Woo's inaugural. Elected president in 1988, Roh had earlier pledged to bring democracy to his country. Jigsaw Productions

Pacific Affairs, had arrived in Seoul with a message from Washington. As he later explained: "I met with President Chun at that time and I made it very clear to him that we believed the use of the Korean military in this situation would be catastrophic. It could lead to serious repercussions in the relations between our two countries."

In the course of his brief visit Sigur saw what Roh obviously saw and even Chun Doo Hwan felt constrained to accept. He explained later: "Korea by 1987 had irrevocably changed. The middle class had become a power. And it could no longer be disregarded. The government wasn't dealing with a handful of left-wing students. They may have been the ones out front, but it was plain that you had strong middle-class support for the demonstrations.

"As one cabinet member said to me, a man not known for his leniency on human rights: 'There is a storm in this country.' And the right word for it is democracy."

The election that followed was a fair one, the first Korea had had in twenty years. Roh Tae Woo won it, but with only 37 percent of the total vote. Had the two opposition candidates, Kim Dae Jung and Kim Young Sam, made common cause, they would easily have won. As things turned out, the election was split three ways.

In Roh's inaugural address he made a memorable statement: "The era when human rights and freedom were neglected in the name of economic growth and security has now ended." This was optimistic. The next four years in Korea would have their instances of government suppression and student-police violence. Given some guarantees of democracy, strikes and other forms of labor unrest multiplied, the more so for the long years of suppression in the past. A corner had been turned, however.

It was not to be a smooth progress. Many contradictory tendencies were at work. If high growth had brought improved living conditions and a sense of popular political confidence, it had also fostered a centralized "Father knows best" kind of bureaucracy. The Korean official's idea of autocratic rule, with its roots deep in an old Confucian tradition, found the give-and-take of democratic politics very harsh medicine. Nationalism of a primitive sort also entered the equation, made more intense by almost a half century of Japanese oppression. So did the urge for national unification, despite the intransigence of the Communist dictatorship in the north. The story of the fight for democracy in Korea is more complex than elsewhere in the Asian-Pacific countries, but because it encompasses so much, it is worth retelling in some detail.

JUST A FEW miles off the heavily traveled Seoul–Pusan Expressway, at the western apex of a rough triangle with the vast Pohang steel complex and the Hyundai shipyards at Ulsan, the small, tidy city of Kyongju sits surrounded by low mountains in the center of fertile farming country. Kyongju has a special meaning to Koreans. If Kwangju to the southwest can be called Korea's modern conscience, Kyongju is the country's abiding soul. For almost a thousand years it was the capital of the Shilla kings, who first unified the country in the seventh century.

The burial mounds over the royal tombs are almost in the city center, the cynosure of unending tours of schoolchildren and other visitors. In the museum some of their gold "flying" crowns can be seen, marvelously crafted artifacts of delicate filigree, unique to their time and place. Not far away stands the great Buddhist temple complex of Pulguksa, whose symmetrically balanced stone bridges and pagodas evoke images of the clouds and flowers for which they are named. First built in A.D. 535, Pulguksa has been officially named Historical Site No. 1.

The Koreans have been a nation for a long time. A Tungusic people of Central Asian origin, they found their way into their peninsula via Manchuria and Mongolia. By the early Bronze Age they had set up a congeries of tribal states throughout the Korean peninsula. They are racially and culturally distinctive. Their Turkic language is unique in East Asia, although Japanese resembles it structurally, and their high cheekbones and rather square-cut features set them apart from both their Chinese and Japanese neighbors.

The Shilla rulers, after finally conquering the armies of their neighbors Paekche and Koguryo, made Kyongju the metropolis of an aristocratic leisure class—albeit one whose leisure was founded on a large population of virtual serfs. Its streets and temples were modeled, like Kyoto's in Japan, after Changan (the present Xian), the sophisticated capital of Tang Dynasty China. Its kings were by no means mere Chinese vassals. In fact, they successfully resisted the efforts of the Tang emperors to turn Korea into a network of Chinese military protectorates. Yet their culture, like Japan's, owed much to Chinese models. Among them was Buddhism, introduced to Korea from China in the fourth century; Kyongju, with its monasteries and temples, was a stronghold of the popular Pure Land sect of Buddhism.

One of the world's great pieces of religious art is the eleven-foot-tall statue of the traditional Sakyamuni Buddha, carved from a single stone and set in the Sokkuram, a grotto hewn out of rock in the mountain behind Pulguksa. Distinguished not only by its serene beauty but also by its tranquil wooded surroundings—in 1991 still free of soft-drink stands and tourist-bus parking places—the Buddha, surrounded by attendant bodhisattvas and disciples, turns its calm stone eyes toward the ocean, unblinking under the first rays of the sun as it comes up over Korea's East Sea (otherwise known as the Sea of Japan).

Some miles out to sea the remains of King Munmu, the ruler who unified the country, still rest inside a large rock now buried beneath the waters. According to old Shilla legend, Munmu stands ready to return to life, possibly reincarnated as a dragon, if invoked by his people to save the nation from foreign invaders.

Reviewing the later history of Munmu's dynasty and the Koryo kingdom—famed for its extraordinary celadon pottery—that supplanted it, one is inclined to think that Munmu, at least in his pre-dragon state, made a serious directional error. For almost a thousand years after his death, invasion threats came not from the sea side but from inland, on the northern and western marches of the peninsula. Khitans, Mongols, and Manchu invaders rode down from the Asian heartland to the north. More disciplined forays came from China. Following the Tang failure to conquer and occupy, each succeeding Chinese dynasty, it would seem, made its own effort to consolidate the vague tributary relationship with Korea—as indeed they did with Vietnam, the other semi-Sinicized nation on China's border.

In the thirteenth century, the Mongols, now ensconced in Beijing as the Yuan Dynasty, arrived in force with their feared cavalry and occupied the entire country. Thereafter Korean soldiers and sailors by the thousands perished during their enforced service as allies in the ill-fated Mongol-Chinese invasion of Japan.

By the late sixteenth century, however, King Munmu's worries about attacks from across the sea were proving out. Hideyoshi's invasion attempts from Japan, as we have seen, ended in failure. Ming troops from China had joined Korean guerrilla bands in harassing the Japanese, while Korea's brilliant admiral, Yi Sun-shin, effectively cut their sea communications and supply lines. But three centuries later a more purposeful assault began. Again the seaborne invaders were Japanese, and their advance into Korea ended this time with total, if temporary colonization.

In fact, the Japanese imperialists, newly modernized after the Meiji Restoration, were only latecomers to the waves of modernization (and colonization) from the West, now lapping at Asia's shores. The same mix of businessmen, missionaries, and proconsuls that had colonized Hong Kong and Singapore and opened China's ports to the opium trade began making overtures to Korea in the mid-nineteenth century. Korea was in no condition to receive them.

SINCE 1392, Korea, then called Choson, had been ruled by kings of the Yi Dynasty, whose military founders built up a new state to replace the vanished glories of Shilla and Koryo. Their state was modeled on China's Confucian society, with the Buddhism of the old Kyongju aristocrats no longer in favor. Instead the country was run by a tight mandarin bureaucracy, painfully status-conscious and hidebound in its reliance on Confucian rites and philosophies. Whereas ingrained Confucian ideas of civic obedience can serve at least temporarily as an aid to strong government—as President Park Chung Hee would later demonstrate—under the late Yi Dynasty oligarchy it gradually ossified Korean society. Authority was centralized, but increasingly inefficient. There were almost no local power centers. People who wanted reform had no recourse but to revolt—and occasional uprisings by the badly used lower classes were bloodily suppressed.

As the Yonsei University historian Kim Dong-gil commented: "The tight control of centralized government in those days made it impossible even to have the kind of feudal system that grew up in medieval Europe or Japan. Feudalism in its way helped educate people. They got used to the idea of contracts, for example. But in Korea, historically speaking, there was no idea of a contract until modern times."

Outside ideas or learning were suppressed by the old Yi government in the name of Confucian orthodoxy. So was Christianity. First brought into Korea from China by French Catholic missionaries, Christian teachings spread quickly in Seoul and other cities. The Confucian mandarinate reacted violently against this "Western" faith, and throughout the nineteenth century thousands of priests and converts were imprisoned or executed. Equally persecuted was a rival Tonghak ("Eastern learning") cult, an eclectic mixture of Christianity, Taoism, and native Korean shamanism, which taught that all men were born equal and deserved equal rights. Tonghak's popularity—understandable in a country where slavery was not finally abolished until 1894—alarmed Choson's Confucian officials, who had inevitably heard much about the populist Taiping Rebellion in neighboring China. Tonghak's founder was executed in 1864, the same year that Hong Xiuquan, the Taiping leader, committed suicide after his final defeat.

IT WAS ABOUT this time that the first Western traders began to knock at the doors of the Hermit Kingdom, as Korea was beginning to be known. The first encounters were not happy. In 1866, when an American merchantman, the *General Sherman,* sailed up to the river port of Pyongyang, it was set on fire and its crew massacred by a Korean mob. Some years later, a small American Navy squadron, thinking to repeat Commodore Perry's "opening" of Japan, tried to force the straits of Kanghwa, at the mouth of the Han River not far from Seoul. Fired on by Korean shore batteries, the Americans landed Marines to capture a local fort, but in the end sailed away, unprepared for prolonged hostilities. A French squadron had landed troops there earlier, with similarly inconclusive result.

Encouraged by the apparent success of this "get-tough" policy, Korea's regent, or *taewongun*, an energetic but very conservative autocrat, set out to enforce a policy of isolation. His timing was disastrously bad. For he acted to close his country just after Japan had been "opened" and its self-modernizing Meiji Restoration had succeeded. In 1875, not averse to doing some opening themselves, the Meiji government sent a Japanese fleet to Korea, with a substantial landing force aboard. The Japanese fleet succeeded where the Americans and French had failed. Bowing to superior force, the Koreans signed the Treaty of Kanghwa with Japan the next year.

The Hermit Kingdom was now open. The United States signed its own commercial treaty in 1882. Other Western nations followed, with the French inserting a clause in theirs allowing the propagation of Christianity. This had important consequences.

Inside Korea, as the extent of "Western learning" finally became known, a struggle began between modernizers and conservatives. Exasperated by decades of increasingly incompetent government, thousands began to join a revived Tonghak movement in the countryside aimed at destroying foreign influences and reviving Korea's native Confucianism. By 1894 a full-scale peasant revolt was sweeping the country. Since government troops proved unable to defeat the Tonghak armies, court factions in desperation called on China and Japan for help.

Each of the two neighbors was eager to help Korea, but on its own terms. The issue was finally decided by Japan's victory in the Sino-Japanese War of 1895, which was largely fought on Korean soil. Japanese troops now put down the last of the Tonghak rebels.

Korea's government was by this time in ruins. Its people impoverished and its army almost nonexistent, the kingdom was in no position to resist annexation by Asia's first homegrown imperialist power. The takeover was formalized after Japan's victory in the Russo-Japanese War a decade later. By 1910, Korea had officially become a government-general of Japan. Even its name was changed, to the Japanese pronunciation of Chosen.

IN HIS INFLUENTIAL book *Korea: The Politics of the Vortex*,[5] Gregory Henderson refers to Japanese rule in Korea as "colonial totalitarianism . . . brief compared to many colonies, but uniquely intense." The intensity was partly due to the marked racial and cultural similarities between Koreans and Jap-

[5] Cambridge: Harvard University Press. In my summaries of Korean history, I have relied heavily on this work, as well as the excellent English updating and revision of Lee Ki-baik's classic *A New History of Korea*, titled *Korea Old and New: A History* (Cambridge, Mass.: Harvard University Press, 1990), authored by Carter J. Eckert, Ki-baik Lee, Young Ick Lew, Michael Robinson, and Edward W. Wagner.

anese. True to the "pan-Asia" thinking of the Meiji era, many Japanese leaders felt that the Koreans, like the Chinese, could be co-opted as fellow Asian allies—albeit very dependent ones. Prince Ito, the Meiji constitution maker, was one of these; ironically, it was his assassination in 1909, by the Korean patriot An Chung-gun, that helped give Japan's Korea policy over to the militarist hard-liners, led by Ito's perennial rival, Yamagata Aritomo.

Yamagata wanted total "Japanization" of the peninsular neighbor. For the first ten years of Japan's rule his generals ruthlessly suppressed not only Korean politics but Korean culture. Korean newspapers were shut down, since even the Korean language was to be superseded by Japanese. Meanwhile mass immigration of Japanese colonists was encouraged. The number of Japanese residents in Korea increased from 42,000 in 1905 to almost 337,000 in 1918. Backed up by a strong gendarmerie imported from Japan, the new imperialists took over lands and businesses. They restructured the government bureaucracy on the Japanese model. Keeping socially to themselves, while setting up a national network of Japanese schools, they made it clear to the Koreans that they were now second-class citizens in their own country.

This was hardly education for democracy. Yet paradoxically the totality of Japanese oppression developed a sense of solidarity, nationalism, and unified dissent among Koreans in all walks of life which had not been present in the days of the Yi Dynasty. Although the nationwide March 1, 1919, independence demonstrations were met by police terror, they nurtured local nationalist movements throughout the country.

Christians were active in them. American Protestants—Presbyterians in particular—had begun intensive missionary work in Korea late in the nineteenth century. The schools and later the colleges they founded had a wide influence; because of their international character, they were partially safe from Japanese repression. Through the years of Japanese rule, to be a Christian in a sense was to make a nationalist statement. It was the tradition of Christian social and political engagement, begun at this time, that later resulted in heavy participation by both Protestants and Catholics in popular protest movements against Korea's own authoritarian rulers after World War II.

Impressed by the strength of Korean protest and worried, as ever, about international public opinion, the Japanese government in Tokyo decided to ease up on its colonial policy. Under a new governor-general, Admiral Saito Makoto, Japan tried out a scheme of "cultural politics" (*bunka seiji*). Korean organizations were encouraged, local advisory councils were permitted, newspapers were allowed to publish, and wider opportunities were given to Koreans both in business and in the schools. Koreans gained considerably from this, just as they could improve their skills by participating in Japanese-led industrialization. Yet they were well aware of getting only the leavings from the Japanese table. When the new Keijo (for Seoul) Imperial University was established, only about 300 Koreans were allowed to study there alongside their Japanese colleagues. Almost every Korean who wanted a university education had to travel to Japan.

As the China Incident of 1937 and subsequent events led to World War II, Japan's militarists were in the ascendant. Even the modest concessions of Admiral Saito's cultural politics were swept away in the interests of harnessing Koreans to fulfill the needs of Japan's wartime garrison state. Hundreds of thousands of men were drafted into hard-labor construction battalions for service in the war zones, while Korean women were taken by the thousands to serve in the *ianbu* ("Comfort Corps") military brothels of the Japanese Army.

Even where Japanese policy was relatively relaxed, the line between independence fighter and Japanese collaborator often ran quite thin. With politics barred to them, the cultural and business spheres were the only places where Koreans could hope to keep nationalism alive—that is, if they chose to work within the context of their society, instead of waging a lonely fight from exile. A case can be made for both alternatives. But to be a political exile is a situation necessarily granted only to a few.

THE LIFE OF Kim Song-su makes an interesting statement about how far a Korean could advance the cause of nationalism within the framework of Japanese rule. The scion of an old *yangban* gentry family in the southwestern province of Cholla, Kim was only fourteen when Japan's victory over the Russians sealed his country's fate. Like other wellborn Koreans of that day, he was educated in Japan, at Tokyo's Waseda University. His family were originally rich landowners, and their wealth increased as they consolidated and expanded their properties. Koreans were denied the right to enter politics in the Japanese-run government-general, but Kim gathered some like-minded associates and set up an informal association, later known as the Posong Group from the name of his native town.

With this, Kim pointed the way for other rich landowners to invest farm revenues in entrepreneurial manufacturing enterprises. A good businessman, he acquired the Kyongsong Spinning and Weaving Company, one of the few large companies of that day under native Korean ownership. He also helped in founding the Honam Bank in his native province as a financing agent for other newly formed Korean companies. He did not shun Japanese protection.

Business was not his only concern, however. Taking advantage of Admiral Saito's lenient governance, he founded in 1920 the *Dong-A Ilbo*, which remains today Seoul's leading newspaper. He paid for the expansion of Posong High School into what is now Korea University. This is, arguably, the most distinguished private university in the country; and Kim Song-su was its founder.

Sokkuram Buddha. This classic statue, dating from the eighth century, stands in the Sokkuram Grotto at Kyongju in the southwest. It is an abiding symbol of Korea's 2,000-year-old history. Korean Overseas Information Service

Kim Sung Soo, founder of the Dong-A Ilbo newspaper and Korea University, helped keep Korean culture alive. Dong-A Ilbo

New building along the Han River suggests the profusion of housing starts in Korea's overcrowded capital metropolis. Peter Bull

Kim's support of education and the press recalls the example of Fukuzawa Yukichi in Meiji Japan. All of Kim's activities, however, had to conform at least superficially to a foreign occupier's set of standards—although there were times when they openly challenged them.[6] To keep his enterprises going, Kim and others like him had to make continual compromises with the Japanese proconsuls. (This was particularly true during World War II, when Korea was run as a vital cog in the Japanese militarists' world order.) But at the same time, in their schools and "Buy Korean" groups like the Korean Production Movement, they gave their countrymen valuable nuclei around which they could meet, exchange ideas, and plan for an independent future. They also offered a beginning for democratic political activity. So did the Korean Christian churches.

Leftist groups also wielded great influence, particularly among the Korean intelligentsia. As we have seen, the Russian Revolution had a powerful effect on the post-1919 Korean independence movement. Korean nationalists who had fled to China and the maritime provinces of Siberia were among the first international Communists. In 1920 Lenin pledged to "support the Korean independence movement with all our strength," making an initial contribution of two million rubles.[7]

Only a minority of Korean leftists could be called Communists. There were Marxists, Christian socialists, and other varieties of "progressive" groups, most of them competing, often violently, against each other.[8] But it is fair to say that socialist or pro-Communist leanings generally prevailed among youth groups, journalists, labor union members (insofar as unions were permitted by the Japanese authorities), and politically conscious nationalist students. At many schools and, interestingly enough, at Keijo (Seoul) Imperial University after its founding, leftist thinking was stimulated by imported Japanese professors. For despite the watchfulness of the *Kempeitai* police and the increasingly right-wing tilt of Japanese governments, some form of egalitarian Marxism remained the "politically correct" faith inside Japanese universities.

Socialism and Communism in particular also gained recruits on a popular level, especially among the hard-pressed farm populations of the northern

[6] During the 1936 Olympics, in which a Korean, running as part of the Japanese team, won a gold medal in track, *Dong-A*'s editors inked out the Japanese flag on the runner's chest in the front-page picture and airbrushed in a Korean flag. For this the newspaper was suspended from circulation.

[7] For this and other background information on Korean Communism, I am indebted to Robert A. Scalapino and Chong-Sik Lee, co-authors of the authoritative *Communism in Korea* (Berkeley: University of California Press, 1972).

[8] The Korean Communist Party was officially organized (with Soviet approval) at a Seoul restaurant on April 17, 1925, only after almost five years of bitter factional infighting, climaxed by a pitched battle between rival Communist military factions in Siberia in 1921.

provinces, who kept in contact with Koreans across the border in China and the Soviet Union. Guerrilla bands also operated in the border regions; fighting against the Japanese, they became popular heroes. For all Koreans, from conservative entrepreneurs to secret Communist Party members, were united in a nationalist resentment against Japan and Japanese rule.

Given Japan's tightening wartime control, with the forcible incorporation of Koreans into the Japanese war effort, there were ever fewer opportunities to express anti-Japanese feelings. By the early 1940s, in fact, a great portion of the country's leadership—whatever their private feelings—could be said to have been successfully co-opted by the Japanese.

It is both facile and unjust, however, to dismiss Kim Song-su and other business leaders of that time as Japanese collaborationists. Kim deserves his characterization as a great cultural nationalist. The university and the newspaper he founded both fostered a sense of Korean identity in the face of a determined Japanese effort, backed by overwhelming power, to turn Koreans into loyal (if still somewhat second-class) Japanese citizens. His company and others like it inevitably had to work within a Japanese economic firmament and accord with Japanese standards. (Among other things, the Kyongsong Spinning and Weaving Company treated its young workers even more harshly than its Japanese counterparts.) Yet without their business experience and leadership it is highly doubtful that the Korean economy could have achieved its rapid takeoff in the sixties. More than half of Park Chung Hee's *chaebol* traced their own or their founders' business beginnings back before 1945.[9]

[9] This information is based principally on a study cited by Carter Eckert in his thoughtful and comprehensive *Offspring of Empire: The Kochang Kims and the Colonial Origins of Korean Capitalism* (Seattle: University of Washington Press, 1991). The study, conducted by Kyu Hyun Kim, concluded that twenty-nine of the founders of the fifty leading *chaebol* had begun their business careers as entrepreneurs or employees of Korean or Japanese companies during the colonial period.

14

The Korean Example

The American way of life cannot survive unless other peoples who want to adopt that pattern throughout the world can do so without fear and in the hope of success.

HARRY S. TRUMAN

The era when human rights and freedom were neglected in the name of economic growth and security has now ended.

ROH TAE WOO

With Japan's surrender in August 1945, the rules of the political game changed spectacularly. Among the newly liberated nations of East Asia, Korea and the Philippines seemed to be in the best position for self-government. Through their forty unpleasant years of Japan's "colonial totalitarianism," Koreans had nonetheless developed modern business and bureaucratic skills to a considerable degree. Education had spread, even if Japanese-dominated, and the peninsula's communications system, as the nerve center of Tokyo's Greater East Asia Co-Prosperity Sphere, was the best on the Asian continent. Native Korean elites were in good supply, including even a core group of young officers educated in military schools in Manchuria and Japan. Across the northern borders in China and Siberia there were hardened groups of Korean guerrilla fighters; whole formations had been organized by both Chinese Nationalists and Communists. Since 1919 long-memoried exiles in the Provisional Government had continued to plot and bide their time in Washington and Chongqing.

All of these groups wanted and expected immediate independence—however imperfect and disparate their plans for implementing it. It was their misfortune to experience instead a joint Soviet-American occupation pledged to enforce a five-year transitional "trusteeship." The resultant confusions, misunderstandings, and confrontations compounded one another. It was, as the Korean saying has it, a case of a shrimp caught between two whales. Nor did it help that both whales were hopelessly myopic and the shrimp was not a very good swimmer.

The history of the Soviet occupation of North Korea can be briefly told. Stalin had agreed at Yalta in 1945 to come into the war against Japan, at American urging. (No one seems to have told the U.S. Joint Chiefs that by 1945 their own submarine blockade and unrestricted air power had already won the war, strategically speaking.) There is little evidence that the Russians looked covetously at Korea the way they looked, for example, at their old Port Arthur base in China. They do not seem to have made detailed preparation for their stewardship, trusting, as they did in Eastern Europe, to the work of pro-Soviet surrogates. When Soviet armies occupied North Korea—after an appalling few weeks of wholesale rape, murder, and robbery perpetrated on both Japanese and Korean inhabitants—they at first gave free rein to a variety of local Korean organizations, under the general direction of a Korean People's Republic. (This provisional government had originally been set up in Seoul at the instigation of the soon-to-retire Japanese governor-general, in an effort to prevent a general massacre of Japanese residents after the surrender.)

The Soviet Army did not establish a formal occupation regime, but its political priorities were soon made clear. Their man for Korea was a thirty-three-year-old anti-Japanese guerrilla leader who took the name of Kim Il Sung. Kim had originally operated with Korean and Chinese partisans in Manchuria, but he had spent the last four years training in Siberia, where he was given the Soviet rank of major. The Russians brought Kim back to Korea in October, welcoming him as "General Kim Il Sung" at a mass rally in Pyongyang, the North Korean capital.

With Soviet help Kim fairly soon established himself as the Party leader, but he proved to be something more than a mere Soviet front man. A brilliant, ruthless, and single-minded political operator—a comparison with Yugoslavia's Tito or Romania's once formidable Nicolae Ceauşescu comes to mind—he used Soviet support to eliminate a considerable number of rival Communist leaders, including Soviet citizens of Korean ancestry who had accompanied the occupying troops. The Russians nonetheless felt quite secure in pulling out the bulk of their troops in 1948. They left behind them a newly created Democratic People's Republic of Korea, complete with Soviet-trained army and secret police, with Kim Il Sung firmly in charge.

As Prime Minister and head of the Korean Workers Party, Kim kept the façade of land reform and other forward-looking measures put through by idealistic leftist committees in the short-lived Democratic People's Republic of 1945. But behind it he organized a totalitarian police state, which has continued to exist under the same "Great Leader's" management. After their formal departure, the Soviets agreed to keep Kim supplied with military advisers and planes, tanks, and artillery. These proved sufficient to start—and almost to win—the Korean War which Kim began in 1950.

THE LATTER half of the 1940s saw two great and impressive American foreign policy achievements—the Marshall Plan in Europe and in Asia the Occupation of Japan. Against these must be balanced two almost total failures. In China the collapse of Marshall's attempts at mediating between Nationalists and Communists only climaxed a disastrous history of attempted accommodation with the corrupt regime of Chiang Kai-shek. In Korea the failure was even worse. Faced with one of the world's most complex cultural and political rehabilitations, the leader of the world's democracies sent in a U.S. Army corps commander and his men with a narrow mission to accept the Japanese surrender, keep order, and "establish orderly government in Korea below the 38th parallel."

Lieutenant General John R. Hodge and his 24th Corps, having fought and won their share of the battle for Okinawa, were hastily ordered to supervise (and indeed to constitute) the U.S. Army Military Government in Korea. Where Douglas MacArthur in Japan (now designated Hodge's superior) had the benefit of several years of intensive study by government planners in Washington and a clear set of directives about the Occupation's goals, Hodge had next to nothing. Washington's World War II planners recognized the strategic importance of Korea, but the problem of Korean independence remained a neglected afterthought. Most of Hodge's military government teams had originally been intended for the Philippines or Japan. He had almost no Korean linguists with him. Even the boundary of his jurisdiction, the 38th parallel, had been rather casually chosen at a Washington conference in August 1945. It was officially proposed to Moscow as a dividing line, in the hopes that the Soviet Army, already on the way to Korea, would stop at this halfway point before overrunning the entire country.

Almost predictably, the Americans made every mistake in the book. Ignoring the newly formed People's Republic and its local committees—nothing about them in the general's orders—Hodge set up a U.S. military government and at first relied for his order keeping on the Japanese police and the existing Japanese-dominated bureaucracy. At one point police fired on crowds coming out to welcome the Americans!

Hodge removed Japanese police administrators, but turned over most local administration to their Korean subordinates. (Japanese and Koreans, Hodge had remarked, looked to him like "the same breed of cat.") The People's Republic committees, generally moderately leftist in character, represented some of the most democratic forces in the country, and they had mobilized considerable spontaneous popular support. By contrast, the police—Koreans as much as Japanese—were generally hated as the symbols of Japanese authority. The resultant anger and confusion in the country was understandable. Violent demonstrations inevitably occurred.

The Americans, trusting in their familiar panacea of "free elections" to purge any political situation of its problems, were perplexed, however, trying to find parties, platforms, and candidates for elections in a country that had never had them. And USAMGIK (for United States Army Military Government in Korea), through its original mistakes, had already lost the support of many Koreans who might have helped.

At this juncture, Syngman Rhee arrived by air from Tokyo, courtesy of friends at MacArthur's headquarters. On October 20, 1945, he was presented to the Korean people, barely a week after his opposite number, Kim Il Sung, had been unveiled by the Soviets in the north. Legislative elections were somehow held late in 1946, with the Korean Democratic Party, recently founded by Kim Song-su and other conservative businessmen, getting a good portion of the vote. Rhee clearly preferred one-man rule, but temporarily aligned himself with the conservative Democrats. National elections were finally held in 1948 under UN supervision. Rhee won them, having elbowed aside most of the plausible alternative candidates. In August of that year, Rhee was proclaimed President—again, the same month as Kim Il Sung was being sworn in as Prime Minister of the People's Republic in the north.

Since the Americans and the Soviets could not agree on any kind of joint trusteeship—the Cold War meanwhile intensifying—each power decided to give its half of the sundered country independence. The Soviet armies formally packed up their bags, leaving North Korea about as independent as its opposite numbers in Eastern Europe. The Americans had to keep their troops in place, thanks to the turbulence of South Korea's politics. These now polarized, assisted both by intensive Communist activity and by the tendency of American military government to regard every nonconservative as a Communist.

Between 1946 and 1950 a pattern of consistent police brutality and oppression drove thousands of Koreans to open revolt. Leftist labor protests had multiplied, a legacy of the oppression of workers under wartime Japanese rule, but neither the military government nor Rhee had done much to improve working conditions.

Late in 1948 the violence escalated. Two regiments of the newly formed Republic of Korea Army mutinied at Yosu, in the southwest. Although

Communist-led, the so-called Yosu-Sunchon uprising attracted much popular support and was suppressed only with considerable bloodshed. For Rhee's dictatorial ways had already alienated large numbers of Koreans. He kept up the pretense of democratic government to satisfy the Americans—they too were preparing to evacuate Korea—but in practice he brooked no opposition. He relied for support increasingly on police power and militant "youth" organizations recruited by his far-right-wing supporters. Many of these were distrusted, if not hated by most Koreans for their prewar collaboration with the Japanese military occupation.

The economy of the new republic was in tatters, dependent on heavy doses of U.S. aid. Partition had left most of the country's natural resources, its power supply, and its industry north of the 38th parallel. The south had by far the greater population; but it was largely agricultural, with only textile and other light industries. The Koreans who had to administer the country were hastily recruited and ill trained, since the Japanese had carefully controlled the infrastructure of their Korean possession, business as well as bureaucracy. (All too many of the few promising local leaders were in Syngman Rhee's jails.) Along with their other problems they had to cope with floods of refugees from the north. As the next four decades would demonstrate, however badly restricted were political freedoms in the south, in Kim Il Sung's northern satrapy opposition was purged with ruthless efficiency.

Meanwhile the U.S. government continued its spectacular corporate indecision over what to do with Korea, now about to join the "free world" community. Faced with an intensified Cold War in Europe—which the Berlin blockade of 1948 only dramatized—and the imminent "loss" of China to Mao Zedong, Pentagon planners wanted to cut their losses. General MacArthur included, the Army did not want Korea inside America's Pacific defense perimeter. Dean Acheson, Harry Truman's new Secretary of State, saw Korea's importance and successfully argued for at least increased economic aid. (In the process, the Americans managed to get a somewhat attenuated land reform law passed, over Rhee's resistance.) It is ironic that Acheson was only reflecting Pentagon opinion when he made the statement in the spring of 1950—later so heavily criticized—that Korea lay "outside" the American strategic perimeter.

By that time the die had been cast. In December 1949, Kim Il Sung arrived in Moscow and asked Stalin to support the reunification of Korea by force. Somewhat reluctantly, Stalin consented, but only on condition that Kim secure Mao Zedong's approval.[1] (Contrary to American opinion at the time,

---

[1] This information, based on the Khrushchev memoirs (*Khrushchev Remembers*, Vols. 1 and 2; Boston: Little, Brown, 1974), has also been corroborated by other Soviet and Chinese sources, including the testimony of former North Korean officials now living in Moscow.

Stalin, a most cautious imperialist, had not prepared much of a "master plan" for this or other conquests.) Based on the turbulence in the south, Kim confidently predicted that a mass uprising would accompany his invasion. Park Hun-young, the veteran Party leader who directed the underground Communists in South Korea (from his headquarters in the north), had assured Pyongyang that 200,000 Communists stood ready to help North Korean forces in the event of an invasion.

Kim seemed to have little doubt of a quick victory. With Stalin's blessing given, he was assured of continuing heavy Soviet armament assistance for his ten divisions. When the war began, he had 250 new Soviet T-34 tanks, some 180 aircraft, and 122-mm heavy artillery. His 150,000-man army, already strengthened with Soviet-trained troops of Korean nationality, had recently been reinforced by several large units of veteran Korean troops who had fought with the People's Liberation Army in China. Well aware of the South Koreans' weakness, he and his generals wanted to attack before they could increase their strength.[2] Most importantly, he took the Americans at their word when they declared Korea to be "outside" their strategic perimeter in Asia.

THE KOREAN WAR was one of those wars that did not have to be fought. From the American point of view, it was, militarily speaking, a series of tactical successes (minus one big disaster) that ended in strategic stalemate. Its lessons were disregarded and its mistakes duplicated in the Vietnam War little more than a decade later. Politically speaking, it was partially effective. At least the Soviet Union and its allies were put on notice that the United States would fight, if necessary, to protect its interests. But it also underlined the limitations of a democracy fighting a war in which its immediate tangible interests were not involved. Even before Dwight Eisenhower's shortsighted, if politically effective "I will go to Korea" speech during the 1952 presidential campaign, public opinion was moving toward disengagement. For most Americans the war was far away.

[2] American academic "revisionist" historians, imaginative as always, have asserted that Kim may have attacked preemptively because he felt threatened by Syngman Rhee's threats to "unify" Korea by force. The incapacity of the Republic of Korea's Army to conduct aggressive warfare, with no air, no armor, and only a small quantity of outranged 105-mm guns, was an open secret at that time. ROK generals even attempted to secure extra small-arms ammunition from Taiwan—since their American suppliers kept them on a very tight leash. I confirmed these deficiencies myself on a reporting trip to Korea in May 1950, just a month before the invasion. Nonetheless, I was sufficiently impressed by the South Korean Army to predict, in *Time* magazine, that "no one any longer thinks that the North could pull off a successful and quick invasion of South Korea, without heavy reinforcements from the Russians or the Chinese." In the end, perhaps, my feckless optimism was proven right.

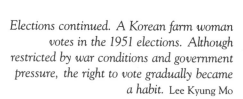

Chinese Communist involvement in the war confirmed a growing freeze in Chinese-American relations, which now intensified on both sides; it was to last for two decades. The Nationalist regime on Taiwan was, of course, saved by the announcement, in the first few days of hostilities, that American sea power would be used to interdict any hostile action from the mainland. Japan, as we have seen earlier, was the war's only real gainer, since American offshore procurement for the war effort primed the pump for Japan's later economic prosperity.

For Korea the war was a disaster. Besides causing almost three million casualties—civilians and military included—it made the division of the country between north and south final, at least for the next four decades. It separated thousands of families, their members scattered between north and south. It condemned the people of the north to life under one of the world's worst Communist dictatorships, whose threats conversely provided justification for continuing authoritarian governments in the south. The north and, for several decades to follow, the Republic of Korea in the south maintained the aspect of garrison states.

IT WAS MY fortune to experience the shock of this war from the beginning. Then a *Time* magazine correspondent in Japan, I managed to fly into Seoul, just three days after the invasion, on the last U.S. Air Force plane sent there to evacuate State Department people and their dependents. This was on June 28, three days after the Soviet T-34 tanks of the North Korean People's Army had crashed over the border and down the Uijongbu corridor into Seoul. The city that I had left barely two months before, just beginning its life as an independent capital, was gripped by terror, as crowds poured through the streets, piling into trucks, buses, and horse-drawn carts heading for the bridges across the Han River and escape to the south.

Alerted by the U.S. Army advisers with whom we were billeted that the North Koreans had broken through, two other newsmen and I drove a borrowed jeep onto the approaches of the largest Han River bridge, now packed with refugees heading south, just as a huge explosion severed the span. Hundreds were killed. The survivors were left to fend for themselves in a city where most of the normal services were grinding to a panicky halt.

We were lucky to find another vehicle and make our crossing on a makeshift ferry farther upstream with the help of some Korean soldiers. As we drove south toward Suwon, the regrouping point for shattered South Korean Army units, our last look at Seoul showed a city ringed by fire. Smoke from bombing and artillery made a wicked halo over the uneven ring of mountains on Seoul's outskirts. At that moment the first North Korean reconnaissance units were probing their way into the city.

Surprise had been complete. Until the last minute even high government and military officials in Pyongyang were not told of its scope. As the former North Korean Deputy Chief of Staff, General Lee Sang-jo, told newsmen in Seoul many years later: "Kim Il Sung planned this invasion with extreme care. South Korean soldiers posted along the front line at that time can vividly testify who provoked this war. North Korean history books are full of distortions about this matter."[3]

The bridge disaster, caused by the premature setting off of demolition charges, had trapped large formations of South Korean troops—about one and a half divisions—still resisting north of the city. Some of the best ROK soldiers, including General Paik Sun-yop and his 1st Division, ultimately had to make their way across the Han without their armament. In any case, the Republic of Korea's fledgling army—denied airplanes, tanks, and heavy artillery by their American allies out of a partly justified concern that too much military aid might have impelled Syngman Rhee's government to attack the north—was no match for the air and armor of Kim Il Sung. Seoul was quickly secured by the Communists, who proceeded systematically to liquidate their enemies in the city.

By July 1, the United States reacted with air and naval support, having secured a United Nations resolution condemning the invasion. (It passed without a veto thanks to the fact that the Soviet representative on the Security Council was then boycotting its proceedings.) Mobilizing troops on the ground was more difficult. Most of the veteran infantrymen who first occupied Japan had long since gone; their poorly trained successors, grown soft on Occupation duty—troop conditioning was not one of General MacArthur's strong points—were scattered throughout Japan in support of various Occupation missions. The strongest force the Eighth Army could scrape up was a reinforced infantry battalion without artillery support, some 500 men.

Task Force Smith, named after its commander, Lieutenant Colonel C. B. Smith, was airlifted to Korea and took up positions near Osan, on the road between Seoul and the southern port city of Pusan, on July 5, 1950. Smith's tired companies were hopelessly outnumbered and outgunned. Bazookas manned by Americans were no more effective against the Soviet T-34 tank than those manned by Koreans. They gave ground with heavy losses. Within the next two weeks most of the 24th Corps had been committed piecemeal, steadily retreating until its commander, Major General William Dean, was taken prisoner in a North Korean breakthrough at the city of Taejon.

---

[3] Lee said this during a visit to Seoul in June 1989 to see relatives. He came from the Soviet Union, where he had been living for many years after escaping Kim Il Sung's intra-Party purge. This testimony corroborates the information about close Soviet–North Korean collaboration given to me by Colonel Pavel Monat, who was Polish military attaché to the Democratic People's Republic of North Korea during the Korean War.

For several weeks I lived with units of the 24th Corps and elements of other units, as they arrived, trying to report this strange new war, in which the Americans were obviously losing. It was an odd sensation for someone who had gone through nothing but victories in the closing years of World War II. The contrasts between resources and availability were sometimes appalling. On one occasion, I drove to the improvised airstrip at Taejon, having just left the outnumbered and wounded survivors of a nasty infantry ambush, caught without artillery to support them, only to watch transport aircraft unloading large quantities of PX supplies, including refrigerated cases of Black Horse ale. While the inexorable American logistics machine was thus started, trained men to use it remained in short supply.

The sacrifices of Task Force Smith and others, however, were not in vain. The North Koreans and their Soviet advisers apparently found it impossible to believe that MacArthur would throw in a battalion to hold off six divisions, air power notwithstanding. So they stopped to reconnoiter and regroup. By stopping they lost what proved to be their only chance to have wound up the Korean War in a hurry. By early August the greater part of three American divisions and a Marine brigade were in place; troops from other members of the United Nations were on their way. A reinvigorated Eighth Army, led by Lieutenant General Walton Walker, one of Patton's World War II tank commanders, had stabilized a defensive line along the Naktong River, while reinforced air power from Japanese bases was bombing the North Korean rear.

On September 15, 1950, U.S. Navy amphibious forces landed an Army and Marine corps at Inchon, Seoul's port. Surprise was total, this time on the American side. Kim Il Sung's army was caught in a classic pincers movement between the landing forces and Eighth Army divisions now breaking out of their perimeter. This was MacArthur at his military best. On September 28, he and Syngman Rhee led what passed for a triumphal procession into the battered, windowless Capitol building, past the still smoldering ruins of Seoul.

I missed the reentry into Seoul. I had landed with the first Marine battalion to attack Inchon, with the mission of securing the island of Wolmi across the causeway from the port. As it happened, I helped Marine intelligence officers interrogate the first prisoners taken. They were not very strong Communists. Poor, young farmers only recently drafted into the North Korean Army, they wanted only to have done with it. ("Don't kill me, I'm a Christian," one had said.) They were tragic living epitomes of the devastation brought on the Korean people by battles they had not sought.

For almost three months prior to Inchon I had covered the fighting as a war correspondent. For most of my colleagues, it was a war. Just that. The civilians who streamed across the battlefield—families uprooted from homes and livelihoods, fleeing tragically southward with what was left of their lives on their

backs—were to most of the Americans, correspondents as well as troops, merely
"gooks," the derogatory name applied to uncommunicable and hence unknowable Asians in Korea, as later in Vietnam and a half century before in the Philippines.

Thanks to my Japanese—then still a lingua franca in Korea—I could talk to them. Each story I heard was a desperate human drama. I saw young soldiers by chance reunited with families they had thought dead, while other people asked me, vainly, if I had seen fathers or mothers or sisters lost in the rush. The facility with which the Communist soldiery could hide in civilian clothes made the Americans understandably jumpy about all civilians. (Although correspondents are noncombatants under international law and not supposed to carry weapons, I kept an automatic in a shoulder holster throughout; Kim Il Sung's troops, whose atrocities became legendary, paid little heed to the Geneva Convention.) Hounded by both sides, families had nothing to cling to but themselves. Living through a war in which so little was done for mere refugees, Koreans intensified a fierceness of family loyalty and a fear of outside authority that would stay with them for many years.

UNFORTUNATELY, the sequel to Seoul's recapture was a series of bad military and political mistakes. The U.S. government, apparently with no concern for the border sensitivity of Communist governments, agreed with Syngman Rhee that the North Korean forces could be pursued north to the Yalu River, with annexation of the area to the Republic of Korea a strong prospect. "Kremlin leaders," Rhee had told me in a July interview, "have destroyed the 38th parallel by invasion. There is no reason why the United States and the United Nations should observe it any longer."

Some of the UN allies expressed doubts on this score. So did cooler heads in Washington. They felt that the safest course was either to return to the 38th parallel boundary or, granting the arbitrariness of this line, to advance into North Korea only as far as a new boundary between Pyongyang and Wonsan on the east coast. For ominous rumblings were coming from the People's Republic of China. Mao Zedong was genuinely worried that MacArthur would go on to invade China.[4] Warnings from Indian diplomats of possible Chinese intervention were confirmed by a variety of reports indicating heavy troop movements toward the Manchurian-Korean border. MacArthur's intelligence staff contemptuously ignored these visible signs of trouble, with predictable results.

The incursion in November of some 300,000 Chinese troops into Korea—

[4] Recent documents made available to scholars suggest that Mao may have decided on intervention in any case.

called, in Communist Newspeak, a spontaneous action of "volunteers"—reversed the military situation. Caught absolutely flat-footed by MacArthur's intelligence failure, the UN forces retreated. Except for the extraordinary breakout of the 1st Marine Division from the Yalu River to the coast, the withdrawal had the semblance of a rout. Seoul was again in the hands of the Communists, but with Marshal Peng Dehuai this time calling the turn, rather than his North Korean allies.

Under a new commander, Lieutenant General Matthew B. Ridgway, the UN forces regrouped and again pushed on north. Seoul was recaptured in March and the UN lines stabilized by April 1951. Now well led, the UN forces were quite capable of advancing farther northward, despite the huge and by no means unskilled military manpower of the Chinese. But over the next two years, while truce negotiations were conducted with the Chinese and Kim Il Sung's reconstituted North Korean Army, the front lines moved but little. By the 1952 election it was abundantly clear that the American public, ill informed as always about its stake in Asia, simply wanted out of the war.

Douglas MacArthur was removed from his command by President Truman because his highly vocal insistence on widening the war, by nuclear bombing if necessary, amounted to insubordination. But the personality clash was actually a side issue of the basic political problem. Ridgway had a far better feel than MacArthur for the realities of pursuing war in a democracy. In his history of the war,[5] he summed it all up: ". . . we could have pushed right on to the Yalu in the spring of 1951, had we been ordered to do so. The price for such a drive would have been far too high for what we would have gained, however. We would have lost heavily in dead and wounded—my estimate at the time was 100,000—fighting against stern resistance across the rugged northern sector of the country . . . At the end of the campaign our battle line would have been stretched from 110 miles to 420 miles and the major responsibility for holding would have been ours, for it would have been far beyond the capability of the ROK army. The questions then would have been: Will the American people support an army of the size required to hold this line? . . . I thought then and I think now that the answer to these questions was 'No.' "

Ridgway was right. The grand old man of the Army, Douglas MacArthur, was wrong in thinking that the American people would support the war's extension. (Even from purely military considerations, there were problems; in line with the "Europe first" strategy of World War II, most available U.S. reserve strength was used to augment Eisenhower's NATO forces.)

If Truman could fire MacArthur, he was not able to fire Syngman Rhee. The inability of the U.S. government to control this autocrat recalled the worst of

---

[5] *The Korean War* (Garden City, N.Y.: Doubleday, 1967).

its problems with Chiang Kai-shek during World War II and foreshadowed the difficulties Americans would later face in coping with the vagaries of Ngo Dinh Diem and, later, Nguyen Van Thieu in Vietnam.

In some ways the American-educated Rhee, an autocrat who thought himself a living symbol of democracy, was the hardest to handle. His long years spent walking the corridors of the Washington bureaucracy had given him a certain talent for influencing U.S. public opinion. In the prevailing mood of the Joe McCarthy fifties, Rhee could play Americans' anti-Communist sentiments like a violin. (Ferdinand Marcos at his manipulative worst did not do a more efficient job of what might be called "American handling.") Rhee continually appealed to the American people, over the heads of their government, to support the "morality" of his hard-line policies.

It is true that Rhee's unyielding resolve had stiffened his country's backbone during the desperate war years. But he and his henchmen used the war situation to settle scores and deal with any opposition, real or fancied, in the most ruthless way. Cloaking his activities under the dubious legitimacy of a National Security Law, he muzzled the elected representatives of the National Assembly. At one point, in 1952, he literally locked them up until they obediently voted his way. Well-meaning conservative politicians like Kim Song-su were brushed aside. Others were assassinated, under suspicious circumstances. The atrocities of Rhee's Youth Corps leader, Lee Bum-suk, and his police chief, "Tiger" Kim, against alleged guerrillas or pro-Communists rivaled the massacres routinely conducted by the Communists of the north.

In the north, Kim Il Sung used military failures in the war as a pretext for liquidating most of his intra-Party opposition. Even such a revered Communist as Park Hun-young, once Deputy Prime Minister of the Democratic People's Republic, was arrested, tortured, and executed in 1953, along with his family, in one of Kim's purges.[6] Unfortunately, the excesses of the police state in the north offered a constant excuse for dictatorial rule in the south—on a domestic as well as an international level.

BY 1960, HOWEVER, after more than a decade of arbitrary and increasingly corrupt rule, Rhee's time had run out. A new country was building itself from the ruins of the war, more urbanized and vastly better educated than before.

---

[6] Park, far more than Kim, was entitled to call himself the archetypal Korean Communist. A delegate to the Far East People's Representative Conference in Moscow in 1922, he faithfully served the Comintern for more than a quarter century, constantly slipping in and out of Korea on his missions. Arrested by the Japanese in Shanghai in 1933, he spent six years in prison. In the immediate postwar period, he organized a strong Communist Party in the south, until forced to flee by the U.S. military government.

The student population in middle schools and high schools had increased from some 120,000 in 1945 to more than 800,000 by 1960; there were now more than 100,000 in college-level institutions, as against 8,000 in 1945. Despite government repression, a national press had begun to voice popular discontents. Kim Song-su's newspaper, *Dong-A Ilbo*, now had a circulation of 400,000. If rural Korea was fairly quiet—thanks to a belated postwar land reform—people in Seoul and the other cities were becoming vocally discontented with Rhee's rule, as bad economically as it was politically. (Few of the new university students had jobs to go to after graduation.)

In April 1960, crowds of demonstrators began to gather in Seoul to protest the blatant rigging of the recent March elections in favor of Rhee's rubber-stamp Liberal Party. In Masan, to the south, more people turned out to denounce the covered-up killing of a protesting student by the police. After police fired on student demonstrators in Seoul—130 were killed in the April 19 riots—a mood of national revulsion set in. The Army refused to back up the venal police. The U.S. government, for its part, finally demanded a real housecleaning. A week after the April 19 demonstrations, the eighty-five-year-old Rhee resigned and left the country shortly thereafter—for exile in Hawaii. He was never to return.

With the end of Rhee's First Republic, Korea was seized by a temporary euphoria. The police were disciplined or disbanded, restrictive political laws repealed, and a new constitution drafted. The government of Chang Myon, the newly elected Prime Minister, was called, with hope, the Second Republic. Chang, an American-educated Catholic, had spent most of his life as the principal of the Catholic Tongsong Commercial School in Seoul. Going into politics after the liberation, he had served as Korea's first ambassador to the United States and later as Rhee's Prime Minister. A man of great probity, he was "caught in the middle," as Han Sun-joo later put it,[7] between student radicals and leftists (those who had survived the Rhee era) calling for sweeping revolution and conservatives who wanted gradual reform, between still powerful Rhee supporters and those who insisted on swift, drastic punishment for old-regime offenders.

Chang was an indecisive leader at a time when tough decisions were demanded. He was unable to mobilize sufficient support for his Democratic Party among the majority, who hoped only for a just, orderly, and anti-Communist government, as against radical student leaders, who had begun to call for unconditional "reunification" with the north. Nor was he able to strike at the nexus of political and business corruption inherited from his right-wing prede-

[7] In his comprehensive study of the 1960–61 period, *The Failure of Democracy in South Korea* (Berkeley: University of California Press, 1974).

cessor. In what would be a recurrent problem for Korean men of goodwill, he seemed to be caught between the radicals and growing pressure from the law-and-order-minded military. For Chang's one sweeping reform—disbanding the old police force—had left the country with something of a public-order problem.

THE MILITARY struck first. In May 1961, a group of officers, led by a dismissed reform-minded colonel, Kim Jong-pil, and a major general named Park Chung Hee, took over the government in a coup d'état. Ruling through a Supreme Council for National Reconstruction, Park went on to dissolve the Assembly, enact strict measures against profiteering, and jail any suspected "Communists" in what he called a new "Korean-style democracy." His rule continued for the next eighteen years.

For more than a quarter century thereafter, until Roh Tae Woo's democratic reforms in 1987, the Republic of Korea's politics was polarized between radical student demonstrators demanding revolutionary change and an authoritarian Army leadership that wanted stability and economic progress, even if accomplished by fiat and at the cost of democratic freedoms. Behind the students was an old Korean tradition. For more than four centuries, from the time young anti-Buddhist Confucian scholars invaded the palace compound to demonstrate in 1519, political-minded students have been thought of as the conscience of the country. Despite the huge expansion of university education since the 1950s, students continued to preserve a kind of elite consciousness—a latter-day evocation, perhaps, of the Confucian literati tradition—which they combined with a visceral anti-establishment leftism. This was by no means unique to their generation—witness the mood of American campuses in the sixties. And considering Korea's ruling structure, the students in Seoul had a great deal to complain about.

Yet the Army's influence cannot be dismissed as merely reactionary. As in other Third World countries, young Army officers in Korea provided the thrust for modernization. The hardships of the war had shaped their thinking. The military, not so incidentally, was one of the few avenues for poor, but bright young people to get an education. The young officers who supported Park's coup regarded themselves, not unreasonably, as populists. To the end Park Chung Hee thought of himself as a reformer.

There was some truth behind his conviction. As we suggested previously, Park was a kind of populist himself, at least in the sense that he was dedicated to improving the lot of the common man. Like Kita Ikki's young Japanese officers in the thirties, he was a poor boy who despised the corruption of the rich and powerful that he saw around him. At one point, he flirted with Communism. Suspected of radical leftist sympathies at the time of the Army's

Yosu-Sunchon rebellion in 1948, Park, then a major, was saved from execution, it is said, by the intervention of his superior, the later Korean War hero, Paik Sun-yop.

More than most young officers in his situation, Park did a lot of reading. He was fascinated by the examples of relatively recent military modernizers like Gamal Abdel Nasser in Egypt or Mustafa Kemal in Turkey, both young officers who came to power at the head of military juntas. Closer to home, he had studied the successes and failures of Sun Yat-sen's 1911 revolution in China and Japan's Meiji Restoration. It was, understandably, the young Meiji reformers who appealed to him most. He could respond not only to their modernizing zeal and their successful mobilization of nationalist patriotism; the Meiji slogan "Enrich the country and strengthen the military" epitomized his own thinking. He also appreciated the Meiji reformers' imaginative use of capitalist enterprise. The German postwar economic *Wirtschaftswunder*—"the miracle on the Rhine," he called it—also impressed him greatly. "With the example of a prosperous Japan before us and a powerful Germany not far away from us, how long are we to sit like this?" he exhorted his countrymen in 1962.

Unlike the Meiji reformers, however, Park and his military junta had to come to terms with their American allies, who not only supported Korea with a vital economic aid program but after their experience with Syngman Rhee were understandably worried, finally, about the prospects for a Korean democracy. If he wanted to have a Meiji-style capitalist development state, Park had to keep up at least the semblance of free elections.

Park won a relatively free presidential election in 1963, after having done everything short of confiscating the ballot boxes, during the last days of the junta, to ensure his ultimate victory. (Among other things, he had banned 4,000 opposition politicians from any political activity for the next six years.) While he dragooned Korea's businessmen into obeying the directives of his economic planners, he went about suppressing political opposition, or even criticism, in every underhanded way possible. Newspapers that opposed him, like *Dong-A Ilbo*, suddenly found their advertising gone, the result of government pressure. His security men were everywhere, spying, reporting, and arresting.

Surveillance was particularly heavy in the university sector, for student demonstrations continued to erupt. Dissident—that is, independent-minded—professors were hounded into resigning. One eminent scholar, on becoming a university president, found his office so full of security personnel and police informers that he was unable to receive visitors. Through it all Park maintained the forms of democracy, causing one Korean scholar friend of mine to comment at the time that "we have the world's only dictatorial, free enterprise, authoritarian democracy."

Which is not to say that Park lacked popular support. For about a decade, probably a majority of Koreans—urban intelligentsia and professional people excepted—saw some virtues in Park's strong central government. Out of economic stagnation and corruption a new economy was emerging, and its benefits were felt in rising incomes. If labor unions were suppressed and political opposition harassed, was sacrifice not necessary to create a prosperous future? If Park's authoritarianism was questioned, government spokesmen—a new Korean growth industry—could always point to the dreadful alternative. As if to oblige, Kim Il Sung's Communist dictatorship in the north continued a pattern of attempted raids and assassinations against the Republic. The heavily mobilized worship of Kim ("Great Leader") by this time eclipsed the worst excesses of the Stalinist personality cult.

By the 1971 election, however, Park's string was running out. Kim Dae Jung, the opposition candidate, took an alarming 45 percent of the vote, with a significant 60 percent in Seoul. Without the conservative countryside behind him, Park would have lost. His response was predictable. The following year he declared martial law and rigged a new constitution that virtually institutionalized his one-man rule. Through this he was able to keep a temporary lid on the country, while his tame technocrats maneuvered the export-driven economy to ever higher GNP growth.

By now, however, too many people were arguing for a greater share in the economy's profits, as well as a greater voice in their own governance. Education levels had continued to rise spectacularly; by 1980 there were some 600,000 college and university students, and this figure would increase to more than one and a half million within the next ten years. Between 1970 and 1980 the high school student population had tripled. With greater education and higher aptitudes came wider concerns; public protests were going beyond groups of elite students. As in the Meiji-era Japan that Park used as a model, a whole society's culture and lifestyle were changing. But in the new world information society a hundred years after Meiji, people were no longer so easy to control.

When Chun Doo Hwan seized power and had himself elected President in 1981, he was already an anachronism. He had none of Park Chung Hee's hold on the voters as the man responsible for their prosperity. Thus Chun's repression, although no crueler than Park's, was resisted more widely. For one thing, Chun created a climate of wholesale corruption. It was based on a network of family and close associates (his wife was popularly known as "the Korean Imelda") that rivaled the misdeeds of Chiang Kai-shek's old Guomindang cronies in China and made the "money politics" of Japan's Tanaka Kakuei and his party bosses in the seventies seem Lincolnesque by comparison. At least Park was personally austere and honest, whatever excesses of money politics were committed in his name.

North Korean prisoners.
Syngman Rhee inspects a
military POW camp in March,
1952. Militant North Korean
Communist POWs later caused
serious trouble in the camps.
Rhee ultimately released
thousands who wished to remain
in the south. Lee Kyung Mo

Park Chung Hee (here shown during Seoul
visit of Henry Kissinger and former
President Gerald Ford) was periodically
nudged toward democratization by his
American allies. Dong-A Ilbo

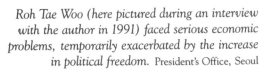

Roh Tae Woo (here pictured during an interview
with the author in 1991) faced serious economic
problems, temporarily exacerbated by the increase
in political freedom. President's Office, Seoul

But there was a more basic reason for Chun's ultimate failure. By the eighties South Korea's people, caught in the satisfying upward spiral of new affluence, had outgrown the neo-Confucian state and society that Park had willed them. Urban Korea was becoming a middle-class society. At least 60 percent of the people identified themselves as such. Koreans worked hard, as they had been used to doing. But by the eighties they wanted to see and enjoy more of the fruits of their labor. A new generation of "yuppies" was growing up in Seoul, confident, free-spending, and numerous. (At the beginning of the nineties more than half of the South Koreans were under thirty.) Consumer demand was far more than a statistic. Both the garrison state and the frugal export-oriented producers who made it were on their way out.

SEOUL IS A CITY I have watched grow up. As it is now—miles of new housing acreage (company, public, and individual) sprawling around huge downtown blocks of glittering glass, concrete, and metal, rows of professionally drab bureaucrats' nests in the government center, splashy department stores that rival Tokyo's, hopelessly jammed traffic animated only by the broken-field running of the world's most aggressive cabdrivers, new subway lines helping to carry people between work and the congeries of restaurants, discos, bars, and movies catering to almost everyone's taste—I find it almost impossible to visualize the rawboned "catch-up" business town of the sixties, still less the dusty former Japanese provincial capital of the late forties. Whenever I visit Seoul now, I find something new—generally something big, brassy, and not very well planned—more like Los Angeles than Singapore. (A fitting parallel, perhaps, since Los Angeles is the headquarters town of the more than one million people of Korean stock who now live in the United States.)

There are, of course, survivals of tradition in all this, and I do not refer merely to the gently landscaped expanse of the Choson Dynasty's Secret Garden, the still-standing two-story East Gate (Tongdaemun), or the solitary serene octagonal pavilion behind the Chosun Hotel. A "Father knows best" bureaucracy, one of the world's most entrenched, remains a bit overfond of dictating its guidance to the real or fancied plebs. A police establishment still reaches out to arrest and hold people with scant warning. (While I was visiting my affiliate Korean company in 1990, an employee suspected of past antigovernment activity was picked up, jailed, and questioned days before anyone was told what had happened, and was tried almost as summarily.) Confucius's ghost remains alive and all too well in the constant disparagement of women—underpaid and discriminated against, although they comprise almost half of the total work force. Not until 1989 did outraged women's groups finally pressure politicians into amending the archaic family law under which women could neither inherit money nor have legal custody of their children.[8]

Yet a new society has appeared—on the farms as well as in the cities—newly conscious of its rights and pressing to enjoy more of its country's wealth. This is not a radical society. The student demonstrators throwing their Molotov cocktails at the police, so beloved by American television and newspaper picture editors, are no longer spearheads of an aroused national protest. Quite like the Japanese student rioters of the early sixties, they have become increasingly violent, as their hard-core leaders find it ever more difficult to get public opinion on their side.

Korea remains, at least in the labor sector, a society of confrontation. Since the 1987 move toward democratization, the long-suppressed unions have staged repeated strikes to get a fairer share of company profits, with significant successes. Their recognition was long overdue and they had to fight for it. Two years of bitter strikes and company lockouts at Hyundai Heavy Industries turned the city of Ulsan—virtually a Hyundai company town—into a battlefield. At one point the government sent in 14,000 police to restore order. In the end the workers got their raises.

Yet like the disastrous Japanese strikes of the fifties, such confrontations are gradually winding down in compromise. The old company paternalism is far from dead and the *chaebol* capitalists remain the heroes of Korea's business-tilted society. The big best-seller of 1989 was the energized Horatio Alger–type advice to the young (*It's a Big World and There's Lots to Be Done*) written by Daewoo's chairman, Kim Woo Choong. The book, interestingly enough, was written in Kim's off-hours, when he was working to settle a potentially crippling strike at the Daewoo shipyards on Koje Island. Kim finally offered to donate a significant sum from his own shareholdings to help meet the workers' demands. Such compromise settlements suggest the start of a new and more equal labor-management relationship.

Citizens' groups have lately been fighting against industrial pollution, just as they have in the United States and Japan. They face a serious problem. In the spring of 1991, an industrial plant of the Doosan group spilled 3,000 tons of toxic chemicals into the Naktong River, temporarily polluting drinking water for wide areas in the country's southeast. Although this had a galvanizing effect on public opinion, it was only one example in a history of virtually unchecked industrial pollution, overlooked by government agencies in the headlong rush

---

[8] The same year that the family law was amended, an appeals court finally reversed the shameful decision by which a Korean woman, raped by an attacker, was sent to prison for "excessive self-defense," while the rapist was acquitted. The legal process took fully five years. Other abuses of this sort still occur.

to expand GNP. But it is citizen activists who are alerting the public and forcing government in turn to act, in the democratic tradition. Change is forcing its way up.

In the spring of 1991 the Republic of Korea held local elections throughout the country—the first such in thirty years. Like the national elections of 1987, they were fair. In 1987, in fact, Roh Tae Woo had been elected President with only 37 percent of the vote, due to a split between the two opposition candidates, Kim Young Sam and Kim Dae Jung. In the National Assembly elections the following year, the government party failed to gain a majority. Its defeat, and subsequent parliamentary reverses, was taken with some grace—amazing grace, one might say, in view of past government behavior in threatening situations.

THE MAN WHO PRESIDED over Korea's democratic transition is one of those people who seem to appear out of nowhere in the course of history, with a previously unsuspected gift for handling difficult political situations. A graduate of the Korean Military Academy, in the same class as Chun Doo Hwan, he was first known as Chun's faithful henchman. It was Roh's troops who safeguarded Chun's power grab in 1980, and there is little doubt of Roh's complicity in the brutal suppression of the Kwangju citizens' uprising.

After retirement from the Army as a four-star general, Roh entered Chun's cabinet first as Minister without Portfolio for Political Affairs, then in 1982 as the Republic's first Minister for Sports. It was his mission to obtain the 1988 Olympics for South Korea. His years of international lobbying, first as a member of government and later as the president of the Seoul Olympic Organizing Committee, proved surprisingly successful. That the Olympics came off in Korea was really his personal triumph.

Even more surprising was his coming forward in June 1987 as the ruling party's presidential candidate, calling for drastic political reform. Was it opportunism to bend with a new wind, after seven years as a supporter of a corrupt autocrat? Or was this a case of a thoughtful, patient man suddenly throwing off the mask? The example of Anwar el-Sadat comes to mind, the obedient Egyptian Army man who, after years as the dictator Nasser's follower, turned his country's policy upside down when he finally came to power. I had known Sadat, and I found many similarities in these two officers. Nor had the comparison escaped Roh himself.

"The tides of history," Roh told me, "brought me to this position." At the time we spoke, in September 1991, in the reception chamber of the newly opened presidential office in the Blue House, he had been three and a half years in office. He spoke quietly, with just a trace of dry wit showing. His 1987 decision, he was quick to say, "was not something that happened overnight. Of course my thinking was influenced by outside events. But I had been pondering this kind of thing for a long time. The decision could not have come by accident. It came after a long period of reflection on the situation in the country and the need for democratic leadership."[9]

Roh, it is said, is the only patient man in Korean politics. In a country whose explosive politicians are wired to traditionally short fuses, he is a planner and a waiter. In January 1990, he surprised the country with the announcement of a merger between his own majority party and two of the major opposition parties, one of them led by Kim Young Sam, his 1987 election opponent. The new majority Democratic Liberal Party—all too readily compared with its swollen Liberal Democratic counterpart in Japan—came into being only after two years of behind-the-scenes negotiations. During this time, I was told, neither of the two opposition parties knew that the other was involved in negotiations. "Once the President has an objective set," one of his aides commented, "he never deviates from it."

One objective successfully attained is his "Northern Policy," a three-year effort to build bridges with the Soviet Union, the People's Republic of China, and other Communist (or once Communist) countries. This diplomacy grew logically out of his experience with the Olympics, in which Chinese and Soviet athletes—despite North Korea's opposition—were conspicuous by their presence. "Going back over ten years," Roh said, "as I went around the world talking to people of different countries, I found that others were as persuaded as I was that harmony is the most important modern political need."

Both China and the Soviet Union had already put aside ideology to develop multibillion-dollar trade relations with South Korea, whose manufactures are well suited to their development needs. In June 1990, Roh made history with his summit meeting with Mikhail Gorbachev in San Francisco, paving the way for the opening of formal diplomatic relations between their countries. In September 1991, the Republic of Korea was finally admitted to the United Nations, along with Communist North Korea, in the separate two-country formula that South Korea had long advocated but Kim Il Sung had long opposed. Double admission was made possible when Beijing refused to veto South Korea's entry, removing the last stumbling block.

In the antechamber outside Roh's reception room hangs a large framed scroll, written in classic Korean *hangul* calligraphy, with the headline "On to Pyongyang." The statement below it is Roh's. Unlike past pronouncements of Korean Presidents on this matter, it is devoid of belligerence. It merely ex-

---

[9] These comments are taken from an interview I had with Roh, which appears in complete form in the Encyclopaedia Britannica's Book of the Year for 1992.

presses the hope, as Roh later said to the UN General Assembly, that "the two Koreas will open a new era of dialogue and cooperation that will lead to our national unity . . . a new era of free exchange of products, information, and people."

THE IMPULSE FOR reunification has grown progressively stronger in this sundered nation, where an estimated ten million Korean family members are divided by the heavily fortified border. In the past Kim Il Sung's demands for instant unification, with all the concessions presumably coming from the south, have been met by almost equally one-sided unifying pronouncements by South Korean leaders. From Syngman Rhee to Chun Doo Hwan, the previous occupants of the Blue House have used the threat from the north as justification for the tightness of their rule. In recent years students and young workers—white- and blue-collar alike—have lobbied for reunification with gathering intensity. To these children of relative affluence, the memory of the north's invasion is dim and the threat of the north's repressive society nonexistent. Many take the North Korean promises of unification at face value. The few students and church people who managed to visit the north illegally were cruelly manipulated by Kim Il Sung's propaganda machine, one of the few efficient organizations in the Democratic People's Republic.

Add to the students' demonstrations the anguish of older Koreans, cut off from parents, siblings, or children in the north by the world's last remaining Iron Curtain. Each autumn, at the Korean thanksgiving holiday of Chusok, families throughout the country bring ceremonial gifts of food to the graves of their ancestors. Those with ancestors' graves in the north must leave the offerings at Imjingak, a monument built for the purpose at the barbed-wire gate to the Demilitarized Zone. Only once, in 1985, were a hundred people permitted to cross the border and search for their relatives.

To take some realistic steps toward unification, Roh unilaterally did away with militant rhetoric on the south's side. Cultural and athletic exchanges have increased; some international teams are now composed of both Koreas. Several conferences have been held between Prime Ministers of the north and the south, and the south has set up a fund to support people exchanges. Some trade between the two Koreas has begun, spurred by the hardship conditions in North Korea's economy.[10] The de-communization of the Soviet Union, as well as China's own economic modernization, has of course facilitated some slight opening gestures by the north.

[10] During my visits to China in the eighties, Chinese friends with relatives in the northeast told me that North Koreans continually cross the border into China in search of food and consumer goods which they lack.

There remain two great obstacles to realizing any meaningful rapport with the north. The first is the character of Kim Il Sung's regime. Despite the efforts of American revisionist historians to paint Kim's father-and-son dictatorship in favorable terms—Bruce Cumings's characterization of the North Korean polity as "revolutionary nationalist corporatism" is probably the most imaginative of the lot[11]—the testimony of most Korean scholars and occasional visitors and refugees from the north has continued to emphasize the rigidity of Kim's monolithic Communism, in which the enforced worship of the dictator and his son and political heir has become a virtual religion (down to families reciting, "Thanks, Great Leader," before they take their meals). Seoul may be untidy, with its noisy welter of competing businesses, gridlocked traffic, and demonstrating students. But it has the untidiness of vitality, political and economic. Pyongyang is neat, clean, and grandiose, with vast, almost carless boulevards, monumental public buildings, and a tightly restricted population. But it has the quiet of a cemetery, a sort of political Forest Lawn, and the largest building projects seem to be unfinished, due to economic problems.

According to former East German ambassador Hans Maretzki: "The system in North Korea is essentially a 'war Communism' such as Stalin maintained, fanning a belligerent psychology among the population—even in the absence of war." Far different from East Germans under Communism, North Koreans have their work, families, and housing rigidly controlled; they are sealed off from contacts, even (or particularly?) with former Communist countries. Repression would seem to continue. Amnesty International and other human rights organizations estimate a total of 100,000 political prisoners in the Great Leader's jails.[12]

Worst of all, Kim's regime apparently continues to build up a nuclear armament capability, which grows dangerous as his regime feels more isolated and hence desperate. (Pyongyang has yet to allow any international inspection of its large nuclear plants.) Although opposition to his reign may be gathering, most observers feel that significant change is impossible while Kim remains in charge.

The other obstacle to early reunification is economic. Its industry obsoles-

[11] As noted in Vol. 2 of his *The Origins of the Korean War* (Princeton, N.J.: Princeton University Press, 1990). This heavily researched work in two volumes, useful for students of Korean politics, is characterized by minute critical detail about postwar developments in the Republic of Korea, but badly flawed by the author's apparent inability to employ his critical faculties in the study of the regime in the north. It has become virtually an occupational failing among American left-wing scholars to take documents and statistics offered by Communist regimes at face value, while making pitiless criticisms of non-Communist countries, where they can move freely and enjoy access to a wide range of research and information. Recent revelations in the Soviet Union, Eastern European countries, and China have offered these scholars, one assumes, considerable food for thought.

[12] The foregoing comment is quoted from the *Far Eastern Economic Review*, May 30, 1991.

cent, its foreign debts unpaid, its food supplies dwindling, and the former Communist allies, China and the Soviet Union, now demanding hard-currency payments in their trade, the Democratic People's Republic of North Korea is virtually bankrupt. To accommodate its people in any kind of economic union, experts reckon, would cost $400 billion, dwarfing the amounts needed to rehabilitate East Germany. So here Seoul's gradual approach is a virtual necessity.

ROH TAE WOO's progressive democratization since 1987 has brought on some problems of its own. They will not easily go away. In the two years after the unions were given freedom to organize and strike, the country experienced about 7,000 labor-management disputes, some of them as violent as the Hyundai strikes at Ulsan. Business and political corruption has by no means disappeared, although it is now under the public scrutiny of an aroused press. Land prices were skyrocketing, as they had in Japan. Nor was Roh's government successful in its efforts to make the huge *chaebol* conglomerates disgorge more of their preempted land for the public's use.

Near the close of Roh's administration—Korean Presidents are allowed only one term in office—police repression was not yet under control. On occasion Roh himself moved harshly against dissent, recalling less happy times. Yet through it all he kept the Army in its barracks. "Civilianization" of the government was almost complete. Most importantly, with local elections proceeding and the stage set for an orderly presidential election in 1992, this former general had institutionalized a democratic succession process in South Korea.

"It's true," he told me, "that people think of the military as being very regimented, apart from the mainstream of civilian life. That's not necessarily true in Korea's case. When our Military Academy was founded, all our textbooks were translations of West Point textbooks—some of them were still in English. At first two-thirds of the faculty were American officers.

"We learned a lot about United States history and the democratic way of life. Our cadets were one of the first groups in Korea to study Western institutions this thoroughly. Indeed, it was the Army that led the modernization of the civilian sector in this country. Outsiders may think of military organizations as intrinsically nondemocratic in nature, but we received many democratic elements as part of our education."

As I spoke with this thoughtful man, my mind went back to the time I last interviewed Syngman Rhee in 1950 and then to 1970, when I talked to Park Chung Hee at an older building in the same Blue House compound. Both Rhee and Park were incorrigible autocrats. The old man, a classic politician in exile, had learned little from his American education, except to use the vocabulary

이제 평양으로 가는 길 을
모스크바로 가는 높은 길이 열린! 이제 평양
으로 가는 길이 열리는 것은 시간문제입니다
평화를 향해·· 통일을 향해 우리가 나아가는
길에 이 세계의 장애는 더 이상 없습니다 이제
우리는 더 큰 희망과 신념을 갖고 전진해야
합니다 자유와 번영의 힘을 더욱 키워 평화와
통일의 길로 힘차게 나아갑시다
소련 방문 귀국 인사

The Road to Pyongyang. To celebrate his trip to Moscow in December 1990—the crowning achievement of his "north politics"—Roh Tae Woo wrote this comment: "Once the road to Moscow is wide open, the way to Pyongyang will be opened in a matter of time. Now there is nothing which blocks our advance into this wide world. We will go forward energetically and clear the way for our bright future and at the same time contribute toward world peace and the prosperity of mankind." Chong Wa Dae (Presidential Office and Residence).

North-south unification came first in sports. Here the unified south-north women's Ping-Pong team celebrated victory at the World Table Tennis Championships in Chiba, Japan, playing under a single flag (top) adopted for the occasion. Yonhap News Agency, Seoul

Downtown Seoul (1991) as seen from the presidential office and residence at Chong Wa Dae. Korean Overseas Information Service

Visitors to Rhiwhachang, Syngman Rhee's old residence in Seoul—now a museum. With the growth of democracy in Korea, the autocratic Rhee has become respected for his early nationalism. Rhee Family

and trappings of democracy, quite cleverly, as a public relations façade. "Why should anything," Rhee had repeated to me, "come between the President and the people?" But he was a President only in title. His idea of governing was closer to the total rule of the Yi Dynasty's old *taewongun* regent.

Park Chung Hee clearly regarded democracy as a nuisance, to be invoked principally when the early U.S. aid programs seemed threatened. He pulled Korea up by its economic bootstraps, it is true; to that extent the country will always remain in his debt. But he was no more a democrat than his opposite number, Kim Il Sung. A variation on an old American saying came to mind. "You might take the boy out of the Japanese military academy," I had thought after meeting him, "but you can't take the Japanese military academy out of that boy."

Roh Tae Woo had gone to a different school. He had learned far more than some of his classmates from that experience, Chun Doo Hwan notably among them. He had gone out to meet statesmen and business leaders of vastly differing systems and traditions throughout the world. He had learned from that experience too. And he was quick to apply these lessons to his own country's situation.

In Korea one found all the elements of developing countries: the economic imperatives, the colonial background, the powerful army, the technocrat bureaucracy, the protesting students, the big businessmen, the government-business connection, the militant workers, the boom in popular education, the heavy baggage of old societal traditions. Out of this mix a new chemistry of responsible nationality had emerged, one capable at some point of taking the captive north along with it. The mixture was volatile. But if severe problems remained, there was every chance that they could be overcome.

Elsewhere in the Asia-Pacific region problems that Koreans were dealing with had yet to be faced. Indonesia and Malaysia had deep worries over succession, not to mention the constant threat of a fundamentalist Islam that seemed intrinsically incapable of acting within a democratic society. Taiwan, under Lee Teng-hui, was on the road to democracy, while the vocally democratic Philippine Republic still had to get its act together. Singapore had yet to escape from under the thumb of Lee Kuan Yew.

Thailand had been kept in equilibrium for years, through a series of comic-opera military coups, by the presence of a useful, if slightly anachronistic monarchy. But the mass civilian protests in May 1992 against the strong-arm tactics of General Suchinda Kraprayoon, the unelected Prime Minister, served notice that their public's patience was wearing thin. When Suchinda's troops fired on the demonstration—killing more than a hundred—they began a time of confrontation, which may bring the end of military rule.

China, its people restless under their brittle gerontocracy, waited; its new goddesses of democracy, if they existed, were yet to be unveiled.

Japan, the oldest Asian democracy—despite its historic flaws—continued to advance its economic legions toward a world empire as yet undefined. But increasingly Japan's own governing processes, their internal crises still masked by a docile electorate, seemed inadequate to bear the strains that economic success had put upon them.

15

The Headquarters Country
and Its Trading-Post Empire

*To do a good job and help one's company grow and prosper—that for so
many of us is what makes life worth living. Our worldly activity and
achievement become part of a religious exercise. It turns into a kind of
religious good. Of course, we do not have a priesthood in this religion of
work. In a sense, it is a priesthood of believers.*

YAMAMOTO SHICHIHEI

*Everything is subsumed unto Tokyo and Tokyo is subsumed unto ev-
erything; and the nation marches victoriously on, untroubled by the
insistence on separateness and difference that troubles so many nations.*

EDWARD SEIDENSTICKER

Its people had developed a new and dynamic form of capitalism. With no
raw material resources other than their own ingenuity, they had transformed a city built on sea-girt marshland into the capital of what the French
scholar Fernand Braudel rightly called "a trading-post empire forming a long
capitalist antenna." From this headquarters their manufacturers and traders
went out to the world, sending back huge inflows of profit from exports and
heavy capital investment. Their merchants were on their way to controlling a
major part of the commodity trade. The gross national product of the city and
its archipelago already rivaled or exceeded that of major continental powers
with much greater area and populations.

More and more foreign businessmen and financiers came to the city, to pay
tribute for their own profit. They were welcomed, as long as they did business
there in the empire's way. Its people had long experience trading with foreigners, operating from cramped enclaves in overseas cities whose customs and
politics were strange to them. And trade they did, however difficult the circumstances. They worked hard, with dedication. Their enemies and even their
friends called them amoral, for they traded with anyone. They were uninter-

ested in taking sides or embracing ideologies. Politics and economics they could easily separate. "Power and wealth," as Braudel put it, "went hand in hand."

Naturally they prospered. "The division of wealth was already very diversified," Braudel wrote, "and the profits from trade were accumulating in a variety of repositories . . . money was constantly being invested and re-invested." Meanwhile the city grew in size and worth, its massive new buildings testimony to what Braudel called "the politics of prestige, which may be, for a city, a state or individual, a way of ruling."

In fact the empire's rule was as diversified as its capital's profit distribution. Although leaders were regularly selected, their freedom of action was extremely limited. Actual power resided in small, interlocking groups of notables, most of them merchants themselves, who ruled over their country and its "world economy" by a kind of running consensus.

With all their wealth the empire's people understandably grew proud and just a bit complacent. Yet they retained a historical memory of major disasters, which dotted their experience like the rise and fall in currency exchanges. They seemed to have triumphed over them all. At least the young thought so. As Braudel noted, "the shadow looming over their country's greatness was that of her greatness itself . . . Leadership of a world-economy is an experience of power which may one day blind the victor to the march of history."

THE BRIEF national character sketch above might have been written about Japan at the onset of the twenty-first century. In fact, it was an encapsuling of comment by Braudel and others on the republic of Venice at the onset of the sixteenth.[1] For several centuries, before the decline that became obvious in the early 1600s, Venice dominated the economic world of the Mediterranean, if not indeed of all Europe; and served as the principal channel of trade to Asia. (It was no accident that Marco Polo was a Venetian.) Although the Venetians combined their economic power with a strong navy, and gave more than they got in the complex land warfare of that period, their preeminence was largely economic.

The parallels with contemporary Japan are not exact, but they generally fit. The innovative manufacturing and trading genius of the Venetians was as powerful a force in the Mediterranean world of the late Middle Ages and early Renaissance as Japan's has become in the Pacific world today. Like the old Venetians, the Japanese do business on an international scale. Equally like the Venetians, the modern Japanese would not win many international popularity contests.

[1] Braudel's remarks are quoted from Chapter 2 of *The Perspective of the World*, Vol. 3 (New York: Harper & Row, 1984).

Aside from drawing an interesting historical analogy—is there anything really new under the sun?—I have cited the example of Venice partly to dramatize the ambivalence of Japanese about their prosperity. It was Japanese scholars, not Americans or Europeans, who pointed to the Venetian analogy—half flattering, half disturbing. Amaya Naohiro, the former MITI vice minister who has become a brilliant commentator on his country's economic role, has used the comparison in urging the Japanese, as the world's only Trading Country Superpower, to defer more to the needs of their customers. (The American political economist Chalmers Johnson, often quoted in these pages, has made much the same point.)

The example of Venice was first cited, to my knowledge, however, by the Kyoto University political scientist Kosaka Masataka, in a remarkably interesting book, *When Civilizations Decay* (*Bunmei ga Suibo suru toki*), published in Japanese in 1981.[2] While Kosaka's examples range from ancient Rome to modern America, he pays particular attention to Venice as the classic "trading nation." He makes implicit and in the end explicit parallels between the experience of Venice and the Netherlands in the sixteenth and seventeenth centuries and that of Japan today. Whether its prosperity comes from the genius of its people or the force of circumstance, he writes, or a fortuitous combination of both, the trading nation is generally disliked. In fact, it becomes the object of suspicion, as its obsession with making money becomes increasingly obvious. This caused trouble for Venice in the past. It can cause trouble for Japan today, he argues. Hence the Japanese should avoid the arrogance that could come from their present prosperity—and look at the examples of decline around them. Japan's decline may come next!

This kind of reflection on success is more common to Japanese than to most peoples. Until recently, at least, Americans have rarely brooded over the problems of prosperity. We are apt to be congenital optimists. Japanese have pessimism in their bones. Possibly it is the cumulative psychological effect of centuries of hard living on their typhoon-swept, volcanic islands. Constantly mindful of their scant natural resources, Japanese play down their material successes. In the very act of pushing their dynamic economy ever faster and further, they subconsciously think back to the long years they have spent trying to "catch up" to the West—and specifically their big friend-enemy-rival-protector-exemplar, the United States. Foreigners grow understandably impatient listening to Japanese spokesmen exculpating the aggressive behavior of a Toshiba or Mitsubishi company overseas by reminding their listeners how poor Japan *really* is.

If this represents a split personality, it is honestly come by. Japan's present

[2] Published by Shinchosha, Tokyo, as part of the Shincho Sensho series of modern classics.

leadership, or most of it, grew up in days of appalling scarcity. Many still have trouble reconciling their traditional islander frugality with the unparalleled affluence in which they are now wallowing. This leads to a feeling that Japan must continue to expand while the going is still good. "We have about ten good prosperous years left—maybe fifteen," one of Japan's best and brightest said to me just a few years back, "so we had better get what we can."

The man who said this has a sophisticated sense of history. He lived through the war and the Occupation; his actions are conditioned by a profound distaste for reliving either period. In Japan's international dealings, he is a pronounced moderate. Unfortunately two new generations of postwar Japanese do not share his historical memory. What they have they take for granted. They are unaccustomed to failure and a bit bored with traditional frugality. More dangerously they live inside the cocoon of a well-insulated monoracial and monocultural society. They have little feel for those outside it, despite their frequent use of buzzwords like "internationalist" and "global" to describe their interests. Even when they journey abroad, secure in their JAL-Pack Japan Airlines tours, happy to shop in the local Paris branches of Mitsukoshi and sample the transplanted Japanese restaurants in New York, it is in the spirit—as an old Japanese friend once remarked—of a guided-tour safari traveling through an African game preserve in air-conditioned buses.

It must have been a bit like that for the prosperous Venetian merchants and their families as they strolled their Canaletto landscapes on the Rialto, living a happy combination of affluence and security. Turkish fleets and Napoleon's armies were far in the future. And they were as yet unaware that a man named Columbus was on his way to discover what he thought were the Indies, in the process making their traditional trade routes to the East nothing more than a piece of history.

WHEN IKEDA HAYATO, the architect of Japan's economic resurgence, died in 1965, the promise of his "income-doubling" policy had been fulfilled. Japan's gross national product, $45 billion in 1960, had exceeded $90 billion by 1965, and by 1980 it would pass the $1 trillion mark. By the 1990s Japan's GNP per capita was well in excess of that of the United States, and Japan's $2.5 trillion total GNP amounted to more than 60 percent of the American. The Japanese were bankers to the world, controlling some 40 percent of international bank assets. From their headquarters in Tokyo the latter-day Venetians ranged across the continents. Their trading places flourished wherever business was done. They dominated the economy of the Pacific as no mere political hegemon could have. Although still sheltered militarily by the American superpower, the need for protection was fading. With the Soviet Union no more and Eastern Europe

Medieval Venice—St. Mark's and the Campanile. Japanese scholars made the Venetian comparison. The Bettmann Archive

Joseph Schumpeter at Harvard. The great economist's idea of "creative destruction" foreshadowed Japan's new capitalism. Courtesy of the Harvard University Archives

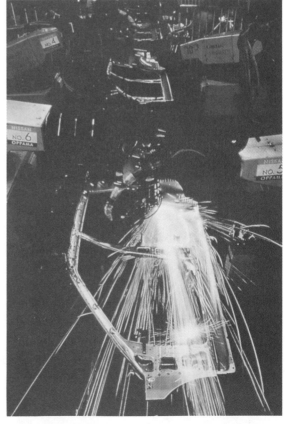

Robotics at Nissan. Although originally dependent on imported technology, Japanese business came to the fore by constructive adaptation. Here robots weld car parts at Nissan's Oppama plant. Richard Kalvar/ Magnum Photos

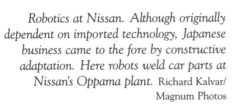

desperately restructuring, the new economic superpower looked out on a world where conventional power definitions had been obliterated. Its only rival, the United States, was heavily in Japan's debt.

Japan's working alliance of bureaucrats and businessmen had produced a dynamic new version of capitalism, a kind of econo-polity, in a world marked by what the economist Leon Hollerman termed "the increased politicization of economic issues." Call it "business society" or "capitalist developmental state," Japan had gone far beyond the parameters that Ikeda and his economic planners had charted. By 1992 it had already become the "headquarters country," as Hollerman put it, dominating an international economic empire.[3] Its closely linked business and financial conglomerates, or *keiretsu*, had written a new chapter in economic history, as had the planner bureaucrats in Tokyo who had charted and accelerated their progress. The Asian Newly Industrializing Countries (NICs) were following in Japan's tradition, although as yet there was no doubt about who was the wing commander in the economic "flying geese" formation. First Americans, then Europeans—Eastern and Western—were queueing up to study Japan's business methods.

Capitalism, Joseph Schumpeter had written, could only survive as a process of "creative destruction" in which good new entrepreneurial ideas and methods displaced and destroyed old ones. Schumpeter, who died in 1950, felt that the classic capitalist entrepreneur was already an endangered species. In his *Capitalism, Socialism and Democracy*[4] he concluded that socialism or some form of state governance would succeed it. That the Japanese could invent a new kind of capitalism and a new kind of group entrepreneurship to go with it was quite beyond his experience.[5]

In this chapter I have endeavored to put Japan's economic successes in some perspective, showing how well Japan's elite business and bureaucracy—and the Japanese, unlike their American contemporaries, do not use "elite" as a pejorative—invented a new kind of economy to deal with twenty-first-century realities, while most of us outside of Japan were still leaning on our mass-production laurels of the mid-twentieth. Whether we refer to Japan's leadership as establishment or oligopoly, it displayed an extraordinary facility at adjusting business tactics to changed conditions. In the process the Japanese invented a

---

[3] Although the term had been used before by Japanese government planners, Hollerman explained and developed its significance in his seminal book, *Japan, Disincorporated* (Hoover Institution, Stanford University Press, 1989). I am indebted to him, as well as to Johnson, for their pioneering work in this area.

[4] New York: Harper, 1942.

[5] In my earlier books *Japan the Fragile Superpower* (New York: Norton / New American Library, 1975; revised 1986) and *Miracle by Design* (New York: Times Books, 1982), I have discussed Schumpeter's ideas more fully.

new kind of capitalism in which words like "stock market," "shareholder," "production," "union," and "free enterprise" took on radically new meanings.

Japan's success was not unalloyed. As with the Venetian and Dutch republics before it, not to mention its American rival, this new business society carried the seeds of future disasters within it. In Japan's case, the continuing problem areas were the inadequacies of its political governance and the determined and disturbing insularity of its people. But even such flaws cannot be appreciated without reviewing the record of the achievement.

THROUGHOUT THE SIXTIES and into the seventies the high-growth boom persisted. True to the spirit of Ikeda's "income-doubling" policy, GNP soared at an average of 12 percent per year between 1965 and 1970. If there was ever a Japan, Inc., at work, it was then. While the trading companies—the nine big *shosha* and their imitators—scoured the world for raw materials to be bought and processed, Japanese business pushed ahead with its export strategies, with their weight shifted from textiles and other light-industry products to big-ticket items like steel, ships, and automobiles. The protective mandarins at the Ministry of Finance and MITI continued to subsidize the fledgling computer industry and other key areas, the while urging Japanese companies to keep acquiring technology from overseas. This they did, with increasing enthusiasm. Between 1961 and 1965, $684 million worth of technology imports came into Japan. The figure for the same period ten years later was fully $3.2 billion.

By far the greatest portion of this technology came from the United States. It was given quite willingly. Most American businesses, still caught up in the euphoria of the fifties and sixties, preferred to concentrate on their own huge domestic market. Expansion overseas was directed principally at familiar trading partners in Latin America and Europe, where Ford and General Motors, among others, had developed large subsidiary companies. For Japan, traditionally remote from their consciousness, they were content with licensing arrangements. With these they could get a good steady return for their patents and inventions—plus business, as it were, without the problems of putting down roots in a largely unknown market.

In any case, the Finance Ministry and the Bank of Japan saw to it that foreign business investment was kept to a minimum. Even the redoubtable IBM, setting up its Japan facilities, was given to understand that its welcome depended on sharing as many of its patents as possible with Japanese companies at reasonable prices. When capital "liberalization" came in the late sixties, as it did in response to continual foreign pressure, it was done grudgingly. Foreign companies quickly found themselves struggling with a variety of unwritten administrative "guidance" requirements and virtually impenetrable networks of local distributors and middlemen of various sorts, even after formal legal barriers to non-Japanese business were withdrawn.

Thus protected at home, the new capitalists of Japan worked out their global marketing strategies. Unlike American companies, who continued to think in terms of their traditional domestic markets, Sony and Toyota started selling to the world. Their first objective was not profits, but market share. The profits could wait until after the market was captured.

Capital they could acquire easily, thanks equally to Japan's high personal savings rates and government support—heavy, if indirect—for investment in export industries. In general, the Bank of Japan kept interest rates low, to promote investment. Whereas the average American company raised money by selling its shares, the average Japanese company—at least in this early Japan, Inc., period—depended almost solely on bank financing. If a company's leading bank was satisfied with its direction, money for long-range development and expansion was easy to obtain. Where American companies were more or less at the mercy of Wall Street financial analysts, pitilessly dissecting each quarterly report, Japanese corporations could afford to take the long view. Their relatively low cost of capital would prove a lasting and often critical competitive advantage.

The *keiretsu* groups of companies, most with their own bank at the center, had the added capability of mobilizing great internal financial resources, where these were needed, in support of any one of their companies or projects. With new modern plants—one good by-product of having the old ones bombed out in the war—Japanese business made a fetish of quality and productivity, constantly working to be more competitive. Generally, industry-wide unions remained weak. But the enterprise union became a fixture of the Japanese economy; its workers, buttressed by seniority systems, were just as anxious as management for the company's success. Given the widespread bonus system—actually a form of profit sharing—they knew they would do well, very well, if the company prospered.

There was another important characteristic of Japan's new modern capitalism: its ancient Confucian sense of hierarchy and group commitment. We have already noted the success of the Confucian capitalists, so called, in Korea, Taiwan, and other areas where the maritime Chinese work. In Japan the Confucian influence was at its strongest, if rarely mentioned; the Japanese needed no public rites to confirm a way of thinking that they had grown up with. Even the great cultural revolution of Meiji, as we have seen, did not uproot the sense of rank and hierarchy that Tokugawa Ieyasu and his heirs had stamped on Japan. The reformers merely ventilated the system—and paradoxically strengthened it by allowing a new social mobility. Instead of an aristocracy, Japan became a meritocracy, subscribing to democratic norms.

The Japanese worker's *ikigai*—that difficult word best translated as "what makes life worth living"—is to better himself and his family, but within the context of his company. In Japan the job is the society. The society is the job.[6] Each person working for a Japanese company becomes a stakeholder in that company, whatever his or her position; most of their lives—the friends they make, the spouses they take—revolve around the corporation. Companies work to foster and strengthen this sense of company identity, and have been successful to the point where a Japanese "salaryman's" most essential article of apparel is the company button in his lapel. Personnel departments recruit college graduates with the patient care of go-betweens at an arranged marriage. They are looking not for specialists—although engineering graduates are in ample supply—but for trainees who can develop into "the whole company man." Unlike most American companies, who buy and sell labor (executives included) like any other commodity, the Japanese company thinks of its work force as precious human capital. Personnel directors prefer to grow their own. As the late William Abernathy of the Harvard Business School once wrote: "Americans buy and sell labor. The Japanese build a productive process around it."

Although somewhat eroded in recent years, the Japanese sense of corporate commitment and identification is, to a foreigner, overwhelming. So is the sense of a ritualized pecking order, reinforced by a company hierarchy that subsumes all the constant communicating and storied group participation of the Japanese workplace. This runs from the obvious rankings of directors, department heads, and the like down to the distinctions between permanent company employees (*seishain*), contract employees (*shokutaku*), and temporary workers.

The same Confucian ranking system obtains with companies themselves. At the top of the heap in Japan's business society come the major first-rank companies—like Nissan, Matsushita, or Fujitsu. It is this top 30 percent of Japanese business that boasts the complete apparatus of job security, seniority systems, and cradle-to-grave benefits (from company recreation resorts and marriage halls down to, in some cases, company funeral facilities). On a level below this are the lower-ranking companies, from small service organizations to subsidiaries and suppliers of big companies. The latter, although constantly trying to improve their status, accept their reduced level in the pecking order. They exist at the mercy of the big corporations, and their risks are greater, since the suppliers and the peripheral contracters are the first to feel the heat of any business downturn.

Rankings in the Japanese corporate hierarchy are not immutable. It is always possible for an Inamori Kazuo to start a technological wonder like the Kyocera

---

[6] I have given a more extensive description of the Japanese work ethic and the workings of Japan's business society in *Japan the Fragile Superpower* and *Miracle by Design*.

industrial ceramics company, for a Nakauchi Isao to build up a Daiei super-market chain, or, for that matter, for a Matsushita Konosuke to found his electronics empire, which began with a radio shop in Osaka. One of the more interesting marks of Japanese business, despite its corporate group culture, is its receptiveness to individual entrepreneurs. Nonetheless, the basic structure is multipyramidal. It takes barely a generation for most one-man companies to assume more traditional corporate form, complete with group decision making, homogenized planning departments, and company directors who can be moved like interchangeable parts.

The classic example of Confucian corporate hierarchy is Toyota. Its head-quarters at Toyota City (once called Koromo), not far from the metropolis of Nagoya, is known in Japan as "an industrial castle town." Recalling in fact the old castle towns of the Tokugawa days, where the local feudal baron lived surrounded by his retainers, Toyota enjoys the services of almost 250 vassal company suppliers, almost all situated within easy driving distance of its head-quarters. (It was just this physical proximity that led Toyota's managers to pioneer the now famous *kamban* or "just in time" inventory system, wherein components from suppliers are brought into the main factory only as they are needed.) As with other large Japanese companies, the primary suppliers are either direct subsidiaries or affiliates bound to the parent by a network of interlocking stock relationships and accustomed to making their components according to Toyota standards. Below these primary suppliers there is a network of secondary suppliers and contractors—in Toyota's case almost 4,000—whose products and work patterns are designed to fit within the Toyota firmament.

Toyota's physical concentration of subsidiaries and suppliers makes it a special case. But other companies developed the same kind of hierarchical relationships, even if geographically more scattered. Where Americans would have chafed at these subsidiary relationships, Japanese who toiled on the lower levels of the corporate pyramids were generally content to wait for their advancement, hoping that continued quality performance would ultimately push their company up to the next level. The general manager at a Tokyo sales company of which I was briefly chairman used the ranking system to good effect, inspiring his Japanese Willy Lomans to ever greater effort. "You are part of a third-rate company now," he would say. "If you work hard, you'll bring us up to second-rate. Someday, conceivably, you may make it up to first-class."[7]

At the very peak of Japan's Confucian business society stand the mandarins of the bureaucracy. From the days of the Heian courts, through the feudal era, the stratifications of Tokugawa, and the young officialdom of the Meiji reformers, Japanese have been heeding their words for the past fifteen centuries. The

---

[7] Alas, they never did.

Toyota assembly line. Toyota Motor Corporation

Computer-aided chassis design at Toyota. Toyota Motor Corporation

Toyota's factory complex at Toyota City (above and top right), with its network of subsidiaries and suppliers, has been called "an industrial castle-town." Here Toyota's engineer executives developed and refined a whole new automobile technology.

Toyota and General Motors workers at the New United Motor Manufacturing (NUMMI) plant in Fremont, California, celebrate the first Nova. Toyota Motor Corporation

Sony's Akio Morita typifies a new breed of internationalist Japanese businessman. Jigsaw Productions

Japan invades Hollywood. Newsweek's *1989 cover suggests the general American concern over Japanese acquisitions.* © 1989 Newsweek, Inc., All rights reserved. Reprinted by permission.

Buy America? Unvarnished cartoon criticism like this showed how Japanese acquisitions disturbed grass-roots Americans. Daily News-Record, Harrisonburg, Va.

bureaucrats in the government ministries—almost alone, as we have seen—were spared in the purges of the U.S. Occupation. Their continuity remained unbroken. Ranked even among themselves—Finance Ministry first, MITI and the Foreign Ministry second, etc.—they are respected as the best and the brightest of Japan's top university graduates. And here again, we have Tokyo University first, Kyoto, Keio, and Hitotsubashi next, and so on through the rankings.

Stronger by far than British Treasury civil servants and French *inspecteurs de finance*, the men in the ministries were the high priests of Japan's high-growth era. Through their avuncular "administrative guidance," they identified and nurtured new growth industries as they helped to phase down and retrain old ones. Through their power to tax and regulate and control money flows, they shaped industries, crated up cartels, and godfathered mergers.

They were by no means omnipotent. Even at the height of the Japan, Inc., phase, they relied on constant playbacks with the industries they were aiding, through the determined antennae rubbing of businessmen and bureaucrats in the *shingikai*, or consultative commissions, threading their way through the economy. As time went on, they would have to share more of their power with politicians of the majority Liberal Democratic Party. Businessmen, as they grew stronger, needed the ministries less. But they have remained the arbiters of Japan's business society, continuing to act as both coach and umpire for Japanese business and finance. In this dual role Japanese find no contradiction.

AMERICANS could be forgiven for regarding Japan's business battalions as a huge infantry army on the march, buying up raw materials and pushing its manufactured exports exponentially, in what seemed like an unending invasion of other people's trade balances. Disquieting, but predictable. Yet in two different years, and in totally different ways, Japanese business and government showed an unexpectedly alert reaction to changed circumstance—changing economic history in the process. The years were 1973 and 1985.

These two years and what they signify mark turning points in Japan's economic strategies. Each represented a break with past performance and aspirations. Each in turn demonstrated the flexibility of Japan's business society. As such they constitute milestones in the transformation of the export-driven Japan, Inc., of the early seventies into the economic superpower of the nineties.

In the fall of 1973, already awash with rising prices, huge union "base-up" salary increases, and an excessive money supply, Japan was hit by the "oil shock" of the OPEC embargo. "Crazy commodity prices" (*kyoran bukka*) soared higher. Land prices were worse. At a 1955 base of 100 they were over 2,000 in 1973, as Japan's large trading companies and big businesses' real estate subsidiaries greedily bought up available land for high-priced development. The premature leakage of Prime Minister Tanaka Kakuei's plans for Rebuilding the Japanese Archipelago turned Japanese real estate speculation, not a fastidious business in the best of times, into a feeding frenzy.

Antipollution demonstrators marched throughout the country. Some groups took to the courts—an unusual step for Japanese, underscoring popular exasperation with an industrial pollution blight that was making some city districts uninhabitable. (Residents of the industry towns of Yokkaichi and Kawasaki were among the worst sufferers.) A 1973 court settlement finally gave some compensation to victims of the Minamata sickness, a crippling bone disease, which had already caused a thousand deaths among people living near the Chisso Company's chemical plants in Kyushu. For the first time in Japan's postwar history, a concerted—and ultimately successful—effort began to cut down industrial pollution on a national level.

As productivity dropped in their factories, Japanese economic planners began to wonder out loud where their future energy and raw material imports would be coming from. One government survey projected that by 1980 Japan would need to take in fully 30 percent of the world's raw material imports to make its high-value-added products. Yet Japan's new plant construction was winding down. The 1974 statistics would show a GNP loss, for the first time in the postwar period.

While alarmed Finance Ministry bureaucrats—the gnomes of Kasumigaseki, as some call them—frantically spun their control levers in the direction of deflation and tight money, the country wallowed in a mood of pessimism. The oil shock had come barely a year after the twin "Nixon shocks," when the United States first forced an upward revaluing of the yen (the while adding a 10 percent surcharge on imports into the United States) and then ignored Japan in its sudden rapprochement with the People's Republic of China. Early in 1974 a new hit movie, *The Sinking of Japan*, based on Komatsu Sakuya's best-selling novel, started playing in Tokyo's first-run theaters. It seemed to encapsule the nation's cumulative concerns. Coming out of the wide-screen disaster film—which portrayed a Japan doomed to sink into the ocean in a vast seismic disturbance—crowds in the Ginza entertainment district wended their way homeward through the emergency brownout imposed on the splashy neon advertising signs, to read increasingly alarmist headlines in the evening papers. "The Economic Sinking of Japan," a special section in a popular monthly, contained articles by the Finance Minister, as well as prominent businessmen and union leaders, pointing out the gravity of Japan's economic situation.

In the midst of the gathering gloom the Ministry of International Trade and Industry published in 1974 its first "long-term vision" for Japanese business. In addition to prescriptions for energy conservation and arguments for internationalizing Japan's economy (and phasing out protectionism), the vision offered one striking new idea. In the future, Japan would become a headquarters country, directing from Tokyo a congeries of processing, converting, and assembling plants throughout the world. Its new industry would be "knowledge-intensive," its principal resource would be information rather than expensive imported energy and raw materials. Labor-intensive industries would be left to others, as Japan moved up the scale. Offshore manufacturing would be part of the new complex, which would be, in accord with MITI tradition, a "plan-directed market economy." Since the beginning of the seventies MITI had been talking about a shift away from "labor-intensive" and "energy-intensive" industry. The ministry had already committed a great deal of funding and other support to the fledgling computer industry. Now its guardians of the economy advised that the road to robots, advanced electronics, and high tech was open.

Japanese businessmen were already headed overseas, in advance of MITI's benediction. Sony had started making TV sets at its San Diego plant in 1972. In 1974 Matsushita opened its Quasar TV plant outside of Chicago. Within a few years Honda would start turning out motorcycles at Marysville, Ohio. Assembly plants for a variety of products were already set up in Southeast Asia. MITI's "vision" served both to sanction and to formalize an important industrial turning point. Official economic "liberalization" measures would soon follow.

By 1975 Japan's economy had been pulled back into shape, but the go-go years of 12 percent annual growth were over. With them went the double-digit annual pay raises, the buy-ups of the world's raw materials, and what was left of Japan's reliance on the labor-intensive industry that for two decades had been the country's major meal ticket. Future growth had to come from investment as well as exports. The businesses of the future would rely on information resources rather than raw materials. (The trading companies themselves would spend more time in information gathering.) More money began to be spent on foreign investments—a good way, it was argued, to counter the protectionist measures other countries had started taking against Japanese exports. With strategic headquarters concentrated in Japan, the search was on for overseas economic bases.

IN SEPTEMBER 1985, slightly more than a decade after MITI's published "vision," another event occurred to expand Japan's economic power and to accelerate the developing "headquarters country" strategy. Here again, paradoxically, it was provoked by outside pressure: principally, American complaints about the $50 billion yearly trade imbalance with Japan. Most international authorities agreed that the U.S. dollar was overvalued in international exchange. Accordingly, at a meeting in New York's Plaza Hotel, the Finance Ministers of Japan, Great Britain, France, Germany, and the United States agreed to strengthen the value of the yen and other major currencies against the overpriced dollar. With a more realistic exchange value operating, American export products, as U.S. Treasury Secretary James Baker proudly explained, would automatically become more attractive in competition. They did throughout the world. Everywhere, that is, except in Japan.

The major Japanese companies, territorialists all, refused to give up their American market share just because of the now expensive yen. Since the oil shock of 1973—which had been followed by a second oil shock in 1979— Japanese industry had embarked on an intensive program of energy saving, cost cutting, and management innovation. No longer so dependent on foreign R&D, Japanese managers had been stressing new technology, quality control, and "slimmed-down management" (*genryo keiei*) to keep unit costs down (and their companies' heads above water) in Japan's cruelly competitive domestic market. Labor cooperated, the successive oil shocks having taught the unions that the age of 30 percent annual raises was over.

The government helped with assistance to structurally depressed industries, continued support for the growing high-tech sector, and macroeconomic fine-tuning ranging from tight-money policies to infrastructure spending, as the occasion demanded. But the initiative was with corporate managements. And they needed no directives from MITI to streamline operations.

Thus when the crunch of the new high yen came, Japanese business was ready. So was the always helpful financial bureaucracy. The Finance Ministry, the Bank of Japan, and MITI cooperated in a massive lowering of interest rates. The monetary stringencies of the past tight-money period were hugely relaxed, as the government did everything the macroeconomy could to stimulate demand. Land prices were allowed to soar, and companies borrowed heavily on their swollen values.

Thus it happened that while American investment bankers and their corporate friends were wasting the republic's substance in a round of unproductive mergers, acquisitions, and leveraged buyouts, Japan's new capitalists began a wave of capital improvement and R&D spending to heighten their productivity. Between 1986 and 1991, some $3.2 trillion dollars was committed to new plant and processes! Far from contracting sales, managers resolved to expand them.

The *keiretsu* combines and their banks made up losses so exporters to the American market could stay competitive. Prices were not raised. In some cases, like that of the DRAM (for dynamic random access computer), major Japanese manufacturers slashed their post-Plaza dollar prices to retain their market share until new offshore plants were available.

Where small or medium-sized companies found the high-yen climate too chilly, they were encouraged to transfer operations offshore, to Southeast Asia or other cheap-labor bases. It was, after all, part of the long-term headquarters strategy that labor-intensive industry should go out to the periphery.

By contrast there was little follow-up to the Plaza Agreement in the United States. The sturdy Adam Smiths of the Reagan administration, dead set against anything that smacked of industrial policy—sat back to watch the lowered dollar restore American trade balances. American carmakers, confident that the high yen would diminish Japanese sales, promptly raised prices themselves—and paid out the usual seven-figure compensation packages to their unsuccessful managers. The Japanese carmakers did not raise theirs. They did, however, speed up work on their new American plants.

For with the new high-value yen in their pockets, American assets suddenly became marvelously attractive to Japanese buyers: investors, financiers, and businessmen alike. Before the eighties, most of Japan's overseas investment had gone to ASEAN or other underdeveloped countries. Japanese businessmen had been rather nervous about acquiring American assets. After the Plaza Agreement, things looked different. A piece of property, be it a building or a corporation, that might have seemed pricey at 250 yen to the dollar suddenly became a prize package at 150. And Japan's headquarters-country strategy took a giant, if unexpected, step forward.

The resultant Japanese boom in American acquisitions, like the slimmed-down management of Japan's businesses, was not ordered up by the government. Japanese investors did not need MITI to tell them that American Treasuries offered a far higher return on their money than they could get at home. Foreign investment was now largely liberalized. From 1986 onward, the pace of Japanese investment in the United States quickened at exponential rates. Some $10 billion poured in through 1986. In 1987, $15 billion was committed; the next year's investment rose to $21 billion. By the end of 1991 total Japanese investment in the United States was well over the $100 billion level.

Although still behind the $120 billion that the British have put into the American economy, Japan was catching up—at least for a time.[8] At the start of the nineties, the United States owed a massive $670 billion in foreign debt—a major share of it to Japan. By contrast Japan's foreign assets were pushing the $400 billion mark. The relationship of the two countries has become a classic case of debtor and creditor, with all that this implies.

The Japanese can hardly be blamed for the sad financial state of the United States. For almost twelve years, throughout the Reagan and Bush administra-

[8] By 1991, however, Japanese investments in the United States began to be cut back, dropping significantly from that of the peak years.

tions, American consumers and their government went heavily into debt. Government spent huge sums on defense, while neglecting both fiscal management and the normal regulatory functions of government over domestic investments, banks, and financial transactions. Wall Street moneymen, aided by hordes of lawyers and investment bankers, presided over a disastrously unproductive series of mergers, leveraged buyouts, and takeovers.

While America's business competitiveness was thus weakened, consumers continued to buy and generally refused to save. (The American rate of personal savings, hovering around 5 percent, remains in sharp contrast to Japan's 18 percent.) With government revenues down, thanks to generous tax cuts, and government spending hugely up, a cheerful group of White House supply-siders apparently counted on Adam Smith's invisible hand to fix up the debt and bail the country out with heavy business investment and more consumer spending. Adam's ghost was slow to respond, but it was soon clear that Japanese banks and corporations were ready to substitute for him. They were understandably eager to buy into a good, interest-paying investment. By the end of 1989, Japanese investors held a sizable percentage of the total $2.25 trillion of U.S. Treasury securities. Simply stated, Japan's loans were paying America's bills.

Setting aside for the moment further consideration of America's profligacy, let us consider here only the corporate side of Japanese investment—that is, the transplanting of Japanese companies to the United States. There is no clearer means of demonstrating the realities of the headquarters-country approach to international business. The motivations for these corporate transplants were impelling, particularly in the areas of electronics and automobiles, Japan's principal export efforts in the United States.

Electronics were the first to move. Protected from foreign competition through their growth period and assisted by government R&D funding, companies like Matsushita and Sony had made rapid progress selling to Americans. Their products were good, new, and reliable. They soon took over the American market, and American competitors either switched product lines or went out of business. (In 1955, there were twenty-seven American television makers; in 1991, only one remained.) Yet rising complaints about floods of Japanese imports—with the well-brandished threat of American protectionism—impelled first Sony, then most of the other Japanese electronics manufacturers to start up factories in the United States.

Japanese business investment, not quite $3 billion in 1978, shot up to $10 billion by 1981. By that time the carmakers had joined in. Honda added automobiles to its Ohio motorcycle plant in 1983, the same year that Nissan began to produce its first trucks at Smyrna, Tennessee. The following year Toyota started its joint venture with General Motors at Fremont, California. Mazda broke ground for its new plant in Michigan in 1985, while the first

Toyota factory in the United States began tooling up in Kentucky in 1987. Thereafter, buoyed by cheap Plaza Agreement dollars and the need to circumvent MITI's voluntary restrictions on the number of cars exported across the Pacific, Japan's car manufacturers led the parade of Japanese industry transplants to the United States.

By 1991, roughly one-third of the new cars sold in the United States were either Japanese imports or products of Japanese transplant factories—made in America by Japan. No longer content with producing small compacts, the Japanese carmakers, like General Motors before them, were going after the luxury end of the market. In the depths of a debt-ridden economic depression, American consumers could look wonderingly at the unending procession of TV commercials lauding the virtues of Toyota's lavishly equipped Lexus, Nissan's elegant Infiniti, or the newer luxury cars available from Mazda, Honda, or Mitsubishi dealers. Fighting their old, but fierce competitive wars on a half-leveled American playing field, these excellent and technically advanced Japanese machines—their new contours often devised by American design studios—offered Americans ever more attractive opportunities to increase their swollen consumer debt.

Here was surely an ultimate irony. America had become the classic consumer society. Starting with Teddy Roosevelt's trust busting, picking up speed with the Keynesian economics of Franklin Roosevelt's New Deal, and supercharged by Lyndon Johnson's Great Society—through Kennedy and Nixon and on to Reagan, the whole economy was inexorably geared toward satisfying consumer needs, real or fancied, and regulating itself according to consumer demand. In the process, the old Roman proverb "Let the buyer beware"—*Caveat emptor,* surviving Latinists may recall—had become reversed to "Let the seller beware." All the appalling modern economic alchemy of advertising and sales promotion—the TV extravaganzas, the telephone marketers, the splashy hoopla of big-name endorsements, and shrieking TV commercials (most of them American inventions)—was concentrated into stimulating consumer demand by satisfying consumer whim. Every resource of government, with its top-heavy scaffolding of consumer-protection laws and institutions, was devoted to helping the consumer pick and choose and buy, ensuring unlimited access to any product from anywhere. This entire consumer-demand mechanism was now brilliantly exploited by the engineers and salesmen of the world's classic producer society—a Japan whose consumers obediently saved before they spent and sanctioned with their votes the ever swelling growth of capital investment and industrial production. Japan's government did everything in its power—from tax breaks to research cartels to export industry targeting—to support ever expansive producers. In Japan's business society, consumers still finished last.

WAS POSTWAR European history repeating itself? "Greater wealth allows them to conduct business faster and more flexibly than their competitors . . . Most striking of all is the strategic character of their penetration. One by one, [they] capture those sectors of the economy most technologically advanced, most adaptable to change, and with the highest growth rates . . . the final handicap European business suffers is the systematic and organized assistance [their] government gives to key industries through its contracts and research grants . . . The best answer [to their competition] is for Europe to unify its industries, encourage scientific research and revise laws governing corporations."

The foregoing comments, which might be echoed in almost any contemporary *American* discussion about *Japanese* competition, were actually made twenty-four years ago by the French journalist Jean-Jacques Servan-Schreiber. He was writing about American industry in Europe. His book *The American Challenge*[9] was written to alert fellow Europeans to the alarming inroads made by large American corporations, whose $14 billion investment in European subsidiaries—hardly a great sum by Japanese standards—threatened, Servan-Schreiber feared, to turn Europe into an American economic dependency.

In the end the American invaders were assimilated. Ford, General Motors, Union Carbide, and other American business satrapies put down roots in Europe. They hired and trained European executives to manage them. They were run from Europe, virtually autonomous, and became part of the competitive landscape, having stimulated European businessmen by their example and inspired a wave of business management courses in Europe's universities.

The later Japanese impact on economic America was ironically similar. The science and technology part of their competition, at least, they had learned from the American book. But the Japanese in America offered some new wrinkles in management and business planning that neither Americans nor Europeans (since the Japanese company is now advancing into the EEC countries) seemed able to cope with. Some of them came from rather old cultural patterns.

The most obvious is the *keiretsu* company itself. When major Japanese corporations set up shop in the United States—some 500,000 Americans now work for them— it was widely assumed that they would behave like American companies in Europe, casting about for local suppliers and handing out business

[9] New York: Atheneum, 1968 (a translation of his widely read French original, *Le Défi Américain*).

on the basis of the most satisfactory bids. Much to the Americans' surprise, however, the Japanese displayed a tendency to bring their own suppliers and affiliated companies with them. Take Toyota, for instance. In his excellent and well-researched *Zaibatsu America*,[10] Robert Kearns counted almost 60 auto-parts facilities, all of them branches of Japanese companies, mobilized to support Toyota's new automobile plant in Georgetown, Kentucky. They represent some of the 240-odd Japanese-controlled auto-parts suppliers now in the United States, which give, as Kearns points out, "a new meaning to the term 'local content.' "

The new Toyota plant itself was built by the Ohbayashi Construction Company, one of Japan's largest. Three Japanese banks, Mitsui, Sanwa, and Tokai, have moved to nearby Lexington, as have two large Japanese insurance companies. While 60 percent of the steel used in the Georgetown plant comes from American companies—the remaining 40 percent is imported—all of them either are partly owned by Japanese steel companies or have close joint-venture relationships with them.

Much the same can be said of the Mitsubishi companies in the United States. Diamond-Star Motors, Mitsubishi's joint venture with Chrysler in Illinois, can buy air conditioners from Mitsubishi in California, glass from Asahi Glass in Ohio, another Mitsubishi affiliate, starters and cruise control from Mitsubishi Electric in Cincinnati, which also supplies machinery for Mitsubishi Semiconductor's new plant in North Carolina.

Such lists could go on indefinitely. It goes without saying that Japanese banks can be relied on for ready financing for the transplant companies. They now hold 12 percent of all banking assets in the United States (U.S. banks have 1 percent of banking assets in Japan) and fully 25 percent of total bank assets in a key state like California. (Overall, of course, Japanese banks' holdings of about 40 percent of international bank assets contrasts with the U.S. share of about 15 percent.) Most of the *keiretsu* transplant companies can count on the services of their main "city bank" and others, based on their relations in Japan.

Only a portion of the companies in a *keiretsu* group are subsidiaries or affiliates. Most are tied together through a system of interlocking shares and constant, if informal consultations between them at their headquarters. In general, they prefer to do business with each other. Communications are simpler and economies of scale can easily be achieved because of their worldwide networking.

Unlike most American overseas subsidiaries, the Japanese transplants are

---

[10] *Zaibatsu America: How Japanese Firms Are Colonizing Vital U.S. Industries* (New York: Free Press, 1991).

tightly run from the home country. Although Americans and other foreign executives are hired, often as company presidents, there is invariably a Japanese adviser in the wings, who is apt to hold the real authority.[11] Japanese companies are happy to hire and train local workers. With some justice they proudly cite their good employment records—although they have tended to put down roots in areas where American minorities are few and trade unions are weak. Local suppliers are often used as well. But the high-value components are generally made either in Japan or by tightly controlled Japanese transplant suppliers. The key goal of these worldwide *keiretsu* is to concentrate information resources, as well as control, in the hands of management in Japan. They are quite happy to delegate most manufacturing tasks to Americans, Europeans, Thais, and Malaysians, since the headquarters country need not concern itself overmuch with nuts and bolts.

Not the least of the *keiretsu* groups' strong points is access to cheap investment capital. Not only do Japanese banks loan lavishly, buttressed by the support of the business-conscious Bank of Japan. But the normal advantages of Japanese corporate borrowers were multiplied by the Plaza Agreement's strong yen. When Sony made its $3.4 billion purchase of Columbia Pictures in 1990, the company borrowed $2.8 billion at very advantageous rates—much of it at what amounted to 1 percent interest. Almost any American company would have had to pay something between 12 and 15 percent for this money at that time.

Similar advantages are available to Japanese companies in highly competitive fields like semiconductors. Recalling his days as counsel for the U.S. Department of Commerce, Clyde Prestowitz cited a conversation with the head of one of Japan's semiconductor companies. "I'm amazed," said Prestowitz. "I know that you are sustaining half a billion dollars in losses this year; yet you say you are expanding your capacity by 40 percent."

"That's right," said the semiconductor executive, a member of the Mitsui Group. "Our group thinks that semiconductors are fundamental to many of their businesses, so we have to stay with this business come what may."

"Between 1985 and 1987," Prestowitz wrote, "the Japanese semiconductor industry lost $4 billion. In that same period the U.S. industry lost $2 billion. In the United States seven or eight companies left the business altogether. About 25,000 people lost their jobs. In Japan no company left the business, no employee lost his job . . . Given their support by government and the banks,

---

[11] This practice might conceivably change over a period of time. American businesses in Japan, for example, were originally run by expatriate executives sent out from the United States. Gradually they were replaced by some Japanese managers—partly for cultural reasons, but largely because expatriate managers and their families cost the American companies, by their reckoning, too much to support.

it is not hard for Japanese executives in those companies to take the long view."[12]

Such grand gestures would, of course, be impossible if Japan did not enjoy such a high savings rate, in addition to its historic government support for targeted industries. The fact remains that, compared to American business-men, Japan's *keiretsu* leaders live in an environment, as Prestowitz put it, "where capital is free."

The Japanese drive for information control and market share—the twin goals of the international "headquarters" strategy—makes no sense in terms of conventional American free enterprise economics. It makes abundant sense, however, when Japan's search for what the late Prime Minister Ohira termed "comprehensive economic security" is seen as a political as much as an eco-nomic goal. Like the Venetian entrepreneurs of another day, Japan's business leaders think of their overseas transplant companies as political because they are commercial necessities useful for the survival of the state. They view these economic outposts not primarily as immediate money earners—although that element helps—but as bases for future operations, part of an interlocking net-work. Just as Americans have been accustomed to think of military bases as the underpinnings of an international military security system, Japan's bases com-prise an economic security chain. For American *military* read Japan's *economic*. Security is spelled the same.

---

[12] From an interview for the television series *The Pacific Century*. Detailed background is given in Prestowitz's book *Trading Places* (New York: Basic Books, 1989), a polemical but well-documented study of Japanese-American business competition.

16

Exporting the Bubble Economy

Japan's current attitudes and policies toward the rest of the world are not completely satisfying, as ever-growing international criticism of Japan suggests. . . . [Yet] better understanding of Japan abroad requires much deeper international interest and concern among the Japanese people. It also requires an environment within Japan which will promote greater and more active international cooperation.

OKITA SABURO

In 1970, during a San Clemente meeting between President Richard M. Nixon and Prime Minister Sato Eisaku, Nixon asked Sato if he would put pressure on Japanese business to cut down on the flood of textile exports into the United States. *"Zensho shimasu,"* Sato replied, roughly translated as "I'll handle it."

To Nixon this meant that the problem was solved. Sato would use his political power to deal with his concern (and thus make things easier for some of Nixon's domestic political supporters in the textile business). But *zensho* is a classically vague Japanese term, meaning something like "I'll do the best I can, but . . ." Mindful of his own domestic supporters in the textile business, Sato was telling Nixon not to expect much of anything, because his power in this case was very limited.

The little mistranslation, writ large, was symptomatic of some deep misconceptions that continue to flaw the relations between the two countries, leaving most such "summit" meetings little more than Reaganesque photo opportunities. Americans tend to think that everybody is like them. Products of a unique, multiracial, pluralist society, a nation united by laws, culture, and shared ideals rather than a single ethnic nationality, Americans assume that their ideas, laws, and lifestyle can work for everybody.

By contrast, Japanese like to think that *nobody* is like them. Monoracial and monocultural, despite their past borrowings, the Japanese dote on the uniqueness of their nation society. They harbor visceral doubts that what works for others can possibly work for them.

Americans think that everything can be accomplished by laws; law is the adhesive that keeps their well-lawyered society together. Japanese believe that laws accomplish little without consensus behind them; that is one reason why so many Japanese laws, antitrust and restraint of trade among them, have little or no provision for enforcement. Americans assume that all cartels or industry groupings are illegal (on the basis of some rather old laws) and hence reprehensible. Japanese find them natural and necessary ways of doing business.

To American businessmen competitive bidding is mandatory, at least officially. Japanese find it unnecessary, as long as you know the people you are doing business with. When Americans talk about research, they think of work done in a university, open to all (even if funded by the Pentagon). Japanese research is mostly proprietary, done by companies, often with MITI's help. American stock shares are held largely by the public, although pension funds and investment bankers hold sizable portions. Japanese shares are 70 percent held by companies and banks, who buy into each other. What is traded publicly on the market is merely the tip of the shareholding iceberg.

The list of differences, dissimilarities, and confusions could go on forever. My point is that these two modern, mutually communicative societies, so outwardly similar, harbor vast structural and societal differences. In economics as in everything else, culture counts.

Some of the worst confusions come from superficial overfamiliarity with each other. The widespread American belief in a monolith called Japan, Inc., is erroneous. Whatever its early postwar past, Japan is now governed by a complex of often warring interests—politicians, bureaucrats, businessmen, and even consumers. The fact that these groups, and subgroups, often cooperate does not mean that their interests are identical. Balancing their priorities has become more difficult—one reason why Japanese Prime Ministers have increasing difficulty in making good on their international promises.

Japanese for their part consistently underrate the regional pulls of American society. Washington is the site of a strong central government with a highly porous superstructure. Japanese business and government spend about $400 million annually on well-paid American lobbyists in efforts to influence it. Yet local, regional, and, most particularly, diverse ethnic and racial influences are stronger than ever before. So are other special constituencies. Worst of all, Japanese businessmen keep assuming that the American market will always be as open as it is today, so that their expansion can continue, be it export or investment. Their fondness for running in packs—note the profusion of real estate and other investment in Hawaii and California—has not helped their reputation.

FOR MORE THAN forty-five years I have lived through different stages of the Japanese-American relationship. As a journalist and a businessman, I have worked in Japan for a total of thirteen years, and I continue to visit Japan constantly as part of my normal round. I speak that language, albeit imperfectly, and have almost as many Japanese friends and associates as I have American. I have watched the two countries move together in so many ways. The very closeness of the relationship has intensified its problems. They have assumed different forms, but they remain essentially the same.

Until very recently Washington saw Japan from a political viewpoint. Japan was first and foremost an ally, a bulwark of the free world, America's anchor in the Pacific against the attacks, real and fancied, of world Communism. As long as Japan gave the United States its unwavering political and diplomatic support—and it did—economic problems should be regarded as secondary. What, after all, is a trade imbalance among friends?

This politics-first view fit in well with several generations of American economists who attributed Japan's extraordinary business success solely to the fact that the Japanese, so to speak, were just building better mousetraps. As a free enterprise economy, they held, Japan operates more or less the same as the United States. They were, of course, against protectionism. Japan, like the United States, should remove any "protectionist" barriers to trade; then all would be well. The subtleties of Japan's nontariff trade barriers, however, eluded American conventional economic wisdom. It was not easy for economists reared in the neoclassical tradition to accept the idea that the Japanese capitalist development state represents a new and unfamiliar economic phenomenon, or that its corporations, not content with being merely competitive, systematically practice what the distinguished scholar of management Peter Drucker has labeled "adversarial trade."[1] Which is to say, Japanese companies set out to dominate an industry and drive the competition out of it. During the high-yen crisis after the Plaza Agreement in 1985, for example, the big *keiretsu* businesses demonstrated their ability to sell products at a heavy loss to keep their overseas markets intact and growing (the while keeping prices up for their home-market consumers in Japan). This was a tactic that Adam Smith and

[1] As outlined in *The New Realities* (New York: Harper & Row, 1989) and numerous other writings.

Motor show in Beijing. Toyota Motor Corporation

TOYOTA AROUND THE WORLD

The headquarters company shows the flag.

Launch of new model Corona in Singapore. Toyota Motor Corporation

Crown Motors Ltd. service center, Hong Kong. Toyota Motor Corporation

Launch of new model Kijang in Indonesia.
Toyota Motor Corporation

Geneva motor show. Toyota Motor Corporation

*Launch of new model Corolla in
New Zealand.* Toyota Motor
Corporation

David Ricardo had not envisioned when they formulated their market-rational economic theories.

American complacency about Japan's unorthodox business strategies was particularly prevalent among White House economic advisers in the wild and woolly West of Reaganomics. Such strategies as targeting key industries for development, a long established canon among MITI bureaucrats in Japan, were nowhere more evident than in computers and semiconductors. Yet they failed to disturb official American economists. One recalls the classic comment of J. Robert Moskin, former White House economic adviser: "If you sell computer chips or potato chips, a hundred dollars is a hundred dollars." So much for developing the industry of the future.

American businessmen, for their part, were equally slow to realize the effectiveness of Japanese business strategies, let alone analyze them. I recall participating in a briefing conference on Japanese business methods, held at General Motors headquarters in Detroit, in the late 1970s. A score or two of GM vice presidents were in attendance. I was depressed to find almost total ignorance about what Japanese business was up to; the General Motors mind-set about Japan was apparently rooted in the Occupation 1940s. My fellow Japanologists and I were in the position of teaching the ABCs of Japanese business practice and industrial policy to carmakers who should have started studying about Toyota and Nissan ten years before. Their ignorance of Japan's automobile industry and the Japanese market was abysmal. Possibly to make sure it stayed that way, my colleagues and I were adjured by the GM man in charge not to say anything about the automobile business in Japan!

Those of us who had worked in Japan were well aware of the global ambitions of the Japanese steel, automotive, and electronics sectors and their near obsession with acquiring and retaining market share. The hardest task my fellow members of the American Chamber of Commerce in Tokyo used to face was convincing their home offices that Japan was worth studying and its markets worth entering. The "arrogance" that American competitors now attribute to Japanese business leaders seemed to have been standard psychological equipment among America's captains of industry in the late sixties and the seventies.

At the time, along with many others, I advocated treating Japanese investors and exporters in the United States just the way Americans were handled in Japan. Such a system of practical "reciprocity" would have proved effective, had it been practiced in the seventies. The few American CEOs I talked to were unenthusiastic, however. I once pointed out to the president of a very large California bank that, while Japanese banks were buying up American banks almost wholesale, it would be impossible for Americans (or any non-Japanese) even to acquire shares in a Japanese bank. "But I don't want to buy a Japanese bank," was his only reply.

Practicing law in Japan was a similarly restrictive proposition. In the United States a foreign lawyer who passes the local state bar examination is admitted to practice. Not so in Japan. After the U.S. Occupation ended, the few loopholes allowing foreigners to practice law in Japan were resolutely sealed off by the Japanese bar association. Despite vigorous protests by swarms of American lawyers—representing as they do one of our nation's few growth industries—the ban on foreign lawyers arguing cases remains largely in force, as of this writing. The Japanese lawyers' defense of their turf rivals the successes of the government tobacco monopoly's bureaucrats in keeping all foreign cigarettes out of Japan, until very recently.[2]

Working in this atmosphere of cultural protectionism was an interesting, if unsettling experience for a foreigner. The press was at best semi-hostile. The American company for which I worked in Tokyo was pilloried by *Asahi,* then Tokyo's largest newspaper, for alleged sales excesses, after accusations by a hoked-up "victims' league" whose credentials the paper never bothered to investigate. Later we started a joint-venture publishing company in which the American partner held a majority—the first such case in the industry. Despite heavy local competition we succeeded, and quite spectacularly. Because of problems at home, we sold our controlling interest to our Japanese partner shortly thereafter.

When we attempted to buy back control, however, with our partner's complete approval, we were blocked by the company's main bank, Mitsubishi, primarily because we represented the dread word *gaishi*—"foreign capital." When a new Japanese partner, a large consumer products company, then bought control, its first act was to conclude a secret agreement with its predecessor—in total violation of our contract—not to sell any significant portion of its remaining stock to the foreigner.

Despite such cases of vest-pocket chauvinism, I found, through ten years as a Japanese company president, that it was by no means impossible for a foreign business to succeed in Japan, given a good product, competent Japanese executives, and long-term commitment to do business in Japan. There are many compensations. Employees are loyal and dedicated. Officials are generally understanding, once they realize that you will play the game their way. Over the years, also, a climate of trust develops with business associates, bankers, and suppliers, which is very comfortable and supportive, at least as long as one remains within Japan's business biosphere.

Many foreign companies have succeeded in Japan as we did. Names like

---

[2] When the famous Surgeon General's report linking smoking with cancer was first published in the United States, quick-thinking Monopoly officials pointed out that carcinogens harmful to foreigners were not necessarily injurious to Japanese.

IBM, National Cash Register, Motorola, Dow, Texas Instruments, and Smith Kline & Beckman come to mind. Some joint ventures like Caterpillar Mitsubishi, Sumitomo 3M, or Merck Banyu have also done well. Yet even in this group companies with cutting-edge products like Motorola and Texas Instruments have had to fight for every yard of market share they got against MITI as well as the competition. The rules of the game were different, and they had to be learned. (IBM, for example, was not allowed to manufacture in Japan until it had agreed to license patents to no fewer than fifteen Japanese companies.) In some cases, like the construction industry, the band-of-brothers relationship between Japan's politically strong builders and their supporters (or, more correctly, supportees) in the majority Liberal Democratic Party made it impossible for American or other non-Japanese competition to get a look-in, despite the easy and profitable access to business given Japan's construction firms in the United States.

As long as I can remember, however, American trade negotiators have had to operate on the assumption that the Japanese negotiate on the same basis that Americans do. By patient argument, American conventional wisdom runs, they can be persuaded to change their business practices. The aim of the American-inspired Structural Impediments Initiative talks at the beginning of the nineties was to force Japan to discard many of its most cherished customs—unwritten cartel arrangements, cumbersome distribution systems, *keiretsu* deals included—in favor of international (for which read American) standards. It is unlikely that this will be done.

Japan's cultural protectionism, with its multitude of vaguely defined "non-tariff" trade barriers, is notably difficult to regulate under GATT conventions. The case for Japanese "uniqueness" is often pushed to the limits of straight-faced absurdity, as in arguments that imported rice is bad for Japanese intestines or foreign skis cannot cope with the peculiar consistency of Japanese snow. There is, however, some substance to cultural protectionism. It is rooted in Japan's present political structure, for one thing. While a streamlined American-type distribution system, for example, would pave the way for more foreign goods in Japan, it would also eliminate the thousands of small "ma and pa" stores that have kept Japan's inner city healthy. A general system of competitive bidding for company purchasing, foreign as well as Japanese, would be desirable. But I see no way it could be enforced. It would damage, if not destroy the pneumatic network of confidence and mutual support on which so much of Japanese business is based.

The Japanese have made great strides in "internationalizing" their tight island economy. Since 1986, when the Maekawa Report commissioned by Prime Minister Nakasone recommended some basic restructuring, the government has pointed the way to an economy less driven by exports than by domestic demand. The country's infrastructure has been built up, consumer spending encouraged, and imports promoted. Still the juggernaut rolls on.

I do not believe the trade imbalance with the United States can be corrected by forcing more changes on Japan. Nor can simple protectionism help. American industry has grown too dependent on Japanese components for that. The United States, however, needs to take a leaf from Japan's book and adopt an industrial policy of its own. This will involve sweeping changes in the way Americans look at economics and a change from the old view of laissez-faire economics. Any reform in this direction will be all the more painful because it is long overdue. And it may well involve surcharges and some discrimination against Japanese products, if the United States wishes to be something more than the major trading post for the headquarters country, Japan.

For Japan, whose people continue to work as a way of life—*karoshi*, "death from overworking," has become a national cause of concern—some stock-taking is necessary. The government can admonish and caution, urging people to import more and spend fewer hours at work, but Japanese companies, secure in their network of foreign economic bases, continue to push forward, exporting not merely their goods and money but a ruthless competitive zeal that sprang from the economy of scarcity in which they were engendered. Now, the world's largest creditor, with its annual capital investment ($660 billion in 1990) greatly exceeding that of the United States,[3] seems desperately intent on "catching up." The territorialists who run Japan's companies are flexible in everything but a braking mechanism. That is one thing that Japanese business totally lacks.

In a thoughtful article in the February 1992 issue of Japan's leading monthly magazine, *Bungei Shunju*, Morita Akio, Sony's chairman—and the closest thing to a statesman Japanese business possesses—questioned whether Japanese corporations' headlong pursuit of market share, to the exclusion of social considerations, the environment, or the quality of life, was not giving Japan a deserved bad name among the nations. "Reform of our management ideals," he wrote, "can be achieved only if the whole economic and social system is changed . . . a painful process."

Shimomura Mitsuko, editor of the cerebral *Asahi Journal* magazine in Tokyo, had earlier underlined the same problem, inherent in the kind of economic machine that Japan has created. "Unfortunately," she wrote, "the machine is so strong and well established that it is hard to overhaul, still less to destroy. How can we create a new machine to aim at new targets? That's the problem at the moment. Everybody knows we are going in a wrong direction, but we don't know how to stop it."[4]

---

[3] For this and other statistics, I am indebted to Kenneth Courtis, senior economic analyst for the Deutsche Bank in the Pacific, one of the world's foremost authorities on Japan's economy.

[4] From an interview in *The Pacific Century* television series.

How indeed? We have noted the success of Japanese business in the United States. To watch Japan's corporations perform in an Asia-Pacific context, let us turn to Southeast Asia. There an economic and voluntary version of the wartime Greater East Asia Co-Prosperity Sphere is alive and well and in some danger of overheating.

"The red rising sun of Japan is coming, to gobble you up. . . . Japan is Here. . . ." As the rock music blares over the sound track, the Japanese rising sun flag turns into a Pacman monster gobbling up land, people, and machines. So ran a popular rock video in Bangkok, circa 1991. For residents of the Thai capital the anti-Japanese sound track was nothing unusual—yet another version of the current hit "The Samurai Have Arrived." But in its flippant way it made an accurate comment on the Japanese accent of Thailand's emergent economic prosperity.

There are some 30,000 Japanese in Thailand, almost an entire transplant society, fully equipped with their own subsidiary companies and joint ventures (roughly 1,000 in number), well-kept housing areas, suburban industrial estates, *karaoke* bars and "sex tours" of the wide-open cabarets in Patpong, MITI representatives, construction companies, more than two million Japanese cars, and some ninety golf courses, most of them new. They can shop in Japanese department stores, handle financial matters at Japanese banks and insurance companies, enjoy the food at Japanese restaurants and hotels, and send their children to special Japanese schools.

Bangkok is the center of all this Japanese activity—like other Asian urban centers, a metropolis pulling an entire country into its vortex. Its population of about nine million has made the city hopelessly overcrowded. Its mass of automobile and motorbike traffic chugs through the streets in a state of almost constant gridlock. Its pollution is arguably the worst in East Asia (which is saying a lot). Once a graceful city of quiet *klong* waterways and gold-roofed Buddhist temples, it is now a forest of newly built ferroconcrete office buildings and shantylike housing developments. Most of the canals have been paved over to become narrow, almost impassable roads, but sewage still flows beneath them. More than a million tons of waste each year—the legacy of haphazard growth—ooze into the silted waters of Bangkok's river, the Chao Phraya, while a hot haze of polluted air hangs perpetually like an aureole around the splashy signs advertising Matsushita, Mitsubishi, Citizen, Nikon, Nissan, Fujitsu, NEC, Mitsui, and other familiar Japanese brands that dominate the Thai economy as effectively as they do the Bangkok skyline. And more than 80 percent of Thailand's industry is located in Bangkok's metropolitan area.

Despite the rock video and an undercurrent of criticism, the Japanese are not deeply resented. For they have brought jobs and prosperity with them. Originally an exporter of commodities (principally rice and rubber), Thailand has developed industrially since the seventies. With a recent growth rate averaging about 10 percent annually and a steadily rising manufacturing component, Thailand is swiftly becoming a Newly Industrialized Country. Japan is Thailand's major trading partner and investor. Japanese industry has put more than $1 billion annually into Thailand over the past four years, while the Japanese government has contributed heavy sums in aid projects.

Over the years, however, the pattern of Japanese economic interaction has changed. The accent is now not on exports to Thailand but investment in offshore plant there. Japanese business overseas still favors its own product for high-quality merchandise. In Thailand and other Southeast Asian countries, for example, Japanese trading companies have established a chain of steel coil "service" centers to import high-value rolled steel direct from Japan. But the emphasis is now on making products that can not only be used in Thailand but also shipped to other countries (Japan itself included). Most Japanese businesses there keep tight control of management, while Thai workers at establishments like the new Toyota plant and the large industrial park at Nava Nakorn are learning new skills and technologies as part of a modern industrial work force.

The mushroom growth of the Thai economy dates from Secretary Baker's optimistic yen raising at the Plaza Hotel in 1985. The graph of Japan's direct investment in Asia looks like the upside of a roller coaster, with the takeoff point between 1985 and 1986. From an annual investment level of under $1 billion, the lines shoot upward toward the $8 billion level. From 1986 to 1991 Japanese corporations invested almost $28 billion in Korea, Taiwan, Hong Kong, and the ASEAN countries. Most of it went into offshore production, to enable Japanese companies to keep their products competitive in the new high-yen era. During the same period the Japanese government disbursed $10 billion in overseas development projects. The bulk of this money went to Southeast Asia.

In his timely book *Asia's New Little Dragons*,[5] Steven Schlosstein, a former American banker in Asia, has analyzed the effect of this industrial restructuring. While direct exports from Japan dropped from 34 percent of total company sales in 1986 to 27 percent in 1989, average production overseas went from 4 percent of sales to 6 percent. With some major export companies, he noted, the percentage of overseas sales jumped even higher—e.g., Hitachi from 20 to 35 percent, Matsushita from 26 to 43 percent, Honda from 29 to 38 percent. In Thailand GNP immediately reflected this implementation of Japan's headquarters-country strategy, as it shot from a 4 percent annual increase in 1985 and 1986 to more than 8 percent in 1987.

In past years, Japanese companies had done a great deal of their offshore

[5] *Asia's New Little Dragons: The Dynamic Emergence of Indonesia, Thailand and Malaysia* (Chicago: Contemporary Books, 1991).

manufacturing in Taiwan, Korea, Hong Kong, and Singapore—the latter two being peculiarly attractive because of their strategic locations and obliging governments. Some of this continued. Yet by the mid-eighties both Korea and Taiwan were becoming more competitors than agents, with relations none too good. Koreans in particular complained that Japan continued to discriminate against Korean exports, while keeping up a huge favorable trade balance with its sales of machinery, tools, and other high-quality items to Korea. ("Why is it," a highly placed Japanese politician friend once complained, "that we can form successful joint ventures everywhere but in Korea?")

Labor costs in the four original NICs were rising—thus defeating the main purpose of Japan's offshore manufacturing. In addition, rising levels of education and industrial capability—Korea being now virtually on a level with Japan in both departments—made both workers and executives in Seoul, Taipei, and Singapore less willing to defer to Japanese bosses. With characteristic candor, Singapore's Lee Kuan Yew commented: "We know that European companies promote Singaporeans faster than the Japanese do. The Japanese for some reason do not believe that Singapore is learning as fast as the Americans or Europeans believe. I can't name one Japanese company where the CEO is a Singaporean."

From Singapore's ASEAN neighbors, however, Japan received no such criticism. Searching for ideal junior partners in development, Japanese corporate planning departments were increasingly attracted to Thailand, Malaysia, and Indonesia. For the directors of a *keiretsu* company group in Tokyo, these three nations represented an almost ideal trade and investment relationship. All three, endowed with rich natural resources, had valuable commodities for sale. Oil, rubber, tin, and timber could flow northward to Japan in return for the computers, cameras, machine tools, and various high-tech products of the global headquarters country. The trade roughly balanced, in 1991 coming to about $20 billion worth each way. All three offer large and willing labor forces, their people only too happy to exchange village life for employment in the new Japanese-run factories. While education levels lag far behind Korea, Taiwan, and Singapore, they are rising, and people are still quite content with the labor-intensive jobs that young Japanese spurn. Add to this the factors of strong central governments and a good supply of Western-educated technocrats to man the bureaucracy. The mix seems the answer to a trading company's prayer.

Yet it would be a mistake to label these three countries as the new "Little Tigers," bounding along in the tracks left by Korea and Taiwan. They have strikingly different cultures and backgrounds. Here reigns no pervasive Confucian ethic. Indonesia and Malaysia are Islamic countries of predominantly Malay race—although Indonesia boasts a considerable degree of cultural and religious diversity (Christians in Sulawesi and Timor, Hindus in Bali) among its 140 million people. The Thais are a separate race altogether, their culture influenced both by China and by India, but most striking in the almost universal Thai adherence to its own brand of Hinayana Buddhism.

In contrast to Koreans and the maritime Chinese of Taiwan and Hong Kong, there is little built-in cultural antipathy to Japan. In Indonesia and Malaysia it is the Chinese influence that has traditionally been feared and resisted. In both countries Chinese have historically dominated business and to an extent intellectual life. Their primacy is a latent source of resentment among the Malay, Javanese, and Sumatran majorities—and one easily stimulated by aggressive local leaders for their own purposes. In 1966, the turmoil over an attempted Communist coup d'état, apparently backed by China, gave rise to a general massacre of Chinese residents, in which almost half a million people died. A similar race war threatened Malaysia in 1969; thousands were killed in anti-Chinese rioting before order was restored.

In a way the Japanese presence is welcomed as a counterweight to this historic economic hegemony of the Chinese merchant and banker. There have been outbreaks of popular anti-Japanese feeling in the recent past. In 1973, Prime Minister Tanaka Kakuei had to be rescued by helicopter from demonstrators in Jakarta. But they were largely the backwash of the wave of Japanese businessmen and their products, which seemed to engulf Southeast Asia in the seventies. There is no historic antipathy. For the past two decades the Japanese government has worked hard and successfully at building good relations with the ASEAN countries. Here the eighties switch from product exports to plant investment has powerfully helped.

FROM A JAPANESE investor's point of view, the political situation in these three ASEAN countries—Indonesia, Malaysia, and Thailand—has seemed gratifyingly stable, with a minimum of problems. Here we might usefully digress for a brief political risk analysis of these countries. In all three democracy has a long way to develop.

Suharto has reigned—the word is used advisedly—as President of Indonesia since his formal takeover from the disgraced Sukarno in 1968. He has run the country on the whole shrewdly, in a paternalistic Javanese tradition. Whereas Indonesians referred to their original dictator as "Bung Karno" ("Brother Sukarno"), Suharto is known more or less affectionately as "Pak Harto" ("Father Harto"). With considerable skill Suharto has kept the country resolutely secular, away from Islamic extremism. His government has also brought the country both stability and a steadily, if slowly rising standard of living. The same Arab-enforced OPEC boycott of 1973 which brought hardship to countries like Japan and Korea represented a windfall for Indonesia, as oil prices soared.

Sudden prosperity brought with it wholesale corruption among Indonesia's government elite, most of them military officers. Managers of the huge oil monopoly, Pertamina, and other semi-government corporations were among the worst offenders. To right the economy Suharto turned increasingly to young technocrats in the government ministries. Known originally as the "Berkeley mafia" from the American university where most received their doctorates, these economic bureaucrats have on the whole charted a responsible course. In recent years they have successfully steered the economy away from the single-product dependence on oil with which postwar Indonesia began. Here, as in other Southeast Asian countries, they have formed working alliances with a variety of Japanese business interests. (Roughly 40 percent of Indonesia's trade is with Japan.)

The leading players in the Indonesian polity (and economy) are military men who came up in the Suharto tradition. From the beginnings of the independence wars, the Army, guided by former Chief of Staff Abdul Haris Nasution and others, set out to become a "social-political force" in the country. This role it never relinquished.

Like China's People's Liberation Army during the Cultural Revolution, the Indonesian Army in the late sixties took over many functions normally performed by political parties, business, or government itself. The reason was the same, structurally speaking. Sukarno's regime had broken up in the wake of the abortive Communist coup against Army conservatives. But whereas China's PLA was mobilized as a kind of backup force behind Mao's far-left Cultural Revolution, the Indonesian Army turned the country to a right-center orientation.

In fact, the Korean government under President Park Chung Hee offers a closer parallel. Both Suharto and Park set about economic revival, under military auspices. By now the Republic of Korea's government under Roh Tae Woo has been largely civilianized, but Indonesia in the early nineties remains more or less comparable to Park Chung Hee's Korea of the late sixties. Its generals and colonels constitute a virtual ruling class.

Thailand is *sui generis*. In recent years the processes of government and economic guidance were relatively untroubled by recurring coups in which one Army Prime Minister generally replaces another. Investors' political risk estimates changed sharply after the huge demonstrations and violence of the Suchinda regime in May 1992. Here, too, however, the monarchy under King Pumiphol, proved itself an anchor of political stability. Changes of political power at the top can still restore the situation.

The Malaysia of Prime Minister Mahathir bin Mohamed is something else again. Far from banking the fires of Islamic separatism, Mahathir stoked them, adroitly stirring up the latent anti-Chinese feeling among Malays for his *bu-*

Indonesian honor guard. In Suharto's country the military still call the turn. Jigsaw Productions

The "Curry Rice Club" meets. Yet even strong leaders like Ikeda (second from right) had to keep their fences mended with continual inner-circle political meetings. Mainichi Shimbun

miputra (literally, "sons of the soil") version of preferential politics. This system puts legal restrictions on educational opportunities for Chinese (and other non-Malays) as well as business participation. The Chinese have not been greatly inconvenienced by this; hiring a Malay bumiputra as a business front man has become a widespread commercial practice. Yet Mahathir's governance in this and other matters is not much of an ad for democracy. Perhaps following in the old Malay tradition of strong-man (orang kuat) leadership, he has moved ruthlessly against opponents, as untroubled by conventional legal safeguards as his neighbor in Singapore, Lee Kuan Yew.

Japanese businessmen are singularly untroubled by authoritarian governments and their violations of human rights. Nor does their government share the ever righteous indignation of Washington at corrupt practices in other countries. Like their Venetian exemplars of the Mediterranean, who traded equally well with Pope and Sultan, the Japanese have a resolutely nonpolitical attitude. Japanese corporations are most favorably impressed, in fact, by Mahathir's "Look East" policy, which he first enunciated shortly after becoming Prime Minister in 1981.

Advising his countrymen to use Japan as a guide, Mahathir released almost all restrictions on foreign investment, and he has gone so far as to advocate an Asian trading bloc, with Japan as its center. Thus far their close economic relationship has proved mutually profitable for Japan and Malaysia. More than 800 Japanese companies are now located in Malaysia, turning out everything from silicon wafers to marine cargo containers. Malaysia's new homemade car, the Proton Saga, is a Mitsubishi clone. Per capita income for the country's 17 million people rose from $1,700 in 1980 to an estimated $2,800 in 1991. As sign and seal on Malaysia's prosperity, it should be known that over the past five years the number of American Express card holders has doubled.[6]

Not surprisingly, when Mahathir in December 1990 proposed creation of his East Asian Economic Group, the Americans were to be excluded. As the nineties dawned, a variety of economists raised the possibility of a "yen bloc" that would be expected to offset both European and North American blocs, real or fancied, as they developed. "The color of our economy is blue," Newsweek quoted Malayan economist Stephen Wong as saying, "because that is the color of a 1,000-yen note. That is fine with us, because that is the reality."

Although Mahathir's trial balloon did not at first ascend very far, the idea could not help but find some support in Japan, where the press has been chewing over the prospect for some years. In 1988, MITI itself wafted a proposal for a regional economic group, under the ambitious heading of "Promoting Comprehensive Economic Cooperation in an International Economic

[6] As noted in Newsweek, August 5, 1991.

Environment Undergoing Upheaval: Toward the Construction of an Asian Network." Here was the headquarters-country idea spelled out in fine print. Japan would be the "first tier" economy, followed by "second tier" economies like Korea, with Indonesia, Malaysia, and Thailand providing the "third tier" base.[7]

The first-tier headquarters, in line with current Japanese business practice, would reserve for itself the most sophisticated types of production, centering on high tech, the "knowledge" industry, and the more sophisticated elements of the mass-production process. Much of this production at interlocking (and descending) levels is already in place, as witness the bewildering cross-hatching of Japanese corporate manufacturing networks in the Pacific Basin.

Interestingly enough, Japanese plans for the Greater East Asia Co-Prosperity Sphere in the thirties and forties envisaged a similar division. Heavy industry was to be concentrated in Northeast Asia. Japan itself, Manchuria, North China, Korea, and Taiwan would constitute the core area. Southeast Asia would serve mainly as a commodity resource. Vietnam, Thailand, and the Philippines would provide food, while Indonesia and Malaysia—then the Netherlands East Indies, Borneo, Singapore, and the Malay States—would keep Japan supplied with oil, rubber, and other useful raw materials. Although much was said about putting the world under one roof (*hakko ichiu*) and, going back to Okakura Tenshin's Meiji era slogan, making Asia one—one imaginative Japanese scholar in the thirties referred to an East Asian Monroe Doctrine— the primary objectives of the Co-Prosperity Sphere were military and economic.[8] In support of the military war effort, Japanese firms were to invest in the other Asian countries—Southeast Asia as well as Korea, Manchuria, and Taiwan—develop their industries, and integrate them into the Co-Prosperity Sphere. All would naturally come under the guidance of the government ministries concerned.

The concept failed in practice. Not only did Japanese industry lack sufficient capital for exploiting other Asian countries' resources, but the U.S. Navy's submarine blockade of Japan left the components of the Greater East Asia

[7] An idea developed by Tokyo University economist Watanabe Toshio, as quoted in Steven Schlosstein's *Asia's New Little Dragons*.

[8] In his 1939 article on the Monroe Doctrine, in fact, the diplomatic historian Kamikawa Hikomatsu wrote: "In the economic sphere the Japanese Monroe Doctrine envisages what may be termed East Asia continentalism, which is none other than a movement based upon the geographical, cultural, and economic solidarity of the countries of East Asia, with the object of bringing about the closest possible intercourse among them. This is not at all an activity of an imperialistic character. It is a joint movement of the East Asiatic peoples." (As quoted in Joyce Lebra's *Japan's Greater East Asia Co-Prosperity Sphere in World War II* [New York: Oxford University Press, 1980].)

empire sundered and unprotected. It was left to Japan's latter-day nationalists to hail the current relationships with other East Asian countries as final vindication of their country's "constructive" wartime intentions. On the other side of the Pacific, many American commentators with an eye on the fiftieth anniversary of the attack on Pearl Harbor began to depict Japan's growing economic hegemony of the nineties as the Greater East Asia Co-Prosperity Sphere revisited.

There are some obvious parallels here. Although eschewing the very idea of political—not to mention military—expansion, the far-ranging economic expansion of Japanese business in Southeast Asia is conducted with the intensity of the strategic military plan. In a world where economic hegemony seems to count for more than military, the Mitsubishi auto assembly plants and the Matsushita electronics factories can readily be called the Clark Fields and Camranh Bays of world economics, bases in Japan's drive for the late Prime Minister Ohira's goal of comprehensive economic security.

The current Japanese presence in Southeast Asia, however, is manifestly not the revived Co-Prosperity Sphere that "Japan bashers" warn against. For one thing, there is the strong element of mutual benefit. This Japan's wartime activities totally lacked. (The propaganda statements of "Asia for the Asiatics" were a far cry from the consistent brutality of Japanese military occupations.) Japanese exports and investments would hardly be tolerated in these strongly nationalist Asian countries if they were not doing the natives a great deal of good. Nor have wartime memories of Japan's political and military aggression disappeared. There is a great difference between Koreans and Singaporeans learning Japanese for business reasons and the spoon-fed doses of "Japanese culture" forced on them half a century ago. Suspicion of Japan's political motives remains very strong.

The Japanese themselves would agree. They have yet to sort out in their minds what role, if any, an Economic Superpower should play in the world. They remain latter-day Venetians. Company by company Japan's business moves into the world, setting up its economic bases and strongpoints as a continuing part of a defensive "catch up" strategy aimed at economic security for one country. But most Japanese have very mixed feelings about exporting their tight island civilization—as opposed to its products. Even more than their medieval Venetian prototypes, who colonized their trading posts while dreaming of a return to their city, the Japanese seem unable to understand why the massed expansion of their business society is viewed by many as a new form of economic aggression.

There is a third and most important obstacle in the way of Japan's becoming a dominant world power. That is the deep flaws and fissures in the Japanese econo-polity. Exemplars of the world's ultimate economic miracle, dispenser of the largest international aid programs, mandatory leading figure at great power economic summits, Japan suffers from the narrow self-interest politics of an insular city-state. Oddly like Venice, and the prototypical city-state of Athens long before it, Japan offers representative democracy to its people, providing in many respects one of the world's most permissive modern governments. But like those long-vanished predecessors, the Japanese democracy stops at the water's edge. Its deepening moral autarchy and its "Japanist" way of public thinking is in ironic contrast to its world reach. Particularly over the last five years, the tremors and rumblings within Japanese society give thoughtful Japanese and their friends an ominous sense of the ground sinking beneath us.

IN JUNE 1988, an article in the local news section of the Tokyo *Asahi* disclosed some improper stock dealings in nearby Kawasaki. Apparently the deputy mayor had accepted a present of some unlisted shares in a company called Recruit in return for a building permit. In modern Japan such sleight of hand in stock dealings barely raises eyebrows, let alone makes news. What regulation exists in Tokyo's Kabuto-cho exchange is almost without punitive powers; speculators and business operators almost constantly play games with it. But the Recruit transactions in Kawasaki turned out to have a long fuse, with some noisy explosives at its end.

Recruit was originally a small job-placement company, with magazines describing employment opportunities for university graduates. But its president, Ezoe Hiromasa, was a master salesman with a talent for energizing both employees and prospects. By 1988 his magazines had a total circulation of almost seven million. He had added a real estate subsidiary to his personnel scouting businesses. More recently he was going into computer communications in a big way, thanks to his friendship with management of Nippon Telephone and Telegraph (NTT), the country's huge communications monopoly. In this he was following the pattern, familiar to Japanese business, of taking his company "high tech."

Money was no problem for Ezoe, who thought big. In the go-go eighties, Japan's already swollen land values soared into the financial stratosphere, bringing bank and company assets (on paper) along with them. Recruit's Cosmos real estate subsidiary was able to borrow $10 billion with ease from obliging banks on the basis of grossly inflated property holdings. Everybody, as the saying goes, was doing it.

Every company did not make a practice of handing out vast quantities of stock shares wholesale to Japanese politicians before going public. Such activities were generally performed discreetly and over a long period of time. Ezoe, however, was a man in a hurry. Anxious to use government and NTT connections to build Recruit's own communications empire, he scattered his shares lavishly and quickly. At least $60 million of Recruit stock went to leaders of the majority Liberal Democratic Party, highly placed bureaucrats, and NTT officials, who disposed of them at vastly inflated prices. As word spread in the newspapers, it became clear that the Kawasaki deputy mayor had some distinguished company.

The Tokyo prosecutor's office began to investigate whether the stock had been given in exchange for preferential treatment. It certainly had. The finger pointed to NTT management and its friends in the Nakasone administration. Whether personally or through intermediaries, virtually the entire party hierarchy seemed to have held pieces of the action.

Within the next year Prime Minister Takeshita Noboru resigned, former Prime Minister Nakasone Yasuhiro (in office at the height of the scandal) left the party, Ezoe himself went to jail, along with the venerable president of NTT. No real reforms were announced for stock-market trading, however. While the bureaucracy sat tight, worried Liberal Democrat politicians—as if to show how badly they needed money—spent roughly $1 billion preparing for the 1989 elections.

In almost any other of the world's democracies, such an explosive scandal would have turned the Liberal Democrats out of office. In Japan almost nothing happened. In the July 1989 elections, it is true, the Socialist Party won temporary control of the largely ceremonial upper house. Since the new party leader was a woman, Doi Takako, and she had persuaded her party leadership to field an unprecedented number of female candidates—Japanese called it the "madonna" election—American pundits were quick to hail the results as a new wave of feminism and clean government in Japan. As always, they were mistaken in assuming that the Japanese, voters and politicians, would behave like Americans in a similar situation.

In fact, the Socialists, perennial political runners-up, were incapable of even aspiring to real leadership. The Japanese electorate over the years has shown little confidence in the Socialists' doctrinaire (and all-male) leadership of old professorial Marxists and union bosses—except as an outlet for occasional protest votes. Since the day of Ikeda Hayato's "income-doubling" policies, the prosperous Japanese electorate has continued to vote its pocketbook and keep the Liberal Democrats in. Hopelessly corrupt and faction-ridden, this one-party government has been supported by a constant flow of funding from Japanese big business. Basing its strength originally on conservative farmers in the countryside—thanks to Japan's curious proportional representation system, which the Liberal Democrats designed, in which one rural vote was generally worth about five city votes—the party had become a permanent fixture.

In 1991, having formally rejoined his party, former Prime Minister Nakasone summed up the situation: "People have nowhere to turn but to the Liberal Democrats. It is true that we had to face highly emotional problems like the Recruit scandal. It was as if the party had been caught in a sudden rain shower. Now the shower is over, the sun is out and our body is dry."

The rainy season was far from over, however. In 1991 it fell out that Nomura Securities, Japan's internationalized super-brokerage and investment firm,[9] had been handing out vast sums in under-the-counter rebates to cover the losses of big *keiretsu* corporate clients in the stock market. This time the police started their research early. Over the preceding two years, investigators learned, Nomura and three other large Japanese brokers had paid out almost $1.5 billion to cover favored customers' losses in the 1990 drop-off in Kabuto-cho. In addition, Nomura and Nikko Securities were accused of funneling money in various guises to favored clients in Japan's *yakuza* underworld.

The shock waves from the Nomura disclosures spread around the financial world, all the more quickly since Nomura had been aggressively muscling its way into the brokerage and investment business in the United States and Europe. The usual resignations of chairmen and presidents followed, but it is widely assumed that the damage done to Nomura was not permanent.

The next problem area appeared in the banks. As with the Nomura disclosures, it came in the backwash of the big stock-market drop late in 1990. The chairmen of the Sumitomo and Fuji banks resigned over bankers' ties to speculators, most particularly in the failure of a textile company that had dropped $6.5 billion in the losses of a real estate subsidiary. The most bizarre banking scandal of all came from the staid Industrial Bank of Japan, the country's major provider of long-term capital. The Industrial Bank and its affiliates had loaned up to $1.8 billion (240 billion yen) to a mysterious Osaka restaurant proprietress named Nui Onoue, who had promptly used their debentures as collateral for a series of disastrous speculations in the falling stock market. Ms. Onoue, believed to have underworld connections, was arrested. Kurosawa Yo, Industrial Bank of Japan's president, explained that the bank had been "fooled."

All this was too much even for Japan's establishment. Unlike the Recruit scandal, the securities and banking improprieties pointed a finger not at the "politicians" but at the citadels of Japan's "best and brightest" bureaucrats: the

---

[9] Founded in 1872 in Osaka as a small rice broker (and money changer), Nomura grew over the years into Japan's and the world's largest securities broker and, at least until recently, Japan's most profitable company. (In 1987 its pretax earnings were $4 billion.) With related activities in real estate, banking, and information gathering, it has also become a powerhouse in international finance. *The House of Nomura* (London: Bloomsbury, 1990) by Al Alletzhauser provides a fascinating study of Nomura and its world.

Finance Ministry and the Bank of Japan. For the Finance Ministry, far from regulating the rebate policy, had encouraged it, in the days of heavy capital investment, based on inflated stock and land prices, after the high-yen Plaza Agreement of 1985. When the ministry, fearing inflation, started to tighten the money supply in 1989, Nomura and other broker colleagues were left holding rather a big bag.

In an August special issue headlined "The Finance Ministry's Failure," *Nikkei Business,* the magazine oracle of Japan's business establishment, denounced the ministry's total failure to regulate the banking and securities industries. "At a time when Japan's economy has become a global resource," the articles began, "it is essential that the Finance Ministry restructure itself now, to use proper controls in rebuilding a healthy market economy for Japan."

Individual critics were harsher. In an article in *Sankei Shimbun,* Makino Noboru, former chairman of the Mitsubishi Research Institute, gave voice to a rising concern over the climate of fraud in Japanese business. He is worth quoting at some length:

> The rash of scandals rocking the nation's finance and trading industries is a sure sign of decline. Scarcely a day goes by without new revelations of foul play. Business peculation is nothing new, of course. But the nature, scale, and frequency of the latest crimes point to a shocking loss of managerial integrity that will ultimately destroy Japanese industry. Steadiness and foresight have been the hallmarks of Japanese management in the postwar era. From the mid-1980s, however, business ethics fell by the wayside as prudent investment gave way to the orgy of speculation and profiteering.
>
> The Big Four brokerage firms spent about $1.3 billion during a two-and-a-half-year period to compensate favored clients for stock-market losses . . . Industry leader Nomura Securities is suspected of share-price manipulation. Nomura and Nikko Securities have admitted lending $268.1 million to an underworld kingpin. Bank officials mocked government regulations by issuing bogus certificates of deposit to serve as collateral for huge loans from credit firms. Major trading company employees have been arrested for fraudulent business schemes or for evading millions of dollars in taxes. Corporate executives, no longer interested in the modest rewards of a hard day's work, want to make a quick killing in stocks or real estate. Business leaders who recently denounced the unscrupulous actions of politicians may be right, but they are hardly in a position to talk . . .
>
> Fiscal policy makers—the Bank of Japan and the Ministry of Finance—kept interest rates low and permitted excess liquidity, causing a runaway rise in stock and land values. Between 1987 and 1989 our gross national product was about $8 trillion. Yet over the same three years, stocks and land increased in value by more than $9 trillion! Big business used funds from new stock

issues to invest in real estate or equities, driving up both markets to unrealistic levels.

By the time the press began warning about the dangers of rampant speculation, the bubble was about to burst . . .

Makino used the word "bubble" advisedly. In the past few years *babbaru keizai*—"bubble economy"—has become common currency in Tokyo and Osaka business circles. The bubble first threatened to burst in October 1990, when the Japanese stock market dropped disastrously, losing more than 40 percent of its value since its top reading the year before. Although its effects were contained, this time, the losses incurred brought the international financial world's attention to the Japanese economy's huge guilty secret: the swollen price of land and the web of interlocking loans and investments dependent on it.

In 1975, in the first edition of my book *Japan the Fragile Superpower*, I expressed shock at the extraordinary rise in property prices. Since that time they have soared almost beyond belief. As of December 1990, to quote the *Economist*, Japan's total stock of property was valued at "a theoretical $2,000 trillion, or five times the size of Japan's gross national product and some four times the total stock of property in America." The rise in property values, which came with Japan's pell-mell urbanization, was furthered by curious zoning restrictions, which among other things set aside huge tracts of metropolitan land for farming purposes. For the past quarter century everyone in Japan has been aware of their dangerous distortions, which make it ever harder for average middle-class Japanese to find remotely adequate housing in the cities. Yet almost nothing has been done by government to bring prices into line.

The reasons are not hard to fathom. Big companies got into the real estate business and profited greatly from high prices. So did the banks and insurance companies. So did politicians who got their voter spending money from business, and by the nineties the level of political spending had unbelievably soared.

In the late eighties, the Finance Ministry and the Bank of Japan had to bring interest rates way down. The government's macroeconomists wanted to keep capital investment up. As the economist Kenneth Courtis summarized: "Policy makers moved to set in place the macroeconomic and financial conditions that transformed Japan's equity market into a money pump. So powerful was the pump that from 1985 to 1990 the largest Japanese companies raised some 85 trillion yen [$600 billion] in virtually free money through the stock market alone."

More and more companies saw their share prices soar on the basis of swollen property values. Banks were happy to loan against property as collateral, and sale of pricey company shares boosted banks' assets, enabling them to sell more.

Since more than two-thirds of the shares on the Tokyo exchange are held by corporations and banks—part of Japan's unique network of interlocking stock ownership—everyone profited from increased values of property owned by the same corporations and banks.

Huge sums of money were made—on paper. Awash in all this liquidity, Japanese *keiretsu* groups borrowed cheap and used their money to buy everything from Malaysian car assembly plants to American record and film companies, cattle ranches (where better to grow export brands of Kobe beef?), and even golf clubs, generally at inflated prices.[10] The ultimate basis for much of their lavish spending was likely as not the hopelessly distended values attached to relatively small chunks of earth, glass, and concrete in downtown Tokyo.

In the old high-growth days, the financial bureaucrats in Tokyo could control such expansion. Now, with regulations relaxed to comport with Japan's internationalized finances, this was not so easy. The Finance Ministry, like other Japanese government organizations, was dedicated to *further* business expansion, not to check it. As the go-go music stopped and the scandals widened, more resignations came. In September 1990, Hashimoto Ryutaro, one of the Liberal Democratic Party's bright boys, had to resign as Finance Minister: he joined the gathering crowd of retirers whose precipitate departures from government and corporate offices suggested a crowd of fleeing samurai pounding down the runway (*hanamichi*) of a provincial *kabuki* theater.

While the resignations were in the best Japanese political tradition ("the quicker you resign, the quicker you can come back"), they hardly represented any kind of solution to a deepening problem. Japanese industrial production could succeed on its own terms—better machines, improved processes, production shortcuts, and all that. But international finance, by definition a transnational world without fixed boundaries, was vastly more complex. As the past five years demonstrated, the world's Economic Superpower had outgrown the capacity of Tokyo's city-state politics to control it.

WITH THE twenty-first century almost upon us, the problem of governance in the economic headquarters country stood out ever more clearly. Just as the American economy had wasted its substance in the eighties of junk bonds, savings and loan scandals, and costly acquisitions, Japan's worldwide business expansion seemed dangerously overextended in the nineties. If there was con-

---

[10] While Japanese purchases in the United States may have been good for American sellers and their brokers, they sometimes proved near disasters for the new owners. Witness the sad story of Isutani Minoru, a big-time developer, who paid $841 million for California's Pebble Beach golf resort in 1990, only to sell it early in 1992, when his development plans ran afoul of local environment ordinances. He lost, it was said, $341 million on the transaction.

stant purposeful advance on the periphery, there seemed to be a great deal of confusion at its core.

Japan is a working democracy. Elections are hard fought. And they can produce surprises. Politicians neglect their constituencies at their peril. In *The Pacific Century* television series which accompanied this volume, our producers followed two competent and public-spirited Diet representatives on their daily round. Kato Koichi, a Liberal Democrat, former head of the Defense Agency and most recently chief cabinet secretary, spends a great deal of his time visiting with the voters in his home constituency of Tsuruoka, in northern Japan. He takes good care of them—farmers and small businesspeople mostly. A man of some influence, he has been responsible for new roads, river dikes, and a rice-husking center. "The most important thing," he is happy to tell us, "is communication. Build roads or raise the price of rice, it means nothing if you can't talk to the people."

Hase Yuriko's constituency is in the heart of Tokyo. Although a Socialist, she is no idealogue. She worked hard on bread-and-butter issues of urban interest—consumer and environment issues are her priority. "Japan," she says, while talking to customers at the bar she owns in Tokyo, "is one large company—a giant company if you count the entire 120 million population as its employees. This company was formed through the work and sacrifice of each laborer and citizen. I don't know who has stolen the fruits of their labor. But we did not become rich as a result of those sacrifices."

Ruling party representative and member of the opposition—each is effective in his or her way. There are many others like them. Millions of Japanese voters listen to them and decide their political fates. Yet Japan's political structure—despite its forms of democracy—has become hopelessly impacted. After more than forty years of one-party rule, the Liberal Democrats have become the preserve of warring factions and disgraceful "money politics," their moves dictated by shadowy kingmakers and influence dispensers. Their only objective is tactical: indulge the people enough so that they won't rock the boat. The ineffective Socialist leadership, frozen in a moribund ideology, is content to take the crumbs from the Liberal Democrats' table—their only influence that of the spoiler. The other opposition parties are equally undistinguished. Even a coalition government would seem to make little change.

Looking at Japan's network of feudal politico-business baronies—powerful enough to obstruct but rarely to act in concert—one wonders how Yoshida Shigeru or Ikeda Hayato would handle this situation. Or, for that matter, Ito Hirobumi, Meiji's great Prime Minister, who, after Okubo fell, restarted and led the marvelous Meiji effort to "catch up" with the advanced West. The irony of Japan's political stalemate is that the "catch up" drive of Ito, Yoshida, and Ikeda—partially military but first and last economic—remains

Whether in rural constituencies like Kato's or big-city worlds like Hase's, Japanese politicians must constantly woo the voter.

Kato Koichi (Liberal Democrat). Jigsaw Productions

Hase Yuriko (Socialist). Jigsaw Productions

the only policy Japanese governments practice. While the economic machine crashes ahead, no one has found where the brakes are. Japan and the world still wait for the Economic Superpower to find political and social outlets for its strength.

The tight alliance of big business, bureaucracy, and one-party politics in Tokyo seems content to stay in power and rake in the profits from its worldwide exports and investments, without worrying much over their effect on the international environment. Shielded for so long by American military power from the need to make international political decisions, Japan's leadership continues to concentrate on making its local voters happy and relatively decision-free. If its work force remained intelligent and able, its younger generation seemed notably less committed to the old work incentives. The new Japanese, the *shinjinrui*—"the new race"—as their elders called them, seemed to be living on the social capital of their past.

In dealing with the rest of the world the Japanese continued to show an appallingly poor grasp of other people's concerns. What other major "power" could agonize for two years over whether to allow a few hundred troops to join a United Nations peacekeeping organization?

One cause of this was the myopia of Japan's ruling establishment. Theirs is a highly selective sense of what to remember. Germans have long since faced up to the horrors of their Nazi past; Russians have spent the past half decade coming to terms suddenly with the misdeeds and human distortions of Communism; Americans keep grappling, however crudely, with the misplaced imperialism of Vietnam and their legacy of racial discrimination. Even China's Deng Xiaoping could concede, on his visit to Japan, that his country "had an ugly face." But in Japan neither young nor old have yet even remotely come to terms with their country's brutal military aggressions of the past—the rapes, massacres, and deportations in China and Southeast Asia, the spoliation of Korea, the needless cruelties of their wartime soldiery.

When Germany's former Chancellor Helmut Schmidt, a keen student of things Japanese, first visited Japan in the seventies, he was struck, above all else, by their "apparent lack of any consciousness of guilt" for the war. If anything, this refusal to come to terms with their not so distant past has intensified with present prosperity. In 1991, former Chief Cabinet Secretary Ishihara Nobuo could state baldly: "It will take decades or even centuries before the correct judgment is delivered on who is responsible for the war."

All of which makes even the best friends of Japan wonder what this nation, so singularly gifted, can ever give. Possibly, while they organize their factories and assembly plants in other Pacific countries, Japanese might reflect a bit on their history with those nations, on their dealings with those different and alien peoples so far from their own tight four islands.

Americans for their part have given considerable time to reflecting on their past relations with Asian peoples—good, bad, and indifferent. Their record, like Japan's, is mixed, although more freely discussed. The story of this record, in which Japan plays an inevitably leading role, is told in the following chapters.

17

The Sentimental Imperialists

Now that the famous expansionist McKinley has been elected President, there is no knowing what big things the United States might not do in the twentieth century.

LIANG QICHAO, 1901[1]

Only a century ago, in the autumn of 1892, a young University of Wisconsin history professor named Frederick Jackson Turner put the finishing touches on the draft of a paper that he was to read at the American Historical Association's meeting the following year. Its title was "The Significance of the Frontier in American History." Its theme was to become a classic: that the constant westward expansion of Americans, taming new frontiers as they went, had played a major part in shaping the national character and building the national society. It is to the frontier, Turner wrote, that "the American intellect owes its striking characteristics. That coarseness of strength combined with acuteness and inquisitiveness, that practical, inventive turn of mind, quick to find expedients, that masterful grasp of material things, lacking in the artistic but powerful to effect great ends, that restless, nervous energy, that dominant individualism working for good and for evil . . ."

---

[1] From the essay "The Development of Imperialism and the Future of the World in the Twentieth Century," as quoted in *Across the Pacific,* by Akira Iriye (New York: Harcourt Brace, 1967).

Turner's thesis was that the national goal of conquering the frontier—as expressed in the constant westward surges of settlers and soldiers, merchants and missionaries—had stamped an indelible mark on American civilization. Our whole national character, he argued, had been built up based on the pioneer premise—that is, there was always land, adventure, and work to be done to the west. America's unique greatness (at least as Americans saw it) was involved with the frontier movement: our optimism, our confidence, the conviction, buttressed by generations of Protestant Christians, that Americans had a mission to teach the rest of the world. The open-ended growth and successes of their still young democracy led Americans to feel that their way—the American way—was a kind of lodestar for the whole world to follow. Since the founding of the Republic, Turner went on, the frontier to the west had offered new fields of opportunity. It represented "a gate of escape from the bondage of the past; the freshness and confidence and scorn of older society, impatience with its restraints and its ideas."

By the 1890s, however, national boundaries reached to the Pacific and they were now fixed. The frontier line, the 1890 census reported noted, "no longer has a place in the census reports."

This loss of the physical frontier, Turner conceded, did not necessarily mean the loss of the frontier spirit. ("He would be a rash prophet who should assert that the expansive character of American life has now entirely ceased. Movement has been its dominant fact . . . and the American intellect will continue to demand a wider field for its exercise.")

Yet his conclusion held a certain note of finality: "What the Mediterranean Sea was to the Greeks, breaking the bond of custom, offering new experiences, calling out new institutions and activities, that, and more, the ever retreating frontier has been to the United States directly and to the nations of Europe more remotely. And now, four centuries from the discovery of America, at the end of a hundred years of life under the Constitution, the frontier has gone, and with its going has closed the first period of American history."

Turner was right and he was wrong. He was right about the power of the frontier mystique, but wrong about its closure. Just as he was drafting his paper, in fact, forces were at work that were to push the frontier farther westward, across the Pacific, in a surge of "coarse strength" and "restless, nervous energy" worthy of Davy Crockett, Daniel Boone, and the Gold Rush. The new Pacific frontier would not only take Americans into a new dimension. It would set the scene for a second century of empire building and breaking, in which the classic virtues and defects of the American character would be displayed and exposed on a global stage.

Within ten years after Turner wrote his essay, the United States had formally annexed the Hawaiian Islands (by act of Congress, in 1898) and, farther to the west, American Samoa. After the jingoistic triumphs of the Spanish-American War, the Philippine Islands were annexed in 1899, along with Puerto Rico and Guam, as U.S. possessions. In 1900, Secretary of State John Hay issued his famous "Open Door" statement to preserve the "territorial and administrative entity" of China; although meaningless in practical terms, it nonetheless gave high public visibility to American concern about free access to the China market. In 1902, Congress passed legislation authorizing the government to build a canal across the isthmus of Panama. Belatedly joining the European powers and Japan, American imperialism was on the march into the Pacific.

The impulse toward the new Pacific frontier encompassed the same drives that Turner had cited in his study of the land frontier. They were in fact an extension of the earlier Pacific strategy of Commodore Perry and the Boston merchants in Canton—only temporarily interrupted by the travail of the Civil War and the later development of the western states. William Seward, Lincoln's (and Andrew Johnson's) Secretary of State, was as convinced as Perry of the need for the United States to expand into the Pacific. He had strengthened the trade-oriented agreements with China and Japan. His purchase of Alaska from Russia in 1867, widely denounced by his countrymen as "Seward's folly," was part of a cooperative Pacific policy that was far ahead of his time. But his work was not pursued.

By the turn of the century, however, the country was stronger than in Perry's or Seward's time, and richer by far. Oil and steel had begun to dominate the economy. Despite the serious growing pains of urban industrialization—big business versus workers and populists, free traders versus protectionists, western farmers versus eastern financiers—the majority of Americans had come to share a new and truculent nationalism. The Manifest Destiny idea of Mexican War days was alive and well. It was now fueled by two unlikely partners. American industry was confidently looking to expand into overseas markets. At the same time an equally confident and increasingly active missionary movement was anxious, as one prominent clergyman of the time put it, "to turn Heathendom into Christendom."

Conventional European imperialism this was not. In September 1898, the war with Spain handily won, an up-and-coming Indiana politician named Albert J. Beveridge made a stirring speech called "The March of the Flag" to his fellow Republicans in Indianapolis. It was peculiarly American in its tone. After working over the nation's frontier past and future—"It is a glorious history our God has bestowed upon His chosen people"—Beveridge epitomized the mood of his fellow citizens. "Shall the American people," he asked, "continue their march towards the commercial supremacy of the world? Shall free institutions broaden their blessed reign as the children of liberty wax in

Frederick Jackson Turner. His American Frontier kept moving westward, across the Pacific.
Library of Congress

Albert J. Beveridge. The Indiana Republican, a classic nineteenth-century American imperialist, thought the "march of the flag" should be continuous.
Library of Congress

Rear Adm. Alfred Thayer Mahan. His ideas on sea power revolutionized an era.
Library of Congress

Brig. Gen. Jacob Smith and staff. "Howling Jake" Smith, third from right, wearing boots, was a leading exponent of "kill and burn" pacification tactics. Library of Congress

Theodore Roosevelt. Taking a leaf from Mahan's book, Roosevelt built up the United States as a Pacific power. Library of Congress

U.S. troops in the Philippines. It took 75,000 U.S. troops to suppress the Filipino "insurrection" between 1899 and 1903. Library of Congress

strength, until the empire of our principles is established over the hearts of all mankind? Have we no mission to perform, no duty to discharge to our fellow man?"

He left little doubt about the answer. As he explained later: "The Philippines are ours forever . . . And just beyond the Philippines are China's illimitable markets. We will not retreat from either . . . We will not abandon our duty in the Orient . . . The Pacific is our ocean . . . and the Pacific is the ocean of the commerce of the future . . . The power that rules the Pacific, therefore, is the power that rules the world."

There were powerful dissenters from this view. They found annexing overseas territories un-American—and probably unconstitutional to boot. Grover Cleveland, a Democrat, refused to sanction Hawaii's annexation while he was President, only to have it reinstated when the Republicans returned to office with William McKinley. The Democratic Party generally took an anti-imperialist position; the Republicans were barely able to get the annexation of the Philippines through the Senate. Other prominent Americans denounced the territorial expansion—President Charles Eliot of Harvard, steelmaker Andrew Carnegie, and labor leader Samuel Gompers among them.

In the election of 1900, the great Democratic populist William Jennings Bryan made an eloquent appeal for granting the Philippines their independence. "Those who would have this nation enter upon a career of empire," he said, "must consider not only the effect of imperialism on the Filipinos, but they must also calculate its effects upon our own nation. We cannot repudiate the principle of self-government in the Philippines without weakening that principle here . . .

"Better a thousand times that our flag in the Orient gave way to a flag representing the idea of self-government than that the flag of this republic should become the flag of an empire."

The protests were of no avail. The Republicans swept the 1900 elections by a bigger majority than before. McKinley won a second term in the White House and Bryan lost, the voters clearly preferring prosperity and the heady drafts of imperialism to moral soul searching. Indeed there were many, pious churchmen among them, who held that American expansion in Asia was another way of doing the Lord's work—and good business, too.

Samuel Capen, president of the American Board of Foreign Missions, clarified this connection between God, expansion, and the economy to his fellow commissioners in a report a few years later: "The business interests of the world are with us. They are recognizing more and more the benefit to themselves which is coming everywhere with the opening of the world to Christianity. When a heathen man becomes a child of God and is changed within, he wants his external life and surroundings to correspond; he wants the Christian dress and the Christian home and the Christian plow and all the other things which distinguish Christian civilization from the narrow and degraded life of the heathen. The merchant knows how the business of the world has already been increased by the progress made by Christianity . . ."[2]

The man who set off the American age of imperialism was not by nature an expansionist. William McKinley was a hardworking Ohio congressman of modest talents who had been put into office by the Republicans' all-powerful political boss, Mark Hanna. As nearly as can be ascertained, God and high tariffs embodied the core of his convictions. About the world outside the United States he knew little. On offering a consular post in Manila to a political office seeker early in his presidency, he confessed that he didn't know exactly where Manila was, since he "hadn't had time to look it up."[3]

When the moment came, during the peace negotiations with Spain, to decide whether or not the Philippines should be annexed, the President resorted to prayer. He later told a visiting group of clergymen about his decision: "I walked the floor of the White House night after night until midnight, and I am not ashamed to tell you gentlemen that I went down on my knees and prayed God Almighty for light and guidance more than one night. And one night late it came to me this way—I don't know how it was, but it came: (1) That we could not give them back to Spain—that would be cowardly and dishonorable; (2) that we could not turn them over to France or Germany—our commercial rivals in the Orient—that would be bad business and discreditable; (3) that we could not leave them to themselves—they were unfit for self-government—and they would soon have anarchy and misrule over there worse than Spain's was; and (4) that there was nothing left for us to do but to take them all and to educate the Filipinos, and uplift and civilize and Christianize[4] them and by God's grace do the very best we could by them as our fellow men for whom Christ also died. And then I went to bed and went to sleep and slept soundly."

While McKinley prayed and slept in the White House, two other Americans of that time set out very purposely to change the map of the Pacific and color it, insofar as possible, red, white, and blue. Theodore Roosevelt, a crusading New York City police commissioner and reform politician, had received, rather grudgingly, an appointment as Assistant Secretary of the Navy in McKinley's administration. On a visit to the new Naval War College at Newport, he had

[2] As quoted by Daniel J. Boorstin in *The Americans: The Democratic Experience* (New York: Random House, 1973).

[3] Cited by Stanley Karnow in *In Our Image: America's Empire in the Philippines* (New York: Random House, 1989).

[4] McKinley apparently knew as little about the religion of the Philippines as he did about the geography. At the time he spoke, most Filipinos had been Catholic for the past three centuries.

made the acquaintance of a studious Navy captain named Alfred Thayer Ma-han. Mahan had published his book *The Influence of Sea Power upon History* in 1890, based on his lectures at the War College. Roosevelt liked the man and the book. Thereafter, through this critical period in American history, the author and the activist, working together, revolutionized the modern concept of sea power. In the process, they re-created the long-neglected American Navy and sailed it back into the Pacific.

Although on its face a study of Anglo-French sea warfare in the years 1660 to 1783, Mahan's book brilliantly dramatized the world primacy of maritime powers over continental land empires. It quickly became an object of intense study among the world's naval strategists. (Its impact was rather like that which Charles de Gaulle's early writing on mechanized warfare would have on tank experts in the years before World War II.) He wrote it, however, principally as a warning to his own countrymen that success in the new world commercial economy depended in the last resort on a Navy that could command the seas. "Whether they will or no," Mahan wrote, "Americans must now begin to look outward."

His thesis was the logical sequel to Turner's frontier theme. As an article in the *Overland Monthly,* discussing Mahan's ideas, expressed it: "The subjugation of a continent was sufficient to keep the American people busy at home for a century. But now that the continent is subdued, we are looking for fresh worlds to conquer; and whether our conservative stay-at-homes like it or not, the colonizing instinct which has led our race in successive waves of immigration . . . is the instinct which is now pushing us out and on to Alaska, to the isles of the sea—and beyond."[5]

Roosevelt hastened to put Mahan's ideas into practice. Taking advantage of the Navy Secretary's temporary absence from the office, the Assistant Secretary ordered Admiral George Dewey and his battleships to Asian waters even before hostilities with Spain broke out. He thus set the stage for the spectacular victory at Manila Bay. When the war began, he resigned his Washington post to form and lead his Rough Riders regiment of volunteer cavalry. He became a national hero for his charge up San Juan Hill during the Cuban fighting.

Back home, TR supported annexation of the Philippines with all the con-siderable rhetoric at his command. ("The guns of our warships have awakened us to new duties. We are face to face with our destiny.") More difficult to handle than ever in domestic politics, now that he was a national hero, the perennial reform candidate in New York was pushed on McKinley by local bosses. This time he became the successful vice presidential candidate. When

[5] As quoted in *The United States Since 1865* by Foster Rhea Dulles (Ann Arbor: University of Michigan Press, 1959).

McKinley was assassinated in 1901, just a year after his reelection, Roosevelt found himself, quite unexpectedly, President of the United States.

President Teddy Roosevelt, as most Americans called him, more than justified Mahan's hopes for an immediate Navy buildup. By 1907, when he dispatched the Great White Fleet on its round-the-world cruise, the United States was recognized as a leading naval power. In 1903 he strong-armed Colombia into accepting the independence of Panama—and Panama into accepting an American-owned Canal Zone for his cherished route across the isthmus. The canal, opened finally in 1914, became the foundation for America's two-ocean Navy—as later expanded into the victorious World War II fighting force by Teddy's young cousin Franklin.

For all his bluster and verbal saber rattling Roosevelt proved himself a shrewd and farseeing modern geopolitician, certainly the most knowledgeable to occupy the White House. In many ways he was ahead of his time. He was the first American statesman to appreciate the growing strategic importance of Japan, a country he alternately feared and admired. As we noted previously, he intervened to arbitrate the peace treaty concluding the Russo-Japanese War, knowing that, despite Japan's military victory,[6] its resources were stretched to the breaking point by the conflict. (He earned the Nobel Peace Prize he was awarded after the Treaty of Portsmouth.) With the callused hand of a veteran big-power diplomat, however, he gave Japan a free hand in Korea (to the everlasting chagrin of pro-American Koreans like Syngman Rhee) in return for Japan's acquiescence in American dominion over the Philippines. In 1908, the last year of Roosevelt's presidency, the Root-Takahira agreement stabilized Japanese-American relations in Asia, guaranteed unrestricted commerce with China included, for the next fifteen years. No mean feat.

Until Roosevelt and Mahan came on the scene, American activities in the Asia-Pacific area had been largely limited to trade. For more than a century, since the days when "King" Derby's Salem ships brought their first cargoes into Canton, buying and selling took priority. The territorial ambitions of Perry and Seward were largely unsupported by American governments.

John Hay was a conscientious Secretary of State, but the Open Door to China he proclaimed in 1900 was little more than a restatement of past policies to keep the most-favored-nation principle the guideline of Pacific trade. Not only were China, Japan, and Korea to hold trade channels open, but European powers were exhorted not to close off equal opportunities for American merchants. The corollary of the Open Door policy, as the historian Tyler Dennett

---

[6] A victory of which he heartily approved. On hearing the news of Admiral Togo's victory at Tsushima, Roosevelt wrote enthusiastically to the Japanese envoy Kaneko Kentaro. "Neither Trafalgar nor the defeat of the Spanish Armada was as complete—as overwhelming."

noted, was "to promote an Asia strong enough to be its own door-keeper."[7]

The policy was strictly economic. There was almost no political or military bite behind the American trader's bark. For most of the nineteenth century, America's "economics-first" policy sheltered in the lee of the political power represented by the British fleet in Asian waters. Ironically enough, the American Pacific role in the nineteenth century most strikingly resembles that of "economics-only" Japan in the latter part of the twentieth—with the political muscle in this case supplied by American sea and air power.

As the twentieth century unfolded, however, the United States became more and more a central, if not *the* central factor in the Pacific Basin—politically, culturally, and economically. As Asia and the Pacific became more important to America, domestic concerns wielded correspondingly greater influence on American foreign policy. These could work to the good, in the case of the powerful American imperatives to teach, to modernize, to educate. Or they could be very bad, as when a vicious and meanspirited racism, overwhelmingly supported by American voters, produced the Exclusion Acts against Asian immigration.

Hardest for non-Americans to understand was the curious combination of personalities, voting blocs, and institutions—businesses and churches conspicuously included—that formed American policy and made it such a pastiche of kindness and brutality, bombast and beneficence. I have called this chapter "The Sentimental Imperialists" after the excellent book of the same name,[8] since this term so well encapsulated the character of the American presence in Asia.

Theodore Roosevelt himself was the classic "sentimental imperialist." In his way an untamed prodigy—certainly the only American President on an intellectual par with Thomas Jefferson (whom Roosevelt, an admirer of Alexander Hamilton, typically disliked)—he combined a lofty strategic vision of the future with a capacity for sudden and often ill-advised political tactics. Well traveled, cosmopolitan and internationalist in his tastes and aspirations, a scholar of considerable ability—his books *The Winning of the West* and *The Naval War of 1812* are classics—he could also be the worst sort of America-first chauvinist. All these qualities showed up in the American occupation of the Philippines. Which is where the record of the sentimental imperialists begins.

[7] As quoted in Dennett's *Americans in Eastern Asia in the Nineteenth Century* (New York: Macmillan, 1922), which remains a classic in its field.

[8] Written by three prominent authorities on Asia—James C. Thomson, Jr., Peter W. Stanley, and John Curtis Perry—*The Sentimental Imperalists* (New York: Harper & Row, 1981) is one of the few books on the American experience in East Asia that is current, academically sound, and highly readable.

* * *

ON FEBRUARY 4, 1899, some nine months after Dewey's victory in Manila Bay, Major General Elwell S. Otis's troops on the Manila perimeter opened fire on Filipino soldiers entrenched around the city. What became known in official American reporting as the Philippine "insurrection" began. Otis, a Harvard-educated Indian fighter, was confident of defeating the Filipinos in a hurry, if indeed they persisted in defying American "sovereignty." His fresh regiments, mostly volunteers eager for action, gunned down the lightly armed opposition mercilessly—"having more fun than a turkey shoot," one trooper put it. By the end of the month General Arthur MacArthur (father of Douglas, who would later make a mark in the Philippines himself) had occupied the provisional Philippine capital at Malolos. Supported by artillery and naval gunfire, the Americans swept north and south of Manila. The enemy, Otis reported to Washington, was "in perilous condition, its army defeated, discouraged and scattered."[9]

The army of General Emilio Aguinaldo was scattered, but it was hardly defeated. Its soldiery was surprised by the sudden American attack. Its leaders were massively disappointed. Aguinaldo, who had been fighting the Spaniards on and off since 1896, at first thought of the Americans as allies who would after a time give the Filipinos back their own sovereignty. In fact, the republic he planned for the Philippines was modeled on that of the United States. He was encouraged in this belief by Americans like Admiral Dewey, who felt that all his country needed from the Filipinos was a naval base or two.

Hoping for a truce with Otis's 24,000 troops, Aguinaldo had steadily given ground to the Americans, after retreating from Manila itself. His troops were numerically superior, however; including auxiliaries, they totaled more than 100,000. They controlled most of Luzon and the other islands. As the Americans landed throughout the islands, they met steady opposition.

By the next year fully 75,000 American troops—the bulk of the American armed forces at that time—were in action against Aguinaldo. The "generalissimo," as he liked to be called, was finally captured in April 1901 after he had waged a long year of exhausting but by no means unsuccessful guerrilla warfare. It was costly on both sides. By the time Theodore Roosevelt declared the war officially over the following year, on the Fourth of July 1902, some 200,000 Filipinos—of whom only about 20,000 were soldiers—had lost their lives. Almost 5,000 American soldiers had been killed in action, while others later succumbed to illnesses contracted in the Philippines. Isolated resistance con-

---

[9] As quoted by Stanley Karnow in *In Our Image*. I have leaned heavily on his account of military operations.

tinued. In 1913, more than a decade after the announced pacification, U.S. troops were still in action against the Muslim Moros in the south.

Unquestionably, open warfare could have been avoided, or at least minimized, if the American government had been clear in its policy. A period of more or less benevolent occupation, followed by autonomy and independence, was finally declared official policy after the Jones Act in 1916. This would not have been hard for most Filipinos to swallow in 1901.

The political situation in their country was complex. While Spain's oppressive rule had ultimately proved unpopular, many among the Filipino gentry would have welcomed an American protectorate. Even Aguinaldo's exemplar, the patriot José Rizal, had at first merely demanded self-government from Spain. Once the Spaniards had been defeated, the mass of the Filipino people, primarily loyal to local leaders, had demonstrated little enthusiasm for total national independence.

The lack of a clear policy in McKinley's first directives reflected a basic contradiction within Americans themselves. How could the land of the free and the home of the brave cancel out another people's freedom? Were the Philippines to be a subject territory, like the European colonies that Americans had long criticized? Or were the Filipinos future citizens of the Republic, willing students of the democratic process? The dilemma was well summarized by historian Peter Stanley: ". . . the United States had stumbled, unawares, to the pragmatic discovery that, of all forms of government, the modern nation-state based on consent is the least suited to empire."[10]

There was little ambiguity about the U.S. Army's behavior, however. Convinced that they were dealing with people of "inferior races," as General MacArthur had it, the troops did their work with a frontier ferocity. The "niggers" or "gugus," as the Filipinos were called, were cut down, burnt out, and tortured like the Indians a generation before. The Filipinos perpetrated atrocities of their own on isolated American detachments. Cruelty escalated, fed by rumor as much as reality. Whole villages were put to the torch as "examples." Civilians were killed indiscriminately. Filipino Catholic churches were shamelessly desecrated by the American volunteers, good Christians all.

Courts-martial for atrocities were few and slackly prosecuted; they gave little indication of the mass cruelty's real extent. For few in Washington wished to believe that "our boys" could get thus out of hand. In the field, however, the directions were unmistakable. "I wish you to kill and burn," Brigadier General Jacob (Howling Jake) Smith told his subordinates, off to avenge the massacre of an American unit on the island of Samar. "The more you kill and burn, the better you will please me."

[10] From Stanley's book *A Nation in the Making* (Cambridge, Mass.: Harvard University Press, 1974).

While Howling Jake and his ilk were still killing and burning, a federal judge from Ohio arrived in the Philippines with a different kind of mission. William Howard Taft, the new governor of the Philippines, announced his policy in this way: "We hold the Philippines for the benefit of the Filipinos, and we are not entitled to pass a single act or approve a single measure that has not that as its chief purpose."

A distinguished American, who would later succeed Roosevelt in the presidency, Taft made his national reputation in the Philippine proconsulship. As the head of a joint Filipino-American commission, appointed from Washington, he presided over an extraordinary effort to remodel the Philippines in the American image. Reconstruction and education were his major objectives. They were unique in the history of colonies. If the Americans had been fully as brutal as the Dutch or French in their pacification efforts, they now began to make massive amends. Harbors were dredged. Roads were built. High standards of health and sanitation—hitherto unknown in the country—were introduced and maintained. Foreshadowing other American efforts later in the century, a widespread aid program set out to revive the war-shattered Philippine economy.

First priority was given to the schools. In August 1901, some five hundred young Americans, male and female, arrived in Manila to take up the teaching mission. Over the next two decades, other American teachers and, later, American-trained Filipinos set out to give the new American dependency an American education, administered in English, dedicated to the proposition, by Horatio Alger out of Jefferson and Lincoln, that all men are created equal, with an equal chance to rise. The very soldiers who had fought the Filipinos were detailed to help in the schools. Many older Filipinos remember being taught English by large, enthusiastic men in khaki uniforms.

The American readers they studied from remain in the islands' folk memory. "This is our town," the lessons read. "My father's name is Mr. Brown. My dog's name is Spot. We live on Main Street." No Spanish or Tagalog or local language was allowed in class. "For every Pilipino word we uttered in school," one contemporary lady recalls, "we had to pay a fine of twenty centavos."

This intensive effort at cultural proselytizing partly worked. But it had a tragic flaw. For all they wanted to teach Filipinos the American way, the Americans never wanted them to join the club. "Our little brown brothers," Taft called them, and so in the American mind they remained. It was even more impossible for Calvinist Americans than it was for the Castilian Catholics before them to transcend their self-imposed barriers of race and culture. After all, wasn't God (almost by definition) on their side? Admiral Dewey's guns had barely cooled when the Presbyterian General Assembly proclaimed: "God has given into our hands, that is, into the hands of American Christians, the Philippine Islands. By the very guns of our battleships, [God] summoned us to go up and possess the land."

William Howard Taft. *The governor-general of the Philippines from 1901 to 1904 (and later twenty-seventh President of the United States) was conciliatory if paternalistic in his administration of the new American colony.* U.S. Army Military History Institute

The Great White Fleet off Yokohama. The U.S. Navy's transpacific cruise was part of Teddy Roosevelt's "Show the Flag" policy. Here the Japanese and U.S. fleets are photographed in Yokohama Harbor, October 1908. Library of Congress

Americans' mixed feelings on colonialism were typified by these contradictory magazine cartoons of the early 1900s. In one, Uncle Sam punishes a presumptuous Filipino leader (Gen. Emilio Aguanaldo), while the second, titled "Really a Financial Investment," shows a U.S. colonial soldier smashing the Constitution. Library of Congress

Liang Qichao, China's great, if unsuccessful, reformer, along with other Asian revolutionaries, took a good bit of his inspiration from the Bill of Rights. Encyclopedia of China

Manila skyline, 1991. Despite basic economic and political problems the ancient "Pearl of the Orient" remains a great metropolis. Steve Vidler/Pacific Press Service

* * *

NOT ALL AMERICANS were jingoists. Many continued to harbor grave doubts about the incompatibility of colonization and American democratic principles—so much so that it became characteristically difficult, over the years, to pass legislation supporting the new colony through Congress. In a memorable piece of advice to W. Cameron Forbes, a proper young Bostonian proconsul, the great pragmatist philosopher William James wrote: ". . . nurse no extravagant ideals or hopes, be contented with small gains, respect the Filipino soul, whatever it prove to be, and try to educe and play on its own possibilities for advance rather than stamp too sudden an Americanism on it. There are abysses of crudity in some of our popular notions in that direction which must make the Almighty shudder."

His words were little heeded. Although Forbes went on to become one of the more capable and dedicated governors of the island dependency, he ruled by his own lights. He considered his job, he wrote years afterward, "to be looking after the interests of the Philippines wherever found and in the manner I felt was best for them, regardless of whether they liked it or not." A stout believer in projecting Turner's frontier theory ever westward, Forbes saw the Philippines as part of a chain of dependencies across the Pacific which might extend as far as a "sister republic" in Siberia.[11]

Academic Marxists of a later day could rightly accuse American businessmen of exploiting Filipino resources, although it can be argued that in the end many gave as good as they got. American business did move into the Philippines, in force, occupying a highly preferential role. Philippine exports in turn were given preferential treatment in the United States. The resulting symbiosis kept the Philippines in the role of a subservient commodity economy, however, trading sugar, copra, hemp, and other local products for American manufactures. Many local American interests—the beet sugar lobby, for example—were opposed to the Philippine relationship altogether, and farmers in California would in time denounce the immigration of "cheap" Filipino labor. The underlying problem remained the lack of any consistent economic development policy for the Philippines. Various American administrations were never able to get major economic programs enacted for their Asian dependency, thanks to Congress's ambivalence on the whole subject.

The Americans' continuing paternalism posed an even more fundamental problem. What fatally besmirched the rather noble vision of Taft and many other Americans, anxious to re-create the Philippines in their own image, was the racial inferiority they attributed to Filipinos. Thus almost by their own

[11] As quoted in Peter Stanley's *A Nation in the Making*.

definition, the ambitious goals the Americans set for their charges could never be achieved. "Americanized without being Americans," Stanley Karnow summed it up.

In the end education stood as the great American contribution. In sharp distinction to the lack of native education in the European Asian colonies, the Americans succeeded in developing and extending a system of basic primary education throughout the islands, later continued at the high school and, to an extent, the college level. The cultural impact was profound.

Native American Protestantism, however, made few gains. Despite their intensive work in education, health, and even sports—"baseball evangelism," the Reverend Frank Laubach called it—the self-righteousness of many American missionaries irritated rather than converted their targets. The McGuffey readers may have won, but Calvin, despite Laubach's strenuous coaching, never got to first base. Caring little for the exhortations of the Protestant clergy to "break the hold of Romanism," the great majority of Filipinos stayed Catholic. Indeed, the Christian social gospel never made serious inroads in the Philippines until the arrival of the American Jesuits, labor priests and all, who revivified Filipino Christianity on its own terms after World War II, at least partly rescuing it from the long-imposed torpor of their racist Hispanic predecessors.

Along with their race prejudice the Americans displayed a corollary tendency to deal principally with the largely Hispanicized Filipino gentry. However much Taft and the other proconsuls talked of democracy, their policy of "attraction" leaned on the cooperation of the ruling landowning *ilustrados*.

Almost all of the Filipino intelligentsia came from this numerically small elite. Urbane, sophisticated, and on the whole very conservative, this was the same oligarchy of wealth and education that had under Spanish rule fastened its hold over the non-Hispanicized Malay majority. The implicit alliance between the American proconsuls and the *ilustrados* held great and unhealthy implications for the future. For all the textbook lessons of self-reliance and democracy that their children now learned in the schools, the peasantry remained largely in thrall to the same rich landowning gentry. What reforms the Americans enacted had to trickle down through the agency of the *ilustrados* who served them.

Nonetheless, much of the American accomplishment—the roads, the schools, the well-dredged harbors, and improved city sanitation—was highly visible, along with the general, if slight economic upturn that accompanied it. A more repressive colonial policy might have worked to crystallize a strong, if anti-American, independence movement. American intentions, however, were too obviously benign, albeit muddled by ineffective execution. (Even the word "colonial" was used most sparingly; more and more it disturbed the American conscience.)

In the late twenties and thirties, in fact, America's deepening sense of isolationism, not to mention economic problems at home, made Congress ever more disposed to grant their "little brown brothers" independence and have done with a continually vexing problem. Manuel Quezon, the first President of the Philippine Commonwealth, was probably his country's ablest politician. Quezon and others like him were hard put to keep publicly advocating total independence, while privately urging their friends on the Hill in Washington to go slow. There were still many Filipinos who would have vastly preferred statehood. "Damn the Americans!" Quezon once expostulated. "Why don't they tyrannize us more?"

I HAVE KNOWN the Philippines and their people in different times and seasons, over almost a half century. My first visit—rather an impromptu one—was in March 1945, when the U.S. Navy transport carrying our small part of the Okinawa invasion force stopped at Leyte. It was almost five months after the first U.S. assault troops had landed there and Douglas MacArthur, corncob pipe at the tilt, had splashed ashore in one of his much photographed "returns." To the north the Sixth Army was pushing back General Yamashita's divisions on Luzon. Manila was already devastated by the last-ditch resistance of Japanese Special Navy Landing Force fanatics—and I use the word advisedly—whose brutalities against helpless Filipino civilians in 1945 rivaled the horrors of the 1937 Rape of Nanjing. Yet there was a mood of relief, if not euphoria among the people on that southern island. The dusty streets of Tacloban, Leyte's provincial capital, were full of families cheerfully setting up houses and businesses again, while dodging the constant traffic of American trucks and jeeps. The Americans were back. The Japanese were gone. Life could begin again. English was spoken. You had the feeling of being welcomed.

In the fall and winter of 1949, I came to Manila, this time as a journalist. Since 1946 the Philippines had been independent—although tied to the United States by a variety of new preferential economic agreements and a ninety-nine-year lease on naval and air bases. The old Dewey Boulevard, the stately palm-lined avenue facing the sea, was now Roxas Boulevard, named after Manuel Roxas, the recently deceased President. Roxas's Vice President, Elpidio Quirino, who had succeeded him, was about to fight and win what proved to be one of the world's most crooked democratic elections. Manila was a montage of conniving politicians, flamboyant gun-toting journalists, glad-handing Rotarian businessmen looking for deals, with a sizable sprinkling of not so fastidious American expatriates in the play. From outside the city came ominous reports of left-wing peasant guerrilla fighters, called the Hukbalahap,[12] who were out to overthrow the government. Within the city, the rich were obviously growing richer, as the opulent restaurants, cars, and elite gambling casinos suggested. The poor were not very much helped. U.S. Secretary of State Dean Acheson and others had begun to worry vocally about some $2 billion of postwar aid that had mostly gone down the drain.

Yet in Manila and on the islands to the south, there were plenty of people to talk to a reporter about democracy and land reform and the need for stronger labor unions. It all sounded very American. After all, we had had our own grafting politicians at home. And Filipinos, alone among peoples in Asia, seemed to have a strong sense of injustice and an American feeling for individual rights. In traveling from Manila south, through Negros and Cebu and those other rich, beautiful islands down to Jolo in the Sulu Sea, I found a feeling of kinship with Filipinos. These were "our people." They had gone to "our schools." They knew what democracy was all about. They could fix things.

In the late sixties and early seventies I came back to the Philippines, this time as a businessman, flying down occasionally from my Tokyo headquarters to watch over the progress of a small sales and publishing company, the Encyclopaedia Britannica's branch in the Philippines. Business seemed better. At least everyone looked more prosperous. Accountants and lawyers—those telltale barnacles of economic success—had increased and multiplied. As a further sign of social, if not economic progress, I found my first job was to deal with not one, but three unions that had taken wing within our small company. All of them were highly vocal.

But there were problems. The big-business sector of Manila, rich in foreign-capital firms, had moved in force to Makati, which had once been a suburb. There a forest of new antiseptic high rises mocked the squalor of the old city and the acres of outlying shantytowns where the poor, the near-poor, and the homeless tried to eke out an existence. The rich, near-rich, and merely prosperous—along with most of the expatriate community—lived in walled-in and heavily guarded enclaves like Forbes Park (an ironic memorial to the prewar governor). Not only was obvious crime rampant, but danger lurked in the form of political assassins, grudge fighters, and people whose emotions might easily

[12] The Hukbalahap—the shortened Tagalog form of People's Anti-Japanese Army—had its origins in guerrilla fighting against the Japanese occupiers during World War II. By the end of the war the Huk bands of landless peasant farmers, led by Communist intellectuals, had become a formidable military force. They assassinated pro-Japanese collaborators and confiscated many large estates to become a power in central Luzon. In 1946, after refusing to surrender their large stores of weapons to the government, they went underground in open revolt. Successful at first, they almost captured Manila. By 1954 they had lost ground to the newly popular government of President Magsaysay; their leader, Luis Taruc, surrendered in that year.

be triggered by real or fancied insults. Most of the better restaurants had counters for checking patrons' guns.

An apparently charismatic politician from the northern province of Ilocos named Ferdinand Marcos had been elected President in 1965. By 1970, he and his wife, a former beauty queen named Imelda, had fastened a tight grip on the country. Although the paraphernalia of democracy—courts, legislatures, and free expression—remained in place, the government was close to dictatorship. Marcos controlled the Army and through a network of cronies was getting his hands on most of the economy as well. Freedom of discussion was still palpably alive in Manila—it would require a herculean type of repression to stifle it completely—but people had begun to fear. A new underground Communist army had taken shape in the provinces; under cover of stamping out the Communists, Marcos and his military were settling many old scores.

Talking to Filipino friends, I felt for the first time a nervousness about their government and its interference in their lives. Corruption, always a factor in the Philippines, was becoming institutionalized, not only through business takeovers by Marcos's people but through various front groups. "Sure, my wife is a member of Imelda's Blue Ladies," a friend of mine told me, referring to a presidential-sponsored "charitable" organization. "She hates those people and what they stand for. But I need the connection for my business."

Throughout this period Marcos received the consistent support of the United States. "My right arm in Asia," Lyndon Johnson rhapsodized at one of their meetings in 1966. Ronald Reagan thought of Marcos as a personal as well as political friend; the Manila party he and Imelda threw for the responsive Reagans in 1969 remains a classic in conspicuous consumption. Years later, long after Marcos had declared martial law in 1972 and cemented his dictatorship, George Bush, then Vice President, lauded him in a formal speech: "We love your adherence to democratic principle and the democratic process."

Such support from Washington was critical to any Philippine politician, as it had been since the days when William Howard Taft began to cooperate with the local *ilustrados*. If anything, it increased rather than diminished during the years of Marcos's rule. In the end, after Corazon Aquino won the 1986 election and Manila's middle class turned out to support her against Marcos's tanks, the American government decisively joined the clamor for Marcos's resignation. By that time both the polity and the economy of the country were in shambles. It would take many years to recover.

How is it that the newly liberated nation of 1945, unique in its popular commitment to democracy and its American support, turned out so badly over the next four and a half decades? The answer to that question tells us as much about America as it does about the Philippines.

Slum kids in Manila. Yet the vast number of poor and needy offers a continual reproach to progress.
Alan Levin

Ferdinand Marcos with Lyndon B. Johnson and his wife. Manipulating American presidents and their policies was not the least of Marcos's skills.
National Archives

Ninoy Aquino just before his assassination. A tragic victim of the Marcos dictatorship. Jigsaw Productions

*   *   *

SINCE THE CLOSE of World War II the United States, as we have seen, invested a great deal of time and money in rehabilitating various countries in the Asia-Pacific region. American motives for doing so were mixed. Democratization (based on American models), economic investment, and international power politics were all involved; the last-named conspicuously included military action. The end results were also mixed. We must include a disaster in Vietnam, a conceivably avoidable war in Korea, and some monumental and destructive miscalculations in China policy. Yet some conspicuous successes were attained. The Occupation of Japan remains a unique achievement. For the dramatic economic upsurge of Korea and Taiwan, along with the later growth of democracy in both countries, American support deserves a large share of credit. Even in the ASEAN countries, if we are to believe Lee Kuan Yew, American economic and military power provided an indispensable platform for growth.

Yet in the Philippines, the Asian country closest to Americans, the land reforms, the economic pump priming, and the political support so successful elsewhere never quite seemed to work. Some can argue that massive American support lacked a strong traditional culture to play against. There was no Confucian ethos, no ancient sense of nationhood to cushion the shock of American modernization and, ultimately, to adapt and work with it.

When the Spaniards colonized the islands, they found a welter of different peoples and languages. (Even now some seventy different languages and dialects are spoken; the national language, Pilipino, is founded on only one of them, Tagalog.) There was no pervasive religion or any authority that ranged beyond a few village kinship groups. As the Encyclopaedia Britannica records in its article on Philippine history: "The Philippines is the only nation in Southeast Asia that became subject to Western colonialism before it had developed either a centralized government ruling over a large territory or an advanced elite culture."

On their Malay subjects—and the Chinese merchants who came to live and trade among them—the Spaniards had imposed an overlay of Hispanic culture, notably their version of Catholicism. They tended to leave native customs and authorities in place, however; education was restricted to the largely Hispanicized local gentry. The Americans stamped their own cultural impress after 1898, pervasive but not very penetrating. As the bitter joke of the Marcos dictatorship days had it: "Three hundred years in a Spanish convent, fifty years of Hollywood, and twenty years of *his* and *hers*."

The Americans' major failing was to take the Americanization of the Filipinos for granted, even though it was, at best, the Americanization of second-class citizenship. The Filipinos, in turn, had trouble growing out of a long dependency relationship. Overall a sense of identification with America persisted—not surprising in view of the basic American education most Filipinos received. Jefferson and Lincoln were Filipino as well as American role models. For Filipinos the classic rich man was Rockefeller, the classic jurist Justice Holmes. Just as Emilio Aguinaldo had admired the democracy of the army that hunted him down, a postwar revolutionary like the Huk leader Luis Taruc, despite his Communist affiliation, continued to idealize America's Presidents; he was proud to have memorized Lincoln's Gettysburg Address.[13]

The hero of them all was MacArthur, virtually deified after his final triumphant "return." His posturing and grandiloquence played beautifully among people to whom style and rhetoric are all-important. When he returned to the Philippines for the last time in 1961, a national holiday was declared.

There was some justice in the tribute. MacArthur's emotional ties to the Philippines were genuine. He inherited them from his father, General Arthur MacArthur, who saw himself as the island dependency's benevolent military viceroy (as well as its conqueror) at the turn of the century. In working out the Pacific strategy for World War II, it is true, he single-handedly swung President Roosevelt toward a costly land invasion of the Philippines, instead of letting Japanese forces there wither on the vine, so to speak, while sea and air power struck directly at the Japanese home islands. There was, Washington conceded, a debt to repay to the only Asian colony whose people had fought for the West.

There were some serious flaws, however, in MacArthur's towering image. His military planning blunders had handed the Japanese an early victory in 1942.[14] Worst of all, on returning to Manila in 1945 he had conspicuously refused to take any action against the considerable number of highly placed Filipinos who had actively collaborated with the Japanese Occupation—most of them from the wealthy *ilustrado* families he knew best. By his order some 5,000 of the worst offenders were freed. With the general's blessing Manuel Roxas, a known collaborator whose alleged ties to the "underground" were highly debatable, was set up as the favored presidential candidate.

Roxas won, in an election characterized by crookedness and bought votes. With this, the old landowning oligarchy of prewar days was restored to power,

[13] As noted in Stanley Karnow's *In Our Image.*

[14] Not only had MacArthur grossly overrated the number of trained Filipino troops available for fighting. Confident that Japan would not invade until mid-1942, he had disastrously dispersed supplies and munitions instead of concentrating them on the future Bataan bridgehead—thereby making a quick defeat inevitable. Conversely, his failure to disperse the sizable American air forces in the Philippines, despite news of the Pearl Harbor attack, enabled the Japanese to destroy almost all American aircraft on the ground in the first few days of combat.

economic as well as political. MacArthur himself left in August 1945 for Japan. He had bigger fish to fry, one assumes, in his shogunal task of Occupation. He visited the Philippines only once again, in 1961, for his triumphal parade.

While the Philippine government, under Roxas and his successor, Quirino, dissolved in a mess of corrupt statehouse politics and gross economic pilferage, Washington congressmen were busy fastening a new network of preferential trade agreements on a complaisant Filipino administration. Their net effect was to keep the newly independent country, as a commodity supplier, in a state of semi-colonial economic dependence on the United States. Shortly thereafter an agreement was also reached for a ninety-nine-year lease on Clark Field, Subic Bay, and other U.S. military bases in the Philippines, on terms highly favorable to the Americans (extraterritoriality included). Senator Robert Taft, President William Howard's son, in summing up the various negotiations, saluted the Philippines as "an American outpost in the Pacific." He added, true to the family tradition: "Certainly we shall always be a big brother, if you please, to the Philippines."[15]

Over the past half century the United States had played three roles in its brotherly governance of the Philippines. They comprised a microcosm of American policy in the Pacific. The first and by far the most credible was that of the Teacher. For all the condescension involved, the Teacher's aspirations were high. American democracy and American know-how were exportables, which we wanted the world to share.

Many of the lessons took. As a reporter and later as a businessman, I encountered over the years Filipinos in many walks of life—crusading editors, rights-conscious lawyers, enlightened businessmen, and dedicated teachers— who tried to live out the lessons in democratic freedoms they had learned in American and Philippine schools. Two Presidents of the Philippines—Corazon Aquino and the tragically short-lived Ramón Magsaysay—were among them. One of the proudest moments of my own life as a peripatetic American came in the middle of a discussion about colonialism with some European and Asian friends. When the Europeans made the point that all colonial regimes were alike, a young Filipina journalist contradicted them. "No one knows the faults of the Americans better than we do. But they did one thing in the Philippines. They educated. They taught us their values. They taught us democracy. They were different from the others."

Protestant Christianity on the American model was often included in the teaching mission. So was the American brand of Catholicism, activist and

---

[15] As quoted in Stanley Karnow's *In Our Image*. In the foregoing comments I have also relied on Karnow's excellent summary of postwar negotiations between the Philippines and the United States.

socially conscious, as more American priests and nuns came to work in the Philippines. Americans of an older generation thought of religion, along with constitutions, the idea of one man–one vote, business schools, and demonstration model railroads, as part of a package deal, albeit haphazardly assembled. Although it is fashionable in the 1990s to denigrate formal religions (generally in favor of unsuspected religion substitutes), it would be a mistake to underrate the positive side of religious belief in what the Americans taught.

The second role was that of the profit-minded Yankee Trader. This was the oldest Pacific policy Americans had, dating back to the clipper ships and the bales of opium piled up in the Canton warehouses. Amoral rather than immoral, the traders wanted big profits, but aimed to give good value, wherever possible. They were interested in politics only insofar as it could help them make better deals. The manufacturers behind them wanted more. They wanted markets for their goods overseas, on terms as favorable as possible.

The third role was that of the big-power imperialist Keeper of the Peace. Although not so set on the pelf of empire as their hungrier European contemporaries—the very word "imperialist," like "colonialist," has always bothered Americans—the urge to carry the flag over the water, first given voice by Teddy Roosevelt, Admiral Mahan, and their followers, remained a powerful one. It brought Americans to the Philippines in the first place. It again became a national concern after the global victory of World War II had finally given Americans a national sense of imperium, intensified by the spread of Communism throughout the world. This challenge prompted a new sense of international mission, an anti-Communist crusade of allies based on military strength. American power would be the guarantor of the "free world's" peace, its bases throughout the world the visible signs of security.

These three roles shifted continually in American policy toward the Philippines. Often one superseded or contradicted the other; the American democracy has a characteristically short attention span. While the image of the Teacher had long predominated, the needs of the Yankee Trader continued to influence votes in Washington. Ultimately the pressures of the Cold War gave Global Peacekeeping the highest priority—which explains why the United States, despite its long investment of people, money, and goodwill in the cause of Philippine democracy, could through four administrations support the cruel and destructive dictatorship of Ferdinand Marcos.

DURING A good part of the Pacific War I was engaged in intelligence work, interrogating Japanese prisoners of war at a camp in Pearl Harbor and in various operational zones, where fighting was going on. American treatment of Japanese war prisoners was on the whole very good—indeed benign if compared with the ghastly brutalities perpetrated on American prisoners by their Japanese captors. Most Japanese prisoners were not very security-conscious. That is, they talked freely. Having been told by their military command to expect torture or death if captured—and reminded that the very fact of their capture would bring disgrace on themselves and their families—they were, if anything, anxious to offer information in return for decent treatment. A few, however, refused to divulge any sort of military information at all. For the most part these were left alone, their silence respected. But in one or two cases interrogators were told that force could be used to find out vital information when many lives were at stake.

Navy Petty Officer Sasaki (not his real name) was one of those. He was not tortured, but he was subjected to a typically American double standard. On orders of the officer in charge, Sasaki was put into a solitary cell normally reserved for infractors of discipline. When he refused to talk, a tough Marine sergeant came into the cell, punched him around, and threatened him with worse. The executive officer at the camp was shocked at this rough treatment. Following the Marine's beating, he visited the cell, apologized to Sasaki for such cruelty, gave him cigarettes, extra rations, and some Japanese reading material. While Sasaki was mulling over this apparent change in his situation, in came the officer in charge and the Marine sergeant, with more threats and punches. The next day the executive officer came in with more cigarettes and candy, and gave Sasaki a pep talk about God and democracy.

In the end, after more of this treatment, Sasaki refused to talk and was returned to the general tent area, presumably more than a little schizophrenic from his experience.

I have come to think of this incident as a capsule of the way the Sentimental Imperialists played out their mutually conflicting roles in the Asia-Pacific region. A traditionally aggressive people, "peace-loving" only on our own terms, we Americans have rarely shrunk from the use of power in our international dealings. But we have always had a bad conscience about it. Even when exercised in a just cause and for apparently the right reasons, force has embarrassed us. From the Korean War stalemate in 1953 to the Gulf War in 1991, we have generally failed to use it as decisively as we might have. We have always been ready to preach—peace, democracy, free enterprise. Possibly because of the high decibel level of the preaching, our practice of these ideals often seems sadly wanting.

The American accomplishment has been nonetheless considerable. Much has been done unselfishly and in the hope that others would follow our example. Our European cousins merely wanted to colonize. Naive in their optimism, the Americans wanted to make other people more "like us." One of Henry R.

Luce's 1942 editorials in *Life* expressed this feeling quite accurately: "Because America alone among the nations of the earth was founded on ideas and ideals which transcend class and caste and racial and occupational differences, America alone can provide the pattern for the future."

If this was an arrogant assumption, it expressed a worthy goal. About the transcendent ideas and ideals there is no mistake. Despite the sniping of a whole generation of "revisionist" historians (Marxist and homegrown), the majority of Americans still believe this. This is doubtless one reason why Ronald Reagan could get so many votes forty years after Luce by evoking John Winthrop's Puritan vision of the God-favored "City on a Hill" in so many of his White House scripts.

The history of the Pacific nations over the past century affords ample evidence that Asian revolutionaries and reformers have taken inspiration from Jefferson and the Declaration of Independence and the Bill of Rights. As we have seen, two different generations of Japanese reformers took the American example as a guide. So did Liang Qichao and Sun Yat-sen in China. Korean reformers, from Syngman Rhee's time onward, found the American ideal central to their thinking—however much it was abused in practice. José Rizal was influenced by the American idea, as was Soetan Sjahrir and a whole generation of nationalist intellectuals in Indonesia. Even as firm a Comintern stalwart as Ho Chi Minh found it useful to cite the Declaration of Independence as a key to his thinking.

Yet such a lofty mission puts a heavy charge on those who try to fulfill it. In this respect, Marxism-Leninism, which we might call the "antimatter" of Jefferson and Madison's ideal, seems to have failed totally—its idealism spent, its few cadres who remained faithful to the ideal of true socialism long since hounded to disgrace or death by Party apparatchiks. The surviving Communist parties of Asia are as devoid of any spark as their fraternal remnants in Europe. In China, North Korea, and Vietnam they are kept alive only by the hired guns of a few old men in power. The principal evidence of their failure, apart from the inconsistencies of their message, was the gap—widening to the point of total contradiction—between the egalitarian ideal and the cynical power seeking of the "New Class" Party leaders who claimed to practice it.

A similar contradiction—although fortunately not so extreme—has flawed the American democracy's Asia dealings. While subscribing to their lofty international (and self-imposed) teaching mission, Americans have also pushed ahead with their tasks of making money—as much and as quickly as possible— and expanding their political and military power over others. The Philippine example shows us how the roles of the Teacher of Democracy, the Yankee Trader, and the Pacific Imperialist have frequently been in conflict.

On a wider stage the noble international goals of the Sentimental Imperialists have continually clashed with national interest, real or fancied, individual greed and ambition, and domestic American prejudices, racial and otherwise. This has been nowhere more evident than in the confused history of America's relations with those two other singular and difficult countries, Japan and China.

18

The Chinese, the Japanese, and Us

In Christ there is no East or West
In Him no South or North
But one great fellowship of love
Throughout the whole wide world.
CHRISTIAN MISSIONARY HYMN

"The Japanese can be tough," Connors said. "They say, 'Business is war,' and they mean it.". . .

Ishigura hissed through his teeth. "Heads will roll," he said.
FROM *RISING SUN,* BY MICHAEL CRICHTON

Over the first decades of contact with China the American image stood up well. The Yankee traders were well regarded, at least by contrast with the more obviously rapacious Europeans. In 1861, Zeng Guofan, the general who conquered the Taiping rebels, drew some distinctions. "Of all Western barbarians," he wrote, "the English are the most crafty, the French next . . . The Americans are of pure-minded and honest disposition and have long been recognized as respectful and compliant toward China . . . When the English and French barbarians attacked the capital of Guangdong, the American chief never assisted the rebels . . . While the American barbarians have always been sincerely steadfast in dealing with China, they have never been in close alliance with the English and French."

Other Chinese observers were less charitable in their views, as it became evident that Americans tended to make common cause with the Europeans and their gunboats. General Zeng's fondness for Americans, also, may have been partly in recognition of the exploits of a remarkable young American soldier of fortune named Frederick Townsend Ward, whose Ever-Victorious Army—a mixed bag of Chinese, European, and American adventurers and British noncom deserters—had pushed back the Taiping rebels from the outskirts of Shanghai. When Ward died in action, aged thirty-one, he had already been given mandarin status and a general's (and admiral's) commission by a grateful court in Beijing.

Ward's most prominent supporter was Anson Burlingame, a Massachusetts politician then serving as American minister to China. One of the first in a long succession of American "China hands," Burlingame brought a delegation of Chinese officials to Washington in 1868. There, under the benevolent expansionist eye of Secretary of State Seward, he pushed through a treaty giving Americans rights to build schools and expand trade in China, as well as allow emigration of Chinese laborers to the United States. Washington also pledged itself not to interfere in China's domestic affairs—welcome words to Chinese already smarting from French, British, and Russian military activity. Burlingame, who later became a trusted councillor of the Beijing government, told an enthusiastic audience of New York businessmen: "The imagination kindles at the future which may be, and which will be, if you will be fair and just to China."

Burlingame's cheerful words were soon drowned out, however, by an angry chorus denouncing Chinese immigrants and Chinese in general. Driven overseas by famine and civil war at home, thousands of poor Chinese men, leaving their families behind, took passage across the Pacific in the 1850s and thereafter. Desperate for work, they readily traveled under slave-ship conditions; by 1872, within four years after Burlingame's treaty, almost 40,000 had arrived in San Francisco. The transcontinental railroad was built largely by some 10,000 "coolie" laborers.[1] After the railroad was completed, a recession followed the post–Gold Rush labor shortage. The Chinese were poor, uneducated, and totally alien to their surroundings, their only wish being to return to their families in China with their savings. Generally unable to communicate in English, they soon became the targets of the most vicious kind of American nativism. They were beaten, robbed, and even lynched by workers, many of them recently arrived immigrants themselves, who felt their jobs threatened.

In San Francisco a local political party was organized with the battle cry "The Chinese Must Go." Labor union bosses denounced the "Orientals." Throughout the 1870s and 1880s, buildings were bombed and burned there and in various other western Chinatowns. In 1878, the citizens of Truckee drove away the whole Chinese population. In 1885, at Rock Springs, Wyoming, twenty-eight Chinese were murdered in one day. Two years later, ten Chinese miners were murdered by vigilantes in Snake River, Oregon.[2]

---

[1] The word "coolie" is an anglicization of the Chinese *kuli,* meaning "hard labor."

[2] For these incidents and the references to Bret Harte and Jack London, which follow, I am indebted to *Americans and Chinese* (Cambridge, Mass.: Harvard University Press, 1963) by Kwang-Ching Liu and *Pacific Destiny* (Boston: Little, Brown, 1969) by Richard O'Connor.

Chinese immigrants to Hawaii. In the latter half of the nineteenth century, thousands of Chinese workers flocked to Hawaii and then California.
Hawaii State Archives

Anti-Chinese reaction. A violent wave of racist indignation, particularly in California, resulted in the Chinese Exclusion Act of 1882. These two cartoons illustrate the bigotry of that period. Cartoon from The San Francisco Illustrated Wasp, *February 21, 1880.* The Eleanor McClatchy Collection, City of Sacramento, Sacramento Archives and Museum Collection Center
Poster for "The Magic Washer." Library of Congress

Western American writers, Mark Twain and Bret Harte among them, wrote eloquent denunciations of these goings-on. "Dead, my reverend friends, dead," Harte memorialized in an obituary for a Chinese named Wan Lee, "stoned to death in the streets of San Francisco in the year of grace 1869, by a mob of half-grown boys and Christian school-children." Their fellow citizens paid them no attention.

In 1882, Congress passed the infamous Chinese Exclusion Act, following a California state election in which more than 150,000 had voted for exclusion, with only 883 against. Ironically, portions of a satirical poem by Harte denouncing the treatment of Chinese (". . . for ways that are dark / And tricks that are vain / The Heathen Chinee is peculiar") were taken literally (and out of context) by anti-Chinese agitators. To Harte's chagrin, the poem quickly became a nationwide best-seller.

The general anti-Chinese feeling was inflamed by intermittent reports of violence against American and European missionaries in China, culminating in the atrocities of the Boxer Rebellion of 1900. American atrocities against Chinese were quickly submerged in the popular subconscious.

By CONTRAST the American relationship with Japan was going swimmingly. At least until the early 1900s the new Pacific partnership had the glow of a honeymoon. Commodore Perry's mission had led to the conclusion of a treaty in 1858, its success largely the result of Consul General Townsend Harris's patient diplomacy. The first official Japanese mission to Washington in 1860 was greeted with general acclaim. Walt Whitman wrote a nice poem about it ("Over the Western sea higher from Niphon come / Courteous, the swart-cheeked two-sword envoys . . .") and *Harper's Weekly* termed them "the British of Asia." Other commentators spoke hopefully of "the Americanization of Japan." While crowds rather boisterously cheered the visitors' procession through the streets of American cities, editorialists were quick to draw favorable distinctions between Japan and China. "We would [not] confound so refined and enlightened a people as the Japanese with so refined and yet degraded a race as the birds' nest and puppy dog eaters." *Frank Leslie's Illustrated Newspaper* advised its readers.

After the Meiji Restoration of 1868 the good feeling continued. Americans comprised by far the greatest number of foreign teachers in Japan, missionaries included. Although the latter made relatively few converts—one complained that the Japanese were anxious to import everything from the West except for opium and Christianity—there was nothing like the anti-Christian rioting that took place in China. Some prominent intellectuals became Christians; many others at least flirted with the idea. Great numbers of American technicians and professional people joined the foreign experts hired by the Meiji government. In fact, many of the early Meiji institutions, as we have seen, were based on American models.

Americans tended to take pride in the accomplishments of this "most Western of Asiatic nations" and looked forward to long and prosperous trading relations. They were flattered at the idea of continuing their teaching relationship, solidified by the founding of Protestant "mission schools" like Doshisha in Kyoto and Rikkyo (St. Paul's) in Tokyo. For all that the Meiji leaders later switched to European political models as more congenial to Japanese ideas of strong central government, Americans continued to command influence in the private sector. The transplanted American author Lafcadio Hearn became the foremost literary interpreter of Japan to Westerners. The art critic Ernest Fenollosa almost single-handedly revived the appreciation of classic Japanese painting, in the face of a pell-mell rush to Western models by Japanese artists of the early Meiji days.

After the turn of the century the climate began to change. Admiral Mahan and President Roosevelt, as we noted, were busy staking out America's claim to an imperialist future as the new Pacific power. At the same time, Japan, with its victory in the Sino-Japanese War had unveiled a program for territorial as well as commercial expansion. Japanese immigrants had already landed in droves on the Hawaiian Islands. By 1900, they already comprised 40 percent of Hawaii's population, and more were coming. In 1897, in fact, a Japanese cruiser had been sent to Honolulu by way of protesting the imminent American annexation of Queen Liliuokalani's realm.

Despite his admiration for the Japanese, Teddy Roosevelt worried about Japan's military threat. On the one hand he supported Japan's rivalry with Russia. He went so far as to work out a de facto arrangement whereby the United States would not interfere with Japanese hegemony over Korea, as long as the United States was left in unthreatened possession of its new colony in the Philippines. Syngman Rhee and other Korean nationalists had put their trust in the United States to oppose the impending annexation and advocate Korea's independence. They rightly regarded this arrangement as a sellout.

Japan's victory in the Russo-Japanese War only increased the gathering tension. American suspicions of Japan deepened: Had they learned so quickly as to threaten their American teachers? To complicate matters, Californians, from the governor on down, were reacting against further Japanese immigration with boycotts, beatings, and insensate brutality. The same arguments used against Chinese immigrants were dusted off again, the same violence resulting. The Japanese—government and private citizens alike—had given more than any other country in relief funds after San Francisco's 1906 earthquake. Yet an official delegation visiting San Francisco for that purpose was stoned by a mob in the city streets.

Unlike the helpless Chinese, Japanese could deploy their power. The anti-

Japanese troops in the Russo-Japanese War. At first American sentiment was with the Japanese, who were regarded as a new progressive force in Asia.
Department of Art History Visual Resources Collection, UCLA

Welcome Americans. This postcard was issued to commemorate the Great White Fleet's visit to Japan in 1908.
Library of Congress

American missionaries, both religious and educational, continued their energetic work in China. Here American nurses preside over a bandaging class at Yale-in-China, Changsha, in 1915. Sophia Smith Collection, Smith College

General Nogi at Port Arthur. Japanese victories by Gen. Nogi Maresuke (here pictured in center with beard) at Port Arthur (Lushun) and Admiral Togo's spectacular naval triumph at Tsushima in 1905 made Americans realize Japan's new Pacific power.
Department of Art History Visual Resources Collection, UCLA

Japanese violence was reported with great detail in the Tokyo press, with predictably angry public reaction. Although the government in Tokyo handled the incidents with great restraint, the very existence of the controversy led excitable California bigots to imagine sinister Oriental spies in every alleyway. "We know," said one prominent Californian, himself a former American naval officer, "that the Japanese in California are soldiers, organized into companies, regiments, and brigades." The steel magnate Andrew Carnegie, visiting Japan for the first time, nervously described his hosts as "demons."

Mori Ogai, one of the giants of Meiji era literature, was also a serving officer in the Imperial Army's medical corps, who had spent many years in Europe. Earlier, during the Russo-Japanese War, he had prophetically described Japan's dilemma: "Win the war and Japan will be denounced as the *yellow peril*; lose the war and Japan will be stigmatized as a country of barbarians."

The American writer Jack London had been a war correspondent during the Russo-Japanese fighting. The nature-loving author of *Call of the Wild* returned to the United States, after some run-ins with Japanese military authorities, a militant white supremacist. As if to fulfill Surgeon General Mori's prophecy, London wrote for the Hearst newspapers an essay entitled "The Yellow Peril." "Handling machines and systems," he wrote, "with remarkable and deadly accuracy, this rejuvenescent Japanese race has embarked on a course of conquest, the goal of which no man knows." All too many Americans believed him. Over his last three years in office Teddy Roosevelt spent a good bit of his time trying to undo the damage done by the "infernal fools" in California, but he was only partially successful.

THUS THE chemistry of Pacific relations changed. Various forces in the United States worked to diminish the decades-long respect and admiration for Japan. By the 1920s the old pro-Japanese feelings were giving way to suspicion, if not outright hostility. Pacific power politics was only one of them. The Yankee trader mentality was also to be reckoned with. Although Japan remained a strong trading partner, with American imports a major factor in its important silk industry, the lure of "huge" China markets kept beckoning. Restatements of John Hay's Open Door policy became the cornerstone of so-called Dollar Diplomacy under William Howard Taft, after he succeeded Roosevelt as President. In most Americans' view the greatest threat to the Open Door was Japan, whose commercial expansion kept pace with its spreading military hegemony in East Asia. By contrast, the Boxer Rebellion's "bloodthirsty hordes" of Chinese fanatics began to fade into a new image of "John Chinaman," the peace-loving victim of Japan's aggression, who was just waiting to take on the faith of American Christianity.

The most active pro-Chinese image makers were a small group of dedicated American missionaries in China. At their peak, in the 1920s, they numbered no more than 5,000. But their missions, dispensaries, and schools were scattered throughout the country; Protestant clergymen presided over a loose network of sixteen Christian colleges and some three hundred high schools. And by the late twenties two Catholic universities were flourishing, with a similar growth in schools and hospitals, most of them American-funded.

Like their colleagues in the Philippines, the missionaries in China were the point men of an extraordinary national effort, which intensified in the 1890s and reached its apogee in the first three decades of the twentieth century. The conversion of China—"Evangelize China in this generation," as the Student Volunteer Movement of 1900 sloganized—was American Protestantism's special version of Manifest Destiny. Securely girt in the armor of their own certitude, churchmen kindled the imagination of young Christians in sermons and lectures throughout the country—some 30,000 each year. "China," the Reverend Frank Rawlinson exhorted his fellow Baptists, "has a glimpse of better things . . . from the light-bearers who follow the Light of the World."[3]

Support was heavy and widespread, from the millions given by rich men like John D. Rockefeller and Edward Harkness to the nickels and dimes in hundreds of thousands of Sunday-school collection boxes. The money bought not only Bibles and hymnbooks—patiently translated by mission scholars into vernacular Chinese—but hospitals, laboratories, and new farm equipment. For most of the new generation of teaching Americans thought of Christianity as inseparable from modern education, public health improvement, and new Western-style constitutions.

Each year the expatriate "light-bearers" in China were joined by fresh reinforcements, like the muscular young Christians of the new Yale-in-China, who arrived in Changsha in 1904 from New Haven to set up their school and hospital. "Get hold of the students, the educated men," wrote their director, Edward Hume (class of '97), "and China will be won." The educated men they got, in various guises. One of the first editors of the new Yale-in-China review was a young radical student named Mao Zedong, who later adopted a similarly unitary approach in his own propaganda work.[4]

It is easy for modern Americans to put down the naive idealism of their pious forebears in China. (Later twenty-first-century generations might look with even greater perplexity at the devout ethnicity that animated U.S. campus

[3] As quoted in *United States Attitudes and Policies Towards China* (Armonk, N.Y.: Sharpe, 1990), edited by Patricia Neils.

[4] The author (Yale, 1945) is indebted for this anecdote to Jonathan Spence's fascinating study *To Change China* (Boston: Little, Brown, 1969).

idealists in the 1990s.) But with all their faults the muscular Christians did make their mark on two generations of Chinese students and intellectuals. They introduced them not merely to modern medicine and technological advances but to the whole Western tradition of empirical scholarship and research, in the humanities as well as in science.

Relatively few Chinese notables followed the revolutionary hero Sun Yat-sen and, later, Chiang Kai-shek in becoming Christians themselves. Many like Hu Shi prided themselves on their strictly modern, John Dewey–style agnosticism. But they retained the lessons they learned. Most of all they were impressed by example. Whether recalcitrant Confucians or newly revolutionary Communists, Chinese intellectuals were touched by the dynamism and self-sacrifice they found among a new generation of mission teachers. The personal example of great missionary educators like Leighton Stuart at Yanjing University made more friends for America than the formal religion they preached. These people were not mandarins. They cared.

Back home in America people warmed to the idea of Christianizing (and Americanizing) China, with little thought given to the vast cultural and ethical obstacles that lay in the path of Western "progress." Whereas Europeans were regarded, often none too pleasantly, as people with sharply different cultures, the "heathen Chinee" were seen as masses sunk in superstition, passively ripe to receive the Christian American message. The turn-of-the-century mission preachers had, it would seem, oversold. Despite the pioneering work of erudite mission scholars like Yale's Kenneth S. Latourette in explaining the complexities of China's culture to their fellow citizens, the average American thought of the Chinese as spiritually and intellectually underprivileged, in need of teachers to point the way. In such a climate was the idea of Americans "winning" or "losing" China born.

SINCE 1904 Chinese had been systematically and legally excluded from immigrating to the United States. Only a few lonely voices had spoken out against this. The great majority of the Sentimental Imperialists apparently found nothing paradoxical in the fact that the Chinese they hoped to convert and enlighten (and sell to) in China were made the victims of the world's most unpleasant racial discrimination within the United States. Now came Japan's turn. Anti-Japanese feeling among Americans had stemmed originally from fear of Japan's growing Pacific power after the Russo-Japanese War. It was exacerbated by Japan's saber rattling in China, which culminated in demands made at the Versailles Peace Conference for the overlordship of China's rich coastal Shandong Province. In the 1920s sensationalist books and magazine articles fanned the flame with predictions of an impending military confrontation. Now popular fear and resentment began to explode, reacting to the increase in Japanese emigration to the United States, first in Hawaii, later in the western states. The ugly local persecutions visited on all Asians in California were now concentrated on the Japanese. From street mobs in San Francisco to state legislators in Sacramento the word was out to "get the Japs."

Since Theodore Roosevelt's time Japanese and American officials had tried, with some success, to curb excesses of anti-Japanese sentiment in the American West. One device was to limit extensive emigration by "gentlemen's agreements," much as Japanese governments a half century later would voluntarily restrict excess exports of automobiles. But in the antiforeign atmosphere of the American twenties, popular pressure, intensified by the anti-Japanese press, the unions, and the ever vigilant American Legion, overcame diplomacy. On July 1, 1924, both House and Senate overwhelmingly passed a restrictive immigration bill incorporating a specific exclusion clause directed against Japan. The weight of opinion in favor of exclusion was heavily regional. (While 80 percent of western newspapers and 45 percent of midwestern papers came out for exclusion, only 5 percent of eastern editorialists were so disposed.) Yet few legislators felt at all strongly about opposing it.

This time the pitch of Japanese popular anger was deafening. No people takes the idea of an international pecking order so seriously as Japan. The Exclusion Act, coming only a few years after the defeat of the racial equality clause by the Versailles treaty makers was an insult of monumental proportions. It would sour Japanese-American relations for the next quarter century.

With polite resilience, however, the diplomats and policy makers in Washington and Tokyo set about to patch up the relationship. Superficially they succeeded. The Washington Conference of 1921–22 set the tone for a series of bravely worded treaties and covenants. It pointed the way toward the later Kellogg-Briand world peace pact of 1929 (which the historian Samuel Eliot Morison justly called an attempt to "keep the peace by incantation"). The principle of the Open Door was nobly restated—with only a few concessions to recent Japanese inroads on Chinese sovereignty. Japan formally accepted the naval superiority of Britain and the United States. Progress was even made on reviving a face-saving immigration quota for Japan, following recommendations from the U.S. Chamber of Commerce and American exporters to Japan.

Violators of the international order were excoriated. When the Japanese Army touched off the conquest of Manchuria in 1931, Secretary of State Henry Stimson denounced this in thundering terms; Japan's peace-loving Foreign Minister Shidehara Kijuro was quick, as always, to apologize. If we look at the diplomatic history of the twenties and thirties, we see a period of vigorous American activity. From Frank Kellogg to Stimson, Secretaries of State continued in the John Hay tradition, laying down the law on China's sovereignty and peace in the Pacific. Indeed, all of them were lawyers. They doted on good negotiations, sweeping agreements, and ringing affirmations—like "safeguarding the rights and interests of China."

IF WE LOOK at the social and political history of the Pacific world in this period, however, we find a totally different picture. Asian revolutionaries may have been galvanized by the noble Wilsonian ideals of "self-determination" expressed at Versailles. Americans at home ultimately rejected them. Congress voted with the country in refusing to join the League of Nations, which Americans themselves had started. Through the twenties the mood of the country turned ever more strongly isolationist. Fourth of July orators abundantly quoted Washington's cautions against "foreign entanglements." The Army and Navy were put on short rations. The lawyers at State knew that there was no real force to back up their pronouncements. Teddy Roosevelt and Admiral Mahan were long dead.

As the Great Depression cast its shadow over the country, few people worried about foreign policy—except for intermittent demands that the European allies pay up on their war debts from 1918. Personally speaking, the Sentimental Imperialists stayed sentimental. Churches still took up their collections for the poor Chinese in the missions. Movie newsreel audiences shook their heads in sympathy at photographs of crying Chinese babies in Shanghai's bombed streets. Editorialists thundered maledictions at the "Jap militarists." But no one wanted to do anything. In the aftermath of the Depression, Franklin D. Roosevelt's New Deal monopolized the national agenda. Even when Roosevelt, a confirmed internationalist, turned his attention to foreign policy, the popular reaction was negative. His famous 1937 "quarantine the aggressors" speech, in which he advocated taking steps to curb Japan as well as Hitler's Germany, was roundly attacked as warmongering. In early 1938, after Japanese forces had invaded China, bombed numerous American mission stations, and sunk an American gunboat, a Gallup poll found 70 percent of Americans in favor of total withdrawal from China—Marines and missionaries included.

In Japan the popular mood worked in the opposite direction. For a belligerent, yet resource-poor country the hard facts of economic depression seemed to point toward expansion rather than isolation. Whereas the American Okies headed west to retrieve their fortunes in California, their Japanese counterparts packed themselves off across the Sea of Japan to Manchuria. The American depression had hit Japan's exports hard. As bad times grew worse, popular resentment increased. America's record of anti-Japanese immigration policies was readily exploited by nationalists, who scornfully contrasted them with Washington's constant preachments against Japan's advances in China. Wasn't it time for Japan to lead the Asian nations in a racial crusade against the West? Made all the bolder by the lack of power behind the State Department's denunciations, Japan's militarists, who didn't think much of laws or lawyers, elbowed aside peacemakers like Shidehara.

The professors and publicists of Japan's ever flexible intelligentsia—Marxists included—began to write articles in favor of the government's newly announced Greater East Asia Co-Prosperity Sphere. Many of them now saw Japan as the protector of Asia against the West, oddly recalling the pronouncements of that enigmatic ideologue Kita Ikki, who had inspired the young rebel officers ten years before with his talk about "revolutionary empire" of Japan and its "Asian Monroe Doctrine."

People in the cities queued up to present their gold jewelry as gifts to the nation. In the countryside farmers and their families gathered at railroad stations to see their conscript sons off to the Army. For greater "spiritual mobilization" Prime Minister Konoe Fumimaro's government ordered labor unions, veterans' organizations, and political parties swept up in one vast Imperial Rule Assistance Association. The nation, not just the militarists, prepared for war.

IT TOOK THE attack on Pearl Harbor to eliminate, for the time, all doubt about the American role in the Pacific. The missions of the teacher and the big-power imperialist fused, as the new standard bearer of the democracies took on the Axis powers. All the ingenuity and hustle of the Yankee trader went into the manufacture of guns, tanks, and airplanes. The tension of the past four decades between America's "moral universalism and political parochialism," as Akira Iriye trenchantly put it,[5] no longer existed. There was now power behind the politics. From that day to this, American attitudes toward the other Pacific nations, as well as United States policy, would be conditioned by an American sense of regional and global interests and responsibilities. All this evolved from the basic wartime commitment. Power flowed "from out of the barrel of a gun" for Franklin D. Roosevelt and Lyndon Johnson as well as for Mao Zedong.

The suddenness of the "sneak attack" on Pearl Harbor, coming after years of well-reported Japanese military atrocities in China, polarized American opinion against "those dirty yellow Japs." All the latent racist Know-Nothingism in American society was mobilized against this obviously sinister enemy. No more cheerful Walt Whitman odes to the "envoys from Niphon"; no more tributes to this "most Western of Asiatic nations."

Some 120,000 Japanese-Americans on the West Coast were rounded up and

[5] In his book on America's Pacific relations, *Across the Pacific* (New York: Harcourt, Brace, 1967).

U.S. troops in Tianjin. Americans also kept up military
appearances in Asia, with garrisons in Tianjin (Tientsin)
China as well as in the prewar Philippines.
The Peabody Museum of Salem

Chiang and Time. Chiang
Kai-shek, here pictured in one
of several Time cover stories,
was a favorite of China-born
editor Henry R. Luce. As
Japanese troops continued their
aggression, Americans' pro-
Chinese sentiments grew
stronger. Copyright © 1948 Time
Warner Inc. Reprinted by
permission.

Japanese-American evacuation. In 1942, shortly after Pearl Harbor, some 170,000 Americans of Japanese ancestry were forcibly evacuated by the U.S. government as "dangerous aliens" and sent to "relocation centers," which were little more than concentration camps. More than forty years later Congress finally awarded some compensation to the survivors of the evacuation—one of the most shameful acts of injustice in American history.
Library of Congress

bundled into "relocation centers" that were little more than concentration camps, allegedly for security reasons. (Nothing whatsoever was done about the recent immigrants from Italy or Germany in similar situations.) Hardly anyone protested against the wrong done to these people, almost all of them loyal Americans. Indeed, leading liberals like the columnist Walter Lippmann were quick to praise the action; Governor Earl Warren of California, later to be praised as the liberal Chief Justice of the Supreme Court, cheerfully assisted Lieutenant General John DeWitt, head of the Western Defense Command and the most vicious of the "Jap haters" in the U.S. military, in this monstrous deed. The prime mover in securing the presidential order for their "evacuation," which FDR dutifully signed, was none other than the old moralist lawyer Henry Stimson, now serving as Roosevelt's Secretary of War. He was energetically assisted by his Assistant Secretary, John McCloy, who praised their action as a "prudent" step. DeWitt, quite a phrasemaker, later summarized the rationale for Stimson and McCloy's decision in the memorable statement: "We will be worried about the Japs all the time until they are wiped off the face of the map."

Certainly the cruelties visited on American prisoners of war by the Japanese were appalling, as were the atrocities perpetrated on civilians throughout the captive nations of the greater East Asia Co-Prosperity Sphere. No amount of postwar Japanese revisionist explanation can erase the horrors of the Bataan death march, the *Kempeitai* tortures in Manila's Fort Santiago and Singapore's Changi jail, the brutal slaughter of Chinese and other Asian civilians, the exploitation of Korean and Indonesian forced laborers, or the beheadings of captured American airmen. The people of Yamato were racists long before America was born. The fact remains that the Sentimental Imperialists fought a similarly dirty war in the Pacific.[6]

I had a unique opportunity to observe the Pacific fighting, having served as a Navy prisoner-of-war interrogator with the Marines in the Palau operation (1944) and the Army and Marines throughout the Okinawa campaign (1945); in addition, I had the chance to question prisoners from Guam, Saipan, and Tarawa at our interrogation center in Pearl Harbor. It was not easy to find and protect prisoners in the field; all too many were shot "trying to escape" by our troops.

For this was a war in which almost no prisoners were taken. Under orders to fight to the end, beleaguered Japanese detachments resisted vastly superior forces with what seemed at the time inhuman tenacity. On a totally unfriendly field of coral reef and tangled jungle, any movement was deemed hostile. The

[6] John H. Dower's *War Without Mercy* (New York: Pantheon, 1986) offers a well-documented, if somewhat narrowly focused account of atrocities on both sides.

very intensity of the fighting dehumanized it. One atrocity would lead to another. Simple accidents, on second or third telling, would become sadistic cruelties. An engineering sergeant shot in the groin by a sniper, while carrying surveying chains, would emerge in a regiment's folklore as a chained-up prisoner slashed and shot in the testicles. Such stories multiplied, with predictable reactions. No veteran of the Pacific fighting would have found the later killings of villagers at Mylai or elsewhere in Vietnam at all surprising.

Japanese soldiers, for their part, had been systematically indoctrinated by the military ideologues of Imperial Headquarters to believe that men with *Nippon seishin* ("Japanese heart and soul") could triumph over the machine power of materialist foreigners. This was the same old samurai myth that the coolheaded Meiji reformers had rejected two generations before! It was central to Imperial Army teaching, moreover, that anyone taken prisoner would be tortured and executed by the bloodthirsty Americans. Tragically, civilians in the Marianas and Okinawa were told the same story. Many men, women, and children committed suicide to avoid capture, out of fear rather than fanaticism.

In defense of the Sentimental Imperialists, however, let it be said that there were many Americans who treated prisoners fairly and with kindness. (Once an enemy had escaped being gunned down, he became a nonhostile curiosity, to be given candy and cigarettes.) An atrocity would be punished if discovered— depending on the unit and commander involved. Unfortunately, in the bitter jungle fighting of the Pacific war there was a thin line between wanton killing and survival. Sometimes, as with our prisoner in Pearl Harbor, the alternation of rough punching with apologies, extra rations, and talks about democracy could be psychologically confusing. But in the U.S. armed forces the rules stipulated fair treatment for prisoners and punishment for brutality. In the Japanese armed forces of World War II—in contrast to the generally well-behaved soldiery of Meiji days—such rules were disregarded as a matter of policy.

In the course of my duties I met and talked, rather extensively, with a great many Japanese, from sophisticated Navy and Army staff officers to seamen, privates, and the petty officers who commanded them. Many of them admitted to having early and deep misgivings about the war, although on the surface they all professed "loyalty to the emperor." Some hated the military and genuinely wanted Japan to take up real democracy. (We had no dearth of volunteers for writing propaganda leaflets.) Most were simple, hardworking people who in peace as in war had tramped along with the mainstream. Some optimists asked—since returned prisoners would not be welcomed in Japan—whether they might get some land in California. Very quickly I got to know them as individuals. Attractive, amusing, boring, offensive—they spanned a wide variety of personalities and types. It was almost impossible to convey this simple fact to the people at home, however, when I returned to America in 1946. To most Americans they were all still "Japs"—part of an ugly, buck-toothed stereotype—not real human beings.

WHILE WARTIME propaganda was transforming the Madame Butterfly people into fiends incarnate, the Chinese had become both innocent victims and heroic fighters for freedom—a far cry from the "bloodthirsty hordes" of the Boxer Rebellion or the lawless bandits who had been harassing mission stations in more recent times. As John Paton Davies, Jr., one of the State Department's real China experts, later wrote: "Bathed in sentimentality about China, and in self-reproach for not having gone to China's rescue when it was first invaded (as Stimson had urged in 1931) the American public and government after Pearl Harbor looked upon the Chinese as needing only American assistance to launch a spirited counteroffensive. Americans attributed to the Chinese the impatient pugnacity then animating themselves. . . . The missionary compulsion to persuade the Chinese of the error of their ways and to walk the straight and narrow path persisted. In World War II the missionary dedication had spread to political and military proselytization. The approach was still high-minded, full of abstract love and concern for the Chinese, and unconsciously self-righteous."[7]

There is something awesome about the continuing American fascination with China. No other people in the world has bought China's own Middle Kingdom myth so thoroughly. Is it the vastness of the country, its antiquity, a faded, seamless garment of dynasty covered with history's unsightly patches, or the remoteness of its culture, so different from ours, that attracts us? Is it a sense of intellectual and cultural inferiority, as we silence the past japes and jeers at the superstitious "heathen Chinee" coolie or the sinister detective-story Fu Manchu to gape at the cool jade or scrolled characters of irreplaceable art? Or is it the challenge posed by this ungovernable civilization-state to the American conviction that our combination of modernity, uplift, and know-how could somehow reform China and make it work?

Whatever the lure, China has attracted the Sentimental Imperialist more powerfully than any other country. Left-winger or right-winger, aesthete, soldier, or earth-moving expert, Americans over the past century and a half have taken the China myth and added their own to it, in a manner hard to separate. Take the "coarseness of strength combined with acuteness and inquisitiveness" which Turner so well described, the "practical, inventive turn of mind," the "restless, nervous energy" of Americans. Combine it with the tradition of the Middle Kingdom and its perennially untapped potential and you have a fateful

---

[7] From Davies's informative book *Dragon by the Tail* (New York: Norton, 1972).

bit of human chemistry. It has worked on the best and brightest of the Sentimental Imperialists.

JOSEPH W. STILWELL was one of these. He was probably the best of America's soldier heroes from World War II. A blunt-spoken, highly practical trainer
and leader of men, he radiated an earthy competence and likability that far
eclipsed the theatrical posturings of Douglas MacArthur or even Eisenhower's
polished assurance. I remember him arriving in Okinawa to take command of
the Tenth Army in late June 1945, a spare figure wearing an outsized prewar
campaign hat and the four stars of a full general. Blunt and abrasive of speech,
with a caustic humor that suffered no fool gladly, "Vinegar Joe" had a dynamism that inspired confidence. We all knew his reputation as possibly the best
on-the-ground infantry commander the Army had. We heard him talk to us at
the headquarters, and we would have followed him anywhere gladly, even
granting the obvious perils of the then anticipated invasion of Japan.

But Stilwell was something more than a soldier. He was the intelligent man's
"China hand," whose homespun affection for the Chinese people was grounded
in a lifetime of eager, curious study. He and his wife took their first trip to
China in 1911, the year of Sun Yat-sen's revolution, on leave from his post in
the Philippines. He learned Chinese as a language officer in the twenties. He
later served with the 15th Infantry in Beijing (that institutionalized survival of
the troops who quelled the Boxer Uprising) and became military attaché to the
Nationalist government (until 1939).

Through years spent tramping the plains and mountains of inland China, he
came to know the country as few foreigners did. He spoke the language well.
He got along well with the people, whom he liked and respected. He wanted
modern China to work. He was convinced that, given a free hand, he could
train and equip many divisions of Chinese Nationalist soldiers to fight the
Japanese. In 1942, with Chiang Kai-shek's grudging consent, he was given
command of all the Chinese armies. Proud of his Chinese troops, he wanted to
build them into the first-rate fighting force he knew they could become.

The generalissimo thought otherwise. Once the Americans were committed
to the war against Japan. Chiang felt confident of the outcome. His objective
was not to have his troops fight, but to conserve them for the ultimate battle
against the Communists. Under Chiang the Guomindang armies were a mass
of corruption, their commanders appointed for political loyalty rather than
military competence. Nonetheless, Stilwell believed that his charter to train
and lead them would be respected. For two and a half years he tried to fight
corruption, promote according to merit, and bring Chinese ground forces to
battle as significant counterweights to the Japanese.

A born reformer, he refused to compromise with Chiang's palace politics. The best of the Chinese generals followed him, and their men revered him. In the desperate jungle battles of Burma, at the thin end of the Allied supply lines, he pushed back the Japanese by sheer force of leadership. In the end he was removed from China for pursuing excellence too strenuously. Chiang demanded his recall, using his prerogatives as a head of state. Roosevelt concurred—he and many in the United States still believing in the fiction, fueled by skilled PR operatives, that Nationalist China was a great power. Had Chiang gone along with Stilwell, it might have become one, but the rot in the Nationalist political leadership had festered too long.

In his autobiographical memoir *In Search of History*, Theodore White, who reported from China at that time, epitomized the failure of Stilwell's mission: "He came of a tradition which has now all but vanished—the tradition of Americans who felt so strongly we were the good people that wherever they went they were convinced they, as Americans, brought virtue. Nor could Stilwell conceive that what was good for America could possibly be bad, or wrong, for other peoples."[8]

IN THE LATE thirties, when Stilwell was military attaché in China, he occasionally met and talked with Agnes Smedley, a nervous, rawboned, talkative American woman who had come out to China in 1928 as a correspondent for the liberal German newspaper *Frankfurter Zeitung*. Like other American journalists of that time, Smedley was quickly disgusted with the corrupt, oppressive behavior of so many of Chiang Kai-shek's Nationalist followers and by contrast fascinated by the apparent dynamism and honesty of Mao Zedong's Communists in Yanan. A radical-causer since her upbringing in a Colorado mining camp—she grew up hating the Rockefellers, who apparently owned the camp—she had already worked for "anti-imperialist" Indian nationalists, established Germany's first state birth control clinic—revolutionary behavior in those days—and been jailed for overenthusiastic demonstrating by the New York police.

In China she became a good friend of Lu Xun and other literary leftists; she successfully agitated for the female poet Ding Ling's release from a Guomindang jail. An ardent feminist, she fought to accompany Chinese Communist troops in combat. Ultimately, among other writings about China, she produced a biography of her friend the "Red Napoleon," Marshal Zhu De. Later Marxist chroniclers lauded the "flaming sincerity" of her fight against injustice wherever

[8] Barbara W. Tuchman's *Stilwell and the American Experience in China* (New York: Macmillan, 1971) gives a thorough and fascinating account of Stilwell's life and times.

she found it. She traveled constantly around China. A tireless extrovert, she taught square dancing to Communist generals and nursed their wounded—anything to help those "fighting and dying for the liberation of the poor."

Like other Americans in China at that time, Smedley was fascinated by Mao Zedong—and he, at least for a time, by her. With an English-speaking Chinese woman as interpreter she and the Chairman had long talks in Yanan. Mao, Zhu De, and other Communist leaders enthusiastically joined in her square-dancing sessions. A violent personal attack on Smedley and her interpreter friend by Mao's first wife, He Zizhen, led to Mao's divorce and, not so incidentally, to Smedley's rebuff by the Communist hierarchy when she asked to join the Chinese Communist Party.[9]

In one way or another Smedley seems to have consorted with most of the leading leftists of that day, Chinese and foreign. (She was for a while the close friend of Richard Sorge, the brilliant Soviet master spy, who was later executed by the Japanese police in Tokyo.) But loyalty to the cause always took precedence with her over personal relationships. Monumentally sentimental, Agnes Smedley was an imperialist in reverse. In a pattern that many idealistic Americans followed throughout the thirties and forties, she blamed every injustice she saw on the financiers and capitalists, those of her own country being the worst of all. To her, Americans—specifically American governments and American capitalists—were the villains of imperialism, along with their European opposite numbers.

The most obvious victims were the Chinese and other exploited peoples. Socialism of the Marxist variety was their one hope. Ultimately the "people" would win, guided by the Communists and like-minded socialist humanitarians who were on the people's side. So ran her version of Holy Writ. "I work about 18 hours a day out here," she once wrote a friend, "and there is no rest even when you do no work, for the poverty of Asia . . . presses in upon you on every side . . . the capitalist system, with its imperialist development, has . . . turned [the human being] into a wolf."[10]

Over the years Smedley's writings increasingly mirrored the Communist Party line of the moment, and in her zeal to make the "people's" side look good, she grew increasingly less troubled by facts. (She described the Soviet Army's postwar looting of Manchuria's industrial plant as a laudable attempt to keep the Americans and the Nationalists from exploiting it.) But no one could question her enthusiasm. In Agnes Smedley all the energy and restless frontier

[9] Full details of this incident are given in a most interesting biography of Smedley, *Agnes Smedley: The Life and Times of an American Radical,* by Janice and Steven MacKinnon (Berkeley: University of California Press, 1988).

[10] As quoted in the MacKinnons' *Agnes Smedley.*

spirit of the American character combined to produce that interesting stereotype, the Sentimental Anti-Imperialist.

There would be many like her. And there would be others, far on the right, who would seek to brand any critic of Nationalist corruption as a Communist. Over the next half century Americans of sharply different political persuasions would find in China, after a bit of effort, exactly the causes they were looking for.

HENRY ROBINSON LUCE took the other side. Born in China in 1898, the son of the Reverend Henry Winters Luce, a missionary intellectual with a particular gift for fund raising, Harry Luce started an upstart weekly magazine called *Time* in 1923, three years after he left Yale. His partner and co-editor was a bright classmate named Britton Hadden. By 1938, when Luce moved his offices to new quarters in New York's Rockefeller Center, his company, Time, Inc.—with its three big-circulation magazines, *Time, Life,* and *Fortune*—had become America's newest, biggest, and most abiding publishing success story.

Luce was an oddity in American life, an idealistic intellectual disguised as a businessman. There was no doubting his competence at running an increasingly complex media corporation, although he had shrewd and powerful executives to help him. But he was above all an editor and an editorialist, to whom ideas and the conflict thereof were the stuff of life.

I worked for Harry Luce for eleven years, first as a *Time* correspondent and editor, later as an editorial and staff writer on *Life.* I got to know him, not well but better than most. Like most of *Time*'s editorial people, I chafed under his often dictatorial leadership. (I was once summarily transferred from my editorial-writing job for unduly roughing up the Republicans in a single commentary on Congress.) On the other hand, if you had a good idea, you could almost always get a hearing at *Time.*

If Luce seemed to possess a set of ironclad convictions, he could paradoxically almost always be reasoned with; at least he could be argued against. He was editorially incorruptible. While Luce ran Time, Inc., the advertising department was kept in its cages. Arrogant and emotionally incoherent as he was, his great redeeming feature was a reporter's curiosity. He was a perennial sucker for a new concept, an unorthodox personality, or an intellectually exciting opinion. On everything, that is, except China.

When it came to the country of his childhood, Luce was the archetypal Sentimental Imperialist. He never lost his father's missionary Presbyterian faith. His whole life was marched to the beat of "Onward, Christian Soldiers"; he was never one to use the word "crusader" with a smile. Rare for his time, he had a feeling for Asia and its traditions. "Racism" was not in his dictionary.

Mao in the Cultural Revolution (1966). Most American China scholars, ignoring the horrors of this period, continued to see Mao's China through rose-colored glasses. Encyclopedia of China

Agnes Smedley. Her view of China was the opposite of Henry Luce's. Here she is pictured in uniform with Communist Fourth Army troops in Anhui in 1939.
Archives and Manuscripts, University Libraries of Arizona State University, Tempe

He loved and admired the Chinese people as much as he loved America. He desperately wanted China to become a democracy—and Christian.

Sadly, Chiang Kai-shek was Harry's man. A converted Methodist general with a beautiful (and Christian) Wellesley-educated wife looked to him like heaven-sent leadership. China's struggle against Japan had the stuff of heroism to Luce—particularly when described in the chattily apocalyptic prose of a *Time* cover story. (Between 1936 and 1955 Chiang drew ten of them.)

Most Americans agreed with him, at least at first. Through the thirties millions of Americans had either read Pearl Buck's *The Good Earth,* a loving, idealized account of Chinese peasant life (whose author also came from a missionary family), or seen the hugely successful movie made from it in 1937— the same year Japan's Kwantung Army started its invasion of China. Americans everywhere identified with the quietly heroic farmer Wang Lung and Olan, his wife, on their way to the local chop suey parlor after the movie. A flood of other books and films drew a glowing picture of the Chinese, down to comic strips and the folksy Charlie Chan movies. (Interestingly, both Charlie Chan and the Chinese couple in *The Good Earth* were played by Westerners.) *Time's* fondness for China was quite representative.

Early in the Pacific war, however, Americans on the scene in China—both journalists and diplomats—began to report that all was not well with the Nationalists. Cruelly wounded by Japanese invasion and occupation, Chiang Kai-shek's government gradually lost control of the country. With its many competent and idealistic bureaucrats and businessmen—the best of the maritime Chinese—uprooted by the Japanese from the modernized coastal cities, Chiang's government grew ever more corrupt, dictatorial, and almost impossible to work with. Americans like General Stilwell found this out the hard way.

By contrast, the Chinese Communists looked good; on their way to power, they were still on their best behavior. They came across, John W. Service, one of the State Department's China-based diplomats, said, as "capable, committed people." An American military mission sent to the Communists' stronghold in Yanan recommended that the United States help them, as well as the Nationalists, in the fight against Japan. Had the Americans worked then with the Communists—or alternatively insisted on Stilwell's prescription for a strong, corruption-free Nationalist Army—history might have turned out differently.

Luce couldn't see it that way. His image of a budding Christian democracy in Nationalist China was too rich and vivid for reality to obscure it. *Time* and *Life* began to steer the news in favor of the Nationalists. Correspondents in the field who disagreed with the Chiang Kai-shek vision had to leave. Through the forties and into the fifties Luce and his magazines became part of an oddly assorted group of influential Americans known as the China Lobby.

Spearheaded in Washington by a former China medical missionary turned congressman named Walter H. Judd—and heavily funded by an unscrupulous right-wing propagandist named Alfred Kohlberg—a variety of like-minded souls tried to convince the United States, government and public, that Chiang Kai-shek, badly maligned by liberals and "pro-Communists," was really doing a good job and had to be supported at all costs. From this position it was easy to move on to a "conspiracy" theory. Many did. Right-wing politicians and journalists were quick to develop the idea that American had somehow "lost" China because of bad propaganda. Had we backed Chiang more heavily, the argument ran, the Nationalists would be winning.

At this point a homemade demagogue named Joseph McCarthy got into the act. Thanks to the vagaries of Wisconsin politics, McCarthy became a United States senator in 1946 and served for two disastrous terms. A quick-witted talker with a flair for publicity, he flung about a series of widely circulated but totally unproven charges about Communists infiltrating the U.S. State Department. Given the temper of the times, with Soviet pressure increasing on Europe and Communist Chinese armies attacking U.S. troops in Korea, he attracted a huge and gullible audience of supporters in his "anti-Communist crusade." He denounced the factual reporting of diplomats like Service, John Carter Vincent, and John Paton Davies, Jr., on the growth and popularity of Mao Zedong's Communists as the work of hidden Communist agents. To the everlasting disgrace of President Dwight Eisenhower and Secretary of State John Foster Dulles, they never publicly questioned this scoundrel's accusations or his motives in making them. (After all, McCarthy's supporters voted Republican.) Thanks in great measure to their silence, McCarthy's random and totally unsubstantiated charges drove Service, Vincent, Davies, and many others from their jobs.

McCarthy was finally formally censured by his fellow senators in 1954 and passed into obscurity. But his witch hunt, abetted by obsessed "anti-Communist" security investigators in the Federal Bureau of Investigation and other government agencies, wrought incalculable damage and injustice. The McCarthyites deprived the country of some of its ablest China experts, at a time when they were most needed.[11]

Harry Luce was no friend of McCarthy. *Time* and his other magazines courageously attacked the witch hunt from the beginning. But Luce continued to push the cause of Chiang, now exiled to Taiwan with the remnants of his

[11] Service and the others were finally vindicated, but only after recourse to the courts. Practically speaking, their careers were ruined by McCarthy's scattershot charges. Other distinguished diplomats, like the late John Emmerson, ironically a Japan rather than a China expert, were denied promotions they would normally have received because of the cloud cast over them by McCarthy's lies.

Nationalist armies. Many Americans, Time, Inc., editorialists among them, continued to believe that the United States had "lost" China because we had withdrawn support from the Nationalists. How else could all those good Nationalist American-educated Christians have gone wrong?

The bulk of public opinion, however, was not with them. As the news came of UN troops cut off by "human wave" attacks of Chinese Communist troops in Korea, the old "horde" images of Boxer Rebellion days were pulled out of the closet. Lost to America, China was now the enemy, caught hopelessly in the vise of international Communism. Mao Zedong and his propagandists reciprocated, their chorus of vituperation even more intense than Foster Dulles's legal maledictions. And so for twenty years the situation remained.

JAPAN, ON THE other hand, had become a friend. The "slant-eyed devils" who had bombed Pearl Harbor and committed unspeakable wartime atrocities were transformed, thanks to MacArthur's Occupation, into friendly apprentices of American democracy. Back came the images of Commodore Perry's eager learners. By the mid-fifties, the Japanese, having apparently repented the error of their ways, were being lauded by American statesmen and editorialists as the new standard bearers of democracy in Asia, a "bridge between East and West," as Vice President Hubert Humphrey later put it.

Americans eagerly read *Windows for the Crown Prince*, the new best-seller by the American Quaker lady who tutored Akihito. Art-theater movie audiences rhapsodized over Kurosawa's *Rashomon*, *Ugetsu Monogatari*, and other Japanese films, while New York crowds enthusiastically visited the new Japanese house at the Museum of Modern Art. Senators praised Japan's stalwart anti-Communism, while sensitive visitors to Japan redoubled their apologies for Hiroshima's A-bomb. The wheel had come full circle. By 1961, the first postwar year when more than 100,000 American tourists visited Japan, *Life* was contentedly running articles on Japanese Zen.

If we had "lost" China, we would seem to have gained Japan. During the Korean War and thereafter, as we have seen, Japan became a new "bastion of democracy" and, not so incidentally, anti-Communism in the Pacific. Despite talk of "equal partnership" at diplomatic conferences, the American political relationship with Japan was clearly that of teacher and learner, leader and follower. It was the story of "our little brown [for which read yellow] brothers" all over again. This time we had everything but the missionaries. Despite the wave of protests from the left in 1960 and 1961, most Japanese became comfortable with the new relationship. They were happy to trade postwar despair for the beginnings of affluence, building up their economy under the protective shield of the Japan–United States Security Treaty.

*   *   *

THE OLD AMERICAN romance with China was not dead, however. The Chinese side of the perdurable America-China-Japan triangle revived, spectacularly, on February 21, 1972, when President Richard M. Nixon stepped out of Air Force One at Beijing Airport, to be greeted by the waiting Chinese Premier, Zhou Enlai. The seemingly strange rapproachement, prepared by Henry Kissinger's exploratory trip the year before, was a logical development in the power politics of the time. Mao had broken with the Soviet Union in 1963, when he publicly denounced Nikita Khrushchev as a "revisionist." Since that time the gap between the two Communist superpowers had widened, to the point of actual fighting along their extensive common borders.

Both China and the United States had much to gain by getting together. China, wasted more than any outsider then realized by the disasters of Mao's socioeconomic experiments and the mindless destruction of the Cultural Revolution, needed economic and technological help from the West. Mao also sought actual security protection against the Soviets. The United States, still hard pressed in Vietnam, was eager to play the strategic "China card" against the Russians. And Nixon, ever the pragmatist, could use a spectacular diplomatic victory.

Machtpolitik by itself, however, was not enough to sell the new transpacific *entente cordiale* to the American people. We had to have a romance, in the best Sentimental Imperialist tradition. There followed a massive outpouring of pro-Chinese sentiment. Right and left collaborated in a rediscovery of China, the new Maoist China, as it happened. The resultant wave of long-husbanded China fascination handily combined anti-Soviet and anti-elitist sentiment— something for everybody. Yet, as events proved, the new China's beauty, as with Chiang Kai-shek's Nationalist Christian country a generation before, resided firmly in the eye of the beholder.

Finally let loose in China after twenty years of turned-down requests for visas, American journalists readily expanded on Nixon's enthusiasm for the trip. The *New York Times* delegation by itself performed prodigies of enthusiastic reporting. Max Frankel, later to become the *Times*'s editor, praised the selfless community spirit of the Cultural Revolution. His colleague Seymour Topping was struck by the "communal democracy" of the Maoist farming communes, while columnist James Reston, after comparing Mao's revolution to "one vast cooperative barn-raising," lauded China's "tremendous effort to bring out what is best in man." Harrison Salisbury, the *Time*'s resident expert on various forms of Communism, saw the Maoist millions typifying "a new spirit among men, a contagious spirit, one on which China could build. But could America match it?" Visiting one of the May Seventh schools for cadres, he described it as "a combination of a YMCA camp and a Catholic retreat."

These were largely social and political judgments. For those American newspaper readers who wanted practical information on the Maoist economy, Harvard's economist John K. Galbraith was there to reassure them. "The Chinese economy," he wrote, "isn't the American or the European future. But it is the Chinese future. And let there be no doubt: for the Chinese, it works."

Galbraith's travel diary of that era, as Sheila Johnson's prescient commentary noted,[12] "consists almost exclusively of descriptions of palaces visited and banquets consumed." Harrison Salisbury's account of his travels reads much the same. ("As each course was served, Mme. Soong rose in her chair . . . and insisted on serving me, as is the Chinese custom . . . Soon we were eating enormous prawns, and then a Peking fish . . .") Travelers to China would learn, over the next two decades, that the capacity of the Maoist "New Class" officialdom for political banqueting and purposefully guided touring was boundless. "One is tempted to conclude from [reading] these recitals," Johnson wrote, "that one of China's great secret weapons is its cuisine."

The banquets and the guided tours concealed from China's visitors (Nixon and Kissinger among them) the grim reality of a country in chaos. In fact, the May Seventh schools proved to be brutally run penal labor camps for ideological "reeducation." The "communal democracy" communes were largely forced resettlements of farming families under tight and ruthless Party control. The effort to create Mao's "new being" had resulted in the ghastly Cultural Revolution. This ten-year-long terror destroyed China's administration and education system, killed hundreds of thousands, and imprisoned or sent into remote rural exile more than 20 million, despite Galbraith's reassurances to his American readers. ("There is a hint in the thought of Mao Zedong that a periodic churning up is necessary.") The economy—both agriculture and industry—was already in ruins after the backyard furnaces and forced plantings of the Great Leap Forward. That portion of the intelligentsia that had survived the 800,000 arrests of Mao's Anti-Rightist campaign had been beaten and vilified during the Cultural Revolution. In the countryside whole counties still mourned the wholesale deaths of the famine of 1960–62, in which at least 20 million paid with their lives for Mao's experiments combining economics with ideologue politics.

A great deal of information about the true state of affairs in China had already been received in the West. Refugees escaping to Hong Kong were a

---

[12] The social anthropologist Sheila Johnson wrote a classic article in *Commentary* (June 1973) titled "To China, with Love," from which some of these quotations are borrowed. Of more recent vintage, Steven W. Mosher's *China Misperceived* (New Republic Books, 1990) summarizes the runaway enthusiasm of American scholars and journalists in their China reporting.

major source of information. But with a few distinguished exceptions—Roderick MacFarquahar, Lucian Pye, Simon Leys, and Ladislav Ladany among them—anything contrary to the newly respectable official China (and Kissinger) line was ignored by most American academic specialists on China. Through the sixties and seventies the normally liberal academic community, its ready sense of injustice powerfully fueled by the Vietnam War, began demonstrating with a vengeance against capitalism, parliamentary democracy, and that body of shared beliefs which as recently as World War II was still called patriotism. Sudden exposure to China gave many of these tenured radicals two surefire exemplars: Marx and Mao. Why can't Americans, the professorial chorus ran, be selfless, moral, and collectively whole like the newly rediscovered Maoist Chinese? Agnes Smedley would have applauded the question.

Even as respected an academic as Harvard's John K. Fairbank, long the dean of American China scholarship, could write in *Foreign Affairs*, after several weeks in China in 1972: "The Maoist revolution is on the whole the best thing that has happened to the Chinese people in many centuries. At least, most Chinese seem now to believe so . . . under Mao the Chinese Revolution has become not only an advance in the industrial arts, creating a new technology and a new class structure, but also a far-reaching moral crusade." According to Professor Fairbank, such phenomena as the Cultural Revolution sought only "to put the process of change into the hands of the People, who were mainly villagers, under the necessary guidance of a new leadership purged of bureaucratic evils." Its "consolidation," as Fairbank then saw it, led to "a sense of relaxation and euphoria that makes 1972 a happy time to be in China."

Less than seven years later, Deng Xiaoping and other survivors of the Cultural Revolution disclosed to the world the miasma of corruption, bureaucratic infighting, vicious persecution, economic disaster, and moral dissolution that lay beneath the surface of Fairbank's "happy time" in China. Faced with the revelation that the pure-minded "anti-elitist" standard bearers of the Cultural Revolution had been beating people to death with lead pipes—with Mao's blessing—the worshipful China scholars began a massive run for cover. It continues to this day. As blind to Mao's defects as the old China Lobby had been to Chiang's, the Reverse Imperialists of "concerned" scholarship have yet to regain their lost credibility.[13] (Some continue to hold that China only started to slip when Deng began to promote economic modernization—for which read capitalism—in violation of Mao's sacred scriptures.) Writing for

[13] Fairbank in later writings denounced the persecution in Maoist labor camps. He was already under attack by savants like James Peck in the Concerned Asian Scholars' bulletin for "his internalization of the rightist world-view, that is the surviving legacy of McCarthyism . . ." The book detailing the Concerned Scholars' report of their trip in the seventies—*China! Inside the People's Republic*—makes amusing reading today.

The New York Review of Books in 1991, Jonathan Mirsky recalled his 1979 meeting with the same guide who had escorted him and fellow members of the Concerned Asian Scholars Committee in 1972. "We wanted to deceive you," the young Chinese Party member admitted, "but you wanted to be deceived."

Deng Xiaoping's reforms provoked yet another wave of good feeling among most Americans, businessmen and Reagan Republicans included—and this time quite justly, for the old image of Mao's Communist Party has been shattered. Yet here again we prematurely tried to project rosy American hopes into the very mixed Chinese reality. The Tiananmen massacre in 1989 was thus far more of a shock than it should have been. The mixed feelings about how to deal with Deng and his last-ditch leadership since that time reflect nothing so much as the classic tension of the Sentimental Imperialists between moral judgment, business as usual, and the needs, real or fancied, of big-power politics. China being China, however, even the faded arrogance of Deng's bureaucrats defending their oppression is treated with a tolerance that Washington hardly displays in other situations. America's romance with the Middle Kingdom continues, even when the love is unrequited.

THE SAME CANNOT be said of Japan. Once again, in the seventies, the pendulum here swung back from affection to animosity. Pride in America's dutiful political apprentice gave way to anger at America's successful economic competitor. The era of "Japan bashing" began in the late seventies and has continued.

I have dealt elsewhere with Japan's rise to Economic Superpowerdom, the resulting vast trade imbalances with the United States, and the oddly symbiotic relationship of the United States and Japan—politically, socially, and culturally. Here I should like to address two major factors: the mounting virulence of Americans' reaction to Japan's economic "aggression" and the concurrent growth in Americans' knowledge for and interest in Japan. They constitute a fascinating paradox.

On July 25, 1985, *The New York Times* devoted most of its Sunday magazine section to an article by Theodore H. White titled "The Danger from Japan." Taking as his point of departure the surrender ceremony aboard the USS *Missouri* on August 2, 1945, forty years before, White set forth his thesis that Japan's government-supported invasion of American consumer markets, while protecting its own industries at home, amounts to total economic warfare. Considering trade surpluses, investment strategies, financial domination, and all, White summarized: "The Japanese provoke American wrath because they are a locked and closed civilization that reciprocates our hushed fear with veiled contempt." It was not a fair commentary. Since reporting on Japan's ruthless invasion of China in the thirties, White had cordially hated the Japanese, to the point of refusing to visit that country after the war.[14] In the article he constantly invoked comparisons to World War II, to the point of warning the Japanese that their trade tactics might meet the same end as the attack on Pearl Harbor. White's article did not deserve the attention given to it. But its timing was deadly. In a sense it set the leitmotif for a steady series of TV and print exposé stories about Japan's economic aggression against the United States.

There was, of course, a good bit of truth in them. Japanese business's elbows-out pursuit of the American market, combined with its heavy cultural and economic protectionism at home, was hard to excuse. But there were many extenuating circumstances, not least of all the tendency of American administrations to overlook economic threat as long as Japan stayed obediently anti-Communist. As we have noted in previous chapters, American business, in contrast, deeply eroded its own competitive worth by its excessive short-term profit taking, its unproductive takeovers, and the greed of its executives.

It is always easier, however, to blame internal trouble on outsiders. The Japanese, clannish and characteristically inarticulate outside their own group society, naturally fitted this role. They started thinking about public relations and corporate citizenship in their American companies roughly fifteen years too late. Meanwhile "Japan bashing" has continued, as more authors and editors warm to their obsessive theme—e.g., *The Japanese Conspiracy* and *The Coming War with Japan*. By the early nineties a new crop of breathless "Japanese world conspiracy" novels had sprouted in the bookstores. There is an underlying racial aspect to this criticism. And it was given a kind of legitimacy not merely by the overassertive tactics of Japanese business leaders but also by the crude and witless remarks of Japanese public figures at home about blacks and other American racial minorities. (One of the drawbacks of instant international communication is the impossibility of restricting political leaders' comment to domestic audiences only; round-the-world playback is now almost inevitable.)

By the nineties, the ninja-world-conspiracy, cloak-and-samurai-sword adventure stories of Eric van Lustbader were succeeded by a smoother variant of the anti-Japanese novel, in which Japanese big businessmen are going about their work of world domination and conquest as relentlessly as Fu Manchu and his Chinese hit men of the thirties.[15] While Clive Cussler's best-selling *Dragon*,

[14] The late Teddy White was a friend of almost forty years' standing. Although he had good things to say about some of my writings on Japan, I found he showed a consistent blind spot about even discussing Japan. His mind-set in this respect remained frozen in the Chongqing (Chung-king) of the thirties.

[15] In *The Japanese Through American Eyes* (Stanford, Calif: Stanford University Press, 1991), Sheila Johnson traces the rise of this literary genre, among other similar phenomena.

with its tale of ultranationalist Japanese businessmen building their own secret A-bombs, can be dismissed as adventuring, such a distinguished stylist as John Updike, in *Rabbit at Rest,* produces his own caricature of the ruthless Japanese businessman. What chance has poor Rabbit as his Toyota franchise is taken away by nasty (but so polite) Mr. Shimada. The Japanese, Shimada assures him, "have great respect for United States. Rike big brother. But in recent times big brother act rike rittle brother. Always cry and comprain . . ."

Michael Crichton's *Rising Sun,* another instant best-seller, is the most sophisticated product of this new cottage industry. A very readable combination of a murder mystery with an exposé of Japanese adversarial business run amok on American soil, his book contains numerous examples of various unsavory Japanese trade practices. Some of them are quite correct when taken in isolation. Their cumulative effect, however, in a book larded with hoked-up Japanese phrases and constant reminders of how "the Japanese" all behave with the predictability of Pavlov's dogs chasing a fox, adds up to a massive half-truth. Reading Updike and Crichton on the Japanese character recalls the way Mrs. Trollope used to go on about the Americans.

They should be taken seriously, however. For they reflect the result of mistakes and heedless behavior by Americans as much as Japanese. When national (and partly racist) criticism leaves the op-ed page and goes into novels, it is time to worry.

There remains some reason to hope that the Japan bashing of the 1990s is less substantial than the racist and denigratory comments of past decades. For every Japan basher, there are more Americans who now know vastly more about Japan than they used to—and show an intelligent, relatively informed interest in the Japanese. Japanese food, Japanese films—this time comedies like *A Taxing Woman* and *Tanpopo* rather than period samurai dramas—Japanese art and architecture have become commonplace on the American scene, as well as the ubiquitous Japanese cars and electronic appliances. An extraordinary amount of Japanese fiction, compared with past years, is being published. Japanese fashions are well reviewed. Japanese students are flocking to the United States for college as well as language study (their elders sometimes buying small American colleges in the process).

In short, Japanese are at last becoming part of the American cast of international characters, along with the Europeans. Good, bad, or indifferent, they have become factors in our lives, rather than objects of exotica. This has always been true of the American presence in Japan. Apart from the obvious fact that Japan and the United States, as we have seen, constitute two halves of a vast macroeconomy, this new cultural affinity, even if admittedly far stronger in the western part of the United States than the eastern, is the best possible anchor for a lasting and mutually beneficial transpacific relationship.

*   *   *

A CENTURY AGO, as we have noted, Frederick Jackson Turner would write of America's western frontier as representing "a gate of escape from the bondage of the past; the freshness and confidence and scorn of older society, impatience with its restraints and its ideas." As Americans have thrust themselves across the Pacific, this same freshness of approach—despite the crime, the drugs, and the moral confusion raging throughout the great Republic—remains a powerful force of attraction to all our transpacific neighbors. There is strength as well as diversity within this pluralist society.

The sense of imperium remains. For all the talk of economic power replacing political, the Sentimental Imperialists, following the decay and defeat of world-aggressive Communism, are the arbiters of international politics.

Harry Luce's famous article, "The American Century," which he wrote for *Life* in February 1941, contained some memorable words. Unjustly maligned for many years, it was written primarily as a plea for Americans to forsake isolationism and take up the cudgels against the Axis powers in World War II, but it is worth reading today.

"In the field of national policy," he wrote, "the fundamental trouble with Americans has been, and is, that whereas their nation became in the 20th century the most powerful and the most vital nation in the world, nevertheless Americans were unable to accommodate themselves spiritually and practically to that fact. Hence they have failed to play their part as a world power—a failure which has had disastrous consequences for themselves and for all mankind. And the cure is this: to accept wholeheartedly our duty and our opportunity as the most powerful and vital nation in the world and in consequence to exert upon the world the full impact of our influence, for such purposes as we see fit and by such means as we see fit."

Modern Americans would argue a lot about the statement. The Sentimental Imperialists are still trying to sort out where international morality and its preachment ends, where power politics and its implementation begins, and how we fit our old ideals to the pulls and pushes of an era in which economic power is in the end more important than military.

Until recently, at least, both the international duty and the opportunity of which Luce wrote have largely been accepted. But as the troubling decade of the nineties unfolds, fast-changing circumstances have made both subject to review and redefinition.

19

Pan-Asians and All-Americans

Of every hue and caste am I, of every rank and religion . . .
FROM "AMERICA," BY WALT WHITMAN

*The Japs have played our game because they have played the game of
civilized mankind . . .*
THEODORE ROOSEVELT, IN A LETTER TO CECIL SPRING-RICE,
WRITTEN IN JUNE 1904, DURING THE RUSSO-JAPANESE WAR

I n the foregoing chapters we have tried to chart the emergence and progress
of a Pacific world. Our object was, in the first instance, to show how the
nations and cultures on the great Pacific's shores have developed, over the past
century and a half, a certain community. This community is based on an
increasingly obvious interdependence of economies, polities, and modern lifestyles, as well as an increasing interplay of beliefs and traditions once thought
hopelessly disparate. Most specifically, we have addressed ourselves to the role
that Americans and their country have played in building this community.

It would have been easier, perhaps, to have concentrated on the dramatic
development of East Asia and its dynamic new economies; on the surface, this
would have seemed of itself a tidy story to tell. But an Asia-Pacific story, if more
discrete, would have been woefully inadequate. For the part played by the
United States in the history of this new and self-conscious region has been vital
and decisive. Indeed, an examination of the resources of the Pacific world and
the regional and global challenges it faces strongly suggests that without the
United States the Pacific world has no future.

The Europeans, it is true, were the first to knock at Asia's Pacific back door.

Their imperialism, based on military firepower and economic exploitation, was rude and intrusive. High-minded cultural colonizers like Ricci and Raffles were exceptions to the rule. The spoliation of China, like the occupation of Indonesia and Vietnam, left a legacy of grievance that lingers. Along with their plantations and proconsuls, however, the Europeans brought the beginnings of modernization. The promise (and threat) of industrial civilization was to agitate East Asia throughout the nineteenth century.

The Japanese were the first to respond to the challenge. But if the massive transformation of the Meiji era was done by the Japanese themselves, it was the American "opening" of Japan that provided the impetus for change. The arrival of Commodore Perry's ships in Tokyo Bay began a complex relationship between Japanese and Americans—respect and fear, teaching and learning, trading and boycotting, which has lasted to this day.

In the twentieth century most of the calls for Asian modernization were made in an American accent. Machines and missionaries were exported from the homeland of Manifest Destiny, with the promise that emulating the American way was the passport to better living in this world, not to mention salvation in the next.

With the people and products came the American political message, the ideal of a working democracy based on the rule of law and individual human rights. From Sun Yat-sen in 1911 to Ho Chi Minh in 1945, reformers quoted the Declaration of Independence as a model for their own people's liberation.

The pervasiveness of this American influence was often little realized by the Americans themselves; judging at least by the scant mention of Asia in his writings and biographies, it is doubtful that Woodrow Wilson knew (or much cared) how explosive a message his Fourteen Points gave to oppressed Koreans and Chinese in 1919. Other Americans, before and after Wilson's time, realized the stake their country had in the Pacific. However much their premises differed, Matthew Perry, William Seward, Theodore Roosevelt, Douglas MacArthur, and Leighton Stuart had shared the same vision. Yet the people as a whole were far from internationalist in their interests. Nativist racism back home made Asians realize the dark and prejudiced side of that word "all-American." The anti-Asian immigration exclusion acts of the early twenties were not very Jeffersonian.

Japan's Meiji revolution of 1868 had a more immediate effect on Asians than American exhortation and example. Not only had the Japanese proved capable of beating the Westerners at their own game. But they had adapted the Western nation-state to fit more familiar Asian standards of authority. Most important for the future, they had worked out the prototype of the development-directed economy that would be the model of East Asia's dynamic Newly Industrializing Countries (NICs) a century later.

Like the export version of America's 1776, Japan's self-modernization developed contradictions that have yet to be solved. On the one hand was the democratic idealism of internationalist thinkers like Fukuzawa Yukichi and Mori Arinori; on the other the emperor-centered "Japanism" of the soldier Yamagata Aritomo and militarist fanatics like Kita Ikki. From victory over the Russians at Port Arthur to attack on the Americans at Pearl Harbor, Japan's twentieth-century ideologues preached "Pan-Asianism," but only with Japan as Asia's racist leader.

Yet here again America intervened. In one of history's great ironies it took an American military occupation to purge the Meiji modernization of its built-in militarist aftereffects and turn the Japanese toward peaceful, albeit aggressive economic aggrandizement.

The Meiji Restoration and the American Revolution shared their influence in the Pacific world, as we have seen, with the more spectacular Russian Revolution. But Russian influence, although sufficient to inspire and train the first generation of Asian Communist leaders, was ultimately rejected as a transplant. It was displaced by Mao's Chinese Communist Revolution, which for a time seemed like the Pacific wave of the future.

Here another irony intervened. Mao proscribed Confucianism from its Chinese homeland. Along with reformers like Lu Xun, he denounced its hierarchical mandarinate as obscurantist. Yet the virtues of ancient "family" Confucianism—its group loyalties, its obsession with education, and its docility before authority—survived as the work ethic of dynamic new maritime Chinese economies in Singapore, Hong Kong, and Taiwan. All three of these countries are Sinic or largely Sinic societies. But if we were to pull up the hood and examine the increasingly fast-purring economic machines in the other ASEAN countries—specifically Indonesia, Malaysia, and Thailand—we would find that there, too, businessmen of Chinese stock predominate. The two largest conglomerates in Indonesia, for example, are owned and operated by Chinese: Liem Sioe Liong's Salim complex (which contributes some 5 percent of the country's national product) and Edward Soeryadjaya's Astra group. Quite a few of Indonesia's best technocrats, as well, are Chinese with Indonesian names.

In recent years tens of thousands of these overseas Chinese have brought their talents across the Pacific to the United States and Canada (where Vancouver contains one of the world's most prosperous Chinese populations). They form the latest wave of the Chinese diaspora. Their ingenuity, engineering skills, and entrepreneurial spirit have given new life to the high-tech R&D emporia in California's Silicon Valley. Back in China the same kind of skilled industry is turning Guangdong and other coastal provinces, well colonized by Hong Kong and Taiwan, into prosperous market economy enclaves strong enough to resist the statist controls remaining to the old Communist mandarins in Beijing.

For all these new market economies the American consumer, as we have noted, has been the engine of Pacific growth, just as American technology has given the impetus for new production. First Japan and then Korea put new-model economies together on the strength of exports to the United States. Singapore depends heavily on offshore outposts of American conglomerates—Taiwan even more so. Almost one-quarter of East Asia's exports continue to go to the United States.

As these East Asian economies grow, they have developed considerable consumer buying power on their own. They offer growing markets for American exports where such exports are promoted and sold. They do not, however, do business the way Americans do. There is little room in their crowded economic temples for Adam Smith's invisible hand, Federal Trade Commissions, or the Sherman Antitrust Act. All of the fast-growing East Asian economies—Thailand, Malaysia, and Indonesia as well as the storied Little Tigers of Korea, Taiwan, Hong Kong, and Singapore—have hewn more or less closely to the Japanese model. Albeit with local variations, they have tended to copy the original alliance of government, business, and finance that powered the catch-up economy of Japan since Meiji. Guided by energetic bureaucracies, private business has generally thrived under authoritarian governments.

Nonetheless, political democracy is on the rise. As people prosper—in what *The Economist* once called "the fastest industrial revolution the world has ever seen"—they have shown more and more concern about their governance. Here American ideals and democratic practice have had considerable influence, even when American diplomacy was wanting. It is hard to underrate the importance of American incentive, for example, in the Republic of Korea's move from authoritarianism toward democracy, impelled by the growth of a middle-class consumer society. We have noted a similar tendency in Taiwan. Even Beijing's rulers have not been heedless of American voices demanding greater respect for basic human rights.

In sum, the United States can take credit for much of the soaring prosperity on the western shores of the Pacific. Free access to American markets, with low preferential tariffs for the underdeveloped, was essential to the success of most of these export-oriented economies, including in the early days Japan's. As we have noted before, the swelling trade imbalances that resulted for the United States were only partly due to the aggressive selling of export-directed, government-assisted Asian economies. An equally important factor was the pious belief of Washington's neoclassical economists and the successive administrations they advised that, despite American industry's falling productivity, international markets would somehow regulate themselves.

Most important of all, however, was the matter of priorities. From the early days of the Cold War the emphasis of American policy in the Pacific was on the political and the military. Economic relationships were seen as merely part of a policy to fight the spread of Communism in the Asia-Pacific countries. Over the span of almost a half century, despite appalling errors and miscalculations, the policy succeeded. It could hardly be called altruistic; American strategic planners thought of bases in Japan or the Philippines as vital to *American* global interests. Yet without this security policy the considerable stability of the region—not to mention its prosperity—would not have been possible.

Let us briefly review that record. In the Cold War forties, East Asia was a primary danger area. Mao Zedong's "liberation" of China had been followed by Kim Il Sung's invasion of South Korea. The Communist insurgency in the Malayan jungles was no sooner settled than the firmament of French control was shattered by Ho Chi Minh in Vietnam. Given the American mind-set of the Cold War, made firmer by the aggressive behavior of Chinese and Soviet regimes, security became the No. 1 priority. To Washington's strategic planners, the national security of the United States became inseparable from containment of an apparently monolithic "world Communism," wherever it was perceived in operation. One country's fall to Communism, it was felt, would bring on another's. The "domino theory," first enunciated by President Dwight Eisenhower at a press conference in 1954, had begun its long life.

Starting with the "reverse course" in Occupation Japan, in which the original objectives of "democratization" were sacrificed in favor of a strong economic and political buildup, Washington as a matter of policy decided to offer every possible bit of aid and trade to the non-Communist nations of East Asia. The objective was to keep the Asia-Pacific countries economically stable so they would remain politically anti-Communist. "Asia," Eisenhower had said, "has already lost some 450 million of its peoples to the Communist dictatorship, and we simply can't afford greater losses."

Even after America's self-imposed disaster in Vietnam, American diplomacy tried to build up Japan, Korea, and the other non-Communist nations in a restored anti-Moscow front. When President Richard Nixon effected his celebrated rapprochement with Mao Zedong in the seventies, Washington strategists saw this primarily as a way to use a "China card" against the Soviet Union.

The national security of the United States was so linked to "free world" solidarity that soaring trade balances unfavorable to America became a secondary consideration. Japan's bureaucrats and businessmen are no fools. At any point over the past fifteen years strong American insistence on reciprocity of treatment in American and Japanese markets could have produced results— much as did the Nixon surcharge on Japanese imports. Yet throughout the eighties no serious consistent measures were taken to deal with this growing economic problem. While U.S. Trade Representatives and Commerce Department negotiators were left to jaw away at unfair Japanese trade practices on specific items—from metal baseball bat imports to Japanese tangerine growers' protectionism—the White House and the State Department continued to assure Japanese governments that anti-Communism and Japan's political solidarity with the free world was all that really mattered.

Over the four and a half decades from 1945 to 1990—and setting aside the staggering expenses for the Vietnam War—the United States contributed some $71 billion in development aid, loans, technical assistance, and other means of economic support to the Asian nations on the western side of the Pacific Rim. The sums were far greater than earlier outlays for the Marshall Plan in Europe. In fact, the American effort in the Asia-Pacific region constituted a second and continuing Marshall Plan in all but name.

Despite wastage, ill-founded assumptions, and false starts, the results in the Asia-Pacific nations were impressive. Technical assistance laid the groundwork for future Asian high-growth economies; so did American insistence on land reform—sadly ineffective, as we have shown, only in the Philippines. Not least of all, generations of postwar Asian students began to take their training in American universities, assisted by liberal U.S. government aid programs. Students with graduate degrees from Harvard, MIT, Princeton, and Berkeley went home to staff the businesses and bureaucracies of the NICs, as indeed they do to this day.

Guaranteeing Pacific economic growth was American military strength: overwhelming air and sea power such as Admiral Mahan hardly dreamed of, backed by the garrisons of U.S. bases off the Asian coast, from Chitose in Hokkaido to Luzon's Subic Bay. Asian nations did not mind being thus protected. A threat did indeed exist. Given the ominous increases in Soviet Pacific forces through the 1970s, plus the aggressive presence of well-armed Soviet surrogates in Vietnam and North Korea, the American security blanket was welcome. And the presence of U.S. forces in Japan obviated any problems, real or fancied, with a "resurgent" Japanese militarism. It was understood by all concerned that accepting cover under the American security blanket also meant ceding political initiative to the Americans who provided it.

UNTIL THE closing years of the eighties this trade-off of possible economic disadvantage for perceived political and military hegemony remained an article of faith in Washington. The few businessmen and economists who warned about Japanese competition and American productivity loss were dismissed as alarmist. But with the thaw in Eastern Europe, followed by the disintegration of Soviet power, the long-established imperatives for America's national policy vanished. The Evil Empire, it was suddenly discovered, had no clothes.

With the world's geopolitical map thus redrawn, it was time to think of a

The Good Old Days? U.S. battleship firing at Japanese positions on Okinawa, just before the landing on April 1, 1945. World War II established American military hegemony in the Pacific.
Library of Congress

Prince Ito. In the newly emerging nations, Japan's Meiji Revolution's example had tremendous influence.
Hagi City Board of Education

Pearl Harbor on V-J Day. But the end of World War II only began four troubled decades of "little wars." U.S. Navy

new set of priorities. People's attitudes had also changed, on both sides of the Pacific. For many years both the brilliance and the persistency of the revolutionary catch-up economics of East Asia had been either ignored or undervalued both by the U.S. government and by most American businesses. Foreign economics—except for aid programs—seems to have been little studied in Washington. Going into the nineties, however, and facing ever grimmer economic statistics, Americans grew far more concerned with exports and unemployment at home than with world strategic superiority. By 1989, American trade with Japan showed an imbalance of $45 billion; the deficit with the NICs—Korea, Taiwan, Hong Kong, and Singapore—had climbed to fully $20 billion. Celebrating the fiftieth anniversary of Pearl Harbor, a variety of American politicians and business leaders were quick to conjure up a Japanese economic menace to replace the shopworn threat of Soviet Communism. Others were already zeroing in on Taiwan or, with more justice, on the People's Republic of China, which by 1990 enjoyed a favorable trade balance of well over $10 billion with the United States (at least a portion of which resulted from the sale of products from its prison camps).

Similarly, a generation of newly prosperous Asians showed increasing impatience with the American military presence. With the Communist threat gone, who needed protection? American denunciations of Japanese and other Asian trade protectionism, however, had aroused considerable resentment. Korean and Japanese farm groups loudly demonstrated against efforts to break their local monopolies, while various Japanese pressure groups—from construction companies to toy manufacturers—fought off spasmodic American efforts to open their markets to international competition.

The final activation of Western Europe's economic union in 1992 posed serious questions of its own for the exporters of East Asia, now doing business on a worldwide scale, and the government strategists behind them. So did the possibility of a North American trade bloc with Canada and Mexico joining the United States. This was viewed by most Asians as a threat (although many Japanese firms, with plants already set up in Mexico, saw it as an enlarged opportunity). With the American presence—militarily and economically—in apparent retreat, what possibilities were open for a new balance of power in the Pacific?

Was the answer, as Malaysia's Mahathir bin Mohamed seemed to think, to enroll in a Japanese-dominated trade and investment bloc, which recalled to many the wartime Greater East Asia Co-Prosperity Sphere? Would this invite Japanese political and cultural domination of Southeast Asia as well? For others in Asia the aggressive advances of Japanese *keiretsu* business, with its networks of banks, subsidiaries, and suppliers, evoked memories of Japanese Army invasions in the thirties and forties.

Alternatively, was a renewed and strengthened kind of Pacific community, an international condominium of sorts, still the best answer? Despite the end of the Cold War, did not some American security presence remain necessary, as well as a dialogue aimed at smoothing the abrasive disputes over Pacific trade? The very mention of the word "Pacific" immediately called to mind the active participation of the North American Pacific nations: the United States, Canada, and Mexico. It also suggested a wider role to be played by Australia and New Zealand.

These two nations have been marginal to our study, for they have not impinged directly on the relationship between Americans and Asians that is our central theme. Basically commodity producers—from wool, lamb, and butter to iron and uranium—they lived somewhat apart from the Asian countries to the north until the coming of World War II. Since the fifties, however, they have been actively involved in the transpacific relationship and provided more than their share of leadership in the nascent Pacific organizations.

Which brings us logically to the matter of Pacific organizations themselves. Do we need them? What is at stake here? Having brought the history of the Pacific world up to date, we should now take time to evaluate the resources of the Pacific nations, the regional and world challenges they face, and the possibilities ahead of us.

"WE ARE NOT making a coalition of countries; we are making a unity of people." So Jean Monnet, the man who inspired and built the European Community, began his memoirs.[1] His exhortation rings even truer when we consider the Pacific community. The Western European nations that finally united in the European Community, after years of preliminary organization and setbacks, are all clearly definable nation-states. Their patriotic pedigrees go back over many centuries. Yet despite their discrete and stubborn nationalisms, their civilization and its tradition are unitary: Roman and Christian. The word "European" means something. Whether Spaniard or German—and for that matter whether Pole, Hungarian, or Russian—there is a shared cultural heritage, generally recognized, a literature, a body of classics, a religion, and common linguistic roots. There is a modern civilization, as well, to which all subscribe.

By contrast, most of the Pacific nation-states are young. With a couple of centuries of independence behind them, the United States, Canada, and Mexico are relative old-timers compared with new states like Malaysia and Singapore. Indonesia is still trying to homogenize its disparate island races into a

[1] *Mémoires* (Paris: Fayard, 1976).

single country. Korea and Vietnam are only a half century away from colonialism. Thailand can trace its modern nationhood back only three centuries. Even Japan, while its imperial line goes back some 2,000 years, can properly date its beginnings as a modern nation-state no further back than the Tokugawa seventeenth century, if not the Meiji nineteenth.

Culturally, of course, they tell a different story. China is far older than Rome's most venerable descendants. Its cultural influence on the rest of Asia is at least as enduring as Europe's Roman traditions. Korea and Vietnam have millennial backgrounds similar to Japan's. Java's and Sumatra's are similarly old, as is the Indic Khmer civilization of Kampuchea. These are the cultures of dynasties and temples and the aristocracies who served them. Their sense of modern popular citizenship is by contrast brand-new; nor should it be confused with ideas of citizenship among Americans and Europeans.

Where the Asia-Pacific countries deal with present-day problems and issues, their overlay of modern civilization is largely a Western graft from America, with a nod in the direction of culturally revolutionary, but seclusive Meiji Japan. Seven-forty-seven jets, horror movies, rock concerts, TV commercials, blue jeans, cocktails, plumbing, banks, and business schools—so many commonplace externals of the life around them are largely American transplants. Their trading transcends their relatively new national boundaries, as does their sense of ideology and politics. Thanks to the computer, the xerographic copier, and the fax machine—not to mention the transnational reach of television—news now travels instantaneously. Even after the Tiananmen massacre, Chinese students and worker dissidents were kept informed of events through international fax transmission. Along with technology and its attendant lifestyles they have mastered the mechanics of the modern nation-state, which is by and large the product of Western philosophy and politics. Their ideas about authority and governance, however, are far different from those of their Western exemplars. So are their concepts of individuals and their relationships to societies. The strength of transnational cultures, religions, and social patterns is far more persistent than in the contemporary West; these are rooted in race and tradition. Whether one's citizenship belongs to Jakarta, Harbin, or Taipei, to cite the classic example, Chinese is still Chinese.

It is true that the revolution of rising expectations has brought a new middle class into existence on the western Pacific littoral. This group—well educated, ambitious, and determinedly urban—is more numerous and prominent in some countries than others, due to the region's different historical time zones. It has some international common denominators. The rising middle class was strong enough to force peaceful revolutions in Korea and the Phlippines; it is becoming a factor in Malaysia and Indonesia; even in avowedly proletarian Chinese towns and cities what the Communist regime calls "bourgeois liberalism" has become highly visible and significant. People of this generation are growing accustomed to a variety of creature comforts that their parents, in their younger days, could hardly have dreamed of. Their lives and attitudes are affected by the changes—family relations and relations between the sexes included.

It would be wrong, however, to conclude, in the grand American manner, that the emerging middle classes of Asia are "just like us." Even in America, the middle class, as we now define it, only appeared in the latter part of the nineteenth century.[2] While all for modernization, and increasingly concerned about political freedoms, the new Asian middle class is far from converted to American-style "look, no hands!" individualism. You will find few courses in "self-esteem" in Singapore or Seoul, but you will find an intensely strong family feeling. Modern Asian businessmen tend to work for the "house," rather than for themselves; their greed, that is, is generally familial or corporate. Almost ritually, they keep on working. Retirement is not worshipped as it is in the United States. If someone retires from a company, the first impulse is to find another job—preferably on contract to the same company. This is conspicuously true in Japan, although Japan's younger generation is far closer to the American than anywhere else in Asia.

Confucius, as we have noted elsewhere, is far from dead in the modern Asian family. People of non-Confucian traditions, like the Javanese or the Malay, continue to foster a similar respect for the senior person and, in particular, the official. The axiom we have quoted before in a Japanese context—"Respect the official and scorn the people" (Kanson minpi)—has its echo everywhere in the Asia-Pacific countries.

Authoritarian regimes have been readily accepted—up to a point—partly because of this tradition, partly because of the spectacular rise in people's material well-being over the past quarter century. And it has been very easy for the technocrats in government ministries to slip into the classic role of the learned mandarin who has passed the examinations and knows what is good for people. Popular democratic protest in both Korea and the Philippines, in fact, succeeded in great part because of strong local Christian populations who could more readily distinguish individual human rights and moral aspirations from the order imposed by the state. It was no accident, during the popular movements of the late eighties, that Cardinal Kim in Seoul and Cardinal Sin in Manila came forth as popular leaders.

Even after the spread of democratic freedoms, we can assume that one-party governments will predominate in the Asia-Pacific countries. The Liberal Democrats in Japan, the People's Action Party in Singapore, and the official Golkar

[2] As Robert Bellah and his co-authors note in *Habits of the Heart* (Berkeley: University of California Press, 1985).

coalition in Indonesia have all ruled for about three decades without interruption. The majority UMNO (for United Malay Nationalist Organization) has enjoyed similar longevity in Malaysia. All are nonideological, although UMNO has an obvious racial bias. Although ridden by corruption and factionalism—as are their counterparts in Korea and Taiwan—they are all for business and increased prosperity, which for most people is not so bad. But they have had to be responsive to popular pressure. Even a would-be Islamic autocrat like Mahathir has had to cater to the voters.

The similarities of lifestyle and politics among these culturally different peoples give Monnet's ideal of the unity of peoples added meaning in an Asian context. Within a single generation millions of Asians have been brought into a transnational world on whose perpetuation their newfound prosperity depends. Here is certainly an argument for some kind of regional organization. Paradoxically, this is made more rather than less necessary by the very fact of their mixed cultural backgrounds. It is here that American participation is once more critical to the success of Pacific regionalism. The pluralist, ethnic-conscious society of the United States, unique in its federalism and racial mixtures, offers, for all its problems, a striking example of unity in diversity.

THE FIRST IDEAS about Pacific cooperation, as in Europe, came from generally realized economic necessities. Not surprisingly, they came from Japan. The distinguished Japanese economist Kojima Kiyoshi sketched out the idea of a Pacific community in a paper written in 1966 advocating a Pacific free trade area. In 1967, primarily for security reasons, five Southeast Asian nations—Singapore, Malaysia, Thailand, the Philippines, and Indonesia—formed the Association of Southeast Asian Nations (ASEAN). (They would later be joined by the small, oil-rich sultanate of Brunei.) Given urgency by the intensification of the Vietnam War, the ASEAN group took some time to work out plans for economic cooperation. Even with their own communication difficulties—they have yet to iron out a welter of intramural trade restrictions—the Southeast Asian Nations' working partnership showed how people of very disparate cultures, races, and political makeup could get together in the common interest.

In 1978 Japan's newly installed Prime Minister, Ohira Masayoshi, became the first statesman to promote the ideas of Kojima and other like-minded economists. China found a strong collaborator in Australia's Prime Minister, Malcolm Fraser. At a 1980 meeting in Canberra, sponsored jointly by the Australians and the Japanese, the promoters of the idea of a working Pacific community took a first step. The present Pacific Economic Cooperation Conference (PECC)—now an organization of twenty Pacific nations—was launched at this meeting.

The United States joined the Canberra Conference and subsequent meetings with slowly gathering enthusiasm. By the early 1980s, in fact, American businessmen and academics were active in two organizations, PECC and the Pacific Basin Economic Council (PBEC). While PBEC consists mainly of businessmen, the national delegations of PECC contain equal numbers of businessmen, academics or professionals, and government officials.

These Pacific Basin groups do not approximate an Organization for Economic Cooperation and Development, and it is not probable that they will ever develop into a counterpart of the European Community. The differences between their member nations—politically, culturally, and economically—are too great. Yet the networking they have set up over the past decade has developed a common internationalist Pacific point of view, which was not there when they began. Starting from trade issues, they have gone on to explore common problems in energy, natural resources, communications, the environment, and human development. Although they have been, almost by definition, diffident in dealing with cultural and social issues, that is a logical next step. In the matter of education alone there is much to be done. (The pioneering work of Japanese and Americans in a joint study of both their national education systems invites wider participation.) In almost every area, the very process of multilateral consultation mitigates the abrasiveness that so often characterizes bilateral negotiating.

Despite the diversity of cultures represented in these councils, they have a certain homogeneity of education and approach. Whereas European Community representatives can claim educational pedigrees as different as Oxford, the Sorbonne, Rome, and Göttingen, the odds are that a quorum of Pacific delegates will have all taken their graduate degrees, at least, from Berkeley or Harvard. English is the invariable lingua franca. (Thanks to the development of different writing and character abbreviation systems over the past half century, even products of the Chinese character-based cultures—Japanese, Taipei and Beijing Chinese, Korean, and Vietnamese—are most comfortable exchanging thoughts in Ronald Reagan's mother tongue.) In the superficial externals of modern lifestyles—as opposed to cultures—most share a grounding in California movies, music, clothing, and other creature comforts.

Although their national objectives may sharply diverge, the delegates to these Pacific Basin forums and specialized task forces are accustomed to working together. Their efforts to reach a consensus on a wide variety of problems, while not always successful, have at least made everyone more considerate of the other person's (or nation's) point of view. As a former U.S. trade negotiator observed: "There is really much more of a discussion process on Pacific trade problems than there is in Europe. When we go to Europe, we are almost immediately involved in confrontational tactics with the EC people. In the

Pacific groups we can talk things over first. This paves the way for some reasonable solutions."

One fruit of such Pacific area conferencing is the progress made in intellectual property protection during the late eighties and early nineties. A decade ago intellectual piracy was a serious problem. It occurred not merely in book publishing or tape sales—the Jolly Roger flew proudly over thousands of small bootleg stores in Taipei and Seoul—but spread into the high-stakes business of computer software. Some governments at first tended to wink at this copyright hijacking. It was, after all, a profitable trade for many of their citizens. But the constant airing of this problem in various Pacific forums reinforced conventional diplomatic pressures for intellectual property rights protection. With local technology innovation everywhere on the rise, it became evident to the NICs that next year's protected patents might be their own.

Regional organizations grew in importance as the economies of the Asia-Pacific countries widened and diversified. Competition from previously underdeveloped countries has increased with greater industrial development and rising worker proficiency. Growing affluence has brought increased consumer demand for goods and services. This includes more imports. In countries like Korea, for example, domestic demand is now very heavy. The growing complexities of the Pacific economies—at once competitive and complementary—cry out for supranational agencies to keep order among them.

In 1989, Australia's Prime Minister, Bob Hawke, proposed an intergovernment organization to take on the job. APEC (for Asia-Pacific Economic Cooperation) began with twelve members: the ASEAN countries, Australia, New Zealand, Canada, Japan, Korea, and the United States. China, Taiwan, and Hong Kong are to join, and it is assumed that the Russian Republic, which inherits virtually all of the old Soviet Union's Pacific real estate, will also enter. This organization now offers the possibility of a pan-Pacific organ at least comparable to the regional economic (and political) institutions that have grown up in Europe. But far more obviously than with the European groups, some of its equal partners will be—to use Orwell's memorable phrase—more equal than others.

IN 1984, HALFWAY through his five-year term as Japan's Prime Minister, Nakasone Yasuhiro offered some cautions when I asked him about the function of Japan and the United States in any Pacific Basin organizations. "America and Japan," he said, "should obviously play key roles. But as big powers, they should walk softly and stay unobtrusive, like the *kuroko* in the theater."

The *kuroko* in the Kabuki theater are the black-clad people who move about adjusting props or scenery onstage. Their plain costumes serve notice that they

Harry Truman and Franklin D. Roosevelt (shortly after the Democratic convention in 1944). In Truman's administration Roosevelt's anticolonial policy in the Pacific was tempered by the Cold War and European policy considerations. AP/Wide World Photos

Korean demonstrations. In Seoul through the eighties anti-American as well as antigovernment slogans filled the air. Jigsaw Productions

The Great Wall. For all the surface modernization, Asians cherish their ancient cultures. Gibney Collection

*Confucian ethics class in Singapore. The new
Asian middle class has its own character.*
Jigsaw Productions

*Nakasone Yasuhiro (with the
author). "The big powers should walk
softly. . . ."* Gibney Collection

Bunraku puppets in Japan. Should the United States and Japan stay backstage?
Japan National Tourist Organization

are not to be noticed. But they set the stage for the actors. In the Bunraku puppet plays, of course, they are even more important, since it is they who manipulate the stylized wooden actors, while their lines are declaimed offstage. In all the new Pacific organizations both Japanese and American delegations have tried to avoid hogging the action—to spare the sensibilities of small nations, most particularly the ASEAN powers. Internationally "hegemony" has become a dirty word. Still, both countries will inevitably be the prime movers in the Pacific world—along with China, to the extent that the current political custodians of the world's oldest continuing civilization can get their modern act together. It is worth considering what roles they can be expected to play and how welcome their prominence can be.

Judging from the economic statistics, there is every reason to assume that Japan would play the leading role in an Asia-Pacific economic bloc. With economic leadership should come cultural and, ultimately, some form of presumed political direction. As the headquarters country of East Asia, Japan would finally take peaceful direction of the same Greater East Asia Co-Prosperity Sphere that Japanese arms failed to stabilize during World War II. Working together in a harmonious division of labor, the East Asian countries of a new "yen bloc" would go on to capture world leadership in the high-tech knowledge industries that will inevitably dominate world trading and investment. If we extrapolate the statistics of the last decade—based on Japanese exports, investment, technological advance, and offshore manufacturing in Southeast Asia—this is a plausible scenario.

It would, interestingly enough, not only realize the expectations of Japan's surviving Pan-Asianists but justify the original game plan of American Occupation strategists in the Korean War days. As John Foster Dulles, then a special State Department envoy, said in September 1950: "We believe there is a big market for Japanese industrial output in Southeast Asia. Things like locomotives, tractors, rails, irrigation equipment and the like can be a very profitable exchange of capital goods from Japan to underdeveloped areas, which can in return give Japan food and raw materials."

Dulles and other Americans of that time hoped to build up Japan into the economic bulwark of the free world in Asia, a strong (but obedient) junior partner in the gathering struggle with Communism in China and the Soviet Union. In the context of Dulles's time it was almost impossible for Americans even to conjure up the Ikeda economic advance a decade later, still less the chain of economic "miracles" wrought not only by Japan but by the nations of the "underdeveloped areas" to which he referred.

With the end of the anti-Communist Cold War, Japan has changed into equal partner and economic adversary. It is not an easy role to play, even for a Kabuki veteran experienced with masks and makeup. Stimulated by the current emphasis on Japanese-American economic rivalry—fast becoming the

Cold War of the nineties—a variety of Japanese businessmen and academic theorists are content to emphasize the adversary aspect. They project the idea of a Pan-Asian bloc capable of realizing an "Asia-Pacific century," which would finally carry out the war aims of the 1940s.

The Japanese who propagate this vision of course receive wide publicity in the United States, comparable to the wide-screen coverage of American Japan bashers in the Tokyo press. They are as yet unrepresentative of Japanese opinion, however. By contrast, cooler heads in Japan are seriously worried about the plight in which the Economic Superpower finds itself. For Japan, as we have suggested earlier, is politically the prisoner of its own economic success.

Let us review the problem. Starting with nothing but the skill and ingenuity of its people, an assist from America, and some striking new and old-new ideas about export marketing, industrial productivity, and government-business cooperation, the Japanese economy transfigured itself within two decades. Its dynamic *keiretsu* conglomerates rewrote the capitalist book. Success begat success. Now world powers in themselves, Japanese companies continued their intensive domestic rivalries on an international scale. Americans, Asians, and Europeans alternatively marveled and shuddered at the phenomenon of Japan, Inc. They were generally mistaken in their identification of Japanese corporate motives as nationalist expansion (the real objective of the classic *keiretsu* world corporation is not to "beat the Americans" but to beat its Mitsubishi or Sumitomo domestic rival). But they were correct in their assumptions about Japanese government support of these microeconomic expansionists.

For Japan's government establishment, with its cross-hatching into business and finance, had by the late eighties constructed an edifice of economic and cultural protectionism in support of its home industry—from tax breaks and open bidding restrictions to inspection and safety standards to local ordinances—that richly deserves the name "mercantilist." The great surge of Japanese prosperity was founded on aggressive penetration of a comparatively free and open American market, without allowing comparable entry for foreign competitors in Japan. The same Japan First mentality dominated Japan's dealings with its developing Asian neighbors.

"Asymmetry," Mark Borthwick writes, "became the dominant feature of Asia-Pacific trade in the later postwar period. The swift resurgence of Japan . . . not only failed to correct this imbalance but added to it. Between 1980 and 1984 the United States absorbed an estimated 71 percent of the growth in manufactured exports from East and Southeast Asia, while Japan took only 9 percent . . ."[3]

---

[3] As quoted in *Pacific Century: The Emergence of Modern Asia* (Boulder, Colo.: Westview, 1992), the textbook that serves as a companion to this volume and the *Pacific Century* television series.

Although Japanese imports have increased in recent years, the imbalance remains a formidable one. Korean and other Asian businessmen have been demanding removal of Japan's mercantilist restrictions as stridently as Americans. Complaints are addressed to the Japanese government, which set up the economic ground rules for Japan's business advances and indeed has made considerable progress in liberalizing formal trade restrictions. But while government economists, as well as the business strategists in the Keidanren, are aware of the wider problem, they can do little to solve it. The time has passed when the officials at Kasumigaseki could act as a bureaucratic superego to check the greed drives of Japan's economic expansionists. While the economic support bureaucracies remain strong, their political clout has lessened. And the world liberalization of money flows has further diminished it. The capacity of Japan's government for prescriptive politico-economic action has never been weaker.

Japan is a working democracy. Governments there stand or fall at the whim of the voters. And Japanese voters—more than 90 percent of whom label themselves contentedly as "middle-class"—do not want to rock the boat. The electorate is a collective *amaembo*—a "creature of dependency"—which, in return for almost a half century's consistent support for a bloated and faction-ridden majority party, expects almost total indulgence of its local creature comforts and prejudices.[4] Largely because of this trade-off, the same country whose corporate spearheads reach out all over the world, trading, investing, and expanding, grows at its core increasingly provincial. Mention international exchange rates or GNP figures and the country's attention is riveted. But in every area but international economic expansion, domestic issues hold priority.

Reading the Tokyo press or watching television, a visitor gets a choked feeling of living in a re-creation of Coolidge America in the 1920s. One recalls Calvin's classic slogan: "The business of this country is business." Or, to reach back into Japan's own history, there was Tokugawa's affluent but isolated Edo society in modern dress. (One wonders what happened to the thrusting internationalism of the early Meiji reformers.) Traders and tycoons may go out to the world to make their deals, but the goal is always to return to the snug womb of Tokyo, where everyone is comfortably and irrevocably Japanese, optimally protected against foreign contamination, and Amaterasu O Mikami's indulged

---

[4] The *amae*, or dependency syndrome, is a singular Japanese cultural characteristic according to which those in authority cater to the needs and demands of those lower-ranking or otherwise dependent on them. Found in government, business, and family life, it is pervasive in Japanese society. It is described at length in Chapter 6 of my book *Japan the Fragile Superpower* (rev. ed. New York: New American Library, 1986).

male children can relax in their favorite *karaoke* bars, after poring over the incoming faxes at the *kaisha*.

"Growing affluence," wrote the distinguished literary critic Kato Shuichi some years back, "has convinced Japanese that we really are No. 1. In the last year, a clear neo-nationalist consensus has reinforced that perception. It's not so much pride in particular national accomplishments as much as a feeling of complacency. 'Ours is a wonderful country—not just a great one, but the best.' "

This kind of self-satisfaction assumes that Japan's gains were made totally on its own, with no sense of obligation or even connection to others. It is the same mind-set that left Japanese as unconcerned about the Gulf War in 1991 as about the history of past Japanese aggressions in East Asia in the thirties and forties. They seem equally remote matters. But rice subsidies and protection of local manufacturers are real, like sumo and *yakuza*. Politicians tamper with them at their peril.

Americans can hardly afford to be supercritical of these Japanese attitudes. Self-satisfied affluence was an American trademark for several postwar decades. Yet with it came strong impulses of international concern and responsibility, sometimes led from Washington, sometimes the result of popular feeling. In postwar Japan there is little room for either. Government is exercised by a combination of bureaucrats and increasingly powerful Liberal Democratic Party politicians, who are all heavily beholden to the local pressure groups that keep electing them. The same can be said of other legislatures—the U.S. Congress for one. But in Japan, with its gerrymandered electoral districts and ingrown party factions, it has proved almost impossible to have a strong executive; every interest must be catered to, including those of the half-docile, half-obstructionist minority parties. In recent years only Nakasone had the temerity to go to the people and attempt to lead, over the heads of his political peers. He was only partially successful. The system is so mired that, to repeat a recent example, the mere mention of sending a few hundred military to join a UN peacekeeping organization—hardly controversial in the world's eyes—was enough to stall the Japanese political process.

The first, though not the final vote, incidentally, came in December 1991, some eight months after the matter of troops for the Gulf War had ceased to be an issue. Few Japanese seemed much concerned over it, although it related directly to the country's sense of international responsibility. In the end Japan paid $13 billion to help defray Gulf War expenses, but only after repeated demands from Washington.

This combination of passivity on international political issues and aggressive economic pursuit of international markets has become almost a national hallmark. For Japan, as the Keio University economist Shimada Haruo has written, "has failed to see, from the perspective of the international community, the problems it is causing the world. And it does not have the leadership to manage its world role from this broader perspective."[5]

The feelings of other Asian countries about Japan's hegemony in an Asia-Pacific sphere are, to put it mildly, mixed. Economic and technological primacy may be generally conceded. But almost everyone harbors grievances about Japan's reluctance to import the manufactures of others (unless produced from offshore Japanese-owned factories). Japanese foreign aid programs—now far more extensive than American—tend to hinge on production of local infrastructure by Japanese companies. Heightened cultural exchange programs, while finally allowing more foreign students to study at Japanese universities and technical institutes, tend to emphasize an Asia-Pacific "organic cultural sphere" in which Japan would call the turn. We are back to the "flying geese" pattern, it would seem, in which the lead Japanese goose would do most of the honking.

Most Asia-Pacific countries continue to be nervous about any extensive Japanese rearmament, with the memory still green of Japanese attack and oppression during World War II. The majority of Japanese themselves still prefer to keep American forces in Japan, under terms of the Japan–United States Security Treaty. But to continue the American military shield over Japan, now that the Soviet menace is removed, is to perpetuate an unhealthy situation. Among the Japanese the American military "umbrella" has fostered over four decades a sense of detachment from any responsibility whatsoever for regional collective security—not to mention support of UN peacekeeping actions on a world scale. At the same time it has increased resentment among Americans at having to offer permanent military protection to their most serious economic competitor.

Even without the threat of Soviet power, there are security problems aplenty. North Korea, Vietnam, and the tangled impasse in Kampuchea remain cause for regional concern, as does the continued domination of China by the Army and state security forces of the failing Mao-Deng Dynasty. (The People's Republic of China, it would seem, continues to provide huge supplies of armaments to rogue regimes like those of Burma, Iran, and the Khmer Rouge faction in Kampuchea.) Political succession problems may yet occur in Malaysia and Indonesia; news of the Army massacre of independence demonstrators in Timor was received as I wrote these lines. While NATO in Europe is pondering its continued existence, a good argument can be made for some kind of Pacific Treaty Organization, with contingents from all the Pacific Basin countries working under an international authority. Here, inevitably, Americans would

---

[5] As translated in *The Journal of Japanese Studies*, Winter 1991.

have to continue to play a leading role. For Japan, even if willing, would seem to be too self-centered and too unsure of itself politically to take any form of leadership—except backstage as Nakasone's self-effacing, but undeniably powerful *kuroko*.

At this point in history neither China nor Russia would seem ready or able to resume the strong positions they once occupied in the Pacific region. They will in time return to center stage, but not until Russia sorts out its economy and China its politics (of which the national economy remains a victim). A democratizing and economically ascendant Korea has to face the staggering task of uniting its own peninsula; it is a far worse problem than Germany's was. Taiwan and the ASEAN countries, like Korea, are supportive of regionalism but not capable of impelling it. Canada and Australia and New Zealand—with the new island nations of the Pacific largely dependent on them—have the capacity for leadership, but without the populations and heavy industrial capacities to back it up. Which brings the responsibility back to the United States.

Here we have a challenge in resources, in initiative, and above all in will. Just a few weeks before this writing, I had a long talk in Seoul with a thoughtful and highly capable member of the Korean cabinet, one of a not inconsiderable number of statesmen in the region who can take the long view beyond current problems. "We see many things wrong with American policy," he said. "We are critical. We have our disputes. Yet the United States remains the one great power that is in no sense a territorialist. That is why the United States is still trusted. It is imperative that the United States remain a strong force in the Asia-Pacific area, because there is no one to replace it. It may be that the Japanese will not rearm, even if forced into a difficult position. But we here do not trust them and other people do not. We may have problems with the United States, but we look to the Americans for our ultimate guarantee of security, as well as the great power of leadership that must on occasion be exerted. This is essential to the stability of this area."

Which raises the final critical question: how ready, willing, and able is a weakened America, divided, soul-searching, and obsessed with its domestic problems, to play a strong senior partner's role in the next Pacific century?

20

America's Pacific Future

*U*ncle Ted," said the late Franklin Delano Roosevelt, "I can't understand what they're doing down there."

The shade of his older cousin replied: "I can't understand it either. You don't gain anything by single, isolated actions. You have to have a coherent plan for dealing with Japan, China, the whole Pacific—especially when Asia is changing so."

It was a quiet Sunday in God's Elysian Fields, and the modest Episcopal service was over. As usual, the two Roosevelt cousins were talking politics. They worried particularly about American performance in the Pacific, for that was a world they both helped create. It was Teddy Roosevelt who carried the big stick of imperialism across the ocean to Manila, then won the Nobel Peace Prize for ending the Russo-Japanese War and fought the good fight against the California vigilantes beating up on Chinese and Japanese immigrants. It was Franklin Roosevelt who sent America's fleets across the ocean to avenge the "day of infamy" and win the Pacific war, backed off, finally, from his support of Chiang Kai-shek's Nationalists and before his death vowed to keep French colonialism from recapturing Vietnam. Why, they kept asking one another, had things gone so wrong lately? And why didn't more of their countrymen seem to care?

"Since I've come up here," said FDR, "our policy for the Pacific seems to have disintegrated. We pulled out of Korea before we should have—and we had that disaster in Vietnam. Perhaps it's lack of popular support. As I told Sam Rosenman once, it's terrible to get out in front and realize that nobody's following you."

"But Franklin, the White House is such a bully pulpit. And the Pacific is our new frontier. I said that down there almost a century ago, long before young Kennedy used the phrase. Remember when I sent the Great White Fleet across? It made them all take notice."

"Wait a minute, Uncle Ted, your Great White Fleet couldn't hold a candle to Halsey's Third Fleet in World War II. My boys turned that ocean into an American lake."

"True enough, Franklin, although I think I could have handled the Japanese problem a lot less expensively. Look at them now. They're top dog again."

"As you know, I've always hated war. But the Japanese seem to be practicing a kind of economic warfare now. What are we doing about that? Or the Chinese Communists? They're more corrupt than that old codger Chiang Kai-shek, who fooled us all for a while. And they don't have much respect for us either."

"The boys down in the White House these days seem to be full of talk. But I don't discern either high ideals or much action. Do we have an effective national policy on anything? This idea of government by pronouncement started—saving your grace—when that cold self-important prig Woodrow Wilson began posturing at Versailles . . ."

"Let's not get partisan, Uncle Ted. I'll never forget the mess I had to clean up after Coolidge and Hoover."

"They weren't my kind of Republican. If you ask me, Franklin, some of our new Presidents seem to be in it just for the job, and it's gone to their heads. Look at those huge White House staffs they have. And imagine a fellow like Bush going on the moving pictures playing golf—with a war and a depression on his hands!"

"Those Yalies were always a dull lot, Uncle Ted—your friend Taft, for example. But I particularly resent Bush and that actor fellow before him literally turning my New Deal inside out."

"Don't forget, I had the Square Deal first. Those were the days when the Republicans took care of the people. We busted the trusts and kept big business in its place."

"The trouble now is that our big business seems to be getting smaller by the day. I could put up with some of those economic royalists as long as they were efficient. And the government—did you see those deficit figures that Hamilton was showing everybody at the ambrosia breakfast? How can those fellows win the Cold War—and bungle the peace? The worst part of it is, they don't seem to understand what's happening right across our ocean, the Pacific . . ."

* * *

WHILE JAPAN'S new Economic Superpower drove on relentlessly in its pattern of economic catch-up, products and investments piling up exponentially with scant thought for the political tomorrow, and while other NICs and their junior competitor-partners—from Korea to Indonesia—were pursuing the revolution of rising expectations with varying degrees of communal fervor, the one surviving Global Superpower was having terrible problems trying to squeeze out of its old tight-fitting Cold War uniform. Staggered by the enormity of its political victory, the United States was clearly in trouble trying to adjust to the new world of competing economies and cultures which that very victory had made possible.

Americans could justly point out the enormous problems of the Russians and other peoples of Eastern Europe as they struggled to hew out a good life. For while now politically free, they had still to reform a mind-set of intellectual serfdom acquired over their half century and more of Communism. Yet Americans themselves were stuck in a similar time warp. A few questers and innovators were pushing ahead with bold discoveries, but the society as a whole had yet to shake off the complacency of the two postwar decades, when American business ruled the economic world as surely as American fleets and missiles dominated world strategy and politics. The complacency had spawned a national tendency to react rather than act, to criticize rather than create, to "stay the course" instead of seeking new directions. Somewhere a sense of national mission had been lost, and with it Americans' sense of national community.

The problems of this national identity crisis were most keenly felt in the Pacific Basin. There the rules of the old game had dramatically changed, as had the character and the behavior of the leading players. It was doubtless easier for Washington to deal with Europe—Eastern and Western—and the always troubled Middle East. There at least Americans had the remains of a consistent policy. But the new growth and dynamism, as we have seen, was happening on the western shores of the Pacific. And there the United States seemed to have no long-range regional policy at all to supplement its variety of bilateral deals. Talk about "keeping the peace" and "equal partnership" no longer sufficed, now that Cold War peace, at least, was a reality and the Asian partners were all doing very well, thank you.

From the time of Woodrow Wilson, American interests in the Asia-Pacific world had enjoyed a distant second priority. In World War II the invasion of Europe was always the principal national concern. The U.S. Navy was fortunately successful in its private sea and air war in the Pacific, although uncritical American support of Chiang Kai-shek in China left a rueful postwar legacy. Prompt action, political and military, in Korea in 1950 was an inevitable casualty of the anti-Soviet buildup in Europe. Concern for America's French ally in Europe—along with the conviction that Asian Communism was merely a Soviet by-product—led directly to the American commitment in Vietnam. The chances for building a solid American relationship with China were damaged, long before the PLA's Tiananmen massacre, by American obsession with playing a military "China card" against Moscow. We have already amply noted the constant sacrifice of American economic interests in favor of keeping Japan's "unsinkable aircraft carrier" firmly welded to the anti-Communist alliance. As for continuing Eurocentrism, it is interesting to recall that until very recently, despite the preeminent world position of Japanese finance (including the fact that vast U.S. deficit borrowings were funded largely by Japanese investors), most American financial pages placed the mark and the pound first in their international exchange reporting, with the yen generally added in the second paragraph.

At the start of the nineties Washington looks particularly careless in its dealings with the Pacific world. Its policy has betrayed the traditional Europe-first outlook: as long as no wars broke out, Asia-Pacific relations could be kept on hold, with traditional Cold War attitudes retained.

It is time to rethink both attitudes and policies. The first order of business, politically speaking, should be to revise the security relationship. The Japan–United States Security Treaty, laudable in its statement of shared objectives, need no longer demand the presence of large U.S. forces on Japanese bases. Japan cannot learn any sooner to protect itself (or not) with its own forces. That should be the prerogative of any sovereign nation. If other Asian nations are worried about the revival of Japanese militarism, they should take up that matter with Tokyo. It is time for the Economic Superpower to cease to rely on, essentially, mercenary American forces to "defend" it. This security relationship, frozen in time, has become a liability to both parties, an outmoded relic of Japan's international "dependency" syndrome.

There is little danger of a resurgent militarism in Japan. The Self-Defense Forces, if technologically strong, have had conspicuous trouble in retaining people, with one of the highest military dropout rates (officers and men) in the world. The fear of a long-dead militarism is fanned by minority parties and myopic sectors of Japan's intelligentsia, who continually cite Article 9 of their American-made Constitution, partly to avoid normal international responsibilities and partly as a reason to justify their existence. They would do well to turn their energies to support a true internationalizing of Japan's trading practices and its school history textbooks, among other things.

Instead of the unitary American base system, the countries of the Pacific Basin should consider a collective security peacekeeping organization, using contingents from all countries willing to participate. There are obvious difficulties—China's People's Liberation Army among them—but it is time to begin moving in that direction. Americans should take the lead in establishing such an organization, which could be useful for disaster-relief and humanitarian as well as military purposes. There is no reason why Siberian Russian forces—and Vietnamese—should not be asked to join. The military danger of the future, as events in Azerbaijan, Georgia, Yugoslavia, and elsewhere demonstrate, will more likely than not come from tribal, religious, or ethnic wars. Against these an international force is the best possible deterrent.

With the security issue out of the way, the United States and Japan would be better able to work out their serious economic differences, as much as possible on the basis of reciprocity and within the context of some general ground rules for regional Pacific trade and investment. The American-Japanese alliance is far more important than a mere military relationship. Despite differences of cultural background, the two peoples share a popular culture and a sense of democracy. They are the inevitable leaders in the region's advancement, and they have a strong obligation to work together in this cause.

The gulf between these two proud countries, we must remember, has been caused as much by American neglect of an industrial policy as by Japan's aggressive reliance on one. It can only be bridged by an intensification of communication and wide cooperation in cultural and technological development. This requires positive leadership on both sides. The two countries already constitute a macroeconomy. Each must realize the implications of that overarching fact.

THE OTHER CENTRAL actor in the Pacific world is China. Here, after some initial success, American foreign policy has done poorly. When we had strong leverage on the Beijing leadership, we failed to use it. Chinese, Communists or otherwise, are hard bargainers. What the current generation of Sentimental Imperialists in Washington saw as persuasive concessions to move the Chinese the right way were viewed by Deng Xiaoping and his coterie as signs of weakness or irresolution.

Up to the time the tanks fired at Tiananmen in 1989, the confrontation between the Communist mandarins and the people of Beijing could have gone either way. The Chinese leadership remains divided, torn between liberal and conservative political alternatives, but generally agreed that continuation of economic reform was their only hope to control a restive population. While Americans were right to condemn the leadership's repression, they overestimated the extent of the democratic resistance. Rural Chinese, who had been most helped by Deng Xiaoping's economic reforms, were little inclined to become freedom fighters. Yet even the bitter old men of the leadership—Deng conspicuously among them—were troubled at the prospect of international displeasure. They were particularly vulnerable in the immediate aftermath of the Tiananmen massacre.

Instead of applying this pressure, President Bush, naively relying on his personal acquaintance with the Beijing hierarchy, went out of his way to assure them, through confidential emissaries, that the American administration, while troubled by their barbarous behavior, nonetheless wanted to keep in friendly contact. With a people for whom gestures often count as actions, his overtures took away much of the considerable political leverage the United States possessed. And with an American President sending secret friendly emissaries to Beijing, it is understandable that the government of Japan—hardly a vigorous international defender of human rights in the best of seasons—would move quickly to restore normal relations.

The Communist mandarins of Zhongnanhai—their ideology bankrupt and their rule sustained by secret police and a half-loyal army—represent a fading dynasty. The analogy with the last days of the Qing is unmistakable. Even their vaunted economic gains, most visible in the countryside and small privatized industry, are being eroded by continued political subsidies to their bloated, deficit-ridden state-run industries. Deng and his coterie are shrewd political traders. But their bluster hardly conceals their insecurity. Not only in the Chinese diaspora outside but within their own administration there are potential Sun Yatsens and Kang Yuweis waiting to take over. There is the vitally important entrepreneurial population of Hong Kong, progressively more nervous about the prospect of 1997. A rich and increasingly confident Taiwan is in growing contact with the mainland cousins—and by now running a good bit of offshore investment there. And Beijing's hold on its own prospering southern provinces is a matter of debate.

In the circumstances the United States needs steady contact with the Chinese—economic and cultural—but fewer face-losing high-level missions. Where possible America should support Hong Kong and Taiwan, as well as the capitalist enclaves inside China itself. Most-favored-nation status should continue on a trading and investment level, but reciprocity of economic treatment should be insisted on. While stressing friendship with the Chinese people—we should use the word "government" as little as possible in this connection—Washington should not be afraid to get tough in its negotiations with the Chinese regime. The old Communist mandarins respect power and little else. What they fear most is their own people's revolution of rising expectations. This continues.

In dealing with the other surviving Asian Communist regimes Washington's diplomacy has earned mixed reviews. Policy toward North Korea has generally followed the lead of President Roh Tae Woo and his successful "northern politics." In an Asian version of the West German *Ostpolitik* initiated by Willy Brandt, Roh succeeded in isolating Kim Il Sung's strange satrapy, first by economic and political trading with the Soviet Union and China, then ultimately by a strong-handed offer to work with the North Koreans toward even-

USS Blue Ridge at Yokosuka. After four decades, it is time to rethink the question of U.S. bases in Japan. Jigsaw Productions

tual unification. The United States has consistently backed up South Korea's policies, to the point of agreeing to withdraw American nuclear weapons from the Korean peninsula once the north permits inspection of its threatening nuclear installations. As a result, an economically destitute north is reluctantly coming to some kind of rapprochement with the prosperous southern neighbor. To make his own nuclear weapon is the Great Leader's last-gasp political ploy. It is admittedly a frightening possibility. Other than that Kim Il Sung has nowhere to go.

In contrast, American policy toward Vietnam in recent years has been almost hopelessly sterile. Nowhere else has the dead hand of Cold War politics been so evident. This is literally so, for the only issue on which the U.S. government deigns to communicate with the People's Republic of Vietnam is the matter of finding the remains of some 2,000 soldiers missing in action—and presumed long dead—in the Vietnam fighting that ended almost two decades ago. Meanwhile an American embargo on trade with Vietnam remains in effect, albeit increasingly flouted by America's onetime anti-Communist allies. And American newspaper readers, well schooled after several *Rambo* films, are periodically regaled with thirdhand "eyewitness" accounts of U.S. prisoners of war still held, for mysterious reasons, in darkest Vietnam's jungle strongholds.

The realities of Vietnam at the outset of the nineties argue for a 180-degree change in this outdated isolation policy. Faced with the same failures of doctrinaire Marxist economics that bedeviled China, the Communist regime in Vietnam, by the end of the eighties, was moving swiftly up the same pragmatist road as Deng Xiaoping. By 1990 agriculture was effectively privatized and most of the country's industry had been opened to local entrepreneurs, where they could find the money. Even before the local Communist hierarchy decided to free their markets, the burgeoning underground trade in foreign commodities had underscored the pending economic victory of the conquered capitalist south over the Marxist north.

The Communist leadership in Hanoi is no friendlier to democracy than their opposite numbers in Beijing, but market economy reformists are in the ascendant; with Soviet aid withdrawn and the country's infrastructure still a shambles, almost any trade and investment overtures from outside would be welcome. Japanese trading companies have already sent their survey teams into Hanoi and Ho Chi Minh City. The opportunities for offshore manufacturing in this country of 67 million are obvious.

The Vietnamese are a gifted people, with a strong Confucian work ethic, whose wartime ingenuity and tenacity could be put to good purpose. Communism has conspicuously failed to eradicate the entrepreneurial flair of Saigon's (sorry, Ho Chi Minh City's) urban population. American journalists and tourists are greeted with some enthusiasm, and there is now considerable contact with the large Vietnamese emigration in the United States. A restored and constructive American relationship with Vietnam could bring this country at least economically into the Pacific community, with a far greater chance for political relaxation to follow. Here is a classic opportunity for Americans—government and business both—to work out a new Pacific policy.

Restored relations with Vietnam would also strengthen the settlement in Kampuchea, which the United States has helped bring about. For some years the greatest threat to a free and ultimately democratic Kampuchea has been not the Vietnamese-backed Hun Sen government but the renewed strength of Pol Pot and the Khmer Rouge, backed as always by the cynical *Machtpolitik* of China. The continuing isolation of Vietnam by the United States has thus far only served to bring closer the desperate Party bosses in Hanoi and Beijing—not normally known to be the best of friends.

America's dismissive treatment of Vietnam differs only in degree from a similar aloofness to the rest of Southeast Asia. Apart from the once colonial Philippines and Singapore, with its carefully planned attractiveness as a base for multinationals' trade and manufacturing, few American businesses have lately shown much interest in Southeast Asia. For the average exporter in the United States, Indonesia, Thailand, and Malaysia are exotic way stations on a Somerset Maugham tour. Yet these countries, as we have seen, are coming up right behind Korea and Taiwan as the NICs of the near future. Increased exports and rising GNP levels are leading to local consumer markets for goods and services. So far Japanese, Korean, and Taiwan businessmen have been the principal purveyors.

Nor has American diplomacy been active in this area. In Japan, where the problem of protectionism has been greatest, the United States has tried hardest to stay friends. This has been true of Korea also. Because of security considerations—and partly because of greater familiarity—the theme of partnership has been continuously stressed. Not so in Southeast Asia. Here, in keeping with their postwar tradition as the regional policeman, American spokesmen have warned against human rights violations, infringement of copyrights, and local protectionism, but without developing any positive programs that could act as a counterweight to the finger wagging.

Yet especially in Thailand and Indonesia, American trade is wanted. Beyond this some expression of cultural, if not political cooperation would be greatly welcomed. The United States has sent some good ambassadors to these countries in the past, but the general silence from Washington has been deafening. Indonesia alone has a population of more than 160 million, a new crop of emergent modern businesses, and a competent bureaucracy determined to reduce the country's dependence on oil exports. It also faces huge educational and cultural challenges in its multiracial makeup. In any American Pacific policy the Indonesian relationship would have to be a key factor.

THERE ARE REASONS for East Asians' consuming interest in Americans. They remain strong enough to outweigh a variety of heedless acts, affronts, and irritants given to them by Americans over long decades. We have alluded to them repeatedly in these pages. But it may be useful to sum up here the basic elements of America's appeal to the other peoples of the Pacific—and the American contribution. They are four:

1. *The Innovative Mind.* By this we mean the impulse and urge to learn by discovery that was embodied in that old, ungainly American term "know-how." Going beyond this is a tradition of support for empirical learning that dignifies testing and experiment rather better than the classical European tradition from which it descended. America is the shrine of discovery and technology, its successful devotees honored whatever their status; this is of special interest to inheritors of the Confucian tradition. Part of this mind-set is a belief in progress, the conviction that modernization will lead to democracy.

2. *The Education Country.* America is the educator of the Pacific Basin. Unlike the exclusionist citadels of Confucian learning—foreigners will not have an easy time getting teaching jobs at Tokyo University—American education is internationalist and all-embracing, its managers shrewd enough to realize that the incoming foreign students will quite possibly give more than they get. Communist mandarins in Beijing or Islamic ideologues in Malaysia, they all cheerfully send their young to study at Yale, Michigan, or Berkeley. For study in America is traditionally nonpartisan, multicultural, and—as far as that concept can be stretched—"objective." It is a marketplace of ideas. It is above all up to date, at the cutting edge of modern scholarship and research.

In 1990, an average year, more than 160,000 students from East Asian countries were enrolled in American colleges and universities. They gave as good as they got; one-fourth of all American doctorates in electrical engineering came from Taiwan alone. Over the years the Fulbright fellowships and similar programs gave graduate-level instruction to tens of thousands of young people who went on to become teachers and leaders in their own countries. For many of different, often hostile ways of thinking, their years of American study marked a turning point in their lives.

Another virtue of American education should be mentioned here: the protection, if not the virtual sanctification of free scientific inquiry and unhampered research. The same sense of academic freedom that brought European scientists to American universities during Hitler's and Stalin's persecutions have attracted two generations of brilliant postwar Asian scholars to the United

States. Chinese have come largely because of political restriction—some Koreans and Southeast Asians as well. Japanese creative scientists, not surprisingly, have found a happier climate for their work in the United States because they are free from the often stultifying group pressures of life in their home universities or corporate research facilities. The two most recent Japanese Nobel Prize winners in science, Ezaki Leona (physics) and Tonegawa Susumu (medicine), both have long had their residences and laboratories in the United States. (Ezaki recently returned to Japan to assume the leadership of the new government "science" university at Tsukuba.)

3. *The Open Society.* America has traditionally been the quintessential open society. The philosopher Karl Popper, who wrote a classic book on the subject,[1] defined this broadly as "the society in which individuals are confronted with personal decisions." The opposite of what Popper termed the closed society (tribalist and collective), the open society puts a premium on individualism, free choice, and the absence of social or political restraints. America exemplifies, in Robert Bellah's words,[2] "aspirations widely shared throughout the world: the ideal of a free society, respecting all its citizens, however diverse, and allowing them to fulfill themselves."

Most Asians' idea of democracy is more collectivist or at least more "communitarian" than the American model. Nonetheless, the individualist democratic ideas of American society, however flawed in practice, have held a historical appeal for the Asia-Pacific peoples. The ideals of free speech, a free press, and free elections—although not necessarily free trade—have worked their magnetism on millions of Asians. As more developing nations have reached for democracy, Americans' support of human rights has struck a responsive chord, for all its preachiness. But transcending any actions of U.S. governments is the old example of the free, good life in America.

The pop culture of America—earthy, irreverent, cacophonous, relentlessly informal—sets the tone for the modern young in the Pacific world, from Vancouver to Vladivostok to Vanuatu. It has done so for Europe as well. The ubiquitous French pundit Régis Debray once commented, prophetically: "There is more power in rock music, videos, blue jeans, fast food, news networks, and TV satellites than in the entire Red Army." This kind of "cococolonization," to borrow the French term of opprobrium, is even more pronounced in East Asia, where American modes and manners are equated with being modern. The new media machines may be Japanese, but the messages they convey are American, and no people are more slavish in their imitation of American lifestyles than the Japanese.

[1] *The Open Society and Its Enemies* (London: Routledge, 1945) has been reprinted many times since.
[2] *Habits of the Heart* (Berkeley: University of California Press, 1985).

However badly skewed the economic trade balances in America's disfavor, the cultural imbalance is overwhelmingly tilted toward the West Coast of the United States. (The American entertainment industry is in fact the country's second-biggest export earner—after aerospace—with an annual trade surplus of $8 billion.) The "Californianization of the free world," as Japan's business commentator Omae Kenichi has it, also extends its reach to the new generation in China and Vietnam. It includes American books in translation as well as the ubiquitous movies, TV series, and commercials. Tangled, unruly, and determinedly anti-authoritarian, America's pop culture influences and attracts.

4. *The Asian-Americans.* In 1965 there was a massive change in U.S. immigration regulations. National-origin quotas, previously weighted in favor of Europeans, were abolished. The new system gave preference to skilled workers and people with family members, regardless of nationality. The number of Asian immigrants soared. Barely one million in 1970, Asian-Americans number something under ten million in 1992.

The economic effects of Asian investment in the United States have already been noted. This is not, incidentally, solely the work of Japanese big business. Maritime Chinese businessmen in Taiwan, Hong Kong, and Southeast Asia, awash in seas of liquidity, have been quick to move capital into American and Canadian ventures and acquisitions. But more important than the infusions of entrepreneurial investment are the entrepreneurs themselves. As individuals and families come to live in the United States, they contribute to this country an immense reserve of talent. Unlike the laborers and indentured farmers of the first Asian immigration a century ago, the new Asian-Americans of the eighties and nineties are apt to be well-educated professionals, eager to play a part in American life. Some 60 percent of Korean immigrants, for instance, are young university graduates. Much of the forced emigrants from Vietnam have been older, with positions of some responsibility behind them. In the American immigrant tradition, they are not afraid of starting out in humble positions and working their way up.

The new immigrants from Asia join the children and grandchildren of the earlier immigration, who by this time have worked and studied their way into the American middle class. Their change in social and economic status is impressive. In 1980, after his first visit to the United States in thirty-five years, one of my scholar friends from Beijing remarked with a wry smile: "When I visited your country first, most of the Chinese I met seemed to be laundrymen or waiters in restaurants. Now they are professors and bosses of computer companies. I hadn't believed such a social evolution possible."

The waves of Asian immigrants have enriched the American pluralist tradition at least as much as they have profited by it. They have had to endure more than their share of discrimination and racial abuse because they are Asian—and hence not so familiar to the average American. But they have the

Lenin uprooted. Like the Russians, Americans face a rethinking of their old Cold War priorities and goals. Jigsaw Productions

Vietnamese countryside. Largely rural and underdeveloped, Vietnam is now eager for trade and investment from the United States.
Peter Bull

Deng Xiaoping. A shrewd political trader to the last.
Encyclopedia of China

advantage of legal protection and a societal tolerance of diversity that seems worlds away from the bigoted treatment of Chinese and Japanese immigrants in the early part of this century.

Representative Gary Locke, chairman of the finance committee in Washington State's legislature, is himself a third-generation Chinese-American. "My grandfather," he recalls, "was here at the turn of the century. Then most Asian-Americans worked on the railroads or they worked the mines, logging timber, or in the fisheries in Alaska. It was hard, physical labor. Most recent immigrants are doing much the same thing—blue-collar work; but because so many barriers of discrimination are knocked down, many are able to go quickly into technical and professional jobs."[3]

The success of these modern immigrants in turn inspires others. Almost all of these new groups, while trying their best to become Americans, have also been quick to build up their own cultural villages—Little Taipei, Little Tokyo, Koreatown, Little Vietnam—in the heart of their adopted cities. Los Angeles is, of course, a prime example. The American journalist Ryszard Kapuscinski, himself a Pole by birth, used the comparison of Vienna at the turn of the century, a mosaic of different cultures and values, where competition between the cultures gave life to the times. "In Los Angeles," he added, "the basis of dynamism is vastly broader. It includes peoples, cultures, and beliefs from other continents and civilizations."[4]

Here is the beginning of a new Pacific culture, a gradual meeting and cross-fertilization of backgrounds, traditions, and ideas which makes the old contrasts of East and West seem tired and out of date. The pluralism of America's open society has helped create the beginnings of this Pacific culture, just as fully as American economic strength offered the springboard for the postwar Asian economic takeoff, and American military and political power the shield behind which it all developed.

It is now time, in conclusion, to look searchingly at the situation of the United States itself as we stand on the threshold of the twenty-first century. Is the world's last Global Superpower fading, in the irreversible decline pattern of older empires before it? Is the great pluralist Republic the casualty of its own successes, the victim of contending factions and their political and economic greed? Or does it have the capacity for self-renewal? And is one key to self-renewal the impact and example of the transnational Pacific world that it helped create?

*　　*　　*

---

[3] As quoted in *The Pacific Century* television series.
[4] From an interview in *New Perspectives Quarterly* (Summer 1988).

To start off the American election year of 1992, President George Bush took the plane to Tokyo. His avowed purpose on his January trip, after stop-overs in Australia, Singapore, and the Republic of Korea, was a simple one: "Jobs, jobs, and jobs." As Bush explained it, a major factor in the current American depression was unfair economic competition from Japan. If the Japanese wanted to avoid American protectionist retaliation—his implicit threat—they had better buy more American products (automobiles in particular), eliminate "structural impediments" to free trade within Japanese society, and cut down their exports to the United States (which at this writing still comprise a good 30 percent of Japan's export total).

Bush brought with him an "action plan" for the Japanese to cut back on American-bound exports, eliminate "unfair" trade practices, and buy American. (Not surprisingly, this was not accepted.) Included in the presidential party was a hastily recruited honor guard of twenty-one American corporate executives—the presidents of Detroit's Big Three carmakers conspicuous among them. It was presumably the job of the airborne CEOs—whose total annual compensation package exceeded $50 million[5]—to dramatize the sorry state of the industries they represented. Bush underlined the purpose of the trip with a well-publicized presidential visit to the recently opened Osaka branch of a large American toy chain.

The same George Bush, just nine months before, had reviewed the victorious troops coming back from America's lightning victory over the Iraqi invaders of Kuwait, announcing the triumphant success of the Global Superpower's world peacekeeping strategy. The abrupt transition from world commander in chief to international toy and car salesman made its own ironic commentary on the changing international emphasis on economic over military power—a central theme of this book. With equal irony, President Bush's desperate scrabbling for Japanese economic aid emphasized a growing tendency in Washington to blame America's economic failings on the Japanese, exactly as we used to ascribe our world political problems to the dastardly dealings of the Soviets.

In a way Bush's demeaning exercise in economic diplomacy was a fit climax to the crescendo of Japan bashing that celebrated the recent fiftieth-anniversary celebration of Japan's World War II attack on Pearl Harbor. The ultimate

[5] Japanese commentators were quick to compare the $3 million annual compensation package of Chrysler's Lee Iacocca, for example, with the far more modest compensation of top executives of Japan's vastly more profitable major carmakers. In his book *In Search of Excess* (New York: Norton, 1991), Graef Crystal, a compensation consultant now teaching at the University of California at Berkeley, offers a disturbing study of how high American top executive salaries have escalated; he estimates the average American CEO's salary as 100 times that of the average worker. While this may be high, the difference in standards is appreciable.

statement of the "blame Japan" argument was contained in the staff report of a CIA-sponsored conference on the Japanese-American relationship earlier in 1991. "The Japanese," the report summarized, "firmly believe that might is right . . . Japan is preparing an economic sneak attack from which the United States may not recover. Our nation and its underlying values are threatened. Economic dominance is their goal."

Throughout these pages we have not stinted on criticism of Japan's intensive, if curiously mindless drive for economic aggrandizement. We have also tried to point out the spasmodic and ineffective response by American business and government to the Asian economic challenge—a challenge of Maritime Chinese, Koreans, and others as well as Japanese. There is no mystery about what *should* be done to restore American economic strength and build for the twenty-first century. The mystery lies in why so little has been done or attempted. For the terrain over which we travel is familiar. The successes of Japan's economic tactics represent a distorted mirror image of what is wrong with America.

Let us consider four major areas of concern: (1) Human Capital, (2) the Quality Imperative, (3) Capital Investment, and (4) Industrial Policy.

1. *Human Capital.* Western economists have tended to think of capital in terms of money, plant, materials, and technology. To this the Japanese added people. The most conspicuous characteristic of postwar Japanese capitalism is its belief that long-term investment in people—which includes training them, partly educating them, and developing them within the company—is more important than long-term investment in plant. Although often ascribed to Japanese cultural homogeneity, the emphasis on human capital evolved partly because of postwar hardships, partly because of a long-term approach to business development, partly because of technological advance. Whereas the typical American corporation sees itself as a purely functional organization, the Japanese think in terms of a "community-company." Whereas the American company hires someone for a specific job, Japanese personnel departments are interested in hiring "the whole person" for a long-term career, moving up slowly by seniority and, wherever possible, the beneficiary of a full-employment policy.

As world economies fast become knowledge-intensive rather than labor-intensive, a qualitative change is taking place in the kind of work to be done and the type of worker needed. In the postindustrial society, as some call it, workers need to be both more flexible and more skilled than they were in the old mass-production days, when factory employees performed very specific and often very rudimentary tasks. Workers themselves become part of technology's upward spiral. The classic American expedient of firing excess people in troubled times—"The first thing we're doing, Mr. Chairman, is to cut costs and lose heads"—can be counterproductive in increasingly high-tech environments.

By contrast, Japanese companies with full-employment policies have had to throw all their energies into technology and productivity improvement as well as searches for new growth areas. Their permanent employees are just that; they are constants, not variables. Managers must make their people more rather than less useful, constantly increasing the value-added portion of their work. This process, as Dr. Johnson said about execution, "wonderfully clears the mind." Workers as well as executives wholeheartedly participate. The stability of this system—which explains why Japanese unions are so peaceful—is a major reason behind Japan's worldwide business expansion.

Takeda Shingen was one of Japan's storied feudal leaders in the turbulent civil wars of the sixteenth century. By all accounts a charismatic figure—he is the hero of Kurosawa's modern film spectacular *Kagemusha*—Takeda, when asked about the condition of his castle strongholds, replied that he had none. "People are my castle," he replied. "People are its walls, people are its moat."

Japan's modern captains of industry are prone to personal comparisons with bygone military heroes, and in recent years Takeda has received more than his share of attention. Their stress on the people factor in their business, however, is no more altruistic than Takeda's. With them, as with Takeda, the development of good, loyal (or at least habitual) people is vital to corporate success.

2. *The Quality Imperative.* In the 1920s and 1930s Japanese manufacturing was known generally as a maker of shoddy and second-rate consumer goods. (Most of the quality production, as later developed, was lavished on heavy industry and military equipment.) Since the fifties, however, the concentration was on quality. It began with cameras. (I remember the astonishment of American photographers when they found that the new Nikon cameras were as good as or better than their cherished Leicas.) It continued with ships, steel, electronic goods, computers, and, above all, cars. In their catch-up business drives, the Japanese were shrewd enough to realize that only superior products could assure them a worldwide reputation. Here, again, came the accent on quality. In making quality the workplace priority, a variety of productivity improvements emerged.

In contrast, American carmakers had grown slack after so many years on top of world markets. While engineers gave way to financial men in the executive suites, promotion and styling became primary concerns, as Detroit, anxious for short-term profit gains, worried little about the long-term technological future. David Halberstam, whose book *The Reckoning*[6] contains telling comparisons of the American and Japanese automobile industries, recalled an incident when a talented Ford engineer ran into Lynn Townsend, then president of Chrysler,

---

[6] New York: Morrow, 1986.

and expressed some concern about the quality of Detroit cars. Townsend assured him that "nobody cares for quality. The only thing people care about is their stock splits." Halberstam concluded: "Detroit regarded as its real customers not the people buying the cars but the people buying the stocks."

3. *Capital Investment and the Long View.* As we have seen, Japanese companies since the sixties have continued to make heavy investments in plant and product improvement, buttressed by a high national savings rate and supportive bank financing. Worrying little about shareholder dividends or short-term profits, they set out to enlarge their market share. In the long run, it is the company dominating the market that can set prices and maximize profits, by developing consumer loyalty. The Japanese manager's principal responsibility is to the community-company, workers included, to all the stakeholders rather than merely to his shareholders. Because of his heavy bank financing, he need not depend for his funding (and, likely as not, his job) on the fickle judgments of the securities markets. He can plan for the far future, sustaining short-term losses, if need be, with support from the *keiretsu* company of which he is a part.

The American manager's primary responsibility is to his shareholders, who are most keenly interested in the current value of their stock. Wall Street analysts are seldom happy about companies investing large sums in research and technology that can only pay off in the far future, for the big players in U.S. stock markets are pension funds and other large institutions uninterested in the companies whose stocks they buy—except as temporary investments. Thus Wall Street rejoices when companies blindly cut costs and close plants in the interests of short-term profitability, thereby presumably proving that they are "lean and mean."

In addition, as we have already pointed out, the cost of investment capital in the United States is high, thanks partly to a tax system that favors spenders rather than savers. It is not easy to build for the far future.

Perhaps understandably, therefore, American managers insist on huge compensation packages, since they cannot count on job security. Whereas Japanese company presidents and chairmen of very large corporations rarely receive more than $500,000 annually in total compensation, thousands of American bosses are well into the seven-figure league. In Graef Crystal's book, previously cited, he recalled a 1991 study in which he calculated the average compensation package of CEOs in 200 major American companies as $2.8 million—if one included stock options and long-term incentive plans. Japanese executives' salaries on the average amount to about 17 times the average worker's salary in their plants; American bosses can receive as much as 100 times their workers' average pay, although the norm will be lower. When business is bad, Japanese executives are the first to take a pay cut. In the United States, by contrast, Crystal's and other studies have shown, top executives' salaries and other compensations keep ascending, whether the company's results are good or bad. American workers are generally paid what the company sets as a fixed wage for a specific job. In Japan, since employees' twice-yearly bonuses depend on their company's performance, a practical version of profit sharing is constantly in effect—a built-in cooperative.

4. *Industrial Policy*. Throughout these chapters we have seen ample evidence of the government support given Japanese companies. Although the simplistic development economy of Japan, Inc., has given way to more complex government-business relationships, Japan's government ministries continue to guide the macroeconomy in the interests of Japanese business, helping corporations plan and attain their long-term goals. (Even closer guidance is exerted on business by the governments of Korea and Singapore.) Government, business, and finance are communicating and cooperating at several levels. This is in sharp distinction to the traditional regulatory, indeed adversary role of the American government in the economy. The mere fact of a President bringing business leaders with him in a table-pounding exercise in Tokyo has little effect on an outmoded system of laws and regulative agencies which, if energetically enforced, brings government into a constant "cops and robbers" relationship with American business. If slackly enforced, there is almost no relationship at all.

SIGNIFICANT cultural differences, we have seen, stand between Japan's business world and America's. America is a multiracial society and pluralist, with many subcultures not only tolerated but encouraged. Japan is monoracial and in one sense monocultural, but with a traditional genius in adapting useful features of other cultures and incorporating them into its own. Neither culture is going to change overnight, but both are historically receptive—with a long and not unsuccessful record of interaction.

Over the past four decades, Japanese adopted American ideas of democracy and capitalist efficiency—from women's suffrage and free trade unions to quality-control circles and transistors. In the 1990s, many Americans are thinking and working in Japanese terms. The 3,500 American employees of Mazda's Flat Rock plant near Detroit work in teams of six to ten people who switch jobs with each other to learn additional skills. There is constant pressure on groups to come up with suggestions that cut costs or boost productivity. *Kaizen*— "change for the good"—the Japanese call this. Mazda's American employees are less congenial to traditional tokens of Japanese groupiness like uniforms and company songs, and their union leaders resent the unrelenting pressure to improve. ("We're elevating each other to a much loftier vicissitude," one said.) But they have adjusted well to a work routine that is reasonable and provides obvious trade-offs.

"We have a no-layoff clause in our contract," one worker told our television interviewers, "which is outstanding. A lot of people want security and Mazda offers them that.

"The company demands a lot—and rightfully so. The quality idea was something I hadn't been exposed to in my previous positions. When they talk about quality, they definitely live it."

Japanese ideas for human capital and workplace improvement can prove out in an American context. Many American companies have demonstrated their worth; some, like Thomas Watson's IBM, seem to have worked on the principle of human capital long before the debut of the Nissan shop uniform or the Matsushita company song. The costs of raising capital in the United States are generally higher than in Japan, partly because of the low rate of savings, but they do not represent an insuperable barrier. The real problem has been the chronic unwillingness of American firms to put a great deal of money into markets without an immediate payoff. Time and time again Japanese competitors—in consumer electronics for one—took over markets when American companies, faced with dwindling profits, simply decided to close the businesses affected and "diversify" into other, less competitive and more immediately profitable areas of endeavor.

In Japanese business this would not have happened. Japan's vaunted MITI—the Ministry for International Trade and Industry—would have taken strong action against foreign competitors, meanwhile extending its support to local companies for long-range research and targeted economic expansion. In consumer electronics, as in other industries, this is exactly what happened. Overtly and covertly MITI and other ministries saw to it that foreign competition was excluded from Japan while they built up local manufacturers with the help of tax breaks and various export and investment credits. At the same time the ministry worked with cartels of Japanese manufacturers to dump their products in the United States. In the late sixties Japanese television sets cost half as much in the United States as they did at home in Japan, whose loyal consumers in effect paid for their country's invasion of the American market.[7]

Playing hardball in support of domestic industry was by no means unknown in the United States. The Pentagon and its civilian contractors had worked out for years on the familiar unlevel playing field of military procurement. But that was for national security. The words "security" and "economy" did not seem to mix. Yet what MITI was doing to support technology for Japan's worldwide economy was exactly what the Pentagon had been doing to stimulate American R&D, in the cause of national defense, for the past forty-five years.

[7] A succinct study of the consumer electronics market is contained in *Made in America*, MIT's survey of American productivity problems (Cambridge: MIT Press, 1990).

In 1956 an American firm called Ampex invented the first videotape recorder. But it took almost twenty years and an enormous investment in R&D to commercialize this technology for the consumer revolution in VCRs. Along the way, Ampex and other American companies dropped out of the play, unwilling or unable to spend the money it took to stay ahead in a market they had pioneered. Today there are more than 250 million videocassette recorders around the world. Most are produced by Japan, Korea, and Taiwan.

Charles Anderson was an engineer on the Ampex team that invented the first video recorder. He now works for a Japanese company, Panasonic—one of some three million Americans whose new jobs were created by foreign investment, principally from the Asia-Pacific countries. "The technology," as he recalls today, "with one exception was all developed back in our lab. The same FM system was used. The present format approximates the early units that we did. It's all there. We just lacked the vision, we lacked the courage to make long-term investments. We walked away from it."

Much the same thing happened earlier with television. American companies first encouraged the new Japanese electronics firms to make parts. They soon began turning out full sets. They were innovative and took risks. For example, while American companies kept making tubes for large, high-quality sets, the Japanese replaced them first with transistors, then semi-conductors. They learned quickly. Starting at the low end of the market, they soon had the experience to make big color sets better and more cheaply in their automated factories.

Aggrieved American electronics firms sued, the while cutting back on their research expenditures, and legal battles raged for almost twenty years, until the Supreme Court in 1986 set aside a lower court's ruling in favor of the Americans. Throughout this period the executive branch was of little help. When Zenith made its final reappeal, the U.S. government joined the Japanese government in opposing it. Some years before, the U.S. Customs Service had indeed ordered the Japanese makers to pay $800 million in duties for "dumping" over a fifteen-year period.[8] At this the Japanese government disclosed that the Carter administration had previously promised to halt the Customs investigations as part of an Orderly Marketing agreement with Japan. In the end the Commerce Department settled the dispute for $78 million in fines and duties— barely a slap on the wrist for years of price fixing.

In electronics and other industries American business kept losing the game

---

[8] It must be noted that "dumping" is a violation only of U.S. law and business practices. In Japan there is nothing wrong with the practice of cutting prices to retain market share in a certain market, then raising prices after the market has been secured. Adam Smith would probably not have objected.

because of short-term thinking, complacency, and an inability to take its Asian competitors seriously—until it was too late. This was nowhere more obvious than with automobiles. Twenty years before Detroit's Big Three chairmen went to Tokyo with George Bush was the time to have started planning economic strategy.

But the complacency of successive American administrations about international competition was even worse. The arsenal of democracy, the keeper of the peace, the leader of the free world—those were the roles Presidents wanted their country to play. And in ensuring the security of the free world, the East Asian countries—Japan in particular—were our allies. Whenever people in the Commerce Department began to make noises about industrial policy and Japanese "targeting" of key American markets, they were countered by an angry State Department pointing to the sanctity of the Japanese alliance—"the most important American bilateral relationship," former ambassador to Japan Mike Mansfield used to put it, "bar none." And with the threat of Soviet power ever present, who could deny the priority of political and strategic over economic relationships?

So the trade-offs continued. The spasmodic American demands for an economic "level playing field" affected the Japanese business boom rather like the occasional thumps on the wall by a neighbor weakly complaining about an all-night party. ("Once the band stops for a few minutes, he'll go back to sleep.") By the eighties, also, the two economies had become so intertwined that it was very difficult to separate them either by embargo or by legislation. The same automobile makers who denounced competition from Japan were using Mitsubishi engines in their new models or working out joint ventures with Mazda or Toyota.

THE WEST COAST of the United States, particularly, was conscious of a close interlocking relationship with its transpacific neighbors. Seattle's Boeing Company is the biggest American exporter, and Asia is its most important overseas market. In 1991 Boeing delivered its seventy-fifth 747 to Japan Air Lines, with sixty-one more 747s either on order or on option. To help develop its new 777 aircraft, Boeing is taking in Japanese aircraft companies as subcontractors and partners.

Another Seattle success story is Microsoft, the world's largest computer software producer. Although ahead of the Japanese in software development, Microsoft, like other American high-tech companies, relies on Japanese hardware producers to pioneer new multimedia technologies.

Increasingly, however, other Asian nations besides Japan have become part of the transpacific connection. Microsoft, for example, produces software in the

Koreatown in Los Angeles. Asian Americans now represent the fastest-growing group of immigrants to the United States. Lisa Romerein/Los Angeles Times

President Bush and Japan's Prime Minister Miyazawa in 1992. The visit of Bush and the Big Three automobile executives to Tokyo was a demeaning exercise in economic diplomacy. Jigsaw Productions

major Asian languages and runs branches in Korea, Singapore, and Taiwan. Taiwan is now third in the world in the production of liquid crystal computer screens and is a key IBM supplier. Korean companies are also extending their Pacific reach. Samsung recently built a chip-making plant in California to supply the American market. Late in 1991, Boeing's old rival, the California-based McDonnell Douglas, hard pressed for funds, was casting about for investment partners. It was a Taiwan firm, Taiwan Air, that offered to buy as much as 40 percent of the company.

In the world of finance, however, Japan remains an all too important American partner. Thanks to heavy borrowings over the past decade, the United States Treasury needs some $10 billion a month merely to service the national debt. Over the past half decade, more than a third of this money has been borrowed from Japanese investors. As of June 1992, the Japanese hold an estimated $250 billion worth of U.S. government bonds, plus additional vast sums in stocks and business investments.

Japanese invested their money in the United States originally because this was profitable, thanks largely to the high yen (dating from the Baker 1985 Plaza Agreement), high interest rates in the United States, and very low interest rates in Japan. Japanese investments are influenced—to put it mildly—by the macroeconomic policies of the government, as well as the interests of the individual investors.

Should Japanese money managers decide to stop investing, the Treasury would have to sell its bills elsewhere—probably to American banks. This could cause great confusion, now that Japanese investors have become part of the American economic landscape. It would, for one thing, mop up a good bit of available investment capital in the United States, with a chain of both monetary and fiscal consequences.

By the spring of 1992 there were many signs that exactly this was happening. Hard hit by the American real estate recession, Japanese investors, many of whom had bought at the height of the market, were looking for the exits. In addition, the collapse of Japan's "bubble economy"—or at least a portion of it—in 1991 and 1992, along with the attendant fall in Tokyo stock prices, had left most banks and corporations in Japan far poorer than they were popularly thought to be. Japanese investments in the United States began to fall off sharply, causing considerable alarm to Americans who had grown dependent on them.

THE DIFFERENCES in economic priorities between Japan and the United States, already great, were widened, disastrously, during the Greed Decade of the 1980s. When Ronald Reagan took office in 1980, he inherited from the

Carter administration a national debt approaching one trillion dollars. When he left office eight years later, the debt exceeded $2.5 trillion. In 1992, given an estimated annual deficit of $350 billion, the Bush administration could reckon on a negative nest egg that approached $3.2 trillion, more than half of America's $5.5 trillion gross national product.

It would be unfair solely to blame Reagan (or his successor) for this extraordinary disfiguring of the economy. Congress and many others share the responsibility. (The origins of the debt expansion, in fact, go back to Lyndon Johnson, who made the mistake of trying to fight the Vietnam War on the expense account.) But it was Reagan whose economic policies—or lack of them—were most immediately responsible.

Reagan came to Washington with an appetizing set of goals. A firm believer in free enterprise, he agreed with a new breed of "supply-side" economists that government's primary role was to remove obstacles in the way of businessmen investing and making money. Accordingly, he would cut taxes and scale down "big government." Thus freed from heavy taxes and (by definition) onerous government regulation, American capitalism would make profits and prosper, its gains "trickling down" to the entire country. In the process, taxes from increased economic activity could balance the budget. International competition posed no problems, as long as it was not Communist. The United States was committed to free trade. At home, however, government regulation of the private sector should be drastically diminished, along with the level of government spending—except for defense. Here America should spend heavily, so the country could "stand tall," facing down the Communist enemy.

These laudable goals, regrettably, were only marginally applicable to the state of the nation during Reagan's years in office. They had deep and unexpected results. While a massive tax cut of almost $800 billion was enacted, it accomplished little for American economic health. Productivity and savings rates continued to fall. But big businessmen and investment bankers—assisted by the first tax cut in a half century to favor the rich—began a feeding frenzy of mergers, unfriendly takeovers, and leveraged buyouts that left some of America's best companies debt-ridden shells. Hundreds of thousands were thrown out of work, as company divisions and subsidiaries were ruthlessly eliminated in the interests of short-term profits and debt reduction.

With government banking regulation greatly weakened in the interests of entrepreneurial freedom, banks lost depositors' money by the buckets in ill-considered commercial dealings. The country's saving and loan associations, hitherto strongholds of small depositors and sober mortgage lending, were triumphantly deregulated by President Reagan early in his administration. Vast numbers of them proceeded to embark on a wave of reckless and sometimes criminal speculative investment, whose effects are still with us. As of the latest reckoning, the U.S. taxpayers have already had to pay out almost $300 billion for this adventure. By the end of the century, the bill will be closer to $400 billion! Meanwhile the ultimate effect of deregulation on air transportation, begun in the Carter administration, was to squeeze out many useful small airlines, concentrating the market in the hands of a few huge survivors, who were now free to carve up the market at will. Similar examples abound.

Continuing a buildup begun by its predecessors, the Reagan administration spent vast sums on the military. Although much of this spending was excessive or downright wasteful—the Navy is now trying to mothball a goodly percentage of the 600-ship fleet thought necessary to overawe the Soviets—it probably had some effect in dampening the Russians' ardor for adversary military spending.[9] The buildup's momentum, plus lessons learned from the bungled invasions of Grenada and Panama, doubtless paved the way for the military success of the later Gulf War.

Yet the military spending, coupled with tax cuts and the bad recession in 1982, only served to swell the deficit. To compensate for defense dollars, government cut heavily into education, health, public works, and nonmilitary research, at a time when more, not less, spending was needed there. Little effort was made to make better sense out of the huge amounts of "entitlement" spending, regarded as politically sacrosanct.

Thanks to tough policies at the Federal Reserve Bank, inflation was checked during the Reagan years. Unemployment figures went down, and there was a boom in service industries. But the recovery was fueled mostly by foreign investment. The new jobs were different: more service-oriented, worse-paying, less permanent. And the growth in GNP was the worst distributed in modern American history. When statisticians began sorting out the gains in 1992, it appeared that fully 60 percent of the growth in American families' income between 1977 and 1989 had gone to the top 1 percent! In after-tax terms, the figure was 75 percent. Middle-income families experienced only very slight gains; the bottom 40 percent of America's families saw their incomes go down. But hordes of investment bankers, high-priced lawyers, and brokers grew almost unbelievably rich, thanks to the swollen profits they made from highly unproductive leveraged buyouts, mergers, and acquisitions.

The economist Robert Kuttner calls the Reagan years the "Great Deferral."[10] By piling up huge deficits, temporarily covered by foreign investment, Reagan's money handlers postponed the need for Americans to face up to their

[9] Washington wags had said, with some truth, that the only people outside of President Reagan to believe in the efficacy of his "Star Wars" antimissile defense were the Soviet General Staff, a group traditionally worshipful of American technological know-how.

[10] In his thought-provoking book *The End of Laissez-Faire* (New York: Knopf, 1991). Robert Reich's *The Work of Nations* (New York: Knopf, 1991), Kevin Phillips's invaluable *The Politics of Rich and Poor* (New York: Random House, 1990), and Adam Smith's *The Roaring Eighties* (New York: Summit, 1988) all offer valuable insights into this period.

national obligations. Corporate debt increased, to the point where it was larger than corporate equities. By easing up on the regulatory and punitive powers of government, the White House encouraged the antics of Wall Street wheeler-dealers like Ivan Boesky, who epitomized an era in his now famous 1986 graduation address at UCLA: "Greed is all right. Greed is healthy. You can be greedy and still feel good about yourself."

With his constant clarion calls to defeat the "Evil Empire" and make America stronger, Reagan obscured the basic change in international economic and hence political realities wrought during his incumbency. For economics was becoming the politics of the twenty-first century impending, and a new estimate of national strength was long overdue.

THE OLD RAILROAD yards outside of Detroit were no longer well kept up, and only a few freight cars stood on a siding. The man in the tower looked down sadly at the tracks below. "When I came here nineteen years ago," he said, "and I'm serious—there used to be a saying—'If I don't like this job, I can just quit and go across the street and get another job.' And that was the truth; you could do that. They needed you. This company here was glad to get you if you were going to be a decent worker. . . .

"In the last ten years they've had the attitude they wished they could get rid of you. Now the cars don't go through here the way they used to. I'll lose this job. I'm assured to end up working for half or less money than I make now. You could end up working anywhere. . . .

"You've got a family to feed. You've got to feed them. My daughter's ten. There's a lot of things she wants to do that she never got to do. When she's fifteen, sixteen years old she'll want a car and I'm facing a minimum wage. It's a bad situation."[11]

The towerman's lament could now be heard throughout America. It was there in the go-go eighties, but by no means was so general. And the erosion of people from traditionally solid blue-collar jobs was overlooked in the flurry of new, if less well-paying opportunities in service industries. By the winter of 1991–92, in the depths of George Bush's depression, the newspapers were headlining the unheard-of: 60,000 to be let go at General Motors, 20,000 at IBM. The doleful litanies continued.

"Competition" was the reason most generally given—and overseas competition in particular. "Money is hard to come by." "Investment has to be watched." So the public relations releases ran, and with no job security some millions of Americans were out on the streets. Estimates in early 1992 noted an unemployment rate of 9 percent.

[11] As interviewed on *The Pacific Century* television series.

Yamaichi Security's New York office. In finance as well as manufacturing, the Japanese influence increases, but not without its problems. Jigsaw Productions

New transpacific airplane for JAL. The Japanese are Boeing's best customers. Jigsaw Productions

U.S. computer conference. In software, the Americans remained ahead. Jigsaw Productions

This was a basic social problem, not merely a matter of economic adjustment. People fired meant families uprooted; families uprooted meant cities uprooted. In a conversation I had with him in the mid-eighties, Doug Fraser, the former president of the UAW–CIO and one of the statesmen of the American labor movement, had said: "When I look at what is happening in Detroit and elsewhere, I can only think: I hope this doesn't mean the end of the blue-collar middle class. For they are the people who built America."

The mass layoffs in American industry—contrasting so sharply with the swollen seven-figure compensation packages of successful (or unsuccessful) corporation CEOs—had no cushion under them, other than the unemployment insurance and welfare payments that were already dragging down state treasuries across the nation. They fell most heavily on the socially and racially disadvantaged; blue-collar jobs in rust-belt factories had long been a magnet for ambitious black workers heading to the cities to better themselves. With tested industries feeling the pinch, there were few retraining programs for taking workers from sunset industries and teaching them new skills. In Japan such courses would have been routine. This was government's job. The free market could not provide such training by itself.

American education in general seemed badly skewed, away from meeting the challenge of changing economies and an information society going commercial. Whereas the Japanese and Koreans were turning out engineers, American college students were setting their sights on being MBAs, with investment banking or financial management their goals—anything but production.

For more than a decade, behind the façade of the world imperium and strategic buildups, strange things had been happening to the American economy. In 1991, the average American worker was making, per hour, about fifty cents less in real dollars than he was in 1970. One out of three jobs in basic American industries has disappeared. Whole communities of people have been destroyed. There are some 40 million people living below the poverty line in the United States of America.

We can't blame those failings on the Japanese. We can, however, profit from the example of Japanese, Koreans, maritime Chinese, and others and try to fashion an industrial policy that will anticipate economic change and direct it, instead of waiting to cope with its consequences. We have every advantage in doing this. The United States retains the leadership in technology, in creative science and research, in higher education. We also have the ideal of individualism, operating within the framework of a pluralist society united by diversity and a shared sense of values.

Filtered as they are by our own experience and tradition, we have kept alive the rational ideals and universal truth-craving of Rome and Greece. We have been the vehicle through which these ideas of Western individualism and democracy came across the Pacific. We should recall, however, that the civilization of China outlasted that of Rome. It is in fact the Chinese idea of the family and the community—as reinterpreted by Japan, Korea, and others—which should give us a new perspective. Economy, in the root meaning of the Greek *oikonomos*, means a stewardship—that is, to manage and distribute the work and goods of a household or community. It is more, far more than the pursuit of private gain.

Conclusion

American society has distinguished itself throughout its history by two great attributes. The first is the ability to take people of widely different backgrounds, cultures, and faiths and assimilate them to the American ideology. This is, essentially, a shared faith in a self-governing polity of citizens, secure in their individual freedoms and equal in their opportunity, but dedicated to safeguard justice and promote the public welfare according to rational principles. Not an easy bill to fill. The second attribute is to adapt their democratic governments, as the historian Samuel Eliot Morison had it, to guide "the changes already wrought and being wrought in American society." The best of these governments, to continue Morison's thought, were "progressives," at least in the sense that "they attempted through government action to curb the arrogance of organized wealth and the wretchedness of poverty amid plenty."

And here we return to the presidential cousins whose conversation we imagined at the outset of this chapter. The two great progressive reforms of our time were initiated, as it happened, by the Roosevelts: first Theodore, next Franklin. Each set of reforms looked both outward, to the development of relations with other countries, and inward, to assuring fair treatment to all and improving the quality of life within the Republic. Each President and the people around him—politicians, academics, businessmen, and journalists—had the foresight and courage to break old precedents and set the Republic's course in new directions.

The first Roosevelt era was most obviously characterized by outward expansion, principally in the Pacific. The Philippines were secured and colonized; the Panama Canal was cut; and America with confidence assumed its role as a world power to be reckoned with. To many, Teddy Roosevelt is remembered as the classic American imperialist. But if he was an imperialist, he was one with a shrewd feel for international political realities and a statesman's sense of national interests and limitations.

He was also a reformer, whose solid domestic achievements outlived his flashier posturings in foreign policy. In Walter Lippmann's words, he was "the first President who shared a new social vision." A self-styled "crusader," Roosevelt believed government should be interventionist. It was not only government's duty to correct imbalances of power and privilege in American society. The national government was also bound to innovate and lead, pointing the way for citizens and local governments to follow.

In this spirit Roosevelt fought against America's huge big-business trusts, the conglomerates of their day, to keep a level playing field, so to speak, within the national economy. Nor did he hesitate to challenge both labor and management when he felt their disputes endangered public welfare. He pioneered consumer protection with the Pure Food and Drug Act, and set up the Interstate Commerce Commission to regulate transportation—"a milestone," as the Encyclopaedia Britannica put it, "on the long road to the modern social-service state."

He was the original ecology President, long before that now well-worn phrase was current. He reclaimed vast portions of land—almost 200 million acres—for national parks and natural resources preserves. He fought corruption in public officials and, with his establishment of presidential commissions, encouraged talented and distinguished Americans to serve on fact-finding panels, studying immigration, farm problems, and other matters of national concern. Roosevelt, as Lippmann later summarized, was "the first President who realized that national stability and social justice had to be sought deliberately and had consciously to be maintained."[12]

Roosevelt's Square Deal had its flaws. But in his seven years in office he set a new course for his country that carried it rather grandly into the twentieth century. Which is to say, he saw new challenges and set about to meet them. In his vision he was far ahead of his time. But his ingrained politician's sense gave him the skill to carry the voters with him, for at least a good part of the way.

In 1932, just one generation after, his fifth cousin Franklin D. Roosevelt[13] became President and began to change history with his New Deal. Faced with the Great Depression, probably the most severe economic downturn in American history, Roosevelt used the full powers of the government to mobilize and reapportion the nation's resources. With massive retraining and public works programs, sweeping agricultural reforms, and public power projects he began a

[12] As quoted in Ronald Steel's *Walter Lippmann and the American Century* (Boston: Atlantic–Little, Brown, 1980).

[13] The relationship proved to be closer than that. Franklin married Theodore Roosevelt's niece, the redoubtable Eleanor Roosevelt. He was a great admirer of Uncle Ted's, at least in his early years. Although a Democrat, he came into politics inspired by Teddy Roosevelt's example, and in his first big post, as Assistant Secretary of the Navy, he followed squarely in Teddy's footsteps.

sustained effort at national planning. Although some of his innovations, like the business-oriented National Recovery Act, backfired, others became part and parcel of modern American tradition and practice. The Wagner Act of 1935 became a new bill of rights for American labor, enforcing collective bargaining and unions' right to strike. The Social Security Act established the American system of unemployment and old-age insurance. The Securities and Exchange Act gave new protection to small investors and set forth strong rules and guidelines for what had hitherto been a lawless stock market. The Works Progress Administration set hundreds of thousands of the unemployed on the road to jobs. The Tennessee Valley Authority became the model program for reviving a depressed area with cheap government power.

It can be argued that much of the New Deal program was ill advised or poorly administered, or that, with many reforms in trouble, the American economy was ultimately bailed out by the huge mass-production spending of World War II. Such criticisms, even where very specific, are historically irrelevant. The effect of the New Deal on the country was total and irreversible. It restored faith in government, by setting government firmly on the side of those who needed help and against entrenched economic power and privilege. It identified government with planning and progress in American life.

The New Deal also created a new internationalism in America. Along with the refocusing of the nation's energies and the redistribution of its wealth came a consciousness of a national mission, which emerged from the victory in World War II. The Marshall Plan for Europe and the American Occupation of Japan grew out of the Roosevelt years.

In many ways FDR carried on the reforms that Theodore Roosevelt had begun. But in the twenty-four years that separated their administrations many of TR's reforms—and those of Woodrow Wilson, it must be added—had been put on hold, compromised, or in fact reversed. Complacent or incompetent Presidents and Congresses were no match for the influence peddlers, the money players, and the political and social reactionaries who prospered in the years of Harding, Coolidge, and Hoover. By the time Franklin D. Roosevelt came to office, it was time to break the mold again and get the society moving.

Much the same can be said today. The America of the 1990s is not the America of Teddy Roosevelt's 1900s or Franklin Roosevelt's 1930s. Much that they did in those times would not be suitable in today's world; while some of their ideas need restatement, others need substantial revision. But change is overdue. We had Eisenhower's updated Era of Good Feeling,[14] the unfulfilled vision of John F. Kennedy, the aborted Great Society of Lyndon Johnson, and the fissuring of the Vietnam years. Since then the screen has been dark.

Now we are faced with another classic opportunity to bring America up to

[14] With apologies to James Monroe and the original.

Seventeenth-century Dutch voyager. Modern communications have made the Pacific a two-way street. The Bettmann Archive

date. It is also a screeching imperative. Before the United States can play the role it should in the world outside, a period of the most intense and sweeping domestic reform is needed. We need an industrial policy for the twenty-first century, not a holding action designed to keep us at the vanished midpoint of the twentieth. In support of this, we need to rebuild our crumbling urban infrastructure. Beyond economics and politics, we need a sense of community that can take the contentious, fractionalizing elements in our society and infuse them with a new sense of common purpose and common destiny. A sense of and for this time.

Under the pressure of modern technology—the technology which we largely invented—our economy has been swiftly changing from the old industrial mass production to a knowledge economy. This is a sweeping change. Our people have made new demands on education, law enforcement, and social justice. But we have continued to live off old social capital, in a society whose laws, school systems, and lifestyles are rooted in the old system.

Instead of reviving this society, we have fractionalized it. We are far from making the national effort necessary to face realities and make the changes that are required. Our political leadership in Washington has been in the hands of cautious timeservers. Big business and big labor have both priced themselves out of the market. Meanwhile the poor proliferate in the midst of plenty; the rich are greedy and increasingly unproductive. And our "instant gratification" society has become the prey of narrow special interest groups, whose clamor grows worse as they are more indulged. We have done everything possible to diminish the risk factor in our society, at precisely the time when we must take risks and rethink our premises—just as we did in the early 1900s and the 1930s. Politicians and public vie in shirking the hard choices.

The Asia-Pacific nations at our doorstep, taking many a cue from our own experience, have not been afraid to take risks. By virtually deifying education they have assimilated new technology, but they have not turned their backs on old values. Over the past half century they have built new dynamic economies, on the ruins of old economic principles. Albeit in varying degrees, they have kept a sense of community identity and community action. To go forward, they need our help and past example.

Equally, we need them. We can learn much from their present achievement, and we must.

Maps

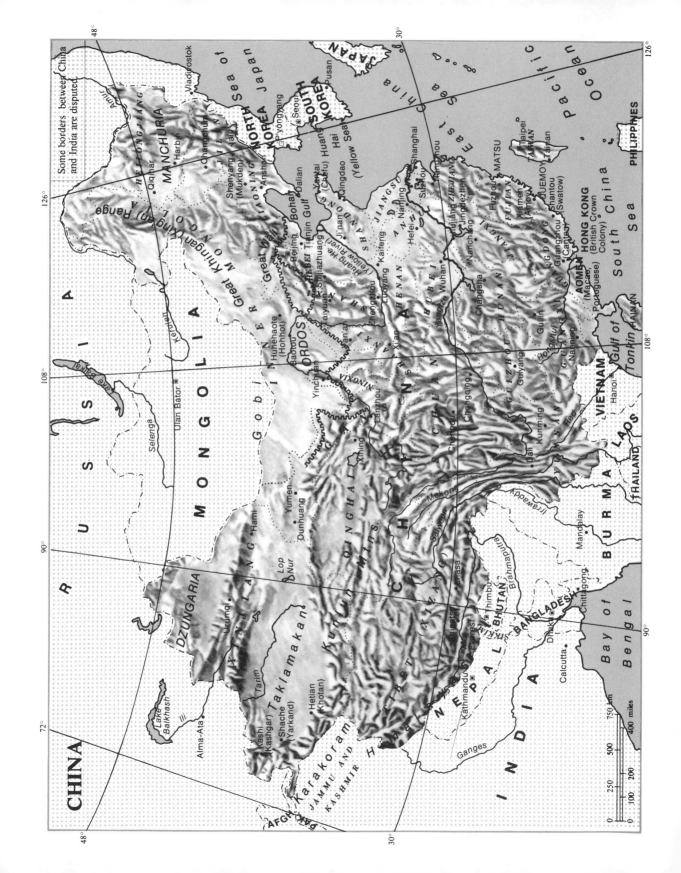

CHINA

Some borders between China and India are disputed

R U S S I A

MONGOLIA

Ulan Bator

Lake Baikal
Selenga
Kerülen

Gobi Desert

MANCHURIA

HEILONGJIANG

Khingan (Xing'an) Range

Greater

Amur
Vladivostok
Sea of Japan
JAPAN

Harbin
Qiqihar
JILIN
Changchun
LIAONING
Shenyang (Mukden)
Anshan
NORTH KOREA
Pyongyang
Yalu
SOUTH KOREA
Seoul
Pusan

Hohhot (Huhehaote)
NEI MONGGOL
Baotou
ORDOS
Great Wall
HEBEI
Beijing
Tianjin Gulf
Bohai
Dalian
Yantai
Qingdao
SHANDONG
(Yellow Sea)
Huang Hai (Yellow Sea)
East China Sea

Yinchuan
NINGXIA
Lanzhou
SHANXI
Taiyuan
Shijiazhuang
Huang He (Yellow River)
Jinan
Kaifeng
HENAN
Zhengzhou
Luoyang
Xi'an
SHAANXI
Yan'an
HUBEI
Wuhan
Yangtze
ANHUI
Hefei
Hefei
JIANGSU
Nanjing
Shanghai
ZHEJIANG
Suzhou
Hangzhou

DZUNGARIA
Ürümqi
XINJIANG
Hami
Lop Nur
Tarim
Taklamakan
Kashi (Kashgar)
Shache (Yarkand)
Hetian (Khotan)
Alma-Ata
Lake Balkhash

Yumen
Dunhuang
QINGHAI
Kunlun Mtns
Xining

SICHUAN
Chengdu
Chongqing
Mekong
Salween

XIZANG
TIBET
Lhasa
Xigatsê
Brahmaputra

HUNAN
Changsha
Hengshui
JIANGXI
Nanchang
Jiujiang
Jingdezhen
FUJIAN
Fuzhou
MATSU
QUEMOY
Xiamen (Amoy)
TAIWAN
Taipei
Tainan

GUIZHOU
Guiyang
GUANGXI
Nanning
GUANGDONG
Guangzhou (Canton)
Gui
Guilin
Hongshui
Xi
Hong

C H I N A

Kunming
Dali
YUNNAN

AOMEN (Macao) (Portuguese)
HONG KONG (British Crown Colony)
South China Sea

VIETNAM
Hanoi
Gulf of Tonkin
HAINAN

LAOS
BURMA
Mandalay
Irrawaddy
THAILAND

NEPAL
Kathmandu
BHUTAN
Thimbu
SIKKIM
Everest
BANGLADESH
Dhaka
Chittagong
Ganges
Calcutta
Bay of Bengal
I N D I A

AFGH.
PAK.
JAMMU AND KASHMIR
Karakoram
H i m a l a y a
Himalayas

PHILIPPINES
Pacific Ocean

0   250   500   750 km
0   100 200   400 miles

48°   126°   30°   126°
72°   90°   108°   108°   90°
48°   30°

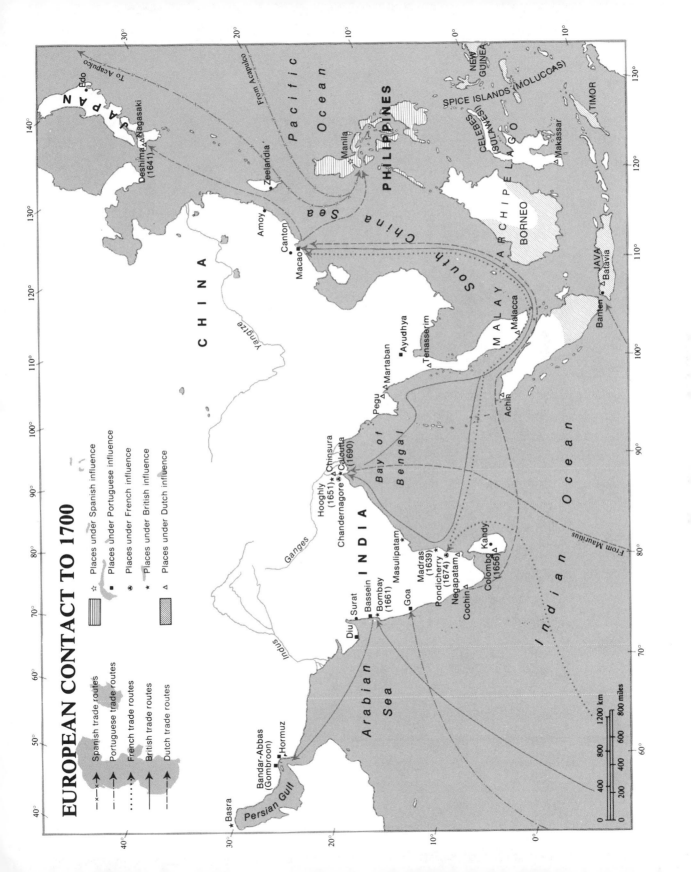

EUROPEAN CONTACT TO 1700

	Spanish trade routes			Places under Spanish influence
–x–		☆		
–·–	Portuguese trade routes	■		Places under Portuguese influence
····	French trade routes	◉		Places under French influence
→	British trade routes	★		Places under British influence
⇢	Dutch trade routes	△		Places under Dutch influence

JAPAN

Edo

Nagasaki
Deshima (1641)

To Acapulco

From Acapulco

Pacific Ocean

CHINA

Yangtze

Amoy

Canton
Macao

Zeelandia

East China Sea

South China Sea

Manila

PHILIPPINES

NEW GUINEA

SPICE ISLANDS (MOLUCCAS)

CELEBES (SULAWESI)

Makassar

TIMOR

MALAY ARCHIPELAGO

BORNEO

JAVA
Batavia

Banten

Malacca

Achin

Ayudhya

Tenasserim

Martaban

Pegu

INDIA

Ganges

Indus

Hooghly (1651)
Chandernagore
Chinsura
Calcutta (1690)

Bay of Bengal

Masulipatam

Madras (1639)

Pondicherry (1674)

Negapatam

Kandy

Colombo (1656)

Cochin

Goa

Bombay (1661)

Bassein

Surat

Diu

Arabian Sea

Indian Ocean

From Mauritius

Persian Gulf

Hormuz

Bandar-Abbas (Gombroon)

Basra

0   200   400   600   800 km
0   400   800   1200 km
0   400   600   800 miles

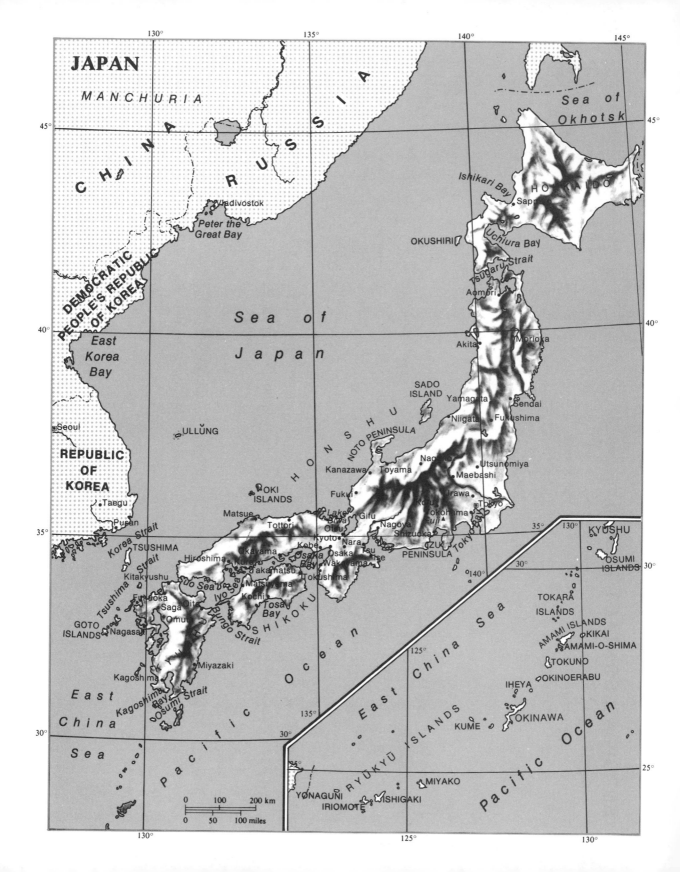

JAPAN

MANCHURIA

CHINA

RUSSIA

Sea of Okhotsk

HOKKAIDO

Vladivostok

Ishikari Bay

Sapporo

Peter the Great Bay

OKUSHIRI

Uchiura Bay

Tsugaru Strait

DEMOCRATIC PEOPLE'S REPUBLIC OF KOREA

Aomori

East Korea Bay

Sea of Japan

Akita

Morioka

SADO ISLAND

Yamagata

Sendai

Seoul

ULLŬNG

Niigata

Fukushima

REPUBLIC OF KOREA

HONSHU

NOTO PENINSULA

Nagano

Utsunomiya

Kanazawa

Toyama

Maebashi

OKI ISLANDS

Urawa

Taegu

Fukui

Kofu

Tokyo

Pusan

Matsue

Lake Biwa

Gifu

Nagoya

Shizuoka

Yokohama

Korea Strait

Tottori

Otsu

Kyoto

Nara

Tsu

Yokohama

TSUSHIMA Strait

Hiroshima

Okayama

Kobe

Osaka

Wakayama

Ise

IZU PENINSULA

Tokyo

Kitakyushu

Kure

Osaka Bay

KYUSHU

OSUMI ISLANDS

Fukuoka

Iyo Sea

Takamatsu

Tokushima

Matsuyama

SHIKOKU

TOKARA ISLANDS

Saga

Oita

Kochi

Tosa Bay

GOTO ISLANDS

Omuta

Bungo Strait

AMAMI ISLANDS

Nagasaki

KIKAI

SAMAMI-O-SHIMA

Miyazaki

TOKUNO

East China Sea

OKINOERABU

Kagoshima

IHEYA

Kagoshima Bay

Osumi Strait

KUME

OKINAWA

East China Sea

Pacific Ocean

RYUKYU ISLANDS

Pacific Ocean

YONAGUNI

MIYAKO

IRIOMOTE

ISHIGAKI

0   100   200 km

0   50   100 miles

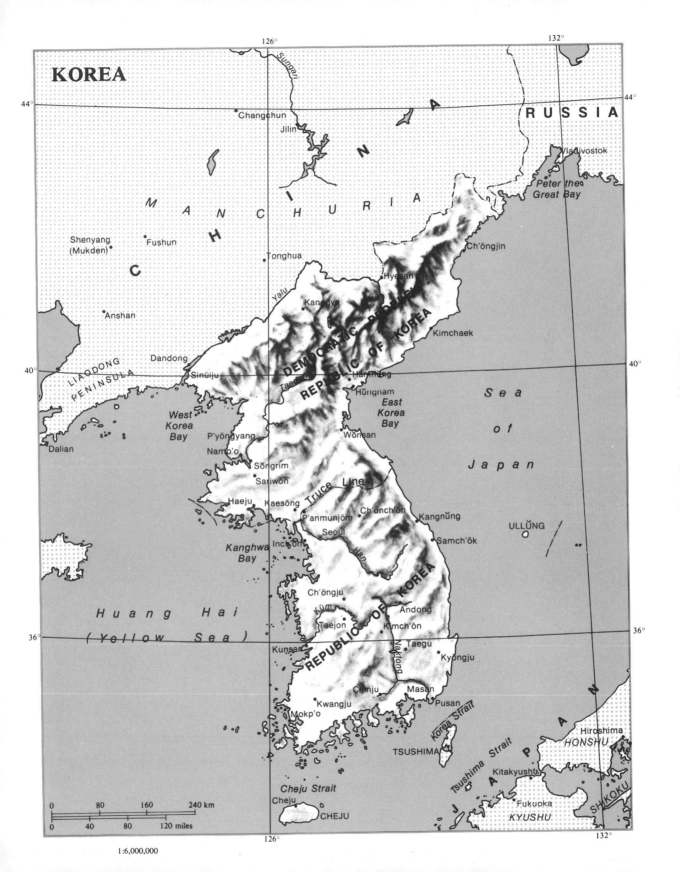

KOREA

CHINA

RUSSIA

MANCHURIA

Changchun
Jilin

Vladivostok

Peter the
Great Bay

Shenyang
(Mukden)
Fushun
Tonghua

Ch'ŏngjin

Hyesan

Kanggye

Yalu

Kimchaek

Anshan

DEMOCRATIC PEOPLE'S

Dandong

LIAODONG
PENINSULA

Sinŭiju

REPUBLIC OF KOREA

Taedong
Hamhŭng

West
Korea
Bay

Dalian

P'yŏngyang

Namp'o

Sŏngrim

Sariwŏn

Haeju

Kaesŏng

Hŭngnam

East
Korea
Bay

Wŏnsan

Sea

of

Japan

Truce
Line

P'anmunjŏm
Seoul

Inch'ŏn

Kanghwa
Bay

Ch'unch'ŏn

Han

Kangnŭng

Samch'ŏk

ULLŬNG

Ch'ŏngju

Kŭm

Huang   Hai
(Yellow   Sea)

Taejŏn

Kunsan

Kwangju

REPUBLIC OF KOREA

Mokp'o

Andong

Kimch'ŏn

Naktong

Taegu

Kyŏngju

Chinju

Masan

Pusan

Korea   Strait

TSUSHIMA

Hiroshima

HONSHU

JAPAN

Tsushima   Strait

Kitakyushu

Cheju   Strait

Cheju

CHEJU

Fukuoka

KYUSHU

SHIKOKU

0   80   160   240 km

0   40   80   120 miles

1:6,000,000

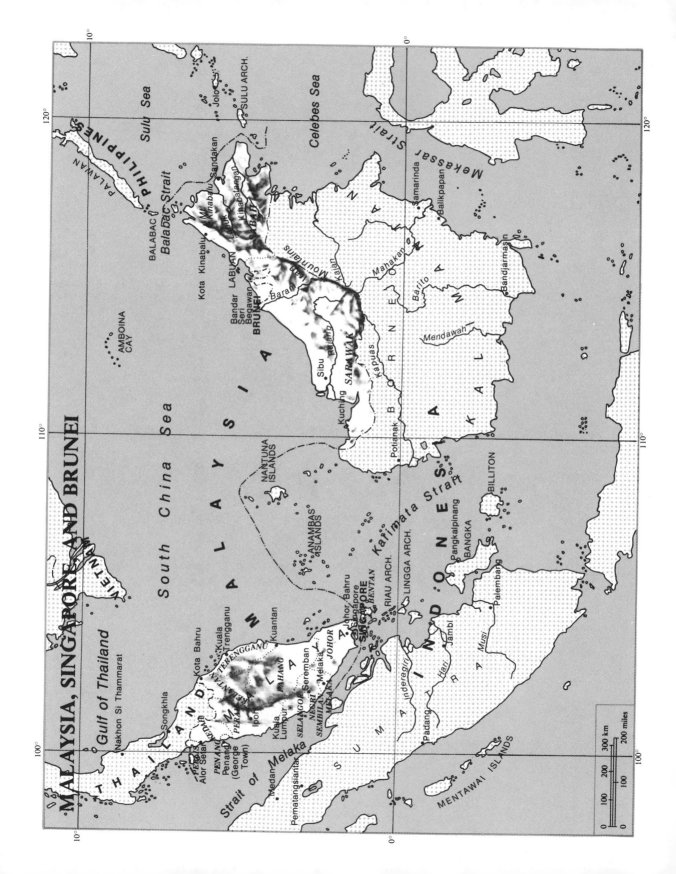

MALAYSIA, SINGAPORE AND BRUNEI

VIETNAM

PHILIPPINES

PALAWAN

Sulu Sea

BALABAC
Balabac Strait

SULU ARCH.
Jolo

Sandakan

Kinabalu

Kota Kinabalu
Bandar
Seri
Begawan
BRUNEI

Celebes Sea

Makassar Strait

Tarakan

Balikpapan

Bandjarmasin

BORNEO

KALIMANTAN

AMBOINA
CAY

Sulu Mountains

Rajang

Baram

Sibu

SARAWAK

Kapuas

Kuching

Barito

Mendawah

Mahakan

Kajan

South China Sea

M A L A Y S I A

NANTUNA
ISLANDS

Potianak

Kalimata Strait

BILLITON

ANAMBAS
ISLANDS

Pangkalpinang

BANGKA

Palembang

RIAU ARCH.

LINGGA ARCH.

BENTAN

Singapore
SINGAPORE

Johor Bahru

Gulf of Thailand

THAILAND

Nakhon Si Thammarat

Songkhla

Kota Bahru

KELANTAN
Kuala
Trengganu
TERENGGANU

KEDAH

Alor Setar

PERAK

PENANG
Penang
(George
Town)

Ipoh

PAHANG

Kuantan

SELANGOR
Kuala
Lumpur

NEGRI
SEMBILAN
Seremban

Melaka
MELAKA

JOHOR

Medan

Pematangsiantar

S U M A T R A

Inderagiri

Padang

Hari

Jambi

R

Musi

MENTAWAI ISLANDS

I N D O N E S I A

Strait of Melaka

Strait of Melaka

0   100   200   300 km
0   100   200 miles

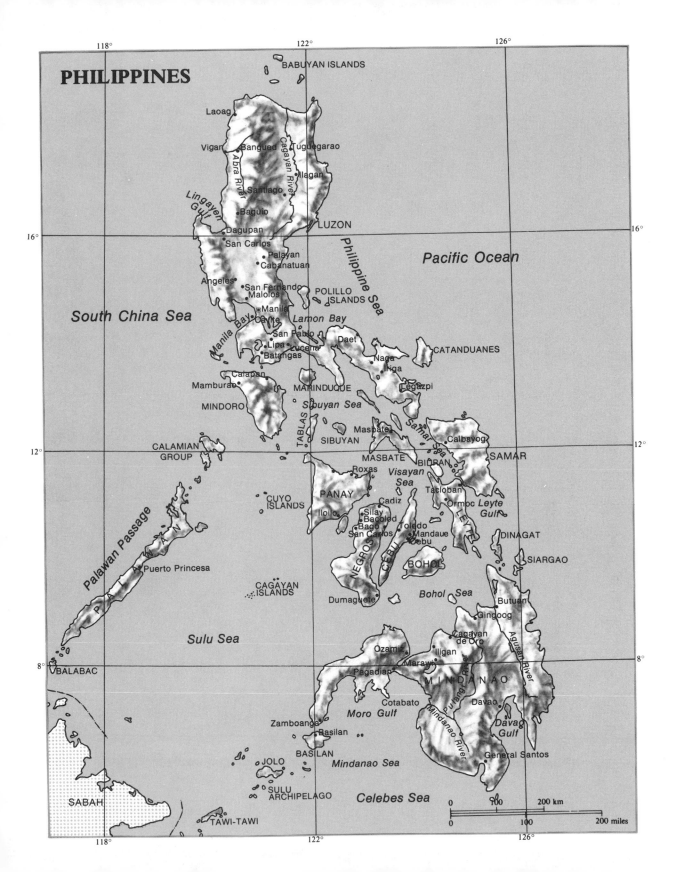

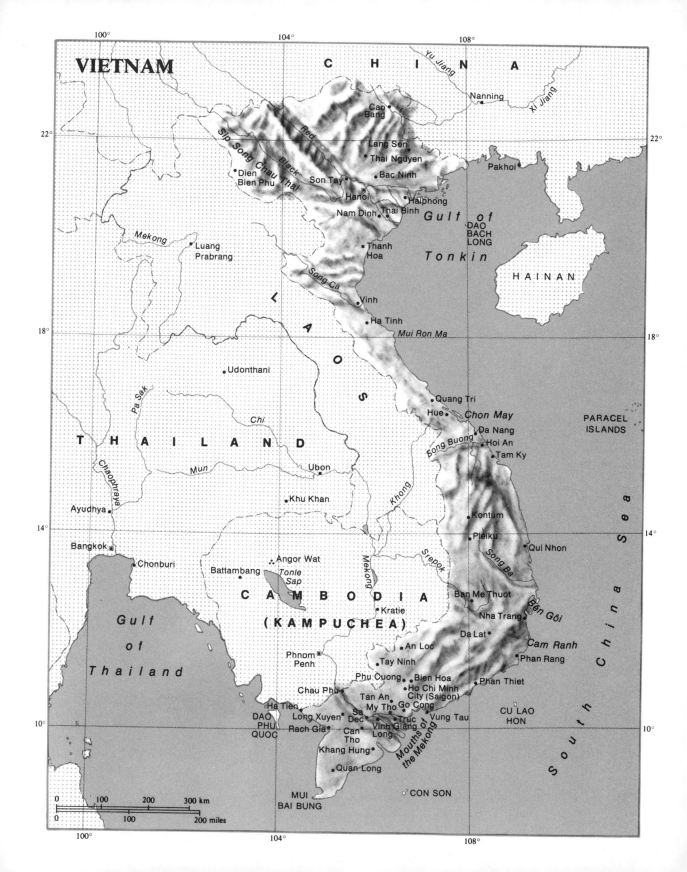

VIETNAM

C H I N A

Yu Jiang

Xi Jiang

Nanning

Cao Bang

Red

Black

Sip Song Chau Thai

Lang Son

Thai Nguyen

Dien Bien Phu

Son Tay

Bac Ninh

Pakhoi

Hanoi

Haiphong

Nam Dinh

Thai Binh

Gulf of

DAO BACH LONG

Mekong

Luang Prabrang

Thanh Hoa

Song Ca

Tonkin

HAINAN

Vinh

Ha Tinh

Mui Ron Ma

L A O S

Udonthani

Pa Sak

Quang Tri

Hue

Chon May

PARACEL ISLANDS

Chi

Da Nang

Hoi An

Song Buong

Tam Ky

T H A I L A N D

Mun

Ubon

Khu Khan

Khong

Kontum

Pleiku

Qui Nhon

Song Ba

Ayudhya

Bangkok

Chonburi

Battambang

Angor Wat

Tonle Sap

Mekong

Srepok

Ban Me Thuot

Ben Gôi

C A M B O D I A

Kratie

Nha Trang

Da Lat

Cam Ranh

(KAMPUCHEA)

An Loc

Gulf of Thailand

Phnom Penh

Tay Ninh

Phu Cuong

Bien Hoa

Ho Chi Minh City (Saigon)

Phan Rang

Phan Thiet

Chau Phu

Ha Tien

Tan An

My Tho

Go Cong

Vung Tau

CU LAO HON

South China Sea

DAO PHU QUOC

Long Xuyen

Rach Gia

Sa Dec

Can Tho

Vinh Long

Truc Giang

Mouths of the Mekong

Khang Hung

Quan Long

CON SON

MUI BAI BUNG

0   100   200   300 km

0   100   200 miles

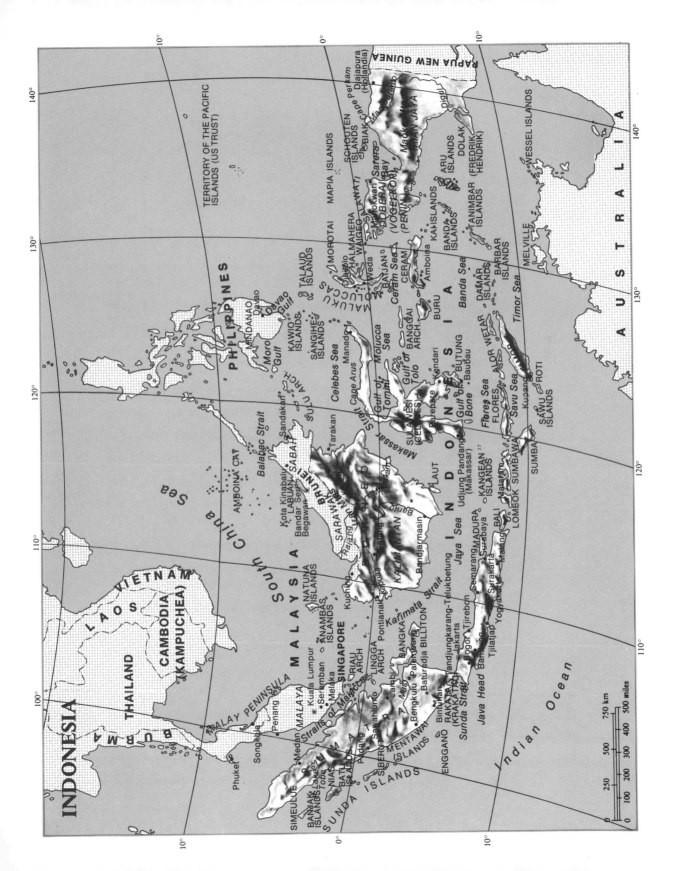

INDONESIA

BURMA

THAILAND

CAMBODIA (KAMPUCHEA)

LAOS

VIETNAM

MALAYSIA

South China Sea

PHILIPPINES

MALAY PENINSULA (MALAYA)

SINGAPORE

BRUNEI

SABAH

SARAWAK

KALIMANTAN

BORNEO

SULAWESI (CELEBES)

MOLUCCAS

MALUKU

HALMAHERA

IRIAN JAYA

PAPUA NEW GUINEA

TERRITORY OF THE PACIFIC ISLANDS (US TRUST)

AUSTRALIA

INDONESIA

Indian Ocean

SUNDA ISLANDS

Java Sea

Flores Sea

Banda Sea

Ceram Sea

Molucca Sea

Celebes Sea

Sulu Sea

Makassar Strait

Timor Sea

Savu Sea

Sâwu

Arafura Sea

Phuket

Songkla

Penang

Medan

SIMEULUE

BANYAK ISLANDS

NIAS

BATU ISLANDS

SIBERUT

MENTAWAI ISLANDS

ENGGANO

Lake Toba

Padang

Sawahlunto

Bengkulu

Palembang

Jambi

Baturadja

Bandar Lampung

Telukbetung

Tandjungkarang

Jakarta

Bogor

Tjirebon

Tjilatjap

Yogyakarta

Surakarta

Semarang

Surabaya

MADURA

BALI

LOMBOK

SUMBAWA

KANGEAN ISLANDS

SUMBA

ROTI

SÂWU ISLANDS

FLORES

ALOR

WETAR

Kupang

TIMOR

BARBAR ISLANDS

DAMAR ISLANDS

BANDA ISLANDS

KAI ISLANDS

TANIMBAR ISLANDS

ARU ISLANDS

DOLAK

BURU

CERAM

Amboina

BUTUNG

Baubau

Kendari

Palembare

Gulf of Bone

Gulf of Tolo

Gulf of Tomini

Cape Arus

Manado

SANGIHE ISLANDS

KAWIO ISLANDS

TALAUD ISLANDS

MOROTAI

Weda

BATJAN

Gulf of Boni

BANGGAI ARCH.

MELVILLE

WESSEL ISLANDS

VOGELKON (PENINSULA)

SALAWATI

WAIGEO

MISOOL

Mt. Okwari Sorong

Geelvink Bay

SCHOUTEN ISLANDS

BIAK

Cape Perkam

Manokwari

Sarera Bay

Maoki

Digul

Djajapura (Hollandia)

MAPIA ISLANDS

Davao

Davao Gulf

MINDANAO

Moro Gulf

BALABAC

Sandakan

Balabac Strait

AMBOINA CAY

Kota Kinabalu

LABUAN

Bandar Seri Begawan

Baram

Kuching

Miri

Rejang

Kapuas

Pontianak

KARIMATA

BILLITON

BANGKA

LINGGA ARCH.

RIAU ARCH.

Kuala Lumpur

Seremban

Melaka

Malacca

Straits of Malacca

NATUNA ISLANDS

ANAMBAS ISLANDS

Barito

Mahakam

Tarakan

Bandjarmasin

Udjung Pandang (Makassar)

Sunda Strait

Java Head

RAKATA (KRAKATAU)

Java

Kahajan

Tjilatjap

SUMATRA

0   100 200 300   400   500   750 km
0   100   200   300   500 miles

Selected References

Amsden, Alice. *Asia's New Giant: South Korea and Late Industrialization.* New York: Oxford University Press, 1989.

Beasley, W. G. *The Meiji Restoration.* Stanford University Press, 1972.

Bellah, Robert N., Richard Madsen, William M. Sullivan, Ann Swidler, and Steven M. Tipton. *Habits of the Heart.* Berkeley: University of California Press, 1985.

Braudel, Fernand. *The Perspective of the World: Civilization and Capitalism, 15th–18th Century* (3 volumes). New York: Harper & Row, 1984.

———. *The Mediterranean and the Mediterranean World in the Age of Philip II* (Volume 1). London: Collins, 1972.

Chang, Jung. *Wild Swans: Three Daughters of China.* New York: Simon & Schuster, 1991.

Clayton, James D. *The Years of MacArthur* (3 volumes). Boston: Houghton Mifflin, 1970.

de Bary, William Theodore. *East Asian Civilization.* Cambridge, Mass.: Harvard University Press, 1988.

Dennett, Tyler. *Americans in East Asia.* New York: Macmillan, 1922.

Dower, J. W. *Empire and Aftermath: Yoshida Shigeru and the Japanese Experience.* Cambridge, Mass.: Harvard University Press, 1979.

Drucker, Peter. *The New Realities.* New York: Harper & Row, 1989.

Eckert, Carter, Ki-baik Lee, Young-Ich Lew, Michael Robinson, and Edward Wagner. *Korea Old and New: A History.* Cambridge, Mass.: Harvard University Press, 1990.

Fairbank, John K. *The Great Chinese Revolution 1900–1985.* New York: Harper & Row, 1986.

Fleming, Peter. *The Siege of Peking.* New York: Oxford University Press, 1983.

Friend, Theodore. *The Blue-Eyed Energy: Japan Against the West in Java and Luzon.* Princeton, N.J.: Princeton University Press, 1988.

Fukui, Haruhiro. *Party in Power: The Japanese Liberal Democrats and Policy-Making.* Berkeley: University of California Press, 1978.

———. *Political Parties of Asia and the Pacific.* Westport, Conn.: Greenwood, 1985.

Gallagher, Louis, S.J. *China in the 16th Century: The Journals of Matthew Ricci.* New York: Random House, 1953.

Gibney, Frank B. *Miracle by Design*. New York: Times Books, 1983.

———. *Japan: The Fragile Superpower*. New York: Norton, 1975; rev. ed., 1986.

———. *Five Gentlemen of Japan*. New York: Farrar, Straus & Young, 1953.

Gluck, Carol. *Japan's Modern Myths*. Princeton, N.J.: Princeton University Press, 1985.

Gold, Thomas B. *State and Society in the Taiwan Miracle*. Armonk, N.Y.: Sharpe, 1988.

Griswold, A. Whitney. *The Far Eastern Policy of the United States*. New York: Harcourt, Brace, 1938.

Halberstam, David. *The Reckoning*. New York: Morrow, 1986.

———. *The New Century*. New York: Morrow, 1991.

Hawks, F. L. *Narrative of the Expedition of an American Squadron to the China Seas and Japan* (Perry Expedition). Washington Senate Printer, 1856.

Hobsbawn, E. J. *The Age of Capital: 1848–1875*. New York: Scribners, 1979.

Hollerman, Leon. *Japan Disincorporated*. Stanford, Calif.: Hoover Institution Press, 1988.

Iriye, Akira. *The Chinese and the Japanese*. Princeton, N.J.: Princeton University Press, 1980.

———. *Across the Pacific: A History of American–East Asia Relations*. Cambridge, Mass.: Harvard University Press, 1967.

Isaacs, Harold. *The Tragedy of the Chinese Revolution*. Stanford, Calif.: Stanford University Press, 1961.

———. *Encounters in China*. Armonk, N.Y.: Sharpe, 1985.

Jansen, Marius B. *Japan and Its World: Two Centuries of Change*. Princeton, N.J.: Princeton University Press, 1988.

———. *The Japanese and Sun Yat-Sen*. Cambridge, Mass.: Harvard University Press, 1954.

———. *Sakamoto Ryoma and the Meiji Restoration*. Princeton, N.J.: Princeton University Press, 1961.

Johnson, Chalmers. *MITI and the Japanese Miracle*. Stanford, Calif.: Stanford University Press, 1982.

———. *Conspiracy at Matsukawa*. Berkeley: University of California Press, 1972.

Johnson, Sheila K. *The Japanese Through American Eyes*. Stanford, Calif.: Stanford University Press, 1991.

Karnow, Stanley. *In Our Image: America's Empire in the Philippines*. New York: Random House, 1989.

———. *Vietnam: A History*. New York: Viking, 1983.

Kuttner, Robert. *The End of Laissez-Faire*. New York: Knopf, 1991.

Kuwabara, Takeo. *Japan and Western Civilization*. Tokyo, 1983.

Ladany, Laszlo. *The Communist Party of China and Marxism 1921–1985*. Stanford, Calif.: Hoover Institution Press, 1988.

Lee, Ki-baik. *A New History of Korea*. Cambridge, Mass.: Harvard University Press, 1984.

Lee, Leo Oufan. *Voices from the Iron House: A Study of Lu Xun*. Bloomington: Indiana University Press, 1987.

Liu, Alan P. L. *Phoenix and the Lame Lion, Modernization in Taiwan Mainland China 1950–1980*. Stanford, Calif.: Hoover Institution Press, 1987.

Liu, Binyan. *A Higher Kind of Loyalty*. New York: Pantheon, 1990.

Lu Xun. *Selected Stories*. Peking: Foreign Language Press, 1960.

Mahan, Alfred T. *The Influence of Sea Power Upon History: 1600–1783*. Boston: Little, Brown, 1898.

Meissner, Maurice. *Mao's China and After*. New York: Free Press, 1985.

Morison, Samuel Eliot. *Old Bruin: Commodore Matthew Calbaith Perry*. New York: Atlantic Monthly, 1987.

———. *Oxford History of the American People*. New York: Oxford University Press, 1975.

Morris, Edmund. *The Rise of Theodore Roosevelt*. New York: Coward, McCann, 1979.

Mosher, Steven W. *China Misperceived*. New York: Basic Books, 1990.

Nakamura, Takafusa. *The Post-War Japanese Economy*. Tokyo: Tokyo University Press, 1981.

Norman, E. H. *Japan's Emergence as a Modern State*. New York: Institute of Pacific Relations, 1940.

Okimoto, Daniel. *Between MITI and the Market*. Stanford, Calif.: Stanford University Press, 1989.

Okita, Saburo. *The Developing Economics and Japan*. Tokyo: University of Tokyo Press, 1980.

Phillips, Kevin. *The Politics of Rich and Poor*. New York: Random House, 1990.

Porter, Michael E. *The Competitive Advantages of Nations*. New York: Free Press, 1990.

Prestowitz, Clyde V., Jr. *Trading Places*. New York: Basic Books, 1988.

Pye, Lucian. *Asian Power and Politics*. Cambridge, Mass.: Harvard University Press, 1985.

Reich, Robert B. *The Work of Nations*. New York: Knopf, 1991.

Reischauer, Edwin O. *The Japanese Today*. Cambridge, Mass.: Harvard University Press, 1988.

———, John K. Fairbank, and Albert O. Craig. *East Asia: The Modern Transformation*. Boston: Houghton Mifflin, 1965.

Sansom, Sir George Bailey. *Japan: A Short Cultural History*. New York: Appleton-Century, 1943.

————. *The Western World and Japan*. New York: Knopf, 1968.

Scalapino, Robert A., with Chung-Sik Lee. *Communism in Korea* (2 volumes). Berkeley: University of California Press, 1972.

————, with George T. Yu. *Modern China and Its Revolutionary Process*. Berkeley: University of California Press, 1985.

Schumpeter, Joseph A. *Capitalism, Socialism and Democracy*. New York: Harper, 1950.

Schwartz, Benjamin. *In Search of Wealth and Power: Yen Fu and the West*. Cambridge, Mass.: Harvard University Press, 1964.

————. *The World of Thought in Ancient China*. Cambridge, Mass.: Harvard University Press/Belknap, 1985.

Servan-Schreiber, Jean Jacques. *The American Challenge*. London: Harnish Hamilton, 1968.

Sjahrir, Soetan. *Out of Exile*. Westport, Conn.: Greenwood, 1969.

Smith, Adam. *The Roaring Eighties*. New York: Summit, 1988.

Spate, O. H. K. *The Pacific Since Magellan* (Volume 1), *Monopolists and Freebooters* (Volume 2), *Paradise Lost and Found* (Volume 3). Minneapolis: University of Minnesota Press, 1979, 1983, 1988.

Stanley, Peter. *A Nation in the Making: The Philippines and the United States*. Cambridge, Mass.: Harvard University Press, 1974.

Storrey, Richard. *The Double Patriots*. London: Chatto & Windus, 1957.

Tuchman, Barbara W. *Stilwell and the American Experience in China*. New York: Macmillan, 1971.

Tu Wei-Ming. *Centrality and Communality—An Essay on Confucian Religiousness*. Albany: State University of New York Press, 1989.

Turnbull, C. Mary. *A History of Singapore*. New York: Oxford University Press, 1988.

Vogel, Ezra. *The Four Little Dragons: The Spread of Industrialization in East Asia*. Cambridge, Mass.: Harvard University Press, 1992.

————. *One Step Ahead in China*. Cambridge, Mass.: Harvard University Press, 1989.

Wade, Robert. *Economic Theory and the Role of Government in East Asian Industrialization*. Princeton, N.J.: Princeton University Press, 1990.

Wild, Colin, and Peter Carey (eds.). *Born in Fire: The Indonesian Struggle for Independence*. London: BBC, 1986.

Wilson, George J. *Radical Nationalism in Japan*. Cambridge, Mass.: Harvard University Press, 1969.

Yoshida, Shigeru. *The Yoshida Memoirs* (trans. by Yoshida Kenichi). Boston: Houghton Mifflin, 1962.

Index

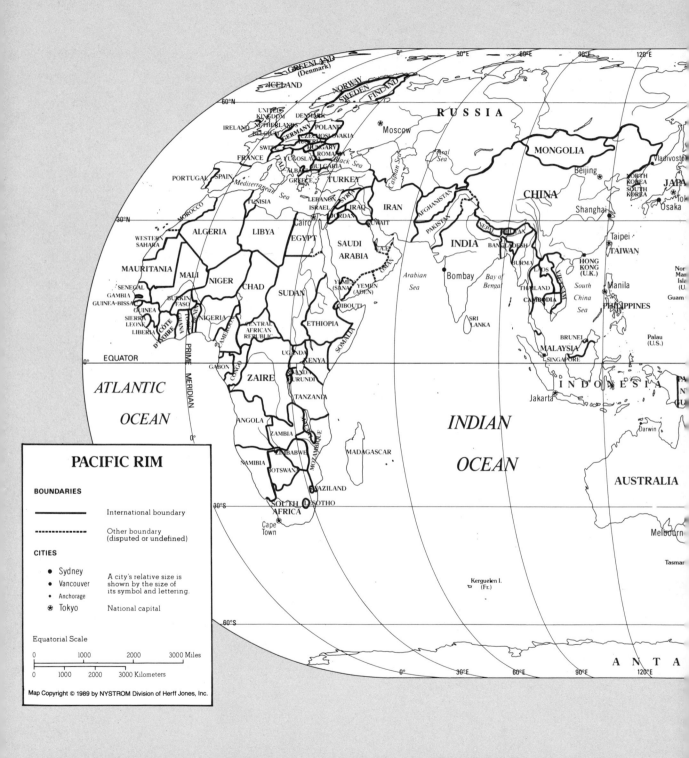

PACIFIC RIM

BOUNDARIES

——————————   International boundary

- - - - - - - - - - -   Other boundary
(disputed or undefined)

CITIES

● Sydney

● Vancouver   A city's relative size is
shown by the size of
· Anchorage   its symbol and lettering.

⊛ Tokyo   National capital

Equatorial Scale

0   1000   2000   3000 Miles

0   1000   2000   3000 Kilometers

Map Copyright © 1989 by NYSTROM Division of Herff Jones, Inc.